*A Dictionary of Quotations about Communication*

# A Dictionary of Quotations about Communication

*compiled and edited by*
Robert A. Nowlan *and*
Gwendolyn L. Nowlan

McFarland & Company, Inc., Publishers
*Jefferson, North Carolina, and London*

**Library of Congress Cataloguing-in-Publication Data**

A dictionary of quotations about communication / compiled and
    edited by Robert A. Nowlan and Gwendolyn L. Nowlan.
        p.      cm.
    Includes indexes.
    ISBN 0-7864-0767-0 (softcover : 50# alkaline paper) ∞
    1. Quotations.    2. Quotations, English.    I. Nowlan, Robert A.
    II.  Nowlan, Gwendolyn Wright, 1945–
    PN6081.D535    2000
    082—dc21                                              00-25240

British Library cataloguing data are available

Cover image © 2000 EyeWire.

Manufactured in the United States of America

*McFarland & Company, Inc., Publishers*
    *Box 611, Jefferson, North Carolina 28640*
        *www.mcfarlandpub.com*

TO OUR PARENTS,
EACH OF WHOM COULD TELL A TALE

AND IN MEMORY OF
EDGAR SCHOONMAKER,
A GENTLEMAN OF MANY STORIES

# Contents

*Introduction*—1

1. Accent—7
2. Achievement—8
3. Action—8
4. Actors—9
5. Advice—10
6. Affectation—11
7. Allegory—11
8. Analogy—12
9. Anecdote—12
10. Angels—13
11. Animals—13
12. Answers—14
13. Antiquity—15
14. Aphorism—16
15. Apology—17
16. Apothegms—18
17. Applause—18
18. Argument—19
19. Art and Artists—21
20. Assumption—22
21. Audience—22
22. Baby and Baby Talk—24
23. Ballads—24
24. Bards and Bardolatry—25
25. Beauty—27
26. Belief—28
27. Bible—29
28. Boasting—30
29. Bon Mots—31
30. Books—32
31. Boredom and Bores—33
32. Boys—34
33. Brain—35
34. Brevity—35

35. Business—36
36. Candor—37
37. Chatter—37
38. Children—38
39. Civilization—39
40. Clarity—40
41. Cleverness—40
42. Cliché—41
43. Comedy—42
44. Communication—42
45. Comparisons—43
46. Complaint—43
47. Compliment—44
48. Concealment—45
49. Conclusion—45
50. Confession—46
51. Conversation—46
52. Courage—48
53. Courtesy—49
54. Criticism—49
55. Cruelty—50
56. Curiosity—50
57. Cursing and Swearing—51
58. Cynics and Cynicism—52
59. Dance—52
60. Death—52
61. Definition—53
62. Devil—54
63. Dialect—54
64. Dialogue—54
65. Differences—55
66. Diplomats and Diplomacy—55
67. Discussion—56
68. Dispute—57
69. Double-Entendre—58
70. Doubt—58

71. Dreams—58
72. Ear—59
73. Echo—60
74. Education—60
75. Eloquence—61
76. Emotion—63
77. Entertainment—64
78. Enunciation—65
79. Epic—65
80. Epigram—65
81. Eulogies and Epitaphs—66
82. Euphemisms—67
83. Exaggeration and Hyperbole—68
84. Excuses—69
85. Experience—69
86. Explanation—70
87. Fable—70
88. Facts—72
89. Fairies—72
90. Fairy Tales—73
91. Fantasy—76
92. Farce—77
93. Fathers—78
94. Fear—78
95. Fiction—79
96. Flattery—80
97. Folk Music—81
98. Folklore—82
99. Fools and Folly—83
100. Forensics—84
101. Generalization—84
102. Gentlemen—85
103. Ghosts—86
104. Giants—86
105. Girls—87
106. God—87
107. Gods—88
108. Gossip—89
109. Grammar—91
110. Griots—92
111. Hearing—93
112. Heart—94
113. Heresy and Heretics—95
114. Heroes—95
115. Historians—96
116. History—96
117. Honesty—98
118. Honor—99
119. Humor—99
120. Hypocrisy—100

121. Iconoclasts—100
122. Ideals and Idealists—101
123. Ideas—101
124. Identity—102
125. Ignorance—102
126. Illusion—103
127. Imagination—104
128. Imitation—105
129. Immortality—106
130. Improvisation—106
131. Indignation—107
132. Information—107
133. Instruction—108
134. Instrument—108
135. Insults—108
136. Interests—109
137. Irony—110
138. Jargon—110
139. Jests and Jesters—111
140. Jokes—112
141. Judgment—113
142. Kindness—114
143. Kings and Queens—115
144. Kisses—115
145. Knowledge—116
146. Ladies—118
147. Language—118
148. Laughter—120
149. Law—122
150. Lawyers—123
151. Lectures—125
152. Legends—127
153. Liars and Lying—128
154. Lies—130
155. Life—130
156. Limericks—132
157. Linguistics—133
158. Listening—134
159. Literature—136
160. Love—137
161. Madness—139
162. Magic—140
163. Man and Men—140
164. Marriage—141
165. Maxims—143
166. Meaning—144
167. Media—145
168. Medicine—146
169. Memory—146
170. Mermaids—147

171. Metaphor—147
172. Mind—148
173. Minstrels—149
174. Miracles—150
175. Monologues—151
176. Moral—151
177. Morality—152
178. Mothers—152
179. Mouth—153
180. Movies—154
181. Music—156
182. Mystery—157
183. Myth—158
184. Mythology—160
185. Name—161
186. Narration—162
187. Nature—163
188. News—164
189. Noise—164
190. Nonsense—165
191. Nostalgia—166
192. Nothing—166
193. Nursery Rhymes—167
194. Oath—168
195. Observation—169
196. Opinion—169
197. Oral Tradition—170
198. Oratory and Orators—171
199. Parables—173
200. Parody—173
201. Pathos—174
202. Pedantry—174
203. People—175
204. Performance—176
205. Persuasion—176
206. Philosophy—177
207. Platitude—178
208. Poetry—179
209. Poets—181
210. Politicians—182
211. Politics—184
212. Power—185
213. Praise—185
214. Prayer—186
215. Preachers—187
216. Preaching—188
217. Prejudice—189
218. Problems—190
219. Professors and Professing—190
220. Pronunciation—192

221. Propaganda—193
222. Prophecy and Prophets—193
223. Prose—194
224. Proverbs—195
225. Puns—196
226. Quarrels—198
227. Questions—199
228. Quotations—200
229. Radio—201
230. Rationalization—202
231. Reading—203
232. Reality—203
233. Reason—204
234. Religion—205
235. Remarks—206
236. Repartee—206
237. Repetition—207
238. Reputation—207
239. Resolution—208
240. Rhetoric—208
241. Rhyme—209
242. Riddles—210
243. Ridicule—210
244. Romance—211
245. Rules—211
246. Rumor—212
247. Sadness—213
248. Sarcasm—213
249. Satire—214
250. Sayings—215
251. Scandal—216
252. Science—217
253. Secret—218
254. Sense—218
255. Sentences—219
256. Sermons—220
257. Sigh—221
258. Silence—221
259. Simile—223
260. Sins and Sinners—223
261. Slander—224
262. Slang—225
263. Sleep—225
264. Society—226
265. Song and Singing—226
266. Sorrow—227
267. Sound—228
268. Speech and Speaking—229
269. Speeches and Speechmaking—230
270. Stories—232

271. Storytelling and Storytellers—236
272. Students and Studies—240
273. Stupidity—241
274. Style—242
275. Subject—243
276. Success—243
277. Syllables—244
278. Symbols—245
279. Sympathy—245
280. Tact—246
281. Tale—247
282. Talk and Talkativeness—250
283. Teachers—252
284. Teaching—253
285. Tears—254
286. Telephone—255
287. Television—255
288. Theater—256
289. Theology—257
290. Thinking—258
291. Thoughts—259
292. Time—260
293. Toasts—262
294. Tongue—262

295. Tradition—264
296. Tragedy—265
297. Trickery—266
298. Truth—266
299. Understanding—269
300. Universe and Universality—270
301. Vanity—271
302. Verbosity—271
303. Verse—272
304. Vocabulary—273
305. Voice—274
306. Wisdom—275
307. Wit—276
308. Witticisms—278
309. Women—279
310. Words—280
311. The World—284
312. Writers—284
313. Writing—285
314. Youth—286

*Index of Authors*—289

*Key Word Index*—311

# Introduction

Our primary goal in preparing this book of quotations is to demonstrate the simple fact that most human communication is still accomplished by means of oral language. Long before email, voice mail, the Internet—before the invention of the printing press, before scribes laboriously copied "books," even before scrolls and inscriptions on stones, before the invention of writing or symbolic representation of ideas, humans spoke and still do. And the greatest part of this use of speech—the greatest part, the most lasting part—was, and still is, to pass on from one generation to the next accumulated knowledge and wisdom.

Those who spoke with this purpose in mind related what was known, believed, theorized, or invented about how things came to be—of the nature of Nature and most importantly of the nature of man.

We might call these individuals storytellers, and indeed they did tell wondrous stories, but they were also scientists, historians, teachers, philosophers, theologians—in fact all of those who strove to understand their world and their place in it—and felt the necessity of sharing their findings and understanding with others who would live long after they were gone.

When we explain our great interest in this kind of "storytelling" many people comment unthinkingly that storytelling is a dying art. They might even observe that it is quaint of us to be interested in something so ancient, so rare, so dead. If we are quaint we share our quaintness with all individuals who search for understanding of the present and direction for the future in examining what has already occurred.

Communication in the oral tradition is not something past. The oral tradition is alive, well, and flourishing—and we suspect it always will be. It is kept vibrant not merely by those who champion folklore and storytelling. Those of us who are fascinated with the power and effectiveness of the oral tradition should not be confused with groups dedicated to preserving something like barbershop harmonizing—although we share their passion.

The oral tradition is and will always be the primary means of communication between human beings. If we should ever reach a point where communication between human beings is no longer important, it will mean humans have been supplanted by machines. (But even so the machines will need to communicate by some means, although we acknowledge it may not be orally.)

This book of quotations is dedicated to and compiled for all those who speak for a living. A pretty good case could be made that this includes just about everyone, save some monks who have taken vows of silence. And while the majority of people enjoy talking—sometimes too frequently and without sufficient reflection—those whom we have most in mind are the individuals in the many professions and occupations who, despite all the written, printed and electronic messages they may transmit, find that their best communicating is done orally, often in an oral give and take with others. To communicate takes at least two: one to speak and one to hear. When communication is most effective these roles are constantly being traded.

The quotations of this book are gathered

for and about those who communicate orally. It embraces the language they use and the subjects upon which they speak. In examining the topic headings readers may find a topic here or there which at first appears strange for inclusion in a book with the declared intentions of this one. But the quotations under that topic heading will convince the reader that the topic belongs here.

When a person speaks he reveals who he is. His choice of words, inflection, use of figures of speech, cliches, complete or incomplete thoughts, and tone of voice combined with his body language, the look in his eyes and other facial expressions tell more of the speaker than do his mere words.

If one reason for speaking is to communicate, however, another is to conceal. But one must be every bit as clever to conceal with speech as to communicate with it—perhaps more so. Speech is used to flatter, to convince, to cajole, to insult, to arouse, to console, to hurt, to interest, to entertain, to instruct, to explain and to counsel.

Creators of songs, poetry, plays, stories, tales and prose have something to say. If some of what they have to say is related in print rather than orally, it is because more can be reached in this way, not because print is a superior mode of expression. Songs must be sung, poems spoken, plays performed, stories and tales told, and prose—well, prose can be a solitary event with one reader seeking a one-way communication with a quiet but present voice. Most of a certain age will recall that one of the most anticipated activities during a schoolday was when a teacher read to the class.

Teachers, who are among those who speak for a living, have their instruction complemented by reading assignments. But for the latter to be effective, the teacher must show students how to read—even those who are already literate. Everything new that is to be learned in any subject has its own peculiar way of being expressed both orally and in written form. It is incumbent on teachers to instruct their students how to hear the lesson, speak of it, write about it and read it. Such instruction is most often done orally.

Every profession or occupation has its own peculiar jargon which to the novice may seem very much a foreign language. Unless someone takes the time to explain, orally, what the words and phrases mean, and how the peculiarities of the language are applied to the field, little true communication will take place.

Attorneys speak for a living. But when they speak in a courtroom in a trial before a jury, it is necessary that a judge preside to rule what the lawyers may legally say and explain the law and what it means to those who must decide the case.

People in the business world speak for a living. We recall a particular television commercial in which the boss announces to his sales force that the company had been "fired" by an old customer who said he didn't know them anymore. The boss decided that the problem was that the sales force had stopped relying on direct contact—in-person, oral contact—with their customers. He informed them that they were going back to visiting customers, and he himself was going to pay a visit to the old customer who had fired them. He understood the importance of face-to-face communication.

Those in the diplomatic service must speak very carefully, less they be too well understood. New diplomats are advised not to say yes, no, maybe, or even to reveal too much by the motion of their head or expressions in their eyes.

Politicians, particularly when trying to get elected, speak for a living. What they say and what they believe may have only a casual relationship as they dare not be too clearly understood lest they risk antagonizing some group of voters. The public has come to expect political rhetoric to be none too informative, and so they listen to politicians with a certain amount of disbelief if not downright suspicion that what is being said is not totally sincere.

Another group of those who speak for a living, members of the media, owe their careers to analyzing for their listeners what politicians, elected officials and others in government have said, have not said, have meant and have not meant. Well meaning as this may be, this instant analysis becomes almost as annoying and superfluous as teams of television sportscasters who not only describe in great detail plays taking place before the eyes of sports fans, but repeat the same play over and over again from any number of angles so they once again can speak the obvious.

Clearly, some of those who speak for a living speak too much or, more accurately, speak of things far too trivial. Not displaying much fluency in oral communication, they speak when they had better remained silent. And this surely applies to all of us.

Silence is an important part of speech, language, communication, and the oral tradition. The best speakers are those who use silence the most effectively. Part of using silence in speaking is "timing," which in speech can be everything. Comedian Jack Benny didn't say funny things all the time or even say things in funny ways. Best known as a master of timing, he could put audiences into convulsions by responding to another's comment with a long pause—just long enough—and finally a simple "Well!"

Many sources of entertainment involve actors, be they in a play, a movie, on radio or television using their splendid voices. While writers are an integral part of these presentations, their words are generally more effective when heard than when read. Shakespeare is credited with being a great playwright, but how much better than reading his plays is to see and hear them performed.

Even the finest novelists are likely to have their masterpieces dramatized and adapted by screenwriters of movies. When this happens, however unfair some may believe it to be, far more people become acquainted with the work by seeing the movie than by reading the novel.

Lest we leave the impression that the use of oral language is limited to the arts and humanities, be assured that the sciences and mathematics are also strongly tied to the oral tradition. The discoveries, inventions and theories of scientists and mathematicians have engendered far more controversy and arguments than any other human inquiry. Those who would explain Nature and its laws are seldom applauded at the beginning. In fact they may be vilified and even punished for suggesting new explanations, especially when there are those who have a vested interest in maintaining earlier explanations.

Galileo is but one example of this situation. The controversies did not necessarily begin when the professor of new knowledge wrote of his findings, but when he and others began speaking of them. It seemed the spoken word was more feared by those in power than the written word. After all, how many people read?

Martin Luther didn't get going with his challenges to certain practices and tenets of the church until he gave dramatic evidence by posting the theses he was willing to debate— that is speak out about—with people who did not read, hearing what he had to say.

Others who speak for a living are orators. We may believe that the age of oratory at least is past, but it has merely evolved. On a less than grand scale, radio call-in shows offer soapboxes upon which grassroots orators may stand and expound their thoughts. Now and then a politician or government official can prove to be a great orator. We think of the likes of Franklin D. Roosevelt and Winston Churchill in their inspired and inspiring addresses to their nations at the time of World War II. On the other side, one must admit that Adolf Hitler was an effective, awesome, spellbinding, albeit evil orator.

Preachers of all denominations and faiths speak for a living. Their messages may be as simple as preaching against sin or as profound as offering their views on living a moral and ethical life. Their sermons may draw their audience's attention to great injustices in the world that must be addressed. These clergymen may lead their flocks to follow the tenets of their established religion, or they may address the roles man must play in dealing with his fellow men.

Then there are the storytellers, whose work includes that of the others who speak for a living. Stories may entertain, but this has hardly ever been their sole purpose. Think of Aesop and his fables, which even today are used to teach morals that still seem significant. The Griots of African cultures were historians of families, tribes, nations, and people, keeping alive the accumulated understanding, beliefs and names of those who had come before. Fairy tales are not just ways of making the Disney company richer. They have lessons to teach, and few were initially intended for children. The myths and mythology of every people have been related by storytellers. The importance of the myths, and the heroes and gods they featured, is by no means limited to those interested in dwelling in the past.

Storytelling can be successfully used in the teaching of anything and everything. Some of the best and most effective teachers and counselors have incorporated storytelling prominently in their practice. If you want people to listen—to do more than listen, to hear and to understand—just announce that you intend to tell them a story.

The format of this book consists of more than three hundred subject headings, each followed by quotations pertinent to the subject. For each quotation, the author of the quotation—using "author" in the broadest sense of the word—is identified, along with its source. Each topic is numbered (for example, "Accent" is topic number 1). Each quotation under the topic has a separate number, preceded by a decimal (.1, .2, .3, etc.). The indexes at the back of the book are keyed to this arrangement; a quotation cited in the index as 147.25 is the twenty-fifth quotation under topic number 147, LANGUAGE. For easy reference, when a topic continues across columns or pages, the topic number is repeated in a small box in the upper left of the column.

In some cases, while the author of the quotation is known, the exact source cannot be found. In this case we say the quotation is "attributed" to the author, or we acknowledge that it is "quoted in" what appears to be a secondary source. This occurs most often when a particular quotation has appeared in print in numerous secondary sources without any identification of a primary source.

After some quotations, comments of an explanatory nature are provided. This is done when we believe that a reference in the quotation should be identified; when an archaic word or phrase requires interpretation; when meaning may not be familiar; or when some interesting circumstance of the quotation can be furnished.

The authors of the quotations are among the most familiar names in history, but also include individuals whose marks on the world

are minimal. The quotations date from 4500 B.C. to the present. Quotations have been chosen to offer a balance in both periods of time and diversity of individuals for each subject. A conscious effort has been made to include many quotations by women and minority groups who have often been underrepresented in quotation books.

Usually the character in a play or a novel who makes a statement included as a quotation is not identified. Instead we give sole credit to the playwright or novelist.

On the other hand, many inspiring statements made by politicians and statesman were probably the work of a team of speech writers. In this case the credit for the quotation is given to the speaker, not the unknown writer. For instance, had we included "Ask not what your country can do for you, ask what you can do for your country," credit would be given to John F. Kennedy, although he may have had some help in the wording of the sentiment.

Sometimes a particular quotation has been attributed to more than one person. In such a case, the alternate candidate is noted, but the source listed is the one current wisdom favors. Some proverbs have been rephrased with only slight modifications by many authors, over many, many years, with none of them the likely first source. When this occurs the author given as the source is merely recording a bit of wisdom with a long anonymous history.

That brings us to the distinction between "anonymous" and "unknown." There are quotations attributed to both, but some of the anonymous authors have clearly chosen to remain so, while those unknown are really unknown. It is a popular theory, which we would like to believe, that many of the anonymous quotations were made by women who dared not identify themselves because they lived in times and circumstances in which women were expected to limit their opinions to husband, family, home and love. While we can find no compelling evidence that this is in fact the case, we can find no fault with those who examine anonymous quotations looking for feminine clues.

For some a book of quotations is a source of material to punch up a speech or to add credence to a bit of research. But we are among those who find that books of quotations make delightful reading for their own sake. One can open a book of quotations to any page and read the wisdom of many who have given serious reflection to a matter and felt obliged to comment upon it. Perusing the contents of books of quotations, it is amazing how frequently one finds himself savoring the author's insight. But then something really remarkable may occur. One thinks beyond what the author has said, and in the process one discovers what he thinks about the matter. The reader comes away enriched with opinions, relative truths and fodder for further reflection. Books of quotations can serve as a university for those who will use them to understand themselves and the nature of the world.

We would like to acknowledge the following friends of communication, language and the oral tradition. They are among those who understand that as long as there are humans on this earth, the best way of relating and passing on information is oral.

Esther Anderson, Mackey Barron, Brian Bemel, Arlene Bielefield, Carol Birch, Judith Black, Tom Buckley, Len Cabral, Tom Callinan, Tom Clarie, Mary and Bill Corcoran, Donald and Merle Davis, Sara deBeer, Carmen Deedy, Leeny Del Seamonds, Pleasant DeSpain, Peter Dolese, John and Gay Evans, Theresa McGoff Ferreira, Heather Forest, A. and Rachel Garcia, Marni Gillard, Jackson Gillman, Linda Goodman, Ken and Elizabeth Grant, Kerry and Sandra Grant, Barbara Hanscom, Melissa Heckler, Katie Hereld, John Hill, Rosalind Hinman, Rita Hughes, Isabel Anna, Tim Jennings, Marty and Steve Johnson, Marybeth and Stephen Johnson, Craig Johnson, Kevin Johnson, Karen Josephson, Nancy Kavanagh, Steve Kardaleff, Grace Kelly, Ruth Kindersley, Susan Klein, Leo Kuczynski, Eve Kyburg, Rod and Sarah Lane, Joe Lawson, Peter Lawson, Ray and Mollie Lawson, Annabel Lee, Tom Lee, Barbara Lipke, Norma Livo, Margaret Reed MacDonald, Jack Maselli, Barbara McBride-Smith, Jeff and Synia McQuillan, Marilyn O'Connor Miller, Wayne Miller, Ethel and Larry Montgomery, Paul and Marilyn Montlick, Danny and Lynne Nowlan, Mary Nowlan, Michael and Kitty Nowlan, Steve and Chris Nowlan, Rocco and Rae Orlando, Jay O'Callahan, Peg O'Sullivan, Daniel and Sharon Ort, Michael Parent, Ted and Liz Parkhurst, Leonard and Marsh Passmore, J. G. Pinkerton, Leanne Ponder, Eleanor Potter, Diane Prunier, Barbara Reed, Connie Rockman, Steve Rosenthal, Lynn and Robert Rubright, Martha Schaff, Aurea Schoonmaker, Josepha Sherman, Pete and Helen Shields, Ann Shapiro, Jimmy Neil Smith, Mary Carter Smith, Phil and Loretta Smith, Lorna Stengel, Ed Stivender, Storycrafters, Laconia (Lot) Therrio, Jackie Torrence, Ellie Toy, Valerie Tutson, Sheila Wartel, Tom Weakley, Teresa Whitaker, Mary and Chris Whited, Mary Williams, Martha Yandle, Linda Yemoto, Jane Yolen.

In addition our lives have been greatly affected and enriched by our departed parents, Marian Shields Nowlan, Dr. Ray N. Lawson and Gertrude Evans Lawson. We are grateful for the love and encouragement of Robert A. Nowlan, Sr.; Dr. Anne Lawson; our children, Robert, Philip, and Edward; Edward's wife, Amy; and our grandchildren, Alexandra, Tommy, John, and Catherine. We also acknowledge Jennifer and her husband, Peter Golanski, Evan Wright, Andrew Wright and his fiancée, Melanie Simpson.

Robert A. Nowlan
and Gwendolyn L. Nowlan

# The Quotations

## 1 Accent

.1 I haven't been abroad in so long that I almost speak English without an accent now.
—Robert Benchley; *After 1903—What?*, 1938

.2 Correct my manners or my waggeries,
But though my accent's not the berries,
Spare my pronunciation vagaries...
—Morris Bishop; "Why and How I Killed My Wife," 1954

.3 We that loved him so, followed him,
honored him,
Lived in his mild and magnificent eye,
Learned his great language, caught his clear accents,
Made him our pattern to live and to die!
—Robert Browning; *Dramatic Romances and Lyrics*, "The Lost Leader," 1845
[The reference is to William Wordsworth.]

.4 Father of Light! Great God of Heaven!
Hear'st thou the accents of despair?
Can guilt like man's be e'er forgiven?
Can vice atone for crimes by prayer?
—Lord Byron; "The Prayer of Nature," 1812

.5 A kind of chanting; all men have accents of their own,—though they only notice that of others.
—Thomas Carlyle; *Critical and Miscellaneous Essays*, 1838

.6 Let others sing of knights and paladins
In aged accents and untimely words.
—Samuel Daniel; *Sonnets to Delia*, "I Must Not Grieve," 1592

.7 Their accents firm and loud in conversation,
Their eyes and gestures eager, sharp and quick
Showed them prepared on proper provocation
To give the lie, pull noses, stick and kick!

And for the very reason it is said
They were so very courteous and well-bred.
—John Hookham Frere; *Prospectus and Specimen of an Intended National Work*, 1798

.8 The twentieth century is only the nineteenth speaking with a slightly American accent.
—Philip Guedalla; Attributed

.9 Since they are not in constant attendance at the cinema their speech is uncorrupted by the slang or accent of Chicago.
—A.P. Herbert; *Misleading Cases*, 1935

.10 The accent of one's country dwells in the mind and the heart, as well on the tongue.
—François de La Rochefoucauld; *Maximes*, 1678

.11 Many Americans feel themselves inferior in the presence of anyone with an English accent, which is why an English accent has become fashionable in television commercials, it is thought to sound authoritative.
—Edwin Newman; *Strictly Speaking*, 1974

.12 Accent is the soul of a language; it gives the feeling and truth to it.
—Jean-Jacques Rousseau; *Emile on Education*, 1762

.13 How many ages hence
Shall this our lofty scene be acted o'er,
In states unborn and accents yet unknown!
—William Shakespeare; *Julius Caesar*, 1599

.14 O, there be players that I have seen play, and heard others praise, and that highly, not to speak it profanely, that, neither having the accent of Christians nor the gait of a Christian pagan, nor man, have so strutted and bellowed that I have thought some of nature's journeymen had made men and not made them well, they imitated humanity so abominably.
—William Shakespeare; *Hamlet*, 1600-1

## 1

.15 It comes to pass oft that a terrible oath, with a swaggering accent sharply twanged off, gives manhood more approbation than ever proof itself would have earned him.
—William Shakespeare; *Twelfth Night*, 1601

.16 When the lute is broken,
Sweet tones are remembered not;
When the lips have spoken,
Loved accents are soon forgot.
—Percy Bysshe Shelley; "When the Lamp Is Shattered," 1822

.17 Our bog is dood, our Bog is dood,
They lisped in accents mild,
But when I asked them to explain
They grew a little mad.
—Stevie Smith; "Our Bog Is Dood"; *Norton Anthology of English Literature*, M.H. Abrams, general ed., 1986

.18 Even though his tongue acquire the Southern knack, he will still have a strong Scots accent of the mind.
—Robert Louis Stevenson; *Memories and Portraits*. "The Foreigner at Home," 1887

.19 By weaker accents, what's your praise
When Philomel her voice doth raise?
—Sir Henry Wotton; "On His Mistress, the Queen of Bohemia," 1624

## 2  Achievement

.1 Now that it's all over, what did you really do yesterday that's worth mentioning?
—Coleman Cox; *Perseverance*, 1922

.2 In his whole life man achieves nothing so great and so wonderful as what he achieved when he learned to talk.
—Otto Jespersen; *Language*, 1904

.3 A man destitute of courage, but boasting of his glorious achievements, imposes on strangers, but is the derision of those who know him.
—Phaedrus; *Fables*, c. 25 B.C.

.4 How my achievements mock me.
—William Shakespeare; *Troilus and Cressida*, 1602

.5 Let's talk sense to the American people. Let's tell them the truth, that there are no gains without pains.
—Adlai E. Stevenson; *Speech during Presidential Campaign*, 1952

## 3  Action

.1 Barking dogs seldom bite.
—Ancient Proverb

.2 The superior man is modest in speech, but surpassing in his actions.
—Confucius; *Analects*, c. 479 B.C.

.3 For as action follows speeches and votes in the order of time, so does it precede and rank before them in force.
—Demosthenes; *Olynthiaca*, c. 384–322 B.C.

.4 People who know how to act are never preachers.
—Ralph Waldo Emerson; *Journals*, 1832

.5 Thought is the blossom;
language the bud;
action the fruit behind it.
—Ralph Waldo Emerson; *Essays, First Series*, 1841

.6 What you do speaks so loud that I cannot hear what you say.
—Ralph Waldo Emerson; *Essays, Second Series*, 1844

.7 Great actions speak great minds.
—John Fletcher; *The Prophetess*, 1647

.8 Give me the ready hand rather than the ready tongue.
—Giuseppe Garibaldi; G.M. Trevelyan, *Garibaldi's Defense of the Roman Republic*, 1907–11

.9 Neither praise nor dispraise thyself, thy actions serve the turn.
—George Herbert; *Jacula Prudentum*, 1640–51

.10 Our actions are like rhymes, to which any one can fit such lines as he chooses.
—François de La Rochefoucauld; *Maximes*, 1678

.11 Sometimes … we have to do a thing in order to find out the reason for it. Sometimes our actions are questions, not answers.
—John Le Carre (David John Moore); *A Perfect Spy*, 1986

.12 Suit the action to the word, the word to the action.
—William Shakespeare; *Hamlet*, 1600–1

.13 Talkers are no good doers.
—William Shakespeare; *Richard III*, 1595

.14 Action is eloquence.
—William Shakespeare; *Coriolanus*, 1608

.15 Speech is the mirror of action.
—Solon; *Apothegm*, c. 600 B.C.

**3**

.16 Actions lie louder than words.
—Carolyn Wells; *Folly for the Wise*, "More Mixed Maxims," 1904

# 4 Actors

.1 Acting is a form of confession.
—Tallulah Bankhead; *Tallulah*, 1952

.2 An actor is a sculptor who carves in snow.
—Lawrence Barrett; Attributed

.3 For an actress to be a success she must have the face of Venus, the brains of Minerva, the grace of Terpsichore, the memory of Macaulay, the figure of Juno, and the hide of a rhinoceros.
—Ethel Barrymore; George Jean Nathan, *The Theatre in the Fifties*, 1953

.4 Actors should be overheard, not listened to, and the audience is fifty percent of the performance.
—Shirley Booth; *News Summaries*, 1954

.5 To be a successful actor … it is necessary to add some eccentricities and mystery to naturalness so that the audience can admire and puzzle over something different from itself.
—Louise Brooks; *Lulu In Hollywood*, 1982

.6 Never meddle with actors, for they are a favored class…. Remember that, as they are merry folk, who give pleasure, everyone favors and protects them.
—Miguel de Cervantes; *Don Quixote*, 1615

.7 Without wonder and insight, acting is just a trade. With it, it becomes creation.
—Bette Davis; *The Lonely Life*, 1962

.8 The question actors most often get asked is how they can bear saying the same things over and over again night after night, but God knows the answer to that is, don't we all anyway; we might as well get paid for it.
—Elaine Dundy; *The Dud Avocado*, 1958

.9 An actor is a kind of guy who if you ain't talking about him ain't listening.
—George Glass; Quoted in Bob Thomas, *Brando*, 1973
[Marlon Brando so liked to repeat this line, that many believe it to be original with him.]

.10 I've often heard it said that an actor can instruct a priest.
—Johann Wolfgang von Goethe; *Faust*, 1808

**4**

.11 On the stage he was natural, simple, affecting; 'Twas only that when he was off he was acting.
—Oliver Goldsmith; *Retaliation*, 1774
[Goldsmith refers to English actor David Garrick.]

.12 Good actors are good because of the things they can tell us without talking. When they are talking they are the slaves of the dramatist. It is what they can show the audience when they are not talking that reveals the fine actor.
—Cedric Hardwicke; *Theatre Arts*, 1958

.13 Life has its heroes and its villains; its soubrettes and its ingenues, and all roles may be acted well.
—Joseph Wood Krutch; *The Modern Temper*, 1929

.14 Acting requires absorption, but not self-absorption and, in the actor's mind, the question must always be "Why am I doing this?," not "How am I doing this?"
—Maureen Lipman; *How Was It for You?*, 1985

.15 "Ham," a poor and generally fatuous performer, was originally "ham fatter," a neophyte in the minstrel ranks, forced to sing "Ham Fat," an old ditty of the George Christy days.
—Edward B. Marks; *They All Sang*, 1919
[The use of "ham" to mean a tenth-rate actor goes back to Shakespeare's days.]

.16 Acting for me was the gospel, the love of the spoken word.
—Jeanne Moreau; Orianna Fallaci, *Limelighters*, 1963

.17 Acting is a masochistic form of exhibitionism. It is not quite the occupation of an adult.
—Laurence Olivier; Quoted in *Time Magazine*, 1978

.18 She ran the whole gamut of the emotions from A to B, and put some distance between herself and a more experienced colleague [Allison Skipworth] lest she catch acting from her.
—Dorothy Parker; Quoted in G. Carey, *Katharine Hepburn*, 1983
[Parker savages Katharine Hepburn's performance opening night of the play *The Lake*, 1933.]

.19 The art of acting consists of keeping the audience from coughing.
—Ralph Richardson; *New York Herald Tribune*, 1946

.20 Acting is to some extent a controlled dream. In one part of your consciousness it really and truly is happening. But, of course, to make it true for the audience all the time, the actor

## 4

must, at any rate some of the time, believe himself that it is really true.
—Ralph Richardson; Gary O'Connor, *Ralph Richardson: An Actor's Life*, 1975

.21 Every writer is a frustrated actor who recites his lines in the hidden auditorium of his skull.
—Rod Serling; *Vogue*, 1957

.22          Like a dull actor now,
I have forgot my part, and I am out,
Even to full disgrace.
—William Shakespeare; *Coriolanus*, 1608

.23 We're actors—we're the opposite of people!...
Think, in your head, now, think of the most ... private ... secret ... intimate thing you have ever done secure in the knowledge of its privacy... Are you thinking of it?... Well, I saw you do it!
—Tom Stoppard; *Rosencrantz and Guildenstern Are Dead*, 1967

.24 I don't like anything about acting. But I did very well by it. I learned the trade well. It's never been very demanding. It doesn't require much brainwork. Acting is not the noblest thing in the world, but there are things lower than acting—not many mind you—but politicians give you something to look down on from time to time.
—Spencer Tracy; Donald Deschner; *The Films of Spencer Tracy*, 1968

.25 I have often wondered, myself, when reading critiques in the papers, what would become of an actor if he tried to follow all the fearfully conflicting advice they contained.
—Mark Twain; *Early Tales and Sketches*, "Answers to Correspondents," 1864–65

.26 In the act of imitation there is the level of no-imitation. When the act of imitation is perfectly accomplished and the actor becomes the thing itself, the actor will no longer have the desire to imitate.
—Ze Ami; *Fushi kadem*, 1400–18

# 5 | Advice

.1 Bad counsel confounds the adviser.
—Aulus Gellius; *Noctes Atticae*, c. A.D. 150

.2 The worst men often give the best advice.
—P.J. Bailey; *Festus: A Village Feast*, 1839

.3 Advice given in the midst of a crowd is disgusting.
—J.L. Burckhardt; *Arabic Proverbs*, 1817

## 5

.4 Who cannot give good counsel? 'Tis cheap, it costs them nothing.
—Robert Burton; *The Anatomy of Melancholy*, 1621

.5 In matters of religion and matrimony, I never give any advice, because I will not have anybody's torments in this world or the next laid to my charge.
—Lord Chesterfield; *Letters to His Son*, Published 1774

.6 We ask advice, but mean approbation.
—C.C. Colton; *Lacon*, 1825

.7 A word to the wise ain't necessary—it's the stupid ones who need the advice.
—Bill Cosby; *Fat Albert's Survival Kit*, 1975

.8 He that will not be counselled can't be helped.
—Thomas Fuller II; *Gnomologia*, 1732

.9 Never give advice unless asked.
—German Proverb

.10 Know when to speak—for many times it brings Danger to give the best advice to kings.
—Robert Herrick; *Caution in Counsel*, 1648

.11 Whatever advice you give, be brief.
—Horace; *Ars Poetica*, c. 19 B.C.

.12 People who have what they want are fond of telling people who haven't what they want that they don't really want it.
—Ogden Nash; quoted in *Kansas City Times*, 1977

.13 It is bad advice that cannot be altered.
—Publilius Syrus; *Sententiae*, c. 1 B.C.

.14 It is not advisable ... to venture unsolicited opinions. You should spare yourself the embarrassing discovery of their exact value to your listener.
—Ayn Rand; *Atlas Shrugged*, 1957

.15 I pray thee, cease thy counsel,
Which falls into mine ears as profitless
As water in a sieve.
—William Shakespeare; *Much Ado About Nothing*, 1598

.16 How is it possible to expect that mankind will take advice, when they will not so much as take warning?
—Jonathan Swift; *Thoughts on Various Subjects*, 1727

.17 For you to ask advice on the rules of love is no better than to ask advice on the rules of madness.
—Terence; *Eunuchus*, c. 160 B.C.

## 5

.18 I have lived some thirty years on this planet, and I have yet to hear the first syllable of valuable or even earnest advice from my seniors.
—Henry David Thoreau; *Walden*; "Economy," 1854

.19 I have found the best way to give advice to your children is to find out what they want to do and then advise them to do it.
—Harry Truman; Quoted by Margaret Truman in TV program *Person to Person*, 1955

.20 He had only one vanity, he thought he could give advice better than any other person.
—Mark Twain; *The Man that Corrupted Hadleyburg and Other Stories and Essays*, 1900

.21 It is always a silly thing to give advice, but to give good advice is absolutely fatal.
—Oscar Wilde; *Portrait of Mr. W.H.*

# 6 Affectation

.1 Universities incline wits to sophistry and affectation.
—Francis Bacon; *Valerius Terminus of the Interpretation of Nature*, 1603

.2 The tenor's voice is spoilt by affectation,
And for the bass, the beast can only bellow.
—Lord Byron; *Don Juan*, 1819–24

.3 An affectation whatsoever in dress implies, in my mind, a flaw in the understanding.
—Lord Chesterfield; *Letters to His Son*, published 1774

.4 A man is never so ridiculous by those qualities that are his own, as by those that he affects to have.
—Benjamin Franklin; *Poor Richard's Almanack*, 1733–35

.5 Some degree of affectation is as necessary to the mind as dress is to the body; we must overact our part in some measure, in order to produce an effect at all.
—William Hazlitt; *Sketches and Essays*, "On Cant and Hypocrisy," 1839

.6 We all wear some disguise, make some professions, use some artifice, to set ourselves off as being better than we are; and yet it is not denied that we have some good intentions and praiseworthy qualities at bottom.
—William Hazlitt; *Sketches and Essays*, "On Cant and Hypocrisy," 1839

## 6

.7 Affectation is always to be distinguished from hypocrisy, as being the art of counterfeiting those qualities which we might with innocence and safety be known to want.
—Samuel Johnson; *The Rambler*, 1750–52

.8 There is pleasure in affecting affectation.
—Charles Lamb; *Detached Thoughts on Books and Reading*, 1822

.9 Affectation is an awkward and forced imitation of what should be genuine and easy, wanting the beauty that accompanies what is natural.
—John Locke; *Some Thoughts Concerning Education*, 1693

.10 Ignorance I can bear without emotion, but the affectation of learning gives me a fit of the spleen.
—Henry Mackenzie; *Julia De Roubigne*, 1777

.11 Can affected ignorance be ever graceful, or a proof of true delicacy.
—Samuel Richardson; *Sir Charles Grandison*, 1749

.12 Affectation is recognized even before it is clear what a man really affects.
—Artur Schopenhauer; "Aphorisms on the Wisdom of Life," 1851

.13 He is too picked, too spruce, too affected too odd, … too peregrinate, as I may call it.
—William Shakespeare; *Love's Labor's Lost*, 1594–95

.14 Affectation is a more terrible enemy to fine faces than the smallpox.
—Richard Steele; *The Spectator*, 1711–12

.15 Humor is odd, grotesque, and wild,
Only by affectation spoil'd;
'Tis nver by invention got,
Men have it when they know it not.
—Jonathan Swift; "To Mr. Delany," 1718

# 7 Allegory

.1 The virtue which we gather from a fable or an allegory, is like the health we get from hunting, as we are engaged in an agreeable pursuit that draws us on with pleasure, and makes us insensible of the fatigue that accompany it.
—Joseph Addison; *The Spectator*, 1711–12

.2 Allegories, when well chosen, are like so many tracts of light in a discourse, that makes everything about them clear and beautiful.
—Joseph Addison; *The Spectator*, 1711–12

.3 The fable is allegorical; its actions are natural, but its agents imaginary.—The tale is fictitious,

**7**

but not imaginary, for both its agents and actions are drawn from the passing scenes of life.—Tales are written mainly for amusement: fables for instruction.
—George Crabbe; *Tales*, 1812

.4 A naked lunch is natural to us,
we eat reality sandwiches.
But allegories are so much lettuce,
Don't hide the madness.
—Allen Ginsberg; "On Burroughs' Work," 1954

.5 A man's life of any worth is a continual allegory—and very few eyes can see the mystery of his life—a life like the scriptures, figurative.
—John Keats; *Letter to George and Georgiana Keats*, 1819

.6 Allegories are fine ornaments and good illustrations, but not proofs.
—Martin Luther; *Letter to Frederick, Elector of Saxony*, 1524

.7 Why, ever since Adam, who has got to the meaning of this great allegory—the world? Then we pygmies must be content to have our paper allegories but ill comprehended.
—Herman Melville; *Letter to Nathaniel Hawthorne*, 1851

.8 Socrates: A young person cannot judge what is allegorical and what is literal; anything that he receives into his mind at that age is likely to become indelible and unalterable; and therefore it is most important that the tales which the young first hear should be models of virtuous thoughts.
—Plato; *Republic*, c. 428 B.C.–347 B.C.

.9 But I cordially dislike allegory in all its manifestations, and always have done so since I grew old and wary enough to detect its presence. I much prefer history, true or feigned, with its varied applicability to the thought and experience of readers.
—J.R.R. Tolkien; *The Fellowship of the Ring*: Forward, 1954

**8** Analogy

.1 Though analogy is often misleading, it is the least misleading thing we have.
—Samuel Butler II; *Notebooks*, "Lord, What Is Man?," 1912

.2 The world is full of hopeful analogies and handsome dubious eggs called possibilities.
—George Eliot (Mary Ann Evans); *Middlemarch*, 1872

**8**

.3 Analogies, it is true, prove nothing, but they can make one feel more at home.
—Sigmund Freud; *New Introductory Lectures on Psychoanalysis*, "The Dissection of the Physical Personality," 1933, tr. James Strachey

.4 O Nature, and O soul of man! how far beyond all utterance are your linked analogies! not the smallest atom stirs or lives on manner, but has its cunning duplicate in mind.
—Herman Melville; *Moby Dick*, 1851

.5 Ultimately the authority of science will always depend on the evidence of sense and on the analogy of familiar objects and events.
—George Santayana; *Realms of Being*, 1937

.6 All perception of truth is the detection of an analogy.
—Henry David Thoreau; *Journal*, 1851

.7 Analogies the past may furnish, but patterns for the future never.
—Albion W. Tourgee; *Murvale Eastman*, 1889

.8 The first man who notices the analogy between a group of seven fishes and a group of seven days made a notable advance in the history of thought.
—Alfred North Whitehead; *Science and the Modern World*, 1925

.9 Important science is not just any similarity glimpsed for the first time. It offers analogies that map the gateways to unexplored terrain.
—Edward O. Wilson; *Biophilia*, 1984

**9** Anecdote

.1 A short anecdote is often a tall tale.
—American Proverb

.2 After a person dies, his biographers feel free to give him a glittering list of intimate friends. Anecdotes are so much tastier spiced with expensive names.
—Louise Brooks; *Lulu in Hollywood*, 1982

.3 When a man fell into his anecdotage it was a sign for him to retire from the world.
—Benjamin Disraeli; *Lothair*, 1870

.4 Anecdotes
The poor man's history.
—Rita Dove; *Grace Notes*, "The Gorge," 1989

.5 The boys of Eton must not be encouraged to dress themselves as swans or wild beasts for

**9**

the purpose of idle and illicit flirtation; but that can be the only effect of these deplorable anecdotes.
  —A.P. Herbert; *Misleading Classes*, 1935
  [Herbert comments on the tendency of the Classical Dictionary *to deprave and corrupt.*]

.6 But oh! the biggest muff afloat
Is he who takes to anecdote.
  —Henry Sambrooke Leigh; "Men I Dislike," 1869

.7 Anecdotes are portable; they can be carried home, they are disbursable at other tables.
  —George Meredith; *Diana of the Crossways*, 1885

.8 Surely an historian's object should not be to amaze his readers by a series of thrilling anecdotes ...
  —Polybius; *Histories*, c. 208 B.C.–126 B.C.

.9 That talk must be very well in hand and under great headway, that an anecdote thrown in front of will not pitch off the track and wreck.
  —Charles Dudley Warner; *Backlog Studies*, "Third Study," 1873

# 10 Angels

.1 Anyone who has ever seen an angel ever mistakes them for a ghost. Angels are remarkable for their warmth and light, and all who see them speak in awe of their iridescent and refulgent light, of brilliant colors, or else of the unbearable whiteness of their being. You are flooded with laughter, happiness.
  —Sophy Burnham; *A Book of Angels*, 1990

.2 The angels all were singing out of tune,
And hoarse with having little else to do,
Excepting to wind up the sun and moon,
Or curb a runaway young star or two.
  —Lord Byron; *The Vision of Judgement*, 1822

.3 When a man dies they who survive him ask what property he has left behind. The angel who bends over the dying man asks what good deeds he has sent before him.
  —The Koran, 610–632

.4 Writ in the climate of heaven, in the language spoken by angels.
  —Henry Wadsworth Longfellow; "The Children of the Lord's Supper," 1849

.5 Speak ye who best can tell, ye sons of light,
Angels, for ye behold him, and with songs

**10**

And choral symphonies, day without night,
Circle his throne rejoicing.
  —John Milton; *Paradise Lost*, 1665, published 1667

.6 I was talking to angels long before they got fashionable.... So maybe you don't believe in angels, that's all right, they don't care. They're not like Tinkerbell, you know, they don't depend on your faith to exist. A lot of people didn't believe the earth was round either, but that didn't make it any flatter.
  —Nancy Pickard; *Confession*, 1994

.7 O, speak again, bright angel; for thou art
As glorious to this night, being o'er my head,
As a winged messenger of heaven.
  —William Shakespeare; *Romeo and Juliet*, 1595

.8 Every time you hear a bell ring, it means that some angel just got his wings.
  —Philip Van Dorn Stern; *It's a Wonderful Life*, 1944
  [In the 1946 film version of Stern's story the line is delivered twice. First apprentice angel Henry Travers says it to James Stewart. It is repeated later, by Karolyn Grimes, playing Stewart's daughter Zuzu. The film was directed by Frank Capra with screenplay by Frances Goodrich, Albert Hackett, Capra and Jo Swerling.]

# 11 Animals

.1 ... the animal shall not be measured by man. In a world older and more complete than ours they move finished and complete, gifted with extensions of the senses we have lost or never attained, living by voices we shall never hear. They are not brethren, they are not underlings; they are other nations, caught with ourselves in the net of life and time.
  —Henry Beston; *The Outermost House*, 1928

.2 An animal's eyes have the power to speak a great language.
  —Martin Buber; *Ich und Du*, 1923, trans. by R.G. Smith as *I and Thou*, 1936

.3 Is it possible that animals have less worries since they live without speech?
  —Elias Canetti; *The Human Province*, Notes from 1942 to 1972, published, 1973

# 11

.4 Animals are such agreeable friends—they ask no questions, they pass no judgements.
—George Eliot; *Mr. Gilfil's Love Story*, 1857

.5 The dumbness in the eyes of animals is more touching than the speech of men, but the dumbness in the speech of men is more agonizing than the eyes of animals.
—Hindustan Proverb

.6 The key [to animal communication] is what the sound means. If you get two roars—one after sex and one during eating—is there anything in the acoustics of those roars that means something specific?
—Harry Hollien; *Language and Linguistics*, 1986

.7 Cats seem to go on the principle that it never does any harm to ask for what you want.
—Joseph Wood Krutch; *The Twelve Seasons*, "February," 1949

.8 Animals were once, for all of us, teachers. They instructed us in ways of being and perceiving that extended our imaginations, that were models for additional possibilities.
—Joan McIntyre; *Mind in the Waters*, 1974

.9 In the faculty of speech man exceeds the brute; but if thou utterest what is improper, the brute is superior.
—Sa'Di (Shaikh-'A-Din); *Gulistan*, 1258

.10 Animals hear about death for the first time when they die.
—Arthur Schopenhauer; *Parerga and Paralipomena*, 1851

.11 My music is best understood by children and animals.
—Igor Stravinsky; *The Observer*, 1961

.12 The best thing about animals is that they don't talk much.
—Thornton Wilder; *The Skin of Our Teeth*, 1942

.13 "Talking to animals" isn't a matter of words used, it is a matter of your thoughts, your expression, and above all the tone of your voice. A harsh voice from me can make my cows jump in terror. I shouted at old Queenie once and she got such a shock that she fell down just as if she'd been shot.
—Barbara Woodhouse; *Talking to Animals*, 1954

.14 Animals have long tongues but can't speak; men have short tongues and shouldn't speak.
—Yiddish Proverb

# 12 Answers

.1 A violent answer sets weapons of fight in motion; speak therefore with the sweetness of affection.
—Ani; *Teaching*, c. 4000 B.C.

.2 If you try to give an on-the-one-hand-or-the-other-hand answer, only one of the hands tends to get quoted.
—Alan Blinder; *Wall Street Journal*, 1995
[Blinder speaks of economic forecasting. Harry Truman once complained that if you asked an economist a question, he would give you such an answer. He observed that what he needed was a one-handed economist.]

.3 The liberally educated person is one who is able to resist the easy and preferred answers, not because he is obstinate but because he knows others worthy of consideration.
—Allan Bloom; *The Closing of the American Mind*, Preface, 1987

.4 Who answers speedily errs easily.
—Judah Bonsenyor; *Dichos y Sentencias*, c. 14th century

.5 The answer is very simple. I don't mean easy, but simple.
—William Faulkner; *Address to Graduating Class, Pine Manor Junior College*, 1953

.6 It's a good answer that knows when to stop.
—Italian Proverb

.7 There have been so many answers they have all been right.
—Deborah Keenan; *Household Wounds*, "Dialogue," 1981

.8 Never answer a question until it is asked.
—Vincent S. Lean; *Collectanea*, 1902–04

.9 She has the answer to everything and the solution to nothing.
—Oscar Levant; *Memoirs of an Amnesiac*, 1965

.10 We have learned the answers, all the answers: It is the question that we do not know.
—Archibald MacLeish; *The Hamlet of A. MacLeish*, 1928

.11 And what a dusty answer gets the soul
When hot for certainties in this our life!
—George Meredith; *Modern Love*, 1862

.12 A soft answer turneth away wrath; but grievous words stir up anger.
—Old Testament: Proverbs

**12**

.13 We will answer all things faithfully.
—William Shakespeare; *The Merchant of Venice*, 1596–97

.14 I can never give a "yes" or a "no." I don't believe everything in life can be settled by a monosyllable.
—Betty Smith; *Maggie—Now*, 1958

.15 Math was my worst subject because I could never persuade the teacher that my answers were meant ironically.
—Calvin Marshall Trillin; *New York Times*, 1990

.16 No answer is also an answer.
—Marcus Weissman-Chajes; *Hokma UMusar*, 1875

.17 For an answer which cannot be expressed the question too cannot be expressed.
—Ludwig Wittgenstein; *Tractatus Logico-Philsophicus*, 1921

.18 To every answer you can find a new question.
—Yiddish Proverb

# **13** Antiquity

.1 Antiquities are history defaced, or some remnants of history which have casually escaped the shipwreck of time.
—Francis Bacon; *Advancement of Learning*, 1605

.2 Woe betide the man who goes to antiquity for the study of anything other than ideal art, logic and general method!
—Charles Baudelaire; Letter published in *The Painter of Modern Life*, 1860

.3 Tell me the tales that to me were so dear,
Long, long ago—long, long ago.
—T.H. Bayly; "Long, Long Ago," 1832

.4 Time which antiquates antiquities, and hath an art to make dust of all things, hath yet spared these minor monuments.
—Sir Thomas Browne; *Hydriotaphia*, 1658

.5 Speak of the moderns without contempt and the ancients without idolatry; judge them all by their merits, and not by their age.
—Lord Chesterfield; *Letters to His Son*, published 1774

.6 O, to bring back the great Homeric time,
The simple manners and the deeds sublime:
When the wise Wanderer, often foiled by Fate,
Through the long furrow drove the ploughshare straight.
—Mortimer Collins: "Letter to Benjamin Disraeli," 1853

**13**

.7 I am not one who was born in the possession of knowledge, I am one who is fond of antiquity, and earnest in seeking it there.
—Confucius; *The Confucian Analects*, c. 479 B.C.

.8 But since men will believe more than they need;
And every man will make himself a creed,
In doubtful questions 'tis the safest way
To learn what unsuspected ancients say.
—John Dryden; *Fables Ancient and Modern*, 1700

.9 Antiquity. And everything to do with it, cliched and boring.
—Gustave Flaubert; *Bouvard et Pecuchet avec un choix des scenarios, du Sottisier, L'Album de la Marquise et Le Dictionnaire des idées recues*, published 1881

.10 The praise of ancient authors proceeds not from the reverence of the dead, but from the competition and mutual envy of the living.
—Thomas Hobbes; *Leviathan: Conclusion*, 1651

.11 Had the Greeks held novelty in such disdain as we, what work of ancient date would now exist?
—Horace; *Epistles*, 20—c. 8 B.C.

.12 You praise the fortune and manners of the men of old, and yet, if on a sudden some god were for taking you back to those days, you would refuse every time.
—Horace; *Satires*, c. 35 B.C.

.13 Asleep in lap of legends old.
—John Keats; *Lamia*, "The Eve of St. Agnes," 1820

.14 When my sonnet was rejected, I exclaimed, "Damn the age, I will write for Antiquity."
—Charles Lamb; Letter to B.W. Procter, 1829

.15 Antiquity surrenders, defeated by new things.
—Lucretius; *De Rerum Natura*, 98 B.C.–c.55 B.C.

.16 With weeping and with laughter
Still is the story told,
How well Horatius kept the bridge
In the brave days of old.
—Thomas Babington Macaulay; *Lays of Ancient Rome*, "Horatius," 1842

.17 Whoever saw old age which did not praise the past time, and blame the present?
—Michel de Montaigne; *Essays*, 1580

.18 In ancient times all things were cheap.
—Martin Parker; *Roxburghe Ballads*, 1841

## 13

.19 Antiquity is not always a mark of verity.
—John Ray; *English Proverbs*, 1670

.20 The ancient people perceived the world and themselves within that world as part of an ancient continuous story composed of innumerable bundles of other stories.
—Leslie Marmon Silko; Quoted in A. Pellowski *The World of Storytelling*, 1977

.21 We extol ancient things, regardless of our own age.
—Tacitus; *Annals*, A.D. 55–c. 120

.22 Ancient histories, as one of our wits has said, are but fables that have been agreed upon.
—Voltaire; *Jeannot et Colin*, 1764

.23 Antiquity is full of eulogies of another more remote antiquity.
—Voltaire; *Philosophical Dictionary*, "Ancients and Moderns," 1764

# 14 Aphorism

.1 But aphorisms, except they should be ridiculous, cannot be made but of the pith and heart of sciences; for discourse of illustration is cut off; recitals of examples are cut off; discourse of order and connexion is cut off; descriptions of practice are cut off. So there remaineth nothing to fill the aphorisms but some good quality of observation.
—Francis Bacon; *The Advancement of Learning*, 1605

.2 The delivering of knowledge in distinct and disjointed aphorisms doth leave the wit of man more free to turn and toss and to make use of that which is so delivered to make several purposes and applications.
—Francis Bacon; *Apothegms New and Old*, 1624

.3 Our life experience, fixed in aphorisms,
    stiffen into cold epigram,
Our heart's blood, as we write with it, turns
    to mere dull ink.
—F.H. Bradley; *Aphorisms*, 1930

.4 The hunter for aphorisms on human nature has to fish in muddy water, and he is even condemned to find much of his own mind.
—F.H. Bradley; *Appearance and Reality*, 1893

.5 The great aphorists read as if they had all known each other well.
—Elias Canetti; *The Human Province*, Notes from 1942 to 1972, published, 1973

.6 The healthy know not of their health, but only the sick: this is the Physician's Aphorism.
—Thomas Carlyle; *Chartism*, 1839

.7 A man of fashion never has recourse to proverbs and vulgar aphorisms.
—Lord Chesterfield; *Letters to His Son*, published in 1774

.8 The aphorisms of one generation become the clichés of the next.
—Lillian Day; *Ninon*, 1957

.9 It's the danger of the aphorism that it states too much in trying to be small.
—George Douglas; *The House with the Green Shutters*, 1901

.10 Aphorisms give you more for your time and money than any other literary form. Only the poem comes near to it, but then most good poems either start off from an aphorism or arrive at one… Aphorisms and epigrams are the corner-stones of literary art.
—Louis Dudek; Collected in *Notebooks 1960–1994*, 1994

.11 An Aphorism is the last link in a long chain of thought.
—Marie von Ebner-Eschenbach; *Aphorisms*, 1893

.12 Most of my writing consists of an attempt to translate aphorisms into continuous prose.
—Northrop Frye; Quoted in Richard Kostelanetz, "The Literature Professors' Literature Professor" in *The Michigan Quarterly Review*, 1978

.13 We all know how old farm folk especially delight in aphorisms of this kind, and in this respect, at all events, show much real wit.
—John Keble; *Lectures on Poetry*, 1835

.14 An aphorism is never exactly truthful. It is either a half-truth or a truth and a half.
—Karl Kraus; *Beim Wort genommen*, 1955, trans. Harry Zohn, *Half-Truths and One-and-a-Half Truths*, 1986

.15 One cannot dictate an aphorism to a typist. It would take far too long.
—Karl Kraus; *Beim Wort genommen*, 1955, trans. Harry Zohn, *Half-Truths and One-and-a-Half Truths*, 1986

.16 If you mean to know yourself, interline such of these aphorisms as affect you agreeably in reading, and set a mark to such as left a sense of uneasiness with you; and then show your copy to whom you please.
—Johann Kaspar Lavater; *Aphorisms on Man*, 1788

# 14

.17 An aphorism
should be
like a burr:
sting,
stick,
and leave
a little soreness
afterwards.
— Irving Layton; *The Whole Bloody Bird*,
"Aphs," 1969

.18 Modern Aphorists are accustomed to make
their phrases a play of wit, flashing antitheti-
cal brilliancies, rather than condensing profound truths.
— George Meredith; *The Ordeal of Richard
Feverel*, 1859

.19 There are aphorisms that, like airplanes, stay
up only while they are in motion.
— Vladimir Nabokov; *The Gift*, 1937

.20 Aphorisms are salted, not sugared, almonds at
Reason's feast.
— Logan Pearsall Smith; *Afterthoughts*,
1931

.21 It is the nature of aphoristic thinking to be always in a state of concluding; a bid to have
the final word is inherent in all powerful
phrase-making.
— Susan Sontag; "Writing Itself: on Roland
Barthes," introduction to *Barthes: Selected Writing*, 1982

# 15 Apology

.1 To apologize is to lay the foundation for a future offense.
— Ambrose Bierce; *Cynic's Word Book*, re-
named *The Devil's Dictionary*, 1906

.2 An apology for the devil: It must be remembered that we have only read one side of the
case. God has written all the books.
— Samuel Butler II; *The Notebooks of
Samuel Butler*, H. Jones, ed., 1912

.3 Never make a defence or apology before you
be accused.
— Charles I; *Letter to Lord Wentworth*, 1636

.4 A stiff apology is a second insult.
— Lord Chesterfield; *Letters to His Son*,
published 1774

.5 Apologies only account for that which they do
not alter.
— Benjamin Disraeli; *Endymion*, 1880

# 15

.6 No sensible person ever made an apology.
— Ralph Waldo Emerson; *Essays; Second
Series*, 1844

.7 Never contradict
Never explain
Never apologize
(Those are the secrets of a happy life!)
— Sir John Fisher; Letter to the *Times*,
1919
["Never apologize; it's a sign of weakness"
was John Wayne's frequent advice in *She
Wore a Yellow Ribbon* (1949)]

.8 Apologizing—a very desperate habit—one
that is rarely cured. Apology is only egotism
wrong side out.
— Oliver Wendell Holmes, Sr.; *The Professor at the Breakfast Table*, 1860

.9 An offense cannot be wiped out by an apology.
If it could, we would substitute apologies for
hangings.
— E.W. Howe; *The Story of a Country
Town*, 1883

.10 A general rule of etiquette is that one apologies for the unfortunate occurrence, but the
unthinkable is unmentionable.
— Judith Martin; *Miss Manners' Guide to
Excruciatingly Correct Behavior*, 1982

.11 The best apology against false accusers is silence and sufferance, and honest deeds set
against dishonest words.
— John Milton; *Apology for Smectymnuus*,
1642

.12 To him she hasted, in her face excuse
Came prologue, and apology too prompt.
— John Milton; *Paradise Lost*, 1665

.13 Apology is a lovely perfume, it can transform
the clumsiest moment into a gracious gift.
— Margaret Lee Runick; *Time for Each
Other*, 1944

.14 A woman springs a sudden reproach upon you
which provokes a hot retort—and then she will
presently ask you to apologize.
— Mark Twain; *Pudd'nhead Wilson's Calendar* 1894

.15 I do not trouble my spirit to vindicate itself
or to be understood,
I see that the elementary laws never
apologize.
— Walt Whitman; *Leaves of Grass*, "Song of
Myself," 1855

.16 It is a good rule in life never to apologize. The
right sort of people do not want apologies, and

## 15

the wrong sort take a mean advantage of them.
—P.G. Wodehouse; *The Man Upstairs*, 1914

# 16 Apothegms

.1  Certainly apothegms are of excellent use. They are pointed speeches. Cicero called them "salinas," salt pits, that you may extract salt out of and sprinkle where you will. They serve to be interlaced in continued speech. They serve to be recited upon occasion of themselves. They serve, if you take out the kernel of them and make them your own.
—Francis Bacon; *Apothegms: Introduction*, 1625

.2  Confucius may indeed be said to have anticipated the apothegm.
—Herbert Giles; *History of Chinese Literature*, late 19th century

.3  Few of the many wise apothegms which have been uttered have prevented a single foolish action.
—Thomas Babington Macaulay; *History of England*, 1848–49

.4  I … try to my fury to find quotations in my own books for Doubleday Doran's *Dictionary of Quotations*. It doesn't work. I am not given to apothegms. My gift is to explain things at length and convey atmosphere.
—Harold Nicolson; Diary entry, 1948

.5  A good apothegm is too hard for the tooth of time, and not worn away by all the centuries although it serves as food for every epoch.
—Freidrich Nietzsche; *Miscellaneous Maxims and Opinions*, 1879

# 17 Applause

.1  Applause: the echo of a platitude.
—Ambrose Bierce; *The Devil's Dictionary*, 1906

.2  The glorious meed of popular applause.
—Lord Byron; *Don Juan*, 1819–24

.3  Since well I've played my part, all clap your hands:
And from the stage dismiss me with applause.
—Caesar Augustus; A.D. 14
[Said to his friends as he lay dying.]

## 17

.4  Applause is the spur of noble minds, the end and aim of weak ones.
—C.C. Colton; *Lacon*, 1820

.5  O Popular Applause! what heart of man
Is proof against thy sweet, seducing charms?
—William Cowper; *The Task*, 1785

.6  The silence that accepts merit as the most natural thing in the world, is the highest applause.
—Ralph Waldo Emerson; *Essays: Second Series*, "Nature," 1844

.7  Just about the only interruption we don't object to is applause.
—Sydney J. Harris; *Clearing the Ground*, "Why I Don't Write About Politics," 1986

.8  The applause of a single human being is of great consequence.
—Samuel Johnson; Boswell's *Life of Samuel Johnson*, 1781

.9  Soul of the Age!
The applause, delight, the wonder of our stage!
—Ben Jonson; "To the Memory of My Beloved, The Author, Mr. William Shakespeare, and What He Hath Left Us," 1623

.10  Anybody's applause is better than nobody's.
—L.E. Landon; *Francesca Carrara*, 1834

.11  Applause that comes thundering with such force you might think the audience merely suffers the music as an excuse for its ovations.
—Griel Marcus; *Mystery Train*, "Elvis Presliad," 1976

.12  There is no reward so delightful, no pleasure so exquisite, as having one's work known and acclaimed by those whose applause confers honor.
—Molière; *Le Bourgeois Gentilhomme*. 1670

.13  There is no applause that so flatters a man as that which he wrings from unwilling throats.
—Ouida; *Pipistrello*, 1881

.14  From the very applause and glad approval of the people any talent can catch the flame.
—Ovid; *Epistalae ex Ponto*, c. 43 B.C.–A.D. 17

.15  Applause is a receipt, not a note of demand.
—Artur Schnabel; *Saturday Review of Literature*, 1951
[The Maestro doesn't feel he owes audiences' encores.]

.16  I would applaud thee to the very echo,
That should applaud again.
—William Shakespeare; *Macbeth*, 1606

**17**

.17 Applause: At the start of a lecture, it is a manifestation of faith. If it comes in the middle, a sign of hope. At the end, it is always charity.
—Fulton J. Sheen; *Peace of Soul*, 1949

.18 I sat down amid the cheers of the uncomprehending little audience.
—Logan Pearsall Smith; *All Trivia*, "The Coming of Fate," 1933

.19 Farewell, and give us your applause.
—Terence; *Eunuchus*, 161 B.C.
[At the end of his play the playwright asks the audience for their signs of appreciation.]

.20 I have been nourished by the sickly food Of popular applause.
—William Wordsworth; *The Borderers*, 1795–96

# 18 Argument

.1 Arguments out of pretty mouths are unanswerable
—Joseph Addison; *The Spectator*, 1711–12

.2 Simplicity ... makes the uneducated more effective than the educated when addressing popular audiences ... Educated men lay down broad general principles; uneducated men argue from common knowledge and draw obvious conclusions.
—Aristotle; *Rhetoric*, 384–322 B.C.

.3 An incisive argument is one which produces the greatest perplexity: for this is the one with the sharpest fang.
—Aristotle; *Rhetoric*, 384–322 B.C.

.4 Some in their discourse, desire rather commendation of wit, in being able to hold all arguments, than of judgement in discerning what is true.
—Francis Bacon; *Essays*: "Of Discourse," 1625

.5 It is not necessary to understand things in order to argue about them.
—Caron de Beaumarchais; *Mariage de Figaro*, 1784

.6 Use soft words and hard arguments.
—H.G. Bohn; *Handbook of Proverbs*, 1855

.7 Somebody has to have the last word. If not, every argument could be opposed by another and we'd never be done with it.
—Albert Camus; *The Fall*, 1956

**18**

.8 The best argument is that which seems merely an explanation.
—Dale Carnegie; *How to Win Friends and Influence People*, 1930

.9 I hate a quarrel because it interrupts an argument.
—G.K. Chesterton; *Generally Speaking*, 1928

.10 When you have no basis for an argument, abuse the plaintiff.
—Cicero; *Pro Flacco*, c. 51 B.C.

.11 The clearness of a cause is diminished by argument.
—Cicero; *De Natura Decorum*, c. 43 B.C.

.12 An argument derived from authority is the greatest force in law.
—Sir Edward Coke; *The First Part of the Institutes of the Laws of England*, "Commentary on Littleton," 1628

.13 Argument is a gift of Nature.
—Charles Dickens; *Barnaby Rudge*, 1841

.14 Never argue. In society nothing must be discussed; give only results.
—Benjamin Disraeli; *Lothair*, 1870

.15 I am bound to furnish my antagonists with arguments, but not with comprehension.
—Benjamin Disraeli; Attributed

.16 A knock-down argument; 'tis but a word and a blow.
—John Dryden; *Amphitryon*, 1690

.17 One hears very sensible things said on both sides.
—George Eliot; *Middlemarch*, 1872

.18 In all disputes, especially about trifles, that party who is most convinced they are right shall always surrender the victory.
—Henry Fielding; *Joseph Andrews*, 1742

.19 Argument seldom convinces anyone contrary to his inclinations.
—Thomas Fuller II; *Gnomologia*, 1732

.20 Her arguments are like elephants. They squash you flat.
—Rumer Godden; *The Battle of the Villa Fiorita*, 1963

.21 I find you want me to furnish you with argument and intellects too.
—Oliver Goldsmith; *The Vicar of Wakefield*, 1766

.22 Don't take the wrong side of an argument just because your opponent has taken the right side.
—Baltasar Gracian; *Handbook-Oracle and the Art of Prudence*, 1647

**18**

.23 Anger is never without an Argument, but seldom with a good one.
—Lord Halifax (George Savile); *Political, Moral and Miscellaneous Thoughts and Reflections*, 1687

.24 The best way I know of to win an argument is to start by being in the right.
—Lord Halisham (Quintin Hogg); *New York Times*, 1960

.25 Argument is powerless against bias or prejudice.
—Thomas Hardy; *A Pair of Blue Eyes*, 1873

.26 If you lose an argument, you can still call your opponent names.
—Elbert Hubbard; *Thousand and One Epigrams*, 1911

.27 You raise your voice when you should reinforce your argument.
—Samuel Johnson; Boswell's *Life of Johnson*, 1781

.28 We may convince others by our arguments; but we can only persuade them by their own.
—Joseph Joubert; *Pensees*, 1842

.29 Of two disputants the warmer is generally in the wrong.
—Charles Lamb; *Essays of Elia*," Popular Fallacies," 1823

.30 Specious and fantastic arrangements of words by which a man can prove a horse-chestnut to be a chestnut horse.
—Abraham Lincoln; *Speech*, 1858

.31 Do we never take up the wrong side of an argument, merely to enliven the conversation?
—Jean Marishall; *The History of Miss Clarinda Cathcart*, 1766

.32 Who is not apt, on occasion to assign a multitude of reasons when one will do? This is a sure sign of weakness in argument.
—Harriet Martineau; *Miscellanies*, "On the Art of Thinking," 1836

.33 My advice to an ordinary religious man … would be to avoid all arguments about religion, and especially about the existence of God.
—Thomas Merton; *The Seven Storey Mountain*, 1948

.34 Con was a thorn to brother Pro—
On Pro we often sicked him:
Whatever Pro would claim to know
Old Con would contradict him!
—Christopher Morley; "The Twins," 1924

.35 You have not converted a man because you have silenced him.
—John Morley; *On Compromise*, 1874

**18**

.36 Who over-refines his argument brings himself to grief.
—Petrarch; *To Laura in Life*, c. 1353

.37 Calling Socrates to an argument is calling cavalry into an open plain.
—Plato; *Theaetetus*, c. 428–c. 348 B.C.
["To challenge cavalry on the open plain" means to challenge a person to do exactly what he wishes to do. Cavalry are pleased to fight on an open plain.]

.38 In a heated argument we are apt to lose sight of the truth.
—Publilius Syrus; *Sententiae*, c 1. B.C.

.39 Discussion is an exchange of knowledge; argument is an exchange of ignorance.
—Robert Quillen; *Syndicated Editorial*, 1932

.40 There is no sense having an argument with a man so stupid he doesn't know you have the better of him.
—John W. Raper; *What the World Needs*, 1945

.41 Trust the man who hesitates in his speech and is quick and steady in action, but beware of long arguments and long beards.
—George Santayana; *Soliloquies in England*, "The British Character," 1922

.42 He draweth out the thread of his verbosity finer than the staple of his argument.
—William Shakespeare; *Love's Labor's Lost*, 1594–95

.43 You are fond of argument, and now you fancy that I am a bag full of arguments.
—Socrates; Plato, *Theaetetus*; c. 428–347 B.C.

.44 The first argument that is brought against every new proposal departing from conventional lines is nearly always that it is impracticable.
—Sir Josiah Charles Stamp; *Fundamental Principles of Taxation*, 1921

.45 Argument is the worst sort of conversation.
—Jonathan Swift; *Thoughts on Various Subjects*, 1711

.46 Arguments only confirm people in their own opinions.
—Booth Tarkington; *Looking Forward to the Great Adventure*, 1826

.47 I am not arguing with you—I am telling you.
—James McNeill Whistler; *The Gentle Art of Making Enemies*, 1890

## 18

.48 How beggarly appear arguments before a defiant deed.
—Walt Whitman; *Leaves of Grass*, "Broad-Axe Song," 1855

.49 Arguments are extremely vulgar, for everybody in good society holds exactly the same opinions.
—Oscar Wilde; *The Importance of Being Earnest*, 1895

.50 Arguments are to be avoided: they are always vulgar and often convincing.
—Oscar Wilde; *The Importance of Being Earnest*, 1895

## 19 Art and Artists

.1 True art selects and paraphrases, but seldom gives a verbatim translation.
—Thomas Bailey Aldrich; *Ponkapog Papers*, "Leaves from a Notebook," 1903

.2 The great artist is the simplifier.
—Henri-Frederic Amiel; *Journal*, 1851

.3 That Art remains the one way possible
Of speaking truth, to mouths like mine at least.
—Robert Browning; *The Ring and the Book*, 1868–69

.4 Art is a form of communication that insinuates. We expect the artist to have more to say than what he communicated and suspect that what he said was a subterfuge for hiding something.
—Nicolas Calas; *Art in the Age of Risk*, 1968

.5 The artistic temperament is a disease that afflicts amateurs. It is a disease which arises from men not having sufficient power of expression to utter and get rid of the element of art in their being.
—G.K. Chesterton; *Heretics*, 1905

.6 An artist cannot speak about his art any more than a plant can discuss horticulture.
—Jean Cocteau; *Newsweek*, 1955

.7 Language is an art, like brewing or baking. ... It certainly is not a true instinct, for every language has to be learnt.
—Charles Darwin; *Descent of Man*, 1871

.8 The divine art is the story.
—Isak Dinesen (Karen Blixen); *Out of Africa*, 1937

.9 The conscious utterance of thought, by speech or action, to any end, is Art.... From its first to its last works, Art is the spirit's voluntary

## 19

use and combination of things to serve its end.
—Ralph Waldo Emerson; *Society and Solitude* "Art," 1870

.10 He is a true enchanter, whose spell operates, not upon senses, but upon the imagination and the heart.
—Washington Irving; *The Sketch Book of Geoffrey Crayon, Gent*, "Stratford on Avon," 1819–20

.11 Art has an enemy called ignorance.
—Ben Jonson; *Every Man Out of His Humor*, 1600

.12 Never trust the artist. Trust the tale. The proper function of the critic is to save the tale from the artist who created it.
—D.H. Lawrence; *Studies in Classic American Literature*, 1924

.13 Art is the retelling of certain themes in a new light, making them accessible to the public of the moment.
—George Lucas; *New York Times*, 1988

.14 Every artist is an unhappy lover. And unhappy lovers want to tell their story.
—Iris Murdoch; *The Black Prince*, 1973

.15 Good art speaks truth, indeed is truth, perhaps the only truth.
—Iris Murdoch; *The Black Prince*, 1973

.16 Whoever learns the work by heart,
Or through the storyteller's art
Becomes acquainted;
His life by sad defeat—although
The king of heaven be his foe—
Is never tainted.
—*Panchatantra*, c. 400 A.D.

.17 Art is a lie that makes us realize the truth.
—Pablo Picasso; Quoted in Dore Ashton, *Picasso on Art*, 1972

.18 In oratory the greatest art is to hide art.
—Jonathan Swift; *Polite Conversation*, 1738

.19 There is no such thing as a dumb poet or a handless painter. The essence of an artist is that he should be articulate.
—Algernon Swinburne; *Essays and Studies*, "Matthew Arnold's New Poems," 1875

.20 An authentic work of art must start an argument between the artist and his audience.
—Rebecca West; *The Count and the Castle*, 1957

.21 When art communicates, a human experience

**19**

is actively offered and actively received. Below this activity threshold there can be no art.
—Raymond Williams; *The Long Revolution*, 1966

.22 Art is communication, imitation, mediation, reorganization, re-creation, innovation, interpretation, reconciliation, and above all, celebration.
—Adele Wiseman; *Old Woman at Play*, 1978

# 20 Assumption

.1 When you assume, you make an "ass" out of "u" and "me."
—Anonymous

.2 The ruling idea of any mind assumes the foreground of thought.
—Amelia Edith Barr; *The Maid of Maiden Lane*, 1900

.3 Assumptions are dangerous things.
—Agatha Christie; *Thirteen Problems*, "The Herb of Death," 1932

.4 It is too often assumed that a person's fancy is a person's real mind.
—Thomas Hardy; *The Hand of Ethelberta*, 1876

.5 We must never assume that which is incapable of proof.
—G.H. Lewes; *Physiology of Common Life*, 1859

.6 There is nothing more effectual in showing us the weakness of any habitual fallacy or assumption than to hear it sympathetically, through the ears, as it were, of a skeptic.
—Margaret Oliphant; *Phoebe Junior*, 1876

.7 Until we can understand the assumptions in which we are drenched we cannot know ourselves.
—Adrienne Rich; *On Lies, Secrets and Silence*, "When We Dead Awaken: Writing as Re-Vision," 1979

.8 That life is worth living is the most necessary of assumptions, and, were it not assumed, the most impossible of conclusions.
—George Santayana; *Life of Reason*, 1905–6

.9 Merely to adopt the most powerful assumption is no more than to assume the more powerful conclusion.
—Robert M. Solow; in the *Journal of Economic Perspectives*, 1994

**20**

.10 I celebrate myself, and sing myself,
And what I assume you shall assume...
—Walt Whitman; *Leaves of Grass*, "Song of Myself," 1855

# 21 Audience

.1 You cannot fool an audience.
—Marian Anderson; *My Lord, What a Morning*, 1956

.2 As half of a poem lies with the reader, so half of an actor's effect lies with his audience, and often then best half.
—Mary Anderson; *A Few Memories*, 1896

.3 It is this simplicity that makes the uneducated more effective than the educated when addressing popular audiences.
—Aristotle; *Rhetoric*, c. 384–322 B.C.

.4 I must have a London audience. I could never preach, but to the educated; to those who were capable of estimating my composition.
—Jane Austen; *Mansfield Park*, 1814

.5 All theories of what is a good play is, or how a good play should be written, are futile. A good play is a play which when acted upon the boards makes an audience interested and pleased. A play that fails in this is a bad play.
—Maurice Baring; *Have You Anything to Declare*, 1925

.6 The theatre must start to take its audience seriously. It must stop telling them stories they can understand.
—Howard Barker; *Guardian*, 1986

.7 The best audience is intelligent, well-educated and a little drunk.
—Alben W. Barkley; Attributed, Recalled at his death, 1956

.8 In the theatre the audience wants to be surprised—but by things they expect.
—Tristan Bernard; Attributed

.9 Your audience gives you everything you need. They tell you. There is no director who can direct you like an audience.
—Fanny Brice; Norman Katkov, *The Fabulous Fanny*, 1952

.10 Nothing is calculated to lose you audience sympathy as too many tears. Move your listeners all you can but let them do the crying.
—Ilka Chase; *Elephants Arrive at Half-Past Five*, 1963

.11 Audiences are always better pleased with a

smart retort, some joke or epigram than with any amount of reasoning.
—Charlotte Perkins Gilman; *The Living of Charlotte Perkins Gilman*, 1935

.12 As thoughts are frozen and utterance benumbed unless the speaker stand in some true relation with his audience, it may be pardonable to imagine that a friend, a kind and apprehensive, though not the closet friend, is listening to our talk; and then, a native reserve being thawed by their genial consciousness, we may prate of the circumstances that lie around us, and even of ourselves, but still keep the inmost Me behind its veil.
—Nathaniel Hawthorne; *The Scarlet Letter*, "Introductory," 1850

.13 In a Persian town they are to be met with in every street. In open sites, such as are often found near market-places, great sheds are erected, open on all sides and furnished with rows of steps capable of seating three or four hundred persons squatting on their heels. In front of the audience is a platform from whence a succession of storytellers repeat their stories to a succession of listeners from morning to night.
—Robert Heath; *Storytelling in All Ages*, 1885

.14 If for the sake of a crowded audience you do wish to hold a lecture, your ambition is no laudable one, and at least avoid all citations from the poets, for to quote them argues feeble industry.
—Hippocrates; *Aphorisms*, c. 460–400 B.C.

.15 Was there ever an audience anywhere, though there wasn't a pair of eyes in it brighter than pickled oysters, that didn't think it was distinguished for intelligence?
—Oliver Wendell Holmes; *Elsie Venner*, 1861

.16 If one talks to more than four people, it is an audience; and one cannot really think or exchange thoughts with an audience.
—Anne Morrow Lindbergh; *North to the Orient*, "The Paper and String of Life," 1935

.17 The audience is not the least important actor in the play and if it will not do its allotted share the play falls to pieces.
—W. Somerset Maugham; *The Summing Up*, 1938

.18 I can never remember being afraid of an audience. If the audience could do better, they'd be

up here on stage and I'd be out there watching them.
—Ethel Merman; Quoted in B. McDowell and H. Umlauf, *Woman's Almanac*, 1977

.19 Sport, as I have discovered, fosters international hostility and leads the audience, no doubt from boredom, to assault and do grievous bodily harm while watching it.
—John Mortimer; *Clinging to the Wreckage*, 1982

.20 What is the main problem of the actor? It is to keep the audience awake, and not let them go to sleep, then wake up and go home feeling they've wasted their money.
—Lord Laurence Olivier; Attributed

.21 I never failed to convince the audience that the best thing they could do was go away.
—Thomas Love Peacock; *Crotchet Castle*, 1831

.22 The audience ... is practically infallible, since there is no appeal from its verdict. It is a little like a supreme court composed of irresponsible minors.
—Agnes Repplier; *Times and Tendencies*, "Actor and Audience," 1931

.23 President Reagan is a rhetorical roundheels, as befits a politician seeking empathy with his audience.
—William Safire; *Language Maven Strikes Again*, 1990

.24 I know two kinds of audience only—one coughing and one not coughing.
—Artur Schnabel; *My Life and Music*, 1962

.25 The audience is the most revered member of the theater. Without an audience there is no theater. Every technique learned by the actor, every curtain, every flat on the stage, every careful analysis by the director, every coordinated scene, is for the entertainment of the audience. They are our guests, our evaluators, and the last spoke in the wheel which can then begin to roll. They make the performance meaningful.
—Viola Spolin; *Improvisation for the Theater*, 1963

.26 I know all about audiences. They believe everything you say—except when you are telling the truth.
—Mark Twain; Letter to *New York Times*, April 15, 1906

.27 To have great poets, there must be great audiences, too.
—Walt Whitman; *Notes Left Over*. "Ventures on an Old Theme," 1881

## 21

.28 The play was a great success, but the audience was a disaster.
—Oscar Wilde; Attributed
[It is said to be his reaction to a poor reception of his play *Lady Windermere's Fan*, 1892.]

.29 There is a sort of men who paint on paper men, birds, animals, insects and so on; the paper is like a scroll and is fixed between two wooden rollers three feet high; at one side these rollers are level with the paper, whilst they protrude at the other side. The man squats down on the ground and places the picture before him, unrolling one part after the other and turning it towards the spectators, whilst in the native language and in a loud voice he gives an explanation of every part; the spectators sit around and listen, laughing or crying according to what he tells them.
—Ying-yai Sheng-lan; 1416; Quoted in Ananada Coomarasaswamy, "Picture Showmen," *Indian Historical Quarterly*, 1929

## 22 Baby and Baby Talk

.1 It's the crying baby that gets the milk.
—American Proverb

.2 Have you not heard the poets tell
How came the dainty Baby Bell
Into this world of ours?
The gates of heaven were left ajar:…
Oh, earth was full of singing-birds
And opening springtime flowers,
When the dainty Baby Bell
Came to this world of ours.
—Thomas Bailey Aldrich; *The Bells*: "The Ballad of Baby Bell," 1855

.3 The most wonderful sound our ears can hear is the sound of a new-born baby.
—Anonymous
[It is an inscription in the room where Lyndon B. Johnson was born.]

.4 Here we have baby. It is composed of a bald head and a pair of lungs.
—Eugene Field; *The Tribune Primer*, 1882

.5 Some admiring what motives to mirth infants meet with in their silent and solitary smiles, have resolved (how truly I know not) that they converse with angels.
—Thomas Fuller I; *A Pisgah Sight of Palestine*, 1650

## 22

.6 The worst feature of a new baby is its mother's singing.
—Kin Hubbard; *Abe Martin's Wisecracks*, 1930

.7 Babies do not want to hear about babies; they like to be told of giants and castles, and of somewhat which can stretch and stimulate their little minds.
—Samuel Johnson; *Miscellanies*, 1784

.8 [Definition of a baby]: A loud noise at one end and no sense of responsibility at the other.
—Ronald Knox; Attributed

.9 Babies and language are the essential ingredients of civilization, and speakers of language no more know where it came from than babies know where they come from.
—Charlton Laird; *Miracle of Language*, 1953

.10 In came … a baby, eloquent as infancy usually is, and like most youthful orators, more easily heard than understood.
—L.E. Landon; *Romance and Reality*, 1831

.11 Hush-a-bye, baby, on the tree top,
When the wind blows, the cradle will rock;
When the bough breaks, the cradle will fall,
And down will come baby, cradle, and all.
—Nursery Rhyme
[Allegedly, this nursery rhyme was the first poem produced on American soil, by a youth who came over on the Mayflower.]

.12 Out of the mouth of babes and sucklings hast thou ordained strength.
—Old Testament: Psalms

.13 They lie flat on their noses at first in what appears to be a drunken slumber, then flat on their backs kicking and screaming, demanding impossibilities in a foreign language.
—Katherine Anne Porter; *The Days Before*, "Marriage Is Belonging," 1952

## 23 Ballads

.1 They'll cry "What expression is in it!"
Don't sing English ballads to me.
—T.H. Bayly; "Don't Sing English Ballads to Me," 1836

.2 And tell prose writers, stories are so stale,
That penny ballads have a better sale.
—Nicholas Breton; *Pasquil*, 1600

.3 The farmer's daughter hath soft brown hair;
(Butter and eggs and a pound of cheese)

**23**

And I met a ballad, I can't say where,
  Which wholly consisted of lines like these.
    —C.S. Calverley; *Ballad*, 1862

.4  Thespis, the first professor of our art,
  At country wakes, sung ballads from a cart.
    —John Dryden; *Sophonisba*: "Prologue,"
    1681

.5  If a man were permitted to make all the ballads, he need not care who should make the
  laws of a nation.
    —Andrew Fletcher of Saltoun; *Political
    Works*, 1706
    [Fletcher claims to have known a wise man
    of the stated opinion. It is believed that
    he refers to the Earl of Cromarty, but
    others feel the "very wise man" is John
    Selden.]

.6  Some people resemble ballads which are only
  sung for a certain time.
    —François de La Rochefoucauld; *Maxi-
    mes*, 1678

.7  Lately our poets loiter'd in green lanes,
  Contend to catch the ballads of the plains;
    —Walter Savage Landor; *Poems*, "Lately
    Our Poets," 1795

.8  A mist of memory broods and floats,
  The border waters flow;
  The air is full of ballad notes
  Borne out of long ago.
    —Andrew Lang; "Twilight on Tweed,"
    1880

.9  He flings a Romany ballad
  Out through his prison bars
  And deaf, he sings of nightingales
  Or blind, he sings of stars.
    —Mary Sinton Leitch; "The Poet," 1922

.10  I have a passion for ballads…. They are the
  gypsy-children of song, born under green
  hedgerows, in the leafy lanes and bypaths of
  literature.
    —Henry Wadsworth Longfellow; *Hyper-
    ion*, 1839

.11  For a ballad's a thing you expect to find lies in.
    —Samuel Lover; *Lyrics of Ireland*, "Paddy
    Blake's Echo," 1858

.12  And I have not ballads made on you all and
  sung to filthy tunes, let a cup of sack be my
  poison.
    —William Shakespeare; *I Henry IV*, 1596–97

.13  He sings several times faster than you'll tell
  money; he utters them as he had eaten ballads
  and all men's ear grew to his tunes.
    —William Shakespeare; *Winter's Tale*, 1609

**23**

.14  A famous man is Robin Hood,
  The English ballad-singer's joy.
    —William Wordsworth; *Rob Roy's Grave*,
    1803

# **24** Bards and Bardolatry

.1  There was singing and music together in accompaniment in presence of Helfdane's war-
  like chieftain; the harp was played and many
  a lay rehearsed, when Hrothgar's bard [scop]
  was to provide entertainment in hall along the
  meadbench…
    —Anonymous, "Beowulf," c. 800

.2  Hear the voice of the Bard!
  Who Present, Past & Future, sees,
  Whose ears have heard
  The Holy Word
  That walked among the ancient trees.
    —William Blake; *Songs of Experience*,
    "Hear the Voice of the Bard," 1794

.3  How have you left the ancient love
  That bards of old enjoyed in you!
  The languid strings do scarcely move!
  The sound is forced, the notes are few!
    —William Blake; *Songs of Innocence*, "To
    the Muses," 1789

.4  The high that proved to high, the heroic for
    earth too hard,
  The passion that left the ground to lose itself
    in the sky,
  Are music sent up to God by the lover and
    the bard;
  Enough that he heard it once; we shall hear
    it by and by.
    —Robert Browning; *Dramatis Personae*,
    "Abt Vogler," 1864

.5  Oh, the bards of olden days, blessed bards in
    song-craft skilled,
  Happy henchmen of the Muses, when the field
    was yet untilled.
    —Choerilus; Aristotle, *Rhetoric*, c. 330 B.C.

.6  Well! If the Bard was weather-wise, who
    made
  The grand old ballad of Sir Patrick Spence.
    —Samuel Taylor Coleridge; *Dejection: an
    Ode*, 1802

.7  The Eighth Commandment was not made for
  bards.
    —Samuel Taylor Coleridge; *Table Talk*,
    1833

**24**

.8 Wine to a gifted bard,
Is a mount that merrily races;
From watered wits
No good has ever grown.
    —Cratinus; *Fragment*, 6th–5th century
    B.C., Quoted by Nicaenetus, fl. 280 B.C.

.9 The Gauls are terrifying in their aspect and
their voices are deep and altogether harsh;
when they meet together they converge with
few words and riddles, hinting darkly at things
for the most part and using one word when
they mean another…. Among them are also to
be found lyric poets whom they call Bards.
These men sing to the accompaniment of instruments which are like lyres, and their song
may be either of praise or of obloquy.
    —Diodorus of Sicily; *Library of History*,
    c. 50 B.C. trans. by C.H. Oldfather

.10 Thy trivial harp will never please
Or fill my craving ear;
Its chords should ring as blows the breeze,
Free, preemptory, clear….
The kingly bard
Must smite the chords rudely and hard,
As with the hammer or with mace.
    —Ralph Waldo Emerson; "Merlin," Ap-
    pears in *An American Anthology, 1787–
    1900*, ed. Edmund Clarence Stedman,
    1900

.11 Olympian bards who sung
Divine ideas below,
Which always finds us young,
And always keep us so.
    —Ralph Waldo Emerson; "The Poet,"
    1844

.12 Among all men on the earth bards have a share
of honor and reverence, because the muse has
taught them songs and loves the race of bards.
    —Homer; *The Odyssey*, c. 700 B.C.

.13 But if you name me among the lyric bards,
I shall strike the stars with my exalted head.
    —Horace; *Odes*, c. 23–13 B.C.

.14 A humble bard, I fashion laborious songs.
    —Horace; *Odes*, c. 23–13 B.C.

.15 'Tis but a cot roofed in with straw, a hovel
    built of clay;
One door shuts out the snow and storm, one
    window greets the day.
And yet I stand within this room and hold all
    thrones in scorn,
For here, beneath this lowly thatch, love's
    sweetest bard was born.
    —R.G. Ingersoll; "The [Robert] Burns
    Cottage in Ayr," *The Works of Robert G.
    Ingersoll*, 1900

**24**

.16 O black and unknown bards of long ago,
How came your lips to touch the sacred fire?
How, in your darkness, did you come to
    know
The power and beauty of the minstrels' lyre?
    —James Weldon Johnson; *St. Peter Relates
    an Incident*, "O Black and Unknown
    Bards," 1917

.17 From Bard to Bard, the frigid Caution crept,
Till Declamation roar'd, while Passion slept.
    —Samuel Johnson; "Prologue Spoken by
    Mr. Garrick," 1747

.18 Bards of Passion and Mirth,
Ye have left your souls on earth!
Have ye souls in heaven too,
Double-lived in regions new?
    —John Keats; "Bards of Passion and of
    Mirth," c. 1637
    [Written on the blank page before Beau-
    mont and Fletcher's *The Fair Maid of the
    Inn*, and thus addressed to these bards in
    particular.]

.19 The bards sublime,
Whose distant footsteps echo
Through the corridors of time.
    —Henry Wadsworth Longfellow; *The
    Waif*, "The Day Is Done," 1844

.20 Poetry is the work of the bard and of the people who inspire him.
    —Jose Marti; *Poesia*, 1891

.21             I will tell you now
What never yet was heard in tale of song,
From old or modern bard, in hall or bower.
    —John Milton; *Comus*, 1634

.22 The bard whom pilfer'd pastorals renown,
Who turns a Persian tale for half-a-crown,
Just writes to make his barrenness appear,
And strains from hard-bound brains eight
lines a year.
    —Alexander Pope; "Epistle to Dr. Ar-
    buthnot," 1735

.23             Bold in thy applause.
The Bard shall scorn pedantic laws.
    —Sir Walter Scott; *Marmion*, 1808

.24 Among the Gallic peoples, generally speaking, there are three sets of men who are held
in exceptional honor: the Bards, the Vates and
the Druids. The Bards are singers and poets;
the Vates, diviners and natural philosophers;
while the Druids, in addition to natural philosophy, study also moral philosophy….
    —Strabo; *Geography*, c. 63 B.C.

# 24

.25 Portraits of famous bards and preachers, all fur
and wool from the squint to the kneecaps.
—Dylan Thomas; *Mrs. Organ Morgan*,
1952

.26 A bard here dwelt, more fat than bard
beseems,
Who, void of envy, guile, and lust of gain,
Of virtue still, and nature's pleasing themes,
Poured forth his unpremeditated strain.
—James Thomson; "The Castle of Indo-
lence," *Poems and Some Letters of James
Thomson*, ed. Anne Ridler, 1963
["A bard here dwelt" refers to Thomson
himself. He claims the following lines
were written by a friend, who may have
been Lord Lylleton.]

.27 I too have written songs. I too have heard the
shepherds call me bard. But I am incredulous
of them; I have the feeling that I cannot yet
compare with Varius or Cinna, but cackle like
a goose among melodious swans.
—Virgil; *Eclogues*, 37 B.C.

.28 Thus roving,
with their devices wander
the gleemen of men
through many lands,
their needs express,
words of thanks utter,
ever south or north
find one
knowing in songs,
liberal of gifts,
who before his court desires
his grandeur to exalt,
valorous deeds achieve,
until all departs
light and life together.
—Unknown: "Widsith," translated by
Benjamin Thorpe, 1962

.29 A great deal, my dear liege, depends
On having clever bards for friends.
What had Achilles been without his Homer?
A tailor, woollen-draper, or a comber!
—John Wolcot; "A Moral Reflection: To
George III," c. 1794

.30 Let other bards of angels sing,
Bright suns without a spot;
But thou art no such perfect thing:
Rejoice that thou art not!
—William Wordsworth; "To—," *Poetical
and Prose Works*, ed. W. Knight, 1896

# 25 Beauty

.1 Even in silence, beauty is eloquent beyond the
power of words.
—Anonymous; *Memoirs of an Oxford
Scholar*, 1756

.2 I must not say that thou wert true,
Yet let me say that thou wert fair;
And they that lovely face who view,
They will not ask if truth be there.
—Matthew Arnold; "Indifference"; *Poeti-
cal Works*, C.B. Tinker and H.F. Lowry,
eds. 1950

.3 It is a blind man's question to ask, why those
things are loved which are beautiful.
—H.G. Bohn; *Handbook of Proverbs*, 1855

.4 Who have not proved how feebly words
essay
To fix one spark of Beauty's heavenly ray?
—Lord Byron; "The Bride of Abydos,"
*Complete Poetical Works*, J.J. McGann,
ed., 1980–81

.5 Beauty is a talisman which works true miracles, and without a fable, transforms mankind.
—Hannah Cowley; *Who's the Dupe?*, 1779

.6 Beauty is part of the finished language by
which goodness speaks.
—George Eliot; *Romola*, 1862–63

.7 The ancients called beauty the flowering of
virtue.
—Ralph Waldo Emerson; *Essays, First Series* "Love," 1841

.8 Beauty is always the first to hear about the
sins of the world.
—Jean Giraudoux; *Pour Lucrece*, 1935,
translated as *Duel of Angels*, 1958

.9 When we speak of beauty, we're speaking of
something we're more or less indifferent to.
—Edith Hamilton; *The Greek Way*, 1930

.10 True beauty dwells on high: ours is a flame
But borrowed thence to light us thither.
Beauty and beauteous words should go
together.
—George Herbert; *The Temple, Sacred
Poems and Private Ejaculations*, "The
Forerunners," published posthumously,
1633

.11 Thou hast not wits to match thy beauty.
—Homer; *Odyssey*, c. 700 B.C.

.12 If a handsome woman allows that another
woman is beautiful, we may safely conclude
she excels herself.
—Jean de La Bruyere, *Characters*, 1688

**25**

.13 Then read from the treasured volume
   The poem of thy choice,
And lend to the rhyme of the poet
   The beauty of thy voice.
   —Henry Wadsworth Longfellow; *The Waif*, "The Day Is Done," 1844

.14 Beauty is the purgation of superfluities.
   —Michelangelo; Quoted by Ralph Waldo Emerson, *Conduct of Life*: "Beauty," 1860

.15 And beauty, making beautiful old rhyme.
   —William Shakespeare; *Sonnets*, 1609

.16 Beauty itself doth of itself persuade
The eyes of men without an orator.
   —William Shakespeare; *The Rape of Lucrece*, 1594

.17 All orators are dumb when beauty pleadeth.
   —William Shakespeare; *The Rape of Lucrece*, 1594

.18 Make me a beautiful word for doing things tomorrow, for that surely is a great and blessed invention.
   —George Bernard Shaw; *Back to Methuselah*, Preface, 1921

.19 I do not know which to prefer,
The beauty of inflections
Or the beauty of innuendoes,
The blackbird whistling
Or just after.
   —Wallace Stevens; *Harmonium*, "Thirteen Ways of Looking at the Blackbird," 1923

.20 Beauty is a mute deception.
   —Theocritus; *Apothegm*, c. 310–250 B.C.

.21 O Beauty, old yet ever new!
   Eternal Voice and Inward Word.
   —John Greenleaf Whittier; "The Shadow and the Light," 1831

.22 The stars of midnight shall be dear
To her; and she shall lend her ear
   In many a secret place
Where rivulets dance their wayward round,
And beauty born of murmuring sound
   Shall pass into her face.
   —William Wordsworth; "Three Years She Grew," 1799

# 26 Belief

.1 A liar will not be believed, even when he speaks the truth.
   —Aesop; *Fables*, c. 570 B.C.

.2 Don't believe that story true that ought to be true
   —American Proverb

**26**

.3 Myths are stories that everyone accepts but no one believes.
   —Anonymous

.4 Society moves by some degree of parricide, by which the children, on the whole, kill, if not their fathers, at least the beliefs of their fathers, and arrive at new beliefs. This is what progress is.
   —Sir Isaiah Berlin; BBC TV Program, *Men of Ideas*, 1978

.5 No iron chain, or outward force of any kind, could ever compel the soul of man to believe or disbelieve.
   —Thomas Carlyle; *Heroes and Hero-Worship*: "The Hero as Priest," 1841

.6 A man lives by believing something; not by debating and arguing about many things.
   —Thomas Carlyle; *Heroes and Hero-Worship*, 1841

.7 Sometimes I've believed as many as six impossible things before breakfast.
   —Lewis Carroll (Charles Dodgson); *Through the Looking Glass*, 1872

.8 Believe nothing rashly.
   —Cato; *Collectio Distichorum*: "Prologues," c. 234–149 B.C.

.9 As a first approximation, I define "belief" not as the object of believing (a dogma, a program, etc.) but as the subject's investment in a proposition, the act of saying it and considering it as true.
   —Michel de Certeau; *The Practice of Everyday Life*, 1974

.10 Nothing is so unbelievable that oratory cannot make it acceptable.
   —Cicero; *Apothegm*, c. 44 B.C.

.11 Such nonsense is often heard in the schools, but one does not have to believe everything one hears.
   —Cicero; *De Divianatione*, c. 44 B.C.

.12 Believe only half of what you see and nothing that you hear.
   —Dinah Mulock Craik; *A Woman's Thoughts*, c. 1880

.13 I make it a rule to believe only what I understand.
   —Benjamin Disraeli; *Infernal Marriage*, 1834

.14 All you've got to do is believe what you hear, and if you do that enough, after a while you'll hear what you believe.
   —Finley Peter Dunne; *Mr. Dooley Remembers: Some Observations by Mr. Dooley*, 1901

**26**

.15 I teach only the truth—but that shouldn't make you believe it.
—Martin Henry Fischer; *Fischerisms*, 1937

.16 Believing: it means believing in our own lies. And I can say that I am grateful that I got this lesson very early.
—Gunter Grass; *Omnibus*, BBC1, November 3, 1992

.17 The believer asks no questions, while no answer can satisfy the unbeliever.
—Hebrew Proverb

.18 I am always at a loss to know how much to believe of my own stories.
—Washington Irving; *Tales of a Traveller*, Preface, 1824

.19 We are inclined to believe those whom we do not know because they have never deceived us.
—Samuel Johnson; Boswell's *Life of Samuel Johnson*, published in 1791

.20 The word "belief" is a difficult thing for me. I don't *believe*. I must have reason for a certain hypothesis. Either I know a thing, and then I know it—I don't need to believe it.
—Carl Jung; interview, 1959, published in *Face to Face*, by Hugh Burnett, 1964

.21 The constant assertion of belief is an indication of fear.
—J. Krishnamurti; Speech, 1929

.22 There was one thing in which the adherents of the scriptures as well as the atheists were agreed: belief in the existence of beings with superhuman powers.
—Nelson Mandela; *Higher Than Hope*, 1991

.23 So far from making it a rule to believe a thing because you have heard it, you ought to believe nothing without putting yourself into the position as if you had never heard it.
—Blaise Pascal; *Pensees*, 1654–62

.24 Whoever has even once become notorious by base fraud, even if he speaks the truth, gains no belief.
—Phaedrus; *Fables*, c. 25 B.C.

.25 Do not believe what I tell you here any more than if it were some tale of a tub.
—Francois Rabelais; *Gargantua and Pantagruel*, 1532

.26 You can make an audience see nearly anything, if you yourself believe in it.
—Mary Renault; *The Mask of Apollo*, 1966

.27 When my love swears that she is made of truth,

**26**

I do believe her, though I know she lies.
—William Shakespeare; *Sonnets*, 1609

.28 The moment we want to believe something, we suddenly see all the arguments for it, and become blind to the arguments against it.
—George Bernard Shaw; *The Intelligent Woman's Guide to Socialism and Capitalism*, 1928

.29 I can believe anything provided it is incredible.
—Oscar Wilde; *The Picture of Dorian Gray*, 1891

# 27 Bible

.1 Holy Bible, book divine,
Precious treasure, thou art mine;
Mine to teach me whence I came,
Mine to teach me what I am.
—John Burton; "Holy Bible, Book Divine," c. 1st half of 18th century

.2 In the poorest cottage are Books: is one Book,
wherein for several thousands of years the spirit
of man has found light, and nourishment, and an
interpreting response to whatever is Deepest in him.
—Thomas Carlyle; "Corn-Law Rhymes," 1832

.3 The sacred book no longer suffers wrong,
Bound in the fetters of an unknown tongue,
But speaks with plainness art could never mend,
What simplest minds can soonest comprehend.
—William Cowper; *Poems*, "Hope," 1782

.4 One day at least in every week,
The sects of every kind
Their doctrines here are sure to seek,
And just as sure to find.
—Augustus De Morgan; *Matter to Spirit*: "Preface," c. 1860

.5 Observing the doctrine of Particular Election … and those who preached it up to make the Bible clash and contradict itself, by preaching somewhat like this: You can and you can't— You shall and you shan't—You will and you won't—And you will be damned if you do— And you will be damned if you don't.
—Lorenzo Dow; *Reflections on the Love of God*, 1836

## 27

.6    The Scriptures, though not everywhere
Free from corruption, or entire, or clear,
Are uncorrupt, sufficient, clear, entire
In all things which our needful faith require.
—John Dryden; *Religio Laici*, 1682

.7    Those who talk of the Bible as a "monument
of English prose" are merely admiring it as a
monument over the grave of Christianity.
—T.E. Eliot: *Religion and Literature*, 1935

.8    The Bible is like an old Cremona; it has been
played upon by the devotion of thousands of
years until every word and particle is public
and tunable.
—Ralph Waldo Emerson; *Letters and Social Aims*: "Quotations and Originality,"
1876

.9    The word unto the prophet spoken
Was writ on tables yet unbroken:
The word by seers or sibyls told,
In groves of oak, or fanes of gold,
Still floats upon the morning wind,
Still whispers to the willing mind.
—Ralph Waldo Emerson; "The Problem,"
*An American Anthology, 1787–1900*, Edmund Clarence Stedman, ed. 1900

.10    The Old Testament is the record of man's conviction that God speaks directly to men.
—Edith Hamilton; *Spokesmen for God*, 1949

.11    The first recorded versions of the creation
story, the flood, the resurrection story, the
story of Job, the story of the prodigal son are
to be found in ancient Egypt.
—W.J. Hardeman; *Kenet and the African
World View*, c. 1980

.12    All is not Gospel that thou does speak.
—John Heywood; *Proverbs*, 1546

.13    The English Bible—a book which if everything else in our language should perish,
would alone suffice to show the whole extent
of its beauty and power.
—Thomas Babington Macaulay; *Essays*:
"John Dryden," 1828

.14    Search the scriptures.
—New Testament; John

.15    But the word of the Lord endureth for ever.
—New Testament; I Peter

.16    Thy word is a lamp unto my feet, and a light
unto my path.
—Old Testament; Psalms

.17    The Bible is literature, not dogma.
—George Santayana; *Introduction to the
Ethics of Spinoza*, 1925

## 27

.18    We pick out a text here and there to make it
serve our turn; whereas, it we take it all together, and considered what went before and
what followed after, we should find it meant
no such thing.
—John Selden; *Table-Talk*: "Scripture,"
published 1689

.19    People who quoted the Scriptures in criticism
of others were terrible bores and usually they
misinterpreted the text. One could prove anything against anyone from the Bible.
—Muriel Spark; *The Mandelbaum Gate*,
1965

.20    The Scripture, in time of disputes, is like an
open town in time of war, which serves
indifferently the occasions of both parties.
—Jonathan Swift; *Thoughts on Various Subjects*, 1727

.21    It is full of interest. It has noble poetry in it;
and some clever fables; and some blood-drenched history; and some good morals; an a
wealth of obscenity; and upwards of a thousand lies.
—Mark Twain; "Letters From the Earth"
in *What is Man? and Other Philosophical
Writings*, Paul Baender, ed., 1973

.22    Jesus loves me! this I know,
For the Bible tells me so.
—Anna Warner; "The Love of Jesus," 1858

.23    The stars, that in their courses roll,
Have much instruction given;
But thy good Word informs my soul
How I may climb to heaven.
—Isaac Watts; *Hymns and Spiritual Songs*,
"The Excellency of the Bible," 1707

.24    The writers of the Bible were ... not cool historians but passionate prophets. They did not
select, organize, and judge facts the way a
modern university professor does.
—Herman Wouk; *This Is My God*, 1959

## 28 Boasting

.1    Brag in thy bravery like a cock beside his hen.
—Aeschylus; *Agamemnon*, c. 525–c. 456
B.C.

.2    Youth, thy words need an army.
—Agesilaus II; Plutarch, *Parallel Lives*, c.
62 B.C.
[To a youth talking boastfully.]

.3    Don't talk too big.
—Aristophanes; *The Frogs*, c. 448–c. 388
B.C.

**28**

.4 If they had not dragged me from under him, I should have killed him.
—Jacob Burckhardt; *Arabic Proverbs*, 1817

.5 Never be boastful; someone may pass who knew you as a child.
—S.G. Champion; *Racial Proverbs*, 1938
[It is a Chinese proverb.]

.6 Cunning egotism. If I cannot brag of knowing something, then I brag of not knowing it. At any rate, brag.
—Ralph Waldo Emerson; *Journals*, 1841

.7 You must stir it and stump it,
And blow your own trumpet,
Or trust me, you haven't a chance.
—W.S. Gilbert; *Ruddigore*, 1887

.8 Yet if thou sin in wine or wantoness,
Boast not thereof; nor make thy shame thy glory.
—George Herbert; *The Temple, Sacred Poems and Private Ejaculations*, "The Church-Porch," published posthumously, 1633

.9 No good thing is it to boast overweeningly.
—Homer; *Iliad*, c. 700 B.C.

.10 What will this boaster produce worthy of such inflated language?
—Horace; *Ars Poetica*, c. 19 B.C.

.11 Do not make yourself so big, you are not so small.
—Jewish Proverb

.12 So much are the modes of excellence settled by time and place, that men may be heard boasting in one street of that which they would anxiously conceal in another.
—Samuel Johnson; *The Rambler*, 1750–52

.13 Nothing ought more to humiliate men who have merited great praise than the care they still take to boast of little things.
—François de La Rochefoucauld; *Maximes*, 1678

.14 He who is self-approving does not shine. He who boasts has no merit. He who exalts himself does not rise high.
—Lao-Tsze; *Tao Te Ching (The Way of Virtue)*, c. 250 B.C., translated by Stephen Mitchell, 1988

.15 He that tooteth not his own horn, the same shall not be tooteth.
—John L. Lewis; Congressional Testimony, 1956

.16 The empty vessel giveth a greater sound than the full barrel.
—John Lyly; *Euphues, or the Anatomy of Wit*, 1578

**28**

.17 Boast not of what thou would'st have done but do
What thou would'st.
—John Milton; *Samson Agonistes*, 1671

.18 An untempted woman cannot boast of her chastity.
—Michel de Montaigne; *Essays*, 1580–95

.19 Boast not thyself of tomorrow, for thou knowest not what a day may bring forth.
—Old Testament; Proverbs

.20 A man destitute of courage, but boasting of his glorious achievements, imposes on strangers but is the derision of those who know him.
—Phaedrus; *Fables*, c. 25 B.C.

.21 He changes a fly into an elephant.
—John Ray; *English Proverbs*, 1670

.22 He who blushes at riding in a rattle-trap, will boast when he rides in style.
—Seneca; *Epistulae ad Lucilium*, c. 4 B.C.–c. A.D. 65

.23 Every braggart shall be found an ass.
—William Shakespeare; *All's Well That Ends Well*, 1604–5

.24 O, I could play the woman with mine eyes
And braggart with my tongue
—William Shakespeare; *Macbeth*, 1606

.25 You will soon find that a boaster and a liar are first cousins.
—C.H. Spurgeon; *John Ploughman's Talk*, 1869

.26 God is ashamed when the prosperous boast of his special favor.
—Rabindranath Tagore; "Stray Birds," 1916

.27 When boasting ends, there dignity begins.
—Edward Young; *Night Thoughts on Life, Death and Immortality*, 1742–45

# 29 Bon Mots

.1 A *bon mot* is a *bon mot* only because it represents a thing which everyone thinks, and expresses it in a lively, delicate, and new manner.
—Anonymous; *The Peregrinations of Jeremiah Grant*, 1763

.2 It is easier to be a lover than a husband, for the same reason that it is more difficult to show a ready wit all day long than to produce an occasional bon mot.
—Honore de Balzac; *The Physiology of Marriage*, 1829

**29**

.3 A happy citation of one *bon mot* is worth any ten offenses.
—Fanny Burney; *Camilla*, 1796

.4 It is not every man that can carry a bon mot.
—William Fitzherbert; Quoted in Boswell's *Life of Johnson*, published in 1791

.5 Genuine bon mots surprise those from whose lips they fall, no less than they do those who listen to them.
—Joseph Joubert; *Pensees*, 1842

.6 A bon mot often runs the risk of being thrown away when quoted as the speaker's own.
—Jean de La Bruyere; *Les Caractères ou les moeurs de ce siècle:* "De la Société et la Conversation," 1688

.7 He liked those literary cooks
Who skim the cream of others' books;
And ruin half an author's graces
By plucking bon-mots from their places.
—Hannah More; *The Bas Bleu*, "Florio," 1784

.8 Her acidic bon mots were the olives of the martini age.
—Unknown, *Vanity Fair*, June 1986
[The reference is to Dorothy Parker.]

# **30** Books

.1 Books are the legacies that a great genius leaves to mankind, which are delivered down from generation to generation, as presents to the posterity of those who are yet unborn.
—Joseph Addison; *The Spectator*, 1711–12

.2 Books will speak plain when counselors blanch.
—Francis Bacon; *Essays*: "Of Counsel," 1625

.3 A book is good company. It is full of conversation without loquacity. It comes to your longing with full instruction, but pursues you never.
—Henry Ward Beecher; *Proverbs from Plymouth Pulpit*, 1887

.4 I take the view, and always have done, that if you cannot say what you have to say in twenty minutes, you should go away and write a book about it.
—Lord Brabazon; *Speech*, House of Lords, 1955

.5 "What is the use of a book," thought Alice, "without pictures or conversations."
—Lewis Carroll; *Alice's Adventures in Wonderland*, 1865

**30**

.6 Next to the author of a good book is the man who makes a good commentary on it.
—Chang Chao; *Yumengying*, c. A.D. 180

.7 No, it'll not do just to read the good old tales out of a book. You've got to tell 'em to make 'em go right.
—Richard Chase; *Grandfather Tales*, 1948

.8 Books do not exhaust words; words do not exhaust thoughts.
—Chinese Proverb

.9 Some read to think,—these are rare; some to write,—these are common; and some to talk—and these form the great majority.
—C.C. Colton; *Lacon*, 1820–25

.10 Books! Bottled chatter! Things that some other simian has formerly said.
—Clarence Day; *Life with Father*, 1935

.11 The reading of all good books is like conversation with the finest men of past centuries.
—Rene Descartes; *Discourse on Method*, 1637

.12 It would be a very big book that contained all the maybes uttered in a day.
—French Proverb

.13 The volumes of antiquity, like medals, may very well serve to amuse the curious; but the works of the moderns, like the current coin of a kingdom, are much better for immediate use.
—Oliver Goldsmith; *The Citizen of the World*, 1762

.14 But certain things have seemed to me to be here as I heard the tongues of those who had speech, and listened to the lips of books.
—Zora Neale Hurston; *Dust Tracks on a Road*, 1942

.15 The memory of having been read to is a solace one carries through adulthood. It can wash over a multitude of parental sins.
—Kathleen Rockwell Lawrence; *The Boys I Didn't Kiss*, 1990

.16 I do not speak wholly without book.
—John Locke; *Toleration*, 1693

.17 His work contains nothing worth quoting; and a book that furnishes no quotations is, *me judice*, no book—it's a plaything.
—Thomas Love Peacock; *Crotchet Castle*, 1831

.18 The lesson intended by an author is hardly ever the lesson the world chooses to learn from his book.
—George Bernard Shaw; *Man and Superman*: "Epistle Dedicatory," 1903

# 30

.19 Books, like proverbs, receive their chief value from the stamp and esteem of ages through which they have passed.
—William Temple; *Ancient and Modern Learning*, 1692

.20 And hold high converse with the mighty dead.
—James Thomson; *Seasons*: "Winter," 1746
[That is, to read books.]

.21 It had been startling and disappointing to me to find out that story books had been written by *people*, that books were not natural wonders, coming up of themselves like grass.
—Eudora Welty; *One Writer's Beginnings*, 1984

# 31 | Boredom and Bores

.1 The man who suspects his own tediousness is yet to be born.
—Thomas Bailey Aldrich; *Ponkapog Papers*, "Leaves from a Notebook," 1903

.2 Perhaps the world's second worst crime is boredom; the first is being a bore.
—Cecil Beaton; *Time Magazine*, 1980

.3 Any subject can be made interesting, and therefore any subject can be made boring.
—Hilaire Belloc; *On Everything*, 1909

.4 Bore: a person who talks when you wish him to listen.
—Ambrose Bierce; *The Devil's Dictionary*, 1911

.5 Bores: People who talk of themselves, when you are thinking only of yourself.
—Countess of Blessington; *Desultory Thoughts and Reflections*, 1839

.6 There are those who need more time to tell than it took the event to happen. These are the farmer-generals of boredom.
—Ludwig Boerne; *Aus Meinem Tagebuche*, 1830

.7 There are few wild beasts more to be dreaded than a communicative man having nothing to communicate.
—Christian Nestell Bovee; *Authors*, Late 19th century

.8 Everyone is a bore to someone. That is unimportant. The thing is to avoid being a bore to oneself.
—Gerald Brenan; *Thoughts in a Dry Season*, 1978

# 31

.9 Society is now one polished horde,
Formed of two mighty tribes, the *Bores* and *Bored*.
—Lord Byron; *Don Juan*, 1819–24

.10 A yawn is a silent shout.
—G.K. Chesterton; *The Wisdom of Father Brown*, 1914

.11 Every improvement in communication makes the bore unbearable.
—Frank Moore Colby; *The Colby Essays*, 1926

.12 I wanted to be bored to death, as good a way to go as any.
—Peter De Vries; *Comfort Me with Apples*, 1956

.13 The true bore is that man who thinks the world is only interested in one subject, because he himself can only comprehend one.
—Benjamin Disraeli; *Vivian Grey*, 1826–27

.14 The bore is usually considered a harmless creature, or of that class of irrational bipeds who hurt only themselves.
—Maria Edgeworth; *Thoughts on Bores*, 1826

.15 Every hero becomes a bore at last.
—Ralph Waldo Emerson; *Representative Men*, 1850

.16 Man is the only animal that can be bored.
—Erich Fromm; *The Sane Society*, 1955

.17 To be bored by essentials is characteristic of small minds.
—Ralph Underwood Johnson; *Poems of Fifty Years*, Preface, 1930

.18 We can forgive those who bore us, but we cannot forgive those who find us boring.
—François de La Rochefoucauld; *Maximes*, 1678

.19 We are nearly always most bored by those whom we bore.
—François de La Rochefoucauld; *Maximes*, 1678

.20 A bore is a man who spends too much time talking about himself that you can't talk about yourself.
—Melville D. Landon; *His Sayings and Doings*, 1875

.21 Virtuous people often revenge themselves for the constraints to which they submit by the boredom which they inspire.
—Gustave Le Bon; *Aphorisms du temps present*, 1913

## 31

.22 It is as cruel to bore a child as to beat him.
—George B. Leonard; *Education and Ecstasy*, 1968

.23 There was one feudal custom worth keeping, at least,
Roasted bores made a part of each well-ordered feast.
—J.R. Lowell; "A Fable for Critics," 1848

.24 A bore is simply a nonentity who resents his humble lot in life, and seeks satisfaction for his wounded ego by forcing himself on his betters.
—H.L. Mencken; "Minority Reports": Collected in *Notebooks*, 1956

.25 The capacity of human beings to bore one another seems to be vastly greater than that of any other animals. Some of their most esteemed inventions have no apparent purpose, for example, the dinner party of more than two, the epic poem, and the science of metaphysics.
—H.L. Mencken; "Minority Reports": Collected in *Notebooks*, 1956

.26 Boredom, after all, is a form of criticism.
—William Phillips; *A Sense of Present*, 1967

.27 A scholar knows no boredom.
—Jean Paul Richter; *Hesperus VIII*, 1795

.28 Boredom is a vital problem for the moralist, since at least half the sins of mankind are caused by the fear of it.
—Bertrand Russell; *The Conquest of Happiness*, 1930

.29 Boredom is a condition which makes men as susceptible to disgust and irritation as headache makes them to noise and glare.
—George Bernard Shaw; *Three Plays for Puritans*: Preface, 1901

.30 If you want to bore an Irishman, play him an Irish melody, or introduce him to another Irishman.
—George Bernard Shaw; Quoted in Michael Holroyd, *Shaw*, 1989

.31 I am one of those unhappy persons who inspire bores to the highest flights of their art.
—Edith Sitwell; Quoted in Elizabeth Salter, *The Last Years of a Rebel*, 1967

.32 Boredom is just the reverse side of fascination: both depend on being outside rather than inside a situation, and one leads to the other.
—Susan Sontag; on *Photography*, "America Seen Through Photography, Darkly," 1977

## 31

.33 A bore is a man, who when you ask him how he is, tells you.
—Bert Leston Taylor; *The So-Called Human Race*, 1922

.34 Somebody's boring me ... I think it's me.
—Dylan Thomas; Quoted in Rayner Heppenstall, *Four Absentees*, 1960

.35 He is an old bore. Even the grave yawns for him.
—Herbert Beerbohm Tree; Quoted in Hesketh Pearson, *Beerbohm-Tree*, 1956 [Tree refers to Israel Zangwill.]

.36 A healthy male adult bore consumes each year one and a half times his own weight in other people's patience.
—John Updike; *Assorted Prose*: "Confessions of a Wild Bore," 1965

.37 The secret of being a bore is to tell everything.
—Voltaire; *Sept discours en vers sur l'homme*, 1738

## 32 Boys

.1 Speak roughly to your little boy,
And beat him when he sneezes:
He only does it to annoy,
Because he knows it teases.
—Lewis Carroll; *Alice's Adventures in Wonderland*, 1865

.2 There is nothing so aggravating as a fresh boy who is too old to ignore and too young to kick.
—Kin Hubbard; *Abe Martin's Wisecracks*, 1930

.3 When I was a beggarly boy
And lived in a cellar damp,
I had not a friend nor a toy,
But I had Aladdin's lamp.
—J.R. Lowell; *Under the Willows and Other Poems*, "Aladdin," 1868

.4 Has any child psychologist ever noted that the talk of small boys among themselves consists almost entirely of boasting.
—H.L. Mencken; "Minority Reports": Collected in *Notebooks*, 1956

.5 The smiles and tears of boyhood's years;
The words of love then spoken.
—Thomas Moore; *National Airs*, "Oft in the Stilly Night," 1815

.6 What are little boys made of?
Frogs and snails
And puppy-dogs' tails,
That's what little boys are made of.
—Nursery Rhyme

**32**

.7  My eyes are dim with childish tears,
    My heart is idly stirred,
    For the same sound is in my ears
    Which in those days I heard.
      —William Wordsworth; "The Fountain,"
      1800

# 33 Brain

.1  Brain, n. An apparatus with which we think
    that we think.
      —Ambrose Bierce; *The Devil's Dictionary*,
      1906

.2  A brain is worth little without a tongue.
      —French Proverb

.3  The left hemisphere became the one to have
    if you were having only one.
      —Howard Gardner; *The Shattered Mind*,
      1975

.4  Half a brain is enough for him who says little.
      —Italian Proverb

.5  There are three kinds of brains; one under-
    stands of itself, another can be taught to un-
    derstand, and the third can neither understand
    of itself or be taught to understand.
      —Niccolo Machiavelli; *The Prince*, 1513

.6  I am a Bear of Very Little Brain, and long
    words Bother Me.
      —A.A. Milne; *Winnie-the-Pooh*, 1926

.7  O that such an imposing appearance should
    have no brain!
      —Phaedrus; *Fables*, c. 25 B.C.

.8  A man's brain is stored powder; it cannot
    touch itself off; the fire must come from out-
    side.
      —Mark Twain; *Mark Twain's Notebooks*,
      Albert Bigelow Paine, ed. 1935

# 34 Brevity

.1  I will discover it with laconic brevity.
      —Francis Beaumont and John Fletcher;
      *The Little French Lawyer*, printed 1647

.2  Say what you will in two
    Words and get through.
    Long, frilly
    Palaver is silly.
      —Marie-Francise-Catherine de Beauveau;
      "Strong Feelings" in Joanna Bankier and
      Deirdre Lashgari, eds. *Women Poets of
      the World*, 1991

**34**

.3  Least said is soonest disavowed.
      —Ambrose Bierce; *The Devil's Dictionary*,
      "Saw," 1906

.4  There's a great power in words, if you don't
    hitch too many of them together.
      —Josh Billings; *Josh Billing's Wit and
      Humor*, 1874

.5  For brevity is very good,
    Where we are, or are not, understood.
      —Samuel Butler I; *Hudibras*, 1663–64

.6  Talk often, but not long: in that case, if you do
    not please, at least you are sure not to tire your
    hearers.
      —Lord Chesterfield; Letter to his son, Oc-
      tober 19, 1748

.7  Brevity is the best recommendation of speech,
    whether in a senator or an orator.
      —Cicero; *De Natura Deorum*, c. 45 B.C.

.8  A good discourse is that from which nothing
    can be retrenched without cutting into the
    quick.
      —St. Francis De Sales; *On Eloquence*, c.
      1602

.9  Speaking much and speaking well are not the
    same thing.... One is almost bound to fall into
    error if one tries to say a great deal.
      —Desiderius Erasmus; *Adages*, 1500

.10  The more you say, the less people remember.
     The fewer the words, the greater the profit.
      —Francois Fenelon; *Dialogues sur l'Elo-
      quence*, c. 1697

.11  When you've got a thing to say,
     Say it! Don't take half a day.
     When your tale's got little in it,
     Crowd the whole thing in a minute!
      —Joel Chandler Harris; *Advice to Writers
      for the Daily Press*, c. 1907

.12  Few were his words, but wonderfully clear.
      —Homer; *The Iliad*, c. 700 B.C.

.13  Every word that is superfluous flows away
     from the full mind.
      —Horace; *Ars Poetica*, c. 19 B.C.

.14  The fewer thy words the fewer thine errors.
      —Solomon Ibn Gabriol; *Choice of Pearls*,
      c. 1050

.15  The fewer the words, the better prayer.
      —Martin Luther; *Of Good Works*, 1520

.16  It is my ambition to say in sentences what
     other men say in whole books—what other
     men do not say in whole books.
      —Friedrich Nietzsche; *The Twilight of the
      Idols*, 1889, trans. by R.J. Hollingdale

**34**

.17 Let thy speech be short, comprehending much in few words.
—Old Testament: Apocrypha: Ecclesiasticus

.18 It is a foolish thing to make a long prologue, and to be short in the story itself.
—Old Testament; Apocrypha: II Maccabees

.19 To make a long story short, I'll tell you in one word.
—Pacuvius; *Ilipna*, c. 160 B.C.

.20 Brevity is the Soul of Lingerie, as the Petticoat said to the Chemise.
—Dorothy Parker; Quoted in Alexander Woollcott, *While Rome Burns*, "Our Mrs. Parker," 1934

.21 In the eloquence of the bar, nothing pleases so much as brevity.
—Pliny the Younger; *Epistles*, c. 200 B.C.

.22 There are things which don't deserve to be said briefly.
—Jean Rostand; *Thoughts of a Biologist*, 1939

.23 As man is now constituted, to be brief is almost a condition of being inspired.
—George Santayana; *Little Essays*, 1920

.24 Therefore, since brevity is the soul of wit,
And tediousness the limbs and outward flourishes,
I will be brief.
—William Shakespeare; *Hamlet*, 1600–1

.25 Give good news in as few words as possible.
—William Gilmore Simms; *The Scout*, 1854

.26 Faith! he must make his stories shorter
Or change his comrades once a quarter.
—Jonathan Swift; *Verses on the Death of Dr. Swift*, 1731

.27 Drop it and come to the point.
—Terence; *Heauton Timorumenos*, 163 B.C.

.28 That's what it means—in a nutshell.
—Lee Thayer; *Persons Unknown*, 1941

.29 Not that the story need be long, but it will take a long while to make it short.
—Henry David Thoreau; *Letter to a Friend*, 1857

# 35 Business

.1 Talk of nothing but business and dispatch that business quickly.

**35**

—Aldus; T.F. Dibdin, *Introduction to the Knowledge of Rare and Valuable Editions of the Greek and Latin Classics*, 1802
[The sentiment appeared on a placard on the door of Aldus' printing office.]

.2 Business tomorrow.
—Archias; Plutarch, *Parallel Lives*: Pelopidas," c. 46–c. 120 A.D. translated by Thomas North, 1759
[According to Plutarch this is the reaction of Archias to a messenger who brought him a letter he said was on a serious matter and should be read immediately. Not wishing to interrupt his banquet, he slipped the message unread under the pillow of his couch. The message was a warning that there was a plot to assassinate him. Sure enough, during the banquet assassins arrived and killed him. The moral, it seems, is that one should never put off attending to business.]

.3 They knew he "meant business," though his words were few.
—G.P. Burnham; *Three Years*, 1875

.4 Business is other people's money.
—Delphine de Girardin; *Marguerite*, 1852

.5 Business today consists in persuading crowds.
—Gerald Stanley Lee; *Crowds*, 1913

.6 He [the businessman] is the only man who is for ever apologizing for his occupation.
—H.L. Mencken; Attributed

.7 You start by saying no to requests. Then if you have to go to yes, OK. But if you start with yes, you can't go to no.
—Mildred Perlman; *New York Times*, 1975

.8 There are two fools in every market; one asks too little, one asks too much.
—Russian Proverb

.9 Everyone lives by selling something.
—Robert Louis Stevenson; "Beggars," 1888, originally published in *Scribner's Magazine*

.10 The single most dangerous word to be spoken in business is "no." The second most dangerous word is "yes." It is possible to avoid saying either.
—Lois Wyse; *Company Manners*, 1987

# 36 Candor

.1 Gracious to all, to none subservient,
Without offence he spake the word he
meant.
—T.B. Aldrich; *The Stillwater Tragedy*,
1880

.2 Affectation, or coldness, or stupid, coarse-
minded misapprehension of one's meaning are
the usual rewards of candor.
—Charlotte Bronte; *Jane Eyre*, 1847

.3 There is no man so friendless but what he can
find a friend sincere enough to tell him disagreeable truths.
—Edward Bulwer-Lytton; *What Will He
Do With It?*, 1857

.4 I was so free with him as not to mince the
matter.
—Miguel de Cervantes; *Don Quixote*, 1605

.5 Candor, my tepid Friend,
Come not to play with me!
The Myrrhs and Mochas of the Mind
Are its Iniquity.
—Emily Dickinson; *Poems*, No. 109, c. 1862

.6 How can a man's candor be seen in all its lus-
tre unless he has a few failings to talk of?
—George Eliot; *Adam Bede*, 1859

.7 Speak boldly, and speak truly, shame the devil.
—John Fletcher; *Wit Without Money*, 1614

.8 Speak out, hide not thy thoughts.
—Homer; *Iliad*, c. 700 B.C.

.9 If you want to get rid of somebody, just tell 'em
something for their own good.
—Kin Hubbard; *Abe Martin's Sayings*, 1915

.10 We talk plainly only to those we love.
—Jean Baptiste Lacordaire; *Conferences*, c.
1835–36

.11 It is the weak and confused who worship the
pseudosimplicities of brutal directness.
—Marshall McLuhan; *The Mechanical
Bride*, "The Tough as Narcissus," 1951

.12 Be not ashamed to say what you are not
ashamed to think.
—Michel de Montaigne; *Essays*, 1580

.13 He hath a heart as sound as a bell, and his
tongue is the clapper, for what his heart thinks
his tongue speaks.
—William Shakespeare; *Much Ado About
Nothing*, 1598

.14 If he persists in saying to me what he likes, he
shall hear what he does not like.
—Terence; *Andria*, c 160 B.C.

.15 Whenever one has anything unpleasant to say
one should always be quite candid.
—Oscar Wilde; *The Importance of Being
Earnest*, 1895

# 37 Chatter

.1 With good and gentle-humored hearts
I choose to chat where'er I come,
Whate'er the subject be that starts;
But if I get among the glum
I hold my tongue to tell the troth
And keep my breath to cool my broth.
—John Byrom; "Careless Content," *Private
Journals and Literary Remains*, published
1854–57

.2 A sort of chit-chat, or small talk, which is the
general run of conversation ... in most mixed
companies.
—Lord Chesterfield; *Letters to His Son*,
published 1774

.3 The evening's chat is not like the morning's
tattle.
—Randle Cotgrave; *Dictionary*: "Parole,"
1611

.4 Follow me and leave the world to chatter: be
as steady as a tower that never bows its head,
however hard the winds may blow.
—Dante Alighieri; *The Divine Comedy*,
1307

.5 The hare-brained chatter of irresponsible friv-
olity.
—Benjamin Disraeli; Speech, 1878

.6 In chatter excellent, but unable quite to speak.
—Eupolis; *Fragments*, c. 5th century B.C.

.7 Their chat on various subjects ran,
But most what each had done for man.
—John Gay; *Fables*, 1727

.8 The meaning doesn't matter if it's only idle
chatter of a transcendental kind.
—W.S. Gilbert; *Patience*, 1881

.9 Chatting to chiding is not worth a chuet.
—John Heywood; *Proverbs*, 1546
[Don't waste your time responding to
scolding.]

.10 'Tis the custom of foolish people ... in their
chit-chat to be always biting people's reputa-
tions behind their backs.
—Samuel Palmer; *Moral Essays on Proverbs*, 1710

.11 I know that we women are all justly accounted
chatterboxes; and then there is that old

proverb, "Never now, nor in any age, such a wonder as a dumb woman."
—Plautus; *Aulularia*, c. 254–184 B.C.

.12 Much chatter, little wit.
—Portuguese Proverb

.13 Teas,
Where small talk dies in agonies.
—Percy Bysshe Shelley; "Peter Bell the Third," 1819

.14 I chatter, chatter, as I flow,
To join the brimming river.
For men may come and men may go,
But I go on forever.
—Alfred, Lord Tennyson; "The Brook," 1855

.15 Who chatters to you will chatter of you.
—R.C. Trench; *On the Lessons in Proverbs*, 1853

.16 For the most of us, if we do not talk of ourselves, or at any rate of the individual circles of which we are the centers, we can talk of nothing. I cannot hold with those who wish to put down the insignificant chatter of the world.
—Anthony Trollope; *Framley Parsonage*, 1860

# 38 Children

.1 Children are voices of immorality to a man, though he be dead.
—Aeschylus; *Libation-Bearers*, c. 458 B.C.

.2 There is hardly any adult ... who admits that he tells stories to his children. Stories ... are considered to be demonic, and of no particular value.
—Hamed Ammar; *Growing Up in an Egyptian Village: Silwa, Promise of Aswan*, 1966

.3 Children are natural mimics—they act like their parents in spite of every attempt to teach them good manners.
—Anonymous

.4 Children should be seen and not heard.
—Aristophanes; *The Clouds*, c. 423 B.C.

.5 ... educational directors, as they are called, should be careful what tales, facts or fiction, children learn.
—Aristotle; *Politics*, c. 400 B.C.

.6 Children have never been very good at listening to their elders, but they have never failed

to imitate them. They must, they have no other models.
—James Baldwin; *Nobody Knows My Name*, "Fifth Avenue, Uptown," 1961

.7 Education commences at the mother's knee, and every word spoken within the hearsay of little children tends towards the formation of character.
—Hosea Ballou; *MS. Sermons*, c. 1834

.8 When the voices of children are heard on the green
And laughing is heard on the hill.
—William Blake; *Songs of Innocence*, "The Echoing Green," 1789–90

.9 There is no end to the violations committed by children on children, quietly talking alone.
—Elizabeth Bowen; *The House in Paris*, 1935

.10 Children can feel, but they cannot analyze their feelings; and if the analysis is partially effected in thought, they know not how to express the result of the process in words.
—Charlotte Bronte; *Jane Eyre*, 1847

.11 A child's own story is a dream, but a good story is a dream that is true for more than one child.
—Margaret Wise Brown; Quoted in Leonard S. Marcus, *Margaret Wise Brown*, 1992

.12 Children and fools speak the truth.
—English Proverb

.13 The child says nothing but what it heard by the fire.
—Thomas Fuller; *Gnomologia*, 1732

.14 Speak when you are spoken to, come when you are called.
—Thomas Fuller II; *Gnomologia*, 1732 [Instructions for children.]

.15 We have a challenge to give children "roots and wings" by sharing folk literature in the classroom.
—Frances S. Goforth and Carolyn V. Spillman; *Using Folklore in the Classroom*, 1994

.16 There is little use to talk about your child to anyone; other people either have one or haven't.
—Don Herold; *There Ought to Be a Law*, 1926

.17 And yet teachers say, "If we get through our workbook, maybe we'll have time for a story." Teachers, the workbook will be forgotten by tomorrow, but the sound, the feel, the sense,

the heart of that story may stay with children as long as they live.
　—Margaret Read MacDonald; *The Story-teller's Start-Up Book*, 1993

.18 When I was a child, I spake as a child, I understood as a child, I thought as a child; but when I became a man, I put away childish things.
　—New Testament: I Corinthians

.19 When you are dealing with a child, keep all your wits about you, and sit on the floor.
　—Austin O'Malley; *Keystones of Thought*, 1914–15

.20 One stops being a child when one realizes that telling one's troubles does not make it better.
　—Cesare Pavese; *The Business of Living: Diaries*, 1935–50

.21 … we begin by telling children stories which though not wholly destitute of truth, are in the main fictitious; and these stories are told them when they are not of an age to learn gymnastics….
　—Plato; *The Republic*, c. 387–367 B.C.

.22 What will a child learn sooner than a song?
　—Alexander Pope; *Imitations of Horace: Epistle*, 1734

.23 It is cruel to compliment children, since they mistake flattery for truth.
　—Ann Radcliffe; *The Mysteries of Udolpho*, 1794

.24 Children pick up words as pigeons peas,
And utter them again as God shall please.
　—John Ray; *English Proverbs*, 1670

.25 I hear of people nowadays who think it is not proper to tell children fairy stories. I am sorry for those children. I wonder what they will give them instead. Algebra perhaps. Nice lot of counting machines we shall have running the century that is to come.
　—Jacob Riis; *The Making of an American*, 1901

.26 Grown-ups never understand anything for themselves, and it is tiresome for children to be always and forever explaining things to them.
　—Antoine de Saint-Exupery; *The Little Prince*, 1943

.27 There's a time when you have to explain to your children why they're born, and it's a marvelous thing if you know the reason by then.
　—Hazel Scott; Quoted in Margo Johnson's "Great (Hazel) Scott!" *Ms.*, 1974

.28 Such wondrous tales as childhood loves to hear.
　—Robert Southey; *Joan of Arc*, 1796

.29 A child should always say what's true,
And speak when he is spoken to,
And behave mannerly at table:
At least as far as he is able.
　—Robert Louis Stevenson; "Whole Duty of Children," 1885

.30 Children are not born knowing the many opportunities that are theirs for the taking. Someone who does know must tell them.
　—Ruth Hill Viguers; Quoted in Joan Peterson *The Horn Book*, "Ruth Hill Viguers," 1991

# 39 Civilization

.1 The true savage is a slave, and is always talking about what he must do; the true civilized man is a free man, and is always talking about what he may do.
　—G.K. Chesterton; *All Things Considered*, "Humanitarianism and Strength," 1908

.2 The civilization of one epoch becomes the manure of the next.
　—Cyril Connolly; *The Unquiet Grave*, 1945

.3 Our civilization is still in the middle stage, scarcely beast, in that it is no longer guided by instinct: scarcely human, in that it is not yet wholly guided by reason.
　—Theodore Dreiser; *Sister Carrie*, 1906

.4 To inflict anyone with a compulsory interview of more than ten minutes indicates a crude state of civilization.
　—Ralph Waldo Emerson; *Uncollected Essays: Social Aims*, 1875

.5 Civilization could not exist until there was written language, because without written language no generation could bequeath to succeeding generations anything but its simpler findings.
　—Charlton Laird; *The Miracle of Language*, 1953

.6 As civilization advances, poetry almost necessarily declines.
　—Thomas Babington Macaulay; *Essays: Mitford's History of Greece*, 1843

.7 Speech is civilization itself. The word, even the most contradictious word, preserves contact—it is silence which isolates.
　—Thomas Mann; *The Magic Mountain*, 1924

## 39

.8   Every advance in civilization has been denounced as unnatural while it was recent.
  —Bertrand Russell; *Unpopular Essays*, "An Author of Intellectual Rubbish," 1950

## 40 Clarity

.1   That's clear as mud.
  —R.H. Barham; *Ingoldsby Legends*: "The Merchant of Venice," 1842

.2   Praised be he who can state a case in a clear, simple and succinct manner, and then stop.
  —Harry H. Belt; Quoted in a Judicial Decision, *Jungwirth v Jungwirth*, 1925

.3   What is conceived well is expressed clearly, And the words to say it will arrive with ease.
  —Nicolas Boileau; *L'Art Poetique*, 1674

.4   In language clearness is everything.
  —Confucius; *Analects*, c. 479 B.C.

.5   The chief virtue that language can have is clearness, and nothing detracts from it so much as the use of unfamiliar words.
  —Galen; *On the Natural Faculties*, c. 175 A.D.

.6   The language of the law must not be foreign to the ears of those who are to obey it.
  —Learned Hand; *The Spirit of Liberty*, 1959

.7   Clear as a London fog.
  —Nathaniel Hawthorne; *The Marble Faun*, "Conclusion," 1860

.8   I strive to be concise, And grow obscure.
  —Horace; *Ars Poetica*, c. 19 B.C.

.9   Some experience of popular lecturing had convinced me that the necessity of making things plain to the uninstructed people was one of the best means of clearing up the obscure corners in own's own mind.
  —T.H. Huxley; *Man's Place in Nature*, 1894

.10   Clarity is an excellent virtue. Like all virtues it can be pursued at ruinous cost. Paid, so far as I am concerned, joyfully.
  —Storm Jameson; *Parthian Words*, 1970

.11   Every man speaks and writes with intent to be understood; and it can seldom happen but he that understands himself might convey his notions to another, if, content to be understood, he did not seek to be admired.
  —Samuel Johnson; *The Idler*, 1758–60

## 40

.12   Crystall clere.
  —John Lydgate; *Minor Poems*, c. 1430

.13   If one cannot state a matter clearly enough so that even an intelligent twelve-year-old can understand it, one should remain within the cloistered walls of the university and laboratory until one gets a better grasp of one's subject matter.
  —Margaret Mead; Quoted in *Redbook*, 1963

.14   A matter than becomes clear ceases to concern us.
  —Friedrich Nietzsche; *Beyond Good and Evil*, 1886

.15   The very first lesson that we have a right to demand that logic shall teach us is, how to make our ideas clear; and a most important one it is, depreciated only by minds who stand in need of it.
  —Charles S. Peirce; "How to Make our Ideas Clear," *Popular Science Monthly*, 1878

.16   If you don't hear the story clearly, don't carry it off with you under your arm.
  —Thai Proverb

.17   Plain clarity is better than ornate obscurity.
  —Mark Twain; in Albert Bigelow Paine's *Mark Twain: A Biography*, 1912

.18   Lucidity adds beauty to profound thoughts.
  —Marquis de Vauvenargues; *Reflexions et Maxims*, 1746

.19   What can be said at all can be said clearly; and whereof one cannot speak, thereon one must keep silent.
  —Ludwig Wittgenstein; *Tractatus Logico-Philosophicus*, 1922

## 41 Cleverness

.1   It is a profitable thing, if one is wise, to seem foolish.
  —Aeschylus; *Prometheus Bound*, c. 478 B.C.

.2   I always did think that cleverness was the art of hiding ignorance.
  —Shelland Bradley; *An American Girl in India*, 1907

.3   If the witty backbiter is blamed and condemned as obnoxious, he is none the less absolved and praised as a clever fellow.
  —Miguel de Cervantes; *Don Quixote*, 1605

**41**

.4 Though I'm anything but clever. I could talk like that for ever.
—W.S. Gilbert; *H.M.S. Pinafore*, 1878

.5 A clever fellow knows how to use the brains of other people.
—George Gissing; *New Grub Street*, 1891

.6 The height of cleverness is to be able to conceal it.
—François de La Rochefoucauld; *Maximes*, 1678

.7 Here is a good rule of thumb;
Too clever is dumb.
—Ogden Nash; *Verses From 1929 On*, "Reflections on Ingenuity," 1959

.8 The Athenians do not mind a man being clever, so long as he does not impart his cleverness to others.
—Plato; *Euthyphro*, c. 375 B.C.

.9 The next best thing to being clever is being able to quote some one who is.
—Mary Pettibone Poole; *A Glass Eye at the Keyhole*, 1938

.10 Mr. Hannaford's utterances have no meaning; he's satisfied if they sound clever.
—Alfred Sutro; *The Walls of Jericho*, 1906

.11 It is never wise to try to appear to be more clever than you are. It is sometimes wise to appear slightly less so.
—William Whitelaw; Attributed

.12 A man likes his wife to be just clever enough to appreciate his cleverness, and just stupid enough to admire it.
—Israel Zangwill; *The Melting Pot*, 1908

# **42** Cliché

.1 At last the secret is out, as it always must come in the end,
The delicious story is ripe to tell to the intimate friend;
Over the tea-cups and in the square the tongue has its desire;
Still waters run deep, my dear, there's never smoke without fire....
—W.H. Auden; *Collected Poems 1933–38*, 1938

.2 Your soul needs to be lonely so that the strangest elements can moil about, curl and growl and jump, fail and get triumphant, all inside you. Sociable people have the most trouble hearing their unconscious. They have

**42**

trouble getting rid of clichés because clichés are sociable.
—Carol Bly; *The Passionate, Accurate Story*, 1990

.3 The cliché is dead poetry. English, being the language of an imaginative race, abounds in clichés, so that English literature is always in danger of being poisoned by its own secretions.
—Gerald Brenan; *Thoughts in a Dry Season*, 1978

.4 Let's have some new clichés.
—Samuel Goldwyn; *The Observer*, "Sayings of the Week," 1948

.5 Clichés are like a cat's fleas. The work in progress is the cat, a living, beautiful creature, but the fleas hop automatically onto the body, and there must be a constant warfare against them.
—Katharine Butler Hathaway; *The Journals and Letters of the Little Locksmith*, 1946

.6 The cliché organizes life; it expropriates people's identity; it becomes ruler, defence lawyer, judge, and the law.
—Vaclav Havel; *Disturbing the Peace*, 1986

.7 Yesterday's avant-garde experience is today's chic and tomorrow's cliché.
—Richard Hofstadter; *Anti-Intellectualism in American Life*, 1963

.8 A Foreign Secretary is forever poised between a cliché and an indiscretion.
—Harold McMillan; *Newsweek*, 1956

.9 The clichés of a culture sometimes tell the deepest truths.
—Faith Popcorn; *The Popcorn Report*, 1991

.10 Man is a creature who lives not upon bread alone, but principally by catchwords; and the little rift between the sexes is astonishingly widened by simply teaching one set of catchwords to the girls and another to the boys.
—Robert Louis Stevenson; *Virginibus Puerisque*, 1881

.11 Love is what makes the world go around—that and clichés.
—Michael Brooke Symons; *Sydney Morning Herald*, 1920

.12 If you want to use a cliché you must take full responsibility for it yourself and not try to job it off on anon., or on society.
—Lewis Thomas; *The Medusa and the Snail*, "Notes on Punctuation," 1979

# 43 Comedy

.1  We never respect those who amuse us, however we may smile at their comic powers.
—Countess of Blessington; *Desultory Thoughts and Reflections*, 1839

.2  Comedy is tragedy that happens to other people.
—Angela Carter; *Wise Children*, 1991

.3  Verbal comedy [is] a way of confronting social ambiguity.
—Ralph Ellison; *Going to the Territory*, 1986

.4  Comedy is an escape, not from truth but from despair; a narrow escape into faith.
—Christopher Fry; quoted in *Time*, November 20, 1950

.5  Great comedy calls large matters into question.
—Penelope Gilliatt; *To Wit*, 1990

.6  Comedy is criticism.
—Louis Kronenberger, *The Thread of Language*, 1952

.7  The test of a real comedian is whether you laugh at him before he opens his mouth.
—George Jean Nathan; *American Mercury*, 1929

.8  A long, exact, and serious comedy;
In ev'ry scene some moral let it teach,
And, if it can, at once both please and teach.
—Alexander Pope; "Epistle to Miss Blount," 1735

.9  Comedy, we may say, is society protecting itself—with a smile.
—J. B. Priestley; *George Meredith*, 1926

.10 Comedy is very controlling—you are making people laugh. It is there in the phrase "making people laugh." You feel completely in control when you hear a wave of laughter coming back at you that you have caused.
—Gilda Radner; *It's Always Something*, 1989

.11 Comedy is the last refuge of the nonconformist mind.
—Gilbert Seldes; *The New Republic*, 1954

.12 And killing time is perhaps the essence of comedy, just as the essence of tragedy is killing eternity.
—Miguel de Unamuno; *San Manuel Bueno*, Prologue, 1931

.13 Comedy is simply a funny way of being serious.
—Peter Ustinov; *Dear Me*, 1977

## 43

.14 The world is a comedy to those that think, a tragedy to those that feel.
—Horace Walpole; *Letter to Horace Mann*, 1747

# 44 Communication

.1  A good message will always find a messenger.
—Amelia E. Barr; *Face Toward the Spring*, 1956

.2  Communication is most complete when it proceeds from the smallest number of words, and indeed of syllables.
—Jacques Barzun; "Simple & Direct," 1977

.3  There can be too much communication between people.
—Ann Beattie, *Secrets and Surprises*, "Weekend," 1978

.4  Self-expression must pass into communication for its fulfillment.
—Pearl S. Buck; Quoted in Helen R. Hull, *The Writer's Book*, 1950

.5  Much unhappiness has come into the world because of bewilderment and things left unsaid.
—Fyodor Dostoyevsky; *Complete Collected Works*, "Critical Articles Introduction," 1895

.6  When the eyes say one thing, and the tongue another, a practised man relies on the language of the first.
—Ralph Waldo Emerson; *The Conduct of Life*, "Behavior," 1860

.7  Why have we the power of speech, but to communicate our thoughts?
—William Godwin; *Caleb Williams*, 1794

.8  No one would talk so much in society, if he only knew how often he misunderstands others.
—Johann Wolfgang von Goethe; *Effective Affinities*, 1808

.9  After all, when you come right down to it, how many people speak the same language even when they speak the same language?
—Russell Hoban; *The Lion of Boaz-Jachin and Jachin-Boaz*, 1973

.10 If nobody was suffered to speak till he had something to say, what pains everybody would take to know something.
—Charles Jenner; *The Placid Man*, 1770

# 44

.11 The more people are reached by mass communications, the less they communicate with each other.
—Marya Mannes; *But Will It Sell*, "The Carriers," 1964

.12 If figures of speech based on sports and fornication were suddenly banned, American corporate communication would be reduced to pure mathematics.
—Jay McInerney; *Brightness Falls*, 1992

.13 Evil communications corrupt good character.
—Menander; *Thais: Fragment*, c. 4th century B.C.

.14 To use the same words is not a sufficient guarantee of understanding; one must use the same words for the same genus of inward experience; ultimately one must have one's experiences in common.
—Friedrich Nietzsche; *The Twilight of the Idols*, 1888

.15 Extremists think "communication" means agreeing with them.
—Leo Rosten; *A Triumph of Reason*, 1970

.16 I distrust the incommunicable; it is the source of all violence.
—Jean-Paul Sartre; *Les Temps Modernes*, "What Is Literature?," 1947

.17 Once a human being has arrived on this earth, communication is the largest single factor determining what kinds of relationships he makes with others and what happens to him in the world about him.
—Virginia Satit; *Peoplemaking*, 1971

.18 Communication is a continual balancing act, juggling the conflicting needs for intimacy and independence.
—Deborah Tannen; *You Just Don't Understand*, 1990

.19 Precision of communication is important, more important than ever, in our era of hair-trigger balances, when a false, or misunderstood word may create as much disaster as a sudden thoughtless act.
—James Thurber; *Lanterns and Lances*, "Friends, Romans and Countrymen, Lend Me Your Ear Muffs," 1961

.20 But humanity is never more sphinxlike than when it is expressing itself.
—Rebecca West; *The Court and the Castle*, 1957

# 45 Comparisons

.1 All comparisons are odious.
—Miguel de Cervantes; *Don Quixote*, 1605

.2 Nothing is good or bad but by comparison.
—Thomas Fuller I; *The Holy State and the Profane State*, 1642

.3 Speeches and fruit should always be fresh.
—Nikki Giovanni; *Sacred Cows ... and Other Edibles*, "In Sympathy with Another Motherless Child," 1988

.4 Talking is like playing on the harp; there is as much in laying the hand on the strings to stop their vibrations as in twanging them to bring out their music.
—Oliver Wendell Holmes; *The Autocrat of the Breakfast Table*, 1858

.5 I murmured because I had no shoes, until I met a man who had no feet.
—Persian Proverb

.6 Comparisons make enemies of our friends.
—Pheilmon; *Fabulae Incarte*, c. 300 B.C.

.7 Comparisons are odious, but they need not be malicious...
—Mark Twain: *A Tramp Abroad*, "German Journals," 1880

.8 Knowing pups are like dogs and kids like goats,
So used I to compare great things with small.
—Vergil; *Ecologues*, c. 70–19 B.C.

# 46 Complaint

.1 To make wail and lament for one's ill fortune, when one will win a tear from the audience, is well worthwhile.
—Aeschylus; *Prometheus Bound*, c. 478 B.C.

.2 Those who do not complain are never pitied.
—Jane Austen; *Pride and Prejudice*, 1813

.3 I think that the insane desire one has sometimes to bang and kick grumblers and peevish persons is a Divine instinct.
—Robert Hugh Benson; *The Average Man*, 1913

.4 Query: Whether it be not delightful to complain? And whether there be not many who had rather utter their complaints than redress their evils?
—Bishop George Berkeley; *The Querist*, 1735

## 46

.5 The wheel that squeaks the loudest is the one that gets the grease.
—Josh Billings; *Josh Billings: His Sayings*, 1865

.6 To complain of the age we live in, to murmur at the present possessors of power, to lament the past, to conceive extravagant hopes of the future, are the common dispositions of the greatest part of mankind.
—Edmund Burke; *Thoughts on the Course of the Present Discontents*, 1770

.7 Complainants are the greatest persecutors.
—Samuel Butler I; *Prose Observations*, 1660–80

.8 Most people complain of fortune, few of nature; and the kinder they think the latter has been to them, the more they murmur at what they call the injustice of the former.
—Lord Chesterfield, *Letters to His Son*, published 1774

.9 Never complain and never explain.
—Benjamin Disraeli; Attributed in John Morley's *Life of Gladstone*, 1903

.10 There is no point in complaining over the past or apologizing for one's fate.
—Ralph Ellison; *Going to the Territory*, "Portrait of Inman Page," 1986

.11 Had we not faults of our own, we should take less pleasure in complaining of others.
—Francois Fenelon; *Concerning the Education of Girls*, 1687

.12 He that always complains, is never pitied.
—Thomas Fuller; *Gnomologia*, 1732

.13 Never admit the pain,
Bury it deep;
Only the weak complain,
Complaint is cheap.
—Dame Mary Gilmore; *The Wild Swan*, "Never Admit the Pain," 1930

.14 Those who complain most are most to be complained of.
—Matthew Henry; *Commentaries*, 1708–10

.15 To have a grievance is to have a purpose in life.
—Eric Hoffer; *The Passionate State of Mind*, 1954

.16 I believe in grumbling; it is the politest form of fighting known.
—Ed Howe; *Country Town Sayings*, 1911

.17 If you are foolish enough to be contented, don't show it, but grumble with the rest.
—Jerome K. Jerome; *Idle Thoughts of an Idle Fellow*, 1886

## 46

.18 There is a small dose of revenge in every complaint; one reproaches those who are different for one's feeling vile, sometimes even with one's being vile.
—Friedrich Nietzsche: *The Gay Science*, 1882–87

.19 We ought not to complain if someone we dearly love behaves now and then in ways we find distasteful, nerve-wracking or hurtful. Instead of grumbling we should avidly hoard up our feelings of irritation and bitterness: they will serve to alleviate our grief on the day when she has gone and we miss her.
—Cesare Pavese; *This Business of Living: Diaries*, 1935–50

## 47 Compliment

.1 Compliments are only lies in court clothes.
—Anonymous

.2 A compliment is a forensic anaesthetic. Many people will complacently undergo a fatal interrogation if they be well flattered all the while; and more men are likely to be caught by a compliment to their ability than be a tribute to their virtue.
—Charles John Darling; *Scintillae Juris*, 1889

.3 Complementing is lying.
—English Proverb

.4 This being in love is great—you get a lot of compliments and begin to think you are a great guy.
—F. Scott Fitzgerald; *The Crack-Up*, 1945

.5 Compliments cost nothing, yet many pay dear for them.
—Thomas Fuller II; *Gnomologia*, 1732

.6 You're exceedingly polite,
And I think it only right
To return the compliment.
—W.S. Gilbert; *H.M.S. Pinafore*, 1878

.7 A compliment is usually accompanied with a bow, as if to beg pardon for paying it.
—J.C. Hare and A.W. Hare; *Guesses at Truth*, 1827

.8 Some people pay a compliment as if they expected a receipt.
—Kin Hubbard; *Abe Martin's Sayings*, 1915

.9 A compliment is something like a kiss through a veil.
—Victor Hugo; *Les Miserables*, 1862

## 47

.10 I much prefer a compliment, insincere or not, to sincere criticism.
  —Plautus; *Mostellaria*, c. 254–184 B.C.

.11 When a man makes a woman his wife, it's the highest compliment he can pay her, and it's usually the last.
  —Helen Rowland; *A Guide to Men*, 1922

.12 Compliment—a thing often paid by people who pay nothing else.
  —Horatio Smith; *The Tin Trumpet*, 1836

.13 It is a grace in flattery to let fall your compliments as that you shall seem to consider them to be a matter of indifference to him to whom they are addressed; for thus one flattery will include another—and that other perhaps the most agreeable—being that of attributing to the party a peculiar absence of self-love.
  —Sir Henry Taylor; *The Statesman*, 1836

.14 I can live for two months on a good compliment.
  —Mark Twain; Letter to Gertrude Natkin, March 2, 1906

.15 The happy phrasing of a compliment is one of the rarest of human gifts, and the happy delivery of it another.
  —Mark Twain; *North American Review*, March 15, 1907

.16 Women are never disarmed by compliments. Men always are.
  —Oscar Wilde; *An Ideal Husband*, 1895

## 48 Concealment

.1 Show me one who boasts continually of his "openness," and I will show you one who conceals much.
  —Minna Thomas Antrim; *At the Sign of the Golden Calf*, 1905

.2 Speech is too often not the art of concealing thought, but of quite stifling and suspending thought, so that there is none to conceal.
  —Thomas Carlyle; *On Heroes and Hero Worship*, 1841

.3 Much truth is spoken, that more may be concealed.
  —Charles John Darling; *Scintillae Juris*, 1877

.4 The true use of speech is not so much to express our wants as to conceal them.
  —Oliver Goldsmith; *The Bee*, 1759

## 48

.5 He was a man who kept his words well to the rear of his possible actions.
  —Thomas Hardy; *A Pair of Blue Eyes*, 1873

.6 For that man is detested by me as the gates of hell, whose outward words conceal his inmost thoughts.
  —Homer; *The Iliad*, c. 700 B.C.

.7 A man had rather have a hundred lies told of him than one truth which he does not wish should be told.
  —Samuel Johnson; Boswell's *Life of Samuel Johnson*, published 1791

.8 Men intend sometimes to conceal their imperfections, or attenuate the opinion of others about them, by frankly acknowledging them. "I am very ignorant," says some man who knows nothing; "I am getting old," says a second above threescore; "I am far from rich," says a third who is wretchedly poor.
  —Jean de La Bruyere; *Characters*, "Of Mankind," 1688

.9 Talking about oneself can also be a means to conceal oneself.
  —Freidrich Nietzsche; *Beyond Good and Evil*, 1886

.10 True genuine contempt remains entirely concealed and gives no hint of its existence. For whoever shows contempt, thereby gives a hint of some regard in so far as he wants to let the other man know how little he esteems him. In this way he betrays hatred which excludes and only feigns contempt.
  —Arthur Schopenhauer; *Parerga and Paralipomena*, "Psychological Remarks," 1851

.11 That I, or any man, should tell everything of himself, I hold to be impossible. Who could endure to own the doing of a mean thing? Who is there that has done none?
  —Anthony Trollope, *An Autobiography*, 1883

.12 Good breeding consists in concealing how much we think of ourselves and how little we think of other persons.
  —Mark Twain; *Notebooks*, published 1935

## 49 Conclusion

.1 I knew a wise man that had if for a by-word, when he saw men hasten to a conclusion, "Stay a little, that we may make the end the sooner.
  —Francis Bacon; *Essays*: "Of Dispatch," 1612

## 49

.2 The shrewd guess, the fertile hypothesis, the courteous leap to a tentative conclusion—these are the most valuable coin of the thinker at work.
—Jerome Seymour Bruner; *The Process of Education*, 1960

.3 Life is the art of drawing sufficient conclusions from insufficient premises.
—Samuel Butler II; *Notebooks: Lord, What Is Man?*, 1912

.4 Say what you have to say and the first time you come to a sentence with a grammatical ending—sit down.
—Winston Churchill; Attributed

.5 A story has been thought to its conclusion when it has taken its worst possible turn.
—Friedrich Durrenmatt; *The Physicists*, "21 Points," 1962

.6 You'd have done fine at track meets. Especially if they'd had an event called Jumping to Conclusions.
—Kristin Hunter; *The Landlord*, 1966

.7 I have come to the conclusion, after many years of sometimes sad experience, that you cannot come to any conclusions at all.
—Vita Sackville-West, *In Your Garden Again*, "May," 1953

.8 But this denoted a foregone conclusion.
—William Shakespeare; *Othello*, 1603–4

## 50 Confession

.1 It is easier to confess a defect than to claim a quality.
—Max Beerbohm; *And Even Now*, 1921

.2 Confession is good for the soul only in the sense that a tweed coat is good for dandruff—it is a palliative rather than a remedy.
—Peter De Vries; *The Tunnel of Love*, 1954

.3 Many think that when they have confessed a fault there is no need of correcting it.
—Marie von Ebner-Eschenbach; *Aphorisms*, 1893

.4 There are some things which men confess with ease, but others with difficulty.
—Epictetus; *Discourses*, c. A.D. 100

.5 His countenance confessed faster than his tongue denied.
—Henry Fielding; *Amelia*, 1751

## 50

.6 We confess our faults in the plural, and deny them in the singular.
—Richard Fulke Greville; *Characters and Reflections*, 1756

.7 It is easy to make a man confess the lies he tells to himself; it's far harder to make him confess the truth.
—Geoffrey Household [Edward West]; *Rogue Male*, 1939

.8 If you can tell anyone about it, it's not the worst thing you ever did.
—Mignon McLaughlin; *The Neurotic's Notebook*, 1963

.9 True confession consists in telling our deed in such a way that our soul is changed in the telling of it.
—Maude Petre; *The Method of Theology*, "Devotional Essays," 1902

.10 Confession of our faults is the next thing to innocence.
—Publilius Syrus; *Sententiae*, c. 1st century B.C.

.11 It is not the criminal things which are hardest to confess, but the ridiculous and shameful.
—Jean-Jacques Rousseau; *Confessions*, 1766–70

## 51 Conversation

.1 Good-nature is more agreeable in conversation than wit, and gives a certain air to the countenance which is more amiable than beauty.
—Joseph Addison; *The Spectator*, 1711–12

.2 "My idea of good company, Mr. Elliot, is the company of clever, well-informed people, who have a great deal of conversation; that is what I call good company." "You are mistaken," said he gently, "That is not good company; that is the best."
—Jane Austen; *Persuasion*, 1818

.3 One evening's conversation with a superior man is better than ten years of study.
—Chinese Proverb

.4 Rhetoricians lay down the rules for oratory, but there are no rules for conversation. I don't really know why there shouldn't be.
—Cicero; *De Officiis*, c. 45 B.C.

.5 A sudden silence in the middle of a conversation suddenly brings us back to essentials: it

reveals how dearly we must pay for the invention of speech.
—E.M. Cioran; *Anathemas and Admirations*, "On the Verge of Existence," 1986

.6 No ingenuous person ever thinks much of the particular subject of conversation.
—James Fenimore Cooper; *Homeward Bound*, 1838

.7 There are few things in life more interesting than an unrestricted interchange of ideas with a congenial spirit; and there are few things more rare.
—Benjamin Disraeli; *Coningsby*, 1844

.8 Conversation is an art in which man has all mankind for competition.
—Ralph Waldo Emerson; *Conduct of Life*, "Considerations by the Way," 1860

.9 In good conversations parties don't speak to the words, but to the meaning of each other.
—Ralph Waldo Emerson; *Letters and Social Aims*, "Social Aims," 1875

.10 Two may talk and one may hear, but three cannot take part in a conversation of the most sincere and searching sort.
—Ralph Waldo Emerson; *Essays: First Series*, "Self Reliance," 1841

.11 Education begins a gentleman, conversation completes him.
—English Proverb

.12 His conversation does not show the minute hand, but he strikes the hour very correctly.
—Benjamin Franklin; *Poor Richard's Almanac*, 1750

.13 Conversation teaches more than meditation.
—Thomas Fuller II; *Gnomologia*, 1732

.14 Discretion in conversation is more important than eloquence.
—Baltasar Gracian; *Oraculo Manual*, 1647

.15 Conversation is the beginning and end of knowledge.
—Stefano Guazzo; *Civil Conversation*, 1574

.16 Silence is one great art of conversation.
—William Hazlitt, *Characteristics*, 1823

.17 The art of conversation is the art of hearing as well as of being heard.
—William Hazlitt; *The Plain Speaker*, "On the Conversations of Authors," 1826

.18 O evenings, and suppers fit for the gods! with which I and my friends regale ourselves in the presence of the household god.... Then conversation arises, not concerning other people's

villas and houses, nor whether Lepos dances well or not; but we debate on what is more to our purpose, and what it is pernicious not to know.... Meanwhile, my neighbor Cervius prates away old stories relative to the subject.
—Horace; *Satires*. c. 35. B.C.

.19 Don't knock the weather; nine tenths of the people couldn't start a conversation if it didn't change once in a while.
—Kin Hubbard; *Comments of Abe Martin*, 1914

.20 That is the happiest conversation where there is no competition, no vanity, but a calm quiet interchange of sentiments.
—Samuel Johnson; *Letter to Lord Chesterfield*, 1775

.21 Conversation is not a search after knowledge, but an endeavour at effect.
—John Keats; *Letter to Benjamin Robert Haydon*, 1817

.22 Confidence causes more conversation than wit.
—François de La Rochefoucauld; *Maxims*, 1678

.23 Polite conversation is rarely either.
—Fran Lebowitz; *Social Studies*, 1977

.24 A single conversation across the table with a wise man is better than ten years' study of books.
—Henry Wadsworth Longfellow; *Hyperion*, 1839
[This is quoted from the Chinese.]

.25 Conversation is like a dear little baby that is brought in to be handed round. You must rock it, nurse it, keep it on the move if you want to keep smiling.
—Katherine Mansfield; *The Dove's Nest*, title story, 1923

.26 Do you know that conversation is one of the greatest pleasures in life? But it wants leisure.
—W. Somerset Maugham; *The Trembling of a Leaf*, "The Fall of Edward Barrond," 1921

.27 Conversation ... is the art of never appearing a bore, of knowing how to say everything interestingly, to entertain with no matter what, to be charming with nothing at all.
—Guy de Maupassant; *On the Water*, 1888

.28 Conversation would be vastly improved by the constant use of four simple words: I do not know.
—Andre Maurois; *De la conversation*, 1921

.29 True conversation is an interpretation of worlds, a genuine intercourse of souls, which doesn't have to be self-consciously profound

## 51

but does have to touch matters of concern to the soul.
—Thomas Moore; *Soul Mates*, 1994

.30 The real art of conversation is not only to say the right thing in the right place, but, far more difficult still, to leave unsaid the wrong thing at the tempting moment.
—Dorothy Nevill, *Under Five Reigns*, 1910

.31 When we talk in company we lose our unique tone of voice, and this leads us to make statements which in no way correspond to our real thoughts.
—Friedrich Nietzsche; *The Gay Science*, 1882–87

.32 Conversation is the socializing instrument par excellence, and in its style one can see reflected the capacities of a race.
—Jose Ortega y Gasset; *Invertebrate Spain*, 1922

.33 Johnson's conversation was by much too strong for a person accustomed to obsequiousness and flattery; it was *mustard in a young child's mouth*.
—Hester Lynch Thrale Piozzi; Quoted in James Boswell's *Life of Johnson*, 1781

.34 Conversation may be divided into two classes—the familiar and the sentimental.
—Ann Radcliffe; *A Sicilian Romance*, 1790

.35 In a conversation, keep in mind that you're more interested in what you have to say than anyone else is.
—Andy Rooney; *Pieces of My Mind*, "A Penny Saved Is a Waste of Time," 1984

.36 Whoever interrupts the conversation of others to make a display of his fund of knowledge, makes notorious his own stock of ignorance.
—Sa'Di; *Gulistan*, c. 1258

.37 Conversation has a kind of charm about it, an insinuating and insidious something that elicits secrets from us just like love or liquor.
—Seneca; *Epistles*, c. 4 B.C.–A.D. 65

.38 Macaulay is like a book in breeches…. He has occasional flashes of silence that make his conversation perfectly delightful.
—Sydney Smith; *Lady Holland's Memoir*, 1855

.39 When you fall into a man's conversation, the first thing you should consider is, whether he has a greater inclination to hear you, or that you should hear him.
—Richard Steele; *The Spectator*, 1711

## 51

.40 It is an impertinent and unreasonable fault in conversation for one man to take up all the discourse.
—Richard Steele; *The Spectator*, 1711–12

.41 Inquisitive people are merely funnels of conversation. They do not take in anything for their own use, but merely pass it on to others.
—Richard Steele; *The Spectator*, 1711–12

.42 Conversation is seldom witty or eloquent in private societies, or anywhere except in very high-flown and ingenious novels.
—William Makepeace Thackeray; *Vanity Fair*, 1847–48

.43 A good memory and a tongue tied in the middle is a combination which gives immortality to conversation.
—Mark Twain; *Roughing It*, 1872

.44 Modest egotism is the salt of conversation; you do not want too much of it, but if it is altogether omitted, everything tastes flat.
—Henry Van Dyke; Edwin Mims, *The Van Dyke Book*, 1905

.45 She never lets ideas interrupt the easy flow of her conversation.
—Jean Webster; *Daddy-Long-Legs*, 1912

.46 She wanted to get away from herself, and conversation was the only means of escape that she knew.
—Edith Wharton; *The House of Mirth*, 1905

.47 If one hears bad music it is one's duty to drown it in conversation.
—Oscar Wilde; *The Importance of Being Earnest*, 1895

.48 Learned conversation is either the affectation of the ignorant or the profession of the mentally unemployed.
—Oscar Wilde; *Intentions: The Critic as Artist*, 1891

## 52  Courage

.1 Courage to ask questions; courage to expose our ignorance.
—Ralph Waldo Emerson; *Letters and Social Aims*, "Social Aims," 1875

.2 When the oldest cask is opened,
And the largest lamp is lit; …
With weeping and laughter
Still is the story told,

## 52

How well Horatius kept the bridge
In the brave days of old.
  —Thomas Babington Macaulay; *Lays of Ancient Rome*, "Horatius," 1842

.3  The most reliable and useful courage is that which arises from the fair estimation of the encountered peril.
  —Herman Melville; *Moby Dick*, 1851

.4  He wants to be taught the difference between courage and bluster.
  —Samuel Richardson; *Clarissa Harlowe*, 1747–48

.5  Had we lived, I should have had a tale to tell of the hardihood, endurance, and courage of my companions which would have stirred the heart of every Englishman. These rough notes and our dead bodies must tell the tale.
  —Robert Falcon Scott; "Message to the Public," *Scott's Last Expedition*, 1913

.6  Hail, Caesar, those who are about to die salute thee.
  —Suetonius; *Life of Claudius*, c. A.D. 70–c. 140
  [The gladiators' salute to the emperor in the arena.]

.7  Courage is resistance to fear, mastery of fear—not absence of fear.
  —Mark Twain; *Pudd'nhead Wilson's Calendar*, 1894

## 53 Courtesy

.1  The small courtesies sweeten life; the greater ennoble it.
  —Christian Nestell Bovee, *Authors*, Late 19th century

.2  Curtsy while you're thinking of what to say. It saves time.
  —Lewis Carroll; *Through the Looking Glass*, 1872

.3  Courtesy is the politic witchery of great personages.
  —Baltasar Gracian; *The Art of Worldly Wisdom*, 1647

.4  To speak kindly does not hurt the tongue.
  —Greek Proverb

.5  There is great force hidden in a sweet command.
  —George Herbert; *Jacula Prudentum*, 1640

.6  Politeness is to do and say
The kindest thing in the kindest way.
  —Ludwig Lewisohn; "Politeness," 1932

## 53

.7  True politeness consists in being easy one's self; and in making every one about one as easy as one can.
  —Alexander Pope; *Thoughts on Various Subjects*, 1727

.8  We require courteous speech from the children at all times and in all circumstances; we owe them the same courtesy in return; and when we fail of it we deserve correction.
  —Mark Twain; *Mark Twain's Which Was the Dream? and Other Symbolic Writings of the Later Years*, John S. Tuckey, ed., 1967

## 54 Criticism

.1  Criticism should be a casual conversation.
  —W.H. Auden; *The Table Talk of W.H. Auden*, comp. Alan Ansen, ed. Nicholas Jenkins, "November 16, 1946," 1990

.2  It is uncommon hard to annihilate a man with words—although it is often undertook.
  —Josh Billings; *Affurisms*, 1865

.3  He who discommendeth others obliquely commendeth himself.
  —Sir Thomas Browne; *Christian Morals*, 1716

.4  We think we are exceptional, and are surprised to find ourselves criticized just like anyone else.
  —Comtesse Diane; *Maximes de la vie*, 1908

.5  Blame-all and praise-all are two blockheads.
  —Benjamin Franklin; *Poor Richard's Almanac*, 1734

.6  Criticism, as it was first instituted by Aristotle, was meant as a standard of judging well.
  —Samuel Johnson; *The Idler*, 1758

.7  There will always be dissident voices heard in the land, expressing opposition without alternatives, finding fault but never favor, perceiving gloom on every side and seeking influence without responsibility. These voices are inevitable.
  —John F. Kennedy; Speech
  [These words were to be a part of the speech that JFK was to give, November 22, 1963, the day of his assassination.]

.8  Criticism is the art of praise.
  —Richard Le Gallienne; *Retrospective Reviews*, 1896

**54**

.9 Criticism of our contemporaries is not criticism; it is conversation.
   —Francois Lemaitre; Quoted by Brander Matthews, *New York Times*, 1922

.10 People ask you for criticism, but they only want praise.
   —W. Somerset Maugham; *Of Human Bondage*, 1915

.11 Critical remarks are only made by people who love you.
   —Federico Mayor; in *The Guardian*, London, June 24, 1988

.12 Criticism is the art of appraising others at one's own value.
   —George Jean Nathan; *The World in Falsehood*, 1923

.13 Criticism, the acid that dissolves images.... Criticism tells us that we should learn to dissolve the idols.
   —Octavio Paz; *Postscript*, 1970

.14 People fed on sugared praises cannot be expected to feel an appetite for the black broth of honest criticism.
   —Agnes Repplier; *Books and Men*, "Curiosities of Criticism," 1888

.15 Your criticism sounds more sincere than your admiration.
   —George Bernard Shaw; *The Irrational Knot*, 1880

.16 Of all the cants that are canted in this canting world, though the cant of hypocrisy may be the worst, the cant of criticism is the most tormenting.
   —Laurence Sterne; *Tristram Shandy*, 1760–7

.17 One mustn't criticize other people on grounds where he can't stand perpendicular himself.
   —Mark Twain; *A Connecticut Yankee in King Arthur's Court*, 1889

.18 On an occasion of this sort it becomes more than a moral duty to speak one's mind; it becomes a pleasure.
   —Oscar Wilde; Attributed

**55** Cruelty

.1 Scarce anything awakens attention like a tale of cruelty.
   —Samuel Johnson; *The Idler*, 1758

.2 Of all cruelties those are the most intolerable that come under the name of condolence and consolation.
   —W.S. Landor; *Letter to Robert Southey*, 1816

**55**

.3 Cruelty is fed, not weakened by tears.
   —Publilis Syrus; *Sententiae*, c. 1st century B.C.

.4 I think that the desire to be cruel and to hurt (with words because any other way might be dangerous to ourself) is part of human nature. Parties are battles (most parties), a conversation is a duel (often). Everybody's trying to hurt first, to get in the dig that will make him or her feel superior, feel triumph.
   —Jean Rhys; *Letters, 1931–1966*, 1984

.5 Opinions which justify cruelty are inspired by cruel impulses.
   —Bertrand Russell; *Unpopular Essays*, "Ideas That Have Harmed Mankind," 1950

.6 I must be cruel only to be kind.
   —William Shakespeare; *Hamlet*, 1601

.7 All cruel people describe themselves as paragons of frankness.
   —Tennessee Williams; *The Milk Train Doesn't Stop Here Anymore*, 1963

**56** Curiosity

.1 A spirit of curiosity is nature's original school of education.
   —Smiley Blanton; *Love or Perish*, 1956

.2 Curiosity always leads to disagreeable questions.
   —Fanny Burney; *Camilla*, 1796

.3 Curiouser and curiouser!
   —Lewis Carroll; *Alice's Adventures in Wonderland*, 1865

.4 I only ask for information.
   —Charles Dickens; *David Copperfield*, 1849–50

.5 It is nothing short of a miracle that the modern methods of instruction have not yet entirely strangled the holy curiosity of inquiry.... It is a very grave mistake to think that the enjoyment of seeing and searching can be promoted by means of coercion and a sense of duty.
   —Albert Einstein; Quoted in George B. Leonard, *Education and Ecstasy*, 1969

.6 The whole art of teaching is only the art of awakening the natural curiosity of young minds for the purpose of satisfying it afterwards.
   —Anatole France; *The Crime of Sylvestre Bonnard*, 1881

## 56

.7 Avoid a questioner, for he is also a tattler.
—Horace; *Epistles*, c. 19 B.C.

.8 Talk to him of Jacob's ladder, he would ask the number of the steps.
—Douglas Jerrold; *A Matter-of-Fact Man*, c. 1850

.9 Keep your mouth shut, and close the doors of sight and sound, and as long as you live you will have no vexation. But open your mouth, or become inquisitive, and you will be in trouble all your life long.
—Lao-Tsze; *The Simple Way*, c. 604–531 B.C.

.10 We are all like Scheherazade's husband, Curiosity is the key to creativity.
—Akio Morita; *Made in Japan*, 1986

.11 We never stop investigating. We are never satisfied that we know enough to get by. Every question we ask leads on to another question. This has become the greatest survival trick of our species.
—Desmond Morris; *The Naked Ape*, 1967

.12 Love of learning is by nature curious and inquisitive, ... prying into everything, reluctant to leave anything, material or immaterial, unexplored.
—Philo; *On the Migration of Abraham*, before A.D. 50

.13 Curiosity begets curiosity.
—Samuel Richardson; *Clarissa Harlowe*, 1747–48

.14 I think, at a child's birth, if a mother could ask a fairy godmother to endow it with the most useful gift, that gift would be curiosity.
—Eleanor Roosevelt; Quoted in *Reader's Digest*, 1983

.15 Curiosity is a willing, a proud, an eager confession of ignorance.
—S. Leonard Rubinstein; "A Habit of Mind," *Reader's Digest*, 1984

.16 Curiosity is one of those insatiable passions that grow by gratification.
—Sarah Scott; *A Description of Millennium Hall*, 1762

.17 Do not be inquisitive. He who asks what has been said about him, who digs out malicious talk, even if it has been private, disturbs his own peace.
—Seneca; *De Ira*, c. 1st century A.D.

.18 He had no curiosity. It was his chief defect.
—Oscar Wilde; *The Picture of Dorian Gray*, 1891

## 57 Cursing and Swearing

.1 'Twas not my mind that swore: my tongue committed a little perjury on its own account.
—Aristophanes; *The Frogs*, 405 B.C.

.2 Don't swear, boy. It shows a lack of vocabulary.
—Alan Bennett; *Forty Years On*, 1969

.3 A little friendly curse of two is a very innocent refreshment to a man's mind.
—Fanny Burney; *Camilla*, 1796

.4 The man who first abused his fellows with swear-words instead of bashing their brains out with a club should be counted among those who laid the foundations of civilization.
—John Cohen; in *The Observer*, November 21, 1965

.5 Swearing is ... learning to the ignorant, eloquence to the blockhead, vivacity to the stupid, and wit to the coxcomb.
—Mary Collyer; *Felicia to Charlotte*, 1744

.6 The best thing about a little judicious swearing is that it keeps the temper. 'Twas intended as a compromise between running away and fighting.
—Finley Peter Dunne; *Observations by Mr. Dooley*, "Swearing," 1902

.7 Grant me some wild expression, Heavens, or I shall burst.
—George Farquhar; *The Constant Couple*, 1699

.8 Curse and be cursed! it is the fruit of cursing.
—John Fletcher; *Rollo*, c. 1616

.9 A curse spoken is like a donkey; it always follows its master.
—Greek Proverb

.10 I shall curse you with book and bell and candle.
—Thomas Malory; *Le Morte d'Arthur*, 1470

.11 He'll swear till he's black in the face.
—John Ray; *English Proverbs*, 1678

.12 Curses, not loud, but deep.
—William Shakespeare; *Macbeth*, 1606

.13 Swearing till my very roof was dry.
—William Shakespeare; *The Merchant of Venice*, 1597

.14 If I ever utter an oath again may my soul be blasted to eternal damnation!
—George Bernard Shaw; *Saint Joan*, 1924

## 57

.15 In certain trying circumstances, desperate circumstances, profanity furnishes a relief denied even to prayer.
—Mark Twain: *Pudd'nhead Wilson's Calendar*, 1894

.16 When it comes down to pure ornamental cursing, the native American is gifted above the sons of men.
—Mark Twain; *Roughing It*, 1872

## 58 Cynics and Cynicism

.1 Cynical speech is characterized by a lengthening of vowel sounds in the syllable that is normally accented, i.e., "Woooonderful." Derivation of this attitude can be traced to the manufacture of the first synthetic fabrics. "That sweater's prooobably acryyyylic."
—Lisa Birnbach; *The Official Preppy Handbook*, 1980

.2 Why should we strive, with cynic frown,
To knock the fairy castles down?
—Eliza Cook; "Oh! Dear to Memory," late 19th century

.3 A cynic can chill and dishearten with a single word.
—Ralph Waldo Emerson; *Society and Solitude* "Success," 1870

.4 A cynic is not merely one who reads bitter lessons from the past; he is one who is prematurely disappointed in the future.
—Sydney Harris; *On the Contrary*, 1962

.5 Cynicism is an unpleasant way of saying the truth.
—Lillian Hellman; *The Little Foxes*, 1939

.6 Cynicism is, after all, simply idealism gone sour.
—Will Herberg; *Judaism and Modern Man*, 1951

.7 If to look truth in the face and resent it when it's unpalatable, and take human nature as you find it, ... is to be cynical, then I suppose I'm a cynic.
—W. Somerset Maugham; *A Writer's Notebook*, 1896, published 1949

.8 Cynicism is the humor of hatred.
—Sir Herbert Beerbohm Tree; quoted in Hesketh Pearson, *Beerbohm-Tree*, 1956

## 59 Dance

.1 A dance is a measured pace, as a verse is a measured speech.
—Francis Bacon; *The Advancement of Learning*, 1605

.2 The truest expression of a people is in its dances and its music.... Bodies never lie.
—Agnes De Mille; *The New York Times Magazine*, 1975

.3 The poetry of the foot.
—John Dryden; *The Rival Ladies*, 1664

.4 Dancing is language given way to movement.
—Brian Friel; *Dancing at Lughnasa*, 1990

.5 Dance is the hidden language of the soul.
—Martha Graham; "Martha Graham Reflects on Her Art and a Life in Dance," *The New York Times Magazine*, 1985

.6 You can't lie when you dance. It's so direct. You do what is in you. You can't dance out of the side of your mouth.
—Shirley MacLaine; James Spada's *Shirley & Warren*, 1985

.7 When we were at school ... many of us have learnt to dance the rumba, or the cha cha, to rock and roll and to twist and even to dance the waltz and the foxtrot. But how many of us can dance, or have even heard of the gombe sugu, the mangala, nyang'umumi, kiduo, or lela mama?
—Julius K. Nyerere; *Tanzania National Assembly Official Reports*, 1962

.8 Dancing is a perpendicular expression of a horizontal desire.
—George Bernard Shaw; *New Statesman*, 1962

## 60 Death

.1 Death's a cruel note,
Set in a mortal throat.
—Leonie Adams; *High Falcon*, "Every Bird of Nature," 1929

.2 No lamentations can loose
Prisoners of death from the grave.
—Matthew Arnold, *Merope*, 1858

.3 Death ... pale priest of the mute people.
—Robert Browning; *Balaustion's Adventure*, 1871

.4 Men are convinced of your arguments, your sincerity, and the seriousness of your efforts only by your death.
—Albert Camus; *The Fall*, 1956

**60**

.5 Death is a displaced name for a linguistic predicament.
  —Paul de Man; quoted in *Signs of Our Times* by David Lehmann, 1991

.6 Any man's death diminishes me, because I am involved in Mankind;
And therefore never send to know for whom the bell tolls; it tolls for thee.
  —John Donne; *Devotions upon Emergent Occasions*, 1624

.7 Someone who talks bravely about death can be reduced to silence by fear of its actual onset.
  —Hans Kung; *Eternal Life?*, 1984

.8 Death is the gentlest of the world's replies.
  —Rose Hawthorne Lathrop; "Give Me Not Tears" in Edmund Clarence Stedman, ed. *An American Anthology*, 1900

.9 Masters, I have to tell a tale of woe,
A tale of folly and of wasted life,
Hope against hope, the bitter dregs of strife,
Ending, where all things end, in death at last.
  —William Morris; *The Beauty of Life*, 1880

.10 Now I lay me down to sleep;
I pray the Lord my soul to keep.
If I should die before I wake,
I pray the Lord my soul to take.
  —New England Primer

.11 Death is the only grammatically correct full-stop...
  —Brian Patten; *Grinning Jack*, "Schoolboy," 1990

.12 I have a rendezvous with Death
At some disputed barricade....
And I to my pledged word am true,
I shall not fail that rendezvous
  —Alan Seeger; "I Have a Rendezvous with Death," *North American Review*, 1916

.13 Do not go gentle into that good night,
Old age should burn and rage at close of day;
Rage, rage, against the dying of the light.
  —Dylan Thomas; "Do Not Go Gentle into That Good Night," 1952

.14 All say, "How hard it is that we have to die,"—a strange complaint to come from the mouths of people who have had to live.
  —Mark Twain; *Pudd'nhead Wilson's Calendar*, 1894

.15 The dead can tell no tales.
  —John Wilson; *Andronicus Comnenius*, 1664

**60**

.16 When the old man died, the shell was lost. In time, the shrine, too, disappeared. All that remained was the story. But that is how it is with all of us; When we die, all that remains is the story.
  —Diane Wolkstein; *White Wave*, "A Chinese Tale," 1980

# 61 Definition

.1 A definition is the enclosing a wilderness of idea within a wall of words.
  —Samuel Butler II; *Note Books*, "Higgledy-Piggledy," 1912

.2 A definition is a sack of flour compressed into a thimble.
  —Remy de Gourmont; "Glory and the Idea of Immortality" in *Le Chemin de Velours*, 1902

.3 We expect definitions to tell us not only what is, but what to do about it.... A label is the first step toward action.
  —Elizabeth Janeway; *Improper Behavior*, 1987

.4 I know not how men, who have the same idea under different names, or different ideas under the same name, can in that case talk to one another.
  —John Locke; *An Essay Concerning Human Understanding*, 1690

.5 I suppose that so long as there are people in the world, they will publish dictionaries defining what is unknown in terms of something equally unknown.
  —Flann O'Brien; *Myles Away from Dublin*, 1990

.6 By speaking, by thinking, we undertake to clarify things, and that forces us to exacerbate them, dislocate them, schematize them. Every concept is in itself an exaggeration.
  —Jose Ortega y Gasset; "In Search of Goethe from Within," in *Partisan Review*, December, 1949

.7 If we are to reclaim our culture, we cannot afford narrow definitions.
  —Starhawk; *The Spiral Dance*, 1979

.8 If you wish to converse with me, define your terms.
  —Voltaire; Attributed

# 62 Devil

.1 Sarcasm I now see to be, in general, the language of the Devil.
—Thomas Carlyle; *Sartor Resartus*, 1834

.2 Let every man speak as he finds and give the devil his due.
—John Dryden; *The Wild Gallant*, 1663

.3 Talk of the devil and he'll appear.
—Gerard Didier Erasmus; *Adagia*, c. 1500

.4 Pray what sort of gentleman is the devil? For I have heard some say there is no such person; and that it is only a trick of the parsons to prevent them being broke; for, if it was publicly known that there was no devil, the parsons would be of no more use than soldiers in peace.
—Henry Fielding; *Tom Jones*, 1749

.5 Speak boldly, and speak truthly,
Shame the Devil.
—John Fletcher; *Wit Without Money*, 1639

.6 The devil is a very successful preacher. He draws a great number after him. No preacher can command hearers like him—he was successful with our first parents—with the old world.
—Lemuel B. Haynes; "Universal Salvation—A Very Ancient Doctrine," 1795

.7 And the Devil said to Simon Legree:
"I like your style, so wicked and free."
—Vachel Lindsay; *Collected Poems*, "A Negro Sermon," 1923

.8 The devil can cite Scripture for his purpose.
—William Shakespeare; *The Merchant of Venice*, 1596–97

.9 All religions issue bibles against him, and say most injurious things about him, but we never hear his side.
—Mark Twain; *Harper's magazine*, 1899

# 63 Dialect

.1 Dialect or the speech of the people is capable of expressing whatever the people are.
A Babylonian dialect
Which learned pedants much affect.
—Samuel Butler I; *Hudibras*, 1663

.2 I once knew a fellow who spoke a dialect with an accent.
—Irvin S. Cobb; *Old Judge Priest*, 1915

.3 But here I sit to toil condemned,
Beside the many-voiced sea;
In sheets of Irish dialect hemmed,

# 63

My temper sadly sawed and phlegmed (new word),
My brow with perspiration gemmed,
My chin unshaved, my hair unkemmed,
My hatred of the world unstemmed,
By doubt distraught, by fear o'erwhelmed,
Oh, this demnition grind be demn'd.
—Finley Peter Dunne; Elmer Ellis' *Mr. Dooley's America*, 1941

.4 Our concern was speech, and speech impelled us
To purify the dialect of the tribe…
—T.S. Eliot; *Four Quartets*, "Little Gidding," 1942

.5 Dialect words—those terrible marks of the beast to the truly genteel.
—Thomas Hardy; *The Mayor of Casterbridge*, 1886

.6 Dialect is the elf rather than the genius of place.
—Alice Meynell; *Essays*, "The Little Language," 1914

.7 Good and much company, and a good dinner; most of their discourse was about hunting, in a dialect I understand very little.
—Samuel Pepys; *Diary*, 1663

.8 Yiddish is sick—but in our history between being sick and dying is a long, long way.
—Isaac Bashevis Singer; *New York Times*, 1978

.9 A language is a dialect that has an army and a navy.
—Max Weinreich; Quoted in Leo Rosten's *The Joy of Yiddish*, 1968

# 64 Dialogue

.1 Regimented minds cannot grasp the concept of confrontation as an open exchange of major differences with a view of settlement through genuine dialogue.
—Sun Kyi Aung San; *Freedom from Fear*, "In Quest of Democracy," 1989

.2 I sometimes almost think that eyes have ears: …
'Tis wonderful how oft the sex have heard
Long dialogues—which pass'd without a word!.
—Lord Byron; *Don Juan*, 1819–24

.3 Death is a dialogue between
The Spirit and the Dust.
—Emily Dickinson; *Complete Poems*, c. 1868, first published 1945

## 64

.4 A fool hath no dialogue with himself, the first thought carrieth him, without the reply of the second.
 —Lord Halifax (George Savile); *Complete Works*, published 1912

.5 Dialogue should simply be a sound among other sounds, just something that comes out of the mouths of people whose eyes tell the story in visual terms.
 —Alfred Hitchcock; quoted in *Hitchcock*, by Francois Truffaut, 1967

.6 The deepest thing I know is that I am living and dying at once, and my conviction is to report that dialogue.
 —Stanley Jasspon Kunitz; Quoted in the *New York Times*, 1987

.7 If you have reason, be brief, 'tis not the time of the moon with me to make one in so slipping a dialogue.
 —William Shakespeare; *Twelfth Night*, 1601

.8 Like a strutting player, whose conceit
 Lies in his hamstring, and doth think it rich
 To hear the wooden dialogue and sound
 'Twixt his stretch'd footing and the scaffoldage.
 —William Shakespeare; *Troilus and Cressida*, 1602

.9 I write plays because dialogue is the most respectable way of contradicting myself.
 —Tom Stoppard; in *The Guardian*, 1973

.10 Dialogue in fiction should be reserved for the culminating moments and regarded as the spray into which the great wave of narrative breaks in curving toward the watcher on the shore.
 —Edith Wharton; *The Writing of Fiction*, 1925

.11 A babe, by intercourse of touch
 I held mute dialogues with my Mother's heart.
 —William Wordsworth; *The Prelude*, 1799–1905, published 1850

.12 Dialogue is a necessary evil.
 —Fred Zinnemann; interview in the *Independent on Sunday*, London, May 31, 1992
 [The Austrian-born U.S. filmmaker prefers the story of a film be carried by the action photographed rather than by words to describe it.]

## 65 Differences

.1 Debate is masculine; conversation is feminine.
 —Amos Bronson Alcott; *Concord Days*, 1872

.2 History tells how it was. A story—how it might have been.
 —Alfred Andersch; "Winterspelt," 1970

.3 The difference between genuine poetry and the poetry of Dryden, Pope, and their school, is briefly this: their poetry is conceived and composed in their wits, genuine poetry is conceived and composed in the soul.
 —Matthew Arnold; *Essays in Criticism*, Second Series, "Thomas Gray," 1888

.4 The frontiers between history and imagination are very little more than Chinese screens, removable at will.
 —Richard Cobb; *The Listeners*, 1978

.5 What is history after all? History is facts which become legend in the end; legends are lies which become history in the end.
 —Jean Cocteau; Interview, 1957

.6 To sum up it would appear that national differences in the manner of storytelling are for the most part superficial.
 —Edwin Sydney Hartland; *The Science of Fairy Tales*, 1891

.7 There is a big difference between what one hears and sees.
 —Japanese Proverb

.8 A man never knows how to say goodbye; a woman never knows when to say it.
 —Helen Rowland; *Reflections of a Bachelor Girl*, 1909

.9 One of the most striking differences between a cat and a lie is that a cat has only nine lives.
 —Mark Twain; *Pudd'nhead Wilson's Calendar*, 1894

.10 The difference between the right word and the almost right word is the difference between lightning and the lightning bug.
 —Mark Twain; Albert Bigelow Paine, ed. *Mark Twain's Notebook*, 1935

## 66 Diplomats and Diplomacy

.1 Diplomacy, n. The patriotic art of lying for your country.
 —Ambrose Bierce; *The Devil's Dictionary*, 1906

## 66

.2  Diplomacy: The art of saying "nice doggie" until you can find a rock.
—Wynn Catlin; Attributed by Bennett Cerf in *The Laugh's on Me*, 1959

.3  I have discovered the art of fooling diplomats; I speak the truth and they never believe me.
—Benso di Cavour; Quoted in William de la Rive, *Reminiscences of Life and Character of Count Cavour*, 1912

.4  All diplomacy is a continuation of war by other means.
—Chou En-Lai; Interview with Edgar Snow, *Saturday Evening Post*, 1954
[Prussian General Karl von Clauswitz (1780–1831) said "War is nothing else but the continuation of state policy with other means. Lenin is quoted in *Selected Works*, "This was always the viewpoint of Marx and Engels, who regarded every war as the continuation of politics of the given interested powers."]

.5  To jaw-jaw is better than to war-war.
—Winston Churchill; Speech, White House, Washington, D.C., 1954

.6  When a diplomat says yes, he means perhaps. When he says perhaps he means no. When he says no, he is not a diplomat. When a lady says no, she means perhaps. When she says perhaps, she means yes. But when she says yes, she is no lady.
—Lord Denning; Speech at Magistrates Association, 1982
[On the difference between a diplomat and a lady.]

.7  To say nothing, especially when speaking, is half the art of diplomacy.
—Will Durant; *Reader Digest*, 1972

.8  There are few ironclad rules of diplomacy but to one there is no exception. When an official reports that the talks were useful, if can safely be concluded that nothing was accomplished.
—J.K. Galbraith; "The American Ambassador," published in *The Foreign Service Journal*, June, 1969

.9  Modern diplomats approach every problem with an open mouth.
—Arthur J. Goldberg; Attributed

.10  Diplomacy is to do and say the nastiest things in the nicest way.
—Isaac Goldberg; *The Reflex*, 1929

.11  Diplomacy: lying in state.
—Oliver Herford; *Neither Here Nor There*, 1922

## 66

.12  Megaphone diplomacy leads to a dialogue of the deaf.
—Lord Geoffrey Howe; Quoted in *The Observer*, 1985

.13  The only decent diplomat is a deaf Trappist.
—John Le Carre; *A Perfect Spy*, 1986

.14  A diplomat is a person who can tell you to go to hell in such a way that you actually look forward to the trip.
—Caskie Stinnett; "Out of the Red," 1960

.15  If a diplomat says *yes*, he means *perhaps*. If he says *perhaps* he means *no*. And if he says *no*, he's a hell of a diplomat.
—Agnes Sligh Turnbull; *The Golden Journey*, 1955

.16  An ambassador is an honest man, sent to lie abroad for the good of his country.
—Henry Wotton; *Reliquiae Wottonianae*, 1651

## 67 Discussion

.1  Democracy means government by discussion, but it is only effective if you can stop people talking.
—Clement Attlee; Speech, 1957

.2  Discussion: a method of confirming others in their errors.
—Ambrose Bierce; *The Devil's Dictionary*, 1906

.3  The mutual confidence on which all else depends can be maintained only by an open mind and a brave reliance upon free discussion.
—Learned Hand; Speech to the Board of Regents, University of the State of New York, 1952

.4  Men are never so likely to settle a question rightly as when they discuss it freely.
—Thomas Babington Macaulay; "Southey's 'Colloquies of Society'," *Edinburgh Review*, 1830

.5  It is good to rub and polish our brain against that of others.
—Michel de Montaigne; *Essays*, "Various Outcomes of the Same Plan," 1580

.6  Discussion in class, which means letting twenty young blockheads and two cocky neurotics discuss something that neither their teacher nor they know.
—Vladimir Nabokov; *Pnin*, 1957

.7  In one case out of a hundred a point is excessively because it is obscure, in the ninety-nine

67

remaining it is obscure because excessively discussed.
—Edgar Allan Poe; *The Pioneer*, "The Rationale of Verse," 1843

.8   The discussion of any subject is a right that you have brought into the world with your heart and tongue. Resign your heart's blood before you part with this inestimable privilege of man.
—Percy Bysshe Shelley; *An Address to the Irish People*, 1812

.9   And friendly free discussion, calling forth
From the fair jewel, Truth, its latent ray.
—James Thomson; *Liberty*, 1734

.10  Discussion in America means dissent.
—James Thurber; *Lanterns and Lances*, "The Duchess and the Boys," 1961

# 68 Dispute

.1   It is labor in vain to dispute with a man, unless somebody be in company, to whose judgement you would both submit.
—Anonymous

.2   The traditional disputes of philosophers are, for the most part, as unwarranted as they are unfruitful.
—Alfred Jules Ayer; *Language, Truth and Logic*, 1936

.3   A good cause need not be patroned by passion, but can sustain itself upon a temperate dispute.
—Thomas Browne; *Religio Medici*, 1643

.4   He'd run in debt by disputation,
And pay with ratiocination.
—Samuel Butler; *Hudibras*, 1663

.5   It is not he who gains the exact point in dispute who scores most in controversy, but he who has shown the most forbearance and the better temper.
—Samuel Butler II; *Notebooks*, "Reconciliation," 1912

.6   No and yes cause long disputes.
—Danish Proverb

.7   It is a fault we may remark in most disputes, that, as truth is the mean between the two opinions that are upheld, each disputant departs from it in proportion to the degree in which he possesses the spirit of contradiction.
—Rene Descartes; *The Principles of Philosophy*, 1644

68

.8   In a philosophical dispute, he gains most who is defeated, since he learns most.
—Epicurus; *Letters, Principal Doctrines, and Vatican Sayings*, "Vatican Sayings," 3rd century B.C.

.9   Some have wondered that disputes about opinions should so often end in personalities; but the fact is, that such disputes begin with personalities; for our opinions are a part of ourselves. Besides, after the first contradiction it is ourselves, and not the thing, we maintain.
—Edward Fitzgerald; *Polonius*, 1852

.10  Many a long dispute among disputes may be thus abridged: It is so. It is not so. It is so. It is not so.
—Benjamin Franklin; *Poor Richard's Almanack*, 1743

.11  They have begun a Dispute, which the Devil will not let them make an End of.
—Thomas Fuller II; *Gnomologia*, 1732

.12  Disputation is the sifter out of the truth.
—Stefano Guazzo; *Civil Conversation*, 1574

.13  Nothing was ever learned by either side in a dispute.
—William Hazlitt; "On the Conversation of Authors," 1820

.14  I never saw an instance of one of two disputants convincing the other by argument. I have seen many, on their getting warm, become rude, & shooting one another.
—Thomas Jefferson; Letter to his Grandson Jefferson Randolph, 1808

.15  Every man will dispute with great good humor upon a subject in which he is not interested.
—Samuel Johnson; Boswell's *Life of Johnson*, 1781

.16  We should have a great many fewer disputes in the world if words were taken for what they are, the signs of our ideas, and not for things themselves.
—John Locke: *An Essay Concerning Human Understanding*, 1690

.17  Young fire-eyed disputants, who deem their swords,
On points of faith, more eloquent than words.
—Thomas Moore; *Lalla Rookh: The Veiled Prophet*, 1817

.18  It were endless to dispute upon everything that is disputable.
—William Penn; *Some Fruits of Solitude*, 1693

**68**

.19 True disputants are like true sportsmen; their whole delight is in the pursuit.
—Alexander Pope; *Thoughts on Various Subjects*, 1727

.20 The partisan, when he is engaged in a dispute, cares nothing about the rights of the question, but is anxious only to convince his hearers of his own assertions.
—Socrates; Plato's *Phaedo*, 4th–3rd century B.C.

# 69 Double-Entendre

.1 There was an old man of Boulogne
Who sang a most topical song.
It wasn't the words
That frightened the birds,
But the horrible double-entendre.
—Anonymous

.2 The marvelous thing about a joke with a double meaning is that it can only mean one thing.
—Ronnie Barker; *Sauce*, "Daddie's Sauce," 1977

.3 And however our Dennises take offence,
A double-meaning shows double sense;
And if proverbs tell truth, A double tooth
Is wisdom's adopted dwelling.
—Thomas Hood; *Whims and Oddities*, 1826–27

# 70 Doubt

.1 No man likes to have his intelligence or good faith questioned, especially if he has doubts about it himself.
—Henry Adams; *The Education of Henry Adams*, 1907

.2 Galileo called doubt the father of invention; it is certainly the pioneer.
—Christian Nestell Bovee; *Summaries of Thoughts*, 1862

.3 They would have been equally horrified at hearing the Christian religion doubted, and at seeing it practiced.
—Samuel Butler II; *The Way of All Flesh*, 1903

.4 If you would be a real seeker after truth, it is necessary that at least once in your life you doubt, as far as possible, all things.
—Rene Descartes; *Principles of Philosophy*, 1644

**70**

.5 We do not know, nor can we know, with absolute certainty that those who disagree with us are wrong. We are human and therefore fallible, and being fallible, we cannot escape the *element of doubt* as to our own opinions and convictions.
—J. William Fullbright; *Address*, Washington, D.C., 1963

.6 I will listen to any one's convictions, but keep your doubts to yourself.
—Johann Wolfgang von Goethe; *Conversations with Eckermann*, 1829

.7 William James used to preach the "will to believe." For my part, I should wish to preach the "will to doubt." … What is wanted is not the will to believe, but the wish to find out, which is the exact opposite.
—Bertrand Russell; *Skeptical Essays*, 1928

.8 Never believe what you cannot doubt.
—Robin Skelton; *A Devious Dictionary*, 1991

.9 Life is doubt. And faith without doubt is nothing but death.
—Miguel de Unamuno; "Salmo II," 1907

.10 When in danger, ponder. When in trouble, delegate. And when in doubt, mumble.
—Robert F. Wagner, Jr.; *New York Times*, 1991

# 71 Dreams

.1 Dreams are the individual's folk-tales and folk-tales are collective dreams.
—Richard Adams; *The Unbroken Web*, 1980

.2 If there were dreams to sell,
Merry and sad to tell,
And the crier rung his bell,
What would you buy?
—T.L. Beddoes; "Dream Pedlary," 1851

.3 People who insist on telling their dreams are among the terrors of the breakfast table.
—Max Beerbohm; *The Works of Max Beerbohm*, 1896

.4 When the legends die, the dreams end. When the dreams end, there is no more greatness.
—Hal Borland; *Sundial of the Seasons*, 1964

.5 This tale's a fragment from the life of dreams.
—Samuel Taylor Coleridge; *Phantom or Fact?*

.6 Very old are we men;
Our dreams are tales
Told in dim Eden

## 71

By Eve's nightingales;
We wake and whisper awhile,
But, the day gone by,
Silence and sleep like fields
Of amaranth lie.
— Walter De La Mare; "All That's Past,"
1912

.7 Thy wise dreams and fables of the sky.
— Homer; *Odyssey*, c. 700 B.C.

.8 …dreams have … in all ages been regarded as
revelations, and have played a large part in furnishing forth mythologies and creating themes
for faith to lay hold upon.
— William James; *Varieties of Religious Experience*, 1902

.9 The firelight of a long, blind, dreaming story
Lingers upon your lips; and I have seen
Firm, fixed forever in your closing eyes,
The Corn King beckoning to his Spring
Queen.
— Randall Jarrell; *Selected Poems*, 1955

.10 Dreams are faithful interpreters of our inclinations; but there is an art required to sort and
understand them.
— Michel de Montaigne; *Essays* "Of Experience," 1580–88

.11 One should not discuss a dream
In front of a simpleton.
— Mu-mon; *The Gateless Gate*, c. 525 B.C.

.12 Stories operate like dreams; both veil what is
to be uncovered; neither is capable of the
cover-up.
— Lore Segal; "Our Dream of the Good
God," Christina Buchmann and Celina
Spiegel, eds. *Out of the Garden*, 1994

.13 Dreams come true; without that possibility,
nature would not incite us to have them.
— John Updike; *Self-Consciousness: Memoirs*, 1989

## 72 Ear

.1 It is the ear that troubles the mouth.
— African Proverb

.2 A man should not permit his ears to hear improper words, because, before all other members of the human body, his ears, being thin
and soft, will be burned first.
— Babylonian Talmud; *Kethuboth*, c. 450

.3 But God has a few of us to whom he
whispers in the ear;

## 72

The rest may reason and welcome; 'tis we
musicians know.
— Robert Browning; *Dramatis Personae*,
"Abt Vogler," 1864

.4 The hearing ear is always found close to the
speaking tongue.
— Ralph Waldo Emerson; *English Traits*,
1856

.5 Better to play with the ears than with the
tongue.
— English Proverb

.6 One pair of ears draws dry a hundred tongues.
— George Herbert; *Jacula Prudentum*, 1640

.7 Little pitchers have wide ears.
— George Herbert; *Jacula Prudentum*, 1640

.8 Went in at the one ear and out the other.
— John Heywood; *Proverbs*, 1546

.9 Hang your ears this way.
— Ben Jonson; *Magnetick Lady*, 1632

.10 I was all ear,
And took in strains that might create a soul
Under the ribs of death.
— John Milton; *Cosmus*, 1637

.11 Where more is meant than meets the ear.
— John Milton "Il Penseroso," 1632

.12 He that hath ears to hear, let him hear.
— New Testament: Mark

.13 Lord, I cry unto thee: make haste unto me;
give ear unto my voice, when I cry unto thee.
— Old Testament: Psalms

.14 If your ears burns, some one is talking about
you.
— Pliny the Elder; *Naturalis Historia*, A.D.
77

.15 The most precious thing a man can lend is his
ears.
— Dagobert D. Runes; *Treasury of Thought*,
1966

.16 Friends, Romans, countrymen, lend me your
ears.
— William Shakespeare; *Julius Caesar*, 1599

.17 She told him stories to delight his ear.
— William Shakespeare; *The Passionate
Pilgrim*, 1599

.18 Take heed what you say. Walls have ears.
— James Shirley; *A Bird in a Cage*, 1633

.19 Ears are eyes to the blind.
— Sophocles; *Oedipus Coloneus*, c. 408 B.C.

.20 They stand by with ears pricked up.
— Virgil; *Aeneid*, 19 B.C.

## 72

.21 The ears don't hear what the mouth utters.
—Yiddish Proverb

.22 We have two ears and only one tongue in order that we may hear more and speak less.
—Zeno; *Maxim*, c. 460 B.C., Diogenes Laertius, *Zeno*

# 73 Echo

.1 Translation is at best an echo.
—George Borrow; *Lavengro*, 1851

.2 The most innocent echo has an impish mockery in it when it follows a gravely persistent speaker.
—George Eliot; *Middlemarch*, 1872

.3 Echo the mimic, the less of the voice, the tail of a word.
—Evodus; *On a Statue of Echo* (Greek Anthology), date unknown

.4 The echo knows all languages.
—Finnish Proverb

.5 Echo is the voice of a reflection in the mirror.
—Nathaniel Hawthorne; *American Note-Books*, 1841–52

.6 Sweet Echo, sweetest nymph, that liv'st unseen
Within thy airy shell
By slow Meander's margent green
And in the violet-embroidered vale.
—John Milton; *Cosmus, A Mask*, 1634

.7 How sweet the answer makes
To music at night,
When, roused by lute or horn, she wakes,
And far away, o'er lawns and lakes,
Goes answering light.
—Thomas Moore; "Echo," 1806

.8 And more than echoes talk along the walls.
—Alexander Pope; "Eloisa to Abelard," 1717

.9 All Classic learning lost on Classic ground;
And last turn'd Air, the Echo of a Sound!
—Alexander Pope; *The Dunciad*, 1742

.10 But her voice is still living immortal,
The same you have frequently heard,
In your rambles in valleys and forests,
Repeating your ultimate word.
—J.G. Saxe; "The Story of Echo," 1850

.12 The shadow of a sound—a voice without a mouth, and words without a tongue.
—Horace Smith; *The Tin Trumpet: Echo*, 1836

## 73

.13 Our echoes roll from soul to soul,
And grow forever and forever.
—Alfred, Lord Tennyson; "The Princess," 1847

.14 My dwelling was small, and I could hardly entertain an echo in it.
—Henry David Thoreau; *Journal*, 1842

# 74 Education

.1 What sculpture is to a block of marble, education is to an human soul.
—Joseph Addison; *The Spectator*, 1711–12

.2 Nothing is to be done in education without steady and regular instruction.
—Jane Austen; *Pride and Prejudice*, 1813

.3 Education, n.: That which discloses to the wise and disguises from the foolish their lack of understanding.
—Ambrose Bierce; *The Devil's Dictionary*, 1906

.4 Education is learning what you didn't know you didn't know.
—Daniel J. Boorstein; *Democracy and Its Discontents*, 1974

.5 To live for a time close to great minds is the best kind of education.
—John Buchan; *Memory Hold the Door*, 1940

.6 Education is, not a preparation for life; education is life itself.
—John Dewey; "My Pedagogic Creed," *The School Journal*, 1897

.7 One might say that the American trend of education is to reduce the senses almost to nil.
—Isadora Duncan; *My Life*, 1927

.8 Education is a progressive discovery of our ignorance.
—Will Durant; *The Story of Philosophy*, 1926

.9 Education is the process of driving a set of prejudices down your throat.
—Martin H. Fischer; *Fischerisms*, 1937

.10 Education is the ability to listen to almost anything without losing your temper or your self-confidence.
—Robert Frost; *Reader's Digest*, 1960

.11 Education makes us more stupid than the brutes. A thousand voices call to us on every hand, but our ears are stopped with wisdom.
—Jean Giraudoux; *The Enchanted*, 1933

**74**

.12 More is often taught by a jest than by the most serious teaching.
—Baltasar Gracian; *The Art of Worldly Wisdom*, c. 1651

.13 The poet is the unsatisfied child who dares to ask the difficult question which arises from the schoolmaster's answer to his simple question, and then the still more difficult question which arises from that.
—Robert Graves; *The White Goddess*, 1948

.14 Poets were the first teachers of mankind.
—Horace; *Ars Poetica*, 19 B.C.

.15 Education is a kind of continuing dialogue, and a dialogue assumes, in the nature of the case, different points of view.
—Robert M. Hutchins; Testimony before House of Representatives committee, 1952

.16 Education is what most people receive, many pass on and few actually have.
—Karl Kraus; *Pro domo et mundo*, 1912

.17 Schooling, instead of encouraging the asking of questions, too often discourages it.
—Madeline L'Engle; *Walking on Water*, 1980

.18 Once you have the cap and gown all you need do is open your mouth. Whatever nonsense you talk becomes wisdom and all the rubbish, good sense.
—Molière; *The Imaginary Invalid*, 1673

.19 And so we discover that education is not something which the teacher does but that it is a natural process which develops spontaneously in the human being.
—Maria Montessori; *The Absorbent Mind*, 1967

.20 Education is what survives when what has been learned has been forgotten.
—B.F. Skinner; "New Methods and New Aims in Teaching," *New Scientist*, 1964

.21 It is scarcely possible to prevent great men from rising up under any system of education.
—Sydney Smith; *Classical Learning*, 1809

.22 To me education is a leading out of what is already there in the pupil's soul. To Miss Mackay it is putting in of something that is not there, and that is not what I call education, I call it intrusion.
—Muriel Spark; *The Prime of Miss Jean Brodie*, 1962

.23 Man is eager to learn and his fondness for tales is a prelude to this quality. It is fondness for tales, then, that induces children to give their

**74**

attention to narrative and more and more to take part in them. The reason for this is that myth is a new language to them—a language that tells them, not of things as they are, but of a different set of things—and what is new is pleasing, and so is what one did not know before, and it is just this that makes men eager to learn. But if you add to this the marvellous and the portentous, you thereby increase the pleasure, and pleasure acts as a charm to incite to learning. At the beginning we must needs make use of such bait for children....
—Strabo; *Geography*, c. 7 B.C.–A.D. 18

.24 What does education often do? It makes a straight-cut ditch of a free, meandering brook.
—Henry David Thoreau; *Journal*, 1850

.25 Education is the acquisition of the art of the utilization of knowledge.
—Alfred North Whitehead; *The Aims of Education*, 1929

.26 Storytelling is the oldest form of education.
—Terry Tempest Williams; *Pieces of White Shell*, 1984

.27 Education has really one basic factor, a *sine qua non*—one must want it.
—George Edward Woodberry; *John Goffer's Mill*, c. 1855–1930

# **75** Eloquence

.1 False eloquence is exaggeration; true eloquence is emphasis.
—William Rounseville Alger; *Poetry of the Orient*, 1856

.2 Eloquence is logic on fire.
—Lyman Beecher; *Works*, 1852

.3 Even the damned may salute the eloquence of Mr. Webster.
—Stephen Vincent Benet; *The Devil and Daniel Webster*, 1936

.4 When a man gets talking about himself, he seldom fails to be eloquent and often reaches the sublime.
—Josh Billings; *Affurisms*, 1865

.5 Brevity is the soul of eloquence, and amplification, the usual fault.
—Hugh Henry Brackenridge; *Modern Chivalry*, 1792–1815

.6 What is eloquence but good sense expressed in clear language?
—Hugh Henry Brackenridge; *Modern Chivalry*, 1792–1815

75

.7 The manner of your speaking is full as important as the matter, as more people have ears to be tickled than understanding to judge.
—Lord Chesterfield; *Letters to His Son*, 1750

.8 He is an eloquent man who can treat humble subjects with delicacy, lofty things impressively, and moderate things temperately.
—Cicero; *De Oratore*, 55 B.C.

.9 Delivery is the management, with grace, of voice, countenance, and gesture.
—Cicero; *De Oratore*, 55 B.C.

.10 Whoever God has given knowledge
and eloquence in speaking,
should not be silent or secretive,
but should willingly show it.
—Marie de France; *Lais*, prologue, c. 1170

.11 I grew intoxicated with my own eloquence.
—Benjamin Disraeli; *Contarini Fleming*, 1832

.12 Eloquence is the child of Knowledge.
—Benjamin Disraeli; *The Young Duke*, 1831

.13 Eloquence is the power to translate a truth into language perfectly intelligible to the person to whom you speak.
—Ralph Waldo Emerson; *Letters and Social Aims: Eloquence*, 1876

.14 The eloquent man is he who is no beautiful speaker, but who is inwardly and desperately drunk with a certain belief.
—Ralph Waldo Emerson; *Journals*, 1845

.15 He that has no silver in his purse should have silver on his tongue.
—Thomas Fuller II, *Gnomologia*, 1732

.16 To the Greeks the Muse gave native wit, to the Greeks the gifts of eloquence in well-rounded phrase.
—Horace; *Ars Poetica*, c. 19 B.C.

.17 There is no more sovereign eloquence than the truth in indignation.
—Victor Hugo; *Les Miserables*, 1862

.18 An idiot's eloquence is silence.
—Japanese Proverb

.19 A man whose eloquence has power
To clear the fullest house in half an hour.
—Soame Jenyns; *Imitations of Horace*, 1747

.20 For they wished to fill the winepress of eloquence not with the tendrils of mere words but with the rich grape juice of good sense.
—St. Jerome; *Letter, 125*, c. 342–420

75

.21 Talking and eloquence are not the same thing: to speak and speak well are two things. A fool may talk, but a wise man speaks.
—Ben Jonson; *Timber, or Discoveries made upon Men and Matter*, 1641

.22 Genuinely good remarks surprise their author as well as his audience.
—Joseph Joubert; *Pensées*, 1847

.23 There is no less eloquence in the tone of the voice, in the eyes and in the air of the speaker, than in his choice of words.
—François La Rochefoucauld; *Maxims*, 1665

.24 True eloquence consists in saying all that should be, not all that could be said.
—François de La Rochefoucauld; *Maxims*, 1665

.25 The finest eloquence is that which gets things done; the worst is that which delays them.
—David Lloyd George; Speech at Paris Peace Conference, 1919

.26 Today it is not the classroom nor the classics which are the repositories of models of eloquence, but the ad agencies.
—Marshall McLuhan; *The Mechanical Bride*, "Plain Talk," 1951

.27 Eloquence is a persuasive thing.
—Menander; *Fragments*, c. 300 B.C.
[Menander elaborates: "But it is really the character of the speaker that does the persuading, not eloquence.]

.28 Copiousness of words, however ranged, is always false eloquence, though it will ever impose on some sort of understanding.
—Mary Wortley Montagu; Letter to Lady Bute, July 20, 1754

.29 Ulysses was not beautiful, but he was eloquent.
—Ovid; *Ars Amatoria*, c. 1 B.C.

.30 Eloquence, which persuades by sweetness, not by authority.
—Blaise Pascal; *Pensees*, 1670

.31 Eloquence is the art of saying things in such a way that those to whom we speak may listen to them with pleasure.
—Blaise Pascal; *Pensees*, 1670

.32 Continuous eloquence wearies.
—Blaise Pascal; *Pensees*, 1670

.33 It is with eloquence as with a flame; it requires fuel to feed it, motion to excite it, and brightness as it burns.
—William Pitt the Younger; Speech, early in 19th century

# 75

.34 He is eloquent enough for whom truth speaks.
—Publilius Syrus; *Sententia*, c. 1st century B.C.

.35 It is the heart which makes men eloquent.
—Quintilian; *De Institutione Oratoria*, c. A.D. 80

.36 You have witchcraft in your lips, Kate. There is more eloquence in a sugar touch of them than in the tongues of the French Council.
—William Shakespeare; *Henry V*, 1598–99
[King Henry woos Catherine.]

.37 I have neither wit, nor words, nor worth,
Action, nor utterance, nor the power of speech,
To stir men's blood; I only speak right on.
—William Shakespeare; *Julius Caesar*, 1599–1600

.38 Faith, that's as well said as if I had said it myself.
—Jonathan Swift; *Polite Conversation*, 1738

.39 Eloquence, smooth and cutting, is like a razor whetted with oil.
—Jonathan Swift; *Thoughts on Various Subjects*, 1714

.40 Great eloquence, like a flame, must have fuel to feed it, motion to excite it, and brightens as it burns.
—Tacitus; *De Oratoribus*, c. A.D. 85

.41 What is called eloquence in the forum is commonly found to be rhetoric in the study.
—Henry David Thoreau; *Walden*, 1854

.42 Noise proves nothing. Often a hen who has merely laid an egg cackles as if she laid an asteroid.
—Mark Twain; *Following the Equator*, 1897

.43 People can always tell well when they are talking what they feel. This is the secret of eloquence.
—Mark Twain, Letter to Olivia Langdon; January 16, 1869

.44 True eloquence does not consist in speech. Words and phrases may be marshalled in every way, but they cannot compass it. It must consist in the man, in the subject, and in the occasion. It comes, if at all, like the outbreaking of a fountain from the earth, or the bursting forth of volcanic fires, with spontaneous, original native force.
—Daniel Webster; *Writings and Speeches*, 1903

.45 A thing said walks in immortality
if it has been said well.
—John Wolcott (Peter Pindar); *Lyric Odes*, 1782–85

# 76 Emotion

.1 Allow me to feel no more than I profess.
—Jane Austen; *Sense and Sensibility*, 1811

.2 Many a man is afraid of expressing honest emotion because the word "sentiment" frightens him.
—Hilaire Belloc; *The Cruise of the Nona*, 1925

.3 They used language concentrating emotion, detail and image until they arrived at a form of dew-like steel.
—Richard Brautigan; *June 30th, June 30th*, 1978
[Speaking of Japanese poets.]

.4 When dealing with people remember you are not dealing with creatures of logic, but with creatures of emotion, creatures bristling with prejudice, and motivated by pride and vanity.
—Dale Carnegie; *How to Win Friends and Influence People*, 1938

.5 He hated people who reeled off their thoughts and emotions to you, who took it for granted that you wanted to know all their inner mechanism. Reserve was always more interesting.
—Agatha Christie; *Sad Cypress*, 1939

.6 Thought is deeper than all speech,
Feeling deeper than all thought.
—Christopher Pearse Cranch; "Thought," 1887

.7 The business of the poet is not to find new emotions, but to use the ordinary ones and, in working them up into poetry, to express feelings which are not in actual emotions at all.
—T.S. Eliot; *The Sacred Wood*, "Tradition and Individual Talent," 1920

.8 Be calm,
dry the living spring of tears that fill
your children's eyes. Console them with stories,
those sweet thieves of wretched make-believe.
—Euripides; *Heracles*, c. 428 B.C.

.9 One feels the excitement of hearing an untold story.
—John Hope Franklin; *Crisis*, "Book Review," 1986

.10 What an instrument is the human voice? How wonderfully responsive to every emotion of the human soul!
—Nathaniel Hawthorne; *The House of the Seven Gables*, 1851

.11 You can't convey an emotion to the public unless you feel it yourself.
—Alfred Hitchcock; interview, August

## 76

1962, published in Francois Truffaut, *Hitchcock,* 1966

.12 All the piteous tales that tears
Have water'd since the world was born.
—Thomas Hood; *Ode to Melancholy,* 1827

.13 If you wish me to weep, you must first feel grief.
—Horace; *Ars Poetica,* c. 19 B.C.

.14 There is no agony like bearing an untold story inside you.
—Zora Neale Hurston; *Dust Tracks on a Road,* 1942

.15 Spilling your guts is exactly as charming as it sounds.
—Fran Lebowitz; *Social Studies,* 1977

.16 There are moments in life, when the heart
is so full of emotion,
That if by chance it be shaken, or into its
depths like a pebble
Drops some careless word, it overflows, and
its secret,
Spilt on the ground like water, can never be
gathered together.
—Henry Wadsworth Longfellow; *The Courtship of Miles Standish,* 1858

.17 The direct speech of feeling is allegorical and cannot be replaced by anything.
—Boris Pasternak; *The Observer,* 1959

.18 My heart is on my lips. I speak just what I think.
—Thomas Love Peacock; *Crotchet Castle,* 1831

.19 Poetry is a form of speech for the better expression of emotional ideas.
—Herbert Spencer; "Origin and Function of Music," 1861

.20 Most of us do not use speech to express thoughts. We use it to express feelings.
—Jennifer Stone; *Stone's Throw,* "The Revisionist Imperative," 1988

.21 Emotions are among the toughest things in the world to manufacture out of whole cloth; it is easier to manufacture seven facts than one emotion.
—Mark Twain; *Life on the Mississippi,* 1883

.22 With the sense of sight, the idea communicates the emotion, with sound, the emotion communicates the idea, which is more direct and therefore more powerful.
—Alfred North Whitehead; *Dialogues of Alfred North Whitehead,* 1943

## 77 Entertainment

.1 A good teacher, like a good entertainer first must hold his audience's attention. Then he can teach his lesson.
—John Henrik Clarke; "A Search for Identity," *Social Casework,* May, 1970

.2 He was a wealthy man, and kindly to his fellow man; for dwelling in a house by the side of the road, he used to entertain all comers.
—Homer; *Iliad,* c. 700 B.C.

.3 A man never does justice to himself as an entertainer when his wife is around.
—Edgar Watson "Ed" Howe; *Country Town Sayings,* 1911

.4 The only way to entertain some folks is to listen to them.
—Kin Hubbard; *Hoss Sense and Nonsense,* 1926

.5 Be not forgetful to entertain strangers: for thereby some have entertained angles unawares.
—Old Testament: Hebrews

.6 Telling stories is among the least costly and yet the most effective means of entertainment available to any family.
—Anne Pellowski; *The Family Storytelling Handbook,* 1987

.7 I am only a public entertainer who has understood his time.
—Pablo Picasso; Quoted in Francoise Gilot and Carlton Lake, *Life with Picasso,* 1964

.8 All entertainment is education is some way, many times more effective than schools because of the appeal to the emotions rather than to the intellect.
—Hortense Powdermaker; *Hollywood, the Dream Factory,* 1950

.9 It seems that the analysis of character is the highest human entertainment. And literature does it, unlike gossip, without mentioning real names.
—Isaac Bashevis Singer; *Isaac Bashevis Singer Talks ... About Everything,* Interview with Richard Burgin, *New York Times Magazine,* November 26, 1978

.10 The essential is to excite the spectators. If that means playing *Hamlet* on a flying trapeze or in an aquarium, you do it.
—Orson Welles; *Les Nouvelles Littéraires,* 1953

# 78 Enunciation

.1 It was one of those plays in which all the actors unfortunately enunciated very clearly.
—Robert Benchley; Attributed

.2 Speak clearly, if you speak at all;
Carve every word before you let it fall.
—Oliver Wendell Holmes, Sr.; "A Rhymed Lesson," John Torrey Morse's *Life and Letters of Oliver Wendell Holmes*, 1896

.3 If you in a tongue utter speech that is not intelligible, how will any one know what is said. For you will be speaking into the air.
—New Testament: I Corinthians

# 79 Epic

.1 I would be the Lyric ever on the lip,
Rather than the Epic memory lets slip.
—Thomas Bailey Aldrich; *Lyrics and Epics*, 1874

.2 At leisure hours in Epic Song he deals,
Writes to the rumbling of his coach's wheels.
—John Dryden; *The Pilgrim*, "Prologue," 1675
[The reference is to Sir Richard Blackmore, a physician who among his many works were four epics. In the preface of one of these he related that they had been written in his coach as he traveled from one professional call to another.]

.3 The first epic poet ... invented the heroic myth. The hero was a man who by himself had slain the father—the father who still appeared in the myth as a totemistic monster. Just as the father had been the boy's first ideal, so in the hero who aspires to his father's place the poet now created the first ego ideal.
—Sigmund Freud; *Totem and Taboo*, 1912–1913

.4 The primitive era was lyrical, the classical era was epic and the modern era is dramatic.
—Victor Hugo; *Cromwell*, preface, 1827
[Hugo's great epics are *The Hunchback of Notre Dame* and *Les Miserables*.]

.5 Boomlay, boomlay, boomlay, Boom,
A roaring, epic, ragtime tune
From the mouth of the Congo
To the mountains of the Moon.
—Vachel Lindsay; *The Congo and Other Poems*, "The Congo," 1914

.6 Who now reads Cowley? if he pleases yet,
His moral pleases, not his pointed wit;

# 79

Forget his epic, nay Pindaric art,
But still I love the language of his heart.
—Alexander Pope; *Epistles: To Augustus*, 1735
[Pope speaks of Abraham Cowley, a Royalist, who contributed to the cause by writing a satire, *The Puritan and the Papist*, 1643 and the political epic, *The Civil War*, 1679.]

.7 The epic disappeared along with the age of personal heroism; there can be no epic with artillery.
—Ernest Renan; *Dialogues et Fragments Philosophiques*, "Probabilities," 1876

.8 In Nature's open book
An epic is the sea,
A lyric is the brook:—
Lyrics for me!
—Frank Dempster Sherman; "Lyrics," 1904

.9 Must not a great history be always an epic?
—W.C. Smith; *Books Which Have Influenced Me*, c. late 19th century

.10 A classic lecture, rich in sentiment,
With scraps of thundrous Epics lilted out
By violet-hooded Doctors, elegies
And quoted odes, and jewels five-words-long,
That on the sketched forefinger of all Time
Sparkle for ever.
—Alfred, Lord Tennyson; "The Princess," 1847

# 80 Epigram

.1 The diamond's virtues well might grace
The epigram, and both excel
In brilliancy in smallest space,
And power to cut, as well.
—George Birdseye; "The Epigram," c. late 19th century

.2 Our live experiences, fixed in aphorisms, stiffen into cold epigram. Our heart's blood, as we write with it, turns to mere dull ink.
—F.H. Bradley; *Appearance and Reality*, 1893

.3 France was long a despotism tempered by epigrams.
—Thomas Carlyle; *History of the French Revolution*, 1837

.4 What is an epigram? A dwarfish whole,
Its body brevity, and wit its soul.
—Samuel Taylor Coleridge; Attributed,

**80**

James Beander Matthews *American Epigrams, Harper's Monthly*, 1903

.5  Rather than waste precious time arguing, I went up and started serving my "sentence" without delay. It was usually about an hour for epigrams; somewhat longer for a paradox.
—Peter De Vries; *Comfort Me with Apples*, 1956

.6  The epigram has been compared to a scorpion, because as the sting of the scorpion lieth in the tail, the force of the epigram is in the conclusion.
—Lilius Gyraldus; *De Poetica Gyraldus*, 1545

.7  The epigram is a beautiful meaning in few and clear words…. It slings at the mark without delay.
—Moses Ibn Ezra; *Shirat Yisrael*, c. 12th century

.8  In general I don't see how an epigram, being a pure bolt from the blue, with no introduction or cue, gets itself writ.
—William James; *Letters*, 1896

.9  The sharp, the rapier-pointed epigram.
—John Keats; *Letters: Epistle to C.C. Clarke*, c. 1820

.10  An epigram is only a wisecrack that's played Carnegie Hall.
—Oscar Levant; *Coronet*, September, 1958

.11  The art of newspaper paragraphing is to stroke a platitude until it purrs like an epigram.
—Don Marquis; Quoted in E. Anthony's *O Rare Don Marquis*, 1962

.12  An epigram is a half-truth so stated as to irritate the person who believes the other half.
—Shailer Mathews; *A Dictionary of Religion and Ethics* (with Gerald B. Smith), 1921

.13  Epigram: a platitude with vine-leaves in its hair.
—H.L. Mencken; *A Book of Burlesques*, 1916

.14  But, with the imprecisive arrow
The acorn fairly struck—
Such is epigram, requiring
Wit, occasion, and good luck.
—Christopher Morley; "The Epigram," *Poems*, 1929

.15  If, with the literate, I am
Impelled to try an epigram,
I never seek to take the credit;
We all assume that Oscar said it.
—Dorothy Parker; *Sunset Gun*, "Oscar Wilde," 1928

**80**

.16  Epigrams succeed where epics fail.
—Persian Proverb

.17  A brilliant epigram is a solemn platitude gone to a masquerade ball.
—Lionel Strachey; Michael Holroyd, *Lionel Strachey*, 1967

.18  No epigram contains the whole truth.
—C.W. Thompson; *Presidents I've Known*, 1929

.19  Somewhere in the world there is an epigram for every dilemma.
—H.W. Van Loon; *Tolerance*, 1925

.20  Epigrams cover a multitude of sins.
—Carolyn Wells; *Folly for the Wise*, 1904

# 81 Eulogies and Epitaphs

.1  Here comes Glib-Tongue: who can out-flatter a Dedication, and lie like ten Epitaphs.
—Benjamin Franklin; *Poor Richard's Almanack*, 1742

.2  A eulogist of bygone days.
—Horace; *Ars Poetica*; c. 19 B.C.

.3  In lapidary inscriptions a man is not under oath.
—Samuel Johnson; Boswell's *Life of Johnson*, 1775

.4  Old soldiers never die, they just fade away.
—General Douglas MacArthur; Address before a joint meeting of U.S. Congress, 1951
[MacArthur quotes an old army ballad in his farewell speech after being fired by President Harry S Truman.]

.5  Pass not, but wonder, and amazed stand
At this sad tomb; for here enclosed lie
such rare perfections that no tongue or hand
Can speak them or portray them to the eye;
Such was her body, such her soul divine!
—Bathsua Makin; "Upon the most lamented death of the Right Honorable, the Lady Elizabeth Langham," 1664

.6  I love eulogies. They are the most moving kind of speech because they attempt to pluck meaning from the fog, and on short order, when the emotions are still ragged and raw and susceptible to leaps.
—Peggy Noonan; *What I Saw at the Revolution*, 1990

**81**

.7 Let no man write my epitaph; let my grave
Be uninscribed, and let my memory rest
Till other times are come, and other men,
Who then may do me justice.
　　—Robert Southey; *Written after Reading
　　the Speech of Robert Emmet*, 1803
　　[Irish patriot Robert Emmet's expressed
　　the exact sentiments in his speech from
　　the dock on the eve of his execution for
　　treason, for leading an abortive uprising
　　against the British.]

.8 Now he belongs to the ages.
　　—Edwin M. Stanton; Comment, April 15,
　　1865
　　[Secretary of War Stanton speaks of assas-
　　sinated President Abraham Lincoln.]

.9 The rarest quality in an epitaph is truth....
Fame itself is but an epitaph; as late, as false,
as true.
　　—Henry David Thoreau; *A Week on the
　　Concord and Merrimack Rivers*, "Mon-
　　day," 1849

.10 Eulogy is invariably dull.
　　—Anthony Trollope; *The Way We Live
　　Now*, 1875

.11 One needs a dash of satire to enliven a eulogy.
　　—Voltaire; Attributed

# **82** Euphemisms

.1 Euphemisms, like fashions, have their day and
pass, perhaps to return at another time. Like
the guests at a masquerade ball, they enjoy social approval only as long as they retain the
capacity for deception.
　　—Freda Adler; *Sisters in Crime*, 1975

.2 It is good to find modest words to express immodest things.
　　—Anonymous

.3 Those expressions are omitted which can not
with propriety be read aloud in the family.
　　—Thomas Bowdler; *Family Shakespeare*,
　　Preface, 1818

.4 The practice of hinting by single letters those
expletives with which profane and violent persons are wont to garnish their discourse, strikes
me as a proceeding which, however well
meant, is weak and futile. I cannot tell what
good it does—what feeling it spares—what
horror it conceals.
　　—Charlotte Bronte; *Wuthering Heights*,
　　Preface, 1847

.5 This instinct of politeness in speech—euphemism, as it is called—which seeks to hint
at an unpleasant or indelicate thing rather than
name it directly, has had much to do with
making words acquire new meanings and lose
old ones.
　　—Robert Chambers; *Information for the
　　People*, c. Early 20th century

.6 Euphemisms are not, as many young people
think, useless verbiage for that which can and
should be said bluntly; they are like secret
agents on a delicate mission, they must airily
pass by a stinking mess with barely so much
as a nod of the head, make their point of con-
structive criticism and continue on in calm
forbearance. Euphemisms are unpleasant
truths wearing diplomatic cologne.
　　—Quentin Crisp; *Manners from Heaven*,
　　1984

.7 The knees of the unmentionables ... soon
began to get alarmingly white.
　　—Charles Dickens; *Sketches by Boz*, 1835

.8 Immodest words admit of no defence,
For want of decency is want of sense.
　　—Wentworth Dillon; *On Translated Verse*,
　　1684

.9 "Interesting condition" was the genteel syn-
onym for pregnancy.
　　—Eleanor Early; *A New England Sampler*,
　　1940

.10 I know uh secret codes. I ain' crazy, I got un
'motional disorder; I ain' got fits, I got uh con-
vulsive disorder; an' I ain' ugly, I plain; an' I ain'
black, I dusky; an' my children ain' bastards,
they—they *love-flowers*!
　　—Joanne Greenberg; *The Monday Voices*,
　　1965

.11 We want to create a sort of linguistic Lourdes,
where evil and misfortune are dispelled by a
dip in the waters of euphemism.
　　—Robert Hughes; *Culture and Complaint*,
　　1993
　　[Hughes speaks of the notion of "political
　　correctness."]

.12 In calling a prostitute an "unfortunate" the
Victorians wished to imply that a prostitute
was someone who had invested in the wrong
stock, in spite of the advice of more experienced investors.
　　—Hugh Kingsmill; *Matthew Arnold*,
　　1928

.13 Any euphemism ceases to be euphemistic after
a time and the true meaning begins to show

## 82

through. It's a losing game, but we keep on trying.
—Joseph Wood Krutch; *If You Don't Mind My Saying So*, Title Essay, 1964

.14 Marian was out powdering her nose.
—Ring Lardner; *Zone of Quiet*, 1926

.15 The trouble with this country is the national passion for euphemisms.
—E.S. Liddon; *The Riddle of the Florentine Folio*, 1935

.16 …Americans do not dissemble what they are up to. They do not seem to feel the need, except through verbiage; *e.g.*, napalm has become "Incinderjell," which makes it sound like Jell-O. And defoliants are referred to as weed-killers—something you use in your driveway. The resort to euphemism denotes, no doubt, a guilty conscience or—the same thing nowadays—a twinge in the public-relations nerve.
—Mary McCarthy; *Vietnam*, "The Home Program," 1967

.17 Excuse me, everybody, I have to go to the bathroom. I really have to telephone, but I'm too embarrassed to say so.
—Dorothy Parker; in Robert E. Drennan's *The Algonquin Wits*, 1968

.18 The ancient Athenians used to cover up the ugliness of things with auspicious and kindly terms, giving them polite and endearing names. Thus they called harlots "companions," taxes "contributions," and the prison a "chamber."
—Plutarch; *Parallel Lives*, "Solon," c. A.D. 100

.19 To rest, the cushion and soft dean invite,
Who never mentions hell to ears polite.
—Alexander Pope; *Moral Essays*, 1731–35

.20 I've heard that breeches, petticoats and smock
Give to the modest mind a grievous shock,
And that my brain (so lucky its device,)
Christ'neth them inexpressible, so nice.
—John Wolcot (Peter Pindar), *A Rowland for an Oliver*, c. 1783

.21 Those comfortably padded lunatic asylums which are known, euphemistically, as the stately homes of England.
—Virginia Woolf; *The Common Reader*, "Outlines: Lady Dorothy Nevill," 1925

## 83 Exaggeration and Hyperbole

.1 In psychoanalysis nothing is true except the exaggerations.
—Theodor Adorno; *Negative Dialectics*, 1966

.2 The speaking in a perpetual hyperbole is comely in nothing but love.
—Francis Bacon; *Essays* "Of Love," 1625

.3 There are people so addicted to exaggeration that they can't tell the truth without lying.
—Josh Billings; *Complete Works*, 1888

.4 The temptation to vivify the tale and make it walk abroad on its own legs is hard to deny.
—Gelett Burgess; *The Romance of the Commonplace*, "Sub Rosa," 1916

.5 What a tale of cock and bull he told my father.
—John Day; *Law Trickes*, 1608

.6 Proportion is almost impossible to human beings. There is no one who does not exaggerate.
—Ralph Waldo Emerson; *Essays: Second Series*, "Nominalist and Realist," 1844

.7 Old wives' foolish tales of Robin Hood.
—Desiderius Erasmus; *Adagia*, 1500

.8 I know exaggeration of both kinds: people whose lies are only picturesque adjectives, and people whose picturesque adjectives are only lies.
—Katharine Fullerton Gerould, *Modes and Morals*, 1920

.9 An exaggeration is a truth that has lost its temper.
—Kahlil Gibran; *The Prophet*, 1923

.10 Exaggeration is a branch of lying.
—Baltasar Gracian; *Oraculo Manual*, 1647

.11 Exaggeration is a prodigality of the judgement which shows the narrowness of one's knowledge or one's taste.
—Baltasar Gracian; *The Art of Worldly Wisdom*, 1647

.12 A tendency to exaggeration was a Roman trait.
—Edith Hamilton; *Mythology*, 1942

.13 We always weaken whatever we exaggerate.
—Jean-Francois de Laharpe; *Melanie*, 1770

.14 Men of great conversational powers almost universally practice a sort of lively sophistry and exaggeration which deceives for the moment both themselves and their auditors.
—Thomas Babington Macaulay; *Essays: On the Athenian Orators*, 1842

## 83

.15 Exaggeration is the cheapest form of humor.
—Elizabeth Peters; *Naked Once More*, 1989

.16 She was neither clear-sighted nor accurate; and in her attempts to describe morals, manners, and even facts, was unable to avoid the pitfalls of exaggeration.
—Anthony Trollope; *Autobiography*, 1883
[Trollope speaks of his mother, Frances Trollope, the author of *The Domestic Manners of the Americans*.]

.17 I play to people's fantasies. People may not always think big themselves, but they can still get very excited by those who do. That's why a little hyperbole never hurts.
—Donald Trump; *Trump: The Art of the Deal*, written with Tony Schwartz, 1987

.18 Exaggeration, the inseparable companion of greatness.
—Voltaire; *Philosophical Dictionary*, "Solomon," 1764

.19 Every man is bound to leave a story better than he found it.
—Mrs. Humphrey Ward; *Robert Elsmere*, 1888

## 84 Excuses

.1  To defend yourself for your fault is to commit another fault.
—Charles Cahier; *Quelques Six Mille Proverbes*, 1856
[An Italian proverb.]

.2  There are reasons, and there are excuses.
—Julia Child; *Julia Child and Company*, 1978

.3  A bad excuse, they say, is better than none at all.
—Stephen Gosson; *The Schoole of Abuse*, 1579

.4  He is witty in nothing but framing excuses.
—Bishop Joseph Hall; *Characters*, "Slothful," 1608

.5  Don't make excuses—make good.
—Elbert Hubbard; *Epigrams*, 1905

.6  Several excuses are always less convincing than one.
—Aldous Huxley; *Point Counter Point*, 1928

.7  He who excuses himself, accuses himself.
—Gabriel Meurier; *Trésor des Sentences*, c. 1575

## 84

.8  When someone gives me three reasons instead of one, I'm inclined not to believe any of them.
—Margaret Millar; *The Fiend*, 1964

.9  Excuses are more than tacit confessions.
—Samuel Richardson; *Sir Charles Grandison*, 1754

.10 An excuse is a lie guarded.
—Jonathan Swift; *Thoughts on Various Subjects*, 1714

.11 Two wrongs don't make a right, but they make a good excuse.
—Thomas Szasz; *The Second Sin*, "Social Relations," 1973

## 85 Experience

.1  I am not afraid of storms for I am learning to sail my ship.
—Louisa May Alcott; Ednah D. Cheney; *Louisa May Alcott, Her Life, Letters, and Journals*, 1889

.2  Experience is a severe mistress, but she makes her scholars truly wise.
—Anonymous; *Memoirs of a Coquet*, 1765

.3  The tongue of experience has most truth.
—Johann Burckhardt; *Arabic Proverbs*, 1817

.4  I don't have to have faith, I have experience.
—Joseph Campbell; *The Power of Myth*, 1988

.5  What I hear, I forget;
What I see, I remember;
What I do, I understand.
—Chinese Proverb

.6  A happy man, and wise is he
By others' harms can warned be.
—John Florio; *Second Fruites*, 1591

.7  Experience teaches slowly, and at the cost of mistakes.
—J.A. Froude; *Short Studies on Great Subjects*: "Party Politics," 1850

.8  Words form the thread on which we string our experiences.
—Aldous Huxley; *The Olive Tree: Words and Behavior*, 1937

.9  We can never describe what we have not seen.
—Samuel Johnson; *Rasselas*, 1759

.10 Experience is a hard teacher because she gives the test first, the lesson afterwards.
—Vernon S. Law; "How to Be a Winner," *This Week*, 1960

## 85

.11 One thorn of experience is worth a whole wilderness of warning.
—James Russell Lowell; *Among My Books: Shakespeare Once More*, 1870

.12 Experience is the only teacher.
—Herman Melville; *The Confidence-Man*, 1857

.13 All is but lip-wisdom which wants experience.
—Sir Philip Sidney; *Arcadia*, 1584

.14 You that woo the Voices—tell them "old experience is a fool."
—Alfred, Lord Tennyson; *Locksley Hall Sixty Years After*, 1886

.15 Believe one who speaks from experience.
—Virgil; *Aeneid*, 19 B.C.

# 86 Explanation

.1 I do loathe explanations.
—J.M. Barrie; *My Lady Nicotine*, 1890

.2 I wish he would explain his explanation.
—Lord Byron; *Don Juan*, Dedication, 1818
[The reference is to Samuel Taylor Coleridge's attempt to explain metaphysics to the nation.]

.3 Explanations take such a dreadful time.
—Lewis Carroll; *Alice's Adventures in Wonderland*, 1865

.4 There is no waste of time in life like that of making explanations.
—Benjamin Disraeli; Speech, "University Education Bill" (Ireland), 1873

.5 I am an enemy of long explanations: they deceive either the maker of the hearer, and usually both.
—Johann Wolfgang von Goethe; *Gotz von Berlichingen*, 1773

.6 You should avoid making yourself too clear even in your explanations.
—Baltasar Gracian; *Handbook-Oracle and the Art of Prudence*, 1647

.7 I am master of everything I can explain.
—Theodor Haecker; *Journal in the Night*, translated 1950

.8 Explaining is generally half confessing.
—Lord Halifax (George Savile); *Political, Moral and Miscellaneous Reflections*, 1750

.9 Never explain. Your friends do not need it and your enemies will not believe you anyway.
—Elbert Hubbard; *Orphic Sayings*, 1900

## 86

.10 No explanation ever explains the need of making one.
—Elbert Hubbard; *Note Book*, 1927

.11 Some unknown natural phenomenon occurs which cannot be explained and a new local demigod is named.
—Zora Neale Hurston; *Dust Tracks on a Road*, 1942

.12 "Are you lost daddy?" I asked tenderly. "Shut up," he explained.
—Ring Lardner; *The Young Immigrants*, 1920

.13 I am one of those unfortunates to whom death is less hideous than explanations.
—D.B. Wyndham Lewis; *Welcome to All This*, 1954

.14 I fear explanations explanatory of things explained.
—Abraham Lincoln; Lincoln-Douglas Debates, 1858
[Lincoln refers to Stephen A. Douglas's explanations during the debates.]

.15 If the poem can be improved by it's author's explanations, it never should have been published.
—Archibald MacLeish; *Poems*, 1933

.16 A little inaccuracy sometimes saves tons of explanation.
—Saki (Hector Hugh Munro); *The Square Egg*, "Clovis on the Alleged Romance of Business," 1924

.17 Shall I tell you why?
Ay, sir, and wherefore; for they say every why hath a wherefore.
—William Shakespeare; *The Comedy of Errors*, 1593

.18 What nuisance can be so great to a man busied with immense affairs, as to have to explain, or attempt to explain, small details to men incapable of understanding them?
—Anthony Trollope; *The Way We Live Now*, 1875

.19 I hate explanations; they fog up so you can't tell anything about it.
—Mark Twain; *A Connecticut Yankee in King Arthur's court*, 1889

# 87 Fable

.1 Fables were the first pieces of wit that made their appearance in the world.
—Joseph Addison; *The Spectator*, 1711–12

.2 Fables take off from the severity of instruction and enforce at the same time that they conceal it.
—Joseph Addison; *The Spectator*, 1711–12

.3 A fable is a bridge which leads to truth.
—Arabian Proverb

.4 I want to tell you a fable they used to relate to me when I was a little boy.
—Aristophanes; *The Birds*, c. 448–c. 388 B.C.

.5 I had rather believe all the fables in Legend, and the Talmud, and the Alcoran, than that the universal frame is without a mind.
—Francis Bacon; *Essays* "Of Atheism," 1625

.6 There are grains of truth in the wildest fable.
—Charlotte Bronte; *Jane Eyre*, 1847

.7 And when life's sweet fable ends,
Soul and body part like friends;
No quarrels, murmurs, no delay;
A kiss, a sigh, and so away.
—Richard Crashaw; *In Praise of Lessius's Rules of Health*, c. 1646

.8 The parents or kinsman were told about these things [at the ceremony after the birth of an Aztec child], having first listened to assurances and then to long, flowery speeches. After this the soothsayers told two dozen lies and fables.
—Fray Diego Duran; *The Ancient Calendar*, 1579

.9 Fables, like parables, are more ancient than formal arguments and are often the most effective means of presenting and impressing both truth and duty.
—Tyron Edwards; Attributed

.10 We walk alone in the world. Friends, such as we desire, are dreams and fables.
—Ralph Waldo Emerson; "Friendship," 1867

.11 I can find my biography in every fable that I read.
—Ralph Waldo Emerson; *Journals*, 1866

.12 Life is eating us up. We shall be fables presently.
—Ralph Waldo Emerson; *Representative Men*, "Montaigne," 1850

.13 Trusting to fables we drift at random.
—Euripides; *Hippolytus*, 428 B.C.

.14 I cannot explain the sadness
That's fallen on my breast.
An old, old fable haunts me,
And will not let me rest.
—Heinrich Heine; "Die Lorelei," 1827

.15 So when or you or I are made
A fable, song, or fleeting shade,
All love, all liking, all delight
Lies drowned with us in endless night.
—Robert Herrick; "Corinna's Going a Maying," 1648

.16 Man is fed with fables through his life, and leaves it in the belief he knows something of what has been passing, when in truth he has known nothing but what has passed under his own eye.
—Thomas Jefferson: *Letter to Thomas Cooper*, 1823

.17            Worse
Than fables yet have feigned, or fear conceived,
Gorgons and Hydras, and Chimeras dire.
—John Milton; *Paradise Lost*, 1667

.18 How many things served us yesterday for articles of faith, which today are fables to us!
—Michel de Montaigne; *Essays*, 1580

.19 Neither give heed to fables and endless genealogies, which minister questions, rather than godly edifying which is in faith.
—New Testament: I Timothy

.20 Refuse profane and old wives fables.
—New Testament: I Timothy

.21 Their pupils should learn to paraphrase Aesop's fables, the natural successors of the fairy-stories of the nursery, in simple and restrained language and subsequently to set down this paraphrase in writing with the same simplicity of style.
—Quintilian; *De Institutione Oratoria*, A.D. 96

.22 The old fable-existences are no more;
The fascinating race has emigrated.
—Johann Friedrich von Schiller; *Wallenstein*, 1798–1801

.23 The fable of Aesop, the cherished and enjoyable book of our youth, was originally related as folklore by a Negro from Ethiopia to the Greeks, who in turn published them.
—Arthur A. Schomburg; *Racial Integrity*, 1913

.24 Read my little fable;
He that runs may read,
Most can raise the flowers now,
For all have got the seed.
—Alfred, Lord Tennyson; "The Flower," 1842

.25 There are no other ancient histories except fables.
—Voltaire; *Letter*, 1764

## 87

.26 History is the recital of facts represented as true. Fable, on the other hand, is the recital of facts represented in fiction.
—Voltaire; *Philosophical Dictionary*, "History," 1764

.27 The bearers of fables are very welcome.
—Monique Wittig; *Les Guerilleres*, 1969

## 88 Facts

.1 Every man has a right to his opinion, but no man has a right to be wrong in his facts.
—Bernard Baruch; *Reader's Digest*, March, 1948

.2 No statement of facts, however honest your people may be, can be relied upon until it has been subjected to the careful study and criticism of people who have a different point of view.
—Louis D. Brandeis; Alfred Lief, ed. *The Social and Economic Views of Mr. Justice Brandeis*, 1934

.3 They demanded facts from him, as if facts could explain anything.
—Joseph Conrad; *Lord Jim*, 1900

.4 The language of facts, that are so often more enigmatic than the craftiest arrangement of words.
—Joseph Conrad; *Lord Jim*, 1900

.6 Facts are stubborn things.
—Ebenezer Elliott; *Field Husbandry*, 1747 [Tobias Smollett used the phrase in his translation of Le Sage's *Gil Blas*, published in 1755.]

.5 Nobody can talk as interesting as the fellow that's not hampered by facts or information.
—Kin Hubbard; *Short Furrows*, 1911

.6 Facts are ventriloquist's dummies. Sitting on a wise man's knee they may be made to utter words of wisdom; elsewhere they say nothing or talk nonsense.
—Aldous Huxley; *Time Must Have a Stop*, 1945

.7 A world of facts lie outside and beyond the world of words.
—T.H. Huxley; *Lay Sermons*, 1870

.8 Fact and fancy look alike across the years that link the past with the present.
—Helen Keller; *The Story of My Life*, 1903

.9 We should not investigate facts by the light of arguments, but arguments by the light of facts.
—Myson of Chen; one of the Seven Sages, c. 600 B.C.

.10 People who mistake facts for ideas are incomplete thinkers; they are gossips.
—Cynthia Ozick; "We Are the Crazy Lady and Other Feisty Feminist Poems," Francine Klagsbrun, ed. *The First Ms. Reader*, 1972

.11 Facts are more powerful than arguments.
—Thomas Paine; *Letter to Abbe Raynal*, 1782

.12 Facts explain nothing. On the contrary, it is fact that requires explanation.
—Marilynne Robinson; *Housekeeping*, 1980

.13 If there is an opinion, facts will be found to support it.
—Judy Sproles; *Omni*, 1979

## 89 Fairies

.1 Up the airy mountain,
Down the rusty glen,
We daren't go a-hunting
For fear of little men;
Wee folk, good folk,
Trooping all together;
Green jacket, red cap,
And white owl's feather.
—William Allingham; "The Fairies," 1850

.2 Do you believe in fairies? If you believe clap your hands. Don't let Tinker die.
—J.M. Barrie; *Peter Pan*, 1904

.3 Every time a child says "I don't believe in fairies," there is a little fairy somewhere that falls down dead.
—J.M. Barrie; *Peter Pan*, 1904

.4 When the first baby laughed for the first time, the laugh broke into a thousand pieces and they all went skipping about, and that was the beginning of fairies.
—J.M. Barrie; *Peter Pan*, 1904

.5 Where little people live in nuts,
And ride on butterflies.
—Abbie Farwell Brown; *The Fairy Book*, 1900

.6 On gossamer nights when the moon is low,
And stars in the mist are hiding,
Over the hill where the foxgloves grow
You may see the fairies riding.
—Mary G.C. Byron, "The Fairy Thrall"; c. late 19th century

**89**

.7 Fairyland is nothing but the sunny country of common sense.
—G.K. Chesterton; *Orthodoxy*, "The Logic of England," 1908

.8 By fairy hands their knell is rung,
By forms unseen there dirge is sung;
There Honor comes, a pilgrim gray,
To bless the turf that wraps their clay,
And Freedom shall awhile repair,
To dwell a weeping hermit there!
—William Collins; "How to Sleep the Brave," 1746

.9 There are fairies at the bottom of our garden!
—Rose Fyleman; *Fairies and Chimneys*, "The Fairies Have Never a Penny to Spend," 1918

.10 'Tis as true as the fairy tales told in the books.
—S.G. Goodrich; "Birthright of the Humming Birds," 1827

.11 Children born of fairy stock
Never need for shirt or frock,
Never want for food or fire,
Always get their heart's desire.
—Robert Graves; "I'd Love to Be a Fairy's Child," 1917

.12 Have ye left the greenwood lone,
Are your steps for ever gone?
Fairy King and Elfin Queen,
Come ye to the sylvan scene,
From your dim and distant shore,
Never more?
—Felicia Dorothea Hemans; *Works*, "Fairy Song," 1839

.13 A little fairy comes at night,
Her eyes are blue, her hair is brown,
With silver spots upon her wings,
And from the moon she flutters down.
—Thomas Hood; "Queen Mab," 1827

.14 Then take me on your knee, mother;
And listen, mother of mine.
A hundred fairies danced last night,
And the harpers they were nine.
—Mary Howitt; "The Fairies of the Caldon Low"; c. 1822–1831

.15 Nothing can be truer than fairy wisdom. It is as true as sunbeams.
—Douglas Jerrold; *Specimens of Jerrold's Wit: Fairy Tales*, 1859

.16 This is Mab, the Mistress-Fairy,
That doth nightly rob the dairy.
—Ben Jonson; *The Satyr: Song*, 1607

.17 The loveliest fairy in the world; and her name is Mrs. Doasyouwouldbedoneby.
—Charles Kingsley; *The Water Babies*, 1863

**89**

.18 There never was a merry world since the fairies left off dancing and the Parson left conjuring.
—John Selden; *Table-Talk: Parson*, 1689

.19 This is the fairy land; O spite of spites!
We talk with goblins, owls and sprites.
—William Shakespeare; *The Comedy of Errors*, 1594

.20 Fairies, black, grey, green, and white,
You moonshine revellers, and shades of night.
—William Shakespeare; *The Merry Wives of Windsor*, 1600–1

.21 The iron tongue of midnight hath told twelve.
Lovers, to bed; 'tis almost fairy time.
—William Shakespeare; *A Midsummer-Night's Dream*, 1595

.22 Ye fairies, from all evil keep her.
—William Wordsworth; *Peter Bell*: "Prologue"

.23     The land of faery,
Where nobody gets old and godly
        and grave,
Where nobody gets old and crafty
        and wise,
Where nobody gets old and bitter of
        tongue.
—William Butler Yeats; *The Land of Heart's Desire*, 1894

# **90** Fairy Tales

.1 Every man's life is a fairy-tale written by God's fingers.
—Hans Christian Andersen; *Works*, Preface, 1843

.2 The unexpurgated *Grimm's Fairy Tales* contain a number of fairy tales in which women are not only the central characters but win by using their own intelligence. Some people feel fairy tales are bad for women. This is true if the only ones they're referring to are those tarted-up French versions of "Cinderella" and "Bluebeard," in which the female protagonist gets rescued by her brothers. But in many of them, women rather than men have the magic powers.
—Margaret Atwood; in Sharon R. Wilson, *Margaret Atwood's Fairy-Tale Sexual Politics*, 1993

.3 Where else could I have gotten the idea, so early in life, that words can change you.
—Margaret Atwood; "Grimms' Remem-

**90**

bered," *The Reception of Grimms' Fairy Tales, Responses, Reactions, Revisions*, 1993
[Atwood has written about the effect on her of having, as a child, read an unexpurgated version of *Grimms Fairy Tales*.]

.4 [The Grimm's fairy tales are] among the few indispensable, common property books upon which Western culture can be founded.... It is hardly too much to say that these tales rank next to the Bible in importance.
—W.H. Auden; "In Praise of the Brothers Grimm," *New York Times Book Review*, November 12, 1944

.5 The fairy tale takes the existential anxieties and dilemmas of a child very seriously and addresses itself directly to them: the need to be loved and the fear that one is thought worthless; the love of life, and the fear of death. Further, the fairy tale offers solutions in ways the child can grasp on his level of understanding.
—Bruno Bettelheim; *The Uses of Enchantment*, 1976

.6 In a fairy tale internal processes are externalized and become comprehensible as represented by the figures of the story and its events.
—Bruno Bettelheim; *The Uses of Enchantment*, 1976

.7 Fairytales represent psychological, not physical triumphs.
—Joseph Campbell: *Grimm's Fairy Tales: Folkloristic Commentary*, 1944

.8 Child of the pure, unclouded brow
And dreaming eyes of wonder!
Through time be fleet and I said thou
Are half a life asunder,
Thy loving smile will surely hail
The love-gift of a fairy tale.
—Lewis Carroll; *Alice in Wonderland*, 1865

.9 The thriller is an extension of the fairy tale. It is melodrama so embellished as to create the illusion that the story being told, however unlikely, could be true.
—Raymond Chandler; *Raymond Chandler Speaking*, 1962

.10 Where the French [fairy] tales tend to be realistic, earthy, bawdy, and comical, the German [fairy tales] veer off toward the supernatural, the poetic, the exotic, and the violent. Of course, cultural differences cannot be reduced to a formula—French craftiness versus German cruelty—but the comparisons make it possible to identify the peculiar inflection that the French give to their stories, and their

**90**

way of telling stories provides clues about their ways of viewing the world.
—Robert Darnton; *The Great Cat Massacre and Other Episodes in French Cultural History*, "Peasant Tall Tales, The Meaning of Mother Goose," 1984

.12 It is possible that our race may be an accident, in a meaningless universe, living its brief life uncared for, on this dark, cooling star: but even so—and all the more—what marvelous creatures we are! What fairy story, what tale from the Arabian Nights of the jinns, is a hundredth part as wonderful as the true fairy tale of the simians!
—Clarence Day; *This Simian World*, 1920

.13 It would be hard to estimate the amount of gentleness and mercy that has made its way among us through these slight channels. Forbearance, courtesy, consideration for the poor and aged, kind treatment of animals, the love of nature, abhorrence of tyranny and brute force—many such good things have been fist nourished in the child's heart by this powerful aid.
—Charles Dickens; "Frauds on the Fairies" in *Household Words: A Weekly Journal*, 1854
[Dickens thought of the myth of fairy tales as a kind of holy scripture.]

.14 We have not formed that ancient world [of fairy tales], it has formed us. We ingested it as children whole, had its values and consciousness imprinted on our minds as cultural absolutes long before we were in fact men and women. We have taken the fairy tales of childhood with us into maturity, chewed but still lying in the stomach, as real identity. Between Snow-white and her heroic prince, our two great fictions, we never did have much of a chance. At some point the Great Divide took place: they (the boys) dreaming of mounting the Great Steed and buying Snow-white from the dwarfs; we (the girls) aspired to become that object of every necrophiliac's lust—the innocent, *victimized* Sleeping Beauty, beauteous lump of ultimate, sleeping good.
—Andrea Dworkin; *Woman-Hating*, 1974

.15 Fairy tales confirm, heal, compensate, counterbalance and criticize the dominating collective attitude, just as dreams confirm, heal, compensate, criticize and complete the conscious attitude of an individual.
—Marie-Louise von Franz; *Individuation in Fairy Tales*, 1977

**90**

.16 Fairy tales represent archetypes in their simplest, barest and most concise form.
—Marie Louise von-Franz; *Interpretation of Fairytales*, 1970

.17 The relation of our typical dreams to fairytales and other fiction and poetry is neither sporadic nor accidental. Sometimes the penetrating insight of the poet has analytically recognized the process of transformation of which the poet is otherwise the instrument, and has followed it up in the reverse direction; that is to say, has traced a poem to a dream.
—Sigmund Freud; *Interpretation of Dreams*, 1900

.18 So long as we have faith in our fairy tales we are none the worse.
—Ellen Glasgow; *The Descendant*, 1897

.19 And in their fairy tales
The warty giant and witch
Get sealed in doorless jails
And the match-girl strikes it rich.
—Anthony Hecht; *Jiggery-Pokery: A Compendium of Double Dactyls*, 1966

.20 I do not know the meaning of my sadness; there is an old fairy tale that I cannot get out of my mind.
—Heinrich Heine; *Book of Songs*, "Homecoming," 1823–24

.21 Fairy tales are most effective when told from memory by a person whose heart is responsive to the tale and to his listeners.
—Julius E. Heuscher; *A Psychiatric Study of Myths and Fairy Tales: Their Origin, Meaning and Usefulness*, 1974

.22 It is not children only that one feeds with fairy tales.
—Gotthold Lessing; *Nathan der Weise*, 1779

.23 These stories suggest a society in which women are as competent and active as men, at every age in every class. Gretel, not Hansel, defeats the Witch; and for every clever young son their is a youngest daughter equally resourceful. The contrast is greater in maturity, where women are often more powerful than men. Real help for the hero or heroine comes more frequently from a fairy godmother or wise woman, and real trouble from a witch or wicked stepmother.... To prepare children for women's liberation therefore, and to protect them against Future Shock, you had better buy at least one collection of fairy tales.
—Alison Lurie; "Fairy Tale Liberation," *New York Review of Books*, December 1970

.24 Discovering these entirely new perspectives in fairy tales was an exciting, fun-filled adventure. And, over and over again, I was stunned to realize how much knowledge about human beings (adults too, not just children) is contained in fairy tales.
—Carl-Heinz Mallet; *Fairy Tales and Children: The Psychology of Children Revealed Through Four of Grimms' Fairy Tales*, 1980

.25 Fairy Tales are popular poetry, for they originated and developed among the people [the folk]. They were born in fusty spinning rooms. Simple people told them to simple people. No one else was interested in these "old wives' tales." No superior authority whether profane or ecclesiastic, exerted any influence. Fairy tales developed outside the great world, beyond the centers of political and cultural power. They absorbed nothing from these areas, no historical events, no political facts, no cultural trends. They remained free of the moral views, behavioral standards, and manners of the various epochs.... Human beings *per se* are the focal point of fairy tales, and people are pretty much alike no matter when or where they have lived.
—Carl-Heinz Mallet; *Fairy Tales and Children: The Psychology of Children Revealed Through Four of Grimms' Fairy Tales*, 1980

.26 The fairy tales of my childhood have a meaning deeper than the truths taught by life.
—Johann von Schiller; *Wallenstein*, 1799

.27 Adults read fairy tales for enjoyment, and also as a way of seeing patterns of meaning in their lives. Fairy tales from the oral tradition offer us a rich resource of symbols and metaphors for psychological interpretation.
—Judy Sierra; *Quests and Spells*, 1994

.28 No fairy tale should be interpreted or analyzed by looking at a single version.
—Judy Sierra; *Quests and Spells*, 1994

.29 Fairy tales register an effort on the part of both women and men to develop maps for coping with personal anxieties, family conflicts, social frictions, and the myriad frustrations of everyday life.
—Maria Tartar; *The Classic Fairy Tales*, "Introduction," 1999

.30 Advanced middle age appears to be a popular time for admitting interest in fairytales. At age fifty-five, George Bernard Shaw declared that he still considered "Grimm" to be the most entertaining of German authors. C.S.

**90**

Lewis confessed to reading fairytales on the sly for years; only after turning fifty did he feel free to acknowledge his addiction to the genre.
—Maria Tatar; *The Hard Facts of the Grimms' Fairy Tales*, Preface, 1987

.31 There is something in them [fairytales] for every age and generation.
—Maria Tatar; *The Hard Facts of the Grimms' Fairy Tales*, Preface, 1987

.32 Here about the beach I wander'd, nourishing a youth sublime
With the fairy tales of science, and the long result of Time.
—Alfred, Lord Tennyson; *Locksley Hall*, 1837–38

.33 Ah, how pleasant to be manipulated, to feel one's heartstrings pulled this way and that—twang, twang again and again, longing, self-pity, nostalgia, remorse—and to let fall the fulsome tear that would be never shed for Grimm.
—P.L. Travers; *What the Bee Knows: Reflections on Myth, Symbol and Story*, 1989
[Travers recalls her response as a child to reading the fairy tales of Hans Christian Andersen.]

.34 On a par with trifles, 'mere old wives' tales' carry connotations of error, of false counsel, ignorance, prejudice and fallacious nostrums—against heartbreak as well as headache; similarly 'fairy tale,' as a derogatory term, implies fantasy, escapism, invention, the unreliable consolations of romance.
—Marina Warner; *From the Beast to the Blonde: On Fairy Tales and Their Tellers*, 1994

.35 [Fairy tales can tell us much about] real conditions in the world of those who told and heard the tales.
—Eugen Weber; "Fairies and Hard Facts: The Reality of Folktales," 1981

.36 With a fairy tale and with a lie you can lull only children to sleep.
—Yiddish Proverb

.37 Fairy tales were first *told* by gifted tellers and were based on rituals intended to endow with meaning the daily lives of members of a tribe. As *oral folk tales*, they were intended to explain natural occurrences such as the change of the seasons and shifts in the weather or to celebrate the rites of harvesting, hunting, marriage and conquest.
—Jack Zipes; "Breaking the Disney Spell," *From Mouse to Mermaid: The Politics of Film, Gender, and Culture*, Elizabeth

**90**

Bell, Lynda Haas, and Laura Sells, eds., 1995

.38 ...the fairy tale may be the most important cultural and social event in most children's lives....
—Jack Zipes; *Fairytales and the Art of Subversion*, 1988

.39 The mass-mediated fairy tales have a technologically produced universal voice and image which impose themselves on the imagination of passive audiences.... The original tale was cultivated by a narrator and the audience to clarify and interpret phenomena in a way that would strengthen meaningful social bonds....
—Jack Zipes; *Breaking the Magic Spell: Radical Theories of Folk and Fairy Tales*, 1979

# 91 Fantasy

.1 If one is lucky a solitary fantasy can totally transform one million realities.
—Maya Angelou; *The Heart of a Woman*, 1981

.2 If you have enough fantasies, you're ready, in the event that something happens.
—Sheila Ballantyne; *Norma Jean the Termite Queen*, 1975

.3 All fantasy should have a solid base in reality.
—Sir Max Beerbohm; *Mainly on the Air*, 1946

.4 We do encourage our children's fantasies; we tell them to paint what they want, or to invent stories. But unfed by our common fantasy heritage, the folk fairy tale, the child cannot invent stories on his own which help him cope with life's problems.
—Bruno Bettelheim; *The Uses of Enchantment*, 1976

.5 How Fancy loves about the world to stray, While Judgement slowly picks his sober way.
—George Crabbe; *The Library*, 1808

.6 When I examine myself and my methods of thought, I come close to the conclusion that the gift of fantasy has meant more to me than my talent for absorbing positive knowledge.
—Albert Einstein; Recalled on 100th anniversary of his birth, February 18, 1979

.7 Fantasies are more than substitutes for unpleasant reality; they are also dress rehearsals,

**91**

plans. All acts performed in the world begin in the imagination.
—Barbara Grizzuti Harrison; "Talking Dirty," *Ms.*, October, 1973

.8 Fantasy is the only truth.
—Abbie Hoffman; *Revolution for the Hell of It*, 1968

.9 A fantasy can be equivalent to a paradise and if the fantasy passes, better yet, because eternal paradise would be very boring.
—Juan Ramon Jimenez; *Selected Writings*, "To Burn Completely," 1957

.10 Dragons are more dangerous, and a good deal commoner, than bears. Fantasy is nearer to poetry, to mysticism, and to insanity than naturalistic fiction. It is a real wilderness, and those who go there should not feel too safe.
—Ursula K. Le Guin; *Language of the Night*, "From Elfland to Poughkeepsie," 1973

.11 Fantasy is the language of the inner self. I will claim no more for fantasy than to say I personally find it the appropriate language in which to tell stories to children—and others.
—Ursula K. Le Guin; *Language of the Night*, 1973

.12 In so far as one denies what is, one is possessed by what is not, the compulsions, the fantasies, the terrors that flock to fill the void.
—Ursula K. Le Guin; *The Lathe of Heaven*, 1971

.13 Round about what is, lies a whole mysterious world of might be, a psychological romance of possibilities and things that do not happen.
—Henry Wadsworth Longfellow; *Driftwood*, "Table-Talk," 1857

.14 Two meanings have our lightest fantasies, One of the flesh, and one of the spirit one.
—James Russell Lowell; *Sonnets, No. 34*, 1874

.15 One's fantasy goes out for a walk and returns with a bride.
—Bernard Malamud; *Long Work, Short Life*, 1961

.16 Safe upon the solid rock the ugly houses stand;
Come and see my shining palace built upon the sand.
—Edna St. Vincent Millay; *A Few Figs from Thistles*, "Second Fig," 1921

.17     A thousand fantasies
Begin to throng into my memory,
Of calling shapes, and beck'ning shadows dire,

**91**

And airy tongues that syllable men's names
On sands and shores and desert wilderness.
—John Milton, *Cosmus*, 1637

.18 I guess I am a fantasy.
—Marilyn Monroe; Quoted in Gloria Steinem, *Outrageous Acts and Everyday Rebellion*, 1984

.19 Fantasy discourages reality, particularly in that reality is, in itself, discouraging.
—Joan Patterson, Conversation, June 19, 1991

.20     True, I talk of dreams,
Which are the children of an idle brain,
Begot of nothing but vain fantasy.
—William Shakespeare; *Romeo and Juliet*, 1594–95

.21 So full of shapes is fancy,
That it alone is high fantastical.
—William Shakespeare; *Twelfth Night*, 1601

.22 If you build castles in the air, your work need not be lost; that is where they should be. Now put the foundations under them.
—Henry David Thoreau; *Walden*, "Conclusion," 1854

.23 The poet is in command of his fantasy, while it is exactly the mark of the neurotic that he is possessed by his fantasy.
—Lionel Trilling; *The Liberal Imagination: Freud and Literature*, 1950

.24 Fantasy is no good unless the seed it springs from is a truth, a truth about human beings.
—Eudora Welty; *The Eye of the Story*, "Fairy Tale of the Natchez Trace," 1978

.25 We had fed our hearts on fantasies,
The heart's grown brutal from the fare;
More substance in our enmities
Than in our love.
—W.B. Yeats; "Meditations in Time of Civil War," 1923

## 92 Farce

.1 Like dreams, farces show the disguised fulfillment of repressed wishes.
—Eric Bentley; *Introduction to Let's Get A Divorce and Other Plays*, "The Psychology of Farce," 1958

.2 Farce is nearer tragedy in its essence than comedy is.
—Samuel Taylor Coleridge; *Table Talk*, entry for August 25, 1833

## 92

.3  Life is a huge farce, and the advantage of possessing a sense of humor is that it enables one to defy fate with mocking laughter.
—George Gissing; *New Grub Street*, 1891

.4  And Tragedy should blush as much to stoop
To the low mimic follies of a farce,
As a grave matron would to dance with girls.
—Horace; *Ars Poetica*, c. 19 B.C.

.5  Comedy speaks for civilization; farce bears an ill-concealed, sometimes unconcealed animus against civilization. Often against civility too.
—Irving Howe; *A Critic's Notebook*, "Farce and Fiction," 1994

.6  Comedy appeals to the collective mind of the audience and this grows fatigued; while farce appeals to a more robust organ, their collective belly.
—W. Somerset Maugham; *The Summing Up*, 1938

.7  If we pretend to be what we are not, women, for whose amusement the farce is performed, will find us out and punish us for it.
—George Meredith; *The Ordeal of Richard Feverel*, 1859

.8  Is it not a noble farce wherein kings, republics, and emperors have for so many ages played their parts, and to which the vast universe serves for a theatre?
—Michel de Montaigne; *Essays*, 1580

.9  Farce is tragedy played at a thousand revolutions per minute.
—John Mortimer; in *The Times*, London, September 9, 1992

.10  What dear delight to Briton farce affords!
Ever the taste of mobs, but now of lords.
—Alexander Pope; *Imitations of Horace*, "Epistles," 1737

.11  Draw the curtain, the farce is played out.
—Francois Rabelais; Said to be his last words, 1553

.12  "What does anything matter!" The farce will go on.
—James Abbott McNeill Whistler; *Gentle Art of Making Enemies*, 1890

## 93

.2  My heart is happy, my mind is free
I had a father who talked with me.
—Hilda Bigelow; Abigail Van Buren's syndicated column "Dear Abby," 1993

.3  Diogenes struck the father when the son swore.
—Robert Burton; *The Anatomy of Melancholy*, 1621

.4  One father is more than a hundred Schoolmasters.
—George Herbert; *Jacula Prudentum*, 1640

.5  I will talk to her like a father.
—J.K. Paulding; *Chronicles of the City of Gotham*, 1830

.6  The sound of his father's voice was a necessity. He longed for the sight of his stooped shoulders as he had never, in the sharpest of his hunger, longed for food.
—Marjorie Kinnan Rawlings; *The Yearling*, 1938

.7  What a father says to his children is not heard by the world, but it will be heard by posterity.
—Jean Paul Richter; "Levana," 1870

.8  It doesn't matter who my father was;
it matters who I remember he was.
—Anne Sexton; journal entry, January 1, 1972, published in "A Small Journal" in *The Poet's Story*, Howard Moss, ed. 1974

.9  If I chance to talk a little wild,
forgive me; I had it from my father.
—William Shakespeare; *Henry VIII*, 1613

.10  All the feelings which my father could not put into words was in his hand—any dog, child or horse would recognize the kindness of it.
—Freya Stark; *Traveler's Prelude*, 1950

.11  Whoever teaches his son teaches not only his son but also his son's son—and so on to the end of generations.
—Talmud; Kiddushin, c. A.D. 500

.12  Fathers should be neither seen nor heard. That is the only proper basis for family life.
—Oscar Wilde, *An Ideal Husband*, 1895

## 93 Fathers

.1  Oh my gloomy father,
why were you always so silent then.
—Ingeborg Bachmann; "Curriculum Vitae," Aliki Barnstone and Willis Barnstone, eds., *A Book of Women Poets from Antiquity to Now*, 1980

## 94 Fear

.1  Fear runs away with my tongue.
—Aeschylus; *Seven Against Thebes*, 467 B.C.

.2  Anastasio having heard all this discourse his hair stood upright like porcupine's quills.
—Giovanni Boccaccio; *Decameron*, 1358

**94**

.3 Fear is an instrument of great sagacity, and the herald of all revolutions.
  —Ralph Waldo Emerson; *Essays, First Series: Compensation*, 1841

.4 Logic and cold reason are poor weapons to fight fear and distrust. Only faith and generosity can overcome them.
  —Jawaharlal Nehru; in Vincent Shean, *Nehru: the Years of Power*, 1960

.5 It was fear that first made gods in the world.
  —Statius; *Thebaid*, c. 1st century A.D.

.6 The poets were not alone in sponsoring myths. Long before them cities and lawmakers had found them a useful expedient…. They needed to control the people by superstitious fears, and these cannot be aroused without myths and marvels.
  —Strabo; *Geography*, c. 7 B.C.–A.D. 18

.7 I shudder as I tell it.
  —Virgil; *Aeneid*; 19 B.C.

.8 Fear no more, says the heart. Fear no more, says the heart, committing its burden to some sea which sighs collectively for all sorrows, and renews, begins, collects, lets fall.
  —Virginia Woolf; *A Room of One's Own*, 1929

.9 Among the Indians he had fought;
And with him many tales he brought
Of pleasures and of fear!
Such tales as told to any Maid
By such a Youth, in the green shade
Were perilous to hear.
  —William Wordsworth; "Ruth; or, The Influence of Nature," in *A Choice of English Romantic Poetry*, Stephen Spender, ed., 1947

# **95** Fiction

.1 If fiction does not show us a better life than reality, what is the good of it?
  —Amelia E. Barr; *All the Days of My Life*, 1913

.2 Fiction is the great repository of the moral sense. The wicked get punished.
  —Anita Brookner; Quoted in Sybil Steinberg, ed. *Writing for Your Life*, 1992

.3 Historical fiction is not only a respectable literary form; it is a standing reminder of the fact that history is about human beings.
  —Helen M. Cam; *Historical Novel*, 1961

**95**

.4 Truth must necessarily be stranger than fiction; for fiction is the creation of the human mind and therefore congenial to it.
  —G.K. Chesterton; *The Club of Queer Trades*, 1905

.5 Novels are to love as fairy tales to dreams.
  —Samuel Taylor Coleridge; *Cervantes*, 1813

.6 Fiction is history without tables, graphs, dates, imports, edicts, evidence, laws; history without hiatus—intelligible, simple, smooth.
  —William Gass; *Habitations of the Word*, 1985

.7 When we risk no contradiction,
It prompts the tongue to deal in fiction.
  —John Gay; *Fables*, 1727

.8 Fiction has not yet outgrown the influence of the stage on which it originated.
  —George Gissing; *New Grub Street*, 1891

.9 The action of a teller is wanted to give due effect to all stories of incident.
  —Thomas Hardy; *The Hand of Ethelberta*, 1876

.10 The main question raised by the thriller is not what kind of world we live in, or what reality is like, but what it has done to us.
  —Ralph Harper; *The World of the Thriller*, "The Emotions," 1969

.11 We must remember, however, that fiction is not falsehood.
  —Arthur Helps; *Friends in Council*, 1849

.12 Fictions meant to please should be close to real.
  —Horace; *Ars Poetica*, c. 19 B.C.

.13 All that non-fiction can do is answer questions. It's fiction's business to ask them.
  —Richard Hughes; *The Fox in the Attic*, 1961

.14 Nothing I have said tis factual except the bits that sound like fiction.
  —Clive James; *Unreliable Memoirs*, 1980

.15 What the detective story is about is not murder but the restoration of order.
  —P.D. James; interview in *The Face*, December, 1986

.16 If science fiction is the mythology of modern technology, then its myth is tragic.
  —Ursula K. Le Guin; "The Carrier Bag Theory of Fiction," 1986, published in *Women of Vision*, Denise M. Du Pont, ed., 1988

## 95

.17 The past exudes legend: one can't make pure clay of time's mud. There is no life that can be recaptured wholly; as it was. Which is to say that all biography is ultimately fiction.
—Bernard Malamud; *Dubin's Lives*, 1979

.18 What makes the poet the potent figure that he is, or was, or ought to be, is that he creates the world to which we turn incessantly and without knowing it and that he gives to life the supreme fictions without which we are unable to conceive of it.
—Wallace Stevens; *The Noble Rider and the Sound of Words*, 1942

.19 Works of fiction, if only well gotten up, have always their advantages in the hearts of listeners over plain, homely truth.
—Harriet Beecher Stowe; *The Pearl of Orr's Island*, 1862

.20 The good end happily, the bad unhappily. That is what fiction means.
—Oscar Wilde; *The Importance of Being Earnest*, 1895

## 96 Flattery

.1 A flatterer is a man that tells you your opinion and not his own.
—Anonymous

.2 It is happy for you that you possess the talent of flattering with delicacy. May I ask whether these pleasing attentions proceed from the impulse of the moment, or are the result of previous study?
—Jane Austen; *Pride and Prejudice*, 1813

.3 Flattery, if judiciously administered is always acceptable, however much we may despise the flatterer.
—Marguerite Blessington; *Desultory Thoughts and Reflections*, 1839

.4 Listening, not imitation, may be the sincerest form of flattery.
—Joyce Brothers; *Reader's Digest*, 1972

.5 No tongue flatters like a lover's.
—Edward George Bulwer-Lytton; *The Last Days of Pompeii*, 1834

.6 Remember to beware of soft and flattering sayings.
—Cato; *Disticha*, c. 175 B.C.

.7 There is no kind of flattery so irresistible as at second hand.
—Henry Fielding; *Tom Jones*, 1749

## 96

.8 A flatterer never seems absurd:
The flatter'd always takes his word.
—Ben Franklin; *Poor Richard's Almanack*, 1740

.9 Flattery sits in the parlor, when plain-dealing is kick'd out of Doors.
—Thomas Fuller II; *Gnomologia*, 1732

.10 Men for the most part, are Flatterers of themselves.
—Stefano Guazzo; *Civil Conversation*, 1574

.11 Who knows not how to flatter knows not how to talk.
—Italian Proverb

.12 A flatterer is a smooth-spoken enemy.
—St. Jerome; *Letters*, A.D. 384

.13 He that is much flattered soon learns to flatter himself: we are commonly taught our duty by fear or shame, and how can they act upon the man who hears nothing but his own praises?
—Samuel Johnson; Boswell's *Life of Samuel Johnson*, 1791

.14 Men are like stone jugs—you may lug them where you like by the ears.
—Samuel Johnson; Boswell's *Life of Samuel Johnson*, 1791

.15 Just praise is only a debt, but flattery is a present.
—Samuel Johnson; *The Rambler*, 1750

.16 Flattery is the incense always offered to female beauty, and love the only language which it hears.
—Charles Johnstone; *The Reverie*, 1763

.17 Every flatterer lives at the expense of his listener.
—Jean de La Fontaine; *Fables*, 1668

.18 We recognize that flattery is poison, but its perfume intoxicates us.
—A.E. Lelievre de La Grange; *Pensees*, 1872

.19 If we did not flatter ourselves, the flattery of others would not harm us.
—François de La Rochefoucauld; *Maxims*, 1665

.20 We sometimes imagine we hate flattery, but we only hate the way we are flattered.
—François de La Rochefoucauld; *Maxims*, 1665

.21 Words really flattering are not those which we prepare but those which escape us unthinkingly.
—Ninon de Lenclos; *Lettres de Ninon de Lenclos*, 1870

**96**

.22 Flattery is praise without foundation.
—Eliza Leslie; *Miss Leslie's Behavior Book*, 1859

.23 I hate careless flattery, the kind that exhausts you in your effort to believe it.
—Wilson Mizner; Edward Dean Sullivan's *The Fabulous Wilson Mizner*, 1935

.24 Avoid flatterers, for they are thieves in disguise.
—William Penn; *Some Fruits of Solitude*, 1693

.25 He is soft-soaping you.
—Plautus; *Menaechmi*, c. 200 B.C.

.26 Our flatterers will tell us anything sooner than our faults, or what they know we do not like to hear.
—Samuel Richardson; *Clarissa Harlowe*, 1747–48

.27 Who flatters you has either cheated you or hopes to do so.
—Rumanian Proverb

.28 What really flatters a man is that you think him worth flattering.
—George Bernard Shaw; *John Bull's Other Island*, 1904

.29 'Tis an old maxim in the schools,
That flattery's the food of fools;
Yet now and then your men of wit
Will condescend to take a bit.
—Jonathan Swift; *Cadenus and Vanerra*, 1713

# **97** Folk Music

.1 A folksinger is someone who sings through his nose by ear.
—Anonymous

.2 A folksinger is an intellectual who sings songs that nobody every wrote.
—Anonymous

.3 The only thing to do with a folk-melody, once you have played it, is to play it louder.
—Anonymous

.4 Folk melodies are a real model of the highest artistic perfection. To my mind, on a small scale, they are masterpieces, just as much as, in the world of large forms, a fugue by Bach or a Mozart sonata.
—Bela Bartok; *Saturday Review*, August 25, 1962

**97**

.5 I guess all songs is folk songs. I never heard no horse sing 'em.
—Big Bill Broonzy; quoted by Charles Keil, *Urban Blues*, 1966
[The quote has also been attributed to Louis Armstrong, appearing in "The Unforgettable Satchmo," *Reader's Digest*, December, 1971.]

.6 While we sit here singing folksongs in our Folksong Club, the folks are somewhere else— singing something different.
—Tony Davis; *Sing Out*, Summer, 1963

.7 All the great musicians have borrowed from the songs of the common people.
—Antonin Dvorak; *Music in America*, 1895

.8 Folk music is a bunch of fat people.
—Bob Dylan; Quoted in David Pickering *Brewer's Twentieth Century Music*, 1994

.9 Nowadays, you go to see a folk singer—what's the folk singer doin'? He's singin' all his own songs. That ain't no folk singer. Folk singers sing those old folk songs…. There's no dedication to folk music now, no appreciation of the art form.
—Bob Dylan; interview in *Rolling Stone*, June, 1984

.10 There is many music. There is almost as many music as there are folk. There are a fantastic number of folk. There is therefore many folk music.
—Mort Goode; Record album notes, 1960

.11 A folk song composes itself.
—Jacob and Wilhelm Grimm; *German Dictionary*, begun in 1854, completed 1954.

.12 Work is the thing. The biggest and best thing you can sing about is work…. Just learn where the work is: that's where you'll find real honest American music and songs being made up.
—Woody Guthrie; "Ear Players," *Common Ground*, 1942

.13 The best way to get to knowing any bunch of people is to go and listen to their music.
—Woody Guthrie; *Woody Sez*, Studs Terkel ed., 1975

.14 Folk songs are written, like all other songs, by individuals. All the folk have to do with them is to choose the ones that are to survive.
—H.L. Mencken; "The Music of the American Negro," *Chicago Sunday Tribune*, November 15, 1928

**97**

.15 Every period which abounded in folk songs has, by the same token, been deeply stirred by Dionysiac currents.
—Friedrich Nietzsche; *The Birth of Tragedy from the Spirit of Music*, translated in 1910

.16 Folk music straightened my spine, and kinked up my hair. It has given me a sense of us as people.
—Odetta, interview, c. 1976

.17 I had thought that folk music was something old, back in the library, and pop music was new—it was something you could hear on the radio. All of a sudden I realized that was a phony distinction. Millions of people were making music which grew out of the old traditions, mostly making up new words to fit old tunes. New words to fit new circumstances. This is what I call the folk process.
—Pete Seeger; quoted in *All You Need Is Love* by Tony Palmer, 1976

.18 Just as the lily, in its glorious and chaste beauty, eclipses the brilliance of brocades and precious stones, so folk music, thanks to its very childlike simplicity, is a thousand times richer and stronger than all the artifices of the learning taught by pedants in the conservatories and musical academies.
—A.N. Serov; *Critical Articles*, Vol. III, 1931

.19 Folk music is the ungarbled and ingenuous expression of the human mind and on that account it must reflect the essential and basic qualities of the human mind.
—Cecil Sharp; *English Folk Song*, 1907

.20 The hackneyed melancholy of street music; a music which sounds like the actual voice of the human Heart, singing the lost joys, the regrets, the loveless lives of the people who blacken the pavements, or jolt along on the buses.
—Logan Pearsall Smith; *Trivia, The Organ of Life*, 1902

.21 A feast of moon and men and barking hounds,
An orgy of some genius of the South
With blood-hot eyes and cane-lipped scented mouths,
Surprised in making folk-songs from soul sounds.
—Jean Toomer; *Cane*, "Georgia Dust," 1923

.22 If I may venture to give my own definition of a folk song. I should call it "an individual flowering on a common stem."
—Ralph Vaughn Williams; *National Music*, 1934

**97**

.23 You got to have smelt a lot of mule manure before you can sing like a hillbilly.
—Hank Williams: Quoted by Christopher S. Wren, *Look*, July 13, 1971

# **98** Folklore

.1 Folk tales are stories that never run out of editions.
—Anonymous

.2 Folklore reveals their [the people's] characteristic efforts to explain and deal with the strange phenomena of nature; to understand and interpret the ways of human beings with each other; and to give expression to deep universal emotions.
—May Hill Arbuthnot; *Children and Books*, 1947

.3 The motifs and themes of traditional folktales still permeate 20th century life…. Names and concepts, such as the golden goose, Cinderella, Hansel and Gretel, Bluebeard, sour grapes or the lion's share elicit emotional responses in us all whether or not we know the "original" tales.
—D.L. Ashliman; *A Guide to Folktales in the English Language*, 1987

.4 Folk tales are an educational "must" for adults, married or single, for the reader [or hearer] who has come once to know and love these tales will never be able again to endure the insipid rubbish of contemporary entertainment.
—W.H. Auden; *The Dyer's Hand*, 1963

.5 The folk tale is the primer of the picture-language of the soul.
—Joseph Campbell; *The Flight of the Gander*, 1958

.6 French folklorists have recorded about ten thousand tales, in many different dialects and in every corner of France and of French-speaking territories.
—Robert Darnton; *The Great Cat Massacre and Other Episodes in French Cultural History*, "Peasant Tall Tales, The Meaning of Mother Goose," 1984

.7 It does not matter whether the children's stories are told well or badly or whether they are read. They constitute for the children the first real encounter with the folktale, and it quite often happens that it is decided then and there who will become, sometimes after many decades, a good storyteller.
—Linda Degh; *Folktales and Society: Storytelling in a Hungarian Peasant Community*, 1968

## 98

.8 Folklore once recorded from the oral tradition does not cease to be, but rather continues on its merry way from raconteur to raconteur, from generation to generation.
　—Alan Dundes; *Little Red Riding Hood: A Casebook*, 1984

.9 The tricky or boastful gods of ancient myths and primitive folk tales are characters of the same kind that turn up in Faulkner or Tennessee Williams.
　—Northrop Frye; *The Educated Imagination*, 1964

.10 All printed texts of folktales are compromises between the written and spoken word, between writers and storytellers.
　—Henry Glassie; *Irish Fairy Tales*, 1985

.11 We have a challenge to give children "roots and wings" by sharing folk literature in the classroom.
　—Frances S. Goforth and Carolyn V. Spillman, *Using Folk Literature in the Classroom*, 1994

.12 Folklore is a collection of ridiculous notions held by other people, but not by you and me.
　—Margaret Halsey; *The Folks at Home*, 1952

.13 Folklore is the boiled-down juice, or potlikker, of human living.
　—Zora Neale Hurston; *Folklore Field Notes*, 1925

.14 As a narrative type, the folktale simultaneously entertains and illuminates the nature of existence.
　—Max Luthi; *The European Folktale*, 1965

.15 In my view the folktale is a narrative of adventures that represents in short form, sublimated and organized, the essential relations of human existence.
　—Max Luthi; *The European Folktale*, 1965

.16 To encourage the art of storytelling and the use of classic and folklore stories in schools and other educational centers; to foster creative work in the arranging and re-writing of stories from various classic and historic sources; to serve as a medium of exchange of stories and experiences in the use of the story; to discover in the world's literature, in history, and in life the best stories for education, and to tell them with love and sympathy for the children, and to bring together in story circles those who love to hear and tell a good story.
　—The National Storyteller's League, 1923

## 98

.17 Travel—away from here, toward a vague and distant destination—is part of our national folklore.
　—David Nichols; *Ernie's America*, "Introduction," January, 1989

.18 Folklore is the product of a special form of verbal art. Literature is also a verbal art, and for this reason the closest connection exists between folklore and literature, between the science of folklore and literary criticism. Literature and folklore overlap partially in their poetic genres.
　—Vladimir Propp; *Theory and History of Folklore*, "Folklore and Literature," 1984

.19 Folklore … presupposes two agents, but different agents, namely, the performer and the listener, opposing each other directly, or rather without a mediating link.
　—Vladimir Propp; *Theory and History of Folklore*, "Folklore and Literature," 1984

.20 the folk-lore
　Of each of the senses; call it, again and again,
　The river that flows nowhere, like a sea.
　—Wallace Stevens; *The Collected Poems of Wallace Stevens*, 1954

.21 Occasions are rare when the best literature becomes, as it were, the folk literature, and generally speaking literature has always been carried on within small limits and under great difficulties.
　—Lionel Trilling; *The Function of the Little Magazine*, 1956

.22 All folk literature, and all literature that keeps the folk tradition, delights in unbounded and immortal things.
　—William Butler Yeats; *The Celtic Element in Literature*, 1902

# 99 Fools and Folly

.1 The treasure of a fool is always in his tongue.
　—Apuleius; *Metamorphoses*, c. A.D. 155

.2 Silence is the virtue of fools.
　—Francis Bacon; *De Dignitate et Augmentis Scientiarum*, 1623

.3 The best way to convince a fool that he is wrong is to let him have his own way.
　—Josh Billings; *Josh Billings: His Sayings*, 1865

.4 Fools and Madmen tell commonly truth.
　—Robert Burton; *The Anatomy of Melancholy*, 1621

## 99

.5 The saddest of all confessions that a man can make—the confession of his own folly.
—Wilkie Collins; *The Woman in White*, 1860

.6 A fool could never hold his peace; for too much talking is ever the indice of a fool.
—Demacatus; Quoted in Ben Jonson, *Explorata, Homer's Ulysses*, 1640

.7 A fool's speech is a bubble of air.
—English Proverb

.8 A fool speaks foolish things.
—Euripides; *Bacchae*, c. 410 B.C.

.9 But fools to talking ever prone,
Are sure to make their follies known.
—John Gay; *Fables*, 1727

.10 If to talk to oneself when alone is folly, it must be doubly unwise to listen to oneself in the presence of others.
—Baltasar Gracian; *Oraculo Manual*, 1647

.11 I have never seen an ass who talked like a human being, but I have met many human beings who talked like asses.
—Heinrich Heine; *Travel Pictures*, 1826–31

.12 There are two kinds of fools: one says, "This is old, therefore it is good"; the other says "This is new, therefore it's better.
—W.R. Inge; *Lay Thoughts of a Dean*, 1926

.13 The wise man who is not heeded is counted a fool, and the fool who proclaims the general folly first and loudest passes for a prophet and Fuhrer, and sometimes it is luckily the other way round as well, or else mankind would long since have perished of stupidity.
—Carl Jung; *Mysterium Coniunctions*, 1955–56

.14 No fools are so troublesome as those who have some wit.
—François de La Rochefoucauld; *Maximes*, 1665

.15 Better to remain silent and be thought a fool than to speak out and remove all doubt.
—Abraham Lincoln; Attributed
[The quote has also been attributed to Mark Twain. It sounds like the kind of observation which may have a long history.]

.16 A long discourse argueth folly, and delicate words incur the suspicion of flattery.
—John Lyly; *Euphues*, 1579

.17 A fellow who is always declaring he's no fool usually has his suspicions.
—Wilson Mizner; Edward Dean Sullivan's *The Fabulous Wilson Mizner*, 1935

## 99

.18 The talk of a fool is like a heavy pack on a journey.
—Old Testament: Apocrypha, Ecclesiasticus

.19 A fool's mouth is his destruction.
—Old Testament; Proverbs

.20 Wise men talk because they have something to say; fools, because they have to say something.
—Plato; *The Apology*, c. 4th century B.C.

.21 A fool's tongue is long enough to cut his own throat.
—John Ray; *English Proverbs*, 1678

.22 Things foolishly worded are not always foolish.
—Charles Reade; *The Cloister and the Hearth*, 1861

.23 They never open their mouths without subtracting from the sum of human knowledge.
—Thomas B. Reed; W.A. Robinson, *Life*, c. early 20th century

.24 *Yes* and *but* are words for fools; wise men neither hesitate nor retract—they resolve and execute.
—Sir Walter Scott; *The Talisman*, 1825

.25 A fool and his words are soon parted.
—William Shenstone; *The Selected Works in Verse and Prose of William Shenstone*, 1770

## 100 Forensics

.1 Forensic speaking either attacks or defends somebody: one or other of these two things must always be done by the parties in the case.
—Aristotle; *Rhetoric*, c. 4th century B.C.

.2 The aim of forensic oratory is to teach, to delight, to move.
—Cicero; *De Optimo Genere Oratorum*, c. 1st century B.C.

.3 Forensics is eloquence and reduction.
—Gertrude Stein; *How to Write*, "Forensics," 1931

## 101 Generalization

.1 For parlor use, a vague generality is a lifesaver.
—George Ade; *Forty Modern Fables*, "The Wise Piker," 1901

.2 Crafty men deal in generalizations.
—Anonymous

**101**

.3 It being the nature of the mind of man, to the extreme prejudice of knowledge, to delight in the spacious liberty of generalities.
—Francis Bacon; *Advancement of Learning*, 1623

.4 To generalize is to be an idiot.
—William Blake; *Annotations* to Sir Joshua Reynolds' Discourses, c. 1798–1809

.5 All generalizations are dangerous, even this one.
—Alexandre Dumas (Fils); Attributed

.6 The cause of all human evils is not being able to apply general principles to special cases.
—Epictetus; *Discourses*, c. 2nd century

.7 We are more prone to generalize the bad than the good. We assume that the bad is more potent and contagious.
—Eric Hoffer; *Reflections on the Human Condition*, 1973

.8 A wise man recognizes the convenience of a general statement, but he bows to the authority of a particular fact.
—Oliver Wendell Holmes; *The Poet at the Breakfast Table*, 1872

.9 All sweeping assertions are erroneous.
—L.E. Landon; *Romance and Reality*, 1831

.10 Generalization is necessary to the advancement of knowledge; but particularly is indispensable to the creations of the imagination.
—Thomas Babington Macaulay; *Milton*, 1834

.11 Men are more apt to be mistaken in their generalizations than in their particular observations.
—Niccolo Machiavelli; *Discourses*, 1531

.12 These people are a specimen of how people talk, the wide world over…. You see how they argue upon the vast interests of vast bodies from the temporary aspect of their own little affairs.
—Harriet Martineau; *Illustrations of Taxation*, 1834

.13 Any general statement is like a cheque drawn on a bank. Its value depends on what is there to meet it.
—Ezra Pound; *ABC of Reading*, 1934

.14 Generalizations are merely conveniences, an attempt to oil the wheels of such civilization as we have. It is exhausting to come newly to everything, to have the same decisions to make over and over again.
—Elizabeth Taylor; *At Mrs. Lippincote's*, 1945

**101**

.15 Intellectual generalities are always interesting, but generalities in morals means absolutely nothing.
—Oscar Wilde; *A Woman of No Importance*, 1893

# **102** Gentlemen

.1. A gentleman is a man who can disagree without being disagreeable.
—Anonymous

.2 To a gentleman—someone who dies without ever pronouncing the word—is a man who climbs Everest, never mentions it to a soul, and listens politely to Pochet's account of how in 1937 in spite of his sciatica, he conquered the Puy de Dome.
—Pierre Daninos; *The Secret of Major Thompson*, 1957

.3 We sometimes meet an original gentleman, who, if manners had not existed, would have invented them.
—Ralph Waldo Emerson; *Essays: Second Series,* "Manners," 1844

.4 A right Gentleman is not borne as the Poet, but made as the Orator … Philosophy received not Plato a Gentleman, but made him one.
—Stefano Guazzo; *Civile Conversation*, 1574

.5 A gentleman is one who is never rude unintentionally.
—H.F. Heard; *A Taste of Honey*, 1941

.6 It is almost a definition of a gentleman to say he is a one who never inflicts pain.
—John Henry Newman; *The Idea of a University*, 1853–58

.7 A gentleman never heard the story before.
—Austin O'Malley; Attributed

.8 The only infallible rule we know is, that the man who is always talking about being a gentleman never is one.
—R.S. Surtees; *Ask Mama*, 1858

.9 No real gentleman will tell the naked truth in the presence of ladies.
—Mark Twain; *Mark Twain's Fables of Man,* "The Secret History of Eddypus," John S. Tuckey, ed., 1972

# 103 Ghosts

.1 Ghosts, like ladies, never speak till spoke to.
—R.H. Barham; *The Ingoldsby Legends: The Ghost*, c. 1840

.2 Ghost: the outward and visible sign of an inward fear.
—Ambrose Bierce; *The Devil's Dictionary*, 1906

.3 The more enlightened our houses are, the more their walls ooze ghosts.
—Italo Calvino; lecture "Cybernetics and Ghosts," November, 1969, published in *The Literature Machine*, 1987

.4 From ghoulies and ghosties and long-leggety beasties
And things that go bump in the night, Good Lord, deliver us!
—Cornish Prayer

.5 No ghost should be allowed to walk
And make such havoc with its talk:
When folks are dead, they should retire—
I have no patience with you, Sire!
—Charles Dalmon; "The Ghost of Hamlet's Father"

.6 I don't believe in ghosts, but I've been afraid of them all my life.
—Charles A. Dana; Quoted by Bert Leston Taylor; *The So-Called Human Race*, c. early 20th century

.7 At first cock-crow the ghosts must go
Back to their quiet graves below.
—Theodosia Garrison; *The Neighbors*, 1909

.8 True love is like ghosts, which everybody talks about and few have seen.
—François de La Rochefoucauld; *Maxims*, 1665

.9 you want to know
whether i believe in ghosts
of course i do not believe in them
if you had known
as many of them as i have
you would not
believe in them either
—Don Marquis; *archy and mehitabel*, "ghosts," 1927

.10 Men say that in this midnight hour,
The disembodied have power
To wander as it liketh them,
By wizard oak and fairy stream.
—William Motherwell; *Midnight*, 1832

.11 Ghosts cannot be put on the witness stand, or have their fingerprints taken. They are completely proof against proof.
—Diana Norman; *The Stately Ghosts of England*, 1963

.12 Your ghosts are very rude unsociable folks.
—Eliza Parsons; *Castle of Wolfenbach*, 1793

.13 An' all us other children, when the supper is done,
We set around the kitchen fire an' has the mostest fun
A-list'nin' to the witch tales 'at Annie tells about
An' the gobble-uns 'at gits you
Ef you
Don't
Watch
Out!
—James Whitcomb Riley; "Little Orphant Annie," *The Complete Works of James Whitcomb Riley*, 1913

.14 Ghosts fear men much more than men fear ghosts.
—William Scarborough; *Chinese Proverbs*, 1875

# 104 Giants

.1 Look, your worship … those things which you see over there are not giants, but windmills.
—Miguel de Cervantes; *Don Quixote*, 1605

.2 Pygmies placed on the shoulders of giants see more than the giants themselves.
—Didacus Stella; Quoted by Robert Burton, *Anatomy of Melancholy*, 1621

.3 Ignorance is a blind giant who, let him but wax unbound, would make it a sport to seize the pillars that hold up the long-wrought of human good, and turn all the places of joy as a buried Babylon.
—George Eliot; *Daniel Deronda*, 1876

.4 A giant will starve with what will surfeit a dwarf.
—Thomas Fuller II; *Gnomologia*, 1732

.5 Even among men, giants are commonly the real dwarfs.
—Baltasar Gracian; *Oraculo Manual*, 1647

.6 If I have seen further than other men it is by standing upon the shoulders of giants.
—Sir Isaac Newton; Letter to Robert Hooke, 1675–76

.7 There were giants in the earth in those days … mighty men which were of old, men of renown.
—Old Testament: Genesis

.8 Far be it from me to tell them of the battles of the giants.
—Plato; *The Republic*, c. 4th century B.C.

## 104

.9  O! it is excellent
To have a giant's strength; but it is
tyrannous
To use it like a giant.
—William Shakespeare; *Measure for Measure*, 1603

## 105 Girls

.1  Girls are so queer you never know what they mean. They say no when they mean yes, and drive a man out of his wits just for the fun of it.
—Louisa May Alcott; *Little Women*, 1869

.2  What are little girls made of?
Sugar and spice, and everything nice;
That's what little girls are made of.
—Anonymous

.3  One of those little prating girls,
Of whom fond parents tell such tedious stories.
—John Dryden; *The Rival Ladies*, 1664

.4  Defiant love sonnets
demanding nude joys
lure girls to be naughty
and live like the boys.
—Alfred Kreymborg; E.S.V.M.—Authors in Epigram, c. 1950

.5  There was a little girl
Who had a little curl
Right in the middle of her forehead;
And when she was good
She was very, very good,
But when she was bad she was horrid.
—Mother Goose; Attributed
[Longfellow's son Ernest W. Longfellow attributes this verse to his father, alleging that they were written about 1856 while the poet was pacing in his garden carrying his second daughter "Edith with the Golden Hair." There is no inclusion of the verse in Longfellow's collection of his works. On the other hand, the verse does not appear in any of the older books of nursery rhymes attributed to Mother Goose.]

.6  You speak like a green girl,
Unsifted in such perilous circumstance.
—William Shakespeare; *Hamlet*, 1600–1

.7  The little rift between the sexes is astonishingly widened by simply teaching one set of catchwords to the girls and another to the boys.
—Robert Louis Stevenson; *Virginibus Puerisque*, 1881

## 106 God

.1  The words that men say are one thing; the things which God doeth are another.
—Amen-em-Apt; *Teaching How to Live*, c. 700 B.C.

.2  god is not
the voice of the whirlwind
god is the whirlwind.
—Margaret Atwood; *The Journals of Susanna Moodie*, "Resurrection," 1970

.3  God is the poet, men but the actors.
—Honore de Balzac; *Christian Socrates*, 1843

.4  What God says is best, is best, though all men in the world are against it.
—John Bunyan; *Pilgrim's Progress*, 1678

.5  God is always more unlike what we say than like it.
—Denise Lardner Carmody; *Virtuous Woman*, 1992

.6  Do not speak of God much. After a very little conversation on the highest nature, thought deserts us and we run into formalism.
—Ralph Waldo Emerson; *Journals*, 1836

.7  Most of the time, God speaks in a whisper.
—Jean Grasso Fitzpatrick; *Something More*, 1991

.8  God is a verb, not a noun.
—R. Buckminster Fuller; "No More Secondhand God," Southern Illinois University, 1963

.9  No statement about God is simply, literally true. God is far more than can be measured, described, defined in ordinary language, or pinned down to any particular happening.
—David Jenkins; Church Times, 1984

.10 Man proposes, but God disposes.
—Thomas A Kempis; *The Imitation of Christ*, c. 1413

.11 God is but a word invented to explain the world.
—Alphonse de Lamartine; *Premiers Meditations poetiques*, 1820

.12 God is love: and he that dwelleth in love dwelleth in God, and God in him.
—New Testament: John

.13 God is an utterable sigh, planted in the depths of the soul.
—Jean Paul Richter; in Thomas Carlyle, "Jean Paul Richter," *Edinburgh Review*, 1827

**106**

.14 I met God. "What," he said, "you already?" "What," I said, "you still?"
—Laura Riding; in Michele Brown and Ann O'Connor, *Hammer and Tongues*, 1986

.15 But who can speak to God, or rather who can't? The question is, who can get an answer?
—William Saroyan; *Chance Meetings*, 1978

.16 Metaphors for God drawn from human experience can easily be literalized. While we are immediately aware that the personal God is not really like a rock or a mother eagle, it is easy to imagine that God is really a king or a father.
—Sandra M. Schneiders; *Women and the World*, 1986

.17 Live among men as if God beheld you; speak to God as if men were listening.
—Seneca; *Epistles*, c. 1st cenury A.D.

.18 You never speak to God; you address a fellow-man, full of his own tempers; and to tell the truth, rightly understood, is not to state the true facts, but to convey a true impression.
—Robert Louis Stevenson; *Virginibus Puerisque*, 1881

.19 Why is it when we talk to God, we're said to be praying—but when God talks to us, we're schizophrenic?
—Lily Tomlin; in Michele Brown and Ann O'Connor, *Hammer and Tongues*, 1986
[It is possible that comedienne Tomlin borrowed this line from U.S. psychiatrist Thomas Szasz who said: If you talk to God, you are praying; if God talks to you, you have schizophrenia. *The Second Sin*, "Schizophrenia," 1973.]

.20 God created man because He loves stories.
—Elie Wiesel; *Souls on Fire*, 1971

# **107** Gods

.1 Zeus, who guided men to think
who laid it down that wisdom
comes alone through suffering.
Still there drips in sleep against the heart
grief of memory; against
our pleasure we are temperate.
—Aeschylus; *Agamemnon*, c. 6th century B.C.

.2 Mother goddesses are just as silly a notion as father gods. If a revival of the myths of these cults gives woman emotional satisfaction, it does so at the price of obscuring the real con-

**107**

ditions of life. This why they were invented in the first place.
—Angela Carter; *The Sadeian Woman*, "Polemical Preface," 1979

.3 We are told that there is no race in the world so uncivilized or barbarous but that it has some intimation of a belief in the gods. It is certain that many men entertain wrong ideas about the gods. This results from a corrupt nature. Nevertheless, all men hold to some divine power and a divine nature, and this is not because of some human agreement of convention. It is commonly accepted that such a unanimity among the world races is according to natural law.
—Cicero; *De Natura Deorum*, c. 1st century B.C.

.4 Human murmurs never touch the gods.
—Claudian; *Epigrams*, c. A.D. 395

.5 All the gods are dead except the god of war.
—Elridge Cleaver; *Soul on Ice*, 1968

.6 Fairest Isle, all isles excelling,
Seat of pleasures, and loves;
Venus here will choose her dwelling,
And forsake her Cyprian groves.
—John Dryden; *King Arthur*, "Song of Venus," 1691

.7 The gods of fable are the shining moments of great men.
—Ralph Waldo Emerson; *Representative Men: Uses of Great Men*, 1850

.8 Do we, holding that the gods exist, deceive ourselves with unsubstantial dreams and lies, while random careless chance and change alone control the world?
—Euripides; *Ion*, c. 425 B.C.

.9 The deities of Olympus, as they are painted by the immortal bard, imprint themselves on the minds which are the least addicted to superstitious credulity. Our familiar knowledge of their names and characters, their forms and attributes, seems to bestow on those airy beings a real and substantial existence; and the pleasing enchantment produces an imperfect and momentary assent of the imagination to those fables which are the most repugnant to our reason and experience.
—Edward Gibbon; *The Decline and Fall of the Roman Empire*, 1776–88

.10 The Persians ... have no images of the gods, no temples nor altars, and consider the use of them a sign of folly. This comes, I think, from

their not believing the gods to have the same nature with men, as the Greeks imagine.
—Herodotus; *The Histories of Herodotus*, c. 440 B.C.

.11 Olympus, where they say there is an abode of he gods, ever unchanging: it is neither shaken by winds nor ever wet with rain, nor does snow come near it, but clear weather spreads cloudless about it, and a white radiance stretches above it.
—Homer; *The Iliad*, c. 700 B.C.

.12 Pluto, the grisly god, who never spares. Who feels no mercy, and who hears no prayers.
—Homer; *Iliad*, c. 700 B.C.

.13 Young friends, no mortal man can vie with Zeus. His home and all his treasures are for ever.
—Homer; *Iliad*, c. 700 B.C.

.14 All ages before ours believed in gods in some form or another. Only an unparalleled impoverishment in symbolism could enable us to rediscover the gods as psychic factors, which is to say, as archetypes of the unconscious. No doubt the discovery is hardly credible as yet.
—Carl Jung; *Collected Works*, 1954

.15 Janus am I; oldest of potentates;
Forward I look, and backward, and below
I count as god of avenues and gates.
—Henry Wadsworth Longfellow; "The Poet's Calendar: January," *Complete Poetical and Prose Works*, 1886

.16 [Human reason] freed men's minds from wondering at portents by wrestling from Jupiter his bolts and power of thunder, and ascribing to the winds the noise and to the clouds the flame.
—Marcus Manilius; *Astronomica*, c. 1st century A.D.

.17 It is convenient that there be gods, and, as it is convenient, let us believe there are.
—Ovid; *Ars Amatoria*, c. 3 B.C.

.18 It is fear that brought gods into the world.
—Petronius; *Satyricon*, c. A.D. 60

.19 Even as the sons of Homer, those singers of deftly woven lays, begin most often with Zeus for their prelude; even so hath our hero laid a first foundation for a tale of achievements in the sacred games by receiving a crown in the sacred grove of Nemean Zeus.
—Pindar; *Odes*, c. 5th century B.C.

.20 Or ask of yonder agent fields above
Why Jove's satellites are less than Jove.
—Alexander Pope; *An Essay on Man*, 1733

**107**

.21 His nature is too noble for the world:
He would not flatter Neptune for his trident,
Or Jove for's power to thunder. His heart's his mouth:
What his breast forges, that his tongue must vent.
—William Shakespeare; *Coriolanus*, 1607–9

.22 See, what a grace was seated on his brow;
Hyperion's curls; the front of Jove himself,
An eye like Mars, to threaten and command,
A station like the herald Mercury
New-lighted on a heaven-kissing hill.
A combination and a form indeed,
Where every god did seem to set his seal,
To give the world assurance of a man.
—William Shakespeare; *Hamlet*, 1600–1

.23 The words of Mercury are harsh after the songs of Apollo.
—William Shakespeare; *Love's Labour's Lost*, 1593–4

.24 The Gods take no thought for our happiness, but only for our punishment.
—Tacitus; *Annals*, c. 115–116

.25 Jupiter laughs at the perjuries of lovers.
—Albius Tibullus; *Elegies*, c. 1st century B.C.

# **108** Gossip

.1 Gossip is irresponsible communication.
—Rita Mae Brown; *A Plain Brown Rapper*, 1976

.2 I don't call it gossip. I call it, "emotional speculation."
—Laurie Colwin; *Happy All the Time*, 1978

.3 While gossip among women is universally ridiculed as low and trivial, gossip among men, especially if it is about women, is called theory, or idea, or fact.
—Andrea Dworkin; *Right-Wing Women*, 1978

.4 Gossip is a sort of smoke that comes from the dirty tobacco-pipes of those who diffuse it; it proves nothing but the bad taste of the smoker.
—George Eliot; *Daniel Deronda*, 1874

.5 Out of some little thing, too free a tongue
Can make an outrageous wrangle.
—Euripides; *Andromache*, c. 426 B.C.

.6 For pines are gossip pines the wide world through
And full of runic tales to sigh or sing.
—James Elroy Flecker; "Brumana," 1913

**108**

.7  Like all gossip—it's merely one of those half-alive things that try to crowd our real life.
—E.M. Forster; *A Passage to India*. 1924

.8  A gossip speaks ill and all of her.
—Thomas Fuller II; *Gnomologia*, 1732

.9  To create an unfavorable impression, it is not necessary that certain things should be true, but that they have been said.
—William Hazlitt; *Characteristics*, 1823

.10  Gossips are frogs—they drink and talk.
—George Herbert; *Jacula Prudentum*, 1640

.11  Gossip is an evil thing by nature, she's a light weight to lift up, oh very easy, but heavy to carry and hard to put down again.
—Hesoid; *Works and Days*, c. 8th century B.C.

.12  Nobody's interested in sweetness and light.
—Hedda Hopper; Quoted in Robert Columbo, *Popcorn in Paradise*, 1979

.13  Gossip is a vice enjoyed vicariously.
—Elbert Hubbard; *Philistine*, 1895

.14  There isn't much to be seen in a little town, but what you hear makes up for it.
—Kin Hubbard; *Abe Martin's Wisecracks*, 1930

.15  When someone says, "I don't wish to mention any names," it ain't necessary.
—Kin Hubbard; *Abe Martin's Wisecracks*, 1930

.16  Men have always detested women's gossip because they suspect the truth: Their measurements are being taken and compared.
—Erica Jong; *Fear of Flying*, 1973

.17  Gossip is the opiate of the oppressed.
—Erica Jong; *Fear of Flying*, 1973

.18  It is merry when gossips meet.
—Ben Jonson; *The Staple of News: Induction*, 1626

.19  Gossip, unlike river water, flows both ways.
—Michael Korda, *Reader's Digest*, June, 1976

.20  Someone who gossips well has a reputation for being good company or even a wit, never for being a gossip.
—Louis Kronenberger; *Company Manners*, 1954

.21  If you haven't got anything good to say about any one come and sit by me.
—Alice Roosevelt Longworth; Michael Teague, *Mrs. L: Conversations with Alice Roosevelt Longworth*, 1981

**108**

.22  Gossip isn't scandal and it's not merely malicious. It's chatter about the human race by lovers of the same.
—Phyllis McGinley; "A New Year and No Resolutions," *Woman's Home Companion*, January, 1957

.23  She poured a little social sewerage into his ears.
—George Meredith; "Love in the Valley," 1883

.24  Another good thing about gossip is that it is within everybody's reach,
And it is much more interesting than any other form of speech.
—Ogden Nash; *I'm a Stranger Here Myself*, " I Have It on Good Authority," 1938

.25  A cruel story runs on wheels, and every hand oils the wheels as they run.
—Ouida (Marie-Louise de La Ramee); *Wisdom, Wit and Pathos: Moths*, 1880

.26  Never ... use the word *gossip* in a pejorative sense. It's the very stuff of biography and has to be woven in. To suggest that the personal life is not an essential element in the creative life is absurd.
—Joan Peyser; *Publishers Weekly*, 1987

.27  The only time people dislike gossip is when you gossip about them.
—Will Rogers; in Paula McSpadden Love's *The Will Rogers Book*, 1961

.28  No one gossips about other people's secret virtues.
—Bertrand Russell; "On Education, Especially in Early Childhood," 1926

.29  That most knowing of persons—gossip.
—Seneca; *Epistles*, c. 1st century A.D.

.30  Gossip is just news running ahead of itself in a red satin dress.
—Liz Smith; *The Dallas Times-Herald*, 1978

.31  Bad gossip drives out good gossip.
—Liz Smith; *Modern Maturity*, 1994

.32  Gossip is a news story with a lot of leeway.
—Liz Smith; *Modern Maturity*, 1994

.33  Gossip, even when it avoids the sexual, bears about it a faint flavor of the erotic.
—Patricia Meyer Spacks; *Gossip*, 1985

.34  There is nothing that can't be made worse by telling.
—Terence; *Phormio*, c. 160 B.C.

**108**

.35 That which is everybody's business is nobody's business.
—Izaak Walton; *Compleat Angler*, 1653

.36 There is only one thing in the world worse than being talked about, and that is not being talked about.
—Oscar Wilde; *The Picture of Dorian Gray*, 1891

.37 It is perfectly monstrous the way people go about nowadays saying things against one, behind one's back, that are absolutely and entirely true.
—Oscar Wilde; *A Woman of No Importance*, 1893

.38 Gossip is hearing something you like about someone you don't.
—Earl Wilson; in *New Woman*, April, 1959

.39 Gossips: sociologists on a mean and petty scale.
—Woodrow Wilson; *An Old Master and Other Political Essays*, 1893

.40 Gossip is the art of saying nothing in a way that leaves practically nothing unsaid.
—Walter Winchell; in St. Clair McKelway's *Gossip: The Life and Times of Walter Winchell*, 1940

# **109** Grammar

.1 "Whom are you?" said he, for he had been to night school.
—George Ade; "The Steel Box," *Chicago Record*, March 16, 1898

.2 Idly inquisitive tribe of grammarians, who dig up the poetry of others by the roots... Get away, bugs that secretly bite the eloquent.
—Antiphanes of Macedonia; Meleager of Gadara, *Greek Anthology* c. 60 B.C.

.3 Once the grammar has been learnt writing is simply talking on paper and in time learning what not to say.
—Beryl Bainbridge; in *Contemporary Novelists*, 1976

.4 Heedless of grammar, they all cried, "That's him!"
—R.H. Barnham; "The Jackdow of Rheims," c. 1837–40

.5 The grammar has a rule absurd
Which I would call an outworn myth:
"A preposition is a word
You mustn't end a sentence with!"
—Berton Braley; *No Rule to Be Afraid Of*, 1904

.6 It is not the business of grammar, as some critics seem preposterously to imagine, to give law to the fashions which regulate our speech. On the contrary, from its conformity to these, and from that alone, it derives all its authority and value.
—George Campbell; *The Philosophy of Rhetoric*, 1776

.7 I will not go down to posterity talking bad grammar.
—Benjamin Disraeli; Attributed; Remark made while correcting proofs of his last Parliamentary Speech, c. 1876

.8 You can be a little ungrammatical if you come from the right part of the country.
—Robert Frost; *The Atlantic*, Jan., 1962

.9 When a thought takes one's breath away, a lesson on grammar seems an impertinence.
—Thomas Wentworth Higginson; Preface to *Poems by Emily Dickinson*, 1890

.10 Invention in language should no more be discouraged than should invention in mechanics. Grammar is the grave of letters.
—Elbert Hubbard; *A Thousand and One Epigrams*, 1923

.11 Grammar is to speech what salt is to food.
—Moses Ibn Ezra; *Shirat Yisrael*, c. 12th century

.12 I have labored to refine our language to grammatical purity, and to clear it from colloquial barbarisms, licentious idioms and irregular combinations.
—Samuel Johnson; *The Rambler*, March 14, 1752

.13 In all the maze of metaphorical confusion.
—Junius; *The Letters of Junius: Dedication to the English Nation*, 1769
[Junius is the pseudonym of an anonymous author, believed to have been, among others, Sir Philip Francis, Lord Shelburne, Lord George Sackville, or Lord Temple.]

.14 Grammar is not a set of rules; it is something inherent in the language, and language cannot exist without it. It can be discovered, but not invented.
—Charlton Laird; *The Miracle of Language*, 1953

.15 And I would fain have any one name to me that tongue, that any one can learn or speak as he should do, by the rules of grammar. Languages were made not by rules or art, but by accident and the common use of people.
—John Locke; *Some Thoughts Concerning Education*, 1693

## 109

.16 It is well to remember that grammar is common speech formulated.
—W. Somerset Maugham; *The Summing Up*, 1938

.17 Grammar, which knows how to control even kings.
—Moliere; *Les Femmes savantes*, 1672

.18 The greater part of the world's troubles are due to questions of grammar.
—Michel de Montaigne; *Essays*, 1580

.19 A man's grammar, like Caesar's wife, must not only be pure, but above suspicion of impurity.
—Edgar Allan Poe; *Marginalia*, 1844

.20 If your four negatives make your two affirmatives, why then, the worse for my friends and the better for my foes.
—William Shakespeare; *Twelfth Night*, 1601

.21 I don't want to talk grammar, I want to talk like a lady.
—George Bernard Shaw; *Pygmalion*, 1916

.22 An aspersion on my parts of speech.
—Richard Brinsley Sheridan; *The Rivals*, 1775

.23 When I read some of the rules for speaking and writing the English language correctly … I think—
    Any fool can make a rule
    And every fool will mind it.
—Henry David Thoreau; *Journal*, February 3, 1860

.24 Perfect grammar—persistent, continuous, sustained—is the fourth dimension, so to speak; many have sought it, but none has found it.
—Mark Twain; *Mark Twain's Autobiography*, Albert Bigelow Paine, ed., 1924

## 110 Griots

.1 Transforming words were placed in the mouths of folk poets from the earliest times in America. Africans in the Americas remembered the storytellers, the griots, who stood in the midst of the children and adults at night and told them rhythmic stories that possessed the special quality of moral and verbal resolution.
—Molefi Asante; *Talk That Talk*, "Folk Poetry in the Storytelling Tradition," 1989

.2 The word griot … has come to be used to denote a specialist musician-cum-narrator of the type found in the Malinke culture zone of

## 110

West Africa…. For millennia, and in all parts of Africa, counterparts … have enlightened and entertained their audiences with songs, stories, admonitions, histories and moral instructions. They have transmitted the classics of African societies and … have served as traditional Africa's informal academy of the humanities.
—Chinweizu; *Voices from Twentieth Century Africa*, Introduction, 1988

.3 I wanted, unskilled weaver that I am with a faltering weaver's shuttle, to put together a few strips so grandmother, if she returned, would find the thread which she was the first to spin, and where the Griot Amadou Koumba would recognize the colors of the beautiful fabrics which he wove for me.
—Birago Diop; *Tales of Amadou Koumba*, "The Stories Which Cradled My Childhood," 1966

.4 Griot singers and storytellers are compared to kings and princes because their memory is a sacred trust that touches every person in their culture.
—William Ferris; *Black Art: Ancestral Legacy*, "Black Art," 1989

.5 When a Griot dies, it is as if a library has burned to the ground.
—Alex Haley; "We Must Honor Our Ancestors," *Ebony*, August, 1986

.6 The griot was the oral historian and educator in any given society. The griot was well respected and very close to kings—in fact, closer to the king than the king's own wife.
—D'Jimo Kouyate; *Talk That Talk*, "The Role of the Griot," 1989

.7 Griots are men of spoken word, and by the spoken word we give life to the gestures of kings. But words are nothing but words; power lies in deeds. Be a man of action, do not answer me any more with your mouth, but tomorrow show me what you will have me recount to coming generations.
—Mali Griot Mamadou Kouyate; *Sundiata: An Epic of Old Mali*, 1217–1237

.8 There is the person who has exhibited the genius of tale telling from childhood…. Among many people he is known as the Griot. According to the Wolof people of Senegal, the true name is gewel. The term Griot is a European adaptation. The Griot (gewel) is that revered individual in the society who is entrusted with the exact cultural history. This exalted position is inherited.
—Pearl Primus; *The Storyteller*, 1989

**110**

.9 The job of the Griot in African society was so important that an error could cost him his life. The Griot began at a very early age to master his technique and information. Like the master drummer, he understudied an elder statesman of the tribe. His training demanded a certain psychological adjustment to the significance of his job—which was to contain and give advice to the cultural "heirlooms of the community."
—Eugene Redmond; *Drumvoice*, 1976

# **111** Hearing

.1 She told him it was terrible to hear such things as he told her and to please go ahead.
—George Ade; *Fables in Slang*, 1898

.2 You have heard what you have heard.
—Aeschylus; *Eumenides*, 458 B.C.

.3 Hearing is not seeing.
—African (Swahili) Proverb

.4 My mother's deafness is very trifling, you see, just nothing at all. By only raising my voice, and saying anything two or three times over, she is sure to hear.
—Jane Austen; *Emma*, 1816

.5 I shall hear in heaven.
—Ludwig van Beethoven; Attributed last words

.6 Men wish to hear no stories but those about the great and powerful, which are of no use to anyone.
—Jacques-Henri Berardin de Saint-Pierre; *Paul et Virginie*, 1788

.7 Hearing a hundred times is not as good as seeing once.
—Selwyn Gurney Champion; *Racial Proverbs*, 1938
[A Japanese proverb.]

.8 We hear with the more keenness what we wish others not to hear.
—George Eliot; *Middlemarch*, 1872

.9 He that hears much and speaks not at all shall be welcome both in bower and hall.
—English Proverb

.10 He that hears one side only, hears nothing.
—English Proverb

.11 From hearing comes wisdom, from speaking, repentance.
—English Proverb

**111**

.12 Hearing he hears not.
—Desiderius Erasmus; *Adagia*, 1523

.13 Every man hears only what he understands.
—Johann Wolfgang von Goethe; *Proverbs in Prose*, 1819

.14 Learning is easier gotten by the ears then by the eyes.
—Stefano Guazzo; *Civile Conversation*, 1574

.15 Less vividly is the mind stirred by what finds entrance through the ears than what is brought before the trusty eyes.
—Horace; *Ars Poetica*, 19 B.C.

.16 None is so deaf as who will not hear.
—Thomas Ingeland; *Disobedient Child*, c. 1560

.17 Would you were come to hear, not see a play....
The maker ... he'd have you wise,
Much rather by your ears than by your eyes.
—Ben Jonson; *The Staple of News: Prologue*, 1626

.18 It is less dishonor to hear imperfectly than to speak imperfectly. The ears are excused: the understanding is not.
—Ben Jonson; *Timber*, "Of Flatterers," 1640

.19 "The more you hear," he said, "the less you'll learn."
—John Masefield; *The Widow in the Bye Street*, 1912

.20 The tale is worth the hearing; and may move Compassion, perhaps deserve your love
And approbation.
—Philip Massinger; *The Unnatural Combat*, c. 1619

.21 Be ye doers of the word, and not hearers only.
—New Testament: James

.22 The man who sees little always sees less than there is to see; the man who hears badly always hears something more than there is to hear.
—Friedrich Nietzsche; *Human, All Too Human*, 1878

.23 The partisan, when he is engaged in a dispute, cares nothing about the rights of the question, but is anxious only to convince his hearers of his own assertions.
—Plato; *The Republic*, c. 360 B.C.

.24 Lord, hear me out, and hear me out this day:
From me to Thee's a long and terrible way.
—Theodore Roethke; "The Marrow," 1964

.25 Romans, countrymen, and lovers! hear me for my cause; and be silent, that you may hear.
—William Shakespeare; *Julius Caesar*, 1599

**111**

.26 All you had to do was tell people what they wanted to hear and they would believe you no matter how implausible your story might be.
—Tom Sharpe; *Wilt*, 1976

.27 For seldom shall she hear a tale
So sad, so tender, yet true.
—William Shenstone; "Jenny Dawson," c. 1742

.28 Hear first and speak afterwards.
—Spanish Proverb

.29 The fellow loved to advise, or rather to hear himself talk.
—Laurence Sterne; *Tristram Shandy*, 1760–67

.30 All speech, written or spoken, is a dead language, until it finds a willing and prepared hearer.
—Robert Louis Stevenson; *Lay Morals*, Edinburgh collection of complete works, 1894–98

.31 Things seen are mightier than things heard.
—Alfred, Lord Tennyson; "Enoch Arden," 1864

.32 If a man does not keep pace with his companions, perhaps it is because he hears a different drummer. Let him step to the music which he hears, however measured of far away.
—Henry David Thoreau; *Walden*, "Conclusion," 1854

.33 If you wish to lower yourself in a person's favor, one good way is to tell his story over again, the way you heard it.
—Mark Twain; "Pudd'nhead Wilson," 1894

# **112** Heart

.1 The heart of a fool is on his tongue; the tongue of a wise man is in his heart.
—Armenian Proverb

.2 Two things are bad for the heart—running up stairs and running down people.
—Bernard M. Baruch; Attributed

.3 I've given my life to storytelling; it's sacred to me. We can touch human hearts forever.
—Brother Blue; in Jimmy Neil Smith's *Homespun: Tales from America's Favorite Storytellers*, 1988

.4 Where hearts are true, Few words will do.
—A.B. Cheales; *Proverbial Folklore*, 1875

.5 A glad heart seldom sighs, but a sorrowful mouth often laughs.
—Danish Proverb

.6 A woman's heart and her tongue are not relatives.
—English proverb

.7 There must be more malice than love in the hearts of all wits.
—B.R. Haydon; *Table Talk*, c. 1840

.8 What is nearest the heart is usually nearest the lips.
—Irish Proverb

.9 The songs of the singer
Are tones that repeat
The cry of the heart
Till it ceases to beat.
—Georgia Douglas Johnson; *The Heart of a Woman*, "The Dreams of the Dream," 1918

.10 When the heart dares to speak, it needs no preparation.
—Gotthold Ephraim Lessing; *Minna von Barnhelm*, 1767

.11 The heart has its reasons which reason knows nothing of.
—Blaise Pascal; *Pensees*, 1670

.12 What the heart thinketh, the tongue speaketh.
—John Ray; *English Proverbs*, 1678

.13 As is your heart, so is your word.
—Russian Proverb

.14 "I have learned," said the Philosopher, "that the head does not hear anything until the heart has listened, and that what the heart knows today the head will understand tomorrow."
—James Stephens; *The Crock of Gold*, 1986

.15 The mouth obeys poorly when the heart murmurs.
—Voltaire; *Tancred*, 1760

.16 An embittered heart talks a lot.
—Yiddish Proverb

.17 I am very glad to demonstrate to you that we also have books; only they are not books with marks in them, but words in our hearts, which have been placed there by our ancestors long ago, even so long ago as when the world was new and young, like unripe fruit.
—Zuni Storyteller: to Frank Hamilton Cushing, 1896

# 113 Heresy and Heretics

.1 They that approve a private opinion, call it opinion; but they that mislike it, heresy, and yet heresy signifies no more than a private opinion.
—Thomas Hobbes; *Leviathan*, 1651

.2 The difference between heresy and prophecy is often one of sequence. Heresy often turns out to have been prophecy—when properly aged.
—Hubert H. Humphrey; speech, Washington, D.C., April 23, 1966

.3 Heresy is what the minority believe; it is the name given by the powerful to the doctrine of the weak.
—R.G. Ingersoll; *Heretics and Heresies*, 1874

.4 A heretic in one generation would have been a saint if he had lived in another, and a heretic in one country would often be a hero in another.
—Rufus M. Jones; *The Church's Debt to Heretics*, 1927

.5 I shall never be a heretic; I may err in dispute, but I do not wish to decide anything finally; on the other hand, I am not bound by the opinions of men.
—Martin Luther; letter, August 28, 1518

.6 There are those who ... have adopted incorrect opinions.... Necessity at certain times impels killing them and blotting out the traces of their opinions lest they should lead astray the ways of others.
—Maimonides; *The Guide of the Perplexed*, 1190

.7 Drunkenness is not a heresy, that a whole sermon should be preached against it.
—Charles Reade; *The Cloister and the Hearth*, 1861

.8 No heretic can learn the language of Heaven.
—Samuel Richardson; *Sir Charles Grandison*, 1749

.9 Among theologians heretics are those who are not backed with a sufficient array of battalions to render them orthodox.
—Voltaire; *Philosophical Dictionary*, 1764

# 114 Heroes

.1 Heroes can be found less in large things than in small ones, less in public than in private.
—James Baldwin; *Nobody Knows My Name*, 1961

.2 I am my own heroine.
—Marie Bashkirtseff; *Journal*, 1887

.3 Who is the hero? The man who conquers his desires.
—Bhartihari; *Niti Sataka*, c. A.D. 100

.4 There are heroes in words as well as heroes in blows.
—Thomas Bridges; *The Adventures of a Bank-Note*, 1770–71

.5 A Hero is someone who has given his or her life to something bigger than oneself.
—Joseph Campbell; *The Hero with a Thousand Faces*, 1949

.6 The history of the world is but the biography of heroes.
—Thomas Carlyle; *On Heroes and Hero-Worship: The Hero as Divinity*, 1840

.7 To believe in the heroic makes heroes.
—Benjamin Disraeli; *Coningsby*, 1844

.8 The real hero is always a hero by mistake; he dreams of being an honest coward like everybody else.
—Umberto Eco; *Travels in Hyper Reality*, 1986

.9 Times of heroism are generally times of terror.
—Ralph Waldo Emerson; *Essays: Heroism*, 1841

.10 A hero cannot be a hero unless in a heroic world.
—Nathaniel Hawthorne; *Journals*, 1850

.11 Heroes know each other.
—Japanese Proverb

.12 Heroes don't need to talk about what they did.
—W.P. Kinsella; *Shoeless Joe*, 1982

.13 Crowds speak in heroes.
—Gerald Stanley Lee; *Crowds*, 1913

.14 Ultimately a hero is a man who would argue with the Gods, and awakens devils to contest his vision.
—Norman Mailer; *Presidential Papers, Special Preface*, 1963

.15 We are the hero of our own story.
—Mary McCarthy; *On the Contrary*, 1961

**114**

.16 Heroes take journeys, confront dragons, and discover the treasure of their true selves.
—Carol Pearson; *The Hero Within*, 1986

.17 The real hero doesn't tell that he is one.
—Philippine Proverb

.18 We can't all be heroes because someone has to sit on the curb and clap as they go by.
—Will Rogers; "A Rogers Thesaurus," *Saturday Review*, August 25, 1962

.19 Hero-worship is strongest where there is least regard for human freedom.
—Herbert Spencer; *Social Statics*, 1851

.20 'Tis sweet to hear of heroes dead,
To know them still alive;
But sweeter if we earn their bread,
And in us they survive.
—Henry David Thoreau; "The Great Adventure" *Journals*, published 1906

.21 We must meet the hero on heroic grounds.
—Henry David Thoreau; *Winter*, February 1, 1852

.22 Our heroes are the men who do things which we recognize, with regret, and sometimes with a secret shame, that we cannot do. We find not much in ourselves to admire, we are always privately wanting to be like somebody else. If everybody was satisfied with himself, there would be no heroes.
—Mark Twain; *Mark Twain's Autobiography*, Albert Bigelow Paine, ed., 1924

# **115** Historians

.1 Historian. A broad-gauge gossip.
—Ambrose Bierce; *The Devil's Dictionary*, 1911

.2 It has been said that though God cannot alter the past, historians can; it is perhaps because they can be useful to Him in this respect that He tolerates their existence.
—Samuel Butler II; *Erewhon Revisited*, 1901

.3 Historians relate not so much what is done as what they would have believed.
—Benjamin Franklin; *Poor Richard's Almanack*, 1732–57

.4 History repeats itself. Historians repeat each other.
—Philip Guedalla; *Supers and Supermen*, "Some Historians," 1920

**115**

.5 Very few things happen at the right time, and the rest do not happen at all; the conscientious historian will correct these defects.
—Herodotus; *History*, c. 5th century B.C.

.6 Historian—an unsuccessful novelist.
—H.L. Mencken; *A Mencken Chrestomathy*, "Sententiae: The Mind of Men," 1949

.7 The talent of historians lies in their creating a true ensemble out of facts which are but half-true.
—Ernest Renan; Preface to the 18th edition of *The Life of Christ*, 1863

.8 Every historian discloses a new horizon.
—George Sand; *Letters of George Sand*, Raphael Ledos de Beaufort, ed., 1886

.9 A historian is a prophet in reverse.
—Friedrich von Schlegel; *Athenaeum: Berlin*, 1799

.10 Ignorance is the first requisite of the historian—ignorance, which simplifies and clarifies, which selects and omits, with a placid perfection unattainable by the highest art.
—Lytton Strachey; *Eminent Victorians*, "Preface," 1918

.11 There is no such thing as a neutral or purely objective historian. Without an opinion a historian would be simply a ticking clock, and unreadable besides.
—Barbara Tuchman; "Can History Be Served Up Hot?," *The New York Times Book Review*, 1964

.12 It should be the historian's business not to belittle but to illuminate the greatness of man's spirit.
—C.V. Wedgewood; *History and Hope*, 1987

.13 To give an accurate description of what has never occurred is not merely the proper occupation of the historian, but the inalienable privilege of any man of parts and culture.
—Oscar Wilde; *The Critic as Artist*, 1891

.14 The historian is the prophet looking backward.
—Carter G. Woodson; *The Story of the Negro Retold*, 1935

# **116** History

.1 History is agreed upon fiction.
—Diane Ackerman; *A Natural History of Love*, 1994

**116**

.2 I have noticed that as soon as you have soldiers the story is called history. Before their arrival it is called myth, folktale, legend, fairy tale, oral poetry, ethnography. After the soldiers arrive, it is called history.
—Paula Gunn Allen; in Judy Grahn, *Queen of Wands*, 1982

.3 History is something that never happened, written by a man who wasn't there.
—Anonymous

.4 Every day of your life is a page of your history.
—Arabic Saying

.5 History is, strictly speaking, the study of questions; the study of answers belongs to anthropology and sociology.
—W.H. Auden; *The Dyer's Hand*, 1962

.6 I am fond of history, and am very well contented to take the false with the true.
—Jane Austen; *Northanger Abbey*, 1818

.7 History. n. An account mostly false, of events mostly unimportant, which are brought about by rulers mostly knaves, and soldiers mostly fools.
—Ambrose Bierce; *The Devil's Dictionary*, 1911

.8 We need history, not to tell us what happened or to explain the past, but to make the past alive so that it can explain us and make a future possible.
—Allan Bloom; *The Closing of the American Mind*, 1987

.9 All true histories contain instructions.
—Anne Bronte; *Agnes Grey*, 1847

.10 History is the essence of innumerable biographies.
—Thomas Carlyle; *Essays*, "On History," 1839

.11 History, a distillation of Rumor.
—Thomas Carlyle; *The French Revolution*, 1837

.12 Woe to them who forget their history
And drug their hearts with false memories.
—Chinweizu; "Admonition to the Black World," *Voices from Twentieth-Century Africa*, 1988

.13 To be ignorant of what occurred before you were born is to remain always a child. For what is the worth of human life, unless it is woven into the life of our ancestors by the records of history?
—Cicero; *De Oratore*, c. 55 B.C.

**116**

.14 The frontiers between history and imagination are very little more than Chinese screens, removable at will.
—Richard Cobb; in *The Listener*, 1978

.15 What is history after all? History is facts which become lies in the end; legends are lies which become history in the end.
—Jean Cocteau; *The Observer*, September 22, 1957

.16 History is like a story in a way; it depends on who's telling it.
—Dorothy Salisbury Davis; "By the Scruff of the Soul" in *Ellery Queen's Mystery Magazine*, 1963

.17 History is the present. That's why every generation writes it anew. But what most people think of us as history is its end product, myth.
—E.L. Doctorow; interview in *Writers at Work*, Eighth Series, George Plimpton, ed., 1988

.18 A book of history is a book of sermons.
—Sir Arthur Conan Doyle; *Micah Clarke*, 1888

.19 I am ashamed to see what a shallow village tale our so-called history is.
—Ralph Waldo Emerson; *Essays: History*, 1841

.20 History … is indeed little more than the register of the crimes, follies, and misfortunes of mankind.
—Edward Gibbon; *The Decline and Fall of the Roman Empire*, 1776–88

.21 American history is a myth and can only be accepted when read with blinders that block out the facts.
—Dick Gregory; *No More Lies*, 1971

.22 History is principally the inaccurate narration of events which ought not to have happened.
—E.A. Hooton; *Twilight of Man*, 1939

.23 History fades into fable; fact becomes clouded with doubt and controversy; the inscription molders from the tablet; the statue falls from the pedestal. Columns, arches, pyramids, what are they but heaps of sand; and their epitaphs, but characters written in the dust?
—Washington Irving; *The Sketch-Book: Westminster Abbey*, 1819–20

.24 Many falsehoods are passing into uncontradicted history.
—Samuel Johnson; in Boswell's *Life of Johnson*, 1799
[Johnson went on to say "Seldom any splendid story is wholly true."]

**116**

.25 All great people glorify their history and look back upon their early attainments with a spiritual vision.
—Kelly Miller; *Voice of the Negro*, 1906

.26 History is a myth, the true myth, of man's fall made manifest in time.
—Henry Miller; *Plexus*, 1949

.27 Much more than a collection of unrelated facts, names, and dates, our history is indeed our story—our interpretation of past events, a reflection of the way we see ourselves and of what we think really matters.
—National Storytelling Press; *Many Voices: True Tales from America's Past*, 1995

.28 History, a far more daring storyteller than romance.
—Charles Reade; *The Cloister and the Hearth*, 1861

.29 A people without history is like the wind on the buffalo grass.
—Sioux Saying

.30 The memories of men are too frail a thread to hang history from.
—John Still; *Gammer Gurton's Needle*, 1566
[Still, Bishop of Bath and Winchester, was believed to be the author of the second oldest English comedy, but the claim of William Stevenson is now more generally favored.]

.31 History as a discipline can be characterized as having a collective forgetfulness about women.
—Clarice Stasz Stoll; *Female and Male*, 1974

.32 To Navajos, a person's worth is determined by the stories and songs she or he knows, because it is by this knowledge that an individual is linked to the history of the entire group.
—Luci Tapahonso; *Culturefront Magazine*, Summer, 1993

.33 History is better than prophecy. In fact history is prophecy. And history says that wherever a weak and ignorant people possess a thing which a strong and enlightened people want, it must be yielded up peacefully.
—Mark Twain; "Pudd'nhead Wilson's New Calendar," 1897

.34 History is all explained by geography.
—Robert Penn Warren; Interview, *Writers at Work: First Series*, 1958

.35 Human history is in essence a history of ideas.
—H.G. Wells; *The Outline of History*, 1920

**116**

.36 There is no life that does not contribute to history.
—Dorothy West; *The Living Is Easy*, 1948

.37 As soon as histories are properly told there is no more need of romances.
—Walt Whitman; *Leaves of Grass*, Preface, 1855–92

**117** # Honesty

.1 An honest man, that cries up his own honesty, acts the honest man, but speaks like a rogue.
—Anonymous

.2 He who says there is no such thing as an honest man, you may be sure is himself a knave.
—George Berkeley; *Maxims Concerning Patriotism*, 1740

.3 An honest man will avow himself and his opinions.
—Hugh Henry Brackenridge; *Modern Chivalry*, 1792–1815

.4 Nobody can boast of honesty till they are tried.
—Susannah Centlivre; *The Perplex'd Lovers*, 1722

.5 An honest man's word is as good as his bond.
—Miguel de Cervantes; *Don Quixote*, 1605

.6 Speaking honestly is a fundamental principle of today's black artist. He has given up the futile practice of speaking to whites, and has begun to speak to his brothers.
—Addison Gayle, Jr.; *The Black Aesthetic*, 1971

.7 Honesty is no greater where elegance is less.
—Samuel Johnson; in Boswell's *Life of Johnson*, 1791

.8 What is more arrogant than honesty?
—Ursula K. Le Guin; *The Left Hand of Darkness*, 1969

.9 There's one way to find out if a man is honest—ask him. If he says "yes," you know he is crooked.
—Groucho Marx; Interview, 1954

.10 People who are brutally honest get more satisfaction out of the brutality than out of the honesty.
—Richard J. Needham; *The Wit and Wisdom of Richard Needham*, 1979

.11 A honest tale speeds best plainly told.
—William Shakespeare; *Richard III*, 1592–1593

**117**

.12 To be honest, one must be inconsistent.
—H.G. Wells; *Outline of History*, 1920

# 118 Honor

.1 No man should break his word of honor.
—Mikhail Bulgakov; *The White Guard*, 1925

.2 Honor's but a word
To swear by only in a Lord.
—Samuel Butler I; *Hudibras*, 1663

.3 The louder he talked of his honor, the faster we counted our spoons.
—Ralph Waldo Emerson; *Conduct of Life: Worship*, 1860

.4 Honor is the word of fools, or of those wiser men who cheat them.
—Henry Mackenzie; *The Man of Feeling*, 1771

.5 Honors never fail to purchase silence.
—Philip Massinger; *The Duke of Milan*, 1620

.6 Well honor is the subject of my story.
I cannot tell what you and other men
Think of this life; but, for my single self,
I had as lief not be as live to be
In awe of such a thing as I myself.
—William Shakespeare; *Julius Caesar*, 1599

.7 On the whole it is better to deserve honors and not have them than have them and not deserve them.
—Mark Twain; *Mark Twain's Notebook*, Albert Bigelow Paine, ed., 1935

# 119 Humor

.1 Even professional humorists seldom enjoy jokes at their own expense.
—Henry Adams; *Esther*, 1884

.2 Mirth is like a flash of lightning, that breaks through a gloom of clouds, and glitters for a moment; cheerfulness keeps up a kind of daylight in the mind, and fills it with a steady and perpetual serenity.
—Joseph Addison; *Spectator*, May 17, 1712

.3 Humor must fall out of a man's mouth like music out of a bobolink.
—Josh Billings; *Proverbial Philosophy*, 1858

.4 There are very few good judges of humor, and they don't agree.
—Josh Billings; *Proverbial Philosophy*, 1858

**119**

.5 Humor comes from self-confidence. There's an aggressive element to wit.
—Rita Mae Brown; *Starting from Scratch*, 1988

.6 In all true humor lies its germ, pathos.
—Edward George Bulwer-Lytton; *The Caxtons*, 1849

.7 Humor is merely tragedy standing on its head with its pants torn.
—Irvin S. Cobb; *Exit Laughing*, 1941

.8 Men will confess to treason, murder, arson, false teeth or a wig. How many of them will own up too a lack of humor?
—Frank Moore Colby; *The Colby Essays*, "Satire and Teeth," 1926

.9 Total absence of humor renders life impossible.
—Colette; *Gigi*, 1952

.10 Humor is by far the most significant activity of the human brain.
—Edward de Bono; in *Daily Mail*, London, January 29, 1990

.11 Humor is an affirmation of dignity, a declaration of man's superiority to all that befalls him.
—Roman Gary; *Promise at Dawn*, 1961

.12 Humor is a rubber sword—it allows you to make a point without drawing blood.
—Mary Hirsch; *View from the Loft*, 1994

.13 Humor very often cuts the knot of serious questions more trenchantly and successfully than severity.
—Horace; *Satires*, c. 35 B.C.

.14 Humor is when the joke is on you but hits the other fellow first—before it boomerangs.
—Langston Hughes; *The Book of Negro Humor*, 1966

.15 The teller of a mirthful tale has latitude allowed him. We are content with less than absolute truth.
—Charles Lamb; *The Last Essays of Elia: Stage Illusions*, 1833

.16 The best definition of humor I know is: humor may be defined as the kindly contemplation of the incongruities of life, and the artistic expression thereof. I think this is the best I know because I wrote it myself.
—Stephen Leacock; *Here Are My Lectures*, 1938

.17 Don't try for wit. Settle for humor. You'll last longer.
—Elsa Maxwell; *How to Do It*, 1957

## 119

.18 Humor is the contemplation of the finite from the point of view of the infinite.
—Christian Morgenstern; *Aphorisms*, c. 1900

.19 Exaggeration is the cheapest form of humor.
—Elizabeth Peters; *Naked Once More*, 1989

.20 Humor hardens the heart, at least to the point of sanity.
—Agnes Repplier; *Under Dispute*, "They Had Their Day," 1924

.21 Everything is funny as long as it happens to somebody else.
—Will Rogers; *The Illiterate Digest*, 1924

.22 It is a difficult thing to like anybody's else ideas of being funny.
—Gertrude Stein; *Everybody's Autobiography*, 1937

.23 Humor is emotional chaos remembered in tranquility.
—James Thurber; *New York Post*, February 29, 1960

.24 Everything human is pathetic. The secret source of Humor itself is not joy but sorrow. There is no humor in heaven.
—Mark Twain; *Following the Equator*, "Pudd'nhead Wilson's New Calendar," 1897

.25 There are several kinds of stories, but only one difficult—the humorous.
—Mark Twain; "How to Tell a Story," 1895

.26 By far the very funniest things that ever happened or were ever said, are unprintable (in our day). A great pity. It was not so in the freer age of Boccaccio and Rabelais.
—Mark Twain; *Mark Twain's Notebooks & Journals*, 1877–1883

.27 Whatever else an American believes or disbelieves about himself, he is absolutely sure he has a sense of humor.
—E.B. White; *Essays of E.B. White*, "Some Remarks on Humor," 1977

.28 Humor is the first of the gifts to perish in a foreign tongue.
—Virginia Woolf; *The Common Reader: First Series*, "On Not Knowing Greek," 1925

## 120 Hypocrisy

.1 I have heard many cry out against sin in the pulpit who yet can abide it well enough in the heart, house, and conversation.
—John Bunyan; *Pilgrim's Progress*, 1678

## 120

.2 Keep thy smooth words and juggling homilies
For those who know thee not.
—Lord Byron; *Sardanapalus*, 1821

.3 Is a Paleface always made with two tongues?
—James Fenimore Cooper; *The Prairie*, 1827

.4 Both religion and virtue have received more real discredit from hypocrites than the wittiest profligates or infidels could ever cast upon them.
—Henry Fielding; *Tom Jones*, 1749

.5 I detest that man, who hides one thing in the depths of his heart, and speaks forth another.
—Homer; *The Iliad*, c. 700 B.C.

.6 A man of forms and phrases and postures.
—Henry James; *The American*, 1877

.7 That character in conversation which commonly passes for agreeable is made up of civility and falsehood.
—Alexander Pope; *Thoughts on Various Subjects*, 1727

.8 A little pretense served the wolf when he had a mind to quarrel with the lamb.
—Samuel Richardson; *Clarissa Harlowe*, 1747–48

.9 How clever you are, my dear!
You never mean a single word you say.
—Oscar Wilde; *A Woman of No Importance*, 1893

.10 Nothing is so provoking as that a man should preach viciously and act virtuously.
—Frances Wright; *A Few Days in Athens*, 1822

## 121 Iconoclasts

.1 There is no rebel like Nature. She is an iconoclast.
—Paul Laurence Dunbar; *The Uncalled*, 1898

.2 A sensible man doesn't tear down idols. Let the world alone and it'll let you alone.
—Ellen Glasgow; *The Descendant*, 1897

.3 Rough work, iconoclasm, but the only way to get at truth.
—Oliver Wendell Holmes, Sr.; *The Professor at the Breakfast Table*, 1860

# 122 Ideals and Idealists

.1 Our ideals are our better selves.
—A.B. Alcott; *Table Talk*, "Habits," 1877

.2 Why should we strive, with cynic frown,
To knock their fairy castles down?
—Eliza Cook; "Oh! Dear to Memory," late
19th century

.3 Mankind has ever been divided into two sects,
Materialists and Idealists; the first founding
on experience, the second on consciousness.
—Ralph Waldo Emerson; *Essays*, "Transcendentalism," 1842

.4 How lovely to think that no one need wait a
moment, we can start now, start slowly changing the world!
—Anne Frank; *Anne Frank's Tales from the
Secret Annex*, Ralph Manheim and
Michel Mok, tr., 1984

.5 Don't use that foreign word "ideals." We have
that excellent native word "lies."
—Henrik Ibsen; *The Wild Duck*, 1884

.6 Idealist: a cynic in the making.
—Irving Layton; *The Wholly Bloody Bird*,
"Aphs," 1969

.7 An idealist is one who, on noticing that a rose
smells better than a cabbage, concludes that it
will also make better soup.
—H.L. Mencken; *A Book of Burlesques*,
"Sententiae," 1920

.8 Only in dreams do men set forth in quest of
the ideal.
—George Moore; *Evelyn Innes*, 1898

# 123 Ideas

.1 If the ancients left us ideas, to our credit be it
spoken that we moderns are building houses
for them.
—A.B. Alcott; *Table Talk: Enterprise*, 1877

.2 One of the greatest pains to human nature is
the pain of a new idea.
—Walter Bagehot; *Physics and Politics*,
1876

.3 One can live in the shadow of an idea without
grasping it.
—Elizabeth Bowen; *The Heat of the Day*,
1949

.4 The raison-d'être of language is an idea to be
expressed. When the idea is expressed, the language may be ignored.
—Chuang-tzu; *On Levelling All Things*, c.
4th century B.C.

.5 Ideas, like ghosts, must be spoken to a little
before they will explain themselves.
—Charles Dickens; *Dombey and Son*, 1846–8

.6 No idea is so antiquated that it was not once
modern. No idea is so modern that it will not
some day be antiquated.
—Ellen Glasgow; Address to Modern
Language Association, 1936

.7 An idea, to be suggestive, must come to the individual with the force of a revelation.
—William James; *The Varieties of Religious
Experience*, 1902

.8 He can compress the most words into the
smallest ideas, of any man I ever met.
—Abraham Lincoln; c. 1859, in Gross'
*Lincoln's Own Stories*
[Lincoln refers to a fellow lawyer.]

.9 We should have a great many fewer disputes
in the world if words were taken for what they
are, the signs of our ideas only, and not for
things themselves.
—John Locke; *Essay Concerning Human
Understanding*, 1690

.10 There are no new ideas. There are only new
ways of making them felt.
—Audrey Lorde; "Poetry Is Not a Luxury"
in *Chrysalis*, 1977

.11 If you are possessed by an idea, you find it expressed everywhere, you even smell it.
—Thomas Mann; *Death in Venice*, 1903

.12 No matter how brilliantly an idea is stated, we
will not really be moved unless we have already half-thought of it ourselves.
—Mignon McLaughlin; *The Neurotic's
Notebook*, 1963

.13 There is no squabbling so violent as that between people who accepted an idea yesterday
and those who will accept the same one tomorrow.
—Christopher Morley; *Religio Journalistici*, c. 1950s

.14 Whenever new ideas emerge, songs soon follow, and before long the songs are leading.
—Holly Near, with Derek Richardson, *Fire
in the Rain ... Singer in the Storm*, 1990

.15 Those for whom words have lost their value
are likely to find that ideas have also lost their
value.
—Edwin Newman; *Strictly Speaking*, 1974

.16 The only listening that counts is that of the
talker who alternately absorbs and expresses
ideas.
—Agnes Repplier; *Compromises*, 1904

**123**

.17 An idea does not pass from one language to another without change.
—Miguel de Unamuno; *Tragic Sense of Life*, Preface, 1913

.18 The only people in the world who can change things are those who can sell ideas.
—Lois Wyse; *The Rosemary Touch*, 1974

# **124** Identity

.1 Tell me what you think you are and I will tell you what you are not.
—Henri Frederic Amiel; *Journal intime*, 1866

.2 Instead of boiling up individuals into the species, I would draw a chalk circle round every individuality, and preach to it to keep within that, and preserve and cultivate its identity.
—Jane Welch Carlyle; *Letters and Memorials*, 1883

.3 I perceive your tongue is English. And what the tongue is, I suppose the man is.
—Charles Dickens; *A Tale of Two Cities*, 1859

.4 Within our whole universe the story only has the authority to answer that cry of heart of its characters, that one cry of heart of each of them: *Who am I?*
—Isak Dinesen; *Last Tales*, "The Cardinal's First Tale," 1957

.5 He who lives like an ass, makes noises like an ass.
—Ethiopian Proverb

.6 Human beings have an inalienable right to invent themselves; when that right is preempted it is called brainwashing.
—Germaine Greer; in *The Times*, London, February 1, 1986

.7 It is thus with most of us; we are what other people say we are. We know ourselves chiefly by hearsay.
—Eric Hoffer; *The Passionate State of Mind*, 1954

.8 Identity is what you can say you are according to what they say you can be.
—Jill Johnston; *The Women's History of the World*, 1988

.9 A poet is the most unpoetical of anything in existence, because he has no identity—he is

**124**

continually infor[ming]—and filling some other body.
—John Keats; Letter to Richard Woodhouse, October 27, 1818

.10 Say that I was a drum major for justice; say that I was a drum major of peace; I was a drum major for righteousness.
—Martin Luther King, Jr.; "The Drum Major Instinct," sermon given at Ebenezer Baptist Church, Atlanta, Georgia, February 4, 1968

.11 People often say that this or that person has not yet found himself. But the self is not something one finds, it is something one creates.
—Thomas Szasz; *The Second Sin*, 1974

.12 To speak as black, female, and commercial lawyer has rendered me simultaneously universal, trendy, and marginal.
—Patricia J. Williams; *The Alchemy of Race and Rights*, 1991

# **125** Ignorance

.1 To be ignorant of one's ignorance is the malady of the ignorant.
—Amos Bronson Alcott; *Table Talk: Discourse*, 1877

.2 An ignorant man will always be the first to be heard.
—Babylonian Talmud: Nedarim, c. 450

.3 I didn't know what she was talking about, so I said "I know that. Who doesn't know that?"
—Lynda Barry; *The Good Times Are Killing Me*, 1988

.4 The trouble ain't that people are ignorant; it's that they know so much that ain't so.
—Josh Billings (Henry Wheeler Shaw); *Encyclopedia of Proverbial Philosophy*, 1880

.5 The man who confesses his ignorance shows it once; the man who tries to conceal it shows it many times.
—Selwyn Gurney Champion; *Racial Proverbs*, 1938
[A Japanese proverb.]

.6 I am not ashamed to confess that I am ignorant of what I do not know.
—Cicero; *Tusculanarum Disputationum*, 45 B.C.

.7 Ignorance never settles a question.
—Benjamin Disraeli; Speech, House of Commons, May 14, 1866

## 125

.8 He who knows little often repeats it.
—Thomas Fuller II; *Gnomologia*, 1732

.9 While all complain of our ignorance and error, everyone exempts himself.
—Joseph Glanvill; *The Vanity of Dogmatizing*, 1661

.10 He knows so little and knows it so fluently.
—Ellen Glasgow; *Barren Ground*, 1925

.11 The little I know, I owe to my ignorance.
—Sacha Guitry; *Toutes Reflexions Faites*, 1947

.12 The recipe for perpetual ignorance is: be satisfied with your opinions and content with your knowledge.
—Elbert Hubbard; *The Philistine*, 1897

.13 Most ignorance is vincible ignorance. We don't know because we don't want to know.
—Aldous Huxley; *Ends and Means: Belief*, 1937

.14 Ignorance, when it is voluntary, is criminal; and he may properly be charged with evil who refused to learn how he might prevent it.
—Samuel Johnson; *Rasselas*, 1759

.15 Nothing in all the world is more dangerous than sincere ignorance and conscientious stupidity.
—Martin Luther King, Jr.; *Strength to Love*, 1963

.16 Most people did not care to be taught what they did not already know; it made them feel ignorant.
—Mary McCarthy; *Birds of America*, 1971

.17 Our knowledge can only be finite, while our ignorance must necessarily be infinite.
—Karl Popper; *Conjectures and Refutations*, 1968

.18 Better be ignorant of a matter than half know it.
—Publilius Syrus; *Moral Sayings*, c. 1st century B.C.

.19 Everybody is ignorant, only on different subjects.
—Will Rogers; *The Illiterate Digest*, 1924

.20 Only the ignorant know everything.
—Dagobert D. Runes; *Treasury of Thought*, 1966

.21 Not ignorance, but ignorance of ignorance is the death of knowledge.
—Alfred North Whitehead; *Dialogues of Alfred North Whitehead*, 1953

## 126 Illusion

.1 Illusion is the dust the devil throws in the eyes of the foolish.
—Minna Antrim; *Naked Truth and Veiled Allusions*, 1902

.2 Beware that you do not lose the substance by grasping at the shadow.
—Aesop; *Fables*, "The Dog and The Shadow," c. 6th century B.C.

.3 We would rather be ruined than changed
We would rather die in our dread
Than climb the cross of the moment
And let our illusions die.
—W.H. Auden; *The Age of Anxiety*, 1948

.4 It is always some illusion that creates disillusion, especially in the young, for whom the only alternative to perfection is cynicism.
—Jacques Barzun; *Teacher in America*, 1944

.5 Perhaps it is better to wake up, rather than to remain a dupe to illusions all one's life.
—Kate Chopin; *The Awakening*, 1899

.6 Every age is fed on illusions, lest men should renounce life early and the human race come to an end.
—Joseph Conrad; *Victory*, 1915

.7 …illusions multiply, and among them there is, I suppose none more ubiquitous than the idea that "you can't change human nature." This ancient platitude might long ago have been relegated to a home for superannuated ideas, were it not so constantly useful.
—Barrows Dunham; *Man Against Myth*, 1947

.8 The highest problem of every art is, by means of appearances, to produce the illusion of a loftier reality.
—Johann Wolfgang von Goethe; *Maxims and Reflections*, "Truth and Poetry," 1818–1827

.9 If you ever do a survey, you'll find that people prefer illusion to reality, ten to one. Twenty, even.
—Judith Guest; *Ordinary People*, 1976

.10 Rob the average man of his life-illusion, and you rob him also of his happiness.
—Henrik Ibsen; *The Wild Duck*, 1884

.11 It is dangerous to let the public behind the scenes. They are easily disillusioned and then they are angry with you, for it was the illusion they loved.
—W. Somerset Maugham; *A Writer's Notebook*, 1949

## 126

.12 Here we wander in illusion.
Some blessed power deliver us from hence!
—William Shakespeare; *The Comedy of Errors*, 1593

.13 "Oh what an artistic animal is our little Man,"
Sneered the wind. "It is wonderful how he can
Invent fairy stories about everything, pit pat,
Will he ever face fact and not feel flat?"
—Stevie Smith; "Will Man Ever Face Fact and Not Fall Flat?," in *Not Waving But Drowning*, 1957

.14 All sorts of allowances are made for the illusions of youth; and none, or almost none, for the disenchantments of age.
—Robert Louis Stevenson; *Virginibus Puerisque*, "Crabbed Age and Youth," 1881

.15 Disillusion comes only to the illusioned. One cannot be disillusioned of what one never put faith in.
—Dorothy Thompson; *The Courage to Be Happy*, 1957

.16 Don't part with your illusions. When they are gone, you may still exist, but you have ceased to live.
—Mark Twain; "Pudd'nhead Wilson's Calendar," 1893

.17 If a man could kill all his illusions he'd become a god.
—Colin Wilson; *Ritual in the Dark*, 1960

.18 Plunge ourselves deep into the sweet illusion.
—Edward Young; *The Revenge*, 1721

## 127 Imagination

.1 Imagination is the child of inherited and living impressions.
—Gertrude Atherton; *The Doomswoman*, 1892

.2 Imagination is the air of the mind.
—P.J. Bailey; *Festus: Another and Better World*, 1839

.3 What is now proved was once only imagined.
—William Blake; *The Marriage of Heaven and Hell: Proverbs of Hell*, 1790

.4 Imagination, which is the Eldorado of the poet and of the novel-writer, often proves the most pernicious gift to the individuals who compose the talkers instead of the writers in society.
—Marguerite Blessington; *The Repealers*, 1833

.5 My kind of theater can be presented anywhere, in any setting, with nothin' but a place to stand—and imagination.
—Brother Blue; in Jimmy Neil Smith, *Homespun: Tales from America's Favorite Storytellers*, 1988

.6 Art is ruled uniquely by the imagination.
—Benedetto Croce; *Esthetic*, 1902

.7 He wants imagination, that's what he wants.
—Charles Dickens; *Barnaby Rudge*, 1841

.8 To make a prairie it takes a clover and one bee,—
One clover, and a bee
And revery.
The revery alone will do
If bees are few.
—Emily Dickinson; *Poems*, No. 97, c. 1858

.9 That fairy kind of writing which depends only upon the force of imagination.
—John Dryden; *King Arthur*, Dedication, 1691

.10 I imagine, therefore I belong and am free.
—Lawrence Durrell; *Justine*, 1957

.11 Imagination is more important than knowledge.
—Albert Einstein; *On Science*, 1950

.12 Imagination is a licensed trespasser; it has no fear of dogs, but may climb over walls and peep in at windows with impunity.
—George Eliot; *Adam Bede*, 1859

.13 A lot of living is done in the imagination.
—Ralph Ellison; *Going to the Territory*, 1986

.14 As a rule, indeed, grown-up people are fairly correct on matters of fact; it is in the higher gift of imagination that they are so sadly to seek.
—Kenneth Grahame; *The Golden Age: The Finding of the Princess*, 1895

.15 He who has imagination without learning has wings and no feet.
—Joseph Joubert; *Pensees*, 1810

.16 Heard melodies are sweet, but those unheard Are sweeter.
—John Keats; "Ode on a Grecian Urn," 1819

**127**

.17 Imagination grows by exercise, and contrary to common belief, is more powerful in the mature than in the young.
—W. Somerset Maugham; *The Summing Up*, 1938

.18 Imagination is the voice of daring. If there is anything Godlike about God it is that. He dared to imagine everything.
—Henry Miller; *Sexus*, 1949

.19 Imagination frames events unknown,
In wild, fantastic shapes of hideous ruin,
And what it fears creates.
—Hannah More; *The Complete Works of Hannah More*, "Belshazzar," 1856

.20 Imagination is the first faculty wanting in those that do harm to their own kind.
—Margaret Oliphant; *Jeanne d'Arc*, "Innocent," 1896

.21 Imagination continually frustrates tradition; that is its function.
—John Pfeiffer; *New York Times*, March 29, 1979

.22 The people who are willing to talk about imagination seldom have much. Imagination is a guilty secret, usually, a possession best kept inside the privacy of one's own skull.
—Margaret Lee Runbeck; *Time for Each Other*, 1944

.23 The lunatic, the lover, and the poet,
Are of imagination all compact.
—William Shakespeare; *A Midsummer Night's Dream*, 1595

.24 Imagination! who can sing thy force?
Or who describe the swiftness of thy course?
—Phyllis Wheatley; *Memoir and Poems of Phyllis Wheatley*, "On Imagination," 1838

.25 Imagination is a contagious disease. It cannot be measured by the yard, or weighed by the pound, and then delivered to the students by members of the faculty. It can only be communicated by a faculty whose members themselves wear their learning with imagination.
—Alfred North Whitehead; *The Aims of Education*, 1929

# **128** Imitation

.1 To refrain from imitation is the best revenge.
—Marcus Aurelius; *Meditations*, c. 2nd century

**128**

.2 One dog barks at something, and a hundred bark at the sound.
—Chinese Proverb

.3 Imitation is the sincerest form of flattery.
—C.C. Colton; *Lacon*, 1820

.4 Imitation, if it is not forgery, is a fine thing. It stems from a generous impulse, and a relative sense of what can and what cannot be done.
—James Fenton; "Ars Poetica," in the *Independent on Sunday*, London, December 16, 1990

.5 What the child imitates he is trying to understand.
—Friedrich Froebel; *The Education of Man*, 1826

.6 The child says nothing, but what is heard by the fire.
—George Herbert; *Jacula Prudentum*, 1640

.7 When people are free to do as they please, they usually imitate each other.
—Eric Hoffer; *The Passionate State of Mind*, 1955

.8 The only good imitations are those that poke fun at bad originals.
—François de La Rochefoucauld; *Maxims*, 1665

.9 Go, and do thou likewise.
—New Testament; Luke

.10 A mere copier of nature can never produce anything great.
—Joshua Reynolds; *Discourses on Painting*, 1774

.11 The talk of the child in the market-place, is either that of his father or his mother.
—Talmud; Sukkah, before A.D. 500

.12 A man never knows what a fool he is until he hears himself imitated by one.
—Herbert Beerbohm Tree; in Hesketh Pearson *Beerbohm-Tree*, 1956

.13 All that I desire to point out is the general principle that Life imitates Art far more than Art imitates Life.
—Oscar Wilde; *Intentions*, "The Decay of Living," 1891

.14 The true aim [of art] is faithfully to represent whatever is imitated.
—Ze Ami; *Fuski kaden*, 1400–18

# 129 Immortality

.1  "Immortals are what you wanted," said Thor in a low quiet voice. "Immortals are what you got."
—Douglas Adams; *The Long Dark Tea-Time of the Soul*, 1988

.2  Biggest affirmative argument I know in favor of "If a man die shall he live again?" is just the way you feel inside you that nothin' can stop you from livin' on.
—Bess Streeter Aldrich; *Song of Years*, 1939

.3  I have brought into his nostrils the life which is everlasting.
—Ani, Papyrus; *Book of the Dead*, c. 4000 B.C.

.4  A good man never dies.
—Callimachus; *Fragments*, c. 3rd century B.C.

.5  To live in hearts we leave
Is not to die.
—Thomas Campbell; "Hallowed Ground," 1825

.6  Immortality is the glorious discovery of Christianity.
—William Ellery Channing; *A Poet's Hope*, "Immortality," c. 1840

.7  If then all souls, both good and bad do teach
With general voice, that souls can never die;
'Tis not man's flattering gloss, but Nature's speech,
Which, like God's oracles can never lie.
—John Davies; *Nosce Teipsum*, 1599

.8  Let him who believes in immortality enjoy his happiness in silence; he has no reason to give himself airs about it.
—Johann Wolfgang von Goethe; Quoted in Johann Peter Eckermann's *Conversations with Goethe*, 1824

.9  From the voiceless lips of the unreplying dead, there comes no word; but in the night of death Hope sees a star, and listening Love can hear the rustle of a wing.
—Robert G. Ingersoll; Tribute to Eben C. Ingersoll, *The Works of Robert G. Ingersoll*, 1900

.10  He ne'er is crowned
With immortality, who fears to follow
Where airy voices lead.
—John Keats; *Endymion*, 1818

.11  If you question any candid person who is no longer young, he is very likely to tell you that, having tasted life in this world, he has no wish to begin again as a "new boy" in another.
—Bertrand Russell; *Unpopular Essays*, "Ideas That Have Harmed Mankind," 1950

# 129

.12  All men think all men mortal, but themselves.
—Edward Young; *Night Thoughts*, 1742–1746

# 130 Improvisation

.1  Improvisation can be either a last resort or an established way of evoking creativity.
—Mary Catherine Bateson; *Composing a Life*, 1989

.2  Improvisation is the essence of good talk, Heaven defend us from the talker who doles out things prepared for us! But let heaven not less defend us from the beautifully spontaneous writer who puts his trust in the inspiration of the moment!
—Max Beerbohm; *Mainly on the Air*, "Lytton Strachey," 1946

.3  He has devoted the best years of his life to preparing his impromptu speeches.
—1st Earl of Birkenhead, Attributed
[The English Conservative politician speaks of Winston Churchill.]

.4  Too much improvisation leaves the mind stupidly void.
—Victor Hugo; *Les Miserables*, 1862

.5  All good verses are like impromptus made at leisure.
—Joseph Joubert; *Pensees*, 1842

.6  A human being tends to believe that the mood of the moment, be it troubled or blithe, peaceful or stormy, is the true, native, and permanent tenor of his existence ... whereas the truth is that he is condemned to improvisation and morally lives from hand to mouth all the time.
—Thomas Mann; *Death in Venice*, "A Man and His Dog," 1918

.7  There's nothing that makes you so aware of the improvisation of human experience as a song unfinished. Or an old address book.
—Carson McCullers; *The Ballad of the Sad Cafe*, 1951

.8  I shall make you an impromptu at my leisure.
—Molière; *Les Precieuses Ridicula*, 1659

.9  Impromptu is truly the touchstone of wit.
—Molière; *Les Precieuses Ridicula*, 1659

.10  Extemporaneous speeches are deft and facile to abundance, but those who make them know neither where to begin nor where to stop.
—Plutarch; *Parallel Lives*, c. 46–c. 120

## 130

.11 Improvisation is too good to leave to chance.
—Paul Simon; quoted in the *International Herald Tribune*, Paris, October 12, 1990

.12 Through spontaneity we are re-formed into ourselves. It creates an explosion that for the moment frees us from handed-down frames of reference, memory choked with old facts and information and undigested theories and techniques of other people's findings. Spontaneity is the moment of personal freedom when we are faced with reality, and see it, explore it and act accordingly. In this reality the bits and pieces of ourselves function as an organic whole. It is the time of discovery, of experiencing, of creative expression.
—Viola Spolin; *Improvisation for the Theater*, 1963

.13 It usually takes me more than three weeks to prepare a good impromptu speech.
—Mark Twain; in Albert Bigelow Paine's *Mark Twain*, 1912

# 131 Indignation

.1 ...the voice of honest indignation is the voice of God.
—William Blake; *The Marriage of Heaven and Hell*, "A Memorable Fancy," 1790–93

.2 A puritan's a person who pours righteous indignation into the wrong things.
—G.K. Chesterton; Attributed

.3 Indignation at literary wrongs I leave to men born under happier stars. I cannot afford it.
—Samuel Taylor Coleridge; *Biographia Literaria*, 1817

.4 Honest indignation does sometimes counsel us wisely.
—Wilkie Collins; *The Legacy of Cain*, 1889

.5 Moral indignation is in most cases two percent moral, forty-eight percent indignation and fifty percent envy.
—Vittorio De Sica; Interview, c. 1960

.6 A good indignation makes an excellent speech.
—Ralph Waldo Emerson; *Journals*, 1841

.7 Indignation does no good unless it is backed with a club of sufficient size to awe the opposition.
—Edgar Watson Howe; *Ventures in Common Sense*, 1919

.8 To be able to destroy with good conscience, to be able to behave badly and call your bad behavior "righteous indignation"—this is the

## 131

height of psychological luxury, the most devilish of moral treats.
—Aldous Huxley; *Chrome Yellow*, 1921

.9 If nature refuses, indignation will produce verses.
—Juvenal; *Satires*, c. 100–128

.10 It is so much easier sometimes to sit down and be resigned than to rise up and be indignant.
—Nellie L. McClung; *Times Like These*, 1915

.11 Hide thyself as it were for a little moment, until the indignation be overpast.
—Old Testament: Isaiah

.12 Humanity is outraged in me and with me. We must not dissimilate nor try to forget this indignation which is one of the most passionate forms of love.
—George Sand; in Raphael Ledos de Beaufort, ed. *Letters of George Sand*, 1886

.13 Moral indignation is jealousy with a halo.
—H.G. Wells; *The Wife of Sir Isaac Harman*, 1914

.14 I was so obsessed and consumed with my grievances that I could not get away from myself and think things out in the light. I was in the grip of that blinding, destructive, terrible thing—righteous indignation.
—Anzia Yezierska; *Hungry Hearts*, "Soap and Water," 1920

# 132 Information

.1 Information can tell us everything. It has all the answers. But they are answers to questions we have not asked, and which doubtless don't even arise.
—Jean Baudrillard; *Cool Memories*, 1987

.2 I am greedy of getting information.
—Callimachus; *Iambi*, c. 250 B.C.

.3 I only ask for information.
—Charles Dickens; *David Copperfield*, 1849

.4 I was brought up to believe that the only thing worth doing was to add to the sum of accurate information in the world.
—Margaret Mead; in *New York Times*, August 9, 1964

.5 Everybody gets so much information all day long that they lose their common sense.
—Gertrude Stein; in Elizabeth Sprigge, *Gertrude Stein*, 1957

**132**

.6  Information appears to stew out of me naturally, like the precious ottar of roses out of the otter.
—Mark Twain; *Roughing It*, "Preface," 1872

# 133 Instruction

.1  It is always safe to learn, even from our enemies—seldom safe to venture to instruct, even our friends.
—C.C. Colton; *Lacon*, 1820

.2  Instruction increases inborn worth and right discipline strengthens the heart.
—Horace; *Odes*, 17–13 B.C.

.3  If you love instruction, you will be well instructed.
—Isocrates; *Ad Daemonicum*, c. 4th century B.C.

.4  It is not often that any man can have so much knowledge of another, as is necessary to make instruction useful.
—Samuel Johnson; *The Rambler*, 1750–52

.5  There are some sages whom we understand less as we hear them longer.
—Samuel Johnson; *Rasselas*, 1759

.6  Instruction in youth is like engraving in stone. Instruction in old age is like engraving in dung.
—Moroccan Proverb

.7  My son, hear the instruction of thy father, and forsake not the law of thy mother.
—Old Testament: Proverbs

.8  Nature's instructions are always slow, those of men are generally premature.
—Jean-Jacques Rousseau; *Emile*, 1762

.9  The villainy you teach me I will execute, and it shall go hard but I will better the instruction.
—William Shakespeare; *The Merchant of Venice*, 1596–97

.10 Age is no better, hardly so well, qualified for an instructor as youth, for it has not profited so much as it has lost.
—Henry David Thoreau; *Journal*, 1950

# 134 Instrument

.1  The attention of the group plays like a wind on the storyteller's instrument. He tunes it and sets the key to fit the particular group in front

**134**

of him; he adjusts his material to the composite listening ear of his group. No two groups are alike nor is the same group in like mood twice running. The art of the storyteller is the most fluid of all the art.
—C. Madeleine Dixon; "Once Upon a Time" in *Storytelling* by the Association for Childhood Education, 1945

.2  And David and all the house of Israel played before the Lord on all manner of instruments made of fir wood, even on harps, and on psalteries, and on timbrels, and on cornets, and on cymbals.
—Old Testament: 2 Samuel

.3  And oftentimes, to win us to our harm,
The instruments of darkness tell us truths,
Win us with honest trifles, to betray's
In deepest consequence.
—William Shakespeare; *Macbeth*, 1606

.4  Let him play the instrument who knows how.
—Spanish Proverb

.5  You are prepared to tell the story, then forget yourself. You are the instrument; the story is the thing.
—Gundrun Thorne-Thomsen; *Storytelling and Stories I Tell*, 1956

.6  The mind of man may be compared to a musical instrument with a certain range of notes, beyond which in both directions we have an infinitude of silence.
—John Tyndall; Lecture, c. 1874

# 135 Insults

.1  If there is anyone here whom I have not insulted, I beg his pardon.
—Johannes Brahms; Attributed
[Said on leaving a gathering of friends.]

.2  Let those who have betrayed him by their adulation, insult him with their malevolence.
—Edmund Burke; *On American Taxation*, 1774

.3  An injury is much sooner forgotten than an insult.
—Lord Chesterfield; Letter to His Son, October 9, 1746

.4  He received insults with a glow most people reserved for compliments.
—Liza Cody, *Dupe*, 1981

.5  He who allows himself to be insulted deserves to be.
—Pierre Corneille; *Heraclius*, 1650

**135**

.6 It is not he who reviles or strikes you who insults you, but your opinion that these things are insulting.
—Epictetus; *Fragments*, c. 1st century

.7 No one can be as calculatedly rude as the British, which amazes Americans, who do not understand studied insult and can only offer abuse as a substitute.
—Paul Gallico; *The New York Times*, January 14, 1962

.8 Each of us carries within himself a collection of instant insults.
—Haim Ginott; *Between Parent and Teenager*, 1969

.9 Insult gives birth to insult.
—Greek Proverb

.10 Fate never wounds more deep the gen'rous heart,
Than when a blockhead's insult points the dart.
—Samuel Johnson; *Sermons*, 1788

.11 This goat-footed bard, this half-human visitor to our age from the hag-ridden magic and enchanted woods of Celtic antiquity.
—John Maynard Keynes; *Essays and Sketches in Biography*, "Mr. Lloyd-George: A Fragment," 1933

.12 There are two insults which no human will endure: the assertion that he hasn't a sense of humor, and the doubly impertinent assertion than he has never known trouble.
—Sinclair Lewis; D.J. Dooley, *The Art of Sinclair Lewis*, 1967

.13 If you can't ignore an insult, top it; if you can't top it, laugh it off, and if you can't laugh it off, it's probably deserved.
—Russell Lynes; *Reader's Digest*, December, 1961

.14 A wise man is superior to any insults which can be put upon him, and the best reply to unseemly behavior is patience and moderation.
—Molière; *The Would-Be Gentleman*, 1670

.15 A graceful taunt is worth a thousand insults.
—Louis Nizer; *My Life in Court*, 1960

.16 If you speak insults, you shall also hear them.
—Plautus; *Psendolus*, c. 195 B.C.

.17 Be prudent, and if you hear, ... some insult or threat, ... have the appearance of not hearing it.
—George Sand; *Handsome Lawrence*, 1872

.18 It is often better not to see an insult than to avenge it.
—Seneca; *De Ira*, c. A.D. 54

**135**

.19 Insults should be well avenged or well endured.
—Spanish Proverb

.20 Insults are like bad coins; we cannot help their being offered to us, but we need not take them.
—C.H. Spurgeon; *Salt-Cellars*, 1885

.21 A husband should not insult his wife publicly, at parties. He should insult her in the privacy of the home.
—James Thurber; *Thurber Country*, 1953

.22 Insults, sneers, and so forth are signs of impotence, not to say cowardice, being substitutes for murder, appeals to others to devalue or destroy. Insults to be effective need outside aid, for in the absence of a third party they lose their sting.
—Paul Valery; *Mauvaises pensées et autres*, 1942

# **136** Interests

.1 If men would avoid that general language and general manner in which they strive to hide all that is peculiar, and would say only what was uppermost in their own minds, after their own individual manner, every man would be more interesting.
—Ralph Waldo Emerson; *Journals*, 1827

.2 Interest will not lie.
—English Proverb

.3 A teacher, like a playwright, has an obligation to be interesting or, at least, brief. A play closes when it ceases to interest audiences. Students close their minds to an over-talkative teacher.
—Haim G. Ginott; *Teacher and Child*, 1972

.4 The test of interesting people is that the subject matter doesn't matter.
—Louis Kronenberger; *Company Manners*, 1954

.5 Interest speaks all sorts of tongues, and plays all sorts of parts, even than of disinterestedness.
—François de La Rochefoucauld; *Maxims*, 1665

.6 To talk easily with people, you must firmly believe that either you or they are interesting. And even then it's not easy.
—Mignon McLaughlin; *The Neurotic's Notebook*, 1963

.7 To know when one's self is interested is the first condition of interesting other people.
—Walter Pater; *Marius the Epicurean*, 1885

## 136

.8   The end of uncertainty is the death of interest.
   —Sir Walter Scott; *The Heart of Midlothian*, 1818

.9   The statements was interesting, but tough.
   —Mark Twain; *The Adventures of Huckleberry Finn*, 1885

## 137 Irony

.1   Irony is the foundation of the character of Providence.
   —Honore de Balzac; *Eugenie Grandet*, 1833

.2   The most perfect humor and irony is generally unconscious.
   —Samuel Butler II; *Life and Habit*, 1877

.3   Men who retain irony are not to be trusted,…. They can't always resist an impulse to tickle themselves.
   —Taylor Caldwell; *Dynasty of Death*, 1938

.4   Irony is a bitter truth wrapped up in a little joke.
   —Hilda Doolittle; *The Walls Do Not Fall*, 1944

.5   Irony and pity are two good counselors: one, in smiling, makes life pleasurable; the other, who cries, makes it sacred.
   —Anatole France; *Le Jardin d'Epicure*, 1894

.6   Calmness and irony are the only weapons worthy of the strong.
   —Emile Gaboriau; *Monsieur Lecoq*, 1869

.7   Irony is an indispensable ingredient of the critical vision; it is the safest antidote to sentimental decay.
   —Ellen Glasgow; *A Certain Measure*, 1943

.8   A sharp sense of the ironic can be the equivalent of the faith that moves mountains. Far more quickly than reason or logic, irony can penetrate rage and puncture self-pity.
   —Moss Hart; *Act One*, 1959

.9   Sentimental irony is a dog that bays at the moon while pissing on graves.
   —Karl Kraus; *Half-Truths and One-and-a-Half Truths*, 1909

.10  Irony is humanity's sense of propriety.
   —Jules Renard; *Journal*, 1892

.11  Humor brings insight and tolerance. Irony brings a deeper and less friendly understanding.
   —Agnes Repplier; *In Pursuit of Laughter*, 1936

## 137

.12  An irony is a nipping jest, or a speech that has the honey of pleasantness in its mouth, and a sting of rebuke in its tale.
   —Edward Reyner; *Rules for the Government of the Tongue*, 1656

.13  Beware of the ironical mood. It is a dangerous instrument.
   —Robert Louis Stevenson; *St. Ives*, 1896–97

.14  Irony is jesting hidden behind gravity.
   —John Weiss; *Wit, Humor, and Shakespeare*, 1876

.15  A taste for irony has kept more hearts from breaking than a sense of humor—for it takes irony to appreciate the joke which is on oneself.
   —Jessamyn West; *To See the Dream*, 1957

.16  Irony is an insult conveyed in the form of a compliment.
   —E.P. Whipple; *Literature and Life: Wit*, 1850

## 138 Jargon

.1   I cannot speak well enough to be unintelligible.
   —Jane Austen; *Northanger Abbey*, 1818

.2   Ours is the age of substitutes: instead of language we have jargon; instead of principles, slogans; and instead of genuine ideas, Bright ideas.
   —Eric Bentley; *The Dramatic Event*, 1954

.3   What's a' your jargon o' your schools,
   Your Latin names for horns an' stools;
   If honest Nature made you fools.
   —Robert Burns; "Death of Dr. Hornbook," 1785

.4   To them the sounding jargon of the schools
   Seems what it is—a cap and bells for fools.
   —William Cowper; *Truth*, 1781

.5   What he whispers sounds like what it is—mere jumble and jargon.
   —Charles Dickens; *Bleak House*, 1852–53

.6   The law of nature is a jargon of words, which means nothing.
   —Henry Fielding; *Tom Jones*, 1749

.7   The patient's ears remorseless he assails;
   Murders with jargon where his medicine fails.
   —Samuel Garth; *The Dispensary*, 1699

.8   Mere jargon; but when nothing else is taught,

## 138

Men think the balderdash is food for thought.
—Johann Wolfgang von Goethe; *Faust, I: Witch's Kitchen*, 1808

.9 I'm bilingual. I speak English and I speak educationese.
—Shirley M. Hufstedler; *Newsweek*, 1980

.10 Jargon is the verbal sleight of hand that makes the old hat seem newly fashionable; it gives an air of novelty and specious profundity to ideas that, if stated directly, would seem superficial, stale, frivolous, or false. The line between serious and spurious scholarship is an easy one to blur, with jargon on your side.
—David Lehman; *Signs of the Times*, 1991

.11 It's the kind of language used extensively in the educational profession. Long words and complex sentences are intended to add importance to something unimportant.
—Jack Mabley; *Detroit Free Press*, November 2, 1981

.12 What's all the noisy jargon of the schools,
But idle nonsense of laborious fools,
Who fetter reason with perplexing rules?
—John Pomfret; *Reason*, c. 1702

.13 Psychobabble is ... a set of repetitive verbal formalities that kills off the very spontaneity, candor, and understanding it pretends to promote. It's an idiom that reduces psychological insight to a collection of standardized observations, that provides a frozen lexicon to deal with an infinite variety of problems.
—Richard Dean Rosen; *Psychobabble: Fast Talk and Quick Cure in the Era of Feeling*, 1977
[Rosen, a U.S. journalist and critic coined the term "psychobabble" to describe speech patterns in the Bay Area of San Francisco.]

.14 She spoke academese, a language that springs like Athene from an intellectual brow, and she spoke it with a nonregional, "good" accent.
—May Sarton; *The Small Room*, 1961

.15 I might not know how to use thirty-four words where three would do, but that does not mean I don't know what I'm talking about.
—Ruth Shays; in John Langston Gwaltney *Drylongso*, 1980

## 139 Jests and Jesters

.1 As for Jest, there be certain things which ought to be privileged from it: namely Religion, Matters of State, Great Persons.
—Francis Bacon; *Essays*, "Of Discourse," 1597

.2 He jests at scars, that never felt a wound.
—William Shakespeare; *Romeo and Juliet*, 1594–95

.3 Jests that give pain are no jests.
—Miguel de Cervantes; *Don Quixote*, 1615

.4 And tells the jest without the smile.
—Samuel Taylor Coleridge; *Youth and Age*, 1823

.5 Nice philosophy
May tolerate unlikely arguments,
But heaven admits no jest.
—John Ford; *'Tis Pity She's a Whore*, 1633

.6 He makes a foe, who makes a jest.
—Ben Franklin; *Poor Richard's Almanack*, 1741

.7 The worst jests are those that are true.
—French proverb

.8 When you see a Jester, a Fool is not far off.
—Thomas Fuller II; *Gnomologia*, 1732

.9 Life is a jest, and all things show it.
I thought so once, and now I know it.
—John Gay; "My Own Epitaph," 1720

.10 The jests of the rich are ever successful.
—Oliver Goldsmith; *The Vicar of Wakefield*, 1766

.11 There's many a true word said in jest.
—T.C. Haliburton; *Wise Saws*, 1843

.12 When thou dost tell another's jest therein
Omit the oaths, which true wit cannot need;
Pick out the tales of mirth, but not the sin.
—George Herbert; "The Church Porch," 1633

.13 A jest breaks no bones.
—Samuel Johnson; Boswell's *Life of Johnson*, 1781

.14 There is no resource for one who cannot laugh at a jest.
—Henry Mackenzie; *Julia De Roubigne*, 1777

.15 The saddest ones are those that wear
The jester's motley garb.
—Don Marquis; "The Tavern of Despair," 1924

.16 If a thing be spoken in jest, it is not fair to take it seriously.
—Plautus; *Amphitruo*, c. 200 B.C.

## 139

.17 The wise make jests and fools repeat them.
—John Ray; *English Proverbs*, 1670

.18 He that makes life not a jest is a sad fellow.
—Samuel Richardson; *Clarissa Harlowe*, 1747–48

.19 A jest loses its point when the jester laughs himself.
—Johann von Schiller; *Fiesco*, 1783

.20 Alas, poor Yorick! I knew him, Horatio: a fellow of infinite jest, of most excellent fancy…. Here hung those lips that I have kissed I know not how oft. Where be your gibes now? your gambols? your songs? your flashes of merriment, that were wont to set the table on a roar? Not one now, to mock your own grinning? quite chap-fallen.
—William Shakespeare; *Hamlet*, 1600–1

.21 The skipping King, he ambled up and down With shallow jesters and rash brain wits.
—William Shakespeare; *I, Henry IV*, 1596–97

.22 Jesters do often prove prophets.
—William Shakespeare; *King Lear*, 1605

.23 I know thee not, old man: fall to thy prayers; How ill white hairs become a fool and jester!
—William Shakespeare; *II, Henry IV*, 1597–98
[The newly crowned Harry rejects his old friend Falstaff.]

.24 A jest's prosperity lies in the ear Of him that hears it, never in the tongue Of him that makes it.
—William Shakespeare; *Love's Labour's Lost*, 1594–95

.25 There's no jest like a true jest.
—Jonathan Swift; *Polite Conversation*, 1738

.26 It is difficult to fashion a jest with a sad mind.
—Tibullus; *Elegies*, 19 B.C.

.27 I myself have heard a very good jest, and have scorned to seem to have so silly a wit as to understand it.
—John Webster; *The Duchess of Malfi*, 1623

## 140 Jokes

.1 A good funeral needs a joke. If mine is not more amusing than my friends', I would rather not go to it.
—Henry Adams; *Esther*, 1884

.2 There are only three basic jokes, but since the mother-in-law joke is not a joke but a very serious question, there are only two.
—George Ade; *Forty Modern Fables*, 1901

.3 The wisest and the best of men, the wisest and best of their actions, may be rendered ridiculous by a person whose first object in life is a joke.
—Jane Austen; *Pride and Prejudice*, 1813

.4 In Milwaukee last month a man died laughing over one of his own jokes. That's what makes it so tough for us outsiders. We have to fight home competition.
—Robert Benchley; R.E. Drennan's *Wit's End*, 1973

.5 I advise comic lecturers, when they lay a warm joke, not to act as a hen doth when she has uttered an egg, but look sorry and let someone else do the cackling.
—Josh Billings; *Proverbial Philosophy*, 1858

.6 The world dwindles daily for the humorist…. Jokes are fast running out, for a joke must transform real life in some perverse way, and real life has begun to perform the same operation perfectly professionally upon itself.
—Craig Brown; *Craig Brown's Greatest Hits*, 1993

.7 There's nothing upon earth I hate like a joke; unless it's against another person.
—Fanny Burney; *Camilla*, 1796

.8 A man must serve his time to every trade Save censure—critics are all ready made. Take hackney'd jokes from Miller, got by rote, With just enough of learning to misquote.
—Lord Byron; *English Bards and Scotch Reviewers*, 1809

.9 Even a joke should have some meaning.
—Lewis Carroll; *Alice's Adventures in Wonderland*, 1865

.10 Vivacity and wit make a man shine in company; but trite jokes and loud laughter reduce him to a buffoon.
—Lord Chesterfield; Letter to his son, February 5, 1750

.11 A good joke is the one ultimate and sacred thing which cannot be criticized. Our relations with a good jest are direct and even divine relations.
—G.K. Chesterton; *All Things Considered*, "Cockneys and Their Jokes," 1908

**140**

.12 When once you have got hold of a vulgar joke, you may be certain that you have got hold of a subtle and spiritual idea.
—G.K. Chesterton; *All Things Considered*, "Cockneys and Their Jokes," 1908

.13 If Adam came on earth again the only thing he would recognize would be the old jokes.
—Thomas Robert Dewar; in George Robey, *Looking Back on Life*, 1933

.14 A chestnut. I have heard you tell the joke twenty-seven times, and I am sure it was a chestnut.
—William Dimond; *The Broken Sword*, 1816

.15 A difference of taste in jokes is a great strain on the affections.
—George Eliot; *Daniel Deronda*, 1874–76

.16 Forgive, O Lord, my little jokes on Thee
And I'll forgive Thy great big one on me.
—Robert Frost; *In the Clearing*, "The Preacher," 1959

.17 A joke never gains over an enemy, but often loses a friend.
—Thomas Fuller II; *Gnomologia*, 1732

.18 It would be a bitter cosmic joke if we destroy ourselves due to atrophy of the imagination.
—Martha Ellis Gellhorn; *The Face of War*, Introduction, 1959

.19 Jokes … are an act of assassination without a corpse, a moment of total annihilation that paradoxically makes anything possible.
—Penelope Gilliatt; *To Wit*, 1990

.20 Some one is generally sure to be the sufferer by a joke.
—William Hazlitt; *Lectures on the English Comic Writers*, 1819

.21 They say the seeds of what we will do are in all of us, but it always seemed to me that in those who make jokes in life the seeds are covered with better soil and with a higher grade of manure.
—Ernest Hemingway; *A Moveable Feast*, 1964

.22 Don't joke about your poverty. That is quite as vulgar as to boast about it.
—Henry James; *The Europeans*, 1878

.23 The increasing seriousness of things—the great opportunity of jokes.
—Henry James; *The Portrait of a Lady*, 1881

.24 The coarse joke proclaims that we have here an animal which finds its own animality either objectionable or funny.
—C.S. Lewis; *Miracles*, c. 1936

**140**

.25 Jokes are grievances.
—Marshall McLuhan; remark made at America Booksellers Association luncheon, Washington D.C., June, 1969

.26 Never joke at funerals, or during business transactions.
—Herman Melville; *Israel Potter*, 1855

.27 Joking decides great things,
Stronglier, and better off than earnest can.
—John Milton; *An Apology for Smectymnuus*, 1642

.28 The aim of a joke is not to degrade the human being but to remind him that he is already degraded.
—George Orwell; *Collected Essays*, "Funny but Not Vulgar," 1968

.29 Whatever is funny is subversive, every joke is ultimately a custard pie.… A dirty joke is not … a serious attack upon morality, but it is a sort of mental rebellion, a momentary wish that things were otherwise.
—George Orwell; *Horizon*, "The Art of Donald McGill," 1941

.30 If we live inside a bad joke, it is up to us to learn, at best and worst, to tell it well.
—Jonathan Raban; *Coasting*, 1986

.31 You could read Kant by yourself, if you wanted; but you must share a joke with some one else.
—Robert Louis Stevenson; *Virginibus Puerisque*, 1881

.32 I tried him with mild jokes, then with severe ones.
—Mark Twain; "A Deception," A.B. Paine, ed. *The Writings of Mark Twain*, 1922–25

.33 That joke was lost on the foreigner—guides cannot master the subtleties of the American joke.
—Mark Twain; *Innocents Abroad*, 1869

# **141** Judgment

.1 No man can justly censure or condemn another, because indeed no man truly knows another.
—Thomas Browne; *Religio Medici*, 1643

.2 Most people suspend their judgement till somebody else has expressed his own and then they repeat it.
—Ernest Dimner; *The Art of Thinking*, 1928

### 141

.3  Hear everything and judge for yourself.
    —George Eliot; *Middlemarch*, 1872

.4  Sound judgement, with discernment, is the best of seers.
    —Euripides; *Helen*, c. 412 B.C.

.5  She had observed that it was from those who had never sailed stormy waters came the quickest and harshest judgements on bad seamanship in heavy seas.
    —Susan Glaspell; *The Visioning*, 1911

.6  I can promise to be sincere but not impartial.
    —Johann Wolfgang von Goethe; *Spruche in Prosa*, 1819

.7  To judge a man means nothing more than to ask: What content does he give to the form of humanity? What concept should we have of humanity if he were its only representative?
    —Wilhelm von Humboldt; *Uber Den Geist Der Menschheit*, 1797

.8  Let those who have not wit enough to speak have judgement enough to hold their tongue.
    —Charles Jenner; *The Placid Man*, 1770

.9  Everyone complains of his memory, and no one complains of his judgement.
    —François de La Rochefoucauld; *Maxims*, 1665

.10 Give your decision, never your reasons; your decisions may be right, your reasons are sure to be wrong.
    —Lord Mansfield; *Advice to Lawyers*, c. 1770

.11 We judge ourselves by our motives and others by their actions.
    —Dwight Morrow; Speech, 1930

.12 Don't judge any man until you have walked two moons in his moccasins.
    —Native American Proverb

.13 Out of thine own mouth will I judge thee.
    —New Testament: Luke

.14 We praise or blame as one or the other affords more opportunity for exhibiting our power of judgement.
    —Friedrich Nietzsche; *Human, All Too Human*, 1878

.15 For their hasty judgement has led many astray, and wrong opinion has caused their thoughts to slip.
    —Old Testament; Apocrypha: Ecclesiasticus

.16 Whoever wants his judgment to be believed, should express it coolly and dispassionately; for all vehemence springs from the will. And

### 141

so the judgments might be attributed to the will and not to knowledge, which by its nature is cold.
    —Arthur Schopenhauer; *The World as Will and Representation*, 1819

.17 Speak of me as I am; nothing extenuate, Nor set down aught in malice.
    —William Shakespeare; *Othello*, 1603–4

.18 Kinder the enemy who must malign us, Than the smug friend who will define us.
    —Anna Wickham; *The Man with a Hammer*, "Traducers," 1916

## 142 Kindness

.1  There is no sickness worse for me than words that to be kind must lie.
    —Aeschylus; *Prometheus Bound*, c. 478 B.C.

.2  Life is short. Let us make haste to be kind.
    —Henri Amiel; *Journal Intime*, December 16, 1868

.3  Kindness is a language the dumb can speak and the deaf can hear and understand.
    —Christian Nestell Bovee; *Summaries of Thought*, 1862

.4  'Twas a thief said the last kind word to Christ: Christ took the kindness and forgave the theft.
    —Robert Browning; *The Ring and the Book*, 1868–69

.5  Little deeds of kindness,
    Little words of love,
    Help to make earth happy
    Like the heaven above.
    —Julia Fletcher Carney; "Little Things," 1845

.6  It is difficult to say how much men's minds are conciliated by a kind manner and gentle speech.
    —Cicero; *De Officiis*, c. 45 B.C.

.7  But what the better are their pious saws To ailing souls, than dry hee-haws, Without the milk of human kindness.
    —Thomas Hood; "Ode to Rae Wilson," 1825

.8  In her tongue is the law of kindness.
    —Old Testament: Proverbs

.9  A word of kindness is better than a fat pie.
    —Russian Proverb

.10 Kind words can be short and easy to speak, but their echoes are truly endless.
    —Mother Teresa; in Georges Gorree and Jean Barbier, *The Love of Christ*

# 143 Kings and Queens

.1 Our converse with kings should be either as rare, or as pleasing, as possible.
  —Aesop; c. 550 B.C. in Plutarch's *Lives*: Solon; c. 1st century A.D.
  [Aesop said this to Solon who had just been banished by Croesus. Solon replied "No, indeed! Either as rare or as beneficial as possible.]

.2 Royalty does good and is badly spoken of.
  —Antisthenes; 5th century B.C., Quoted in Diogenes Laertius *Lives and Opinions of Eminent Philosophers*, c. 3rd century A.D.

.3 Everyone likes flattery; and when you come to
  Royalty you should lay it on with a trowel.
  —Benjamin Disraeli; Quoted in G.W.E. Russell, *Collections and Recollections*, 1880s

.4 I am your anointed Queen. I will never be by violence constrained to do anything. I thank God I am endued with such qualities that if I were turned out of the Realm in my petticoat I were able to live in any place in Christendom.
  —Elizabeth I of England; Speech, 1566

.5 You should be a king of your word.
  —James Ferguson; *Scottish Proverbs*, c. 1595

.6 It is the misfortune of kings that they will not hear the truth.
  —Johann Jacoby; to King Frederick Wilhelm IV of Prussia, November 2, 1848

.7 The noble history of the Sangreal, and of the most renowned Christian king … King Arthur.
  —Thomas Malory; *Le Morte d'Arthur*, 1470

.8 Uneasy lies the head that wears a crown.
  —William Shakespeare; *II Henry IV*, 1578–79

.9 Kings are commonly said to have long hands; I wish they had as long ears.
  —Jonathan Swift; *Thoughts on Various Subjects*, 1727

.10 Here lies our Sovereign Lord, the King
  Whose word no men relies on:
  He never said a foolish thing
  Nor ever did a wise one.
  —John Wilmot, Second Earl of Rochester, "The King's Epitaph," 1677
  [The verse was written on the door of Charles II's bedchamber. The King allegedly agreed with its sentiments, saying "This is very true: for my words are

# 143

my own, and my actions are my ministers."]

# 144 Kisses

.1 A kiss is a lovely trick designed by nature to stop speech when words become superfluous.
  —Ingrid Bergman; Attributed

.2 She that will kiss, they say, will do worse.
  —Robert Davenport; *The City Night-Cap*, 1661

.3 One fond kiss before we part,
  Drop a tear and bid adieu.
  —Robert Dodsley; "The Parting Kiss" in R. Strauss' *Dodsley: Poet, Publisher and Playwright*, 1910

.4 "Kiss me. Again. Once more." Commands to be obeyed when issued by a woman.
  —Lawrence Durrell; *Monsieur*, 1974

.5 Kissing is a prologue to a play. There is no woman who grants that, but will grant more.
  —Henry Fielding; *Joseph Andrews*, 1742

.6 Oh what lies lurk in kisses!
  —Heinrich Heine; *The Romantic School*, 1833

.7 The sound of a kiss is not so loud as that of a cannon, but its echo lasts a great deal longer.
  —Oliver Wendell Holmes; *The Professor at the Breakfast Table*, 1860

.8 Jenny kissed me when we met,
  Jumping from the chair she sat in;
  Time, you thief, who love to get
  Sweets in your list, put that in!
  Say I'm weary, say I'm sad,
  Say that health and wealth have missed me:
  Say I'm growing old, but add
  Jenny kissed me.
  —Leigh Hunt; "Jenny Kissed Me," 1838
  [Jenny was Jane Walsh Carlyle.]

.9 And out lips found ways of speaking
  What words cannot say,
  Till a hundred nests gave music,
  And the East was gray.
  —Frederic Lawrence Knowles; *A Memory*, c. late 19th century

.10 Sweet Helen, make me immortal with a kiss.
  —Christopher Marlowe; *Doctor Faustus*, 1694

.11 When women kiss it always reminds one of prize-fighters shaking hands.
  —H.L. Mencken; *Chrestomathy*, 1949

## 144

.12 Kisses are first, and cusses come later.
—Mexican Proverb

.13 A kiss can be a comma, a question mark, or an exclamation point. That's basic spelling that every woman ought to know.
—Mistinguett; *Theatre Arts*, December, 1955

.14 Some men kiss and do not tell, some kiss and tell; but George Moore told and did not kiss.
—Susan Mitchell; in Oliver St. John Gogarty *As I Was Going Down Sackville Street*, 1937

.15 A kiss, when all is said, what is it?
An oath that's given closer than before;
A promise more precise; the sealing of
Confessions that till then were barely breathed;
A rosy dot placed on the i in loving.
'Tis a secret told to the mouth instead of the ear.
—Edmond Rostand; *Cyrano De Bergerac*, 1897

.16 Speak cousin, or if you cannot, stop his mouth with a kiss.
—William Shakespeare; *Much Ado About Nothing*, 1598

.17 Kiss me Kate, we will be married o' Sunday.
—William Shakespeare; *The Taming of the Shrew*, 1592

.18 Come, swear to that, kiss the book.
—William Shakespeare; *The Tempest*, 1611

.19 As a gentleman, I do not kiss and tell.
—George Bernard Shaw; *Misalliance*, 1910

.20 Lord! I wonder what fool it was that first invented kissing.
—Jonathan Swift; *Polite Conversation*, 1738

## 145 Knowledge

.1 All men by nature desire knowledge.
—Aristotle; *Metaphysics*, c. 4th century B.C.

.2 For knowledge too, is itself power.
—Francis Bacon; *Religious Meditations*, "Of Heresies," 1597

.3 I am not young enough to know everything.
—J.M. Barrie; *The Admirable Crichton*, 1902

.4 Men are called fools in one age for not knowing what they were called fools for averring in the age before.
—Henry Ward Beecher; *Life Thoughts*, 1858

.5 All human knowledge takes the form of interpretation.
—Walter Benjamin; *One Way Street and Other Writings*, "Under the Sign of Saturn," 1978

.6 The real community of man ... is the community of those who seek the truth, of the potential knowers.
—Allan Bloom; *The Closing of the American Mind*, 1987

.7 What I wanted to do was take what I knew and break it down for those who didn't have the literary teeth to chew it, so they could at least gum it.
—Brother Blue; in Jimmy Neil Smith, *Homespun: Tales from America's Favorite Storytellers*, 1988

.8 We are told in the language of Jewish myth that in his mother's womb man knows the universe and forgets it at birth.
—Martin Buber; *I and Thou*, 1970

.9 The great impediments to knowledge are, first, the want of a common language; and next, the short duration of existence.
—Edward George Bulwer-Lytton; *Zanoni*, 1842

.10 What cruel maxims are we taught by a knowledge of the world!
—Fanny Burney; *Evelina*, 1778

.11 Well didst thou speak, Athena's wisest son!
"All that we know is, nothing can be known."
—Lord Byron; *Childe Harold's Pilgrimage*, 1812

.12 To know how to say what others only know to think is what makes men poets or sages; and to dare to say what others only dare to think makes men martyrs or reformers or both.
—Elizabeth Charles; *Chronicle of the Schonberg-Cotta Family*, 1863

.13 A man does not know what he is saying until he knows what he is not saying.
—G.K. Chesterton; *All Things Considered*, 1908

.14 What man knows is not to be compared with what he does not know.
—Chuang-tze; *Philosophy*, c. 400 B.C.

.15 The essence of knowledge is, having it, to apply it; not having it, to confess your ignorance.
—Confucius; *Analects*, c. 500 B.C.

.16 Without knowing the force of words, it is impossible to know men.
—Confucius; *Analects*, c. 500 B.C.

.17 Knowledge is a polite word for dead but not buried imagination.
—E.E. Cummings; "Jottings" in *Wake, no. 10*, 1951

.18 We do not know one millionth of one per cent about anything.
—Thomas A. Edison; *Golden Book*, April, 1931

.19 "I may not know much"—another form of locution often favored by her. The tone in which it was spoken utterly belied the words; the tone told you that not only did she know much, but all.
—Edna Ferber; *Show Boat*, 1926

.20 Everything is not known but everything is said.
—Anatole France; *The Literary Life*, 1888

.21 Tell me what you *Know* is True;
I can *Guess* as well as you.
—Arthur Guiterman; *A Poet's Proverbs*, 1924

.22 All knowledge is ambiguous.
—J.S. Habgood; *The Observer*, April 14, 1991

.23 Ole Man Know-all died last year.
—Joel Chandler Harris; *Plantation Poets*, 1880

.24 All knowledge is remembrance.
—Thomas Hobbes; *Human Nature*, 1651

.25 It is the province of knowledge to speak, and it is the privilege of wisdom to listen.
—Oliver Wendell Holmes; *The Poet at the Breakfast Table*, 1872

.26 Tell me, and then again show me, so I can know.
—Zora Neale Hurston; *Moses, Man of the Mountain*, 1939

.27 You cannot teach what you don't know. You cannot give energy if you're not on fire on the inside.
—Jesse Jackson; in "Reverend Jesse Jackson, *Ebony Man*, December, 1986

.28 Knowledge is nothing but as it is communicated.
—Samuel Johnson; *Rasselas*, 1759

.29 But I am bound to say something in defense of those who originally invented myths; I think they wrote them for childish souls; and I liken them to nurses who hang leathern toys to the hands of children when they are irritated and teething…. So those mythologists wrote for the feeble soul whose wings are just

beginning to sprout, and who, though still incapable of being taught, is yearning for further knowledge….
—Julian; *Greek Anthology*, c. 60 B.C.

.30 Let the fools talk, knowledge has its value.
—Jean de La Fontaine; *Fables*, 1678

.31 Knowledge is what we get when an observer, preferably a scientifically trained observer, provides us with a copy of reality that we can all recognize.
—Christopher Lasch; "The Lost Art of Political Argument," in *Gannett Center Journal*, Spring, 1990

.32 Nothing can be loved or hated unless it is first known.
—Leonardo Da Vinci; *Notebooks of Leonardo Da Vinci*, Irama A. Ritcher, ed. 1977

.33 Teach thy tongue to say "I do not know."
—Maimonides; Letter, c. 1190

.34 A good listener is not only popular everywhere, but after a while he knows something.
—Wilson Mizner; in A. Johnson, *The Legendary Mizners*, 1953

.35 Those who know least are the greatest scoffers.
—Samuel Richardson; *Clarissa Harlowe*, 1747–48

.36 I hate books; they only teach us to talk about things we know nothing about.
—Jean-Jacques Rousseau; *Emile*, 1762

.37 Nobody tells all he knows.
—Senegaleze Proverb

.38 He said he knew what is what.
—John Skelton; *Why Come Ye Not to Count*, c. 1520

.39 To know that we know what we know, and that we do not know what we do not know, that is true knowledge.
—Henry David Thoreau; *Walden*, 1854

.40 The things we know best are the things we haven't been taught.
—Luc, Marquis de Vauvenargues, *Reflexions et Maximes*, 1746

.41 What a fellow doesn't know doesn't hurt him.
—Eugene Walter; *The Easiest Way*, 1908

.42 There are only two kinds of people who are really fascinating—people who know absolutely everything, and people who know absolutely nothing.
—Oscar Wilde; *The Picture of Dorian Gray*, 1891

# 146 Ladies

.1  Such a perfect lady! She never raises her voice, she never fidgets, she never contradicts, she never gets untidy.
—Elizabeth Bibesco; *The Fir and the Palm*, 1924

.2  A lady is one who never shows her underwear unintentionally.
—Lillian Day; *Kiss and Tell*, 1931

.3  A lady is nothing very specific. One man's lady is another man's woman; sometimes, one man's lady is another man's wife. Definitions overlap but they almost never coincide.
—Russell Lynes; "Is There a Lady in the House?," *Look*, July 22, 1958

.4  A lady, that is an enlightened, cultivated, liberal lady—the only kind to be in a time of increasing classlessness—could espouse any cause: wayward girls, social diseases, unmarried mothers, and/or birth control, with impunity. But never by so much as the shadow of a look should she acknowledge her own experience with the Facts of Life.
—Virgilia Peterson; *A Matter of Life and Death*, 1961

.5  But the typical lady everywhere tends to the feudal habit of mind. In contemporary society she is an archaism, and can hardly understand herself unless she knows her own history.
—Emily James Putnam; *The Lady*, "Introduction," 1910

.7  Ladies are just those of us who have been silenced.
—Jennifer Stone; *Mama Bears News and Notes*, 1994

.8  Give us that grand word "woman" once again,
And let's have done with "lady"; one's a term
Full of fine force, strong, beautiful, and firm,
Fit for the noblest use of tongue or pen;
And one's a word for lackeys.
—Ella Wheeler Wilcox; *Poems of Pleasure*, "Woman," 1888

.9  Women all want to be ladies, which is simply to have nothing to do, but listlessly to go they scarcely care where, for they cannot tell what.
—Mary Wollstonecraft; *A Vindication of the Rights of Women*, 1792

# 147 Language

.1  Language. I loved it. And for a long time I would think of myself, of my whole body, as an ear.
—Maya Angelou; *New York Times*, 1993

# 147

.2  All true language
is incomprehensible,
Like the chatter
of a beggar's teeth.
—Antonin Artaud; "Ci-Git," 1947

.3  Language is a mixture of statement and evocation.
—Elizabeth Bowen; *Afterthoughts*, "Advice," 1962

.4  A silly remark can be made in Latin as well as Spanish.
—Miguel de Cervantes; *Don Quixote*, 1605

.5  I speak Spanish to God, Italian to women, French to men and German to my horse.
—Holy Roman Emperor Charles V; Attributed

.6  Speak the language of the company that you are in; speak it purely, and unguarded with any other.
—Lord Chesterfield; Letter to His son, February 22, 1748

.7  Wherever you go, speak the language of that place.
—Chinese Proverb

.8  Language is a process of free creation; its laws and principles are fixed, but the manner in which the principles of generation are used is free and infinitely varied. Even the interpretation and use of words involves a process of free creation.
—Noam Chomsky; Lecture, "Language and Freedom," January, 1970

.9  The raison-d'être of language is an idea to be expressed. When the idea is expressed, the language may be ignored.
—Chuang-tzu; *Philosophy*, c. 4th–3rd century B.C.

.10  In language clearness is everything.
—Confucius; *Analects*, c. 500 B.C.

.11  Curiously enough, it seems to be only in describing a mode of language which does not mean what it says that one can actually say what one means.
—Paul de Man; "The Rhetoric of Temporality," in *Interpretation*, Charles Singleton, ed. 1969

.12  The voice of the inanimate! Who shall translate for us the language of the stones?
—Theodore Dreiser; *Sister Carrie*, 1900

.13  I have been a believer in the magic of language since, at a very early age, I discovered that

some words got me into trouble and others got me out.
—Katherine Dunn; in Susan Cahill, ed. *Growing Up Female*, 1993

.14 Language is a city to the building of which every human being brought a stone.
—Ralph Waldo Emerson; *Letters and Social Aims: Quotations and Originality*, 1876

.15 ...for the most human thing we have is language, and we've got it, so that we can speak.
—Theodor Fontane; *Irretrievable*, 1891

.16 Write with the learned, pronounce with the vulgar.
—Benjamin Franklin; *Poor Richard's Almanack*, 1723

.17 The chief merit of language is clearness, and we know that nothing detracts so much from this as do unfamiliar terms.
—Galen; *On the Natural Faculties*, c. 2nd century A.D.

.18 Because everyone uses language to talk, everyone thinks he can talk about a language.
—Johann Wolfgang von Goethe; *Maxims and Reflections*, 1823

.19 Whoever is not acquainted with foreign languages knows nothing of his own.
—Johann Wolfgang von Goethe; *Proverbs in Prose*, 1819

.20 Like a diaphanous nightgown, language both hides and reveals.
—Karen Elizabeth Gordon; *Intimate Apparel*, 1989

.21 Language—human language,—after all is but little better than the croak and cackle of fowls, and other utterances of brute nature—sometimes not so adequate.
—Nathaniel Hawthorne; *American Note-Books*, July 14, 1850

.22 That is not a good language that all understand not.
—George Herbert; *Jacula Prudentum* 1640

.23 After all, when you come right down to it, how many people speak the same language even when they speak the same language.
—Russell Hoban; *The Lion of Jachin-Boaz and Jachin-Boaz*, 1973

.24 Every language is a temple, in which the soul of those who speak is enshrined.
—Oliver Wendell Holmes; *The Professor at the Breakfast Table*, 1859

.25 Language is the picture and counterpart of thought.
—Mark Hopkins; Address, December 1, 1841

.26 Language is by its very nature a communal thing; that is, it expresses never the exact thing but a compromise—that which is common to you, me, and everybody.
—T.E. Hulme; *Speculations*, "Romanticism and Classicism," 1923

.27 Well-chosen phrases are a great help in the smuggling of offensive ideas.
—Vladimir Jabotinsky; *The War and the Jew*, 1942

.28 Language is the most imperfect and expensive means yet discovered for communicating thought.
—William James; *Thought and Character*, 1907

.29 Accuracy of language is one of the bulwarks of truth.
—Anna Jameson; *A Commonplace Book*, 1855

.30 Language is memory and metaphor.
—Storm Jameson; *Parthian Words*, 1970

.31 Language is the dress of thought.
—Samuel Johnson; *Lives of the Poets: Cowley*, 1779

.32 Language, as symbol, determines much of the nature and quality of our experience.
—Sonia Johnson; *The Ship That Sailed Into the Living Room*, 1991

.33 Language is a living thing. It must survive in men's minds and on their tongues if it survives at all.
—Charlton Laird; *The Miracle of Language*, 1953

.34 The only living language is the language in which we think and have our being.
—Antonio Machado; *Juan De Mairena*, 1943

.35 Our native language is like a second skin, so much a part of us we resist the idea that it is constantly changing, constantly being renewed.
—Casey Miller and Kate Swift; *The Handbook of Nonsexist Writing*, 1980

.36 We die. That may be the meaning of our life. But we do language. That may be the measure of our lives.
—Toni Morrison; Nobel Prize acceptance speech, 1993

**147**

.37 He mobilized the English language and sent it into battle to steady his fellow countrymen and hearten those Europeans upon which the long dark night of tyranny had descended.
—Edward R. Murrow; Broadcast, 1954 [Speaking of Winston Churchill during WWII.]

.38 Language, as we know, is full of illogicalities.
—Gunnar Myrdal; *Beyond the Welfare State*, 1960

.39 What a great language I have, it's a fine language we inherited from the fierce Conquistadors.... They carried everything off and left us everything.... They left us the words.
—Pablo Neruda; *Memoirs*, 1974

.40 Therefore is the name of it called Babel; because the Lord did there confound the language of all the earth.
—Old Testament: Genesis

.41 Newspeak was the official language of Oceania.
—George Orwell; *Nineteen Eighty-Four*, 1949

.42 Mere elegance of language can produce at best but an empty renown.
—Petrarch; *Letter to Posterity*, 1367–72

.43 The sum of human wisdom is not contained in any one language, and no single language is capable of expressing all forms and degrees of human comprehension.
—Ezra Pound; *The ABC of Reading*, 1934

.44 If you want to tell the untold stories, if you want to give voice to the voiceless, you've got to find a language. Which goes for film as well as prose, for documentary as well as autobiography. Use the wrong language and you're dumb and blind.
—Salman Rushdie; "Songs Don't Know the Score," book review in *The Guardian*, January 12, 1987

.45 There was language in their very gesture.
—William Shakespeare; *The Winter's Tale*, 1610

.46 Language is not neutral, It is not merely a vehicle which carries ideas. It is itself a shaper of ideas.
—Dale Spender; *Man Made Language*, 1980

.47 Language is the main instrument of man's refusal to accept the world as it is.
—George Steiner; "After Babel," 1975

**147**

.48 Perhaps of all the creations of man language is the most astonishing.
—Lytton Strachey; *Words and Poetry*, 1922

.49 Where shall we look for standard English, but to the words of a standard man?
—Henry David Thoreau; *A Week on the Concord and Merrimack Rivers*, "Sunday," 1849

.50 What is the real function, the essential function, the supreme function, of language? Isn't it merely to convey ideas and emotions?
—Mark Twain, Speech, New York City, September 19, 1906

.51 I personally think we developed language because of our deep inner need to complain.
—Jane Wagner; *The Search for Signs of Intelligent Life in the Universe*, 1985

.52 Language, as well as the faculty of speech, was the immediate gift of God.
—Noah Webster; *American Dictionary of the English Language*, Preface, 1828

.53 We were taught as the chief subjects of instruction Latin and Greek. We were taught very badly because the men who taught us did not habitually use either of these languages.
—H.G. Wells; *The New Machiavelli*, 1911

.54 Language ... is not an abstract construction of the learned, of the dictionary-makers, but is something arising out of the work, needs, tears, joys, affections, tastes, of long generations of humanity, and has its bases broad and low, close to the ground.
—Walt Whitman; *November Boughs*, "Slang in America," 1888

.55 The limits of my language mean the limits of my world.
—Ludwig Wittgenstein; *Tractatus Logico-Philosophicus*, 1922

# **148** Laughter

.1 Man is distinguished from all other creatures by the facility of laughter.
—Joseph Addison; *The Spectator*, September 26, 1712

.2 In the language of screen comedians four of the main grades of laugh are the titter, the yowl, the belly laugh and the boffo. The titter is just a titter. The yowl is a runaway titter. Anyone who has ever had the pleasure knows

**148**

all about a belly laugh. The boffo is the laugh that kills.
—James Agee; "Comedy's Greatest Era," *Life Magazine*, September 5, 1949

.3 The greatest enemy of authority; therefore is contempt, and the surest way to undermine it is laughter.
—Hannah Arendt; *On Violence*, 1969

.4 Among those whom I like or admire, I can find no common denominator, but among those I love I can: all of them make me laugh.
—W.H. Auden; *The Dyer's Hand*, 1962

.5 For what do we live, but to make sport for our neighbors, and laugh at them in our turn?
—Jane Austen; *Pride and Prejudice*, 1813

.6 I hasten to laugh at everything, for fear of being obliged to weep.
—Pierre-Augustin de Beaumarchais; *Le Barbier de Seville*, 1775

.7 Laughing is the sensation of feeling good all over, and showing it principally in one spot.
—Josh Billings (H.W. Shaw); *Sayings: Laffing*, 1858

.8 There was a kind of leer about his lips; he seemed laughing in his sleeve.
—Charlotte Bronte; *Shirley*, 1849

.9 Laughter's never an end, it's a by-product.
—Struthers Burt; *Festival*, 1931

.10 No man who has once heartily and wholly laughed can be altogether irreclaimably bad.
—Thomas Carlyle; *Sartor Resartus*, 1833–34

.11 For me, a hearty "belly laugh" is one of the most beautiful sounds in the world.
—Bennett Cerf; *An Encyclopedia of Modern American Humor*, Forward, 1954

.12 The most completely lost of all days is that on which one has not laughed.
—Sebastien De Chamfort; *Maximes et Pensées*, 1794

.13 What was significant about the laughter ... was not just the fact it provides internal exercise for a person ... —a form of jogging for the innards—but that it creates a mood in which the other positive emotions can be put to work, too.
—Norman Cousins; *Anatomy of an Illness*, 1979

.14 One can know a man from his laugh, and if you like a man's laugh before you know anything of him, you may confidently say that he is a good man.
—Fyodor Dostoyevsky; *The House of the Dead*, 1862

**148**

.15 I am especially glad of the divine gift of laughter; it has made the world human and lovable, despite all its pain and wrong.
—W.E.B. Du Bois; *Dusk of Dawn: An Essay Toward an Autobiography of Race Concept*, 1940

.16 Men show their characters in nothing more clearly than in what they think laughable.
—Johann Wolfgang von Goethe; *Spruche in Prosa*, c. 1825

.17 Though the clown is often deadpan, he is a connoisseur of laughter.
—Mel Gussow; on Avner Eisenberg in his one-man show *Avner the Eccentric*, *New York Times*, September 21, 1984

.18 If you don't learn to laugh at trouble, you won't have anything to laugh at when you're old.
—Ed Howe; *Country Town Sayings*, 1911

.19 He deserves Paradise who makes his companions laugh.
—The Koran, c. 610–632

.20 Laughter is an orgasm triggered by the intercourse of reason with unreason.
—Jack Kroll; *Newsweek*, 1976

.21 The sound of laughter is like the vaulted dome of a temple of happiness.
—Milan Kundera; *The Book of Laughter and Forgetting*, 1978

.22 It's possible to forgive someone a great deal if he makes you laugh.
—Caroline Llewellyn; *Life Blood*, 1993

.23 We must laugh or we die; to laugh is to live. Not to laugh is to have the tetanus. Will you weep? then laugh while you weep. For mirth and sorrow are kin; are published by identical nerves.
—Herman Melville; *Mardi*, 1849

.24 Hostility is expressed in a number of ways. One is laughter.
—Kate Millett; *Sexual Politics*, 1969

.25 I can usually judge a fellow by what he laughs at.
—Wilson Mizner; A. Johnston, *The Legendary Mizners*, 1953

.26 It is a strange job making decent people laugh.
—Molière; *L'Ecole des Femmes*, 1662

.27 Laughter is pleasant, but the exertion is too much for me.
—Thomas Love Peacock; *Nightmare Abbey*, 1818

.28 If anyone represents men of worth as overpowered by laughter we must accept not it, much less if gods.
—Plato; *Republic*, c. 375 B.C.

**148**

.29 He who laughs, lasts.
—Mary P. Poole; *A Glass Eye at the Keyhole*, 1938

.30 One inch of joy surmounts of grief a span,
Because to laugh is proper to man.
—François Rabelais; *Gargantua and Pantagruel*, 1532

.31 A maid that laughs is half taken.
—John Ray; *English Proverbs*, 1670

.32 We are in the world to laugh. In purgatory or hell we shall no longer be able to do so. And in heaven it would not be proper.
—Jules Renard; *Journal*, June 1907

.33 We cannot really love anybody with whom we never laugh.
—Agnes Repplier; *American and Others*, 1912

.34 Laughter springs from the lawless part of our nature.
—Agnes Repplier; *In Pursuit of Laughter*, 1936

.35 [What makes life worth living is] to be born with the gift of laughter and a sense that the world is mad.
—Rafael Sabatini; *Scaramouche*, 1921

.36 There is a great difference between seeking how to raise a laugh from everything, and seeking in everything what may justly be laughted at.
—Lord Shaftesbury; *Sensus Communis: An Essay on the Freedom of Wit and Humor*, 1709

.37 There are few who would not rather be hated than laughed at.
—Sydney Smith; *Sketches of Moral Philosophy*, 1805

.38 You will make one die of laughing.
—Jonathan Swift; *Polite Conversation*, 1738

.39 A good laugh is sunshine in a house.
—William Makepeace Thackeray; *Sketches: Love, Marriage*, 1863

.40 Laughter need not be cut out of anything, since it improves everything.
—James Thurber; Helen Thurber and Edward Weeks, eds. *Selected Letters of James Thurber*, 1981

.41 Now you can laugh but on one side of your mouth, friend.
—Torriano; *Piazza Universale*, 1666

.42 Laughter which cannot be suppressed is catching. Sooner or later it washes away our defences, and undermines our dignity, and we

**148**

join in it—ashamed of our weakness, and embittered against the cause of its exposure, but no matter, we have to join in, there is no help for it.
—Mark Twain; *Mark Twain's Which Was the Dream? and Other Symbolic Writings of the Later Years*, "Indiantown," John S. Tuckey, ed., 1967

.43 Laughter would be bereaved if snobbery died.
—Peter Ustinov; in *Observer*, March 13, 1955

.44 He laughs best that laughs last.
—Sir John Vanbrugh; *The Country House*, 1706

.45 Laughter or crying is what a human being does when there's nothing else he can do.
—Kurt Vonnegut, Jr.; *Playboy*, 1973

.46 The laughter of man is the contentment of God.
—John Weiss; *Wit, Humor, and Shakespeare*, 1876

.47 A good time for laughing is when you can.
—Jessamyn West; *Except for Me and Thee*, 1969

.48 Laugh and the world laughs with you;
Weep, and you weep alone.
—Ella Wheeler Wilcox; *Poems of Passion: Perdita, and Other Stories*, "Solitude," 1886

.49 She had a penetrating sort of laugh. Rather like a train going into a tunnel.
—P.G. Wodehouse; *The Inimitable Jeeves*, 1923

# 149 Law

.1 Law is a pledge that citizens of a state will do justice to one another.
—Aristotle; *Politics*, c. 322 B.C.

.2 The magistrate is a speaking law, but the law is a silent magistrate.
—Cicero; *De Finibus*, c. 50 B.C.

.3 The law is simply expediency wearing a long white dress.
—Quentin Crisp; *Manners from Heaven*, 1984

.4 No written laws can be so plain, so pure,
But wit may gloss and malice may obscure.
—John Dryden; *The Hind and the Panther*, 1687

**149**

.5  The law is only a memorandum.
—Ralph Waldo Emerson; *Essays: Second Series*, "Politics," 1844

.6  The life of the law has not been logic; it has been experience.
—Oliver Wendell Holmes, Jr.; *The Common Law*, 1881

.7  When a law is made the way to avoid it is found out.
—Italian Proverb

.8  I know law too well in practice to be moved by any theories about it.
—Charles Kingsley; *Alton Locke*, 1850

.9  The business of the law is to make sense of the confusion of what we call human life—to reduce it to order but at the same time to give it possibility, scope, even dignity.
—Archibald MacLeish, "Apologia" in the *Harvard Law Review*, June, 1972

.10 The law is blind, and speaks in general terms.
—Thomas May; *The Heir*, c. 1620

.11 Law is experience developed by reason and applied continually to further experience.
—Roscoe Pound; *Christian Science Monitor*, April 24, 1963

.12 To succeed in the other trades, capacity must be shown; in the law, concealment of it will do.
—Mark Twain; *Following the Equator*, "Pudd'nhead Wilson's New Calendar," 1897

# **150** Lawyers

.1  The public regards lawyers with great distrust. They think lawyers are smarter than the average guy but use their intelligence deviously. Well, they're wrong; usually they are not smarter.
—F. Lee Bailey; *Los Angeles Times*, January 9, 1972

.2  There is never a deed so foul that something couldn't be said for the guy; that's why there are lawyers.
—Melvin Belli; *Los Angeles Times*, December 18, 1981

.3  Lawyer, n. One skilled in circumvention of the law.
—Ambrose Bierce; *The Devil's Dictionary*, 1906

.4  Doctors ... still retain a high degree of public confidence because they are perceived as heal-

**150**

ers. Should lawyers not be healers? Healers, not warriors? Healers, not procurers? Healers, not hired guns?
—Warren E. Burger; to American Bar Association, February 12, 1984

.5  Our wrangling lawyers ... are so litigious and busy here on earth, that I think they will plead their client's causes, hereafter, some of them in hell.
—Robert Burton; *Anatomy of Melancholy*, 1621

.6  Doctors purge the body, preachers the conscience, lawyers the purse.
—Charles Cahier; *Quelques Six Mille Proverbes*, 1856

.7  The best trained, most technically skilled and ethically most responsible lawyers are reserved for the upper reaches of business and society. This leaves the least competent, least well-trained, and least ethical lawyers to the lower-income individuals.
—Jerome E. Carlin; *Lawyer's Ethics*, 1966

.8  He saw a lawyer killing a viper
On a dunghill hard by his own stable;
And the Devil smiled, for it put him in mind
Of Cain and his brother Abel.
—Samuel Taylor Coleridge; "The Devil's Thoughts," 1799

.9  One hires lawyers as one hires plumbers, because one wants to keep one's hands off the beastly drains.
—Amanda Cross; *The Question of Max*, 1976

.10 Lawyers and painters can soon change white to black.
—Danish Proverb

.11 Shyster lawyers—a set of turkey-buzzards whose touch is pollution and whose breath is pestilence.
—G.G. Foster; *New York in Slices*, 1849

.12 To some lawyers, all facts are created equal.
—Felix Frankfurter; *Felix Frankfurter Reminisces*, 1960

.13 God works wonders now and then; behold, a lawyer, an honest man.
—Benjamin Franklin; *Poor Richard's Almanack*, 1733

.14 He [a good lawyer] is one that will not plead that cause wherein his tongue must be confuted by his conscience.
—Thomas Fuller I; *Holy and Profane States: The Good Advocate*, 1642

**150**

.15 I know you lawyers can, with ease,
'Twist words and meanings as you please.
—John Gay; *Fables*, 1727

.16 No poet has ever interpreted nature as freely as a lawyer interprets reality.
—Jean Giraudoux; *Tiger at the Gates*, 1935

.17 Lawyers are always more ready to get a man into troubles than out of them.
—Oliver Goldsmith; *The Good-Natured Man*, 1768

.18 Lawyers are like morticians—we all need one sooner or later, but better later than sooner.
—Eileen Goudge; *Garden of Lies*, 1989

.19 The lawyer must either learn to live more capaciously or be content to find himself continuously less trusted, more circumscribed, till he becomes hardly more important than a minor administrator, confined to a monotonous round of record and routine, without dignity, inspiration, or respect.
—Learned Hand; *The Spirit of Liberty*, 1959

.20 Lawyers spend a great deal of time shovelling smoke.
—Oliver Wendell Holmes, Jr.; Attributed

.21 A man may as well open an oyster without a knife, as lawyer's mouth without a fee.
—Barten Holyday; *Technogamia*, 1618

.22 Clergymen can marry you, but if you find you have made a mistake, in order to get unmarried, you have to hire a lawyer.
—Elbert Hubbard; *Philistine*, 1908

.23 Every once in a while you meet a fellow in some honorable walk of life that was once admitted to the bar.
—Kin Hubbard; "Books Received," c. 1900

.24 Lawyers earn a living by the sweat of their browbeating.
—James G. Huneker; *Painted Veil*, 1920

.25 My definition of utter waste is a coachload of lawyers going over a cliff, with three empty seats.
—Lamar Hunt; Attributed

.26 How can expectation be expected from a body [Congress] which we have saddled with a hundred lawyers, whose trade is talking?
—Thomas Jefferson; *Writings*, Henry A. Washington, ed. 1853–54

.27 I would be loath to speak ill of any person who I do not know deserves it, but I am afraid he is an attorney.
—Samuel Johnson; in Mrs. Piozzi, *Johnsoniana*, 1768.

**150**

.28 Lawyers may say anything for their fee.
—Charles Johnstone; *The Reverie*, 1763

.29 So wise, so grave, of so perplex'd a tongue,
And loud withal, that would not wag, nor scarce
Lie still without a fee.
—Ben Jonson; *Volpone*, 1605–6

.30 What is the price of your voice?
—Juvenal; *Satires*, c. A.D. 120

.31 No other profession is subject to the public contempt and derision that sometimes befalls lawyers. … the bitter fruit of public incomprehension of the law itself and its dynamics.
—Judge Irving R. Kaufman; Quoted in San Francisco *Examiner & Chronicle*, April 17, 1977

.32 I think we may class the lawyers in the natural history of monsters.
—John Keats; Letter to G. Keats, March 13, 1819

.33 He is no lawyer who cannot take two sides.
—Charles Lamb; Letter to Samuel Rogers, December, 1833

.34 Two attorneys can live in a town, when one cannot. i.e. they make work for each other.
—V.S. Lean; *Collectanea*, 1902

.35 The law does not exist for the lawyers though there are some of us who seem to think that it does. The law is for all the people and the lawyers are only its ministers.
—Robert A. Leflar; Speech, American Judicature Society, *Wall Street Journal*, May 27, 1971

.36 It is unfair to believe everything we hear about lawyers—some of it might not be true.
—Gerald F. Lieberman; Attributed

.37 Discourage litigation. Persuade your neighbors to compromise whenever you can…. As a peace-maker the lawyer has a superior opportunity of being a good man. There will still be business enough.
—Abraham Lincoln; Notes for Law Lecture, July, 1850

.38 Apologists for the profession contend that lawyers are as honest as other men, but this is not very encouraging.
—Ferdinand Lundberg; in Kenneth Redden, *Modern Legal Glossary*, 1983

.39 Lawyers are men who hire out their words and anger.
—Martial; *Epigrams*. c. 1st century A.D.

## 150

.40 Three Philadelphia lawyers are a match for the Devil.
—New England Proverb

.41 Woe unto you also, ye lawyers! for ye lade men with burdens grievous to be borne, and ye yourselves touch not the burdens with one of your fingers.
—New Testament; Luke

.42 Most lawyers who win a case advise their clients that "we have won" and, when justice has frowned upon their cause, that "you have lost."
—Louis Nizer; *My Life in Court*, 1960

.43 A lawyer with a briefcase can steal more than a thousand men with guns.
—Mario Puzo; *The Godfather*, 1969

.44 Lawyers are operators of the toll bridge across which anyone in search of justice has to pass.
—Jane Bryant Quinn; *Newsweek*, October 9, 1978

.45 What we lawyers want to do is to substitute courts for carnage, dockets for rockets, briefs for bombs, warrants for warheads, mandates for missiles.
—George Rhyne; *Wall Street Journal*, June 27, 1963
[Rhyne's comments were made at the World Conference on World Peace through Law.]

.46 You want the unvarnished and ungarnished truth, and I'm no hand for that. I'm a lawyer.
—Mary Roberts Rinehart; *The Man in Lower Ten*, 1909

.47 About half the practice of a decent lawyer consists in telling would-be clients that they are damned fools and should stop.
—Elihu Root; in Martin Mayer, *The Lawyers*, 1967

.48 Why is there always a secret singing
When a lawyer cashes in?
Why does the hearse horse snicker
Hauling a lawyer away?
—Carl Sandburg; *The Lawyers Know Too Much*, 1920

.49             O perilous mouths,
That bear in them one and the self-same tongue,
Either of condemnation or approve;
Bidding the law make court'sy to their will;
Hooking both right and wrong to the appetite,
To follow as it draws.
—William Shakespeare; *Measure for Measure*, 1603

## 150

.50 The first thing we do, let's kill all the lawyers.
—William Shakespeare; *II Henry VI*, 1590

.51 Shun going to law as you would shun the devil; and look upon all attorneys as devouring sharks or ravenous fish of prey.
—Tobias Smollett; *Peregrine Pickle*, 1751

.52 I do believe that half a dozen commonplace attorneys could so mystify and misconstrue the Ten Commandments, and so confuse Moses' surroundings on Mount Sinai, that the great law-giver, if he returned to this planet, would doubt his own identity, abjure every one of his deliverances, yea, even commend the very sins he so clearly forbade his people.
—Elizabeth Cady Stanton; in Theodore Stanton and Harriet Stanton Blatch, eds. *Elizabeth Cady Stanton as Revealed in Her Letters and Reminiscences*, 1922

.53 The lawyer hummed and hawed, not because he had any real objections but because it is a lawyer's business to consider remote contingencies, and a straightforward agreement to anything would be wildly unprofessional.
—Josephine Tey; *A Shilling for Candles*, 1936

.54 Next to the confrontation between two highly trained, finely hones batteries of lawyers, jungle warfare is a stately minuet.
—Bill Veeck; *The Hustler's Handbook*, 1965

.55 Lawyers' work required sharp brains, strong vocal chords, and an iron butt.
—Jessamyn West; *The Massacre at Fall Creek*, 1975

.56 An incompetent attorney can delay a trial for years or months. A competent attorney can delay one even longer.
—Evelle J. Younger; *Los Angeles Times*, March 3, 1971

## 151 Lectures

.1 He was then lying under the discipline of a curtain lecture.
—Joseph Addison; *The Tatler*, 1710
[A curtain lecture is a lecture given a wife to her husband when they are in bed at night.]

.2 The effect which lectures produce on a hearer depends on his habits, for we demand the language we are accustomed to, and that which is different from this seems not in keeping but somewhat unintelligible and foreign because

**151**

of its unwontedness. For it is the customary that is intelligible.
—Aristotle; *Metaphysics*, c. 4th century B.C.

.3 Lecturer: one with his hand in your pocket, his tongue in your ear, and his faith in your patience.
—Ambrose Bierce; *The Devil's Dictionary*, 1911

.4 Here we have a saying: a good friend is someone who visits you when you are in prison. But a really good friend is someone who comes to hear your lectures.
—Malcolm Stanley Bradbury; *Rates of Exchange*, 1983

.5 Poets and painters are outside the class system, or rather they constitute a special class of their own, like the circus people and the gipsies. For the sake of their moral health they should be relatively poor and should mix mainly with their own kind. When they are short of money it is better for them to practise shop-lifting than to give lectures.
—Gerald Brenan; *Thoughts in a Dry Season*, 1978

.6 Stand still, and I will read to thee
A lecture, Love, in love's philosophy.
—John Donne; *Songs and Sonnets*, "A Lecture Upon the Shadow," 1611

.7 Do not go lightly or casually to hear lectures; but if you do go, maintain your gravity and dignity and do not make yourself offensive.
—Epictetus; *Enchiridion*, c. A.D. 110

.8 One performs autopsies on corpses. The idea of lecturing on a living poet is all wrong.
—Robert Graves; in *Esquire*, 1970

.9 If for the sake of a crowded audience you do wish to hold a lecture, your ambition is no laudable one, and at least avoid all citations from the poets, for to quote them argues feeble industry.
—Hippocrates; *Precepts*, c. 5th century B.C.

.10 Fill'd with trouble of my own—
A Wife who preaches in her gown,
And lectures in her night-dress!
—Thomas Hood; "The Surplice Question," 1845

.11 Some experience of popular lecturing had convinced me that the necessity of making things plain to uninstructed people was one of the very best means of clearing up the obscure corners in one's own mind.
—T.H. Huxley; *Man's Place in Nature*, "Preface," 1894

**151**

.12 In every university there are admirable investigators who are notoriously bad lecturers. The reason is that they never spontaneously see the subject in the minute articulate way in which the student needs to have it offered to his slow reception.
—William James; *Talks to Teachers on Psychology*, 1890

.13 Lectures which please only while they were new, to become new again, must be forgotten.
—Samuel Johnson; *Rasselas*, 1759

.14 Most people tire of a lecture in ten minutes; clever people can do it in five. Sensible people never go to lectures at all. But the people who do go to a lecture and who get tired of it, presently hold it as a sort of grudge against the lecturer personally. In reality his sufferings are worse than ours.
—Stephen Leacock; *My Discovery of England*, 1922

.15 They will get it straight one day at the Sorbonne.
We shall return at twilight from the lecture
Pleased that the irrational is rational.
—Wallace Stevens; *Notes Toward a Supreme Fiction*, "It Must Give Pleasure," 1942

.16 A classic lecture, rich in sentiment,
With scraps of thundrous Epic lilted out
By violet-hooded Doctors, elegies
And quoted odes, and jewels five-words-long,
That on the stretched forefinger of all Time
Sparkle for ever.
—Alfred, Lord Tennyson; *The Princess*, 1847

.17 I fear that to the last women's lectures will demand mainly courtesy from men.
—Henry David Thoreau; *Winter*, December 31, 1851

.18 Lecturing is an institution.
—Anthony Trollope; *He Knew He Was Right*, 1869

.19 There's a great moral difference between a lecture and a speech … for when you deliver a lecture you get good pay, but when you make a speech you don't get a cent.
—Mark Twain; Speech, Hartford, Connecticut, October 26, 1880

.20 It is not necessary to be able to lecture in order to go into the lecture field.
—Mark Twain and Charles Dudley Warner; *The Guilded Age*, 1889

.21 Behold, I do not give lectures or a little charity,
When I give I give myself.
—Walt Whitman; "Song of Myself," 1855

## 151

.22 The first duty of a lecturer—to hand you after an hour's discourse a nugget of pure truth to wrap up between the pages of your notebooks and keep on the mantelpiece for ever.
　　—Virginia Woolf; *A Room of One's Own*, 1929

.23 Brilliant lecturers shouldn't be wasted in lecture rooms: they should appear on TV. We need black market universities, in which people just help each other, and which don't leave out the poor.
　　—Theodore Zeldin; Quoted in Christina Hardyment "Zeldin and the Art of Human Relationships" in *Oxford Today*, 1995

# 152 Legends

.1 Legends have always played a powerful role in the making of history…. Without ever relating facts reliably, yet always expressing their true significance, they offered a truth beyond realities, a remembrance beyond memories.
　　—Hannah Arendt; *Origins of Totalitarianism*, 1951

.2 People surrounded by a legend rarely look the parts they have been assigned.
　　—James Baldwin; *Nobody Knows My Name*, 1961

.3 Every legend contains its residuum of truth, and the root function of language is to control the universe by describing it.
　　—James Baldwin; *Notes of a Native Son*, 1955

.4 It's always seemed to me … that legends and yarns and folktales are as much a part of the real history of a country as proclamations and provisos and constitutional amendments.
　　—Stephen Vincent Benet; in Charles A. Fenton *Stephen Vincent Benet: The Life and Times of an American Man of Letters*, 1958

.5 What a dull world this would be if every imaginative maker of legends was stigmatized as a liar!
　　—Heywood Broun; *Pieces of Hate*, 1922

.6 Legend is the consecration of fame.
　　—Coco Chanel; in Marcel Haedrich, *Coco Chanel, Her Life, Her Secrets*, 1971

.7 A legend is an old man with a cane known for what he used to do. I'm still doing it.
　　—Miles Davis; in *International Herald Tribune*, Paris, July 17, 1991

.8 It takes a certain brashness to attack the accepted economic legends but none at all to perpetuate them. So they are perpetuated.
　　—John Kenneth Galbraith; *The Liberal Hour*, 1960

.9 There are times when reality becomes too complex for Oral Communication. But Legend gives it a form by which it pervades the whole world.
　　—Jean-Luc Godard; *Alphaville*, 1965
　　[At the beginning of the film written and directed by Godard, the computer Alpha 60, expresses this sentiment.]

.10 Legends die hard. They survive as truth rarely does.
　　—Helen Hayes; *On Reflections*, with Sanford Dody, 1968

.11 Facts are fine, fer as they go … but they're like water bugs skittering atop the water. Legends, now—they go deep down and bring up the heart of a story.
　　—Marguerite Henry; *Misty of Chincoteague*, 1947

.12 No truth is strong enough to defeat a well-established legend.
　　—Winifred Holtby; *Pavements at Anderby*, "The Murder of Madame Mollard," 1930

.13 Legend adheres to artists whose deaths seem the corollaries of their works.
　　—Joyce Johnson; *Minor Characters*, 1983

.14 Asleep in lap of legends old.
　　—John Keats; *The Eve of St. Agnes*, 1820

.15 These are the stories that never, never die, that are carried like seed into a new country, are told to you and me and make in us new and lasting strengths.
　　—Meridel Le Sueur; *Nancy Hawks of Wilderness Road*, 1949

.16 Should you ask me, whence these stories? Whence these legends and traditions?
　　—Henry Wadsworth Longfellow; *The Song of Hiawatha*, 1855

.17 The past exudes legend: one can't make pure clay of time's mud. There is no life that can be recaptured wholly; as it was. Which is to say that all biography is ultimately fiction.
　　—Bernard Malamud; *Dubin's Lives*, 1979

.18 Men must have legends, else they die of strangeness.
　　—Les A. Murray; "Noonday Axeman," 1965

## 152

.19 Sometimes legends make reality, and become more useful than the facts.
—Salman Rushdie; *Midnight's Children*, 1981

.20 As Michael read the Gaelic scroll
It seemed the story of the soul;
And those who wrought, lest there should fail
From earth the legend of the Gael,
Seemed warriors of Eternal Mind
Still holding in a world gone blind,
From which belief and hope had gone,
The lovely magic of its dawn.
—George William Russell (AE), *The Interpreters*, "Michael," 1922

.21 Half-legend, half-historic.
—Alfred, Lord Tennyson, *The Princess*, "Prologue," 1847

# 153 Liars and Lying

.1  A liar will not be believed, even when he speaks the truth.
—Aesop; *Fables*, "The Shepherd's Boy," c. 6th century B.C.

.2  At first the throne is set up for the liar, but at last his lies shall find him out, and they shall spit in his face.
—Ahikar; *Teachings*, c. 550 B.C.

.3  I have not lied willingly. I have not done aught with a false heart.
—Ani; *Papyrus: Book of the Dead*, c. 4000 B.C.

.4  When they speak the truth they are not believed.
—Aristotle; c. 340 B.C., Diogenes Laertius, *Aristotle*
[Aristotle's answer when asked "What is the reward of liars?"]

.5  Homer has taught all other poets the art of telling lies skillfully.
—Aristotle; Diogenes Laertius, *Aristotle*, c. 200

.6  This is the punishment of a liar; He is not believed, even when he speaks the truth.
—Babylonian Talmud: Sanhedrin, c. 450

.7  Liars begin by imposing upon others, but end in deceiving themselves.
—H.G. Bohn; *Handbook of Proverbs*, 1855

## 153

.8  Any fool can tell the truth, but it requires a man of some sense to know how to tell a lie well.
—Samuel Butler II; *Note Books*, "Truth and Consequence," 1912

.9  The best liar is he who makes the smallest amount of lying go the longest way.
—Samuel Butler II; *The Way of All Flesh*, 1903

.10 Do not tell everything, but never lie…. You may always observe that the greatest fools are the greatest liars.
—Lord Chesterfield; Letter to his son, February 17, 1754

.11 She lied with fluency, ease and artistic fervor.
—Agatha Christie; *They Came to Baghdad*, 1951

.12 Lying is the only art form that the public sanctions and instinctively prefers to reality.
—Jean Cocteau; *Diary of an Unknown*, 1952

.13 Of course I lie to people. But I lie altruistically—for our mutual good. The lie is the basic building block of good manners. That may seem mildly shocking to a moralist —but then what isn't?
—Quentin Crisp; *Manners from Heaven*, 1984

.14 Lying is father to falsehood, and grandsire is perjury; fraud (with two faces) is his daughter, a very monster; treason (with hairs like snakes) is his kinsman.
—Thomas Dekker; *The Seven Deadly Sins of London*, 1606

.15 A good portion of speaking well consists in knowing how to lie.
—Gerard Didier Erasmus; *Colloquia: Philetymus and Psuedocheus*, 1524

.16 Some men were born to lie, and women to believe them!
—John Gay; *The Beggar's Opera*, 1727

.17 Ask me no questions, and I'll tell you no fibs.
—Oliver Goldsmith; *She Stoops to Conquer*, 1773

.18 He entered into the territory of lies without a passport for return.
—Graham Greene; *The Heart of the Matter*, 1948

.19 The most mischievous liars are those who keep sliding on the verge of truth.
—Augustus William Hare; *Guesses at Truth*, 1827

**153**

.20 Liar: one who tells an unpleasant truth.
 —Oliver Herford; *The Herford Aesop*, 1921

.21 It is better to be lied about than to lie.
 —Elbert Hubbard; *The Philistine*, 1901

.22 They certainly lied up a mess. The men would start telling stories and one man would stop another and say, "Wait a minute, let me put my dime on your dollar."
 —Zora Neale Hurston; *Mules and Men*, 1935

.23 Cunning has effect from the credulity of others rather than from the abilities of those who are cunning. It requires no extraordinary talents to lie and deceive.
 —Samuel Johnson; in Boswell's *Life of Johnson*, 1781

.24 It is an art to have so much judgement as to apparel a lie well, to give it a good dressing.
 —Ben Jonson; *Explorata*: "Mali Choragi Fuere," 1636

.25 There is nothing so pathetic as a forgetful liar.
 —F.M. Knowles; *A Cheerful Year Book*, c. 1870

.26 I never lied save to shield a woman or myself.
 —Ring Lardner; *Ex Parte*, 1926

.27 He shall not prosper who deviseth lies.
 —Mohammed; *Koran*, c. 625

.28 He who does not need to lie is proud of not being a liar.
 —Friedrich Nietzsche; *Nachgelassene Fragmente*, 1882–89

.29 There are people who lie simply for the sake of lying.
 —Blaise Pascal; *Pensees*, c. 1660

.30 Equivocation is half-way to lying, as lying is the whole way to hell.
 —William Penn; *Some Frutis of Solitude*, 1693

.31 There is a difference between telling a falsehood and lying. One who lies is not himself deceived, but tries to deceive another; he who tells a falsehood is himself deceived. One who lies deceives, as far as he is able; but one who tells a falsehood does not himself deceive, any more than he can help. A good man ought to take pains not to lie; a wise man, not to tell what is false.
 —Publius Nigidius; *Fragments*, Aulius Gellius, *Noctes Atticae*, c. 2nd century A.D.

.32 There is no doubt about the truth of the proverb that a liar should have a good memory.
 —Quintilian; *Institutionis Oratoriae*, c. A.D. 80

**153**

.33 Lying is done with words, and also with silence.
 —Adrienne Rich; *On Lies, Secrets and Silence*, "Women and Honor: Some Notes on Lying," 1979

.34 People lie because they can't help making a story better than it was the way it happened.
 —Carl Sandburg; *The People, Yes*, 1936

.35 If I tell thee a lie, spit in my face, call me a horse.
 —William Shakespeare; *I Henry IV*, 1596–7

.36 Optimistic lies have such immense therapeutic value that a doctor who cannot tell them convincingly has mistaken his profession.
 —George Bernard Shaw; *Misalliance*, "Preface," 1914

.37 As universal a practice as lying is, and as easy a one as it seems, I do not remember to have heard three good lies in any conversation, even from those who were most celebrated in that faculty.
 —Jonathan Swift; *Thoughts on Various Subjects*, 1711

.38 The young ought to be temperate in the use of this great art until practice and experience shall give them that confidence, elegance, and precision which alone can make the accomplishment graceful and profitable.
 —Mark Twain; Address to Saturday Morning Club, Boston, April 15, 1882

.39 There are 869 different forms of lying, but only one of them has been squarely forbidden. Thou shalt not bear false witness against thy neighbor.
 —Mark Twain; "Pudd'nhead Wilson's New Calendar," 1893

.40 A liar is a man who doesn't know how to deceive.
 —Luc de Clapiers de Vauvenargues; *Reflexions*, 1746

.41 He will lie even when inconvenient, the sign of the true artist.
 —Gore Vidal; *Two Sisters*, 1970

.42 The aim of the liar is simply to charm, to delight, to give pleasure. He is the very basis of a civilized society.
 —Oscar Wilde; *The Decay of Lying*, c. 1890

.43 The only form of lying that is absolutely beyond reproach is lying for its own sake.
 —Oscar Wilde; *The Decay of Lying*, c. 1890

.44 I am going to tell you a story, and though its outside dress is false, I hope the inside is true, and of such lies may we all be guilty.
 —Nancy Willard; *Telling Time*, 1993

## 153

.45 Someone who knows too much finds it hard
not to lie.
—Ludwig Wittgenstein; Journal entry,
1947

## 154 Lies

.1  A lie always needs a truth for a handle to it.
—Henry Ward Beecher; *Proverbs from Plymouth Pulpit*, 1887

.2  The devil is the father of lies, but he neglected
to patent the idea, and the business now suffers
from competition.
—Josh Billings; *Josh Billings, His Works
Complete*, 1880

.3  There are lies so simple and lovely that saints
may speak them gracefully.
—Clare Boothe; *Kiss the Boys Good-Bye*,
Introduction, 1939

.4  Truth is no man's slave—but lies—what magnificent servants they make.
—Phyllis Bottome; *The Life Line*, 1946

.5  Better a noble lie than a miserable truth.
—Robertson Davies; in Alan Twigg, *Con-
versations with Twenty-four Canadian
Writers*, 1981

.6  There are three kinds of lies; lies, damn lies,
and statistics.
—Benjamin Disraeli; Quoted by Mark
Twain in his *Autobiography*, 1924

.7  No lie ever grows old.
—Euripides, c. 425 B.C. Quoted by Pon-
tanus, *Collectie Proverbiorum*
[The meaning of the assertion is that a lie
is perpetually young.]

.8  Without lies humanity would perish of despair and boredom.
—Anatole France; *The Bloom of Life*, "Af-
terword," 1922

.9  It's not a lie, it's a terminological inexactitude.
—Alexander Haig; TV Interview, 1983

.10 Maybe half a lie is worse than a real lie.
—Lillian Hellman; *Another Part of the Forest*, 1947

.11 Sin has many tools, but a lie is the handle that
fits them all.
—Oliver Wendell Holmes, Sr.; *The Autocrat of the Breakfast Table*, 1858

.12 A lie turned topsy-turvy, can be prinked and
tinselled out, decked in plumage new and fine,
till none knows its lean old carcass.
—Henrik Ibsen, *Peer Gynt*, 1867

## 154

.13 Good lies need a leavening of truth to make
them palatable.
—William McIlvanney; *The Papers of Tony
Veitch*, 1983

.14 A lie grows in size as it is repeated.
—Ovid; *Metamorphoses*, A.D. 7

.15 A red hot lie is the best kind.
—Plautus; *Mostellaria*, c. 220 B.C.

.16 There is no lie so reckless as to be without
some proof.
—Pliny the Elder; *History*, c. A.D. 70

.17 The famous maxim of *Mein Kampf* is that any
lie will be believed, if it is big enough.
—Herman Rausching; *The Revolution of
Nihilism*, 1939

.18 The only thing that ever came back from the
grave that we know of was a lie.
—Marilla M. Ricker; *The Philistine*, 1908

.19 That's a lie with a lid on.
—C.H. Spurgeon; *John Ploughman's Pictures*, 1880

.20 A lie is an abomination unto the Lord, and a
very present help in trouble.
—Adlai E. Stevenson; Speech, Springfield,
Illinois, January, 1951

.21 The cruellest lies are often told in silence.
—Robert Louis Stevenson; *Virginibus
Puerisque: Truth of Intercourse*, 1874

.22 A false story has seven endings.
—Swahili Proverb

.23 It often happens that, if a lie be believed only
for an hour, it has done its work, and there is
no further occasion for it.
—Jonathan Swift; *The Examiner*, 1715

.24 One falsehood treads on the heels of another.
—Terence; *Andria*, 166 B.C.

.25 Lies are the mortar that bind the savage individual man into the social masonry.
—H.G. Wells; *Love and Mr. Lewisham*,
1900

## 155 Life

.1  I don't want to get to the end of my life and
find that I just lived the length of it. I want to
have lived the width of it as well.
—Diane Ackerman; *Newsweek*, 1986

.2  Life loves to be taken by the lapel and told: "I
am with you kid. Let's go."
—Maya Angelou; *Wouldn't Take Nothing
for My Journey Now*, 1993

**155**

.3 Life is a handful of short stories, pretending to be a novel.
—Anonymous

.4 Life is a wonderful thing to talk about, or to read about in history books—but it is terrible when one has to live it.
—Jean Anouilh; *Time Remembered*, 1939

.5 Stories are important. They keep us alive. In the ships, in the camps, in the quarters, fields, prisons, on the road, on the run, underground, under siege, in the throes, on the verge—the storyteller snatches us back from the edge to hear the next chapter. In which we are the subjects.
—Toni Cade Bambara; "Salvation Is the Issue," Evans, ed., *Black Woman Writers*, 1984

.6 The life of every man is a diary in which he means to write one story, and writes another; and his humblest hour is when he compares the volume as it is with that he vowed to make it.
—J.M. Barrie; *The Little Minister*, 1891

.7 If it were possible to talk to the unborn, one could never explain to them how it feels to be alive, for life is washed in the speechless real.
—Jacques Barzun; *The House of Intellect*, 1959

.8 Life comes before literature, as the material always comes before the work. The hills are full of marble before the world blooms with statues.
—Phillips Brooks; *Literature and Life*, c. 1892

.9 Life is a drama, not a monologue.
—Edward George Bulwer-Lytton; *The Caxtons*, 1849

.10 Myths are clues to the spiritual potentialities of the human life.
—Joseph Campbell; *The Power of Myth*, 1988

.11 Life is a tragedy when seen in close-up, but a comedy in long-shot.
—Charles Chaplin; Quoted in his obituary, *The Guardian*, December 28, 1977

.12 We tell ourselves stories in order to live.
—Joan Didion; *The White Album*, 1979

.13 In three words I can sum up everything I've learned about life. It goes on.
—Robert Frost; Attributed

.14 There's only one story, the story of your life.
—Northrop Frye; in John Ayre, *Northrop Frye: A Biography*, 1989

**155**

.15 Life is a verb, not a noun.
—Charlotte Perkins Gilman; *Human Work*, 1904

.16 When I hear somebody sigh that "Life is hard," I am always tempted to ask, "Compared to what?"
—Sydney J. Harris; *A Majority of One*, 1957

.17 Real life never arranges itself exactly like a romance.
—Nathaniel Hawthorne; *The Blithedale Romance*, 1852

.18 Life is made up of sobs, sniffles and smiles, with sniffles predominating.
—O. Henry; *The Four Million*, "The Gift of the Magi," 1906

.19 Our whole life is like a play.
—Ben Jonson; *Explorata*, "De Piis et Probis," 1636

.20 The great question of all choosers and adventurers is "Was it worth while?"—and whatever else you may expect of life, don't expect an answer to that.
—Sheila Kaye-Smith; *A Challenge to Sirius*, 1917

.21 Life can only be understood backwards; but it must be lived forwards.
—Soren Kierkegaard; *Stages on Life's Way*, 1845

.22 The best lessons, the best sermons are those that are lived.
—Yolanda King; *Ebony*, August, 1987

.23 My candle burns at both ends;
It will not last the night;
But, ah, my foes, and, oh, my friends—
It gives a lovely light.
—Edna St. Vincent Millay; *A Few Figs from Thistles*, "First Fig," 1920

.24 Life is a foreign language; all men mispronounce it.
—Christopher Morley; *Thunder on the Left*, 1925

.25 Those stories do recount what life has been since time immemorial while *The Chronicles of Japan* depicts only incidents thereof. It is in the former that the principles are treated in detail.
—Shikibu Murasaki; *The Tale of Genji*, c. 1000

.26 All life is a stage and a play, so learn to play your part.
—Palladas; *Epigram*, c. A.D. 425

## 155

.27 We live beyond any tale we happen to enact.
—V.S. Pritchett; Attributed

.28 Life is a school, and the lesson never done.
—Charles Reade; *The Cloister and the Hearth*, 1861

.29 Life is the farce in which every one must take a part.
—Arthur Rimbaud; *Une Saison en Enfer*, 1873

.30 The first half of life gives us the text; the next thirty supply the commentary on it.
—Arthur Schopenhauer; *Parerga und Paralipomena*, 1851

.31 It is more fitting for a man to laugh at life than to lament over it.
—Seneca; *Moral Essays*, "On Peace of Mind," c. 1st century A.D.

.32 As is a tale, so is life, not how long it is, but how good it is, is what matters.
—Seneca; *Ad Lucilium*, c. A.D. 64

.33 Life's but a walking shadow, a poor player
That struts and frets his hour upon the stage
And then is heard no more; it is a tale
Told by an idiot, full of sound and fury
Signifying nothing.
—William Shakespeare; *Macbeth*, 1605–6

.34 Life is as tedious as a twice-told tale,
Vexing the dull ear of a drowsy man.
—William Shakespeare; *King John*, 1596

.35 Life is a tragedy wherein we sit as spectators for a while, and then act our part in it.
—Jonathan Swift; *Thoughts on Various Subjects*, 1711

.36 Life is far too important a thing ever to talk seriously about.
—Oscar Wilde; *Vera, or the Nihilists*, 1883

## 156  Limericks

.1 The limerick's admitted a verse form:
A terse form: a curse form: a hearse form.
It may not be lyric
And at best it's Satyric,
And a whale of a tail in perverse form.
—Conrad Aiken; *A Seizure of Limericks*, 1964

.2 The limerick's an art form complex
Whose contents run chiefly to sex;
It's famous for virgins
And masculine urgin's
And vulgar erotic effects.
—Anonymous

## 156

.3 The limerick packs laughs anatomical
Into space that is quite economical.
But the good ones I've seen
So seldom are clean
And the clean ones so seldom comical.
—Anonymous

.4 The Marquis de Sade and Genet
Are most highly thought of today;
But torture and treachery
Are not my sort of lechery
So I've given my copies away.
—W.H. Auden; *The New York Review of Books*, May 12, 1966

.5 The limerick is furtive and mean;
You must keep her in close quarantine,
Or she sneaks to the slums
And promptly becomes
Disorderly, drunk and obscene.
—Morris Bishop; *Spilt Milk*, 1942

.6 There once was an artist named Lear
Who wrote verses to make children cheer.
Though they never made sense,
Their success was immense,
And the Queen thought that Lear was a dear.
—H.I. Brock; "A Century of Limericks," *The New York Times Magazine*, November 17, 1946

.7 Mark Twain was a mop-headed male,
Whose narratives sparkled like ale;
And this Prince of the Grin
Who once fathered Huck Finn
Can still hold the world by the tale.
—Mrs. W.S. Burgess, 1940s
[Mrs. Burgess of Fullerton, Nebraska, was the winning entry when the Mark Twain Society instituted a nationwide contest for the best limerick on Twain.]

.8 Oh, my name is John Wellington Wells,
I'm a dealer in magic and spells,
In blessings and curses,
And ever-filled purses,
In prophecies, witches, and knells.
—W.S. Gilbert; *The Sorcerer*, 1877

.9 Well, it's partly the shape of the thing
That gives the old limerick wing;
These accordion pleats
Full of airy conceits
Take it up like a kite on a string.
—Francis B. Gummere; *The Popular Ballad*, 1894

.10 A goddess capricious is Fame.
You may strive to make noted your name.
But she either neglects you

## 156

Or coolly selects you
For laurels distinct from your aim!
—Edward Lear; *A Book of Nonsense*, 1845

.11 All hail to the town of Limerick
Which provides a cognomen, generic,
    For species of verse
    Which, for better or worse,
Is supported by layman and cleric.
—H. Langford Reed; *The Compleat Limerick Book*, 1925

.12 A canner, exceedingly canny,
One morning remarked to his granny,
    "A canner can can
    Anything that he can,
But a canner can't can a can, can he?
—Carolyn Wells; "The Canner," *Book of American Limericks*, 1925

# 157 Linguistics

.1 The terms "Aryan" and "Semitic" have no racial significance whatsoever. They simply denote linguistic families.
—American Anthropological Association Resolution, 1938

.2 Because words pass away as soon as they strike upon the air, and last no longer than their sound, men have by means of letters formed signs of words. Thus the sounds of the voice are made visible to the eye, not of course as sounds, but by means of certain signs.
—Saint Augustine of Hippo; *Confessions*, c. 395

.3 Every living language, like the perspiring bodies of living creatures, is in perpetual motion and alteration; some words go off, and become obsolete; others are taken in, and by degrees grow into common use; or the same word is inverted to a new sense and notion, which in tract of time makes as observable a change in the air and features of a language as age makes in the lines and mien of a face.
—Richard Bentley, *Letter to Mill*, 1691

.4 Examine language; what, if you except some few primitive elements [of natural sound], what is it all but Metaphors, recognized as such, or no longer recognized.
—Thomas Carlyle; *Sartor Resartus*, 1833–4

.5 It is quite natural to expect that a concern for language will remain central to the study of human nature, as it has been in the past. Anyone concerned with the study of human nature and human capacities must somehow come to

## 157

grips with the fact that all normal humans acquire language.
—Noam Chomsky; *Current Issues in Linguistic Theory*, 1964

.6 Language is a process of free creation; its laws and principles are fixed, but the manner in which the principles of generation are used is free and infinitely varied. Even the interpretation and use of words involves a process of free creation.
—Noam Chomsky; "Language and Freedom," lecture Loyola University, Chicago, January 1970

.7 Usage, in which lies the decision, the law, and the norm of speech.
—Horace; *Ars Poetica*, c. 19 B.C.

.8 Language is the only instrument of science, and words are but the signs of ideas.
—Samuel Johnson; *A Dictionary of the English Language*, "Preface," 1755

.9 Custom is the most certain mistress of language, as the public stamp makes the current money.
—Ben Jonson; *Explorata*, 1636

.10 God having designed man for a social creature, furnished him with language, which was to be the great instrument and cementer of society.
—John Locke; *Essay Concerning Human Understanding*, 1690

.11 Language is neither innocent nor neutral. Linguistic habits condition our view of the world and hinder social change.
—Carmen Martinez Ten; in *Espana 91*, 1991

.12 Before linguistics, before the literal link of language, there was listening.
—Hannah Merker; *Listening*, 1994

.13 Linguistics becomes an ever eerier area, like I feel like I'm in Oz,
Just trying to tell it like it was.
—Ogden Nash; *The Old Dog Barks Backwards*, "What Do You Want, a Meaningful Dialogue or a Satisfactory Talk," 1972

.14 After a speech is fully fashioned to the common understanding, and accepted by consent of a whole country and nation, it is called a language.
—George Puttenham; *The Art of English Poesie*, 1589

.15 The notion of really independent of language is carried over by the scientist from his

**157**

earliest impressions, but the facile reification of linguistic features is avoided or minimized.
—Willard Van Orman Quine; *Word and Object*, 1960

.16 Language study is a route to maturity. Indeed, in language study as in life, if a person is the same today as he was yesterday, it would be an act of mercy to pronounce him dead and to place him in a coffin, rather than in a classroom.
—John A. Rassias; *Quote*, May 26, 1974

.17 This is your devoted friend, sir, the manifold linguist.
—William Shakespeare; *All's Well That Ends Well*, 1604–5

.18 Linguistic analysis. A lot of chaps pointing out that we don't always mean what we say, even when we manage to say what we meant.
—Tom Stoppard; *Professional Foul*, 1978

# **158** Listening

.1 When one listens to a story, one is being creative. The listener adds to it with his or her imagination.
—Arthur T. Allen; "The Ethos of the Teller of Tales," *Readings on Creativity and Imagination in Literature and Language*, L.V. Kosinski, ed., 1968

.2 We are a tongued folk. A race of singers. Our lips shape words and rhythms which elevate our spirits and quicken our blood…. I have spent over fifty years listening to my people.
—Maya Angelou; "Shades and Slashers of Light," in Evans, ed., *Black Women Writers*, 1984

.3 She seldom listens to anybody for more than half a minute.
—Jane Austen; *Pride and Prejudice*, 1813

.4 To talk to someone who does not listen is enough to tense the devil.
—Pearl Bailey; *Talking to Myself*, 1971

.5 Many men use their ears as a boltingcloth, only to catch the bran and let the flour go.
—Henry Ward Beecher; *Proverbs from Plymouth Pulpit*, "Man," 1887

.6 It seemed rather incongruous that in a society of supersophisticated communication, we often suffer from a shortage of listeners.
—Erma Bombeck; *If Life Is a Bowl of Cherries, What Am I Doing in the Pits?*, 1971

**158**

.7 Sit back and relax, dear listeners, and let the joy bells ring in your receptive minds as I attempt to do my thing.
—J. Mason Brewer; *American Negro Folktales*, 1968

.8 But yet she listen'd—'tis enough—
Who listens once will listen twice.
—Lord Byron; *Mazeppa*, 1817

.9 If people are unwilling to hear you, better it is to hold your tongue than them.
—Lord Chesterfield; *Letters to His Son*, published 1774

.10 Listens like a three years' child.
—Samuel Taylor Coleridge; *The Ancient Mariner*, 1798

.11 Were we as eloquent as angels, yet we should please some men, some women, and some children much more listening, than by talking.
—C.C. Colton; *Lacon*, 1820

.12 He listens to good purpose who takes note.
—Dante Alighieri; *The Divine Comedy: Inferno*, c. 1314

.13 Listen more often
To Things than to Beings,
Hear the voice of fire,
Hear the voice of water.
Listen in the wind to
The bush that is sobbing:
This is the ancestors breathing
Is the breathing of our forefathers.
—Birago Diop; "Spirits," 1967

.14 People ought to listen more slowly!
—Jean Sparks Ducey; *Christian Science Monitor*, December 9, 1986

.15 Speak your truth quietly and clearly; and listen to others, even the dull and ignorant; they too have their story.
—Max Ehrmann; *Desiderata*, 1927

.16 Listeners never hear anything good.
—Paul Leicester Ford; *The Great K. & A. Train Robbery*, 1897

.17 Someone to tell it to is one of the fundamental needs of human beings.
—Miles Franklin; *Childhood at Brindabella*, 1963

.18 He that listens after what People say of him, shall never have Peace.
—Thomas Fuller; *Gnomologia*, 1732

.19 The most difficult thing of all, to keep quiet and listen.
—Aulus Gellius; *Noctes Atticae*, c. A.D. 150

**158**

.20 Everything has been said before, but since no-body listens we have to keep going back and beginning all over again.
—Andre Gide; *Le traite du Narcisse*, 1891

.21 I'm glad I understand that while language is a gift, listening is a responsibility.
—Nikki Giovanni; *Racism 101*, "Griots," 1994

.22 There are people who instead of listening to what is being said to them are already listening to what they are going to say themselves.
—Albert Guinon; Comment, c. 1900

.23 It takes a great man to make a good listener.
—Sir Arthur Helps; *Brevia*, c. 1870

.24 Blessed
are those who listen
when no one is left to speak.
—Linda Hogan; *Calling Myself Home*, "Blessing," 1978

.25 It is the province of knowledge to speak and it is the privilege of wisdom to listen.
—Oliver Wendell Holmes; *The Poet at the Breakfast Table*, 1872

.26 No man would listen to you talk if he didn't know it was his turn next.
—Edgar Watson "Ed" Howe; *Plain People*, 1929

.27 Listen and you will learn.
—Solomon Ibn Gabriol; *Choice of Pearls*, c. 1050

.28 No one cares to speak to an unwilling listener. An arrow never lodges in a stone: often it re-coils upon the sender of it.
—St. Jerome; *Letters*, A.D. 370

.29 You seldom listen to me, and when you do you don't hear, and when you do hear you hear wrong, and even when you hear right you change it so fast that it's never the same.
—Marjorie Kellogg; *Tell Me That You Love Me, Junie Moon*, 1968

.30 Give us grace to listen well.
—John Kreble; *The Christian Year: Palm Sunday*, 1827

.31 The opposite of talking isn't listening. The opposite of talking is waiting.
—Fran Lebowitz; *Social Studies*, 1977

.32        Listen, every one
That listen may, unto a tale
That's merrier than the nightingale.
—Henry Wadsworth Longfellow; *Tales of a Wayside Inn*, "The Sicilian's Tale," 1863

.33 Folks will always listen when the tale is their own.
—Henry Mackenzie; *The Man of Feeling*, 1771

.34 My father used to say to me: "Son, you do all right in this world if you just remember that when you talk you are only repeating what you already know—but if you listen you may learn something."
—J.P. McEvoy; *Charlie Would Have Loved This*, 1956

.35 No one really listens to anyone else, and if you try it for a while you'll see why.
—Mignon McLaughlin; *The Second Neurotic's Notebook*, 1966

.36 Listening is a magnetic and strange thing, a creative force. The friends who listen to us are the ones we move forward toward, and we want to sit in their radius. When we are listened to, it creates us, makes us unfold and expand.
—Karl A. Menninger; *Love Against Hate*, 1942

.37 As anyone with a speech or hearing disability can tell you, listening is not always auditory communication.
—Hannah Merker; *Listening*, 1994

.38 Many public speakers are good extemporaneous listeners.
—Edgar Wilson "Bill" Nye; F.W. Nye, *Bill Nye: His Own Life Story*, 1926

.39 To listen acutely is to be powerless, even if you sit on a throne.
—Cynthia Ozick; *Metaphor & Memory*, "Italo Calvino: Bringing Stories to Their Senses," 1989

.40 We only consult the ear because the heart is wanting.
—Blaise Pascal; *Pensees*, c. 1670

.41 It is fairly well established that in a normal conversation the hearer really hears only about fifty per cent of the sounds produced by the speaker, and supplies the rest out of his own sense of the context.
—Mario Pei; *The Story of Language*, 1947

.42 The grace of listening is lost if the listener's attention is demanded not as a favor, but as a right.
—Pliny the Younger; *Epistles*, c. 1st century

.43 To listen well is a second inheritance.
—Publilius Syrus; *Sententiae*, c. 43 B.C.

.44 Listeners never hear good of themselves.
—John Ray; *English Proverbs*, 1678

## 158

.45 A man who listens because he has nothing to say can hardly be a source of inspiration. The only listening that counts is that of the talker who alternately absorbs and expresses ideas.
    —Agnes Repplier; *Compromises*, "The Luxury of Conversation," 1904

.46 The earliest instruction was imparted orally, a system still extant in Africa and the Orient. It trains the mind to listen.
    —Arthur A. Schomburg; in *Racial Integrity*, 1923

.47 Teach me half the gladness
    That thy brain must know,
    Such harmonious madness,
    From my lips would flow,
    The world should listen then,
        as I am listening now.
    —Percy Bysshe Shelley; *To a Skylark*, 1821

.48 To listen is an effort, and just to hear is no merit. A duck hears also.
    —Igor Stravinsky; News summaries, June 24, 1957

.49 I know how to listen when clever men are talking. That is the secret of what you call my influence.
    —Hermann Sudermann; *Es Lebe das Leben Liv*, c. 1889

.50 No syren did ever charm the ear of a listener, as the listening ear has charmed the soul of the syren.
    —Sir Henry Taylor; *The Statesman*, 1836

.51 He began to realize the deep truth that no one, broadly speaking, ever wishes to hear what you have been doing.
    —Anglea Thirkell; *The Old Bank House*, 1949

.52 The first duty of love is to listen.
    —Paul Tillich; recalled on his death, October 22, 1965

.53 They are a very decent generous lot of people out here and *they don't expect you to listen....* It's the secret of the social ease in this country. They talk entirely for their own pleasure. Nothing they say is designed to be heard.
    —Evelyn Waugh; *The Loved One*, 1948
    [British novelist Waugh's British expatriate Sir Francis Hinsley speaks of southern California.]

.54 A good listener tries to understand thoroughly what the other person is saying. In the end he may disagree sharply, but before he disagrees, he wants to know exactly what it is he is disagreeing with.
    —Kenneth A. Wells; *Guide to Good Leadership*, 1953

## 158

.55 A good listener is not someone who has nothing to say. A good listener is a good talker with a sore throat.
    —Katherine Whitehorn; Attributed

## 159 Literature

.1 Literature by its very nature is committed to questioning yesterday's assumptions and today's commonplaces ... one prime aim of scholarship is to promote uncertainty.
    —Robert Martin Adams; Quoted in *Contemporary Literary Critics*, Elmer Borklund, ed. 1977

.2 The writer in western civilization has become not a voice of his tribe, but of his individuality. This is a very narrow-minded situation.
    —Aharon Appelfeld; in the *International Herald Tribune*, Paris, August 10, 1989

.3 Storytelling as an art means recreating literature—taking the printed words in a book and giving them life.
    —Anthony Bonner; ed. and tr. *Songs of the Troubadours*, 1972

.4 For the beginning of literature is myth, and in the end as well.
    —Jorge Luis Borges; *Labyrinths*, "Parable of Don Quixote," 1962

.5 The folk literature of the American Negro has a rich inheritance from its African background. They brought with them no material possessions to aid in preserving the arts and customs of their homelands. Yet though empty-handed perforce, they carried on their minds and hearts a treasure of complex musical forms, dramatic speech, and imaginative stories, which they perpetuated through the vital art of expression. Wherever the slaves were ultimately placed, they established an enclave of African culture that flourished in spite of environmental disadvantages.
    —J. Mason Brewer; *American Negro Folktales*, 1968

.6 I believe all literature started as gossip.
    —Rita Mae Brown; *Starting from Scratch*, 1988

.7 The struggle of literature is in fact a struggle to escape from the confines of language; it stretches out from the utmost limits of what can be said; what stirs literature is the call and attraction of what is not in the dictionary.
    —Italo Calvino; "Cybernetics and Ghosts," lecture, Turin, November, 1969, published in *The Literature Machine*, 1987

## 159

.8 Speak of the moderns without contempt, and of the ancients without idolatry.
—Lord Chesterfield; Letter to his son, 1748

.9 He set out seriously to describe the indescribable. That is the whole business of literature, and it is a hard row to hoe.
—G.K. Chesterton; *All I Survey*, 1933

.10 The greatest masterpiece in literature is only a dictionary out of order.
—Jean Cocteau, "Le Potomak," c, 1940s

.11 Another special feature of Indian literature which was to be adopted as a regular feature in the Chinese ... was the mixture of prose and verse. The stories liberally included in their scriptures by the Indians, who are born storytellers, contributed to the development of literature in China.
—Paul Demieville; "Translations of Buddhist Literature," in *Dictionary of Oriental Literatures*, Jaroslav Prusek and Zbigniew Slupski, eds., 1974

.12 Literature is conscious mythology: as society develops, its mythical stories become structural principles of story-telling, its mythical concepts sun-gods and the like, become habits of metaphoric thought. In a fully mature literary tradition the writer enters into a structure of traditional stories and images.
—Northrop Frye; *The Bush Garden*, "Conclusion," 1971

.13 The land of literature is a fairy land to those who view it at a distance, but, like all other landscapes, the charm fades on a nearer approach, and the thorns and briars become visible.
—Washington Irving; *Tales of a Traveller*, "Notoriety," 1824

.14 National literature begins with fables and ends with novels.
—Joseph Joubert; *Pensees*, 1810

.15 Literature is my Utopia. Here I am not disfranchised. No barrier of the senses shuts me out from the sweet, gracious discourse of my book-friends. They talk to me without embarrassment or awkwardness.
—Helen Keller; *The Story of My Life*, 1902

.16 Literature exists for the sake of the people—to refresh the weary, to console the sad, to hearten the dull and the downcast, to increase man's interest in the world, his joy of living, and his sympathy in all sorts of conditions of man.
—M.T. Manton; dissenting U.S. Courts of

## 159

Appeals, opinion, *U.S. v One Book Called "Ulysses,"* 1934

.17 Black literature is taught as sociology, as tolerance, not as a serious, rigorous art form.
—Toni Morrison; "The Pain of Being Black," *Time Magazine*, May 22, 1989

.18 Great literature is simply language charged with meaning to the utmost possible degree.
—Ezra Pound; *How to Read*, 1931

.19 Literature: proclaiming in front of everyone what one is careful to conceal from one's intermediate circle.
—Jean Rostand; *Journal d'un caractere*, 1931

.20 Literature is the immortality of speech.
—August Wilhelm von Schlegel; Attributed

.21 Literature is the memory of humanity.
—Isaac Bashevis Singer; *U.S. News & World Report*, November 6, 1978

.22 The critics will say as always that literature is decaying, From the time of the first critic up to now they have said nothing else.
—Osbert Sitwell; "What It Feels Like to Be an Author," 1963

.23 Literature is simply the appropriate use of language.
—Evelyn Waugh; Letter to Ann Fleming, 1960

.24 The art of literature, vocal or written, is to adjust the language so that it embodies what it indicates.
—Alfred North Whitehead; in *The Faber Book of Aphorisms*, 1964

.25 Literature is the orchestration of platitudes.
—Thornton Wilder; *Time*, January 12, 1953

## 160 Love

.1 Everyone admits that love is wonderful and necessary, yet no one can agree on what it is.
—Diane Ackerman; *A Natural History of Love*, 1994

.2 To love without criticism is to be betrayed.
—Djuna Barnes; *Nightwood*, 1937

.3 To try to write love is to confront the muck of language: that region of hysteria where language is both *too much* and *too little*, excessive ... and impoverished.
—Roland Barthes; *A Lover's Discourse*, 1977

**160**

.4 Love ceases to be a pleasure when it ceases to be a secret.
—Aphra Behn; *The Lovers' Watch*, "Four O'Clock, General Conversation," 1686

.5 How do I love thee? Let me count the ways.
I love thee to the depth and breadth and height
My soul can reach.
—Elizabeth Barrett Browning; *Sonnets from the Portuguese*, 1850

.6 Lover's vows do not reach the ears of the gods.
—Callimachus; *Epigrams*, c. 3rd century B.C.

.7 In love, everything is true, everything is false; and it is the one subject on which one cannot express an absurdity.
—Sebastien Nicolas Roche Chamfort, *Maximes et pensees*, 1805

.8 Words are the weak support of cold indifference; love has no language to be heard.
—William Congreve; *The Double-Dealer*, 1694

.9 Grumbling is the death of love.
—Marlene Dietrich; *Marlene Dietrich's ABC*, 1962

.10 I am two fools, I know, for loving, and for saying so.
—John Donne; *Songs and Sonnets*, "The Triple Fool," 1633

.11 Hearing your voice is pomegranate wine
I live by hearing it.
Each look with which you look at me
Sustains me more than food and drink.
—Egyptian Verse

.12 And were an epitaph to be my story
I'd have a short one ready for my own.
I would have written of me on my stone:
I had a lover's quarrel with the world.
—Robert Frost; "The Lesson for Today," 1942

.13 Everyone talks of what he loves.
—Thomas Fuller II; *Gnomologia*, 1732

.14 When Silence speaks for Love she has much to say.
—Richard Garnett; *De Fiagello Myrteo*, 1905

.15 There is no question for which you are not the answer.
—Bonnie Zucker Goldsmith; "Credo," *The Spoon River Poetry Review*, 1993

.16 Love makes all men orators.
—Robert Greene; *Works*, 1583

**160**

.17 Words have no language which can utter the secrets of love; and beyond the limits of expression is the expounding of desire.
—Hafiz; *Ghazals from the Divan*, c. 14th century

.18 Under certain circumstances a woman will tolerate a man's conversation about his love for another woman, but the whole emphasis must lie on love, not on the object of that love.
—Hugo von Hofmannsthal; *The Book of Friends*, 1922

.19 Love is sparingly soluble in the words of man, therefore they speak much of it; but one syllable of woman's speech can dissolve more of it than a man's heart can hold.
—Oliver Wendell Holmes, Sr.; *The Autocrat of the Breakfast Table*, 1857–58

.20 I love thee—I love thee!
'Tis all that I can say;
It is my vision in the night,
My dreaming in the day.
—Thomas Hood; "I Love Thee," c. 1843

.21 Love, I find is like singing. Everybody can do enough to satisfy themselves, though it may not impress the neighbors as being very much.
—Zora Neale Hurston; *Dust Tracks on a Road*, 1942

.22 Love is a cruel conqueror.
Happy is he who knows him through stories
And not by his blows.
—Jean de la Fontaine; *Fables*, "Le lion amoureux," 1688

.23 That was the first sound in the song of love!
Scarce more than silence is, and yet a sound.
—Henry Wadsworth Longfellow; *The Spanish Student*, 1843

.24 True love lacketh a tongue.
—John Lyly; *Euphues*, 1579

.25 No word is used with more meanings than this term, most of the meanings being dishonest in that they cover up the real underlying motives in the relationship.
—Rollo May; *Love and Will*, 1969

.26 [The passion wherewith] we lash ourselves into the persuasive speech distinguishing us from the animals.
—George Meredith; *Diana of the Crossways*, 1885

.27 Love talked about can be easily turned aside, but love demonstrated is irresistible.
—W. Stanley Mooneyham; *Come Walk the World*, 1978

## 160

.28 When a man talks of love, with certain caution trust him;
But if he swears, he'll certainly deceive thee.
—Thomas Otway; *The Orphan*, 1680

.29 It is the way of love and glory,
Each tongue best tells his own story.
—Thomas Overbury; *Of the Choice of a Wife*, 1614

.30 Pleasant words are the food of love.
—Ovid; *Ars Amatoriae*, c. 1 B.C.

.31 By the time you swear you're his,
Shivering and sighing,
And he vows his passion is
Infinite—undying—
Lady, make note of this;
One of you is lying.
—Dorothy Parker; *Enough Rope*, "Unfortunate Coincidence," 1926

.32 To be able to say how much you love is to love but little.
—Francesco Petrarch; *Sonetti in Vita Madonna Laura*, c. 1350

.33 But I in love, was mute and still.
—Alexander Pushkin; *Eugene Onyegin*, 1823–31

.34 Love is not dumb. The heart speaks many ways.
—Jean Racine; *Britannicus*, 1669

.35 We may, without undue tension of speech, speak of Goodness as Love in conduct; of Truth as Love in thought; of Beauty as Love in self-expression, in whatever medium.
—Richard Roberts; in Newton, *My Idea of God*, 1946

.36 Love that is wise
Will not say all it means.
—Edwin Arlington Robinson; "Tristram," 1927

.37 Love makes a poet of the veriest boor.
—Sappho; *Fragment*, c. 610 B.C.

.38 Love makes mutes of those who habitually speak most fluently.
—Madeleine de Scudery; *Choix de pensees*, "de l'amour," c. 17th century

.39 Love means never having to say you're sorry.
—Erich Segal; *Love Story*, 1970

.40 And swearing till my very roof was dry
With oaths of love.
—William Shakespeare; *The Merchant of Venice*, 1600

.41 Speak low, if you speak love.
—William Shakespeare; *Much Ado About Nothing*, 1600

## 160

.42 Love's best habit is a soothing tongue.
—William Shakespeare; *The Passionate Pilgrim*, 1599

.43 When my love swears that she is made of truth,
I do believe her, though I know she lies.
—William Shakespeare; *Sonnets*, 1609

.44 They love indeed who quake to say they love.
—Philip Sidney; *Astrophel and Stella*, 1591

.45 Who are wise in love, Love most, say least.
—Alfred, Lord Tennyson; "Merlin and Vivien," 1832

.46 Jove laughs at lovers' perjuries, and bids the winds carry them away without fulfillment.
—Tibullus; *Elegies*, 19. B.C.

.47 Love is a talkative passion.
—Thomas Wilson; *Sacra Privata*, c. 1755

.48 Why is it that the most unoriginal thing we can say to one another is still the thing we long to hear? "I love you" is always a quotation.
—Jeanette Winterson; *Written on the Body*, 1992

## 161 Madness

.1 There is in every madman a misunderstood genius whose idea, shining in his head, frightened people, and for whom delirium was the only solution to the strangulation that life had prepared for him.
—Antonin Artaud; *Van Gogh, The Man Suicided by Society*, 1947

.2 When confronting madness it is best to hold one's peace.
—James Baldwin; *Nobody Knows My Name*, 1961

.3 We are all born mad. Some remain so.
—Samuel Beckett; *Waiting for Godot*, 1952

.4 Every man is mad once or twice in his life.
—Charlotte Bronte; *Shirley*, 1849

.5 Men are mad most of their lives; few live sane, fewer die so.... The acts of people are baffling unless we realize that their wits are disordered. Man is driven to justice by his lunacy.
—Edward Dahlberg; *The Carnal Myth*, 1976

.6 Whom the gods wish to destroy, they first make mad.
—Euripides; *Fragments*, c. 5th century B.C.

## 161

.7 It is his reasonable conversation which mostly frightens us in a madman.
—Anatole France (Jacques-Anatole-Francois Thibaut); *Historie contemporaine*, 1897–1901

.8 There is a supreme lucidity, which is the precisely calculated awareness which is called madness.
—Martha Graham; *The Notebooks of Martha Graham*, 1973

.9 Insanity is often the logic of an accurate mind overtasked.
—Oliver Wendell Holmes, Sr.; *The Autocrat of the Breakfast Table*, 1858

.10 All power of fancy over reason is a degree of insanity.
—Samuel Johnson; *Rasselas*, 1759

.11 Did the hospital specialize in poets and singers, or was it that poets and singers specialized in madness? ... What is it about meter and cadence and rhythm that makes their makers mad?
—Susanna Kaysen; *Girl, Interrupted*, 1993

.12 If only no one had told them I was mad. Then I wouldn't be.
—Kate Millett; *The Looney-Bin Trip*, 1990

.13 The usefulness of madmen is famous: they demonstrate society's logic flagrantly carried out down to its last scrimshaw scrap.
—Cynthia Ozick; "The Hole/Birth Catalog" published in *The First Ms. Reader*, Francine Klagsbrun, ed., 1972

.14 I am but mad north-north-west: when the wind is southly I know a hawk from a handsaw.
—William Shakespeare; *Hamlet*, 1600–1

.15 We must remember that every 'mental' symptom is a veiled cry of anguish. Against what? Against oppression, or what the patient experiences as oppression. The oppressed speak a million tongues.
—Thomas Szasz; *The Second Sin*, 1973

.16 You're only given a little spark of madness. You mustn't lose it.
—Robin Williams; quoted in *Funny Business*, David Housham and John Frank-Keyes, 1992

## 162 Magic

.1 Magicians can do more by means of faith than physicians by the truth.
—Giordano Bruno; *Degli Eroici Furori*, 1585

## 162

.2 The magic of the tongue is the most dangerous of all spells.
—Edward George Bulwer-Lytton; *Eugene Aram*, 1832

.3 Words and magic were in the beginning one and the same thing, and even today words contain much of their magical power.
—Sigmund Freud; *A General Introduction to Psychoanalysis* (twenty-eight lectures), 1916–17

.4 The masterless man, ... afflicted with the magic of the necessary words.... Words that may become alive and walk up and down in the hearts of the hearers.
—Rudyard Kipling; Speech, February 14, 1923

.5 Words divested of their magic are but dead hieroglyphs.
—Henry Miller; *The Books in My Life*, 1951

.6 Love passed, the muse appeared, the weather of mind got clearly newfound; now free, I once more weave together emotion, thought, and magic sound.
—Alexander Pushkin; *Eugene Onegin*, 1823

.7 It seems like whenever stories and storytellers are together; there's a little magic ... a little magic that happens.
—Jay Stailey; *The National Association for the Preservation and Perpetuation of Story-Telling Board Retreat*, 1993

.8 Magic is the craft of shaping, the craft of the wise, exhilarating, dangerous—the ultimate adventure. The power of magic should not be underestimated. It works, often in ways that are unexpected and difficult to control.
—Starhawk; *The Spiral Dance*, 1979

.9 Know ye a man who can tell me tales of the deeds of magicians? Then the royal son Khafra stood forth and said, "I will tell thy Majesty a tale of the days of thy forefather, Nebka..."
—Westcar Papyrus; c. 2000–1300 B.C.

## 163 Man and Men

.1 The life of every man is a diary in which he means to write one story, and writes another; and his humblest hour is when he compares the volume as it is with what he vowed to make it.
—James M. Barrie; *The Little Minister*, 1891

.2 By God, if women had but written stories, As have these clerks within their oratories,

## 163

They would have written of men more wickedness
Than all the race of Adam could redress.
—Geoffrey Chaucer; *The Canterbury Tales*, c. 1387

.3 Man has been defined as a talking animal.
—M.D. Conway; *The Earthward Pilgrimage*, 1870

.4 A man said to the universe:
"Sir, I exist!"
"However," replied the universe,
"The fact has not created in me
A sense of obligation."
—Stephen Crane; "War Is Kind," 1899

.5 I decline to accept the end of men ... I believe that man will not merely endure: he will prevail. He is immortal not because he alone among creatures has an inexhaustible voice but because he has a soul, a spirit capable of compassion and sacrifice and endurance.
—William Faulkner; Nobel Prize Acceptance Speech, December 10, 1950

.6 Neanderthal man listened to stories, if one may judge by the shape of his skull.
—E.M. Forster; *Aspects of the Novel*, "The Story," 1927

.7 Man is a make-believe animal—he is never so truly himself as when he is acting a part.
—William Hazlitt; *Notes on a Journey Through France and Italy*, 1826

.8 And first the golden race of speaking men
Were by the dwellers in Olympus made;
They under Cronos lived, when he was king
In heaven. Like gods were they, with careless mind,
From toil and sorrow free, and nought they knew
Of dread old age.
—Hesiod; *Works and Days*, c. 8th century B.C.

.9 Language most shows a man: Speak, that I may see thee.
—Samuel Johnson; Boswell's *Life of Johnson*, 1791

.10 [Man] is the only one in whom the instinct of life falters long enough to enable it to ask the question "Why?"
—Joseph Wood Krutch; *The Modern Temper*, "The Genesis of a Mood," 1928

.11 Man is a fallen god who remembers the heavens.
—Alphonse de Lamartine; *Meditations*, 1820

.12 God made man merely to hear some praise
Of what He'd done on those Five Days.
—Christopher Morley; *Fons et Origo*, 1922

## 163

.13 And God said, Let us make man in our image, after our likeness; and let them have dominion over the fish of the sea, and over the fowl of the air, and over the cattle, and over all the earth, and over every creeping thing that creepeth upon the earth.
—Old Testament: Genesis

.14 I wish I loved the Human Race;
I wish I loved its silly face;
I wish I liked the way it walks;
I wish I liked the way it talks;
And when I'm introduced to one
I wish I thought what jolly fun!
—Walter Raleigh the Younger; "Impromptu," 1914

.15 "When you say Man," said Oedipus, "you include women too. Everyone knows that." She said, "That's what you think."
—Muriel Rukeyser; *Breaking Open*, "Myth," 1973

.16 What a piece of work is a man! How noble in reason! how infinite in faculty! in form and moving how express and admirable! in action how like an angel! in apprehension how like a god! the beauty of the world! the paragon of animals! And yet, to me, what is this quintessence of dust? man delights not me—no, nor women neither.
—William Shakespeare; *Hamlet*, 1600–1

.17 I like a man who talks me to death, provided he is amusing; it saves so much trouble.
—Mary Shelley; Letter, 1840

.18 The fish in the water is silent, the animal on the earth is noisy, the bird in the air is singing. But Man has in him the silence of the sea, the noise of the earth and the music of the air.
—Rabindranath Tagore; *Stray Birds*, 1916

.19 The whole world loved man when he smiled. The world became afraid of him when he laughed.
—Rabindranth Tagore; *Stray Birds*, 1916

.20 We must cherish our old men. We must revere their wisdom, appreciate their insight, love the humanity of their words.
—Alice Walker; *In Search of Our Mothers' Gardens*, 1983

## 164 Marriage

.1 A woman seldom asks advice before she has bought her wedding clothes.
—Joseph Addison; *The Spectator*, September, 1712

## 164

.2 It is better to marry a quiet fool than a witty scold.
—Anonymous; *Politeuphuia*, 1669

.3 It is easier to be a lover than a husband for the simple reason that it is more difficult to be witty every day than to say pretty things from time to time.
—Honore de Balzac; *La Physiologie du mariage*, 1826

.4 Courtship to marriage, as a very witty prologue to a very dull play.
—William Congreve; *The Old Bachelor*, 1693

.5 The particular charm of marriage is the duologue, the permanent conversation between two people who talk over everything and everyone till death breaks the record. It is this back-chat which, in the long run makes a reciprocal equality more intoxicating than any form of servitude or domination.
—Cyril Connolly; *The Unquiet Grave*, 1944

.6 Misses! the tale that I relate
This lesson seems to carry—
Choose not alone a proper mate,
But proper time to marry.
—William Cowper; *Pairing Time Anticipated: Moral*, c. 1780s

.7 Novels often end in marriage, yet real life frequently begins there.
—Frances Marion Crawford; *A Rose of Yesterday*, 1897

.8 I have tried both marriage and single life, and I cannot recommend either.
—John W. De Forest; *Miss Ravenel's Conversion from Secession to Loyalty*, 1867

.9 Marriage is to courtship as humming is to singing.
—Peter De Vries; *Consenting Adults*, 1980

.10 Married life requires shared mystery even when all the facts are known.
—Richard Ford; *The Sportswriter*, 1986

.11 Marriage, to him, was an institution for producing children and eliminating small talk.
—Helen Hudson; *Tell the Time to None*, 1966

.12 One can't explain one's marriage.
—Henry James; *The Portrait of a Lady*, 1881

.13 A poet may praise many he would be afraid to marry.
—Samuel Johnson; *Lives of the Poets*, "Waller," 1783

## 164

.14 Sometimes it was worth all the disadvantages of marriage just to have that: one friend in an indifferent world.
—Erica Jong; *Fear of Flying*, 1973

.15 It has been discovered experimentally that you can draw laughter from an audience anywhere in the world, of any class or race, simply by walking on the stage and uttering the words "I am a married man."
—Ted Kavanaugh; *News Review*, July 10, 1947

.16 A doleful music—an ancient tale of wrong—the Song of the Brides!
—George Alfred Lawrence; *Guy Livingstone*, 1857

.17 We might knit that knot with our tongues, that we shall never undo with our teeth.
—John Lyly; *Euphues*, 1579

.18 Comedies and romances always end with a marriage, because, after that, there is nothing to be said.
—Henry Mackenzie; *Julia De Roubigne*, 1777

.19 One of the best hearing aids a man can have is an attentive wife.
—Groucho Marx; *The Groucho Phile*, 1976

.20 When you speak of other people's marriage, you are, of course, saying something about your own.
—Carol Matthau; *Among the Porcupines*, 1992

.21 Always the same old story
Father Time and Mother Earth,
A marriage on the rocks.
—James Merrill; "The Broken Home," 1966

.22 Often the difference between a successful marriage and a mediocre one consists of leaving about three or four things a day unsaid.
—Harlan Miller; Attributed

.23 There are two kind of marriages—where the husband quotes the wife, or where the wife quotes the husband.
—Clifford Odets; *Rocket to the Moon*, 1938

.24 Quarrels are the dowry which married folk bring one another.
—Ovid; *The Art of Love*, c. A.D. 8

.25 Maybe being married is talking to oneself with one's other self listening.
—Ruth Rendell; *A Sleeping Life*, 1978

.26 A good marriage is that in which each appoints the other guardian of his solitude.
—Ranier Maria Rilke; *Letters*, 1892–1910

**164**

.27 Woe to the house where the hen crows and the rooster keeps still.
—Spanish Proverb

.28 Marriage is one long conversation, chequered by disputes.
—Robert Louis Stevenson; *Memories and Portraits*, "Talk and Talkers," 1882

.29 Venus, a beautiful, good-natured lady, was the goddess of love; Juno, a terrible shrew, the goddess of marriage: and they were always mortal enemies.
—Jonathan Swift; *Thoughts on Various Subjects*, 1711

.30 Marriage is the one subject on which all women agree and all men disagree.
—Oscar Wilde; *Lady Windemere's Fan*, 1892

# **165** Maxims

.1 It is with some an unalterable maxim, that the good-natured man must be a fool.
—Anonymous; *The Birmingham Counterfeit*, 1772

.2 The mind of man, when its daily maxims are put before it, revolts from anything so stupid, so mean, so poor.
—Walter Bagehot; *Literary Studies*, c. 1877

.3 A good maxim is never out of season.
—H.G. Bohn; *Handbook of Proverbs*, 1855

.4 The best maxim that ever came into the mind of man: *one thing at once*.
—Hugo Henry Brackenridge; *Modern Chivalry*, 1792–1815

.5 Let every man speak his maxim.
—Fanny Burney; *Cecilia*, 1782

.6 Most maxim-mongers have preferred the prettiness to the justness of a thought, and the turn to the truth.
—Lord Chesterfield; Letter to his son, January 15, 1753

.7 Mean narrow maxims which enslave mankind,
Ne'er from its bias warp thy settled mind.
—Charles Churchill; *The Prophecy of Famine*, c. 1764

.8 The maxim of the British people is "Business as usual."
—Winston Churchill; Speech at the Guildhall, November 9, 1914

**165**

.9 A man of maxims only is like a Cyclops with one eye, and that eye placed in the back of the head.
—Samuel Taylor Coleridge; *Table Talk*, June 24, 1827

.10 Jane borrow'd maxim from a doubting school,
And took for truth the test of ridicule;
Lucy saw no virtue in a jest,
Truth was with her of ridicule the test.
—George Crabbe; *Tales of the Hall*, 1819

.11 The gods respect and the demons adore the maxims of the sages.
—Justus Doolittle; *Chinese Proverbs*, 1872

.12 It is a good maxim to trust a person entirely or not at all; for a secret is often innocently blabbed by those who know but half of it.
—Henry Fielding; *Amelia*, 1751

.13 There are words and maxims whereby you may soothe the pain and cast much of the malady aside.
—Horace; *Epistles*, 20. B.C.

.14 A maxim is the exact and noble expression of an important and unquestionable truth.
—Joseph Joubert; *Pensees*, 1810

.15 There is ... only a single categorical imperative and it is this: Act only on that maxim through which you can at the same time will that it should become a universal law.
—Immanuel Kant; *Outline of the Metaphysics of Morals*, 1785

.16 I ought never to act in such a way that I can also will that my maxim should become a universal law.
—Immanuel Kant; *Outline of the Metaphysics of Morals*, 1785

.17 Nothing is so useless as a general maxim.
—Thomas Babington Macaulay; "Machiavelli," *Edinburgh Review*, March, 1827

.18 Maxims are the condensed good sense of nations.
—James Mackintosh; c. 1832, Quoted on the title page of Broom's *Legal Maxims*

.19 A new maxim is often a brilliant error.
—Chretien de Malesherbes; *Pensées et maximes*, mid–18th century

.20 A maxim is only a proverb in its caterpillar stage.
—D.E. Martin; *The Antiquity of Proverbs*, 1922

.21 That grounded maxim
So rife and celebrated in the mouths

## 165

Of wisest men; that to the public good
Private respects must yield.
—John Milton; *Samson Agonistes*, 1671

.22 All the good maxims already exist in the world; we just fail to apply them.
—Blaise Pascal; *Pensees*, 1670

.23 A maker of maxims is synonymous with a pessimist.
—Joseph Roux; *Meditations of a Parish Priest: Prelude*, c. 1870

.24 O, I see thee old and formal, fitted to thy petty part,
With a little hoard of maxims preaching down a daughter's heart.
—Alfred, Lord Tennyson; *Locksley Hall*, 1837–38

.25 If a mean person uses a wise maxim, I bethink me how it can be interpreted so as to commend itself to his meanness; but if a wise man makes a commonplace remark, I consider what wiser construction it will admit.
—Henry David Thoreau; *Walden*, 1854

.26 It is more trouble to make a maxim that it is to do right.
—Mark Twain; *Following the Equator*, "Pudd'nhead Wilson's New Calendar," 1897

.27 The maxims of men reveal their character. The Indian proverb says: "Speak that I may know you."
—Marquis de Vauvenargues; *Reflections and Maxims*, 1746

.28 Few maxims are true in every respect.
—Marquis de Vauvenargues; *Reflections and Maxims*, 1746

.29 'Tis my maxim, he's a fool that marries, but he's a greater fool that does not marry a fool.
—William Wycherley; *The Country Wife*, 1675

## 166 Meaning

.1 Storytelling reveals meaning without committing the error of defining it.
—Hannah Arendt; *Men in Dark Times*, 1959

.2 She understood as women often do more easily than men, that the declared meaning of a spoken sentence is only its overcoat, and the real meaning lies underneath its scarves and buttons.
—Peter Carey; *Oscar and Lucinda*, 1987

## 166

.3 "Then you should say what you mean. "The March Hare went on. "I do," Alice hastily replied; "at least—at least I mean what I say—that's the same thing, you know." "Not the same thing a bit!" said the Hatter. "Why you might as well say that 'I see what I eat' is the same thing as 'I eat what I see'!"
—Lewis Carroll; *Alice's Adventures in Wonderland*, 1865

.4 "The question is," said Alice, "whether you can make words mean so many different things." "The question is," said Humpty Dumpty, "which is to be master—that's all."
—Lewis Carroll; *Through the Looking Glass*, 1872

.5 Worthy audience, we pray you, take things as they are meant.
—Richard Edwards; *Damon and Pithias: Prologue*, 1571

.6 Poets in our civilization, as it exists at present, must be difficult.... The poet must become more and more comprehensive, more allusive, more indirect, in order to force, to dislocate if necessary, language into its meaning.
—T.S. Eliot; *The Metaphysical Poets*, 1921

.7 First learn the meaning of what you say, then speak.
—Epictetus; *Discourses*, Late 1st century A.D.

.8 If sentences have little meaning when they are writ, when they are spoken they have less.
—Henry Fielding; *Joseph Andrews*, 1742

.9 Meanings are discovered, not invented.
—Viktor Frankl; *The Will to Meaning*, 1969

.10 She says what she means, and means what she says.
—Erle Stanley Gardner; *The D.A. Cooks a Goose*, 1942

.11 The deeper the experience of an absence of meaning—in other words, of absurdity—the more energetically meaning is sought.
—Vaclav Havel; *Disturbing the Peace*, 1986

.12 Two meanings have our lightest fantasies,
One of the flesh, and of the spirit one.
—J.R. Lowell; *Sonnets*, 1844–48

.13 Meaning, subtle as odor.
—George Meredith; *The Adventures of Harry Richmond*, 1871

.14 Long-worded, long-winded, obscure, affirmatizing by negatives, confessing by implication!—Where's the beginning and end of you, and what's your meaning?
—George Meredith; *Vittoria*, 1867

# 166

.15 A story has to have muscle as well as meaning, and the meaning has to be in the muscle.
—Flannery O'Connor; in *The Habit of Being*, Sally Fitzgerald, ed., 1979

.16 The belief that words have a meaning of their own account is a relic of primitive word magic, and it is still a part of the air we breathe in nearly every discussion.
—C.K. Ogden and I.A. Richards; *The Meaning of Meaning*, 1923

.17 The same meaning changes with the words which express it. Meanings receive their dignity from words instead of giving it to them.
—Blaise Pascal; *Pensées*, c. 1670

.18 Social criticism begins with grammar and the re-establishing of meaning.
—Octavio Paz; *The Other Mexico: Critique of the Pyramid*, 1972

.19 Eternal truths will be neither true nor eternal unless they have fresh meaning for every new social situation.
—Franklin D. Roosevelt; Address at the University of Pennsylvania, September 20, 1940

.20 Learn, my son, to listen, not to the sounds of words that weave the wind, not to reasonings that throw dust in your eyes. Learn to look farther.
—Antoine de Saint-Exupery; *The Wisdom of the Sands*, 1950

.21 What is the short meaning of this long harangue?
—Johann von Schiller; *Die Piccolomini*, 1799

.22 I will tell you my drift.
—William Shakespeare; *Much Ado About Nothing*, 1598

.23 Mr. Hannaford's utterances have no meaning; he's satisfied if they sound clever.
—Alfred Sutro; *The Walls of Jericho*, early 20th century

.24 Where shall we seek for meaning?
In wisdom's court
Or in a life of sorrow?
—Sajida Zaidi; "New Angles," *Women Writing in India*, Susie Tharu and K. Lalita, eds.

# 167 Media

.1 What the mass media offer is not popular art, but entertainment which is intended to be

# 167

consumed like food, forgotten, and replaced by a new dish.
—W.H. Auden; *The Dyer's Hand*, "The Poet and the City," 1962

.2 The media transforms the great silence of things into its opposite. Formerly constituting a secret, the real now talks constantly. News reports, information, statistics, and surveys are everywhere.
—Michel de Certeau; *The Practice of Everyday Life*, 1974

.3 The United States is unusual among the industrial democracies in the rigidity of the system of ideological control—'indoctrination', we might say—exercised through the mass media.
—Noam Chomsky; *Language and Responsibility*, "Politics," 1979

.4 When distant and unfamiliar and complex things are communicated to great masses of people, the truth suffers a considerable and often a radical distortion. The complex is made over into the simple, the hypothetical into the dogmatic, and the relative into the absolute.
—Walter Lippmann; *The Public Philosophy*, 1955

.5 Can one really distinguish between the mass media as instruments of information and entertainment, and as agents of manipulation and indoctrination?
—Herbert Marcuse; "One Dimensional Man," 1968

.6 The medium is the message. This is merely to say that the personal and social consequences of any medium—that is, of any extension of ourselves—result from the new scale that is introduced into our affairs by each extension of ourselves, or by any new technology.
—Marshall McLuhan; *Understanding Media*, 1964

.7 The Medium is the Legend.
—Malcolm Muggeridge; *Esquire*, 1968

.8 We are given in our newspapers and on TV and radio exactly what we, the public, insist on having, and this very frequently is mediocre information and mediocre entertainment.
—Eleanor Roosevelt; *My Day*, 1959

.9 [The word] *media* is the plural of *mediocre*.
—Rene Saguisag; *New York Times*, January 22, 1987
[Saguisag's remark was prompted by the press coverage of Philippines President Corazon C. Aquino's administration.]

## 167 | Medicine

.10 The media. It sounds like a convention of spiritualism.
—Tom Stoppard; *Might and Day*, 1978

## 168 Medicine

.1 Medicine does not depend on the incantations of the sorcerer.
—African Proverb (Annang)

.2 Medication without explanation is obscene.
—Toni Cade Bambara; *The Sea Birds Are Still Alive*, "Christmas Eve at Johnson's Drugs N Goods," 1982

.3 When the patient is dead, it was the disease killed him, not the doctor. Dead men tell no tales.
—Hugo Henry Brackenridge; *Modern Chivalry*, 1792–1815

.4 Doctors are so opinionated, so immovable in their dry, materialistic view.
—Charlotte Bronte; *Villette*, 1853

.5 Stories are medicine.
—Clarissa Pinkola Estes; *Women Who Run with the Wolves*, 1992

.6 In medicine as in statecraft and propaganda, words are sometimes the most powerful drugs we can use.
—Sara Murray Jordan; *The New York Times*, 1959

.7 One of the most difficult things to contend with in a hospital is the assumption on the part of the staff that because you have lost your gall bladder you have also lost your mind.
—Jean Kerr; *Please Don't Eat the Daisies*, "Operation Operation," 1957

.8 To discuss medicine before the ignorant is of one piece with teaching the peacock to sing.
—Rudyard Kipling; *Kim*, 1900

.9 I can't stand the whispering. Every time a doctor whispers in the hospital, next day there's a funeral.
—Paul Simon; *The Gingerbread Lady*, 1970

.10 The art of medicine consists of amusing the patient while Nature cures the disease.
—Voltaire; Attributed

## 169 Memory

.1 How we remember, what we remember, and why we remember form the most personal map of out individuality.
—Christina Baldwin; *One to One*, 1977

.2 It's a poor sort of memory that only works backward.
—Lewis Carroll; *Through the Looking Glass*, 1872

.3 Memory is the thing you forget with.
—Alexander Chase; *Perspectives*, 1966

.4 A storyteller is a person who has a good memory and hopes other people haven't.
—Irvin S. Cobb; *Old Judge Priest*, 1915

.5 All stimulation generates a memory—and these memories have to go somewhere, Our bodies are essentially diskettes.
—Douglas Coupland; *Microserfs*, 1995

.6 Some call her Memory,
And some Tradition; and her voice is sweet,
With deep mysterious accords.
—George Eliot; *The Spanish Gypsy*, 1868

.7 Imagination and memory are but one thing which for divers considerations hath divers names.
—Thomas Hobbes; *Leviathan*, 1651

.8 Every man's memory is his private literature.
—Aldous Huxley; *Collected Essays*, 1959

.9 The true art of memory is the art of attention.
—Samuel Johnson; *The Idler*, 1758

.10 How is it that we remember the least triviality that happens to us, and yet not remember how often we have recounted it to the same person.
—François de La Rochefoucauld; *Maxims*, 1678

.11 The surest way not to be remembered is to talk about the way you want to be.
—Norman Mailer; Interview, *Playboy*, 1968

.12 The selective memory isn't selective enough.
—Blake Morrison; in the *Independent on Sunday*, London, June 16, 1991

.13 I hold it a noble task to rescue from oblivion those who deserve to be eternally remembered.
—Pliny the Younger; *Epistles*, early 2nd century

.14 For memories of days that nothing can recall,
To song or tears is dead and voiceless now.
—Alexander Pushkin; *Elegy*, 1826

## 169

.15 The Right Honorable gentleman is indebted to his memory for his jests and to his imagination for his facts.
—Richard B. Sheridan; Speech, House of Commons, in Moore *Memoirs of the Life of Sheridan*, 1825
[Sheridan replies to a Mr. Dundas.]

.16 Sometimes what we call "memory" and what we call "imagination" are not so easily distinguished.
—Leslie Marmon Silko; *Storyteller*, 1981

.17 Story-telling is subject to two unavoidable defects—frequent repetition and being soon exhausted; so that whoever values this gift in himself, has need of a good memory, and ought frequently to shift his company.
—Jonathan Swift; *Thoughts on Various Subjects*, 1911

.18 I would speak if only I had memories. Go on—don't tell me who I was like yesterday. I console myself with being mortal here; tomorrow very soon absence will come to my black brow.
—Tchigaya U Tam'si; "Headline to Summarize a Passion," *Epitome*, 1962

.19 Memory … is the diary that we all carry about with us.
—Oscar Wilde; *The Importance of Being Earnest*, 1895

## 170 Mermaids

.1 According to the constitution of mermaids, so much of a mermaid as is not a woman must be a fish.
—Charles Dickens; *Barnaby Rudge*, 1841

.2 Go, and catch a falling star,
Get with child a mandrake root,
Tell me, where all past years are,
Or who cleft the Devil's foot.
Teach me to hear mermaids singing.
—John Donne; Song "Go and Catch a Falling Star," c. 1610–11

.3 I have heard the mermaids singing, each to each/ I do not think that they will sing to me.
—T.S. Eliot; "The Love Song of J. Alfred Prufrock," 1917

.4 What a top is a lovely woman, ends below in a black and ugly fish.
—Horace; *Ars Poetica*, c. 19 B.C.

.5 O, train me not, sweet mermaid, with thy note.
—William Shakespeare; *The Comedy of Errors*, 1594

## 170

.6 Since once I sat upon a promontory,
And heard a mermaid on a dolphin's back
Uttering such dulcer and harmonious breath
That the rude sea grew civil at her song,
And certain stars shot madly from their spheres
To hear the sea-maid's music.
—William Shakespeare; *A Midsummer Night's Dream*, 1595

.7 As if some mermaid did their ears entice.
—William Shakespeare; *The Rape of Lucrece*, 1594

.8 Who would be a mermaid fair,
Singing alone, Combing her hair?
—Alfred, Lord Tennyson; "The Mermaid," 1830

.9 Slow sail'd the weary mariners and saw,
Betwixt the green brink and the running foam,
Sweet faces, rounded arms, and bosoms prest
To little harps of gold; and while they mused,
Whispering to each other half in fear
Shrill music wash'd them on the middle sea.
—Alfred, Lord Tennyson; "The Sea Fairies," 1832

## 171 Metaphor

.1 No metaphor should of necessity run like a coach on four wheels.
—Thomas Adams; *Sermons*, 1861

.2 The greatest thing in style is to have a command of metaphor.
—Aristotle; *Poetics*, c. 4th century B.C.

.3 The simile has been superseded by the metaphor and the metaphor is often reduced to the image or the symbol.
—Louise Bogan; "Reading Contemporary Poetry," *College English*, February, 1953

.4 I hate to hunt down a tired metaphor.
—Lord Byron; *Don Juan*, 1819–24

.5 Examine language; what, if you expect some few primitive elements (of natural sound), what is it all but Metaphors, recognized as such, or no longer recognized.
—Thomas Carlyle; *Sartor Resartus*, 1833–34

.6 The coldest word was once a glowing metaphor.
—Thomas Carlyle; *Past and Present*, 1843

.7 All slang is metaphor, and all metaphor is poetry.
—G.K. Chesterton; *The Defendant*, "A Defense of Slang," 1901

## 171

.8 When I can't talk sense, I talk metaphor.
—John Philpot Curran; in Moore *Life of Sheridan*, 1825

.9 Metaphors are much more tenacious than facts.
—Paul de Man; *Allegories of Reading*, 1979

.10 It is astonishing what a different result one gets by changing the metaphor!
—George Eliot; *The Mill on the Floss*, 1860

.11 Dead metaphors make strong idols.
—Marcia Falk; "Notes on Composing New Blessings" in Judith Plaskow and Carol P. Christ, eds. *Weaving the Visions*, 1989

.12 Nothing can make the metaphor that the stage is a picture of life more strong, than the observing every theatrical performance spoiled by the great desire each performer shows of playing the top part.
—Sarah Fielding; *The Adventures of David Simple*, 1744

.13 I love metaphor the way some people love junk food.
—William Gass; Interview in *Writers at Work*, 1981

.14 The golden light of metaphor, which is the intelligence of poetry, was implicit in alchemical study. To change, magically, one substance into another, more valuable one is the ancient function of metaphor, as it was of alchemy.
—Patricia Hampl; *A Romantic Education*, 1981

.15 Farewell sweet phrases, lovely metaphors.
—George Herbert; "The Forerunners," 1633

.16 Yesterday's daring metaphors are today's clichés.
—Arthur Koestler; *The Heel of Achilles*, 1974

.17 Metaphors are not to be trifled with. A single metaphor can give birth to love.
—Milan Kundrea; *The Unbearable Lightness of Being*, 1984

.18 The metaphor is far more intelligent than its author, and this is the case with many things. Everything has its depths. He who has eyes sees something in everything.
—Georg Christoph Lichtenberg; *Aphorisms*, 1764–99

.19 Most of our expressions are metaphorical— the philosophy of our forefathers lies hidden in them.
—Georg Christoph Lichtenberg; *Aphorisms*, 1764–99

## 171

.20 I love metaphor. It provides two loaves where there seems to be one. Sometimes it throws in a load of fish.
—Bernard Malamud; Interview in *Writers at Work*, 1984

.21 There's nothing like a metaphor for an evasion.
—George Meredith; *Beauchamp's Career*, 1876

.22 Metaphor is the energy charge that leaps between images, revealing their connections.
—Robin Morgan; *The Anatomy of Freedom*, 1982

.23 The metaphor is perhaps one of man's most fruitful potentialities. Its efficacy verges on magic, and it seems a tool for creation which God forgot inside one of His creatures when He made him.
—Jose Ortega y Gasset; *The Dehumanization of Art*, 1925

.24 A beau and wilting perish'd in the throng, One died in metaphor, and one in song.
—Alexander Pope; *The Rape of the Lock*, 1714

.25 Mr. Speaker, I smell a rat; I see him forming in the air and darkening the sky; but I'll nip him in the bud.
—Boyle Roche; Attributed
[A classic example of mixed metaphors.]

.26 The motive for metaphor, shrinking from
The weight of primary noon,
The ABC of being,
The ruddy temper, the hammer
Of red and blue, the hard sound—
Steel against intimation—the sharp flash,
The vital, arrogant, fatal, dominant X.
—Wallace Stevens; "The Motive for Metaphor," 1947

## 172 Mind

.1 Old minds are like horses; you must exercise them if you wish to keep them in working order.
—John Quincy Adams; *The Memoirs of John Quincy Adams*, 1874–77

.2 Great minds discuss ideas, average minds discuss events, small minds discuss people.
—Anonymous

.3 All I can say about my mind is that, like a fire carefully laid by a good housemaid, it is one that any match will light.
—Margot Asquith; *More or Less About Myself*, 1934

**172**

.4 Men converse by means of language, but words are formed at the will of the generality, and there arises from a bad and unapt formation of words a wonderful obstruction to the mind.
—Francis Bacon; *Advancement of Learning*, 1605

.5 I had rather believe all the fables in the Legend and the Alcoran, than that this universal frame is without a mind.
—Francis Bacon; *Essays*: "Of Atheism," 1625

.6 When I was a boy, they used to say that "only a mule and a milepost never changed its mind."
—Bernard M. Baruch; Meyer Berger, *New York*, 1960

.7 Wit is the lightning of the mind, reason the sunshine, and reflection the moonlight.
—Countess Blessington; *Desultory Thoughts and Reflections*, 1839

.8 The great secret of managing the mind of man is to find employment for it.
—Hugh Henry Brackenridge; *Modern Chivalry*, 1792–1815

.9 So I sat talking with my mind.
—Robert Browning; "Christmas Eve," c. 1860s

.10 I shook the sermon out of my mind.
—John Bunyan; *Grace Abounding*, 1666

.11 The voice of the intellect is a soft one, but it does not rest until it has gained a hearing.
—Sigmund Freud; *The Future of an Illusion*, 1928

.12 It is not enough for poems to be fine; they must charm, and draws the mind of the listener as well.
—Horace; *Ars Poetica*, c. 19 B.C.

.13 Do not say the first thing that comes to your mind.
—Ivory Coast Saying

.14 The perversion of the mind is only possible when those who should be heard in its defence are silent.
—Archibald MacLeish; *The Irresponsibles*, 1940

.15 When the mind is thinking, it is talking to itself.
—Plato; *Philebus*, c. 4th century B.C.

.16 There is nothing like desire for preventing the thing one says from bearing any resemblance to what one has in one's mind.
—Marcel Proust; *A la recherche du temps perdu, Le Cote de Guermantes*, 1921

**172**

.17 He seemed to have more in his head than could come out at his mouth.
—Samuel Richardson; *Clarissa Harlowe*, 1747–48

.18 Can the mind forget the history of its own life?
—Anthony Trollope; *He Knew He Was Right*, 1869

.19 There is nothing in the world like a persuasive speech to fuddle the mental apparatus.
—Mark Twain; Attributed

# **173** Minstrels

.1 I want to feel the surging
Of my sad people's soul
Hidden by a minstrel-smile.
—Gwendolyn A. Bennett; "Heritage," 1923

.2 No command of art,
    No toil can help you hear;
    Earth's minstrelsy falls clear
But on the listening heart.
—John Vance Cheney; "The Listening Heart," 1880

.3 Of myself I will say this much, that once I was minstrel of the Heodeningras, my master's favorite. My name was Deor. For many years I had a goodly office and a generous lord, till now Heorrenda, a skillful bard, has received the estate which the protector of warriors gave to me in days gone by.
—Deor, A.D. 35–41, Bruce Dickins, tr.

.4 A wandering minstrel I—
A thing of shreds and patches,
Of ballads, songs and snatches,
And dreamy lullaby!
—W.S. Gilbert; *The Mikado*, 1885

.5 When Pan sounds up his minstrelsy;
His minstrelsy! O base! This quill,
Which at my mouth with wind I fill,
Puts me in mind, though her I must
That still my Syrinx' lips I kiss.
—John Lyly; "Midas"

.6 The swan murmurs sweet strains, with failing tongue, itself the minstrel of its own death.
—Martial; *Epigrams*, c. 1st century A.D.

.7 Negro minstrels are apt to overdo the ebony; exemplifying the old saying, not more just than charitable, that "the devil is never so black as he is painted."
—Herman Melville; *The Confidence-Man*, 1857

## 173

.8 The Minstrel Boy to the war is gone,
In the ranks of death you'll find him;
His father's sword he has girded on,
And his wild harp slung behind him.
—Thomas Moore; *Irish Melodies*, "The
Minstrel Boy," 1807

.9 The minstrel, by whatever name he or she was
known, did continue to narrate stories in verse,
chant, or song, as one of a number of enter-
tainments. Other skills they displayed included juggling, tumbling, and acrobatics, and
short dramatic skits.
—Anne Pellowski; *The World of Storytelling*, 1977

.10 Sing, minstrel, sing us now a tender song
Of meeting and parting, with the moon in
it.
—Stephen Phillips; *Ulysses*, 1902

.11 The way was long, the wind was cold,
The Minstrel was infirm and old;
His wither'd cheek, and tresses gray,
Seemed to have known a better day...
—Sir Walter Scott; *The Lay of the Last
Minstrel*, 1805

.12 Ring out the want, the care, the sin,
The faithless coldness of the times;
Ring out, ring out my mournful rhymes,
But ring the fuller minstrel in.
—Alfred, Lord Tennyson; *In Memoriam
A.H.H.*, 1850

.13 Knight-errant of the Never-ending Quest,
And minstrel of the Unfulfilled Desire;
For ever tuning thy frail earthly lyre
To some unearthly music.
—Henry Van Dyke; "Shelley," late 19th
century

.14 Ethereal minstrel! pilgrim of the sky!
In mid whirl of the dance of Time ye start,
Start at the cold touch of Eternity,
And cast your cloaks about you, and depart:
The minstrels pause not in their minstrelsy.
—William Watson; *Epigrams*, c. 1602

.15 Dost thou despise the earth where cares
abound?
Or, while the wings aspire, are heart and eye
Both with thy nest upon the dewy ground?
Thy nest which thou canst drop into at will,
Those quivering wings composed, that music
still!
—William Wordsworth; "To a Skylark,"
1827

## 174 Miracles

.1 As far the narrations touching the prodigies
and miracles of religions, they are either not
true, or not natural; and therefore impertinent
for the story of nature.
—Francis Bacon; *Essays*, 1625

.2 The church speaks of miracles because it
speaks of God. Of eternity in time, of life in
death, of love in hate, or forgiveness in sin, or
salvation in suffering, or hope in despair.
—Dietrich Bonhoeffer; *No Rusty Swords*,
1965

.3 The most serious doubt that has been thrown
on the authenticity of the miracles is the fact
that most of the witnesses in regard to them
were fishermen.
—Arthur Brinstead; Attributed

.4 There is in every miracle a silent chiding of the
world, and a tacit reprehension of them who
require, or need miracles.
—John Donne; *Sermons*, 1627

.5 Miracles exist as ancient history merely; they
are not in the belief, nor in the aspiration of
society.
—Ralph Waldo Emerson; *Nature, Addresses, and Lectures*, 1844

.6 Such is the progress of credulity, that miracles,
most doubtful on the spot and at the moment,
will be received with implicit faith at a convenient distance of time and space.
—Edward Gibbon; *The Decline and Fall of
the Roman Empire*, 1766–88

.7 A miracle: an event described by those to
whom it was told by men who did not see it.
—Elbert Hubbard; *Epigrams*, 1895

.8 Miracles are the children of mendacity.
—R.G. Ingersoll; Speech, New York, April
25, 1881

.9 Miracles seem impossible, just because they
break the laws of Nature. There seems something blasphemous in supposing that God can
mar His own order.
—Charles Kingsley; *Alton Locke*, 1850

.10 For those who believe in God no explanation
is needed; for those who do not believe in
God, no explanation is possible. [Of the cures
at Lourdes]
—Father John Lafarge; Quoted in Franz
Werfel's *The Song of Bernadette*, 1942

.11 A miracle entails a degree of irrationality—
not only because it shocks reason, but because
it makes no appeal to it.
—Emmanuel Levinas; "Ethics and Spirit,"
1952, reprinted in *Difficult Freedom*, 1990

**174**

.12 A miracle cannot prove what is impossible; it is useful only to confirm what is possible.
  —Moses Maimonides; *Guide of the Perplexed*, 1190

.13 Is to dispute well, logic's chiefest end? Affords this art no greater miracle?
  —Christopher Marlowe; *Doctor Faustus*, c. 1592

.14 Every miracle can be explained after the event. Not because the miracle is no miracle, but because explanation is explanation.
  —Franz Rosenzweig; *Judah ha-Levi*, 1927

.15 Men talk about Bible miracles because there is no miracle in their lives. Cease to gnaw the crust. There is ripe fruit over your head.
  —Henry David Thoreau; *Journal*, June, 1850

# 175 Monologues

.1 A monologue is not a decision.
  —Clement Attlee; in Francis Williams, *A Prime Minister Remembers*, 1961

.2 Life is a drama, not a monologue.
  —Edward George Bulwer-Lytton; *The Caxtons*, 1849

.3 Most conversations are simply monologues delivered in the presence of a witness.
  —Margaret Millar; *The Weak-Eyed Bat*, 1942

.4 There is no such thing as conversation. It is an illusion. There are interesting monologues, that is all.
  —Rebecca West; *There Is No Conversation*, 1935

# 176 Moral

.1 People want to be amused, not preached at, you know. Morals don't sell nowadays.
  —Louisa May Alcott; *Little Women*, 1868

.2 There is no moral truth, the weight of which can be felt without experience.
  —Hugh Henry Brackenridge; *Modern Chivalry*, 1792–1815

.3 Though sages may pour out their wisdom's treasure,
There is no sterner moralist than Pleasure.
  —Lord Byron; *Don Juan*, 1819–24

**176**

.4 Everything's got a moral, if you can only find it.
  —Lewis Carroll; *Alice's Adventures in Wonderland*, 1865

.5 For though myself be a full vicious man,
A moral tale yet I you telle can.
  —Geoffrey Chaucer; *The Canterbury Tales*, 1387

.6 He cursed the canting moralist,
Who measures right and wrong.
  —John Davidson; "A Ballad of a Poet Born," 1894

.7 Too many moralists begin with a dislike of reality.
  —Clarence Day; *This Simian World*, 1920

.8 There's a moral in everything.
  —Charles Dickens; *Dombey and Son*, 1848

.9 Whate'er the story be, the moral's true.
  —John Dryden; *University of Oxford*, "Prologue," 1673

.10 And many a holy text around she strews
That teach the rustic moralist to die.
  —Thomas Gray; *Elegy Written in a Country Churchyard*, 1751

.11 I like a story with a bad moral … all true stories have a coarse touch or a bad moral, depend upon it. If the storytellers could ha' got decency and good morals from true stories, who'd have troubled to invent parables?
  —Thomas Hardy; *Under the Greenwood Tree*, 1872

.12 A story with a moral appended is like the bill of a mosquito. It bores you, and then injects a stinging drop to irritate your conscience.
  —O. Henry; *Strictly Business*, "The Gold That Glittered," 1910

.13 And now, dear little children, who may this story read,
To idle, silly, flattering words, I pray you ne'er give heed:
Upon an evil counselor close heart, and ear, and eye,
And take a lesson from the tale of the Spider and the Fly.
  —Mary Howitt; "The Spider and the Fly," 1834

.14 His fall was destined to a barren strand,
A petty fortress, and a dubious hand;
He left the name, at which the world grew pale,
To point a moral, or adorn a tale.
  —Samuel Johnson; *The Vanity of Human Wishes*, 1748

## 176

.15 To denounce moralizing out of hand is to pronounce a moral judgment.
—H.L. Mencken; *Prejudices*, 1924

.16 I moralize two meanings in one word.
—William Shakespeare; *Richard III*, 1597

.17 Come, you are too severe a moraler.
—William Shakespeare; *Othello*, 1604

.18 And is there any moral shut
Within the bosom of the rose?
—Alfred, Lord Tennyson; *The Day-Dream*, "Moral," 1835

.19 Persons attempting to find a motive in this narrative will be persecuted; persons attempting to find a moral in it will be banished; persons attempting to find a plot in it will be shot.
—Mark Twain; *The Adventures of Huckleberry Finn*, "Introduction," 1884

.20 A man who moralizes is usually a hypocrite, and a woman who moralizes is invariably plain.
—Oscar Wilde; *Lady Windemere's Fan*, 1892

.21 Moral truth, resting entirely upon the ascertained consequences of actions, supposes a process of observation and reading.
—Frances Wright; *A Few Days in Athens*, 1822

## 177 Morality

.1 All the rules of morality are but maxims of prudence.
—Hugh Henry Brackenridge; *Modern Chivalry*, 1792–1815

.2 Morality was held a standing jest,
And faith a necessary fraud at best.
—Charles Churchill; *Gotham*, 1764

.3 Morality, said Jesus, is kindness to the weak; morality, said Nietzsche, is the bravery of the strong; morality, said Plato, is the effective harmony of the whole. Probably all three doctrines must be combined to find a perfect ethic; but can we doubt which of the elements is fundamental?
—Will Durant; *The Story of Philosophy*, 1926

.4 Men talk of "mere Morality," which is much as if one should say "Poor God, with nobody to help Him."
—Ralph Waldo Emerson; *Conduct of Life*, "Worship," 1860

## 177

.5 Morality comes with the sad wisdom of age, when the sense of curiosity has withered.
—Graham Greene; *A Sort of Life*, 1971

.6 Moralizing and morals are two different things and are always found in entirely different people.
—Don Herold; *Strange Bedfellows*, 1930

.7 Veracity is the heart of morality.
—Thomas Henry Huxley; *Universities Actual and Ideal*, 1893–94

.8 Teachers of mortality discourse like angels, but they live like men.
—Samuel Johnson; *Rasselas*, 1759

.9 I find the doctors and the sages
Have differ'd in all climes and ages,
And two in fifty scarce agree
Of what is pure morality.
—Thomas Moore; "Morality," 1813

.10 Morality, like language, is an invented structure for conserving and communicating order.
—Jane Rule; *Lesbian Images*, 1975

.11 We have, in fact, two kinds of morality side by side; one which we preach but do not practice, and another which we practice but seldom preach.
—Bertrand Russell; *Skeptical Essays*, "Eastern and Western Ideals of Happiness," 1928

.12 Without doubt the greatest injury of all was done by basing morals on myth. For, sooner or later, myth is recognized for what it is, and disappears. Then morality loses the foundation on which it has been built.
—Lord Samuel; Romances Lecture, 1947

.13 Every fool believes what his teachers tell him, and calls his credulity science or morality as his father called it divine revelation.
—George Bernard Shaw; *Maxims for Revolutionists*, 1903

## 178 Mothers

.1 What the mother sings to the cradle goes all the way to the coffin.
—Henry Ward Beecher; *Proverbs from Plymouth Pulpit*, "Human Life," 1887

.2 I learned your walk, talk, gestures and nurturing laughter. At that time, Mama, had you swung from bars, I would, to this day, be hopelessly, imitatively, hung up.
—S Diane Bogus, "Mom de Plume," 1977, in *Double Switch*, Patricia Bell-Scott, et al., eds., 1991

**178**

.3 The lullaby is the spell whereby the mother attempts to transform herself back from an ogre to a saint.
—James Fenton; "Ars Poetica," *Independent on Sunday*, March 11, 1990

.4 When the strongest words of what I have to offer come out of me sounding like words I remember from my mother's mouth, then I either have to reassess the meaning of everything I have to say now, or re-examine the worth of her old words.
—Audre Lorde; *Zami: A New Spelling of My Name*, 1982

.5 The best academe, a mother's knee.
—James Russell Lowell; *The Cathedral*, 1870

.6 Treetalk and windsong are
the language of my mother
her music does not leave me.
—Barbara Mahone; *Sugarfield*, title poem, 1970

.7 I am all the time telling about you, and bragging to one person or another. I am like the Ancient Mariner, who had a tale in his heart he must unfold to all. I am always button-holing somebody and saying, "Someday you must meet my mother." And then I am off. And nothing stops me till the waiter closes up the cafe. I do love you so much, my mother.... If I didn't keep calling you mother, anybody reading this would think I was writing to my sweetheart. And he would be quite right.
—Edna St. Vincent Millay; *Letters of Edna St. Vincent Millay*, Allan Ross, ed., 1952

.8 Hindered characters
seldom have mothers
in Irish stories, but they all have grandmothers.
—Marianne Moore; *What Are Years?*, "Spenser's Ireland," 1941

.9 Where are those songs
my mother and yours
always sang
fitting rhythms
to the whole
vast span of life?
—Micere Githae Mugo; *Daughter of My People, Sing*, "Where Are Those Songs?," 1976

.10 My mother is a woman who speaks with her life as much as with her tongue.
—Kesaya E. Noda; "Growing Up Asian in America," in Asian Women United in California, ed. *Making Waves*, 1989

**178**

.11 Most mothers are instinctive philosophers.
—Harriet Beecher Stowe; *The Writings of Harriet Beecher Stowe*, 1896

.12 Who ran to help me when I fell,
And would some pretty story tell,
Or kiss the place to make it well?
My Mother.
—Ann Taylor; "My Mother," 1804
[Charles Dickens quoted these lines in *The Old Curiosity Shop*, 1841. It has been estimated as the best-known English poem.]

.13 Mother is the name for God in the lips and hearts of little children.
—William Makepeace Thackeray; *Vanity Fair*, 1847–48

.14 No song or story will bear my mother's name. Yet, so many of the stories I write, that we all write, are my mother's stories. Only recently did I fully realize this, that through years of listening to my mother's stories of her life, I have absorbed not only the stories themselves, but something of the manner in which she spoke, something of the urging that involves the knowledge that her stories—like her life—must be recorded.
—Alice Walker; *In Search of Our Mother's Gardens*, title essay, 1974

# 179 Mouth

.1 Keep watch over thy mouth, lest it be thy destruction.
—Ahikar; *Teachings*, c. 550 B.C.

.2 I don't let my mouth say nothing my head can't stand.
—Louis Armstrong; *Life Magazine*, April 15, 1956

.3 Now hold your mouth.
—Geoffrey Chaucer; *Sir Thopas*, c. 1386

.4 The mouth utters lilies.
—Justus Doolittle; *Chinese Vocabulary*, 1872
[That is, excellent discourse. On the other hand "to make mouth-flowers" means to utter mere words.]

.5 Lo, I am silent and curb my mouth.
—Euripides; *Andromache*, c. 430 B.C.

.6 When you speak to a man, look on his eyes; when he speaks to you, look on his mouth.
—Benjamin Franklin; *Poor Richard's Almanack*, 1732–57

## 179

.7  He has a mouth for every matter.
—Thomas Fuller II; *Gnomologia*, 1732

.8  The wise hand doth not all that the foolish mouth speaks.
—George Herbert; *Jacula Prudentum*, 1640

.9  Take some care of what goes into the mouth, but much more of what comes out of it.
—T.E. Hulme; *Proverb Love*, 1902

.10  Just because my mouth opens up like a prayer book it does not have to flap like a Bible.
—Zora Neale Hurston; *Dust Tracks on a Road*, 1942

.11  A lying mouth is a stinking pit.
—Ben Jonson; *Explorata: Veritas Proprium Hominis*, 1616

.12  You never open your mouth, but you put your foot in it.
—P.W. Joyce: *English as We Speak It*, 1910

.13  Keep your trap shut for a minute.
—Bayard Kendrick; *The Odor of Violets*, 1941

.14  There you go, shooting off your mouth.
—N.P. Langford; *Vigilante Days and Ways*, 1890

.15         From whose mouth issu'd forth Mellifluous streams that water'd all the schools
Of Academics old and new.
—John Milton; *Lycidas*, 1638

.16  The words of his mouth were smoother than butter, but war was in his heart: his words were softer than oil, yet were they drawn swords.
—Old Testament: Psalms

.17  Keep your mouth shut and your eyes open.
—Samuel Palmer; *Moral Essays on Proverbs*, 1710

.18  For God's sake, shut your bazoo.
—Westbrook Pegler; *Fair Enough*, March 31, 1941

.19  A wise head hath a close mouth to it.
—John Ray; *English Proverbs*, 1678

.20  That which goes out of your mouth enters other people's ears.
—William Scarborough; *Chinese Proverbs*, 1875

.21  Had I such a mouth as Hydra, such an answer would stop them all.
—William Shakespeare; *Othello*, 1604

.22  All is lost that goes beside your mouth.
—Jonathan Swift; *Polite Conversation*, 1738

## 180  Movies

.1  People have been modeling their lives after films for years, but the medium is somehow unsuited to moral lessons, cautionary tales, or polemics of any kind.
—Renata Adler; *A Year in the Dark*, 1969

.2  My movie is born first in my head, dies on paper; is resuscitated by the living persons and real objects I use, which are killed on film but, placed in a certain order and projected on to a screen, come to life again like flowers in water.
—Robert Bresson; *Times*, London, November 1, 1990

.3  There are no rules in filmmaking. Only sins. And the cardinal sin is dullness.
—Frank Capra; Quoted in *People*, February 9, 1987

.4  Motion pictures need sound as much as Beethoven symphonies need lyrics.
—Charles Chaplin; Quoted in Lois and Alan Gordon *American Chronicle*, 1987

.5  Movies suddenly become "film" and "cinema," an "art form" and terribly chic.... Film criticism becomes the means whereby a stream of young intellectuals could go straight from the campus film society into the professionals' screening room without managing to get a glimpse of the real world in between.
—Judith Crist; *The Private Eye, the Cowboy and the Very Naked Girl*, 1968

.6  Any movie that makes you a little uncomfortable is good news to me, because it means you're experiencing things that you are not familiar with.
—Brian DePalma, interview, *Sight and Sound*, December, 1992

.7  It struck me that the movies had spent more than half a century saying, "They lived happily ever after" and the following quarter-century warning that they'll be lucky to make it through the weekend. Possibly now we are now entering a third era in which the movies will be sounding a note of cautious optimism. You know it just might work.
—Nora Ephron; Quoted in *Los Angeles Times*, July 27, 1989

.8  Ninety percent of the moving pictures exhibited in America are so vulgar, witless and dull that it is preposterous to write about them in any publication not intended to be read while chewing gum.
—Wolcott Gibbs; *Esquire*, 1968

.9  Black and white are the most ravishing colors of all in film.
—Penelope Gilliat; *Three-Quarter Faces*, 1980

# 180

.10 All you need for a movie is a gun and a girl.
—Jean Luc Godard; quoted in *Projections*, John Boorman and Walter Donohue, eds., 1992

.11 Pictures are for entertainment, messages should be delivered by Western Union.
—Sam Goldwyn; Arthur Marx, *Goldwyn*, 1976

.12 We don't need books to make films. It's the last thing we want—it turns cinema into the bastard art of illustration.
—Peter Greenaway; Quoted in the *Independent on Sunday*, July 10, 1994

.13 I discovered early in my movie work that a movie is never any better than the stupidest man connected with it. There are times when this distinction may be given to the writer or director. Most often it belongs to the producer.
—Ben Hecht; *A Child of the Century*, 1954

.14 Good movies make you care, make you believe in possibilities again.
—Pauline Kael; *Going Steady*, 1968

.15 The words "Kiss Kiss Bang Bang" which I saw on an Italian movie poster, are perhaps the briefest statement imaginable of the basic appeal of movies. This appeal is what attracts us, and ultimately what makes us despair when we begin to understand how seldom movies are more than this.
—Pauline Kael; *Kiss Kiss Bang Bang*, "A Note on the Title," 1968

.16 All my movies are about strange worlds that you can't go into unless you build them and film them. That's what's so important about film to me. I just like going into strange worlds.
—David Lynch; interview, *Premiere*, September, 1990

.17 Adding sound to movies would be like putting lipstick on the Venus de Milo.
—Mary Pickford; recalled on her death, May 29, 1979

.18 Other than life experience, nothing left a deeper imprint on my formative self than the movies.
—Letty Cottin Pogrebin; *Deborah, Golda, and Me*, 1991

.19 It isn't what the movies put in that makes them so wonderful—it's what they leave out.
—Ernie Pyle; Quoted in Richard Dyer MacCann *Film and Society*, 1964

# 180

.20 There's only one thing that can kill the movies, and that's education.
—Will Rogers; *The Autobiography of Will Rogers*, 1949

.21 Movies have always been a form of popular culture that altered the way women looked at the world and reflected how men intended to keep it.
—Marjorie Rosen; *Popcorn Venus*, 1973

.22 The motion picture is the people's Art.
—Adela Rogers St. Johns; *Love, Laughter, and Tears*, 1978

.23 Movies are about people who do things. The number one fantasy of the cinema is that we can do something—we are relatively impotent in our lives so we go to movies to watch people who are in control of their lives.
—Paul Schrader; interview, *Schrader on Schrader*, Kevin Jackson, ed., 1990

.24 In this business we make movies. American movies. Leave the films to the French.
—Sam Shepard; *True West*, 1980

.25 Movies have mirrored our moods and myths since the century began. They have taken on some of the work of religion.
—Jennifer Stone; *Mind Over Media*, "Epilogue," 1988

.26 The motion picture presents our customs and our daily life more distinctly than any other medium and therefore, if we were to come back a thousand years from today and tried to find some form of expression that would more clearly, more perfectly explain how we live today, it would have to be the motion picture, because there is no medium of today that so universally must please as great a number of people....
—Irving Thalberg; in Richard Dyer MacCann *Film and Society*, 1964

.27 Movies are, like sharp sunlight, merciless; we do not imagine, we view.
—John Updike; *Odd Jobs*, "Being on TV-II," 1991

.28 Nobody should come to the movies unless he believes in heroes.
—John Wayne; quoted in *The Official John Wayne Reference Book* by Charles John Kieskalt, 1993

# 181 Music

.1 He knew music was Good, but it didn't sound right.
—George Ade; *Fables in Slang*, 1900

.2 A tale out of season is as music in mourning.
—American Proverb

.3 For music any words are good enough.
—Aristophanes; *Birds*, 1846

.4 What I like about music is its ability to be convincing, to carry an argument through successfully to the finish, though the terms of the argument remain unknown quantities.
—John Ashbery; Quoted in *New York Times Magazine*, May 23, 1976

.5 A verbal art like poetry is reflective; it stops to think. Music is immediate, it goes on to become.
—W.H. Auden; *The Dyer's Hand*, "Notes on Music and Opera," 1962

.6 Modern music, a language a thousand times richer than the language of words, is to speech what thought is to utterance; it arouses sensations and ideas in their primitive form, in that part of us where sensations and ideas have their birth, but leaves them as they are in each of us. That power over our inmost being is one of the grandest facts in music.
—Honore de Balzac; *Massimmilla Doni*, 1839

.7 Music … can name the unnameable and communicate the unknowable.
—Leonard Bernstein; *The Unanswered Question*, 1976

.8 Chamber music—a conversation between friends.
—Catherine Drinker Bowen; in *The Music Lover's Book*, Kathleen Kimball, Robin Petersen and Kathleen Johnson, eds., 1990

.9 Music is well said to be the speech of angels: in fact, nothing among the utterances allowed to man is felt to be so divine. It brings us near the infinite.
—Thomas Carlyle; *The Opera*, 1832

.10 Words are wearisome and worn, while the arabesques of music are forever new.
—Colette; *My Apprenticeship*, 1936

.11 If the music doesn't say it, how can the words say it for the music?
—John Coltrane; Quoted in *Jazz* by Nat Hentoff, 1976

.12 It is only that which cannot be expressed otherwise that is worth expressing in music.
—Frederick Delius; *At the Crossroads*, September, 1920

.13 Music is the eye of the ear.
—Thomas Draxe; *Bibliotheca*, 1616

.14 Music is the only language in which you cannot say a mean or sarcastic thing.
—John Erskine; Quoted in *Reader's Digest*, April, 1934

.15 Music is nothing but wild sounds civilized into time and tune.
—Thomas Fuller I; *Worthies of England*, 1662

.16 Music is the most disagreeable and the most widely beloved of all noises.
—Theophile Gautier; *Le Figaro*, October 20, 1863

.17 The other arts persuade us, but music takes us by surprise.
—Eduard Hanslick; *The Beautiful in Music*, 1854

.18 Where words leave off, music begins.
—Heinrich Heine; Quoted by Peter Ilyich Tchaikovsky in a letter to Nadezhda Filaaretovna von Meck, March 1, 1878

.19 People always sound so proud when they announce they know nothing of music.
—Lillian Hellman; *Another Part of the Forest*, 1947

.20 Music is meaningless noise unless it touches a receiving mind.
—Paul Hindemith; *A Composer's World*, 1961

.22 Music expresses that which cannot be said and on which it is impossible to be silent.
—Victor Hugo; *Les Rayons et les ombres*, 1840

.23 After silence that which comes nearest to expressing the inexpressible is music.
—Aldous Huxley; "Music at Night," 1931

.24 Of all the noises, I think music the least disagreeable.
—Samuel Johnson; *Morning Chronicle*, August 16, 1816

.25 Music is our myth of the inner life.
—Susanne K. Langer; *Philosophy in a New Key*, 1942

.26 Music is Love in search of a word.
—Sidney Lanier; *The Symphony*, 1875

.27 Music is not a species of language, but language is a species of music.
—Sidney Lanier; *The Science of English Verse*, 1880

**181**

.28 Music ... is a language, but a language of the intangible, a kind of soul-language.
—Edward MacDowell; *Critical and Historical Essays*, 1912

.29 Music is the art of expressing sensations by modulated sounds.
—C.F. Michaelis; *Uber den Geist der Tonkunst*, 1800

.30 Music relates sound and time and so pictures the ultimate edges of human communications.
—Iris Murdoch; *The Black Prince*, 1973

.31 Wagner's music is better than it sounds.
—Bill Nye; Attributed

.32 Pour not out words where there is a musician.
—Old Testament; Apocrypha, Ecclesiasticus

.33 [Music]: The only universal tongue.
—Samuel Rogers; *Italy: Bergamo*, 1822–28

.34 If music could be translated into human speech, it would no longer need to exist.
—Ned Rorem; *Music from Inside Out*, 1967

.35 Music is a kind of harmonious language.
—Gioacchino Rossini; Quoted by Antonio Zanolini in *Biografia di Gioacchino Rossini*, 1875

.36 Music is "Ordered Sound."
—Harold Samuel; *The Mystery of Music*, 1977

.37 Here will we sit and let the sounds of music Creep into our ears.
—William Shakespeare; *The Merchant of Venice*, 1600

.38 Music is the effort we make to explain to ourselves how our brains work. We listen to Bach transfixed because this is listening to a human mind.
—Lewis Thomas; *The Medusa and the Snail*, "On Thinking About Thinking," 1979

.39 Music is the crystallization of sound.
—Henry David Thoreau; *Journal*, February 5, 1841

.40 Pop music is collective music; it is as archaic as tribal music without the innocence of tribal music, and as impregnated with warning and somnambulism as Wagner at his worst.
—Laurens van der Post; *A Walk with a White Bushman*, 1986

.41 The language of tones belongs equally to all mankind, and melody is the absolute language in which the musician speaks to every heart.
—Richard Wagner; *Beethoven*, 1870

**181**

.42 Where the speech of man stops short, then the art of music begins.
—Richard Wagner; *A Happy Evening*, 1840

.43 If verbal language and its development has to be considered one of the most admirable achievements of the human spirit, then we must admire, in the creation of musical language, a prodigious feat of the human soul...
—Bruno Walter; *Of Music and Music-Making*, 1957

.44 Good music is wine turned to sound.
—Ella Wheeler Wilcox; *Poems of Progress*, "The Choosing of Esther," 1909

# 182 Mystery

.1 But now the mystic tale that pleas'd of yore Can charm an understanding age no more.
—Joseph Addison; *The Spectator*, 1712

.2 What is the modern detective story but an extension of the medieval morality play?
—Catherine Aird; "The Devout Benefit of Clergy," in Dilys Winn, *Murder Ink*, 1977

.3 I talk like a Sphinx.
—Charlotte Bronte; *Jane Eyre*, 1847

.4 To know, to get into the truth of anything, is ever a mystic act, of which the best logics can but babble on the surface.
—Thomas Carlyle; *On Heroes, Hero-Worship and the Heroic in History*, 1841

.5 Silence hovers over all the mountain peaks. The world is aflame with grandeur. Each flower is an outpouring of love. Each being speaks for itself. Man alone can speak to all beings. Human living alone enacts the mystery as a drama.
—Abraham Joshua Heschel; *Who Is Man?*, 1965

.6 Listen to the voices in the upper air, Nor lose thy simple faith in mysteries.
—Henry Wadsworth Longfellow; "The Castle-Builder," 1845

.7 Seek not to mystify the mystery.
—Herman Melville; *Pierre*, 1852

.8 We spend our lives talking about this mystery: our life.
—Jules Renard; *Journal*, April 1984, tr. Elizabeth Roget

### 182

.9   Plain truth will influence half a score of men at most in a nation, or an age, while mystery will lead millions by the nose.
—Henry St. John; Letter, July 28, 1721

.10  You can tear a poem apart to see what makes it technically tick…. You're back with the mystery of having been moved by words. The best craftsmanship always leaves holes and gaps in the works of the poem so that something that is not in the poem can creep, crawl, flash, or thunder in.
—Dylan Thomas; *Dylan Thomas's Poetic Manifesto*, in the Texas Quarterly, Winter, 1961

.11  A mystery is good for nothing if it remains always a mystery.
—Anthony Trollope; *Phineas Finn*, 1869

.12  Some mystery should be left in the revelation of character in a play, just as a great deal of mystery is always left in the revelation of character in life, even in one's own character to himself.
—Tennessee Williams; Stage Directions for *Cat on a Hot Tin Roof*, 1955

.13  Visionary power
Attends the motions of the viewless winds,
Embodied in the mystery of words.
—William Wordsworth; *The Prelude*, 1799–1805

### 183  Myth

.1   Myth is neither a lie nor a confession: it is an inflexion.
—Roland Barthes; *Mythologies*, 1957

.2   A myth contains the story that is preserved in popular memory and that helps bring to life some deep stratum buried in the depths of the human spirit.
—Nicholas Berdyaev; *New Middle Ages*, 1924

.3   A myth is far truer than a history, for a history only gives a story of the shadows, whereas a myth gives a story of the substances that cast the shadows.
—Annie Besant; *Esoteric Christianity*, 1901

.4   For in the beginning of literature is myth, and in the end as well.
—Jules Luis Borges; *Labyrinths*, "Parable of Don Quixote," 1962

.5   The Jew of antiquity cannot tell a story in any other way than mythically, for to him an event

### 183

is worth telling only when it has been grasped in its divine significance.
—Martin Buber; *On Judaism*, 1967

.6   Myth is the hidden part of every story, the buried part, the region that is still unexplored because there are as yet no words to enable us to get there…. Myth is nourished by silence as well as by words.
—Italo Calvino; Lecture "Cybernetics and Ghosts," 1969

.7   Myths, so to say, are public dreams: dreams are private myths.
—Joseph Campbell; *Myths to Live By*, 1990

.8   Myths are clues to the spiritual potentialities of the human life.
—Joseph Campbell; *The Power of Myth*, 1988

.9   Myths deal in false universals, to dull the pain of particular circumstances.
—Angela Olive Carter; *The Sadeian Woman*, "Polemical Preface," 1979

.10  A myth is a fixed way of looking at the world which cannot be destroyed because, looked at through the myth, all evidence supports that myth.
—Edward de Bono; *PO, Beyond Yes and No*, 1977

.11  Every myth, whatever its nature, recounts an event that took place *in illo tempore*, and constitutes as a result, a precedent and pattern for all the actions and 'situations' later to repeat that event. Every ritual, and every meaningful act that man performs, repeats a mythical archetype.
—Mircea Eliade; *Myth and Reality*, 1963

.12  It were better to follow the myths about the gods than to become a slave to the Destiny of the natural philosophers; for the former suggests a hope of placating the gods by worship, whereas the latter involves a necessity which knows no placation.
—Epicurus; *Aphorisms*, c. 34th century B.C.

.13  The tricky or boastful gods of ancient myths and primitive folk tales are characters of the same kind that turn up in Faulkner or Tennessee Williams.
—Northrop Frye; *The Educated Imagination*, 1964

.14  Nothing is more difficult that competing with a myth.
—Francoise Giroud; *I Give You My Word*, 1974

# 183

.15 The art of mythmaking has been transferred from the subject-matter of the work to the artist himself as the content of his art.
  —Richard Hamilton; "For the Finest Art Try—POP," *Gazette*, No. 1, 1961

.16 If the creation story, the virgin birth, and the resurrection are only myths, then I'm myth-taken and myth-tified and myth-erable.
  —Vance Havner; *Pepper 'n' Salt*, 1966

.17 Myths there must be, since visions of the future must be clothed in imagery. But there are myths which displace truth and there are myths which give wings to truth.
  —William Ernest Hocking; *The Meaning of Immortality in Human Experience*, 1957

.18 There is nothing truer than myth: history, in its attempt to "realize" myth distorts it, stops halfway; when history claims to have "succeeded," this is nothing but humbug and mystification. Everything we dream is "realizable." Reality does not have to be: it is simply what it is.
  —Eugene Ionesco; "Experience of the Theatre," *Nouvelle N.R.F.*, No. 62, 1958

.19 Myths are early science, the result of men's first. The bearers of the myth of every decade seem to carry in their hands the axe and the spade to execute and inter the myth of the previous one.
  —Murray Kempton; Column, *New York Post*, 1965

.20 With reference both to the 'first things' and to the 'last things', therefore, we cannot dispense with *demythologizing, not to eliminate but to interpret.*
  —Hans Kung; *The Church*, 1967

.21 When the genuine myth rises into consciousness, that is always its message. You must change your life.
  —Ursula K. Le Guin; "Myth and Archetype in Science Fiction," 1976, *Language of the Night*, 1979

.22 When myth meets myth, the collision is very real.
  —Stanislaw Lec; *Unkempt Thoughts*, 1962

.23 I therefore claim to show, not how men think in myths, but how myths operate in men's minds without their being aware of the fact.
  —Claude Levi-Strauss; *The Raw and the Cooked*, "Overture," 1964

# 183

.24 It is a sure sign that a culture has reached a dead end when it is no longer intrigued by its myths.
  —Greil Marcus; *Mystery Train*, "Elvis: Presliad," 1976

.25 When a myth becomes a daydream it is judged, found wanting, and must be discarded. To cling to it when it has lost its creative function is to condemn oneself to mental illness. I do not say we must learn to live without myths … but we must at least get along without evasions. A daydream is an evasion.
  —Thomas Merton; *Conjectures of a Guilty Bystander*, 1966

.26 History is the myth, the true myth, of man's fall made manifest in time.
  —Henry Miller; *Plexus*, 1949

.27 A myth is whatever concept or truth or reality a whole people have arrived at over years of observation. It cannot be manufactured by a handful of people. It must be the collective creation of—and acceptance by—hordes of anonymous people.
  —Toni Morrison; "Behind the Making of the Black Door," *Black World*, February 19, 1974

.28 A myth always rises to fill a need.
  —Gloria Naylor; "The Myth of the Matriarch," *Life*, Spring, 1988

.29 The primary function of myth is to validate an existing social order. Myth enshrines conservative social values, raising tradition on a pedestal. It expresses and confirms, rather than explains or questions the sources of cultural attitudes and values.... Because myth anchors the present in the past it is a sociological charter for a future society which is an exact replica of the present one.
  —Ann Oakley; *Woman's Work: The Housewife, Past and Present*, 1974

.30 Contemporary man has rationalized the myths, but he has not been able to destroy them.
  —Octavio Paz; *The Labyrinth of Solitude*, Appendix," 1950

.31 Science must begin with myths, and with the criticism of myths.
  —Sir Karl Popper; "Philosophy of Science: A Personal Report," in *British Philosophy in the Mid-Century*, ed. C.A. Mace, 1957

.32 One of the great inventions of the twentieth century was the studied, methodical engineering of myth for political ends.
  —Caryl Rivers; "Mythogony" in *Quill*, 1985

## 183

.33 Myths galvanize people and direct their form of culture, They are the fullness and depth of the people. Myths are the projections of their learned fears, anxieties, frustrations, hopes, and the deepest unconscious contradictions of a civilization.
—Pat Robinson, Interview, c. 1988

.34 Myths make history. The mythic symbol taps unconscious reservoirs of energy in all of us, winning our assent and motivating action by its imaginative power. Perhaps nothing has more to do with determining what we will decide to regard as truth than the force of an empowered symbol superbly projected upon the cultural stage.
—Theodore Roszak; *Where the Wasteland Ends*, 1972

.35 A myth is, of course, not a fairy tale. It is the presentation of facts belonging to one category in the idioms appropriate to another. To explode a myth is accordingly not to deny the facts but to re-allocate them.
—Gilbert Ryle; *The Concept of Mind*, "Introduction," 1949

.36 There's myth in the sense of a lie. There's myth in the sense of fantasy. There's myth in all those senses. But the traditional meaning of myth is that it served a purpose in our life. The purpose had to do with being able to trace ourselves back through time and follow our emotional self…. And that's been destroyed. Myth in its truest form has been demolished…. All we have is fantasies about it.
—Sam Shepard; Interview, 1990

.37 The test of a true myth is that each time you return to it, new insights and interpretations arise.
—Starhawk; *The Spiral Dance*, 1989

.38 There was a muddy centre before we breathed
There was a myth before the myth began,
Venerable and articulate and complete.
—Wallace Stevens; *Notes Toward a Supreme Fiction*, "It Must Be Abstract," 1942

.39 Myths reveal their content to other levels of awareness than merely logical or reasoning mental processes; in some cases they leap beyond these processes to convey truth.
—R.J. Stewart; *The Elements of Creation Myth*, 1989

.40 Myths and the characters whose stories they are, live in the quiet of mountains and valleys, forests and meadows, rocks and springs, until someone comes along and thinks to tell them. They have other hiding places too, inside the

## 183

language we use every day, in the names of the places where they happened, or in the names of trees or days on the calendar.
—Dennis Tedlock; *Breath on the Mirror: Mythic Voices and Visions of the Living Maya*, 1993

.41 Freud becomes one of the dramatis personae, in fact, as discoverer of the great and beautiful modern myth of psychoanalysis. By myth, I mean a poetic, dramatic expression of a hidden truth; and in placing this emphasis, I do not intend to put into question the scientific validity of psychoanalysis.
—D.M. Thomas; *The White Hotel*, author's note, 1981

.42 Myths and legends die hard in America. We love them for the extra dimension they provide, the illusion of near-infinite possibility to erase the narrow confines of most men's reality. Weird heroes and mould-breaking champions exist as living proof to those who need it that the tyranny of "the rat race" is not yet final.
—Hunter S. Thompson; "Those Daring Young Men in Their Flying Machines," *Pageant*, 1969

.43 Myths hook and bind the mind because at the same time they set the mind free; they explain the universe while allowing the universe to go on being unexplained.
—Jeanette Winterson; *Boating for Beginners*, 1985

.44 A glorious place, a glorious age, I tell you! A very Neon Renaissance—And the myths that actually touched you at that time—not Hercules, Orpheus, Ulysses and Aeneas—but Superman, Captain Marvel, Batman.
—Tom Wolfe; *The Electric Kool-Aid Acid Test*, 1968

# 184 Mythology

.1 Mythology is the body of primitive people's beliefs concerning its origins, early history, heroes, deities … as distinguished from the true accounts which it invents later.
—Ambrose Bierce; *The Devil's Dictionary*, 1906

.2 Mythology is the mother of religions, and grandmother of history.
—Zsuzsanna E. Budapest; "Herstory" in *Sister*, 1974

.3 Mythology is the use of imagery to express the otherworldly in terms of this world, and the

**184**

divine in terms of human life, the other side in terms of this side.
—Rudolf Bultmann; *The World and Beyond*, 1960

.4 Mythology is the womb of mankind's initiation to life and death.
—Joseph Campbell; *The Power of Myth*, 1988

.5 Only the fortunate can take life without mythology.
—Will and Ariel Durant; *The Age of Reason Begins*, 1961

.6 Mythology is nothing other than psychological processes projected into the outer world.
—Sigmund Freud; "Philosophy of Life," 1932

.7 Literature is conscious mythology: as society develops, its mythical stories become structural principles of story-telling, its mythical concepts, sun-gods and the like, become habits of metaphoric thought. In a fully mature literary tradition the writer enters into a structure of traditional stories and images.
—Northrop Frye; *The Bush Garden*, "Conclusion," 1971

.8 Neither the violence of Antiochus, nor the arts of Herod, nor the example of the circumjacent nations, could ever persuade the Jews to associate with the institutions of Moses the elegant mythology of the Greeks.
—Edward Gibbon; *The Decline and Fall of the Roman Empire*, 1776–88

.9 The Gospels were … written for people thinking mythologically at a time of mythological thinking.
—Hans Kung; *On Being a Christian*, 1976

.10 Mythology is much better stuff than history. It has form; logic; a message.
—Penelope Lively; *Moon Tiger*, 1987

.11 No more masks! No more mythologies!
—Muriel Rukeyser; *The Speed of Darkness*, "The Poem as Mask," 1968

.12 Children are natural mythologists: they beg to be told tales, and love not only to invent but to enact falsehoods.
—George Santayana; *Dialogues in Limbo*, 1925

.13 What counted was the mythology of self, Blotched out beyond unblotching.
—Wallace Stevens; *Harmonium*, "The Comedian as the Letter C," 1923

**184**

.14 One may as well preach a respectable mythology as anything else.
—Mary Agusta Ward; *Robert Elsmer*, 1888

.15 Mythology is what grown-ups believe, folklore is what they tell children, and religion is both.
—Cedric Whitman; Letter to Edward Tripp, February 28, 1969

.16 I made my song a coat
Covered with embroideries
Out of old mythologies
From heel to throat.
—William Butler Yeats; "A Coat," *Collected in Responsibilities*, 1914

# **185** Name

.1 For my name and memory, I leave it to men's charitable speeches, and to foreign nations, and the next ages.
—Francis Bacon; From his Will, 1626

.2 He said true things but called them by wrong names.
—Robert Browning; "Bishop Blougram's Apology," c. 1875

.3 The glory and the nothing of a name.
—Lord Byron; "Churchill's Grave," c. 1813

.4 Must a name mean something?
—Lewis Carroll; *Through the Looking Glass*, 1872

.5 The beginning of wisdom is to call things by their right names.
—Chinese Proverb

.6 Listen how they say your name. If they can't say that right, there's no way they're going to know how to treat you proper, either.
—Rita Dove; *Through the Ivory Gate*, 1992

.7 Of all eloquence a nickname is the most concise; of all arguments the most unanswerable.
—William Hazlitt; *Essays*, "On Nicknames," published 1839

.8 He left the name at which the world grew pale,
To point a moral, or adorn a tale.
—Samuel Johnson; *Vanity of Human Wishes*, 1748

.9 We don't know when our name came into being or how some distant an ancestor acquired it. We don't understand our name at all, we don't know its history and yet we bear it with exalted fidelity, we merge with it, we

**185**

like it, we are ridiculously proud of it as we had thought it up ourselves in a moment of brilliant inspiration.
—Milan Kundera; *Immortality*, 1991

.10 Sleep on, O brave-hearted, O wise man that kindled the flame—
To live in mankind is far more than to live in a name.
—Vachel Lindsay; *The Eagle That Is Forgotten*, 1913

.11 I pray you
you (if any open this writing)
Make in your mouths the words that were our names.
—Archibald MacLeish; "Epistle to Be Left in the Earth," *Chief Modern Poets of Britain and America*, 1970

.12 The name that dwells on every tongue,
No minstrel needs.
—Don Jose Manrique; "Coplas de Manrique," 1476, Henry Wadsworth Longfellow, tr., 1833.

.13 Sticks and stones may break my bones, but names will never hurt me.
—Margaret Millar; *Wall of Eyes*, 1943

.14 From antiquity, people have recognized the connection between naming and power.
—Casey Miller and Kate Swift; *Words and Women*, 1976

.15 Names, once they are in common use, quickly become mere sounds, their etymology being buried, like so many of the earth's marvels, beneath the dust of habit.
—Salman Rushdie; *The Satanic Verses*, "Ayesha," 1988

.16 What's in a name? that which we call a rose
By any other name would smell as sweet.
—William Shakespeare; *Romeo and Juliet*, 1595

.17 What we name must answer to us; we can shape it if not control it.
—Starhawk; *Dreaming in the Dark*, 1982

.18 We have lost the faculty of giving lovely names to things. Names are everything.
—Oscar Wilde; *The Picture of Dorian Gray*, 1891

# **186** Narration

.1  We construct a narrative for ourselves, and that's the thread we follow from one day to the

**186**

next. People who disintegrate as personalities are the ones who lose that thread.
—Paul Auster; *Sunday Times*, April 16, 1989

.2  The eagerness of a listener quickens the tongue of a narrator.
—Charlotte Bronte; *Jane Eyre*, 1847

.3  The narrative impulse is always with us; we couldn't imagine ourselves through a day without it.
—Robert Lowell Coover; *Time*, May 7, 1986

.4  There is no longer any such thing as fiction or nonfiction; there's only narrative.
—E.L. Doctorow; *New York Times Book Review*, January 27, 1988

.5  Honest John [Bunyan] was the first that I know of who mixed narration and dialogue; a method of writing very engaging to the reader.
—Benjamin Franklin; *Autobiography*, 1868

.6  Merely corroborative detail, intended to give artistic verisimilitude to a bald and unconvincing narrative.
—W.S. Gilbert; *The Mikado*, 1885

.7  Chiefs who no more in bloody fights engage,
But, wise thro' time, and narrative with age,
In summer-days like grasshoppers rejoice,
A bloodless race, that send a feeble voice.
—Homer; *Iliad*, c. 700 B.C.

.8  The history of mankind is little else than a narrative of designs which have failed, and hopes that have been disappointed.
—Samuel Johnson; *Works*, A.T. Hazen and J.H. Middendorf, eds., published in 1960s

.9  We breathe, we think, we conceive of our lives as narratives.
—Christopher Charles Herbert Lehmann-Haupt; On Peter Brooks, "Reading for Plot," 1984, *New York Times*,, May 29, 1989

.10 Never think that any narrative, which is not confuted by its own absurdity, is without one argument at least on its side.
—Charlotte Lennox; *The Female Quixote*, 1752

.11 Let us not forget the condition of life as narration: that we can never see the whole picture at once—unless we propose to throw overboard all the God-conditioned forms of human knowledge.
—Thomas Mann; *The Magic Mountain*, 1924

**186**

.12 The symmetry of form attainable in pure fiction cannot so readily be achieved in a narration essentially having less to do with fable than with fact. Truth uncompromisingly told will always have its ragged edges; hence the conclusion of such a narration is apt to be less finished than an architectural finial.
—Herman Melville; *The Works*, 1922–24

.13 The pleasant narrator in the first person is the happy bubbling fool, not the philosopher who has come to know himself and his relations toward the universe. The words of this last are one to twenty; his mind is bent upon the causes of events rather than their progress.
—George Meredith; *The Adventures of Harry Richmond*, 1871

.14 Suspense is the soul of narrative.
—Charles Reade; *The Cloister and the Hearth*, 1861

.15 Most people who have the narrative gift—that great and rare endowment—have with it the defect of telling their choice things over the same way every time, and this injures them and causes them to sound stale and wearisome after several repetitions.
—Mark Twain; *Joan of Arc*, 1896

.16 At present, nothing is talked of, nothing admired, but what I cannot help calling a very insipid and tedious performance: it is a kind of novel, called *The Life and Opinions of Tristram Shandy*; the great humor of which consists in the whole narration always going backward.
—Horace Walpole; Letter to Sir David Dalrymple, 1760

# **187** Nature

.1  About nature consult nature herself.
—Francis Bacon; *De Augmentis Scientiarum*, 1605

.2  We cannot command Nature except by obeying her.
—Francis Bacon; *Novum Organum*, 1605

.3  Nature ever has a voice.
—Emerson Bennett; *The Prairie Flower*, 1849

.4  The universal mother, Nature.
—Charlotte Bronte; *Jane Eyre*, 1847

.5  To him who in the love of Nature holds Communion with her visible forms, she speaks A various language.
—William Cullen Bryant; *Thanatopsis*, 1811

**187**

.6  The book of nature is a catechism. But, after it answers the first question with "God," nothing but questions follow.
—George Washington Cable; *Madame Delphine*, 1881

.7  The only words that ever satisfied me as describing Nature are the terms used in fairy books, "charm," "spell," "enchantment." They express the arbitrariness of the fact and its mystery.
—G.K. Chesterton' *Orthodoxy*, "The Logic of Elfland," 1908

.8  He conceived Nature to be a woman with a deep aversion to tragedy.
—Stephen Crane; *The Red Badge of Courage*, 1895

.9  Nature will tell you a direct lie if she can.
—Charles Robert Darwin; *The Origin of Species by Means of Natural Selection*, 1859

.10 Nature's silence is its one remark, and every flake of world is a chip off that old immutable block.
—Annie Dillard; *Teaching a Stone to Talk*, 1982

.11 Nature has a language of her own, which she uses with strict veracity.
—George Eliot; *Adam Bede*, 1859

.12 Nature tells every secret once.
—Ralph Waldo Emerson; *Nature*, 1836

.13 The language of nature is the universal language.
—Christoph Gluck; "Haweis," *Music and Morals*, 1967

.14 Never does Nature say one thing and Wisdom another.
—Juvenal; *Satires*, c. 100

.15 Education altereth nature.
—John Lyly; *Euphues: The Anatomy of Wit*, 1579

.16 Speak to the earth, and it shall teach thee.
—Old Testament: Job

.17 Those honor Nature well, who teach that she can speak on everything, even on theology.
—Blaise Pascal; *Pensees*, 1670

.18 Nature is the common, universal language, understood by all.
—Kathleen Raine; *Selected Poems*, 1988

.19 Whether man is disposed to yield to nature or to oppose her, he cannot do without a correct understanding of her language.
—Jean Rostand; *Thoughts of a Biologist*, 1939

## 187

.20 Nature speaks in symbols and in signs.
—John Greenleaf Whittier; "To Charles Summer," c. 1863

.21 Though all the bards of earth were dead,
And all their music passed away,
What Nature wishes should be said
She'll find the rightful voice to say.
—William Winter; "The Golden Silence," 1891

# 188 News

.1 It is an ill office to be the first to herald ill.
—Aeschylus; *Persians*, 472 B.C.

.2 News, news, news, my gossiping friends, I have wonderful news to tell.
—Edward George Bulwer-Lytton; "News," 1855

.3 It is an old saying that Ill News hath wings and Good News no legs.
—Margaret Cavendish; *Sociable Companions*, c. 1660

.4 Tydings make either glad or sad.
—John Clarke; *Paroemiologia*, 1670

.5 News is the first rough draft of history.
—Philip L. Graham; attributed
[The aphorism has also been attributed to Ben C. Bradlee.]

.6 Good news may be told at any time, but ill in the morning.
—George Herbert; *Jacula Prudentum*, 1640

.7 And that's the news from Lake Wobegon, where all the women are strong, all the men are good-looking, and all the children are above average.
—Garrison Keillor; Tag line on his radio show "A Prairie Home Companion" 1974–87 and in the 1990s.

.8 When distant and unfamiliar and complex things are communicated to great masses of people, the truth suffers a considerable and often a radical distortion. The complex is made over into the simple, the hypothetical into the dogmatic, and the relative into an absolute.
—Walter Lippmann; *The Public Philosophy*, 1955

.9 For evil news rides post, while good news baits.
—John Milton; *Samson Agonistes*, 1671

.10 How beautiful upon the mountains are the feet of him that bringeth good tidings.
—Old Testament: Isaiah

## 188

.11 My ears await your tidings.
—Plautus; *Asinaria*, c. 200 B.C.

.12 The conflict between the men who make and the men who report the news is as old as time. News may be true, but it is not truth, and reporters and officials seldom see it the same way…. In the old days, the reporters or couriers of bad news were often put to the gallows; now they are given the Pulitzer Prize; but the conflict goes on.
—James Reston; *The Artillery of the Press*, "The Tug of History," 1966

.13 The nature of bad news infects the teller.
—William Shakespeare; *Antony and Cleopatra*, 1606

.14 Yet the first bringer of unwelcome news
Hath but a losing office, and his tongue
Sounds ever after as a sullen bell,
Remembered knolling a departed friend.
—William Shakespeare; *II Henry IV*, 1598

.15 The messenger of good news is always an object of benevolence.
—Sydney Smith; *Sketches of Moral Philosophy*, 1849

.16 Nobody likes the bringer of bad news.
—Sophocles; *Antigone*, c. 440 B.C.

.17 It takes your enemy and your friend, working together, to hurt you to the heart; the one to slander you and the other to get the news to you.
—Mark Twain; *Following the Equator*, "Pudd'nhead Wilson's New Calendar," 1897

# 189 Noise

.1 For twenty-five centuries, Western knowledge has tried to look upon the world. It has failed to understand that the world is not for the beholding. It is for hearing. It is not legible, but audible. Our science has always desired to monitor, measure, abstract and castrate meaning, forgetting that life is full of noise and that death alone is silent: work noise, noise of man, and noise of beast. Noise bought, sold, or prohibited. Nothing essential happens in the absence of noise.
—Jacques Attali; *The Political Economy of Music*, 1977

.2 A good man makes no noise over a good deed, but passes on to another as a vine to bear grapes again in season.
—Marcus Aurelius; *Meditations*, c. 2nd century A.D.

## 189

.3  Everybody has their taste in noises as well as in other matters.
    —Jane Austen; *Persuasion*, 1815

.4  I have felt and hoped to have led other people to feel that the sounds of their environment constitute a music which is more interesting than the music which they would hear if they went into a concert hall.
    —John Cage; Interview, *Soho Weekly News*, September 12, 1974

.5  The world is never quiet, even its silence eternally resounds with the same notes, in vibrations which escape our ears. As for those that we perceive, they carry sounds to us, occasionally a chord, never a melody.
    —Albert Camus; *The Rebel*, 1951

.6  A noise like of a hidden brook
    In the leafy month of June,
    That to the sleeping woods all night
    Singeth a quiet tune.
    —Samuel Taylor Coleridge; *The Rime of the Ancient Mariner*, 1789

.7  A noisy man is always in the right.
    —William Cowper; *Poems*, "Conversation," 1782

.8  For children is there any happiness which is not also noise?
    —Frederick W. Faber; *Spiritual Conferences*, 1858

.9  He who sleeps in continual noise is wakened by silence.
    —William Dean Howells; Attributed

.10 Noise has one advantage. It drowns out words.
    —Milan Kundera; *The Unbearable Lightness of Being*, 1984

.11 The trumpet does not more stun you by its loudness, than a whisper teases you by its provoking inaudibility.
    —Charles Lamb; *Essays of Elia*, 1823

.12 And learn, my sons, the wondrous power of Noise,
    To move, to raise, to ravish ev'ry heart.
    —Alexander Pope; *The Dunciad*, 1743

.13 It is with narrow-souled people as with narrow-necked bottles; the less they have in them the more noise they make in pouring out.
    —Alexander Pope; *Miscellanies*, 1727

.14 Noise is the most impertinent of all forms of interruption.
    —Arthur Schopenhauer; *Parerga and Paralipomena*, "On Noise," 1851

## 189

.15 We like no noise unless we make it ourselves.
    —Marie de Sevigne; *Letters of Madame de Sevigne and Her Friends*, vol. 2, 1811

# 190  Nonsense

.1  You're talking nonsense.
    —Aristophanes; *Plutus*, 388 B.C.

.2  To appreciate nonsense requires a serious interest in life.
    —Gelett Burgess; *The Romance of the Commonplace*, "The Sense of Humor," 1916

.3  For daring nonsense seldom fails to hit,
    Like shattered shot, and pass with some for wit.
    —Samuel Butler I; *On Modern Critics*, c. 1678

.4  Learned nonsense has a deeper Sound,
    Than easy Sense, and goes for more profound.
    —Samuel Butler I; *Remains*, c. 1680

.5  Such nonsense is often heard in the schools, but one does not have to believe everything one hears.
    —Cicero; *De Divinatione*, c. 44 B.C.

.6  Made still a blund'ring kind of melody;
    Spurred boldly on, and dashed through thick and thin,
    Through sense and nonsense, never out nor in.
    Free from all meaning, whether good or bad,
    And in one word, heroically mad.
    —John Dryden; *Absalom and Achitophel*, pt. II, 1682

.7  The learned Fool writes his Nonsense in better Language than the unlearned; but still 'tis Nonsense.
    —Benjamin Franklin; *Poor Richard's Almanack*, July, 1754

.8  It is a far, far better thing to have a firm anchor in nonsense than to put out on the troubled seas of thought.
    —John Kenneth Galbraith; *The Affluent Society*, 1958
    [Economist Galbraith refers to the resistance of conventional wisdom to the "economics of affluence."]

.9  I express many absurd opinions, but I am not the first man to do it; American freedom consists largely in talking nonsense.
    —Edgar Watson "Ed" Howe; *Plain People*, 1929

**190**

.10 Even God has been defended with nonsense.
—Walter Lippmann; *A Prelude to Politics*,
"The Golden Rule and After," 1914

.11 No one is exempt from talking nonsense; the
misfortune is to do it solemnly.
—Michel de Montaigne; *Essays*, 1595

.12 If you're a preacher, you talk for a living, so
even if you don't make sense, you learn to make
nonsense eloquently.
—Andrew Young; "Words of the Week,"
*Jet*, March 7, 1988

# 191 Nostalgia

.1 Is it possible to be nostalgic about old fears?
—Peter Ackroyd; *English Music*, 1992

.2 The nostalgia—
not of memories
But of what has never been!
—Zoe Akins; *The Hills Grow Smaller*, "The
Tomorrows," 1937

.3 Nostalgia is the realization that things weren't
as unbearable as they seemed at the time.
—Anonymous

.4 In every age 'the good old days' were a myth.
No one ever thought they were good at the
time. For every age has consisted of crises that
seemed intolerable to the people who lived
through them.
—Brooks Atkinson; "Once Around the
Sun," 1951

.5 Nostalgia is a seductive liar.
—George W. Ball; *Newsweek*, 1971

.6 Understanding is the last recourse of nostalgia.
—Yves Bonnefoy; "L'improbable," 1977

.7 The remembrance of past pleasures affects us
with a kind of tender grief, like what we suffer
for departed friends; and the ideas of both may
be said to haunt our imagination.
—Henry Fielding; *Tom Jones*, 1749

.8 Nostalgia is a dangerous emotion, both because it is powerless to act in the real world,
and because it glides so easily into hatred and
resentment against those who have taken our
Eden from us.
—Carolyn G. Heilbrun; *The New York
Times*, December 25, 1992

.9 The Japanese are described as "the most nostalgic people on earth," but I think possibly
the remark applies to all island people, who
have the spirit of adventure, but also the feel-

**191**

ing of being secure on a small place among the
waters.
—Robin Hyde; "I Travel Alone: My Trans-
Siberian Journey to England," *Mirror*,
1938

.10 Few cultures have not produced the idea that
in some past era the world ran better than it
does now.
—Elizabeth Janeway; *Man's World, Woman's
Place*, 1971

.11 Time has lost all meaning in that nightmare
alley of the Western world known as the
American mind. We wallow in nostalgia but
manage to get it all wrong. True nostalgia is
an ephemeral composition of disjointed memories … but American style nostalgia is about
as emphemeral as copywrited deja vu.
—Florence King; *Reflections in a Jaundiced
Eye*, "Deja Views," 1989

.12 A society that has made "nostalgia" a mar-
ketable commodity on the cultural exchange
quickly repudiates the suggestion that life in
the past was in any important way better than
life today.
—Christopher Lasch; *The Culture of Nar-
cissism*, 1979

.13 It was the last nostalgia: that he
Should understand.
—Wallace Stevens; "Esthetique du Mal,"
1947

.14 The deeper the nostalgia and the more complete the fear, the purer, the richer the word
and the secret.
—Elie Wiesel; *Legends of Our Times*, 1968

# 192 Nothing

.1 Sometimes speech is no more than a device
for saying nothing—and a neater one than silence.
—Simone de Beauvoir; *The Prime of Life*,
1960

.2 Drawing on my fine command of language, I
said nothing.
—Robert Benchley; *Chips Off the Old
Benchley*, 1949

.3 He is considered the most graceful speaker
who can say nothing in most words.
—Samuel Butler II; *Notebooks*, 1912

.4 When you have nothing to say, say nothing.
—C.C. Colton; *Lacon*, 1820

# 192

.5 Nothing is often a good thing to say, and always a clever thing to say.
—Will Durant; *New York World-Telegram and Sun*, June 6, 1958

.6 He has a rage for saying something when there's nothing to be said.
—Samuel Johnson; Boswell's *Life of Johnson*, 1780

.7 You ain't heard nothin' yet, folks.
—Al Jolson; Catch Phrase
[The great entertainer echoed his promise at just about every performance, including in his starring role in the first talking picture, *The Jazz Singer*, 1927.]

.8 One cannot create an art that speaks to men when one has nothing to say.
—Andre Malraux; *Man's Hope*, 1938

.9 He's a wonderful talker who has the art of telling you nothing in a great harangue.
—Molière; *Le Misanthrope*, 1666

.10 From a mere nothing springs a mighty tale.
—Propertius; *Elegies*, c. 1st century B.C.

.11 To say nothing, to do nothing, to know nothing, and to have nothing.
—William Shakespeare; *All's Well That End's Well*, 1602

.12 O my Antonio, I do know of these,
That therefore only are reputed wise
For saying nothing.
—William Shakespeare; *The Merchant of Venice*. 1596–97

.13 In fact, nothing is said that has not been said before.
—Terence; *Eunuchus*, "Prologue," c. 150 B.C.

.14 I have heard, indeed, that two negatives make an affirmative, but I never heard before that two nothings every made anything.
—George Villiers, second Duke of Buckingham; Speech, House of Lords, c. 1680

.15 One always speaks badly when one has nothing to say.
—Voltaire; Attributed

.16 He knew the precise psychological moment when to say nothing.
—Oscar Wilde; *The Picture of Dorian Gray*, 1891

# 193 Nursery Rhymes

.1 Bye, baby bunting,
Daddy's gone a-hunting,
Gone to get a rabbit skin
To wrap the baby bunting in.

.2 Fee, fi, fo, fum,
I smell the blood of an Englishman;
Be he alive or be he dead,
I'll grind his bones to make my bread.

.3 Georgie Porgie, pudding and pie,
Kissed the girls and made them cry;
When the boys came out to play,
Georgie Porgie ran away.

.4 Hey diddle diddle,
The cat and the fiddle,
The cow jumped over the moon;
The little dog laughed
To see such sport,
And the dish ran away with the spoon.

.5 Humpty Dumpty sat on a wall,
Humpty Dumpty had a great fall.
All the king's horses,
And all the king's men,
Couldn't put Humpty together again.

.6 Jack and Jill went up the hill
To fetch a pail of water;
Jack fell down and broke his crown,
And Jill came tumbling after.

.7 Jack Sprat could eat no fat,
His wife could eat no lean,
And so between them both, you see,
They licked the platter clean.

.8 Little Bo-peep has lost her sheep,
And can't tell where to find them;
Leave them alone, and they'll come home,
Bringing their tails behind them.

.9 Little Jack Horner
Sat in the corner
Eating a Christmas pie;
He put in his thumb,
And pulled out a plum,
And said, What a good boy am I!

.10 Mary, Mary, quite contrary,
How does you garden grow?
With silver bells and cockle shells,
And pretty maids all in a row.

.11 Old King Cole
Was a merry old soul,
And a merry old soul was he;
He called for his pipe,
And he called for his bowl,
And he called for his fiddlers three.

.12 Old Mother Hubbard
Went to the cupboard,

**193**

To fetch her poor dog a bone;
But when she came there
The cupboard was bare
And so the poor dog had none

.13 Pat-a-cake, pat-a-cake, baker's man,
Bake me a cake as fast as you can;
Pat it and prick it, and mark it with a B,
Put it in the oven for baby and me.

.14 The Queen of Hearts
She made some tarts,
All on a summer's day;
The Knave of Hearts
He stole the tarts,
And took them clean away.

.15 Rock-a-bye, baby, on the tree top,
When the wind blows the cradle will rock;
When the bough breaks the cradle will fall,
Down will come baby, cradle, and all.

.16 Sing a song of sixpence,
A pocket full of rye;
Four and twenty blackbirds,
Baked in a pie.

.17 There was a crooked man, and he walked a
    crooked mile,
He found a crooked sixpence against a
    crooked stile;
He bought a crooked cat, which caught a
    crooked mouse,
And they all lived together in a little
    crooked house.

.18 Three blind mice, see how they run!
They all ran after the farmer's wife,
She cut off their tails with a carving knife,
Did you every see such a thing in your life,
As three blind mice.

.19 Tom, Tom, the piper's son,
Stole a pig and away he run.
The pig was eat,
And Tom was beat,
And Tom went howling down the street.

.20 Who killed Cock Robin?
I, said the Sparrow,
With my bow and arrow,
I killed Cock Robin.

# **194** Oath

.1 Oaths are not surety for a man, but the man
for the oaths.
—Aeschylus; *Fragments*, c. 458 B.C.

.2 Oaths are but words, and words but wind.
—Samuel Butler I; *Hudibras*, 1664

**194**

.3 You may depend upon it, the more oath-tak-
ing, the more lying.
—Samuel Taylor Coleridge; *Table Talk*,
May 25, 1830

.4 A liar is always lavish of oaths.
—Pierre Corneille; *Le Menteur*, 1642

.5 My tongue has sworn it, but my mind is
unsworn.
—Euripides; *Hippolytus*, c. 428 B.C.

.6 Would have their tale believed for their
oaths,
And are like empty vessels under sail.
—George Herbert; *The Church-Porch*, 1633

.7 I swear by Apollo Physician, by Asclepius, by
Health, by Panacea, and by all the gods and
goddesses, making them my witnesses, that I
will carry out, according to my ability and
judgment, this oath and this indenture.... I
will use treatment to help the sick according
to my ability and judgment, but never with a
view to injury and wrongdoing ... I will keep
pure and holy both my life and my art.... In
whatsoever houses I enter, I will enter to help
the sick, and I will abstain from all intentional
wrongdoing and harm, especially from abus-
ing the bodies of man or woman, bond or free.
And whatsoever I shall see or hear in the
course of my profession in my intercourse with
men, if it be what should not be published
abroad, I will never divulge, holding such
things to be holy secrets. Now if I carry out
this oath, and break it not, may I gain forever
reputation among all men for my life and for
my art; but if I trangress it and forswear myself, may the opposite befall me.
—Hippocrates; *The Physician's Oath*, c. 420
B.C.

.8 The Erinyes, who exact punishment of men
underground if one swears a false oath.
—Homer; *The Iliad*, c. 700 B.C.

.9 God will not take you to task for vain words
in your oaths, but He will take you to task for
what your hearts have amassed.
—The Koran

.10 Deceive boys with toys, but men with oaths.
—Lysander; Quoted in Francis Bacon, *The
Advancement of Learning*, 1605

.11 Oaths are the flash-notes of speech.
—D.C. Murray; *Tales*, 1898

.12 An oath, an oath, I have an oath in heaven:
Shall I lay perjury on my soul?
No, not for Venice.
—William Shakespeare; *The Merchant of
Venice*, 1600

# 195 Observation

.1 Observation is a passive science, experimentation an active science.
  —Claude Bernard; *Introduction a l'Etude de la Medecine Experimenatale*, 1865

.2 Nothing exists until or less it is observed. An artist is making something exist by observing it. And his hope for other people is that they will also make it exist by observing it. I call it "creative observation," Creative viewing.
  —William Burroughs; *Painting and Guns*, 1992

.3 The eyes believe themselves, the ears believe other people.
  —German Proverb

.4 Since the measuring device has been constructed by the observer... We have to remember that what we observe is not nature in itself but nature exposed to our method of questioning.
  —Werner Karl Heisenberg; *Physics and Philosophy*, 1958

.5 I am a camera with its shutter open, quite passive, recording, not thinking.
  —Christopher Isherwood; *Goodbye to Berlin*, 1939

.6 The lower classes of men, though they do not think it worthwhile to record what they perceive, nevertheless perceive everything that is worth noting; the difference between them and a man of learning often consists in nothing more that the latter's facility for expression.
  —G.C. Lichtenberg; *Aphorisms*, 1764–99

.7 Observation—activity of both eyes and ears.
  —Horace Mann; *Lectures on Education*, 1845

.8 You are all right and all are wrong:
  When next you talk of what you view,
  Think others see as well as you.
  —Rev. James Merrick; "The Chameleon," c. 1740

.9 Seeing many things, but thou observest not; opening the ears, but he heareth not.
  —Old Testament: Isaiah

.10 There is no more difficult art to acquire than the art of observation, and for some men it is quite as difficult to report an observation in brief and plain language.
  —William Osler; *Aphorisms from His Bedside Teachings and Observations*, William Bennett Bean, ed., 1950

## 195

.11 One must always tell what one sees. Above all, which is more difficult, one must always see what one sees.
  —Charles Peguy; *Basic Verities*, 1943

.12    He read much;
  He is a great observer, and he looks
  Quite through the deeds of men.
  —William Shakespeare; *Julius Caesar*, 1599

# 196 Opinion

.1 Nothing is more common than to endeavor to make proselytes to our opinion.
  —Anonymous; *Private Letters from an American in England*, 1769

.2 Some men are just as sure of the truth of their opinions as are others of what they know.
  —Aristotle; *Nicomachean Ethics*, c. 4th century B.C.

.3 To be positive: to be mistaken at the top of one's voice.
  —Ambrose Bierce; *The Devil's Dictionary*, 1906

.4 We are greatly inclined to think nobody in the right, but those who are of the same opinion with ourselves.
  —Frances Moore Brooke; *The History of Emily Montague*, 1769

.5 Men get opinions as boys learn to spell,
  By reiteration chiefly.
  —Elizabeth Barrett Browning; *Aurora Leigh*, 1856

.6 No man's opinions can be worth holding unless he knows how to deny them easily and gracefully upon occasion in the cause of charity.
  —Samuel Butler II; *The Way of All Flesh*, published in 1903

.7 If every man were straightforward in his opinions, there would be no conversation.
  —Benjamin Disraeli; Attributed

.8 Stiff in opinion, always in the wrong.
  —John Dryden; *Absalom and Achitophel*, 1681

.9 A prig is a fellow who is always making you a present of his opinions.
  —George Eliot; *Middlemarch*, 1872

.10 Every opinion reacts on him who utters it.
  —Ralph Waldo Emerson; *Essays: Compensation*, 1841

**196**

.11 Stay at home in your mind. Don't recite other people's opinions.
—Ralph Waldo Emerson; *Letters and Social Aims: Social Aims*, 1875

.12 Our own opinion is never wrong.
—Thomas Fuller; *Gnomologia*, 1732

.13 Men who borrow their opinions can never repay their debts.
—Lord Halifax; *Miscellaneous Thoughts and Reflections*, late 17th century

.14 People do not seem to talk for the sake of expressing their opinions, but to maintain an opinion for the sake of talking.
—William Hazlitt; *Table Talk*, 1821–22

.15 It is not often that an opinion is worth expressing, which cannot take care of itself.
—Oliver Wendell Holmes, Sr.; *Medical Essays*, 1885

.16 A man's opinions are generally of much more value than his arguments.
—Oliver Wendell Holmes, Sr.; *The Professor at the Breakfast Table*, 1860

.17 Those who never retract their opinions love themselves more than they love truth.
—Joseph Joubert; *Pensées*, 1810

.18 Opinion! which on crutches walks,
And sounds the words another talks.
—David Lloyd; "The Poet," c. 1792

.19 Opinions cannot survive if one has no chance to fight for them.
—Thomas Mann; *The Magic Mountain*, 1924

.20 What is asserted by a man is an opinion: what is asserted by a woman is opinionated.
—Marya Mannes; *But Will It Sell?*, "The Singular Woman," 1964

.21 I disapprove of what you say, but I will defend to the death your right to say it.
—Voltaire; Attributed
[The famous line is actually S.G. Tallentyne's summary of Voltaire's attitude towards Helevetius following the burning of the latter's *Denl'Esprit* in 1759. In *The Friends of Voltaire*, 1907.]

.22 The chief effect of talk on any subject is to strengthen one's own opinions, and, in fact, one never knows exactly what he does believe until he is warmed into conviction by the heat of attack and defence.
—Charles Dudley Warner; *Backlog Studies*, "Sixth Study," 1873

.23 It is just when opinions universally prevail and we have added lip service to their authority

**196**

that we become sometimes most keenly conscious that we do not believe a word that we are saying.
—Virginia Woolf; *Letters*, Nigel Nicholson and J. Trautmann, eds., 1975–80

**197** # Oral Tradition

.1 In the past, researchers have consistently set up their studies of Cajun and Creole oral traditions as would be autopsies, yet its vital signs seem to be quite healthy. It is, in fact, difficult to avoid hearing, in groups of two or more in South Louisiana bars, barbershops and bareques, "T'as entendu le conte pout..." (Have you heard the one about...?)
—Barry J. Ancelet: *Cajun and Creole Folktales: The French Oral Tradition of South Louisiana*, 1994

.2 It is pure illusion to think that an opinion which passes down from century to century, from generation to generation, may not be entirely false.
—Pierre Bayle; *Thoughts on the Comet*, 1682

.3 Tradition—which sometimes brings down truth that history has left slip, but is oftener the wild babble of the time, such as was formerly spoken at the fireside, and now congeals in newspapers—tradition is responsible for all contrary averments.
—Nathaniel Hawthorne; *The House of Seven Gables*, 1851

.4 They recreated history, giving it life through the words and voices.
—Kenyan Saying

.5 I heard recalled the lofty deeds of my father's ancestors and their names from the earliest times. As the couplets were reeled off it was like watching the growth of a great genealogical tree that spread its branches far and wide and flourished its boughs and twigs before my eyes.
—Camara Laye; *The Dark Child*, 1954

.6 In my youth in the Transkei, I listened to the elders telling stories of the old days ... tales of wars fought by our ancestors in defense of the fatherland. The names of Dingane, Bambata, Hintsa, and Makana, Squngatha and Dalasile, Moshoeshoe, and Sekukhuni were praised as the pride and glory of the entire African nation. I wanted to serve my people ... this is what motivated me.
—Nelson Mandela; *Higher Than Hope*, 1991

**197**

.7 Storytelling was first practiced by ordinary persons gifted in poetic speech, which had been discovered in play; gradually this playful aspect of poetic tale telling was grafted onto religious rituals, historical recitations, educational functions, and the like.
—Anne Pellowski; *The World of Storytelling*, 1977

.8 My ancestors in Africa reckoned sound of major importance; they were all great talkers, great orators, and where writing was unknown, folk-tales and an oral tradition kept the ears rather than the eyes sharpened.
—Paul Robeson; "An Exclusive Interview with Paul Robeson," *West Africa Review*, August 1936

.9 The earliest instruction was imparted orally, a system still extant in Africa and the Orient. It trains the mind to listen.
—Arthur A. Schomburg; *Racial Integrity*, 1923

.10 When the last red man shall have perished from the earth and his memory among the white men shall have become a myth, these stories shall swarm with the invisible dead of my tribe. At night when the streets of your cities and villages shall be silent, and you think them deserted, they will throng, with the returning hosts that once filled and still love this beautiful land.
—Chief Seathe of the Duwamish Indians, c. 1855

.11 Something had happened, and even as we sat listening, we knew we would return the next year and the next. It was if an ancient memory had been jogged—of people throughout time, sitting together, hearing stories: a congregation of listeners. We were taken back to a time when the story, transmitted orally, was all there was. How had we wandered so far from the oral tradition? What had pulled us away?
—Jimmy Neil Smith; *"Homespun" Tales from America's Favorite Storytellers*, 1988

.12 The first foundations of all history are the recitals of the father to the children, transmitted afterward from one generation to another; at their origin they are at the very most probable, when they do not shock common sense, and they lose one degree of probability in each generation. With time the fable grows and the truth grows less; from this it comes that all the origins of people are absurd.
—Voltaire; *Essai sur les Moeurs*, 1756

.13 The evangelists knew they had to write down Christ's teachings, in order to continue the process of passing them on by word of mouth, for preachers to use. But the sacred appeal of oral transmission remains crucial. The memory or the fancy of the story's origins inspires the stimulation of a storyteller's voice in the literary text, and this performance modifies the narrative, it solicits the audience.
—Marina Warner; *From the Beast to the Blonde*, 1994

.14 While the literary fairy tale was being institutionalized at the end of the seventeenth and beginning of the eighteenth century in France, the oral tradition did not disappear, nor was it subsumed by the new literary genre. Rather the oral tradition continued to feed the writers with material and was now also influenced by the literary tradition itself.
—Jack Zipes; "Breaking the Disney Spell," *From Mouse to Mermaid: The Politics of Film, Gender, and Culture*, Elizabeth Bell, Lynda Haas and Laura Sells, eds., 1995

# **198** Oratory and Orators

.1 An orator is a man who says what he thinks and feels what he says.
—William Jennings Bryan; in Paxton Hibben's *The Peerless Leader*, 1929

.2 An orator is a good man who is skilled in speaking.
—Marcus Porcius Cato; Quoted in Quintilian *Institutio Oratoria*, c. 1st cent A.D.

.3 He mouths a sentence as curs mouth a bone.
—Charles Churchill; *The Rosciad*, 1761

.4 The best orator is the one whose address instructs, delights, and moves the minds of the hearers. The orator is obliged to instruct, while pleasure is a gratuity granted to the audience. But to stir the emotions is indispensable.
—Cicero; *De Optimo Genere Oratorum*, c. 1st century B.C.

.5 A Man never becomes an orator if he has anything to say.
—Peter Finley Dunne; *The Gift of Oratory*, 1901

.6 Every great orator ought to be accompanied by an orchestra or, at worst, a pianist, who would

**198**

play trills while the artist was refreshing himself with a glass of water.
—Peter Finley Dunne; *Mr. Dooley on Making a Will*, "On the Gift of Oratory," 1919

.7 Here comes the orator, with his flood of words and his drop of reason.
—Benjamin Franklin; *Poor Richard's Almanack*, 1735

.8 Some for fear their orations should giggle, will not let them smile.
—Thomas Fuller I; *The Holy State and the Profane State*, 1642

.9 Commencement oratory ... must eschew anything that macks of partisan politics, political preference, sex, religion or unduly firm opinion. Nonetheless, there must be a speech: Speeches in our culture are the vacuum that fills a vacuum.
—John Kenneth Galbraith; Commencement address at American University, Washington D.C., *Time*, June 18, 1984

.10 An orator can hardly get beyond commonplaces: if he does, he gets beyond his hearers.
—William Hazlitt; *The Plain Speaker*, "On the Difference Between Writing and Speaking," 1826

.11 The great orator always shows a dash of contempt for the opinions of his audience.
—Elbert Hubbard; *Philistine*, 1909

.12 The nature of oratory is such that there has always been a tendency among politicians and clergymen to oversimplify complex matters. From a pulpit or a platform even the most conscientious of speakers finds it very difficult to tell the whole truth.
—Aldous Huxley; *Collected Essays*, 1959

.13 Amplification is the vice of the modern orator.... Speeches measured by the hour die with the hour.
—Thomas Jefferson; Letter to David Harding, April 20, 1824

.14 Oratory is the power of beating down your adversary's arguments, and putting better in their place.
—Samuel Johnson; Boswell's *Life of Johnson*, May 8, 1781

.15 Oratory will not work against the stream, or on languid tides.
—George Meredith; *Beauchamp's Career*, 1876

.16 The greatest orator [Cicero], save one, of antiquity, has left it on record that he always

**198**

studied his adversary's case with as great, if not still greater, intensity than even his own.
—John Stuart Mill; *On Liberty*, 1859

.17 What the orators want in depth, they give you in length.
—Charles Louis Montesquieu; *Lettres persanes*, 1721

.18 All that is necessary to raise imbecility into what the mob regards as profundity is to lift it off the floor and put it on a platform.
—George Jean Nathan; "Profundity," *American Mercury*, September, 1929

.19 Oratory is just like prostitution: you must have little tricks.
—Vittorio Emanuele Orlando; *Time*, December 8, 1952

.20 Political oratory is the art of saying platitudes with courtesy and propriety.
—Armando Palacio Valdes; *Literary Testament*, "Politics," 1929

.21 The capital of the orator is the bank of the highest sentimentalities and the purest enthusiasms.
—Edward G. Parker; *The Golden Age of American Oratory*, 1864

.22 He possesses the utmost facility and copiousness of expression, and though always extempore, his discourses have all the propriety and elegance of the most studied and elaborate compositions.
—Pliny the Younger; *Epistles*, c. A.D. 98

.23 I am no orator, as Brutus is;
But, as you know me all, a plain blunt man, ...
For I have neither wit, nor words, nor worth,
Action, nor utterance, nor the power of speech,
To stir men's blood: I only speak right on.
—William Shakespeare; *Julius Caesar*, 1599

.24 The orator is he who can speak on every question with grace, elegance, and persuasiveness, suitably to the dignity of his subject, the requirements of the occasion, and the taste of his audience.
—Tacitus; *A Dialogue on Oratory*, c. A.D. 81

.25 Charm us orator, till the lion look no larger than the cat.
—Alfred, Lord Tennyson; *Locksley Hall, Sixty Years After*, 1886

.26 Voice and manner were perhaps too much in the foreground of a speaker's thoughts in the old days of elocutions and flowing oratory. I

**198**

suspect that we have gone too far in neglect of them.
—Norman Thomas; *Great Dissenters*, 1962

.27 A very dangerous thing, for often the wings which take one into clouds of oratorial enthusiasm are wax and melt up there, and down you come.
—Mark Twain; Speech, New York City, May 14, 1908

# 199 Parables

.1 It is not usually possible in a poem or a story to make the relationship between particular and universal fully explicit. Those who try to do so end up writing parables.
—John Peter Berger; *Pig Earth*, "Historical Afterward," 1979

.2 Sound words, I know, Timothy's is to use,
And old wives' fables he is to refuse;
But yet grave Paul him nowhere did forbid
The use of parables; in which lay hid
That gold, those pearls, and precious stones that were
Worth digging for, and that with greatest care.
—John Bunyan; *The Pilgrim's Progress*, "The Author's Apology for His Book," 1678

.3 Here the parable ends, as all parables end—incomplete, disappointing.
—Henry Francis Keenan; *The Money-Makers*, 1884

.4 Seest thou not how God hath coined a parable? A good work is like a good tree whose root is firmly fixed, and whose top is in the sky. And it produces its edible fruit every season, by permission of its Lord.... And a corrupt word is like a corrupt tree which has been torn off the ground, and has no fixity. God makes those who believe stand firm in this life and the next by His firm Word.
—The Koran, c. 610–632

.5 Therefore speak I to them in parables: because they seeing see not; and hearing they hear not, neither do they understand.
—New Testament: Matthew

.6 I will open my mouth in a parable: I will utter dark sayings of old.
—Old Testament; Psalms

.7 I am the Tathagata [Buddha], o ye gods and men! ... and the Tathagata who knows the difference as to the faculties and energy of

**199**

those beings, produces various Dharmaparya-yas, tells many tales, amusing, agreeable, both instructive and pleasant, tales by means of which all beings not only become pleased with the law in this present life, but also after death will reach happy states.... Therefore, Kasyapa, I will tell thee a parable, for men of good understanding will generally readily enough catch the meaning of what is taught under the shape of a parable.
—Sacred Books of the East

.8 Parables are not lies because they describe events which never happened.
—George Bernard Shaw; *Saint Joan*, 1924

.9 Forgotten mornings when he walked with his mother
Through the parables
Of sunlight
And the legend of the green chapels.
—Dylan Thomas; "Poem in October," 1946

.10 One special kind of literature, parable, conveniently combines story and projection. Parable serves a laboratory where great things are condensed in a small space. To understand parable is to understand root capacities of the everyday mind, and conversely.
—Mark Turner; Attributed

.11 Parable is the projection of story.
—Mark Turner; Attributed

# 200 Parody

.1 The style is the man; and some will add that, this unsupported, it does not amount to much of a man. It is a sort of fighting and profane parody of the Old Testament.
—G.K. Chesterton; *The Victorian Age*, 1912 [Chesterton refers to Algernon Swinburne.]

.2 Parody is homage gone sour.
—Brendan Gill; *Here at the New Yorker*, 1975

.3 Parodies and caricatures are the most penetrating of criticisms.
—Aldous L. Huxley; *Point Counter Point*, 1928

.4 So much contemporary art and design is a parody, a joke, and full of allusions to the past. It's like that because it is the end of an era, like the end of the nineteenth century. Not such a comfortable period to live in. Everything must

## 200

be a kind of caricature to register, everything must be larger than life.
—Christian Lacroix; Quoted in *The Sunday Times*, London, October, 1987

.5    Parody is just originality in a second-hand suit.
—Eugenio Montale; in the *Listener*, June 7, 1990

.6    Satire is a lesson, parody is a game.
—Vladimir Nabokov; Interview in *Wisconsin Studies in Contemporary Literature*, Spring, 1967

.7    It's simply that I believe that parody has been displaced and that it now invades all gestures and actions. Where there used to be events, experiences, passions, now there are nothing but parodies. This is what I tried to tell Marcelo so many times in my letters: that parody had completely replaced history.
—Ricardo Piglia; *Artificial Respiration*, 1994

.8    To equip a dull, respectable person with wings would be but a parody of an angel.
—Robert Louis Stevenson; *Virginibus Puerisque*, "Crabbed Age and Youth," 1881

## 201 Pathos

.1    In all true humor lies its germ, pathos.
—Edward George Bulwer-Lytton; *The Caxtons*, 1849

.2    It is certainly trying to a man's dignity to reappear when he is not expected to do so: a first farewell has pathos in it, but to come back for a second lends an opening to comedy.
—George Eliot; *Middlemarch*, 1872

.3    The pathos of life is worse than the tragedy.
—Ellen Glasgow; *Barren Ground*, 1925

.4    The pathos of distance.
—Freidrich Nietzsche; *Beyond Good and Evil*, 1886

.5    Nothing but the infinite pity is sufficient for the infinite pathos of human life.
—Joseph H. Shorthouse; *John Inglesant*, 1881

.6    By some subtle law all tragic human experiences gain in pathos by the perspective of time.
—Mark Twain; *The Man Who Corrupted Hadleyburg and Other Stories and Essays*, "My Debut as a Literary Person," 1990

## 201

.7    And the infinite pathos of human trust
In a God whom no one knows.
—William Watson; "Churchyard in the Wold," 1890

## 202 Pedantry

.1    Where men shall not impose for truth
and sense,
The pedantry of courts and schools.
—George Berkeley; *Verses on the Prospect of Planting Arts and Learning in America*, 1758

.2    Plague take all your pedants, say I!
—Robert Browning; "Sibrandus Schafraburgebsis," 1844

.3    Though a scholar is often a fool, he is never a fool so supreme, so superlative, as when he is defacing the first unsullied page of human history, by entering into it the commonplaces of his own pedantry.
—Edward George Bulwer-Lytton; *The Caxtons*, 1849

.4    I love the man who knows it all,
From east to west, from north to south,
Who knows all things, both great and
small,
And tells it with his tiresome mouth.
—Robert Joseph Burdette; *The Silver Trumpets*, 1911

.5    A Babylonia dialect
Which learned pedants much affect…
—Samuel Butler I; *Hudibras*, 1663

.6    Pedantry consists in the use of words unsuitable to the time, place and company.
—Samuel Taylor Coleridge; *Biographia Litearia*, c. 1817

.7    Pedantry crams our heads with learned lumber, and takes out our brains to make room for it.
—Charles Caleb Colton; *Lacon*, 1820

.8    Aye, 'tis well enough for a servant to be bred at an University. But the education is a little too pedantic for a gentleman.
—William Congreve; *Love for Love*, 1695

.9    The pedant can hear nothing but in favor of the conceits he is amorous of, and cannot see but out of the grates of his prison.
—Joseph Glanvill; *The Vanity of Dogmatizing*, 1661

.10    Pedants may cry out loud
or frown at me,

**202**

but I must say it: Cervantes
usually puts me to sleep.
—Manuel Gonzales Prada; *Grafitos*, "Hom-
bres y libros," 1937

.11 There is an honest unwillingness to pass off
another's observations for our own, which
makes a man appear pedantic.
—Augustus Hare; *Guesses at Truth*, 1827

.12 Pedantry is to suppose that there is no knowledge in the world but that of books.
—William Hazlitt; *The Round Table*, 1817

.13 Pedantry is the dotage of knowledge.
—Holbrook Jackson; *The Anatomy of Bibliomania*, 1930

.14 Pedantry is the unseasonable ostentation of
learning.
—Samuel Johnson, *The Rambler*, 1751

.15 A pedant is always throwing his system in your
face, and applies it equally to all things, times,
and places, just like a tailor who would make
a coat out of his own head, without any regard
to the bulk or figure of the person who must
wear it.
—Mary Wortley Montagu; Letter to Lady
D., January 13, 1716

.16 I acquired a certain pedantic presumption and
the slightest touch of ostentation, which subsequently, thank goodness, I've completely
cured myself of.
—Benito Perez Galdos; *El Amigo Manso*,
1882

.17 Whoever interrupts the conversation of others
to make a display of his fund of knowledge,
makes notorious his own stock of ignorance.
—Sa'Di; *Gulistan*, 1258

.18 Bold in thy applause,
The Bard shall scorn pedantic laws.
—Walter Scott; *Marimon*, "Introduction,"
1808

.19 How fiery and forward our pedant is!
—William Shakespeare; *The Taming of the
Shrew*, 1593

.20 The vacant skull of a pedant, generally furnishes out a throne and a temple of vanity.
—William Shenstone; *Of Men and Manners*, 1764

.21 Aristotle was a pedantic blockhead, and still
more knave than fool.
—Tobias Smollett; *Sir Launcelot Greaves*,
1760–61

**202**

.22 Pedantry is properly the over-rating of any
kind of knowledge we pretend to.
—Jonathan Swift; *A Treatise on Good Manners*, c. 1745

.23 The intellectual world is divided into two
classes—dilettantes, on the one hand, and
pedants, on the other.
—Miguel de Unamuno; *The Tragic Sense of
Life*, 1912

# **203** People

.1 A people's voice is a mighty power.
—Aeschylus; *Agamemnon*, 458 B.C.

.2 The voice of the people is the voice of God.
—Alcuin; *Admonitiv ad Carolum Magnum*,
c. A.D. 800

.3 Do not wonder if the common people speak
more truly than those of higher rank; for they
speak with more safety.
—Francis Bacon; *De Augmentis Scientiarum*, 1605

.4 Some people are so dry that you might soak
them in a joke for a month and it would not
get through their skins.
—Henry Ward Beecher; *Proverbs From
Plymouth Pulpit*, 1867

.5 What kind of people we become depends cru-
cially on the stories we are nurtured on; which
is why every sensible society takes pains to
prepare its members for participation in its
affairs by, among other things, teaching them
the best and the most instructive from its inheritance of stories. These are ... drawn from
both the factual and the imaginative literature
bequeathed by its ancestors, namely, its songs,
poems, plays, myths, epics, fables, histories....
—Chinweizu; *Voices from Twentieth-Century Africa*, "Introduction," 1988

.6 To despise the popular talk.
—Horace; *Odes*, c. 23 B.C.

.7 The difference between mad people and sane
people ... is that sane people have variety
when they talk-story. Mad people have only
one story that they talk over and over.
—Maxine Hong Kingston; *The Woman
Warrior*, 1976

.8 People can say anything.
—Russian Proverb

.9 The views of the mob are neither bad nor
good.
—Tacitus; *Annals*, c. A.D. 100

# 204 Performance

.1  I think it's the height of arrogance to go on-stage and *not* be extraordinary and brilliant. It's the height of arrogance to make average music. You know, people are listening.
   —Brett Anderson; quoted in *New Musical Express*, London, 1992

.2  They who are to be judges must also be performers.
   —Aristotle; *Politics*, c. 4th century B.C.

.4  The ultimate sin of any performer is contempt for the audience.
   —Lester Bangs; in *Village Voice*, August 29, 1977

.5  To others we are not ourselves but a performer in their lives cast for a part we do not even know that we are playing.
   —Elizabeth Bibesco; *The Fir and the Palm*, 1924

.6  I come out before an audience and maybe my house burned down an hour ago, maybe my husband stayed out all night, but I stand there.... I got them with me, right there in my hand and comfortable. That's my job, to make them comfortable, because if they wanted to be nervous they could have stayed home and added up the bills.
   —Fanny Brice; in Norman Katkov, *The Fabulous Fanny*, 1952

.7  The most difficult performance in the world is acting naturally, isn't it? Everything else is artful.
   —Angela Carter; *Fireworks*, "Flesh and Mirror," 1974

.8  When you perform ... you are out of yourself—larger and more potent, more beautiful. You are for minutes heroic. This is glory on earth. And it is yours, nightly.
   —Agnes de Mille; in *The New York Times*, 1963

.9  There is no strong performance without a little fanaticism in the performance.
   —Ralph Waldo Emerson; *Journals*, 1859

.10 Teaching is, in one of its aspects, a performing art.
   —Joseph Epstein; "A Classic Act," *Quest*, September, 1981

.11 Performance is an act of faith.
   —Marya Mannes; *The New York I Know*, 1961

.12 All words,
   And no performance!
   —Philip Massinger; *The Parliament of Love*, 1624

# 204

.13 A bad performance haunts the artist like a nightmare for days and days, and the memory of it is erased only by a good performance.
   —Gerald Moore; *Am I Too Loud? A Musical Autobiography*, 1962

.14 It is in performance that the sudden panic hits, that we beg for release from our destiny and at the same time court the very experience that terrifies us.... A well-meaning friend says, "There's nothing to get nervous about," and it almost helps, because the desire to strangle distracts us for the moment.
   —Eloise Ristad; *A Soprano on Her Head*, 1982

.15 The awful consciousness that one is the sole object of attention to that immense space, lined as it were with human intellect from top to bottom, and on all sides around, may perhaps be imagined but can not be described.
   —Sarah Siddons; *The Reminiscences of Sarah Kemble Siddons, 1773–1785*, 1942

# 205 Persuasion

.1  Persuasion's only shrine is eloquent speech.
   —Aristophanes; *The Frogs*, 405 B.C.

.2  Of the modes of persuasion furnished by the spoken word there are three kinds. The first kind depends on the personal character of the speaker; the second on putting the audience into a certain frame of mind; the third on the proof, or apparent proof, provided by the words of the speech itself.
   —Aristotle; *Rhetoric*, c. 4th century B.C.

.3  The rhetoric wherewith I persuade another cannot persuade myself: there is a depraved appetite in us, that will with patience hear the learned instructions of reason, but yet perform no further than agrees to its own irregular humor.
   —Sir Thomas Browne; *Religio Medico*, 1643

.4  No printer's type can record ... the persuasion of his silvery tongue.
   —Edward George Bulwer-Lytton; *What Will He Do with It?*, 1858

.5  If you would convince others, seem open to conviction yourself.
   —Lord Chesterfield; *Letters to His Son*, 1774

.6  If one word does not succeed, ten thousand are of no avail.
   —Chinese Proverb

**205**

.7  He who wants to persuade should put his trust not in the right argument, but in the right word. The power of sound has always been greater than the power of sense.
—Joseph Conrad; *A Personal Record* "A Familiar Preface," 1912

.8  He spake, and straight
Upon his lips Persuasion sate.
—Eupolis; *Doemoi*, c. 446–411 B.C.

.9  "For your own good" is a persuasive argument that will eventually make a man agree to his own destruction.
—Janet Frame; *Faces in the Water*, 1961

.10  Would you persuade, speak of interest, not of reason.
—Benjamin Franklin; *Poor Richard's Almanack*, 1734

.11  One may be confuted yet not convinced.
—Thomas Fuller; *Gnomologia*, 1732

.12  He, from whose lips divine persuasion flows.
—Homer; *Iliad*, c. 700 B.C.

.13  The persuasion of a friend is a strong thing.
—Homer; *Iliad*, c. 700 B.C.

.14  Persuasive speech, and more persuasive sighs, Silence that spoke, and eloquence of eyes.
—Homer; *Iliad*, c. 700 B.C.

.15  Yet hold it more humane, more heav'nly, first,
By winning words to conquer willing hearts,
And make persuasion do the work of fear.
—John Milton; *Paradise Lost*, 1671

.16  There is nothing that you may not get people to believe in if you will only tell it them loud enough and often enough, till the welkin rings with it.
—Ouida; *Wisdom and Pathos*, 1884

.17  Men can resist the remonstrances that wound them, and so irritate them, better than they can those gentle appeals that rouse no anger, but soften the whole heart.
—Charles Reade; *Griffith Gaunt*, 1866

.18  One of the best ways to persuade others is with your ears—by listening to them.
—Dean Rusk; in *Reader's Digest*, July, 1961

.19  Use a sweet tongue, courtesy, and gentleness, and thou mayest manage to guide an elephant with a hair.
—Sa'Di; *Gulistan*, 1258

.20  We are always on the side of those who speak last.
—Marie de Sevigne; *Letters of Madame de*

**205**

*Sevigne to Her Daughter and Her Friends*, vol. 1, 1811

.21  I see
that everywhere among the race of men
it is the tongue that wins and not the deed.
—Sophocles; *Philoctetus*, 409 B.C.

.22  It is impossible to persuade a man who does not disagree, but smiles.
—Muriel Spark; *The Prime of Miss Jean Brodie*, 1961

.23  Persuasion hung upon his lips.
—Laurence Sterne; *Tristram Shandy*, 1759

.24  An infallible method of making fanatics is to persuade before you instruct.
—Voltaire; *Philosophical Dictionary: Oracles*, 1764

.25  There is a danger in being persuaded before one understands.
—Thomas Wilson; *Maxims of Piety*, c. 1755

# 206 Philosophy

.1  Philosophy: unintelligible answers to insoluble problems.
—Henry Brooks Adams; Attributed by Bert Leston Taylor in *The So Called Human Race*, 1920

.2  What I have gained from the study of philosophy is the ability to hold converse with myself.
—Antisthenes; *Apothegm*, c. 375 B.C.

.3  The philosophy of life is nothing but an accurate ocular knowledge of the vicissitude of all things.
—Karl Friedrich August; *Horrid Mysteries*, 1797

.4  As for the philosophers ... their discourses are as the stars, which give little light, because they are so high.
—Francis Bacon; *On the Advancement of Learning: Civil Knowledge*, 1605

.5  The Socratic manner is not a game at which two can play.
—Max Beerbohm; *Zuleika Dobson*, 1911

.6  All are lunatics, but he who can analyze his delusion is called a philosopher.
—Ambrose Bierce; *The Devil's Dictionary*, 1906

.7  They talk like philosophers and live like fools.
—H.G. Bohn; *Handbook of Proverbs*, 1855

## 206

.8   There is nothing so strange and so unbelievable that it has not been said by one philosopher or another.
—Rene Descartes; *Discours de la Methode*, 1637

.9   All philosophy lies in two words, sustain and abstain.
—Epictetus; *Discoures*, c. A.D. 100

.10  You can't do without philosophy, since everything has its hidden meaning which we must know.
—Maxim Gorky; *The Zykons*, 1914

.11  The difference between gossip and philosophy lies only in one's way of taking a fact.
—Oliver Wendell Holmes, Jr.; "The Bar as a Profession," *Youth's Companion*, 1896

.12  Philosophical disputes don't often affect the price of fish or wine.
—Elizabeth Janeway; *Improper Behavior*, 1987

.13  Philosophy is about the asking of questions.
—Charles Johnson; *The World and I*, 1991

.14  Whence? wither? why? how?—these questions cover all philosophy.
—Joseph Joubert; *Pensées*, 1842

.15  Philosophizing is a process of making sense out of experience.
—Suzanne K. Langer; *Philosophical Sketches*, 1962

.16  Wonder is the foundation of all philosophy, inquiry the progress, ignorance the end.
—Michel de Montaigne; *Essays*, 1580

.17  In other words, apart from the known and the unknown, what else is there?
—Harold Pinter; *The Homecoming*, 1965

.18  I am safe, he is not philosophizing.
—Plautus; *Psuedolus*, c. 3rd century B.C.

.19  Philosophers are as jealous as women; each wants a monopoly of praise.
—George Santayana; *Dialogues in Limbo*, 1925

.20  The greater the philosopher, the harder it is for him to answer the questions of common people.
—Henryk Sienkiewicz; *Quo Vadis*, 1911

.21  Our most visible philosophies—visible in the sense of the media—are arcane juggleries. They play with words.
—George Steiner; Lecture "Modernity, Mythology, and Magic," Salzburg, 1994

## 206

.22  Philosophy has a fine saying for everything.
—For Death it has an entire set.
—Laurence Sterne; *Tristram Shandy*, 1759–67

.23  Say, Not so, and you will out circle the philosophers.
—Henry David Thoreau; *Journal*, June 26, 1840

.24  When he who hears doesn't know what he who speaks means, and when he who speaks doesn't know what he himself means—that is philosophy.
—Voltaire; *Candide*, 1759

## 207 Platitude

.1   The word *corruption* is the father of more platitudes than any word in the American language.
—Gertrude Atherton; *Senator North*, 1900

.2   A platitude is simply a truth repeated until people get tired of hearing it.
—Stanley Baldwin; Speech, House of Commons, May 29, 1924

.3   It is strange how long we rebel against a platitude until suddenly in a different lingo it looms up again as the only verity.
—Ruth Benedict; in Margaret Mead, *An Anthropologist at Work*, 1959

.4   To higher and higher platitudes.
—Richard J. Daley; *Life*, February 8, 1960 [Chicago's first mayor Daley cites goals for the future.]

.5   Where in this small-talking world can I find A longitude with no platitude?
—Christopher Fry; *The Lady's Not for Burning*, 1949

.6   I am not fond of uttering platitudes In stained-glass attitudes.
—W.S. Gilbert; *Patience*, 1881

.7   Thou say'st an undisputed thing In such a solemn way.
—Oliver Wendell Holmes, Sr.; "To an Insect"

.8   The platitude turned on its head is still a platitude.
—Norman Mailer; *Advertisements for Myself*, 1961

.9   The art of newspaper what else is to stroke a platitude until it purrs like an epigram.
—Don Marquis; in W. Anthony *O Rare Don Marquis*, 1962

## 207

.10 Work should begin with wine and generous joking,
And in the places of penalties for smoking
Let us have fines for platitudes and croaking.
—John Shaw Neilson; *Collected Poems*, "To a Blonde Typist," 1934

.11 A platitude is a truth we are tired of hearing.
—Godfrey Nicholson; Attributed

.12 Hail to Martin Farquhar Tupper!
Who when he bestrides the crupper
Of Pegasus, gets the upper
Hand of poets more renowned; ...
Suited to all times and latitudes,
By the everlasting platitudes.
—Richard Henry Stoddard; "Proverbial Philosophy," 1871

.13 Platitudes? Yes, there are platitudes. Platitudes are there because they are true.
—Margaret Thatcher; in *London Times*, 1984

.14 The immortal axiom-builder, who used to sit up nights reducing the rankest old threadbare platitudes to crisp and snappy maxims that had a nice, varnished, original look in their regimentals...
—Mark Twain; *"The Last Words of Great Men," Collected Tales, Sketches, Speeches and Essays, 1852–1890*, Louis J. Budd, ed., 1992
[Twain refers to Benjamin Franklin.]

.15 Is there anything more terrible than a "call"? It affords an occasion for the exchange of the most threadbare commonplaces. Calls and the theatre are the two great centers for the propagation of platitudes.
—Miguel de Unamuno; *Essays and Soliloquies*, 1924

.16 In modern life nothing produces such an effect as a good platitude. It makes the whole world kin.
—Oscar Wilde; *An Ideal Husband*, 1895

## 208 Poetry

.1 Poetry is simply the most beautiful, impressive, and widely effective mode of saying things, and hence its importance.
—Matthew Arnold; *Essays in Criticism*, "Heine," 1888

.2 Poetry is where the language is renewed.
—Margaret Atwood; in Alan Twigg, *For Openers*, 1981

## 208

.3 Poetry makes nothing happen: it survives
In the valley of its saying.
—W.H. Auden; *Another Time*, "In Memory of W.B. Yeats," 1940

.4 Poetry is one of the destinies of speech.... One would say that the poetic image, in its newness, opens a future to language.
—Gaston Bachelard; *The Poetics of Reverie*, "Introduction," 1960

.5 Poetry is life distilled.
—Gwendolyn Brooks; *Augusta Chronicle*, 1976

.6 Poetry is a friend to whom you can say too much.
—Gwendolyn Brooks; in *Black Poetry Writing*, 1975

.7 I have nothing to say
and I am saying and that is
poetry.
—John Cage; "Lecture on Nothing," in *Silence*, 1961

.8 When you are describing
A shape, or sound, or tint;
Don't state the manner plainly,
But put it in a hint;
And learn to look at all things
With a sort of mental squint.
—Lewis Carroll; "Poeta Fit, Non Nascitur," 1869

.9 "I can repeat poetry, as well as other folk if it comes to that—" "Oh, it needn't come to that!" Alice hastily said.
—Lewis Carroll; *Through the Looking Glass*, 1872

.10 Poetry is but the shadow or reflection of chivalry, heroism, action. First an age of deeds, and then an age of song.
—William Alexander Caruthers; *The Kentuckian in New York*, 1834

.11 Poetry, the eldest sister of all arts, and parent of most.
—William Congreve; *The Way of the World*, "Dedication," 1700

.12 Genuine poetry can communicate before it is understood.
—T.S. Eliot; *Dante*, 1929

.13 Poetry is the only verity—the expression of a sound mind speaking after the ideal, not after the apparent.
—Ralph Waldo Emerson; *Letters and Social Aims*, "Poetry and Imagination," 1875

## 208

.14 The great art of all poetry is to mix truth with fiction, in order to join the credible with the surprising.
—Henry Fielding; *Tom Jones*, 1749

.15 Poetry is what is lost in translation. It is also what is lost in interpretation.
—Robert Frost; Quoted in Louis Untermeyer, *Robert Frost: A Backward Look*, 1964

.16 Poetry is the renewal of words forever and ever. Poetry is that by which we live forever and ever unjaded. Poetry is that by which the world is never old.
—Robert Frost; Letter to R.P.T. Coffin, February 24, 1938

.17 Poetry is the language in which man explores his own amazement ... says heaven and earth in one word ... speaks of himself and his predicament as though for the first time. It has the virtue of being able to say twice as much as prose in half the time, and the drawback, if you do not give it your full attention, of seeming to say half as much in twice the time.
—Christopher Fry; *Readers' Digest*, April, 1970

.18 If there's no money in poetry, neither is there poetry in money.
—Robert Graves; Speech, London School of Management, December 6, 1963

.19 Poetry is the sung voice of accurate perception.
—Patricia Hampl; in Kate Green, *If the World Is Running Out*, 1983

.20 If Galileo had said in verse that the world moved, the Inquisition might have let him alone.
—Thomas Hardy; in F.E. Hardy, *The Later Years of Thomas Hardy*, 1930

.21 Poetry cannot be explained, it must be lived.
—Anne Hebert; *Poems*, "Poetry Broken Solitude," 1960

.22 A verse may find him who a sermon flies,
And turn delight into sacrifice.
—George Herbert; *The Temple*, "The Church-Porch," 1633

.23 Poetry is not the thing said but a way of saying it.
—A.E. Housman; *The Name and Nature of Poetry*, 1933

.24 My poems are indelicate. But so is life.
—Langston Hughes; in the *Pittsburgh Courier*, 1927

## 208

.25 Poetry is a spoken and not a written art.
—*Imagist Manifesto*, 1915

.26 Lying and poetry are always friends.
—Jean de La Fontaine; *Fables*, 1668

.27 A poem is usually a highly professional artificial thing, a verbal device designed to reproduce a thought or emotion indefinitely.
—Philip Larkin, Letter, March 12, 1965

.28 A poem should not mean But be.
—Archibald MacLeish; "Ars Poetica," 1926

.29 Poetry is the language of a state of crisis.
—Stephane Mallarme; *Vers et Prose*, 1893

.30 Poetry is an expression, through human language restored to its essential rhythm, of the mysteriousness of existence; it endows our life with authenticity and constitutes our only spiritual task.
—Stephane Mallarme; Letter to M. Leo d'Orfer, June, 27, 1884

.31 Poetry is what Milton saw when he went blind.
—Don Marquis; "The Sun Dial," *New York Sun*, 1912–22

.32 When a poem says something that could not have been said in any other way, in music, prose, sculpture, movement or painting, then it is poetry.
—Sybil Marshall; *An Experiment in Education*, 1963

.33 Not reading poetry amounts to a national pastime here.
—Phyllis McGinley; Attributed

.34 Poetry is a comforting piece of fiction set to more or less lascivious music.
—H.L. Mencken; *Prejudices*, 1919

.35 All poetry is of the nature of soliloquy.
—John Stuart Mill; *Thoughts on Poetries and Its Varieties*, 1859

.36 We have let rhetoric do the job of poetry.
—Cherrie Moraga; "La Guera" in Cherrie Moraga and Gloria Anzaldua, eds. *This Bridge Called My Back*, 1983

.37 Poetry heals the wounds inflicted by reason.
—Novalis; *Detached Thoughts*, c. late 18th century

.38 Prose—it might be speculated—is discourse; poetry ellipsis. Prose is spoken aloud; poetry overheard.
—Joyce Carol Oates; "The Romance of Emily Dickinson's Poetry," *(Woman) Writers: Occasions and Opportunities*, 1988

## 208

.39 Poetry is adolescence fermented and thus pre-served.
— Jose Ortega y Gasset; "In Search of Goethe from Within, Letter to a German," *Partisan Review*, December, 1949

.40 Poetry comes fine-spun from a mind at peace.
— Ovid; *Tristia*, c. A.D. 8

.41 To read a poem is to hear it with our eyes; to hear it is to see it with our ears.
— Octavio Paz; *Alternating Current*, "Recapitulations," 1973

.42 With me poetry has not been a purpose, but a passion.
— Edgar Allan Poe; *The Poetic Principle*, 1850

.43 Poetry is the revelation of a feeling that the poet believes to be interior and personal but which the reader recognizes as his own.
— Salvatore Quasimodo; in *The New York Times*, May 14, 1960

.44 Poetry is a language that tells us, through a more or less emotional reaction, something that cannot be said.
— E.A. Robinson; in Mark Van Doren's *Edwin Arlington Robinson*, 1927

.45 Poetry, the language of the gods.
— Samuel Rogers; *Italy*, c. 1820

.46 Poetry is *subconscious conversation*, it is as much the work of those who understand it and those who make it.
— Sonia Sanchez; "Ruminations/Reflections" in Evans, ed. *Black Women Writers*, 1984

.47 Poetry is the opening and closing of a door, leaving those who look through to guess what is seen during a moment.
— Carl Sandburg; "Ten Definitions of Poetry" in *Modern American Poetry*, Louis Untermeyer, ed., 1936

.48 In poetry there is always fallacy, and some-times fiction.
— Sir Walter Scott; *The Bride of Lammermoor*, 1819

.49 It is as unseeing to ask what is the *use* of poetry as it would be to ask what is the use of religion.
— Edith Sitwell; *The Outcasts*, 1962

.50 Poetry is the natural language of all worship.
— Madame de Stael; *Germany*, 1810

.51 After all, the commonplaces are the great poetic truths.
— Robert Louis Stevenson; *Virginibus Puerisque*, 1881

## 208

.52 If you want a definition of poetry, say: "Poetry is what makes you laugh or cry or yawn, what makes my toenails twinkle, what makes me want to do this or that or nothing" and let it go at that.
— Dylan Thomas; letter to a student, 1951

.53 Poetry is trouble dunked in tears.
— Gwyn Thomas; Attributed

.54 Poetry is nothing but healthy speech.
— Henry David Thoreau; *Journal*, September 4, 1841

.55 Poetry is usually false. The difficulty is to know when it is false and when it is true.
— Anthony Trollope; *Phineas Finn*, 1869

.56 The poem—that prolonged hesitation be-tween sound and sense.
— Paul Valery; in *Tel quel*, 1943

.57 The poetry of a people comes from the deep recesses of the unconscious, the irrational and the collective body of our ancestral memories.
— Margaret Walker; in *Black World*, December 1971

.58 For what is a poem but a hazardous attempt at self-understanding: it is the deepest part of autobiography.
— Robert Penn Warren; Attributed

.59 We make out of the quarrel with others, rhetoric, but of the quarrel with ourselves, poetry.
— W.B. Yeats; *Essays*, "Anima Hominis," 1924

.60 I think poetry should be alive. You should be able to dance to it.
— Benjamin Zephaniah; in *The Sunday Times*, August 23, 1987

## 209 Poets

.1 How strangely should we be deceived, if we should take a poet in the literal sense?
— Anonymous; *The Temple-beau*, 1754

.2 A poet is, before anything else, a person who is passionately in love with language.
— W.H. Auden; *The New York Times*, October 9, 1960

.3 Now comes the public and demands that we tell it what the poet desires to say. The answer to this is: If we knew, he wouldn't be one.
— Hermann Bahr; *Studien zur Kritik der Moderne*, 1894

**209**

.4 Poets are all who love, who feel great truths,
And tell them.
—P.J. Bailey; *Festus: Another and a Better World*, 1839

.5 Wise poets that wrapt Truth in tales,
Knew her themselves through all the veils.
—Thomas Carew; *Poems*, "Ingrateful Beauty Threatened," 1640

.6 The worst tragedy for a poet is to be admired though misunderstood.
—Jean Cocteau; *Le Rappel a l'orde*, "Le Cog et l'Arlequin," 1926

.7 To a poet, silence is an acceptable response, even a flattering one.
—Colette; *Earthly Paradise*, "The Occupation," 1966

.8 The mission of the poet is to soothe.
—Mrs. Rebecca Harding Davis; *Waiting for the Verdict*, 1868

.9 Time was, when a poet sat upon a stool in a public place, and mused in the sight of men.
—Charles Dickens; *A Tale of Two Cities*, 1859

.10 Poets, the first instructors of mankind.
—Wentworth Dillon; *De Arte Poetica*, 1680

.11 A Black poet is a preacher.
—Henry Dumas; in *Drumvoice*, 1976

.12 We Poets of the proud old lineage
Who sing to find your hearts, we know not why,—
What shall we tell you? Tales, marvelous tales
Of ships and stars and isles where good men rest.
—James Elroy Flecker; "The Golden Journey to Samarkland," epilogue, 1913

.13 We all write poems; it is simply that poets are the ones who write in words.
—John Fowles; *The French Lieutenant's Woman*, 1969

.14 A very good or a very bad poet is remarkable; but a middling one who can bear?
—Thomas Fuller; *Gnomologia*, 1732

.15 The difference between a common man and a poet is, that one has been deluded, and cured of his delusion, and the other continues deluded all his days.
—Thomas Hardy; *Desperate Remedies*, 1871

.16 All men owe honor to the poets—honor and awe, for they are the dearest to the Muse who puts upon their lips the ways of life.
—Homer; *Ars Poetica*, c. 13 B.C.

**209**

.17 O Black and unknown bards of long ago,
How came your lips to touch the sacred fire?
—James Weldon Johnson; "O Black and Unknown Bards," *The Book of American Negro Poetry*, 1931

.18 To a poet nothing is useless.
—Samuel Johnson; *Rasselas*, 1759

.19 Poets ... are liberal-minded men who will squeeze a word till it hurts.
—Archibald MacLeish; "Apologia," in the *Harvard Law Reviews*, June, 1972

.20 There is no advice to give young poets.
—Pablo Neruda; Attributed

.21 Poets utter great and wise things which they do not themselves understand.
—Plato; *Ion*, c. 385 B.C.

.22 The void yields up nothing. You have to be a great poet to make it ring.
—Jules Renard; *Journal*, December, 1906

.23 I wanted to choose words that even you would have to be changed by.
—Adrienne Rich; *Leaflets*, "Implosions," 1969

.24 This is what all poets do: they talk to themselves out loud; and the world overhears them.
—George Bernard Shaw; *Candida*, 1895

.25 A poet is a nightingale, who sits in darkness and sings to cheer its own solitude with sweet sounds.
—Percy Bysshe Shelley; "A Defense of Poetry," 1821

.26 The poet is the priest of the invisible.
—Wallace Stevens; *Opus Posthumous*, "Adagia," 1957

.27 There were *skalds* [poets] with Harald and the Fairhaired and men still their poems, and the poems about all the kings who have since ruled Iceland. And we take our statements most of all from what is said in those poems.
—Snorri Sturluson; *Heimskringla*, "Prologue," c. 1225

.28 All poets who, when reading from their own works, experience a choked feeling, are major.
—E.B. White; *Quo Vadimus?* "How to Tell a Major Poet," 1939

**210 Politicians**

.1 A politician is an animal who can sit on a fence and yet keep both ears to the ground.
—Anonymous

**210**

.2 If the Senate makes a weak man weaker, it makes a strong man stronger, owing to the very temptations he must resist from the day he enters, the compromises he is forced to make, and the danger to his convictions from the subtler brains of older men.
—Gertrude Atherton; *Senator North*, 1900

.3 There is one fact that the second-rate politician never grasps. That is, that the true American respects convictions; no matter how many fads he may conceive nor how loud he may clamor for their indulgence, when his mind begins to balance methodically again, he respects the man who told him he was wrong and imperilled his own reelection rather than vote against his convictions.
—Gertrude Atherton; *Senator North*, 1900

.4 The politician is an acrobat. He keeps his balance by saying the opposite of what he does.
—Maurice Barres; *Mes Cahiers*, 1896–1932

.5 Vote for the man who promises least; he'll be the least disappointing.
—Bernard Baruch; quoted by Meyer Berger, *Meyer Berger's New York*, 1960

.6 It only takes a politician believing in what he says for the others to stop believing him.
—Jean Baudrillard; *Cool Memories*, 1987

.7 The people-pleaser is not always the friend of the people.
—Hugh Henry Brackenridge; *Modern Chivalry*, 1792–1815

.8 It is dangerous for a national candidate to say things that people might remember.
—David Broder; *Washington Post*, 1973

.9 [A politician is] little other than a *red-tape* talking machine, and unhappy bag of parliamentary eloquence.
—Thomas Carlyle; Attributed

.10 A politician is an arse upon which everyone has sat except a man.
—E.E. Cummings; *100 Selected Poems*, 1926

.11 You campaign in poetry. You govern in prose.
—Mario Cuomo; in *New Republic*, April 8, 1985

.12 Since a politician never believes what he says, he is surprised when others believe him.
—Charles De Gaulle; *Newsweek*, October 1, 1962

.13 A politician is a man who can be verbose in fewer words than anyone else.
—Peter DeVries; Attributed

**210**

.14 Demagogues are the mob's lacqueys.
—Diogenes; *Diogenes Laertius*, "Diogenes," c. 3rd century A.D.

.15 It is our experience that political leaders do not always mean the opposite of what they say.
—Abba Eban; Quoted in *The Observer*, December 5, 1971

.16 A "penchant for telling the truth" can cripple a candidate's chances faster than being caught *in flagrante delicto* with the governor's wife.
—Sidney J. Harris; *Clearing the Ground*, "Honesty Not the Best Policy for Winning Votes," 1986

.17 He was a power politically for years, but he has never got prominent enough to have his speeches garbled.
—Kin Hubbard; *Abe Martin's Broadcast*, 1930

.18 A politician is required to listen to humbug, talk humbug, condone humbug. The most we can hope for is that we don't actually believe it.
—P.D. James; *A Taste for Death*, 1986

.19 A politician ought to be born a foundling and remain a bachelor.
—Claudia ("Lady Bird") Johnson; *Time*, December 1, 1975

.20 Politicians are the same all over. They promise to build a bridge even where there is no river.
—Nikita Khrushchev; Comment to reporter, Glen Cove, New York, 1960

.21 Don't write anything you can phone, don't phone anything you can talk face to face, don't talk anything you can smile, don't smile anything you can wink and don't wink anything you can nod.
—Earl Long; Attributed

.22 The politicians were talking themselves red, white and blue in the face.
—Clare Boothe Luce; Speech, 1960

.23 A candidate for office can have no greater advantage than muddled syntax, no greater liability than a command of language.
—Marya Mannes; *More in Anger*, 1958

.24 did you ever
notice that when
a politician
does get an idea
he usually
gets it all wrong.
—Don Marquis; *Archy's Life of Mehitabel*, "Archygrams," 1933

**210**

.25 A politician divides mankind into two classes: tools and enemies.
—Friedrich Nietzsche; *Human, All-Too Human*, 1878

.26 Never lose your temper with the Press or the public is a major rule of political life.
—Christabel Pankhurst; *Unshackled*, 1959

.27 People start parades—politicians just get out in front and act like they're leading.
—Dana Gillman Rinehart; quoted in *The Observer*, May 22, 1988

.28 The most successful politician is he who says what everybody is thinking most often and in the loudest voice.
—Theodore Roosevelt; in J.B. Bishop, *Theodore Roosevelt and His Time Shown in His Own Letters*, 1920

.29 He knows nothing; he thinks he knows everything—that clearly points to a political career.
—George Bernard Shaw; *Major Barbara*, 1905

.30 A politician is a statesman who approaches every question with an open mouth.
—Adlai E. Stevenson; Quoted in *The Fine Art of Political Wit*, Leon Harris, 1964

.31 ...suppose you were an idiot. And suppose you were a member of Congress. But I repeat myself.
—Mark Twain; *Letters from the Earth*, Bernard DeVoto; 1962

.32 One of the most fascinating aspects of politician—watching is trying to determine to what extent any politician believes what he says.
—Gore Vidal; *Reflections Upon a Sinking Ship*, 1969

.33 You won't be able to find such another pack of poppycock gabblers as the present Congress.
—Artemus Ward; *Travels: Things in New York*, 1865

.34 A politician's words reveal less about what he thinks about his subject than what he thinks about his audience.
—George Will; Quoted in Richard Reeves, *A Ford, Not a Lincoln*, 1975

# **211** Politics

.1 There is no political gain in silence and submission.
—Sidney Abbott; *Sappho Was a Right-On Woman*, with Barbara J. Love, 1972

**211**

.2 All political parties die at last of swallowing their own lies.
—John Arbuthnot; Quoted in Richard Garnett's *Life of Emerson*, 1887

.3 From politics, it was an easy step to silence.
—Jane Austen; *Northanger Abbey*, 1818

.4 Politics are usually the executive expression of human immaturity.
—Vera Brittain; *The Rebel Passion*, 1964

.5 Finality is not the language of politics.
—Benjamin Disraeli; speech, House of Commons, February 28, 1859

.6 Mediocrity in politics is not to be despised. Greatness is not needed.
—Hans Magnus Enzensberger; *The Late Show*, BBC2, November 5, 1990

.7 Politics is the art of the possible. It consists of choosing between the disastrous and the unpalatable.
—John Kenneth Galbraith; *Ambassador's Journal*, 1969

.8 Politics us the science of how who gets what, when and why.
—Sidney Hillman; *Political Primer*, 1944

.9 The purification of politics is an iridescent dream.
—John Ingalls; Article in *New York World*, 1890

.10 In politics all abstract words conceal treachery.
—C.L.R. James; *The Black Jacobins*, 1963

.11 Politics is the enemy of the imagination.
—Ian McEwan; *Vietnam*, 1967

.12 In political discussion heat is in inverse proportion to knowledge.
—J.G.C. Minchin; *The Growth of Freedom in the Balkan Peninsula*, 1933

.13 A valuable qualification of a modern politician seems to be a capacity for concealing or explaining away the truth.
—Dorothy Nevill; *My Own Times*, 1912

.14 In our time, political speech and writing are largely the defense of the indefensible.
—George Orwell; *Shooting an Elephant*, "Politics and the English Language," 1950

.15 Politics is just like show business ... a hell of an opening, you coast for a while, you have a hell of an ending.
—Ronald Reagan; in *The New York Times*, April 23, 1995

# 211

.16 All politics is based on the indifference of the majority.
—James Reston; "New York," *The New York Times*, June 12, 1968

.17 I tell you folks, all Politics is Apple Sauce.
—Will Rogers; *The Illiterate Digest*, 1924

.18 Politics in a work of literature are like a pistol-shot in the middle of a concert, something loud and vulgar and yet a thing to which it is not possible to refuse one's attention.
—Stendhal; *La Chartreuse de Parme*, 1839

.19 Politics is perhaps the only profession for which no preparation is thought necessary.
—Robert Louis Stevenson; *Familiar Studies of Men and Books: Yo Shida-Torajiro*, 1882

.20 Politics is one subject that goes to the vitals of every rural American; and a Hoosier will talk politics after he is dead.
—Booth Tarkington; *The Gentleman from Indiana*, 1899

.21 In politics if you want something said, ask a man. If you want something done, ask a woman.
—Margaret Thatcher; *People*, September 15, 1975

.22 Politics in America is the binding secular religion.
—Theodore H. White; *Time*, December 29, 1986

# 212 Power

.1 I believe in the power of the spoken word.
—Anita Baker; Interview, c. 1987

.2 I call the discourse of power any discourse that engenders blame, hence guilt, in its recipient.
—Roland Barthes; inaugural lecture at College de France, January 7, 1977.

.3 We want to internalize the story, like a musician who has played "My Funny Valentine" a zillion times. And when the story is internalized, we're on automatic. Now, we're free to give the story power—to give ourselves over to the tale and the tellin'.
—Brother Blue; in Jimmy Neil Smith *Homespun: Tales from America's Favorite Storytellers*, 1988

.4 There is a weird power in a spoken word.
—Joseph Conrad; *Lord Jim*, 1900

# 212

.5 Speech is power: speech is to persuade, to convert, to compel.
—Ralph Waldo Emerson; *Journals*, Waldo Emerson Forbes, ed., 1909–14

.6 Power consists to a large extent in deciding what stories will be told.
—Carolyn Heilbrun; *Writing a Woman's Life*, 1988

.7 Laughter and tears are meant to turn the wheels of the same sensibility; one is wind-power and the other water-power, that is all.
—Oliver Wendell Holmes; *The Autocrat of the Breakfast Table*, 1858

.8 Great power constitutes its own argument, and it never has much trouble drumming up friends, applause, sympathetic exegesis, and a band.
—Lewis Lapham; *Imperial Masquerade*, 1990

.9 There is a homely adage which runs: "Speak softly and carry a big stick; you will go far."
—Theodore Roosevelt; Speech, Minnesota State Fair, September 2, 1901

# 213 Praise

.1 None are more apt to praise others extravagantly, than those who desire to be praised themselves.
—Anonymous

.2 We often praise and dispraise in conversation, rather than the company should have a good opinion of our judgment, than for any love or hatred to the persons we mention.
—Anonymous

.3 There is no such whetstone to sharpen a good wit and encourage a will to learning as is praise.
—Roger Ascham; *The Schoolmaster*, 1570

.4 Just as it is always said of slander that something always sticks when people boldly slander, so it might be said of self-praise (if it is not entirely shameful and ridiculous) that if we praise ourselves fearlessly, something will always stick.
—Francis Bacon; *Apothegms*, c. 1626

.5 A man who does not love praise is not a full man.
—Henry Ward Beecher; *Proverbs from Plymouth Pulpit*, 1887

.6 Praise undeserved is satire in disguise.
—Broadhurst; *To the Celebrated Beauties of the British Court*, c. 1700

**213**

.7  Praise out of season, or tactlessly bestowed, can freeze the heart as much as blame.
—Pearl S. Buck; *To My Daughter, with Love*, 1967

.8  The advantage of doing one's praising to oneself is that one can lay it on so thick and exactly in the right places.
—Samuel Butler II; *The Way of All Flesh*, 1903

.9  Nothing so soon the drooping spirits can raise
As praises from the men, whom all men praise.
—Abraham Cowley; "Ode Upon a Copy of Verses of My Lord Broghill's," 1663

.10  Praise requires constant renewal and expansion.
—Doris Grumbach; *Coming Into the End Zone*, 1991

.11  Praise to the face is open disgrace.
—T.C. Haliburton (Sam Slick), *Wise Saws*, 1943

.12  Generally we praise only to be praised.
—François de La Rochefoucauld; *Maximes*, 1665

.13  A child is fed with milk and praise.
—Mary Lamb; "The First Tooth," 1809

.14  The deafest man can hear praise, and is slow to think of any excess.
—Walter Savage Landor; *Imaginary Conversations*, "Milton and Marvel," 1824–1853

.15  Bravos but induce flatulency.
—Herman Melville; *Mardi*, 1849

.16  Praise is always pleasing, let it come from whom, or upon what account it will.
—Michel de Montaigne; *Essays*, "On Vanity," 1580

.17  Praise, of course, is best: plain speech breeds hate.
But ah the Attic honey
Of telling a man exactly what you think of him!
—Palladas; Quoted in *Greek Anthology*, c. 10th century A.D.

.18  Get someone else to blow your horn and the sound will carry twice as far.
—Will Rogers; *The Illiterate Digest*, 1924

.19  We bestow on others praise in which we do not believe, on condition that in return they bestow upon us praise in which we do.
—Jean Rostand; *Le Carnet d'un biologiste*, 1962

**213**

.20  We find it easy to believe that praise is sincere; why should anyone lie in telling the truth?
—Jean Rostand; *Le Carnet d'un biologiste*, 1962

.21  Say nothing good of yourself, you will be distrusted; say nothing bad of yourself, you will be taken at your word.
—Joseph Roux; *Meditations of a Parish Priest*, c. 1870

.22  I will praise any man who will praise me.
—William Shakespeare; *Antony and Cleopatra*, 1606

.23  Praise shames me, for I secretly beg for it.
—Rabindranath Tagore; *Stray Birds*, 1916

.24  Men sometimes feel injured by praise because it assigns a limit to their merit.
—Luc de Clapiers Vauvenargues; *Maxims and Reflections*, 1746

.25  The sweetest of all sounds is praise.
—Xenophon; *Memorabilia*, c. 375 B.C.

# **214** Prayer

.1  Prayer is the language of the heart.
—Grace Aguilar; *The Spirit of Judaism*, 1842

.2  The best prayers have often more groans than words.
—John Bunyan; *The Pilgrim's Progress*, 1678

.3  Do not make long prayers; always remember that the Lord knows something.
—Joseph H. Choate; *American Addresses*, 1911

.4  Prayer is conversation with God.
—Clement of Alexandria; *Stromateis*, c. 2nd cent A.D.

.5  Prayer is translation. A man translates himself into a child asking for all there is in a language he has barely mastered.
—Leonard Cohen; *Beautiful Losers*, 1970

.6  Think over your prayers; for He to whom you make them knows all tongues; that of the heart as well as those of the mouth.
—James Fenimore Cooper; *The Last of the Mohicans*, 1826

.7  For the happy man prayer is only a jumble of words, until the day when sorrow comes to explain to him the sublime language by means of which he speaks to God.
—Alexandre Dumas; *The Count of Monte Cristo*, 1884

## 214

.8 Ejaculations are short prayers darted up to God on emergent occasions.
—Thomas Fuller I; *Good Thoughts in Bad Times*, 1642

.9 Prayer is the voice of faith.
—Richard Hengest Horne; *Orion*, 1843

.10 Certain thoughts are prayers. There are moments when, whatever the attitude of the body, the soul is on its knees.
—Victor Hugo; *Les Miserables*, 1862

.11 Prayer does not change God, but it changes him who prays.
—Soren Kierkegaard; *The Present Age*, 1962

.12 In saying my prayers, I discovered the voice of an innermost self, the raw nerve of my identity.
—Gelsey Kirkland; *Dancing on My Own Grave*, 1986

.13 Being mortal, never pray for an untroubled. life; But ask the gods to give you an enduring heart.
—Menander; *Fragment*, c. 342–292 B.C.

.14 Prayer is power within us to communicate with the desired beyond our thirsts.
—George Meredith; *Lord Ormand and His Aminta*, 1984

.15 A god when angry is moved by the voice of prayer.
—Ovid; *Ars Amatoria*, c. 43 B.C.–A.D. 17

.16 Do not pray for yourself: you do not know what you need.
—Pythagoras; *Axiom*, c. 525 B.C.

.17 We know what to pray for when we pray, that God's will may be done, and that we may be resigned to it.
—Samuel Richardson; *Clarissa Harlowe*, 1747–48

.18 What men usually ask for when they pray to God is, that two and two many not make four.
—Russian Proverb

.19 Common people do not pray; they only beg.
—George Bernard Shaw; *Misalliance*, 1910

.20 Our prayers should be for blessings in general, for God knows what is good for us.
—Socrates; Quoted in Diogenes Laertius, *Lives*, c. 3rd century A.D.

.21 Pray as if everything depended on God, and work as if everything depended upon man.
—Francis Cardinal Spellman; Attributed

## 214

.22 Complaint is the largest tribute Heaven receives, and the sincerest part of our devotion.
—Jonathan Swift; *Thoughts on Various Subjects*, 1711

.23 You can't pray a lie. I found that out.
—Mark Twain; *Huckleberry Finn*, 1884

.24 I have never made but one prayer to God, a very short one: "O Lord make my enemies ridiculous," And God granted it.
—Voltaire; *Letter to M. Damilliville*, April 16, 1767

.25 The Lord's Prayer contains the sum total of religion and morals.
—Duke of Wellington; Attributed

# 215 Preachers

.1 The test of a preacher is that his congregation goes away saying, not "What a lovely sermon" but, "I will do something."
—St. Francis de Sales; *Introduction to the Devout Life*, 1609

.2 I would have every minister of the gospel address his audience with the zeal of a friend, with the generous energy of a father, and with the exuberant affection of a mother.
—Francois Fenelon; *Dialogues des morts*, 1712–30

.3 Great sermons lead the people to praise the preacher. Good preaching leads the people to praise the Saviour.
—Charles G. Finney; *Autobiography*, 1876

.4 There are many preachers who don't hear themselves.
—German Proverb

.5 The best of all the preachers are the men who live their creeds.
—Edgar A. Guest; *Sermons We See*, 1934

.6 What do our clergy lose by reading their sermons? They lose preaching, the preaching of the voice in many cases, the preaching of the eye almost always.
—Augustus William Hare; *Guess at Truth*, 1827

.7 A country clergyman with a one story intellect and a one-horse vocabulary.
—Oliver Wendell Holmes, Sr.; *The Autocrat of the Breakfast Table*, 1858

.8 A preacher is one who works orally.
—Elbert Hubbard; *A Thousand and One Epigrams*, 1911

## 215

.9 Woe to those preachers who listen not to themselves.
—T.E. Hulme; *Proverb Love*, 1902

.10 Why is it that a great proportion of our pastors seem to conspire together with one consent to make the periodical duty of listening to them as hard as possible.
—George Alfred Lawrence; *Guy Livingstone*, 1857

.11 As a marksman aims at the target and it's bull's-eye, and at nothing else, so the preacher must have a definite point before him, which he has to hit.
—John Henry Newman; *The Idea of a University*, 1960

.12 Preachers say, do as I say, not as I do. But if the physician had the same disease upon him that I have, and he should bid me do one thing, and himself do quite another, could I believe him?
—John Selden; *Table-Talk: Preaching*, c. 1654

.13 Some ministers would make good martyrs: they are so dry they would burn well.
—Charles Haddon Spurgeon; *Gems from Spurgeon*, 1859

.14 A great preacher is a great artist. Words are his tubes of paint. Verse, his brush. The souls of men the canvas on which he portrays the truths caught in moments of inspiration. The God-man is a man of imagination.
—Marvin P. Tolson; "Portrait of Jesus, the Young Radical," *Washington Tribune*, July 4, 1938

.15 God's true priest is always free;
Free, the needed truth to speak,
Right the wronged, and raise the weak.
—John Greenleaf Whittier; "The Curse of the Charter-Breakers," *The Writings of John Greenleaf Whittier*, 1894

.16 The number of good preachers may have decreased. But so has the number of good listeners.
—Spencer Wilson; Letter to the editor, *London Times*, August 20, 1968

.17 If you're a preacher, you talk for a living, so even if you don't make sense, you learn to make nonsense eloquently—Andrew Young; in "Words of the Week," *Jet*, March 7, 1988

## 216 Preaching

.1 He that does not know how wisely to meddle with public affairs in preaching the gospel, does not know how to preach the gospel.
—Henry Ward Beecher; *Proverbs from Plymouth Pulpit*, 1887

.2 The world is dying for want, not of good preaching, but of good hearing.
—George Dana Boardman; Attributed

.3 Let us, even to the wearing of our tongues to the stumps, preach and pray.
—John Bradford; *On Repentance*, c. 1654

.4 He preaches well that lives well.
—Miguel de Cervantes; *Don Quixote*, 1615

.5 I am not to preach, but to relate.
—Daniel Defoe; *Roxana*, 1724

.6 I like the silent church before the service begins, better than any preaching.
—Ralph Waldo Emerson; *Essays, First Series: Self-Reliance*, 1841

.7 My preaching at its best has itself been personal counseling on a group scale.
—Harry Emerson Fosdick; Recalled on his death, October 5, 1969

.8 Sir, a woman's preaching is like a dog's walking on his hind legs. It is not done well: but you are surprised to find it done at all.
—Samuel Johnson; Boswell's *Life of Johnson*, July 31, 1763

.9 Begin low, speak slow;
Take fire, rise higher;
When most impressed
Be self-possessed;
At the end wax warm,
And sit down in a storm.
—Rev. John Leifchild; "Lines on Public Speaking," 1850

.10 For it is of great advantage to human nature that the most virtuous men can hardly ever fully say why they are virtuous, and while they believe they are preaching their faith they are not really preaching it at all.
—Georg Christoph Lichtenberg; *Aphorisms*, 1764–99

.11 When I hear a man preach, I like to see him act as if he were fighting bees.
—Abraham Lincoln; Attributed

.12 Preaching is heady wine. It is pleasant to tell people where they get off.
—Arnold Lunn; Attributed

.13 Only the sinner has the right to preach.
—Christopher Morley; "Tolerance," 1928

## 216

.14 An ounce of practice is worth a pound of preaching.
—John Ray; *English Proverbs*, 1670

.15 Men of talents are sooner to be convinced by short sentences than by long preachments.
—Samuel Richardson; *Clarissa Harlowe*, 1747–48

.16 To preach long, loud and damnation, is the way to be cried up. We love a man that damns us, and we run after him again to save us.
—John Selden; *Table-Talk: Damnation*, c. 1654

.17 That we should practice what we preach is generally admitted; but anyone who preaches what he and his hearers practise must incur the gravest moral disapprobation.
—Logan Pearsall Smith; *Afterthoughts*, "Life and Human Nature," 1931

.18 He deserves to be preached to death by wild curates.
—Sydney Smith; Quoted in Lady Holland *Memoir*, 1855

.19 To preach, to show the extent of our reading, of the subtleties of our wit—to parade in the eyes of the vulgar with the beggarly accounts of a little learning, tinselled over with a few words which glitter, but convey little light and less warmth—is a dishonest use of the poor single half hour in a week which is put into our hands. 'Tis not preaching the gospel, but ourselves. For my own part, continued Yorick, I had rather direct five words point-blank to the heart.
—Laurence Sterne; *Tristram Shandy*, 1760–1767

.20 He preached his sermon in the manner which men are wont to use when they know that they are preaching in vain. There is a tone of refusal, which, through the words used may be manifestly enough words of denial, is in itself indicative of assent.
—Anthony Trollope; *Ayala's Angel*, 1881

.21 Preach not because you have to say something, but because you have something to say.
—Richard Whatley; *Apothegms*, 1828

## 217 Prejudice

.1 The prejudice of education goes a great way, and it is not the work of an hour to remove it.
—Anonymous; *The Fruitless Repentance*, 1769

## 217

.2 A prejudice is a vagrant opinion without visible means of support.
—Ambrose Bierce; *The Devil's Dictionary*, 1911

.3 Prejudices, it is well known, are most difficult to eradicate from the heart whose soil has never been loosened or fertilized by education; they grow, firm as weeds among stones.
—Charlotte Bronte; *Jane Eyre*, 1847

.4 When dealing with people, remember you are not dealing with creatures of logic, but with creatures of emotion, creatures bristling with prejudice and motivated by pride and vanity.
—Dale Carnegie; *How to Win Friends and Influence People*, 1930

.5 We hate some persons because we do not know them; and will not know them because we hate them.
—Charles Caleb Colton; *Lacon*, 1820

.6 People of poor capacities are apt to be deluded by vulgar prejudices.
—William Donaldson; *The Life and Adventures of Sir Bartholomew Sapskull*, 1768

.7 Prejudices are the props of civilization.
—Andre Gide; *Counterfeiters*, 1926

.8 Race prejudice can't be talked down, it must be lived down.
—Francis James Grimke; *Stray Thoughts and Meditations*, 1914

.9 Learn never to conceive a prejudice against others, because you know nothing of them. It is bad reasoning, and makes enemies of half the world.
—William Hazlitt; *Sketches and Essays*, "On Prejudice," 1839

.10 Opinions founded on prejudice are always sustained with the greatest violence.
—Lord Francis Jeffrey; *Edinburgh Review*, 1814

.11 Prejudice squints when it looks and lies when it talks.
—Laure Junot; *Memoirs of Madame Junot*, 1883

.12 I am, in plainer words, a bundle of prejudices—made up of likings and unlikings.
—Charles Lamb; *Essays of Elia*, 1823

.13 Everyone is a prisoner of his own experiences. No one can eliminate prejudices—just recognize them.
—Edward R. Murrow; Broadcast, December 31, 1955

## 217

.14 It is hard to remove early-taken prejudices, whether of liking or distaste: people will hunt for reasons to confirm first impressions, in compliment to their own sagacity: nor is it every mind that has the ingenuousness to confess itself mistaken, when it finds itself to be wrong.
—Samuel Richardson; *Clarissa Harlowe*, 1747–48

.15 When orators and auditors have the same prejudices, those prejudices run a great risk of being made to stand for incontestable truths.
—Joseph Roux; *Meditations of a Parish Priest*, 1886

.16 We all decry prejudice, yet we are all prejudiced.
—Herbert Spencer; *Social Statics*, 1851

.17 There is too much bigotry in the old holding back the spirit of togetherness of the young.
—Leon Sullivan; *Crisis*, March, 1983

## 218 Problems

.1 Myths are a way of solving the problem of making intelligible to the marketplace conclusions arrived at in the ivory tower.
—Adesanya Adebayo; Talk, 1958

.2 I have yet to see any problem, however complicated, which, when you looked at it in the right way, did not become more complicated.
—Poul Anderson; in the *New Scientist*, September 25, 1969

.3 You are either part of the solution or part of the problem.
—Eldridge Cleaver; Speech, San Francisco State, 1969

.4 Problems are messages.
—Shakti Gawain; *Living in the Light*, 1986

.5 A problem that presents itself as a dilemma carries an unfortunate prescription: to argue instead of act.
—Elizabeth Janeway; *Improper Behavior*, 1987

.6 Any solution to a problem changes the problem.
—R.W. Johnson; in *The Washingtonian*, November, 1979

.7 Some people always assume that if you mention a problem, you caused it.
—Sonia Johnson; *Going Out of Our Minds*, 1987

## 218

.8 Problems are only opportunities in work clothes.
—Henry J. Kaiser; Maxim, recalled at his death, August 24, 1967

.9 His [Isaac Newton's] peculiar gift was the power of holding continuously in his mind a purely mental problem until he had seen through it.
—John Maynard Keynes; *Essays in Biography*, 1933

.10 When one's own problems are unsolvable, and all best efforts frustrated, it is life-saving to listen to other people's problems.
—Suzanne Massie; in Robert and Suzanne Massie, *Journey*, 1975

.11 There is always an easy solution to every human problem—neat, plausible, and wrong.
—H.L. Mencken; *Prejudices*, 1922

.12 The problems of this world are only truly solved in two ways: by extinction or duplication.
—Susan Sontag; *I, Etcetera*, "The Dummy," 1978

## 219 Professors and Professing

.1 A professor is one who talks in someone else's sleep.
—W.H. Auden; Attributed

.2 Being a professor of poetry is rather like being a Kentucky colonel. It's not really a subject one can profess—unless one hires oneself out to write pieces for funerals or the marriages of dons.
—W.H. Auden; *The Dyer's Hand*, 1962

.3 The professors laugh at themselves, they laugh at life; they long ago abjured the bitch-goddess Success, and the best of them will fight for his scholastic ideals with a courage and persistence that would shame a soldier. The professor is not afraid of words like *truth*; in fact he is not afraid of words at all.
—Catherine Drinker Bowen; *Adventures of a Biographer*, 1946

.4 The hawk-nosed, high-cheek-boned Professor....
The sallow, virgin-minded, studious Martyr to mild enthusiasm.
—Robert Browning; "Christmas-Eve," 1850

| 219 |
|-----|

.5  Respectable Professors of the Dismal Sciences.
   —Thomas Carlyle; *Latter Day Pamphlets*, 1850
   [Carlyle refers to political economy and social science.]

.6  Professors in every branch of the sciences prefer their own theories to truth; the reason is that their theories are private property, but truth is common stock.
   —Charles Caleb Colton; *Lacon*, 1825

.7  A college professor is in the business of teaching. His business is not to give information.
   —Bronson Cutting; Speech in the U.S. Senate, June 14, 1934

.8  When eras die, their legacies
   Are left to strange police.
   Professors in New England guard
   The glory that was Greece.
   —Clarence Day; *Thoughts Without Words*, "Thoughts on Death," 1928

.9  Antiquity was perhaps created to provide professors with their bread and butter.
   —Jules De Goncourt; *Journal*, January 6, 1866

.10 I found that the most professing men were the greatest objects of interest: and that their conceit, their vanity, their want of excitement, and their love of deception all prompted to these professions, and were all gratified by them.
   —Charles Dickens; *David Copperfield*, 1849–1850

.11 If the science professors knew as little about their jobs as the literary ones the University would have been blown up long ago!
   —Louis Esson; in Vance Palmer, *Louis Esson and the Australian Theatre*, 1948

.12 The poet should be a professor of hope.
   —Jean Giono; *L'Eau Vive*, 1944

.13 Professors of literature, our present masters, are always more ridiculous when they take up today's or yesterday's avant-garde.
   —Geoffrey Grigson; *The Private Art*, 1982

.14 A mere professor, spite all his cant, is
   Not a whit better than a Mantis,—
   An insect, of what clime I can't determine,
   That lifts its paws most parson-like, and thence,
   By simple savages—thro' sheer pretence—
   Is reckon'd quite a saint amongst the vermin.
   —Thomas Hood; "Ode to Rae Wilson," 1825

| 219 |
|-----|

.15 Now owls are not really wise—they only look that way. The owl is sort of a college professor.
   —Elbert Hubbard; *Thousand and One Epigrams*, 1911

.16 State a moral case to a ploughman and a professor. The former will decide it as well, and often better than the latter, because he has not been led astray by artificial rules.
   —Thomas Jefferson; Letter to Peter Carr, August 10, 1787

.17 The more insignificant an art or science is, the more vain the professors of it are of their knowledge.
   —Charles Jenner; *The Placid Man*, 1770

.18 If a professor thinks what matters most
   Is to have gained an academic post
   Where he can earn a livelihood, and then,
   Neglect research, let controversy rest,
   He's but a petty tradesman at the best,
   Selling retail the work of other men.
   —Kalidasa; *Sakuntala*, c. 5th century

.19 *The Two Ways*: One is to suffer; the other is to become a professor of the fact that another suffered.
   —Soren Kierkegaard; in Auden *Kierkegaard Anthology*, 1952

.20 Take away paradox from the thinker and you have the professor.
   —Soren Kierkegaard; in *The University and the Modern World*, Arnold S. Nash, ed., 1943

.21 Why then I'll fit you, say no more.
   When I was young, I gave my mind
   And plied myself to fruitless poetry:
   Which though it profit the professor naught
   Yet it is passing pleasing to the world.
   —Thomas Kyd; *The Spanish Tragedy*, 1594

.22 I am what is called a *professor emeritus*—from the Latin *e*, 'out,' and *meritus*, 'so he ought to be.'
   —Stephen Leacock; *Here Are My Lectures*, 1938

.23 Few professors, real ones, ever complete their work: what they give to the world is fragments. The rest remains. Their contributions must be added up, not measured singly. Every professor has his "life work" and sometimes does it, and sometimes dies first.
   —Stephen Leacock; *Model Memoirs: On the Need for a Quiet College*, 1942

.24 The horse, the mass of human intelligence, draws along the cart of history in which stands

**219**

the professor, looking backward and explaining the scenery.
—Stephen Leacock; *My Remarkable Uncle: Who Canonizes the Classics?*, 1942

.25 Whenever the cause of people is entrusted to professors it is lost.
—Nikolai Lenin; *Political Parties and the Proletariat*, 1917

.26 Our American professors like their literature clear, cold, pure and very dead.
—Sinclair Lewis; Address, *Swedish Academy*, December 12, 1930

.27 All professors of the arts love to fraternize.
—Herman Melville; *Omoo*, 1847

.28 The Liberals are the professors of the practicable in politics.
—George Meredith; *Beauchamp's Career*, 1876

.29 Profess not the knowledge ... that thou hast not.
—The Old Testament: Apocrypha, Ecclesiasticus

.30 The education of youth is professed by many, but executed by few.
—James Ridley; *The History of James Lovegrove*, 1761

.31 People would compose music skillfully enough if only there were no professors in the world.
—George Bernard Shaw; *Music in London, 1890–94*, 1931

.32 A practitioner in panegyric, or, to speak more plainly, a professor of the art of puffing.
—Richard Brinsley Sheridan; *The Critic*, 1779

.33 If the authority to which he [professor] is subject resides in the body corporate, the college, or university, of which he himself is a member, and in which the greater part of the other members are, like himself, persons who either are or ought to be teachers, they are likely to make a common cause, to be all very indulgent to one another, and every man to consent that his neighbor may neglect his duty, provided he himself is allowed to neglect his own.
—Adam Smith; *The Wealth of Nations*, 1776

.34 Seven pupils in the class
Of Professor Callias,
Listen silent while he drawls.—
Three are benches, four are walls.
—Henry Van Dyke; *Poems*, "The Professor," 1911

**219**

.35 Culture is an instrument wielded by professors to manufacture professors, who, when their time comes will manufacture professors.
—Simone Weil; *The Need for Roots*, 1949

.36 Perhaps there is something innate that in the first place disposes a man to become a University teacher or specialist. He is, I suspect, more often than not by nature and instantly afraid of the uproar of things. Visit him in college and you will see that he does not so much live there as lurk.
—H.G. Wells; *The World of William Clissold*, 1926

.37 I consider it a monstrous presumption that university lecturers should think themselves competent to go on talking year after year to young men, students, while holding themselves aloof from the opportunity of learning from eager youths, which is one of the most valuable things on earth.
—Alfred North Whitehead; *Dialogues*, as recorded by Lucien Price, 1953

.38 To discharge the duties of a professor means to be willing to make ... ideas accessible to anyone, anywhere, at any time. It means to consider scholarship not as a property, but as a devotion, a sacrament.
—Norbert Wiener; *Boston Sunday Herald*, October 30, 1960

.39 Professors of literature, who for the most part are genteel but mediocre men, can make but a poor defense of their profession, and the professors of science, who are frequently men of great intelligence but of limited interests and education, feel a politely disguised contempt for it; and thus the study of one of the most pervasive and powerful influences on human life is traduced and neglected.
—Yvor Winters; *In Defense of Reason*, "Foreword," 1960
[U.S. literary critic Winters speaks of literature.]

**220** Pronunciation

.1 If you take care to pronounce correctly the words usually mispronounced, you may have the self-love of the purist, but you will not sell any goods.
—George Ade; *Fables in Slang*, 1899

.2 Everyone has a right to pronounce foreign names as he chooses.
—Winston Churchill; *The Observer*, "Sayings of the Week," 1951

# 220

.3  He pronounced some of his words as if they were corks being drawn out of bottles.
    —Winston Graham; in *Readers' Digest*, November, 1981

.4  Speak the speech, I pray you, as I pronounced it to you, trippingly on the tongue; but if you mouth it, as many of your players do, I had as lief the towncrier spoke my lines.
    —William Shakespeare; *Hamlet*, 1600–1

.5  They spell it Vinci and pronounce it Vinchy; foreigners always spell better than they pronounce.
    —Mark Twain; *Innocents Abroad*, 1869

.6  The educated Southerner has no use for an *r*, except at the beginning of a word.
    —Mark Twain; *Life on the Mississippi*, 1883

# 221 Propaganda

.1  It is sometimes necessary to lie damnably in the interests of the nation.
    —Hilaire Belloc; Letter to G.K. Chesterton, December 12, 1917

.2  Propaganda is that branch of the art of lying which consists in nearly deceiving your friends without quite deceiving your enemies.
    —F.M. Cornford; Quoted in *New Statesman*, London, September 15, 1978

.3  Propaganda has done more to defeat the good intentions of races and nations than even open warfare.
    —Marcus Garvey; *Philosophy and Opinions of Marcus Garvey*, 1923

.4  As soon as by one's own propaganda even a glimpse of right on the other side is admitted, the cause for doubting one's own right is laid.
    —Adolf Hitler; *Mein Kampf*, 1925

.5  Propaganda doesn't deceive people; it merely helps them deceive themselves.
    —Eric Hoffer; *The Passionate State of Mind*, 1955

.6  The propagandist's purpose is to make one set of people forget that certain other sets of people are human.
    —Aldous Huxley; *The Olive Tree*, 1937

.7  All our advertising is propaganda, of course, but it has become so much a part of our life, is so pervasive, that we just don't know what it is propaganda *for*.
    —Pauline Kael; *I Lost It at the Movies*, 1965

# 221

.8  Education by means of prefabricated ideas is propaganda.
    —Mordecai M. Kaplan; *Reconstructionist*, April, 1950

.9  Loud peace propaganda makes war seem imminent.
    —D.H. Lawrence; *Pansies*, "Peace and War," 1929

.10  All propaganda is lies, even when one is telling the truth.
    —George Orwell; Diary entry, March 14, 1942

.11  Why is propaganda so much more successful when it stirs up hatred than when it tries to stir up friendly feelings?
    —Bertrand Russell; *The Conquest of Happiness*, 1930

.12  The whites told only one side. Told it to please themselves. Told much that is not true. Only his own best deeds, only the worst deeds of the Indians, has the white man told.
    —Yellow Wolf of the Nez Perce; in McWhorter *Yellow Wolf: His Own Story*, 1940

# 222 Prophecy and Prophets

.1  How can you pretend to foretell the affairs of others when you cannot foresee your own?
    —Aesop; *Fables*, "Mantis," c. 570 B.C.
    [Of the soothsayer who, while prophesying in the forum, was interrupted and informed that his house had been broken into and robbed.]

.2  Study prophecies when they are become histories.
    —Sir Thomas Browne; *Religio Medici*, 1642

.3  Of all the horrid, hideous notes of woe, ...
    Is that portentous phrase, "I told you so,"
    Utter'd by friends, those prophets of the past.
    —Lord Byron; *Don Juan*, 1824

.4  The best prophet of the future is the past.
    —Lord Byron; *Journal*, January 28, 1821

.5  The people who were honored in the Bible were the false prophets. It was the ones we call the prophets who were jailed and driven into the desert, and so on.
    —Noam Chomsky; interview, *The Guardian*, November 23, 1992

**222**

.6  I shall always consider the best guesser the best prophet.
—Cicero; *De Divinatione*, 44 B.C.

.7  Ancestral voices prophesying war.
—Samuel Taylor Coleridge; "Kubla Khan," 1816

.8  A prophet is a man who foresees trouble.
—Finley Peter Dunne; *Rising of the Subject Races*, 1901

.9  Among all forms of mistake, prophecy is the most gratuitous.
—George Eliot; *Middlemarch*, 1871–72

.10 He is the best diviner who conjectures well.
—Euripides; *Fragments*, c. 420 B.C.

.11 The best qualifications of a prophet is to have a good memory.
—Lord Halifax (George Savile); *Maxims, Works*, 1693

.12 Thy voice sounds like a prophet's word;
And in its hollow tones are heard
The thanks of millions yet to be.
—Fitz-Greene Halleck; *Marco Bozzaris*, 1855

.13 God has granted to every people a prophet in his own tongue.
—Mohammed; *The Koran*, c. 625

.14 A prophet is not without honor, save in his own country.
—New Testament: Matthew

.15 To be a prophet it is sufficient to be a pessimist.
—Elsa Triolet; *Proverbes d'Elsa*, 1971

.16 Prophecies boldly uttered never fall barren on superstitious ears.
—Mark Twain; *Personal Reflections of Joan of Arc*, 1896

.17 The wisest prophets make sure of the event first.
—Horace Walpole; Letter to Thomas Walpole, February 9, 1785

**223** Prose

.1  Prose is when all the lines except the last go on to the end. Poetry is when some of them fall short of it.
—Jeremy Bentham; Quoted in M. St. J. Packe *The Life of John Stuart Mill*, 1954

**223**

.2  He who writes prose builds his temple to Fame in rubble; he who writes verse builds in granite.
—Edward George Bulwer-Lytton; *The Caxtons*, 1849

.3  That mild apostate from poetic rule,
The simple Wordsworth, framer of a lay
As soft as evening in his favorite May,...
Who, both by precept and example, shows
That prose is verse, and verse is merely prose.
—Lord Byron; *English Bards and Scotch Reviewers*, 1809

.4  I wish our clever young poets would remember my homely definitions of prose and poetry; that is, prose,—words in their best order; poetry,—the best words in their best order.
—Samuel Taylor Coleridge; *Table Talk*, July 12, 1827

.5  Is not the noblest poetry of prose fiction the poetry of everyday truth?
—Wilkie Collins; *Basil*, "Letter of Dedication," 1852

.6  Prose books are the show dogs I breed and sell to support my cat.
—Robert Graves; *New York Times*, July 13, 1958
[Graves claims he writes novels to support his love of writing poetry.]

.7  Mediocre prose might be read as an escape, might be spoken on television by actors, or mouthed in movies. But mediocre poetry did not exist at all. If poetry wasn't good, it wasn't poetry. It was that simple.
—Erica Jong; *How to Save Your Own Life*, 1977

.8  Prose on certain occasions can bear a great deal of poetry: on the other hand, poetry sinks and swoons under a moderate weight of prose.
—Walter Savage Landor; *Imaginary Conversations of Greeks and Romans*, "Archdeacon Hare and Walter Landor," 1853

.9  The borderline between prose and poetry is one of those fog-shrouded literary minefields where the wary explorer gets blown to bits before ever seeing anything clearly. It is full of barbed wire and the stumps of dead opinions.
—Ursula Le Guin; *Dancing on the Edge of the World*, 1989

.10 The early morning always has this touch ... whisper ... gleam ... beat of wings of eden. Prose can paint evening and moonlight, but poets are needed to sing the dawn. Prose is equal to melancholy stuff. Gladness requires

**223**

the finer language. Otherwise we have it coarse—anything but a reproduction.
—George Meredith; *Diana of the Crossways*, 1885

.11 For more than forty years I have been speaking prose without knowing it.
—Molière; *Le Bourgeois Gentilhomme*, 1670

.12 You can always count on a murderer for a fancy prose style.
—Vladimir Nabokov; *Lolita*, 1955

.13 Good prose is like a window pane.
—George Orwell; *Collected Essays*, "Why I Write, *1968*

.14 Poetry must be *as well written as prose.*
—Ezra Pound; Letter to Harriet Monroe, January, 1915

.15 What a lumbering poor vehicle prose is for the conveying of great thought!… Prose wanders around with a lantern & laboriously schedules & verifies the details & particulars of a valley & its frame of crags & peaks, then Poetry comes & lays bare the whole landscape with a single splendid flash.
—Mark Twain; Letter to W.D. Howells, February 25, 1906

.16 Poetry is to prose as dancing is to walking.
—John Barrington Wain; BBC radio broadcast, January 13, 1976

.17 Most people become bankrupt having invested too heavily in the prose of life. To ruin one's self over poetry is an honor.
—Oscar Wilde; *The Picture of Dorian Gray*, 1891

.18 The poet gives us his essence, but prose takes the mold of the body and mind entire.
—Virginia Woolf; *The Captain's Death Bed*, "Reading," 1950

# **224** Proverbs

.1 A proverb is the horse of conversation; when the conversation lags, a proverb will revive it.
—African Saying

.2 Solomon made a book of proverbs, but a book of proverbs never made a Solomon.
—Anonymous

.3 The genius, wit, and spirit of a nation are discovered in its proverbs.
—Francis Bacon; Essays, c. 1616

.4 A wise heart discerneth the proverbs of the wise.
—Ben Sira; *Book of Wisdom*, c. 190 B.C.

**224**

.5 Proverbs are the deductions of experience, and to which we assent as soon as expressed; containing in them an obvious truth, which the simplest understand.
—Hugh Henry Brackenridge; *Modern Chivalry*, 1792–1815

.6 A proverb is a short sentence based on long experience.
—Miguel de Cervantes; *Don Quixote*, 1605

.7 I do not say a proverb is amiss when aptly and seasonably applied; but to be forever discharging them, right or wrong, hit or miss, renders conversation insipid and vulgar.
—Miguel de Cervantes; *Don Quixote*, 1615

.8 A proverb is a racial aphorism which has been, or still is, in common use, conveying advice or counsel, invariably camouflaged figuratively, disguised in metaphor or allegory.
—S.G. Champion; *Racial Proverbs*, "Introduction," 1938

.9 Proverbs may be called the literature of the illiterate.
—F.S. Cozzens; *Sayings*, 1870

.10 Proverbs are the daughters of daily experience.
—Dutch Proverb

.11 Proverbs, like the sacred books of each nation, are the sanctuary of the intuitions.
—Ralph Waldo Emerson; *Essays, First Series* "Compensation," 1841

.12 A proverb does not tell a lie; an empty pipe does not burn.
—Estonian Proverb

.13 Proverbs: short aphorisms, in which men of great genius have wrapt up some egregious discovery, either in nature or science, making it thus easily portable for the memory which is apt to fail under the burden of voluminous erudition.
—Henry Fielding; *Jonathan Wild*, 1743

.14 A proverb is much matter decocted into few words.
—Thomas Fuller I; *Worthies*, c. 1661

.15 Constant popping off of proverbs will make thee a byword thyself.
—Thomas Fuller II; *Introductio ad Prudentium*, 1731

.16 Don't quote your proverb until you bring your ship into port.
—Gaelic Proverb

.17 Proverbs are all old. If they're new they're not proverbs.
—Eugene Healy; *Mr. Sandeman Loses His Life*, 1940

**224**

.18 [Proverbs are] Stories and sayings they will well remember.
—George Herbert; *Priest to the Temple*

.19 The proverbs of a nation furnish the index to its spirit.
—J.G. Holland; *Gold-Foil: An Exordial Essay*, c. 1881

.20 Proverbs may not improperly be called the philosophy of the common people.
—James Howell; *Lexicon: English Proverbs*, 1659

.21 Proverbs … are short sayings made out of long experience.
—Zora Neale Hurston; *Moses, Man of the Mountains*, 1939

.22 Proverbs are always platitudes until you have personally experienced the truth of them.
—Aldous Huxley; Attributed

.23 A proverb is no proverb to you till life has illustrated it.
—John Keats; *Letters*, c. 1821

.24 Truth comes in a well rubbed-down state in the form of the sayings of the ancestors.
—Khati, King of Egypt; *Teaching*, c. 2500 B.C.

.25 Proverbs, the ready money of human experience.
—James Russell Lowell; *My Study Windows*, 1871

.26 He took to proverbs; sure sign of the sere leaf in a man's mind.
—George Meredith; *Beauchamp's Career*, 1876

.27 A proverb is the halfway house to an ideal; and the majority rest there content: can the keeper of such a house be flattered by his company?
—George Meredith; The Ordeal of Richard Feverel, 1859

.28 A proverb is an Instructive Sentence, in which more is generally Design'd than is Express'd, and which has pass'd into Common Use and Esteem either among the Learned or Vulgar.
—Samuel Palmer; *Moral Lessons on Proverbs*, 1710

.29 Wise men make Proverbs, but Fools repeat 'em.
—Samuel Palmer; *Moral Lessons on Proverbs*, 1710

.30 Proverbs put old heads on young men's shoulders.
—Charles Reade; *The Cloister and the Hearth*, 1861

**224**

.31 Proverbs are the wisdom of whole nations and ages collected into a small compass.
—Samuel Richardson; *Clarissa Harlowe*, 1747–8

.32 Proverbs often contain more wisdom in them than the tedious harangues of most parsons and moralists.
—Samuel Richardson; *Clarissa Harlowe*, 1747–48

.33 Proverbs may be set against proverbs.
—Samuel Richardson; *Sir Charles Grandison*, c. 1749

.34 A proverb is the wisdom of many and the wit of one.
—Lord John Russell; *Apothegm*, c. 1850

.35 Proverbs beautify speech.
—Russian Proverb

.36 The proverb is something musty.
—William Shakespeare; *Hamlet*, 1600

.37 Patch grief with proverbs.
—William Shakespeare; *Much Ado About Nothing*, 1598

.38 The proverbist knows nothing of the two sides of a question. He knows only the roundness of answers.
—Karl Shapiro; *The Bourgeois Poet*, 1964

.39 What is a proverb, but the experience and observation of several ages, gathered and summed up into one expression?
—Robert South; *Sermons*, c. 1716

.40 Proverbs … receive their chief value from the stamp and esteem of ages through which they have passed.
—Sir William Temple; *Of Ancient and Modern Learning*, 1692

# **225** Puns

.1 The seeds of punning are in the minds of all men, and though they may be subdued by reason, reflection, and good sense, they will be very apt to shoot up in the greatest genius.
—Joseph Addison; *The Spectator*, 1711

.2 A pun is a short quip followed by a long groan.
—Anonymous

.3 Good poets have a weakness for bad puns.
—W.H. Auden; "The Truest Poetry is the Most Feigning," 1963

.4 It was so quiet you could hear a pun drop.
—Arthur "Bugs" Baer; Attributed

225

.5 I consider punning a sort of literary prostitution in which future happiness is swapped up for the pleasure of the moment.
—Josh Billings (Henry W. Shaw), *Josh Billings on Ice*, 1868

.6 I think no innocent species of wit or pleasantry should be suppressed; and that a good pun may be admitted among the smaller excellencies of lively conversation.
—James Boswell; *Life of Samuel Johnson*, 1791

.7 The Window has four Little Panes;
   But One have I—
   The Window Panes are in its Sash;
   I Wonder Why!
—Gelett Burgess; "Panes," c. 1913

.8 A turn for punning, call it Attic salt.
—Lord Byron; *English Bards and Scotch Reviewers*, 1809
["Attic salt" is a term for refined wit.]

.9 But still a pun I do detest, ...
   They who've least wit can make them best.
—William Combe; *Dr. Syntax in Search of the Picturesque*, 1812

.10 It requires a genius to make a good pun—some men of bright parts can't reach it.
—Hannah Cowley; *The Belle's Stratagem*, c. 1780s

.11 A man who could make so vile a pun would not scruple to pick a pocket.
—John Dennis; Remark, c. 1693

.12 Rare compound of oddity, frolic, and fun!
   Who relish'd a joke, and rejoic'd in a pun.
—Oliver Goldsmith; *Retaliation*, 1774

.13 A pun or a ludicrous expression frequently has more weight with the vulgar than the most solid argument.
—Richard Graves; *The Spiritual Quixote*, 1773

.14 My sense of sight is very Keen,
   My sense of hearing weak.
   One time I saw a mountain pass,
   But could not hear its peak.
—Oliver Herford; "My Sense of Sight," c. 1921

.15 A pun is prima facie an insult to the person you are talking with. It implies utter indifference to or sublime contempt for his remarks, no matter how serious.
—Oliver Wendell Holmes, Sr.; *The Autocrat of the Breakfast Table*, 1858

.16 A good pun deserves to be drawn and quoted.
—Ronald L. Holter; Quoted by L.M. Boyd, *Detroit Free Press*, April 24, 1982

225

.17 Ben Battle was a soldier bold,
   And used to war's alarms;
   But a cannon-ball took off his legs,
   So he laid down his arms.
—Thomas Hood; "Faithless Nelly Gray," c. 1821–23

.18 A quibble, poor and barren as it is, gave [Shakespeare] such delight that he was content to purchase it by the sacrifice of reason, propriety and truth. A quibble was to him the fatal Cleopatra for which he lost the world and was content to lose it.
—Samuel Johnson; *Shakespeare*, 1765

.19 The pun is two strings of thought tied with an acoustic knot.
—Arthur Koestler; Quoted in "Take My Word for It," Frank Muir and Denis Norden, 1978

.20 A pun is a noble thing per se. O never bring it in as an accessory! ... it fills the mind; it is as perfect as a sonnet; better.
—Charles Lamb; Letter to Samuel Taylor Coleridge, c. 1810

.21 A pun is a pistol let off at the ear, not a feather to tickle the intellect.
—Charles Lamb; *Last Essays of Elia*, "Popular Fallacies, That the Worst Puns Are the Best," 1833

.22 I wish to draw my last breath through a pipe and exhale it in a pun.
—Charles Lamb; Letter to W. & D. Wordsworth, September 28, 1805

.23 It often happens that a bad pun
   Goes farther than a better one.
—W.S. Landor; "Last Fruit Off an Old Tree," 1795

.24 Many of us can still remember the social nuisance of the inveterate punster. This man followed conversation as a shark follows a ship.
—Stephen Leacock; *The Boy I Left Behind Me*, 1947

.25 A pun is the lowest form of humor—when you don't think of it first.
—Oscar Levant; *Memoirs of an Amnesiac*, 1965

.26 The goodness of the true pun is in the direct ratio of its intolerability.
—Edgar Allan Poe; *Marginalia*, 1844–49

.27 Of puns it has been said that they who most dislike then are least able to utter them.
—Edgar Allan Poe; *Marginalia*, 1844–49

## 225

.28 I am thankful that my name is obnoxious to no pun.
—William Shenstone; "Egotisms," 1742

.29 Puns are in very bad repute.... The wit of words is so miserably inferior to the wit of ideas that it is very deservedly driven out of good company.
—Sydney Smith; *Sketches of Moral Philosophy*, 1805

.30 When the Rudyards cease from Kipling And the Haggards Ride no more.
—J.K. Stephen, *Lapsus Calami*, 1891

.31 Punning is a talent which no man affects to despise but he that is without it.
—Jonathan Swift; *Polite Conversation*, 1738

.32 Every poet knows the pun is Pierian, that it springs from the same soil as the Muse ... a matching and shifting of vowels and consonants, an adroit assonance sometimes derided as jackassonance.
—Louis Untermeyer; *Bygones*, 1965

.33 Punning is a low species of wit.
—Noah Webster; *An American Dictionary of the English Language*, 1828

## 226 Quarrels

.1 The quarrels of friends are the opportunities of foes.
—Aesop; *Fables*, "The Lions and the Bulls," c. 6th century B.C.

.2 Quarrels can end but words spoken never die.
—African Saying

.3 When two quarrel, he who keeps silence first is the most praiseworthy.
—Babylonian Talmud: Kiddushin, c. 450

.4 Quarrel not with a loud-tongued man, and lay not wood on fire.
—Ben Sira; *Book of Wisdom*, c. 190 B.C.

.5 In time they quarreled, of course, and about an abstraction —as young people often do, as mature people almost never do.
—Willa Cather; *Youth and the Bright Medusa*, "Coming, Aphrodite!," 1920

.6 People generally quarrel because they cannot argue.
—Gilbert K. Chesterton; Attributed

.7 It is better to quarrel with a knave than a fool.
—C.C. Colton; *Lacon*, 1820

## 226

.8 They had quarreled about this single, solitary sore point: their life.
—Annie Dillard; *The Living*, 1992

.9 In all private quarrels the duller nature is triumphant by reason of its dullness.
—George Eliot; *Felix Holt, The Radical*, 1866

.10 When we quarrel, how we wish we had been blameless.
—Ralph Waldo Emerson; *Journal*, c. 1870

.11 A quarrelsome Man has no good Neighbors.
—Benjamin Franklin; *Poor Richard's Almanack*, 1746

.12 Those who in quarrels interpose, Most often wipe a bloody nose.
—John Gay; *Fables*, "The Mastiff," 1727

.13 Most quarrels amplify a misunderstanding.
—Andre Gide; *Journals*, 1920

.14 No Quarrel ever stirred Before the second Word.
—Arthur Guiterman; *A Poet's Proverb*, 1924

.15 Every quarrel begins in nothing and ends in a struggle for supremacy.
—Elbert Hubbard; *One Thousand and One Epigrams*, 1911

.16 A world of dew: Yet within the dewdrops— Quarrels.
—Kobayashi Issa; c. 1880, Geoffrey Bownas and Anthony Thwaite, trs.

.17 Though a quarrel in the streets is a thing to be hated, the energies displayed in it are fine, the commonest man shows a grace in his quarrel.
—John Keats; Letter, 1819

.18 Quarrels do not last long if the wrong is only on one side.
—François de La Rochefoucauld; *Maximes*, 1665

.19 He does not quarrel, therefore no one in the world can quarrel with him.
—Lao-Tsze; *The Way of Virtue*, c. 550 B.C.

.20 How easily that man must pass his time who sits, like a spider in the midst of his feeling web, ready to catch the minutest occasion for quarrel and resentment.
—Henry Mackenzie; *The Man of the World*, 1773

.21 I have noticed when chickens quit quarrelling over their food they often find that there is

# 226

enough for all of them. I wonder if might not be the same with the human race.
  —Don Marquis; *Archy's Life of Mehitabel,* "Random Thoughts by Archy," 1933

.22 Above all, avoid quarrels caused by wine.
  —Ovid; *Ars Amatoriae,* c. 1 B.C.

.23 In quarrelling the truth is always lost.
  —Publilius Syrus; *Maxims,* c. 1st century

.24 A married couple are well suited when both partners usually feel the need for a quarrel at the same time.
  —Jean Rostand; *Le Mariage,* 1927

.25 In a false quarrel there is no true valor.
  —William Shakespeare; *Much Ado About Nothing,* 1598

.26 The test of a man or woman's breeding is how they behave in a quarrel.
  —George Bernard Shaw; *The Philanderer,* 1893

.27 The quarrel is a very pretty quarrel as it stands; we should only spoil it by trying to explain it.
  —Richard Brinsley Sheridan; *The Rivals,* 1775

.28 Bad quarrels come when two people are wrong. Worse quarrels come when two people are right.
  —Betty Smith; *Tomorrow Will Be Better,* 1948

.29 It takes two to make a quarrel.
  —Socrates; *Apothegm,* c. 406 B.C.

.30 A dignity which has to be contended for is not worth a quarrel; for it is of the essence of real dignity to be self-sustained, and no man's dignity can be asserted without being impaired.
  —Sir Henry Taylor; *The Statesman,* 1836

.31 How finely some people can hang up quarrels—or pop them into a drawer—as they do their work, when dinner is announced, and take them out again at a convenient season!
  —William Makepeace Thackeray; *Lovel the Widower,* c. 1860s

.32 We make out of the quarrel with others, rhetoric, but of the quarrel with ourselves, poetry.
  —W.B. Yeats; *Per Amica Silentia Lunae,* "Anima Hominis," 1917

# 227 Questions

.1 The first key to wisdom is this—constant and frequent questioning ... for by doubting we

# 227

are led to question and questioning we arrive at the truth.
  —Pierre Abelard; *Sic et Non,* c. 1120

.2 To ask the hard question is simple.
  —W.H. Auden; "The Question," 1963

.3 A prudent question is one-half of wisdom.
  —Francis Bacon; *Essays,* 1625

.4 Hypothetical questions get hypothetical answers.
  —Joan Baez; *Daybreak,* 1966

.5 Every sentence I utter must be understood not as an affirmation, but as a question.
  —Niels Bohr; *New York Times Book Review,* October 20, 1957

.6 He who asks a question is a fool for five minutes; he who does not ask a question remains a fool forever.
  —Chinese Proverb

.7 Always the beautiful answer who asks a more beautiful question.
  —E.E. Cummings; *Collected Poems,* "Introduction," 1938

.8 Questions are always easy.
  —Benjamin Disraeli; *Sybil,* 1845

.9 He that nothing questioneth, nothing learneth.
  —Thomas Fuller; *Gnomologia,* 1732

.10 The power to question is the basis of all human progress.
  —Indira Gandhi; *Speeches and Writings,* 1975

.11 Bromidic though it may sound, some questions don't have answers, which is a terribly difficult lesson to learn.
  —Katharine Graham; in Jane Howard, "The Power That Didn't Corrupt," *Ms.,* October, 1974

.12 A wise man's question contains half the answer.
  —Solomon Ibn Gabriol; *Choice of Pearls,* c. 1050

.13 Don't ask questions of fairy tales.
  —Jewish Proverb

.14 Questioning is not a mode of conversation among gentleman.
  —Samuel Johnson; Boswell's *Life of Johnson,* 1776

.15 It is better to debate a question without settling it than to settle a question without debating it.
  —Joseph Joubert; *Pensees,* 1810

## 227

.16 I keep six honest serving-men
(They taught me all I knew);
Their names are What and Why and
When
And How and Where and Who.
—Rudyard Kipling; *Just So Stories*, "The
Elephant's Child," 1902

.17 If we would have new knowledge, we must get
a whole new world of questions.
—Susanne K. Langer; *Philosophy in a New
Key*, 1957

.18 The only questions that really matter are the
ones you ask yourself.
—Ursula Le Guin; in *The Writer*, 1992

.19 The impulse to ask questions is among the
more primitive human lusts.
—Rose Macaulay; *A Casual Commentary*,
"Into Questions and Answers," 1926

.20 ...questions are the breath of life for a con-
versation.
—James Nathan Miller; *Reader's Digest*,
September, 1965

.21 There is really nothing more to say—except
why. But since why is difficult to handle, one
must take refuge in how.
—Toni Morrison; *The Bluest Eye*, 1970

.22 Good questions outrank easy answers.
—Paul A. Samuelson; *Newsweek*, August
21, 1978

.23 By nature's kindly disposition most questions
which it is beyond a man's power to answer do
not occur to him at all.
—George Santayana; *The Life of Reason*,
1905–6

.24 We should never accept anything reverently
without asking it a great many very searching
questions.
—George Bernard Shaw; Attributed

.25 No man really becomes a fool until he stops
asking questions.
—Charles Steinmetz; *The Apple Cart*,
"Preface," 1929

.26 It is better to ask some of the questions than
to know all the answers.
—James Thurber, *Fables for Our Times*,
1940

.27 Judge a man by his questions rather than his
answers.
—Voltaire; *Dictionnaire philosophique*, 1764

.28 Questions are never indiscreet; answers sometimes are.
—Oscar Wilde; *An Ideal Husband*, 1895

## 228 Quotations

.1 One must be a wise reader to quote wisely and
well.
—A.B. Alcott; *Table Talk* "Quotations,"
1877

.2 It needs no dictionaries of quotations to remind me that the eyes are the windows of the
soul.
—Max Beerbohm; *Zuleika Dobson*, 1911

.3 Quoting: the act of repeating erroneously the
words of another.
—Ambrose Bierce; *The Devil's Dictionary*,
1911

.4 Life itself is a quotation.
—Jorge Luis Borges; quoted in Jean Baudrillard's *Cool Memories*, 1987

.5 Shake(speare) was a dramatist of note who
lived by writing things to quote.
—Henry Cuyler Bunner; "Shake, Mulleary
and Go-ethe" c. 1896

.6 With just enough of learning to misquote.
—Lord Byron; *English Bards and Scotch Reviewers*, 1809

.7 A quotation, like a pun, should come un-
sought, and then be welcomed only for some
propriety of felicity justifying the intrusion.
—Robert William Chapman; *The Portrait
of a Scholar: The Art of Quotation*, 1920

.8 It is a good thing for an uneducated man to
read books of quotations.
—Winston Churchill; *My Early Life*, 1930

.9 To be apt in quotation is a splendid and dangerous gift. Splendid, because it ornaments a
man's speech with other men's jewels; dangerous, for the same reason.
—Robertson Davies; "Dangerous Jewels,"
*Toronto Daily Star*, October 1, 1960

.10 Quotations are useful in periods of ignorance
or obscurantist beliefs.
—Guy Debord; *Panegyric*, 1989

.11 Quotations, like much better things, has its
abuses. One may quote till one compiles.
—Isaac D'Israeli; *Curiosities of Literature:
Quotation*, 1791–1823

.12 Sometimes it seems the only accomplishment
my education ever bestowed on me, the ability to think in quotations.
—Margaret Drabble; *The Summer Birdcage*,
1977

.13 The everlasting quotation-lover dotes on the
husks of learning.
—Maria Edgeworth; *Thoughts on Bores*,
1826

**228**

.14 By necessity, by proclivity—and by delight, we all quote.
—Ralph Waldo Emerson; *Letters and Social Aims*, "Quotations and Originality," 1876

.15 I hate quotations. Tell me what you know.
—Ralph Waldo Emerson; *Journals*, 1849

.16 Quotations confess inferiority.
—Ralph Waldo Emerson; *Letters and Social Aims*, "Quotations and Originality," 1876

.17 I just want to know who said it. And also when he said it, and where he said it, and what it was he said, and whether he said it at all or whether I've merely imagined it.
—Michael Frayn; *Alphabetical Order*, 1977

.18 Every Quotation contributes something to the stability or enlargement of the language.
—Samuel Johnson; *Dictionary*, "Preface," 1755

.19 He wrapped himself in quotations—as a beggar would enfold himself in the purple of emperors.
—Rudyard Kipling; *Many Inventions*, 1893

.20 Quotations judiciously chosen and properly introduced elucidate and heighten discourse.
—Herbert Lawrence; *The Contemplative Man*, 1771

.21 In England only uneducated people show off their knowledge; nobody quotes Latin or Greek authors in the course of conversation, unless he has never read them.
—George Mikes; *How to be an Alien*, 1946

.22 I quote others only in order the better to express myself.
—Michel de Montaigne; *Essays*, 1580

.23 The next best thing to being clever is being able to quote some one who is.
—Mary Pettibone Poole; *A Glass Eye at the Keyhole*, 1938

.24 He ranged his tropes, and preached up patience; Backed his opinions with quotations.
—Matthew Prior; *Paulo Purganti and His Wife*, 1708

.25 A fine quotation is a diamond on the finger of a man of wit, and a pebble in the hand of a fool.
—Joseph Roux; *Meditations of a Parish Priest*, 1886

.26 I always have a quotation for everything—it saves original thinking.
—Dorothy Sayers; *Have His Carcase*, 1932

**228**

.27 I often quote myself; it adds spice to my conversation.
—George Bernard Shaw; Quoted in *Reader's Digest*, 1943

.28 To be occasionally quoted is the only fame I care for.
—Alexander Smith; *Dreamthorp*, "Men of Letters," 1863

.29 It is better to be quotable than honest.
—Tom Stoppard; in *Guardian*, March 21, 1973

.30 Famous remarks are seldom quoted correctly.
—Simeon Strunsky; *No Mean City*, 1945

.31 One has to secrete a jelly in which to slip quotations down people's throats and one always secretes too much jelly.
—Virginia Woolf; *Leave the Letters Till We Are Dead*, 1981

.32 Some for renown, on scraps of learning dote, And think they grow immortal as they quote.
—Edward Young; *Last of Fame*, 1728

# **229** Radio

.1 Radio in the 30's was a calm and tranquil medium. Oleaginous-voiced announcers smoothly purred their commercial copy into the microphone enunciating each lubricated syllable. Tony Wrons was cooing his soothing poems. Bedtime stories were popular. Radio was one unruffled day from Cheerio in the early morning through to Music to Read By at midnight. Radio was fraught with politeness.
—Fred Allen; *Treadmill to Oblivion*, 1954

.2 TV just feeds you. Radio involves you.
—Himan Brown; *Newsweek*, 1974

.3 Radio wasn't outside our lives. It coincided with—and helped to shape—our childhood and adolescence. As we slogged toward maturity, it also grew up and turned into television, leaving behind, like dead skin, transistorized talk-radio and non-stop music shows.
—Vincent Canby; *New York Times*, January 30, 1987
[Critic Canby speaks of the golden age of radio.]

.4 People in America when listening to radio, like to lean forward. People in Britain like to lean back.
—Alistair Cooke; Quoted in *Celebrity*

**229**

Register, Cleveland Amory and Earl Blackwell, eds., 1963

.5   The power of the radio is not that it speaks to millions, but that it speaks intimately and privately to each one of those millions.
—Hallie Flanagan; *Dynamo*, 1943

.6   From talk radio to insult radio wasn't really that much of a leap.
—Leonore Fleischer; *The Fisher King*, 1991

.7   The transistor radio is the modern leper's bell.
—Ian Fleming; Quoted in 1970

.8   The radio … goes on early in the morning and is listened to at all hours of the day, until nine, ten and often eleven o'clock in the evening. This is certainly a sign that the grown-ups have infinite patience, but it also means that the power of absorption of their brains is pretty limited, with exceptions, of course—I don't want to hurt anyone's feelings. One or two news bulletins would be ample per day! But the old geese, well—I've said my piece!
—Anne Frank; *The Diary of a Young Girl*, 1947, entry for March 27, 1944

.9   It is astonishing how articulate one can become when alone and raving at a radio. Arguments and counter-arguments, rhetoric and bombast flow from one's lips like scurf from the hair of a bank manager.
—Stephen Fry; *Paperweight*, 1992

.10  Public radio is a ghetto of good taste.
—Garrison Keillor; "National Public Radio Broadcast," February 9, 1991

.11  Radio news is bearable. This is due to the fact that while the news is being broadcast the disc jockey is not allowed to talk.
—Fran Lebowitz; "Metropolitan Life," 1978

.12  The ideal voice for radio should have no substance, no sex, no owner, and a message of importance for every housewife.
—Edward R. Murrow; *The Observer*, 1969

.13  TV gives everyone an image, but radio gives birth to a million images in a million brains.
—Peggy Noonan; *What I Saw at the Revolution*, 1990

.14  A discovery that makes it possible for a man to deliver a speech and not only bore those nearby, but others hundreds of miles away.
—Agnes Repplier; in Emma Repplier, *Agnes Repplier*, 1957

.15  Radio is the creative theater of the mind.
—Wolfman Jack Smith; *Newsweek*, 1973

**229**

.16  Simply a radio personality who outlived his prime.
—Evelyn Waugh; Christopher Sykes, *Evelyn Waugh*, 1975
[Waugh speaks of Winston Churchill.]

.17  One of the chief pretenders to the throne of God is radio itself, which has acquired a sort of omniscience. I live in a strictly rural community, and people here speak of "The Radio" in the large sense, with an over-meaning. When they say "The Radio" they don't mean a cabinet, an electrical phenomenon, or a man in a studio, they refer to a pervading and somewhat godlike presence which has come into their lives and homes.
—E.B. White; "Sabbath Morn," February, 1939

.18  The radio is now something people listen to while they are doing something else.
—Tom Wolfe; *The Kandy-Kolored Tangerine-Flake Streamline Baby*, 1965

# **230** Rationalization

.1   How quick come the reasons for approving what we like!
—Jane Austen; *Persuasion*, 1818

.2   He was of that pleasant temperament which believes whatever it is comfortable to believe; he was always able to explain facts to suit his mental necessities.
—Margaret Deland; *Around Old Chester*, "The Third Volume," 1915

.3   Who supposes that it is an impossible contradiction to be superstitious and rationalizing at the same time?
—George Eliot; *Daniel Deronda*, 1876

.4   We do what we can and then make a theory to prove our performance the best.
—Ralph Waldo Emerson; *Journals*, 1834

.5   Two things cannot be reduced to rationalizing: time and beauty.
—Czeslaw Milosz; *Beginning with My Streets*, 1992

.6   There's nothing people can't contrive to praise or condemn and find justification for doing so, according to their age and their inclinations.
—Molière; *The Misanthrope*, 1666

# 231 Reading

.1 Reading is to the mind what exercise is to the body.
—Joseph Addison; *The Tatler*, 1709

.2 Reading is a basic tool in the living of a good life.
—Mortimer J. Adler; *How to Read a Book*, 1940

.3 To read is to translate, for no two person's experiences are the same.
—W.H. Auden; *The Dyer's Hand*, 1962

.4 Read not to contradict and confute, nor to believe and take for granted, nor to find talk and discourse, but to weigh and consider.
—Francis Bacon; *Essays*, "Of Studies," 1597

.5 When we read a story, we inhabit it. The covers of the book are like a roof and four walls. What is to happen next will take place within the four walls of the story. And this is possible because the story's voice makes everything its own.
—John Berger; "Ev'ry Time We Say Goodbye" in *Expressen*, Stockholm, November 3, 1990

.6 Because we all know how to read, we imagine that we know what to read. Enormous fallacy!
—Aldous Huxley; *Music at Night*, 1931

.7 We read to say what we have read.
—Charles Lamb; *New Times*, January 13, 1825

.8 What is reading but silent conversation?
—Walter Savage Landor; *Imaginary Conversations; Aristotle and Callisthenes*, 1824–53

.9 The unread story is not a story; it is little black marks on wood pulp. The reader, reading it, makes it live: a live thing, a story.
—Ursula Le Guin; *Dancing at the Edge of the World*, 1989

.10 What a writer asks of his reader is not so much to like as to listen.
—Henry Wadsworth Longfellow; *Complete Poetical and Prose Works*, 1886

.11 There are two motives for reading a book: one, that you enjoy it; the other, that you can boast of it.
—Bertrand Russell; *The Conquest of Happiness*, 1930

.12 We shouldn't teach great books; we should teach a love of reading.
—B.F. Skinner; in R. Evans *B.F. Skinner: The Man and His Ideas*, 1968

# 231

.13 To pass from hearing literature to reading it is to take a great and dangerous step.
—Robert Louis Stevenson; *Random Memories*, 1887

.14 When I am reading a book, whether wise or silly, it seems to me to be alive and talking to me.
—Jonathan Swift; *Thoughts on Various Subjects*, 1711

.15 For what are the classics but the noblest recorded thoughts of man? They are the only oracles which are not decayed.
—Henry David Thoreau; *Walden*, "Reading," 1854

.16 Ever since I was first read to, then started reading to myself, there has never been a line read that I didn't hear. As my eyes followed the sentence, a voice was saying it silently to me. It isn't my mother's voice, or the voice of any person I can identify, certainly not my own. It is human, but inward, and it is inwardly that I listen to it. It is to me the voice of the story or the poem itself.
—Eudora Welty; *One Writer's Beginnings*, "Listening," 1934

.17 As I read, my ears are opened to the magic of the spoken word.
—Richard Wright; *12 Million Black Voices*, 1941

# 232 Reality

.1 Illusion and reality often merged.
—Peter Abrahams; *Tell Freedom*, 1954

.2 They took me on strange adventures among strange people. And there were no words between me and the story, only the story, which was the reality.
—Peter Abrahams; *Tell Freedom*, 1954

.3 Beware that you do not lose the substance by grasping the shadow.
—Aesop; *Fables*, "The Dog and the Shadow," c. 6th century B.C.

.4 Stories ought not to be just little bits of fantasy that are used to while away an idle hour; from the beginning of the human race stories have been used—by priests, by bards, by medicine men—as magic instruments of healing, of teaching, as a means of helping people come to terms with the fact that they continually have to face insoluble problems and unbearable realities.
—Joan Aiken; *The Way to Write for Children*, 1982

**232**

.5 Given that external reality is a fiction, the writer's role is almost superfluous. He does not need to invent fiction because it is already there.
—J.G. Ballard; interview in *Friends*, London, October 30, 1970

.6 If it were possible to talk to the unborn, one could never explain to them how it feels to be alive, for life is washed in the speechless real.
—Jacques Barzun; *The House of Intellect*, 1959

.7 It is not easy to free
Myth from reality
or rear this fellow up
to lurch, lurch with them
in the tranced dancing of men.
—Earle Birney; "The Bear on the Delhi Road" in *Modern Canadian Verse*, A.J.M. Smith, ed., 1967

.8 Words, as is well known, are the great foes of reality.
—Joseph Conrad; *Under Western Eyes*, "Prologue," 1911

.9 He who confronts the paradoxical exposes himself to reality.
—Friedrich Durrenmatt; *The Physicists*, "21 Points on the Physicists," 1962

.10 The stories that we tell ourselves and our children function to order our world, serving to create both a foundation upon which each of us constructs our sense of reality and a filter through which we process each event that confronts us every day.
—Henry Louis Gates, Jr.; in Goss and Barnes, eds., *Talk That Talk*, 1989

.11 How our story has been divided up among the truth-telling professionals! Religion, philosophy, history, poetry, compete with each other for our ears; and science competes with all together. And for each we have a different set of ears. But, though we hear much, what we are told is as nothing: none of it gives us ourselves, rather each story-kind steals us to make its reality of us.
—Laura Riding Jackson; *The Telling*, 1972

.12 Reality leaves a lot to the imagination.
—John Lennon; *The Way It Is*, CBC-TV, June, 1969

.13 To mention a loved object, a person, or a place to someone else is to invest that object with reality.
—Anne Morrow Lindbergh; *North to the Orient*, "Baker's Lake," 1935

**232**

.14 Reality is not the same to the doer as to the sayer.
—Haki Madhubuti; in *Black Poetry Writing*, 1975

.15 We live in a fantasy world, a world of illusion. The great task in life is to find reality.
—Iris Murdoch; in Rachel Billington, "Profile: Iris Murdoch," *The London Times*, 1980

.16 You too much not count overmuch on your reality as you feel it today, since, like that of yesterday, it may prove an illusion for you tomorrow.
—Luigi Pirandello; *Six Characters in Search of an Author*, 1921

.17 Reality can easily become the current fantasy.
—Judith Rossner; *August*, 1983

.18 A myth is a story which describes and illustrates in dramatic form certain deep structures of reality.
—Denis de Rougemont; *Love in the Western World*, 1939

.19 Language helps form the limits of our reality.
—Dale Spender; *Man Made Language*, 1980

# 233 Reason

.1 Reason is the only argument that belongs to man.
—Hugh Henry Brackenridge; *Modern Chivalry*, 1792–1815

.2 Between craft and credulity, the voice of reason is stifled.
—Edmund Burke; Letter to the Sheriff of Bristol, 1777

.3 He reasoned me out of my reason.
—Daniel Defoe; *Moll Flanders*, 1722

.4 Poor men's reasons are not heard.
—English Proverb

.5 Reason, however we flatter ourselves, hath not such despotic empire in our minds, that it can, with imperial voice, hush all our sorrow in a moment.
—Henry Fielding; *Jonathan Wild*, 1743

.6 If you will not hear reason, she will surely rap your knuckles.
—Benjamin Franklin; *Poor Richard's Almanack*, 1758

.7 'Tis vain to speak reason where 'twill not be heard.
—Thomas Fuller II; *Gnomologia*, 1732

## 233

.8 I'll not listen to reason. Reason always means what someone else has got to say.
—Elizabeth Gaskell; *Cranford*, 1853

.9 Man is a reasoning rather than a reasonable animal.
—Alexander Hamilton; *Works*, 1904

.10 Hearken to reason, or she will be heard.
—George Herbert; *Jacula Prudentum*, 1640

.11 Why and Wherefore set out one day,
To hunt for a wild Negation.
They agreed to meet at a cool retreat
On the point of Interrogation.
—Oliver Herford; "Metaphysics," 1898

.12 Why can't they let people have a chance to behave reasonably in stories.
—William Dean Howells; *The Rise of Silas Lapham*, 1885

.13 I asked for reasons, not sermons.
—Charles Kingsley; *Hereward the Wake*, 1866

.14 His tongue
Dropt manna, and could make the worse appear
The better reason.
—John Milton; *Paradise Lost*, 1665

.15 Human beings are the only creatures who are able to behave irrationally in the name of reason.
—Ashley Montagu; Quoted in *New York Times*, September 30, 1975

.16 There is a way of asking us for our reasons that leads us not only to forget our best reasons but also to conceive a stubborn aversion to all reasons. This way of asking makes people very stupid and is a trick used by tyrannical people.
—Friedrich Nietzsche; *The Gay Science*, 1882–87

.17 Most of our so-called reasoning consists in finding arguments for going on believing as we already do.
—James Robinson; *The Mind in the Making*, 1921

.18 The intelligible forms of ancient poets,
The fair humanities of old religion,
The power, the beauty, and the majesty
That had their haunts in dale or piny mountain,
Or forest by slow stream, or pebbly spring,
Or chasms and watery depths,—all these have vanished;
They live no longer in the faith of reason.
—Johann von Schiller; *On Naive and Reflective Poetry*, 1795–96

## 234 Religion

.1 Religion tends to speak the language of the heart, which is the language of friends, lovers, children, and parents.
—E.S. Ames; Newton, *My Idea of God*, 1959

.2 Religion is so far from being understood, that it is rendered by some explainers the most doubtful and disputable thing in the world.
—Thomas Amory; *The Life of John Buncle*, 1756

.3 Religion—that voice of the deepest human experience.
—Matthew Arnold; *Culture and Anarchy: Sweetness and Light*, 1869

.4 And is it true? And is it true,
This most tremendous tale of all,
Seen in a stained-glass window's hue,
A Baby in an ox's stall?
The Maker of the stars and sea
Became a Child on earth for me?
—Sir John Betjeman; *A Few Late Chrysanthemums*, "Christmas," 1954

.5 I expect you remember Bultmann's essay on the 'demythologizing' of the New Testament? My view of it today would be, not that he went 'too far', as most people thought, but that he didn't go far enough. It is not only the 'mythological' concepts such as miracle, ascension, and so on (which are not in principle separable from the concepts of God, faith, etc.) but 'religious' concepts generally, which are problematic.
—Dietrich Bonhoeffer; *Letters and Papers from Prison*, 1944

.6 The religions of the world are the ejaculations of a few imaginative men.
—Ralph Waldo Emerson; *Essays, Second Series*, 1849

.7 The religions we call false were once true.
—Ralph Waldo Emerson; *Essays, Second Series*, "Character," 1844

.8 Many have quarreled about religion that have never practiced it.
—Benjamin Franklin; *Poor Richard's Almanack*, 1753

.9 Religion is an illusion and it derives its strength from the fact that it falls in with our instinctual desires.
—Sigmund Freud; *New Introductory Lectures on Psychoanalysis*, "A Philosophy of Life," 1932

# 234

.10 Mythology is not religion. It may rather be re-garded as the ancient substitute, the political counterpart for dogmatic theology.
—William Hare; *Guesses and Truth*, 1827

.11 Religion is the most widely debated and least agreed upon phenomenon of human history.
—Georgia Harkness; *Conflicts in Religious Thought*, 1929

.12 Religion is a way of walking, not a way of talking.
—W.R. Inge; *Outspoken Essays*, 1919

.13 Myth is someone else's religion.
—Caroline Llewellyn; *The Lady of the Labyrinth*, 1990

.14 When the Europeans came, they said we were nonbelievers. They denied the validity of our ancient religions.
—Miriam Makeba; *My Story*, 1987

.15 Each religion, by the help of more or less myth which it takes more or less seriously, proposes some method of fortifying the human soul and enabling it to make its peace with its destiny.
—George Santayana; *Persons and Places: My Host the World*, 1953

.16 Mythology is the religious sentiment growing wild.
—Friedrich von Schelling; *Philosophie der Kunst*, 1800

.17 Religion is like love. It flourishes best in silence, and is to be felt, not spoken of.
—Olive Schreiner; *Undine*, 1876, published 1928

.18 There is only one religion, though there are a hundred versions of it.
—George Bernard Shaw; *Arms and the Man*, "Preface," 1894

# 235 Remarks

.1 Our pride hinders us from being made wise by the remarks of our friends.
—Anonymous; *The Ladies Advocate*, 1749

.2 Just enough truth to make the remark unbearable.
—Thomas Hardy; *Desperate Remedies*, 1871

.3 A fool's remark is like a thorn concealed in mud.
—Irish Proverb

.4 Their qualifying remarks showed in their very dispraises too much liking.
—Samuel Richardson; *Clarissa Harlowe*, 1747–48

# 235

.5 Remarks are not literature.
—Gertrude Stein; *The Autobiography of Alice B. Toklas*, 1930
[Said to Ernest Hemingway.]

.6 Famous remarks are very seldom quoted correctly.
—Simeon Strunsky; *No Mean City*, 1944

.7 Often a quite assified remark becomes sanctified by use and petrified by custom; it is then a permanency, its term of activity a geologic period.
—Mark Twain; "Does the Race of Man Love a Lord?," *Collected Tales, Sketches & Essays, 1891–1910*, Louis J. Budd, ed., 1992

# 236 Repartee

.1 I cannot think of any repartee
I simply wag my great, long, furry ears.
—E.C. Bentley, "Ballade of Plain Common Sense," 1905

.2 Violence is the repartee of the illiterate.
—Alan Brien; *Punch*, 1973

.3 Repartee is what you wish you'd said.
—Heywood Broun; in Robert E. Drennan; *The Algonquin Wits*, 1968

.4 Silence is the unbearable repartee.
—G.K. Chesterton; Attributed

.5 A majority is always the best repartee.
—Benjamin Disraeli; *Tancred*, 1847

.6 Repartee is a duel fought with the point of jokes.
—Max Eastman; *Enjoyment of Laughter*, 1936

.7 A genius for repartee is a gift for saying what a wise man thinks only.
—Thomas Hardy; *The Collected Letters of Thomas Hardy*, 1978

.8 Repartee: any reply that is so clever that it makes the listener wish he had said it himself.
—Elbert Hubbard; *The Philistine*, 1895

.9 Repartee is something we think of twenty-four hours too late.
—Mark Twain; *Mark Twain Speaking*, Paul Fatout, ed., 1976

.10 There are men who fear repartee in a wife more keenly than a sword.
—P.G. Wodehouse; *Jill the Reckless*, 1922

# 237 Repetition

.1 That which is repeated too often becomes insipid and tedious.
  —Nicolas Boileau-Despreaux; *The Art of Poetry*, 1674

.2 She says the same thing over and over again thinking repetition will substitute for proof.
  —Rita Mae Brown; *In Her Day*, 1976

.3 There are only two or three human stories, and they go on repeating themselves as fiercely as they had never happened before.
  —Willa Cather; *O Pioneers!*, 1913

.4 If you don't say anything, you won't be called on to repeat it.
  —Calvin Coolidge; Saying, c. 1925

.5 What if one does say the same things,—of course in a little different form each time,—over and over? If he has anything to say worth saying, that is just what he ought to do.
  —Oliver Wendell Holmes, Sr.; *Over the Teacups*, 1891

.6 What so tedious as a twice-told tale?
  —Homer; *Odyssey*, c. 9th century B.C.

.7 A meaningless phrase repeated again and again begins to resemble truth.
  —Barbara Kingsolver; *Animal Dreams*, 1990

.8 A truth does not become greater by frequent repetition.
  —Maimonides; *Tehiyat HaMethim: Respona*, prior to 1204

.9 I hope that we are like the Jews in that we never get tired of telling our story and that people will be around to tell it over and over again.
  —Melba Moore; "The Making of a Black Legacy in Film," *Ebony*, March, 1985

.10 Use not vain repetitions.
  —New Testament: Matthew

.11 Repetition is the mother, not only to study, but also of education. Like the fresco-painter, the teacher lays colors on the wet plaster which ever fade away, and which he must ever renew until they remain and brightly shine.
  —Jean Paul Richter; *Levana*, 1807

.12 Repetition is the only form of permanence that nature can achieve.
  —George Santayana; *The Life of Reason*, 1905–6

.13 There is no absurdity so palpable but that it may be firmly planted in the human head if you only begin to inculcate it before the age of

five, by constantly repeating it with an air of great solemnity.
  —Arthur Schopenhauer; *Studies in Pessimism*, "Psychological Observations," 1851

.14 A good tale is none the worse for being twice told.
  —Sir Walter Scott; *Old Mortality*, 1816

.15 What the first philosopher taught the last will have to repeat.
  —Henry David Thoreau; *Walden*, 1854

.16 After people have repeated a phrase a great number of times, they begin to realize it has meaning and may even be true.
  —H.G. Wells; *The Happy Turning*, 1946

# 238 Reputation

.1 'Tis better never to be named than to be ill spoken of.
  —Susannah Centlivre; *The Basset Table*, 1705

.2 There are two modes of establishing our reputation; to be praised by honest men, and to be abused by rogues.
  —Charles Caleb Colton; *Lacon*, 1825

.3 The invisible thing called a Good Name is made up of the breath of numbers that speak well of you.
  —Lord of Halifax (George Savile), *Works*, 1750

.4 What people say behind your back is your standing in the community in which you live.
  —Edgar Watson Howe; *Country Town Sayings*, 1911

.5 Many a man's reputation would not know his character if they met on the street.
  —Elbert Hubbard; *The Philistine*, 1897

.6 Woe unto you, when all men shall speak well of you!
  —New Testament: Luke

.7 At every word a reputation dies.
  —Alexander Pope; *Rape of the Lock*, 1714

.8 Do you want to injure someone's reputation? Don't speak ill of him, speak too well.
  —Andre Siegfried; *Some Maxims*, 1950s

.9 To be mis-spoken and mis-seen of men, Which is not for high-seated hearts to fear.
  —Algernon Swinburne; *Bothwell*, 1874

# 238

.10 One man lies in his words and gets a bad reputation; another in his manners, and enjoys a good one.
—Henry David Thoreau; *Journal*, June 25, 1852

.11 The only way to compel men to speak good of us is to do it.
—Voltaire; Attributed

.12 There is only one thing in the world worse than being talked about, and that is not being talked about.
—Oscar Wilde; *The Picture of Dorian Gray*, 1891

# 239 Resolution

.1 Resolved to take fate by the throat and shake a living out of her.
—Louisa May Alcott; in Edna D. Cheney, ed. *Louisa May Alcott: Her Life, Letters, and Journals*, published 1889

.2 Resolution is necessary to decision unequivocal and satisfactory, unawed by forensic opinion or the influence of individuals.
—Hugh Henry Brackenridge; *Modern Chivalry*, 1792–1815

.3 Resolve to perform what you ought; perform without fail what you resolve.
—Benjamin Franklin; *Autobiography*, 1791

.4 A resolution to avoid an evil is seldom framed till the evil is so far advanced as to make avoidance impossible.
—Thomas Hardy; *Far from the Madding Crowd*, 1874

.5 Every man naturally persuades himself that he can keep his resolutions, nor is he convinced of his imbecility but by length of time and frequency of experiment.
—Samuel Johnson; *Prayers and Meditations*, 1785

.6 He who breaks a resolution is a weakling;
He who makes one is a fool.
—F.L. Knowles; *A Cheerful Yearbook*, c. 1880

.7 Resolutions are easily formed when the heart suggests them.
—Charlotte Lenox; *Henrietta*, 1758

.8 It is always during a passing state of mind that we make lasting resolutions.
—Marcel Proust; *The Maxims of Marcel Proust*, 1948

# 239

.9 Never tell your resolution before hand.
—John Selden; *Table-Talk: Wisdom*, c. 1654

.10 Good resolutions are simply checks that men draw on a bank where they have no account.
—Oscar Wilde; *The Picture of Dorian Gray*, 1891

.11 Good resolutions are useless attempts to interfere with scientific laws.
—Oscar Wilde; *The Picture of Dorian Gray*, 1891

# 240 Rhetoric

.1 Rhetoric may be defined as the faculty of observing in any given case the available means of persuasion.
—Aristotle; *Rhetoric*, c. 322 B.C.

.2 For all a rhetorician's rules
Teach nothing but to name his tools.
—Samuel Butler I; *Hudibras*, 1663

.3 His speech was a fine example, on the whole,
Of rhetoric, which the learn'd call "*rigmarole.*"
—Lord Byron; *Don Juan*, 1818

.4 The Orator persuades and carries all with him, he knows not how; the Rhetorician can prove that he ought to have persuaded and carried all with him.
—Thomas Carlyle; *Critical and Miscellaneous Essays*, "Characteristics," 1839

.5 Eloquence is the language of nature, and cannot be learned in the schools; but rhetoric is the creature of art, which he who feels least will most excel in.
—Charles Caleb Colton; *Lacon*, 1820

.6 Sweet, silent rhetoric of persuading eyes,
Dumb eloquence, whose power doth move the blood
More than the words of wisdom of the wise.
—Samuel Daniel; "The Complaint of Rosamond," 1592

.7 A sophistical rhetorician, inebriated with the exuberance of his own verbosity, and gifted with an egotistical imagination that can at all times command an interminable and inconsistent series of arguments to malign an opponent and glorify himself.
—Benjamin Disraeli; Speech, July 27, 1878

.8 I confess to some pleasure from the stinging rhetoric or a rattling oath.
—Ralph Waldo Emerson; *Journals*, 1840

240

.9 His sober lips then did he softly part,
Whence of pure rhetoric whole streams
outflow.
—Edward Fairfax; *Godfrey of Bullogne*,
1600

.10 Spare your Rhetoric and speak Logic.
—Thomas Fuller II; *Gnomologia*, 1732

.11 He needs to acquire the art of seeming to
pluck, as he goes along in the progress of his
speech, as by the wayside, some flower of
rhetoric.
—Benjamin Harrison; Speech, New England Society of Pennsylvania, December 22, 1893

.12 The strongest figure in female rhetoric to excite compassion is a flood of tears.
—Charles Jenner; *The Placid Man*, 1770

.13 Rhetoric takes no real account of the art in literature and morality takes no account of the
art in life.
—Joseph Wood Krutch; *The Modern Temper*, 1929

.14 You have to persuade men to action not by
reasoning, but by rhetoric.
—W. Somerset Maugham; *Christmas Hol-
iday*, 1939

.15 Rhetoric in a worthy cause has good chances
of carrying the gravest.
—George Meredith; *The Tragic Comedians*, 1880

.16 Enjoy your dear wit and gay rhetoric, That
hath so well been taught her dazzling fence.
—John Milton; *Cosmus*, 1634

.17 Today violence is the rhetoric of the period.
—Jose Ortega y Gasset; *The Revolt of the
Masses*, 1959

.18 There is a Truth and Beauty in Rhetoric; but
it oftener serves ill turns than good ones.
—William Penn; *Some Fruits of Solitude*,
1693

.19 Rhetoric, or the art of speaking, is an enchantment of the soul.
—Plato; *The Greek Anthology*, c. 10th century A.D.

.20 Rhetoric is the art of ruling the minds of men.
—Plato; *Phaedrus*, c. 385 B.C.

.21 Rhetoric without logic is like a tree with leaves
and blossoms, but no root; yet more are taken
with rhetoric than logic, because they are
caught with fine expressions which they understand not reason.
—John Selden; *Table-Talk: Preaching*, c.
1654

240

.22 The heavenly rhetoric of thine eyes.
—William Shakespeare; *Love's Labour's
Lost*, 1595

.23 Practice rhetoric in your common talk.
—William Shakespeare; *The Taming of the
Shrew*, 1594

.24 I can do you blood and love without the
rhetoric, and I can do you blood and rhetoric
without the love and I can do you all three
concurrent or consecutive but I can't do you
love and rhetoric without the blood. Blood is
compulsory—they're all blood you see.
—Tom Stoppard; *Rosencrantz and Guildenstern Are Dead*, 1967

.25 Flowers of rhetoric, in sermons and serious
discourses, are like the blue and red flowers in
corn, pleasing to them who come only for
amusement, but prejudicial to him who would
reap profit.
—Jonathan Swift; *Thoughts on Various Subjects*, 1714

.26 What is called eloquence in the forum is commonly found to be rhetoric in the study.
—Henry David Thoreau; *Walden*, 1854

# 241 Rhyme

.1 The misliking of rhyming beginneth not now
of any newfangle singularity, but hath been
long misliked of many, and that of men of the
greatest learning and deepest judgment.
—Roger Ascham; *The Schoolmaster*, 1570

.2 I'm tired of Love: I'm still more tired of
Rhyme.
But Money gives me pleasure all the time.
—Hilaire Belloc; *Sonnets and Verse*, "Fa-
tigue," 1923

.3 Be the subject lighthearted or sublime,
sense always should agree with rhyme.
—Nicolas Boileau-Despreaux; *L'Art Poetique*, 1674

.4 For rhyme the rudder is of verses,
With which like ships they steer their
courses.
—Samuel Butler; *Hudibras*, 1662–80

.5 The mighty master of unmeaning rhyme.
—Lord Byron; *English Bards and Scotch Re-
viewers*, 1809
[Byron speaks of Erasmus Darwin.]

.6 Rhymes are scarce in this world of ours.
—Charles Stuart Calverley; "Lovers, and a
Reflection," 1862

## 241

.7 Abandoning rhyme and fixed rules in favor of other intuitive rules brings us back to fixed rules and to rhyme with renewed respect.
—Jean Cocteau; *Professional Secrets*, 1922

.8 When you write in prose you say what you mean. When you write in rhyme you say what you must.
—Oliver Wendell Holmes, Sr., *Over the Teacups*, 1891

.9 The troublesome and modern bondage of Rhyming.
—John Milton; *Paradise Lost*, 1667

.10 The more rhyme there is in poetry the more danger of its tricking the writer into something other than the urge in the beginning.
—Carl Sandburg; Quoted in *The Complete Poems of Carl Sandburg*, "Notes for a Preface," 1986

.11 Verse without rhyme is a body without a soul.
—Jonathan Swift; "Advice to a Young Poet," December 1, 1720

.12 But here I am in Kent and Christendom, Among the Muses, where I read and rhyme.
—Sir Thomas Wyatt the Elder; "Mine own John Poins," 1536

.13 Rhyme often makes mystical nonsense pass with the critics for wit.
—William Wycherley; *The Plain-Dealer*, 1676

## 242 Riddles

.1 I cannot forecast to you the action of Russia. It is a riddle wrapped in a mystery inside an enigma.
—Winston Churchill; Radio Talk, October 1, 1939

.2 All is riddle, and the key to a riddle is another riddle.
—Ralph Waldo Emerson; *The Conduct of Life*, "Illusions," 1860

.3 Life's perhaps the only riddle That we shrink from giving up.
—W.S. Gilbert; *The Gondoliers*, 1889

.4 The novelist who could interpret the common feelings of commonplace people would have the answer to "the riddle of the painful earth" on his tongue.
—William Dean Howells; *The Rise of Silas Lapham*, 1885

.5 Women, as they are like riddles in being unintelligible, so generally resemble them in this,

## 242

that they please us no longer once we know them.
—Alexander Pope; *Thoughts on Various Subjects*, 1727

.6 When on the road to Thebes, Oedipus met the Sphinx, who asked him her riddle, his answer was: *Man*. This simple word destroyed the monster. We have many monsters to destroy. Let us think of Oedipus' answer.
—George Seferis; Speech upon receiving the Nobel Prize, 1963

.7 Although a subtler Sphinx renew Riddles of death Thebes never knew.
—Percy Bysshe Shelley; *Selected Poems*, published, 1977

.8 I talk in riddles. I'd rather speak plainly. But some ways are still unmapped.
—Elizabeth Smart; *In the Meantime*, "All I Know About Why I Write," 1984

.9 You love to speak in riddles.
—Sophocles; *Oedipus the King*, c. 409 B.C.

.10 We live amongst riddles and mysteries.
—Laurence Sterne; *Tristram Shandy*, 1760–67

## 243 Ridicule

.1 The talent of turning men into ridicule, and exposing to laughter those one converses with, is the qualification of little ungenerous tempers.
—Joseph Addison; *The Spectator*, December 15, 1711

.2 To make fun of a person to his face is a brutal way of amusing one's self; be delicate and cunning, and keep your laugh in your sleeve, lest you frighten away your game.
—Gelett Burgess; *The Romance of the Commonplace*, "The Use of Fools," 1916

.3 There is hardly any mental misery worse than that of having our own serious phrases, our own rooted beliefs, caricatured by a charlatan or a hireling.
—George Eliot; *Felix Holt, The Radical*, 1866

.4 We grow tired of everything but turning others into ridicule, and congratulating ourselves on their defects.
—William Hazlitt; *The Plain Speaker*, 1826

.5 Mockery is often poverty of wit.
—Jean de La Bruyere; *Characters*, 1688

.6 The most effective way of attacking vice is to expose it to public ridicule. People can put up

## 243

with rebukes but they cannot bear being laughed at: they are prepared to be wicked but they dislike appearing ridiculous.
—Molière; *Tartuffe*, "Preface," 1664

.7  Ridicule may be a shield, but it is not a weapon.
—Dorothy Parker; in John Keats, *You Might As Well Live*, 1970

.8  Ridicule often checks what is absurd, and fully as often smothers that which is noble.
—Sir Walter Scott; *Quentin Durward*, 1823

.9  Shall quips and sentences and these paper bullets of the brain awe a man from the career of his humor?
—William Shakespeare; *Much Ado About Nothing*, 1598

.10  Scoffing come not of wisdom.
—Sir Philip Sidney; *Apologie for Poetrie*, "Objection Stated," 1595

.11  A bigot delights in public ridicule, for he thinks he is a martyr.
—Sydney Smith; *Peter Plymley Letters*, 1807

.12  Mockery is the fume of little hearts.
—Alfred, Lord Tennyson; "Guinevere," 1869

.13  Love can bear anything better than ridicule.
—Caitlin Thomas; *Leftover Life to Kill*, 1957

.14  An ounce of ridicule is often more potent than a hundred-weight of argument.
—Anthony Trollope; *The Eustace Diamonds*, 1873

## 244 Romance

.1  She had been forced into prudence in her youth, she learned romance as she grew older—the natural sequence of an unnatural beginning.
—Jane Austen; *Persuasion*, 1818

.2  The essence of romantic love is that wonderful beginning, after which sadness and impossibility may become the rule.
—Anita Brookner; *A Friend from England*, 1987

.3  Love stories are only fit for the solace of people in the insanity of puberty. No healthy adult human being can really care whether so-and-so does or does not succeed in satisfying his

## 244

physiological uneasiness by the aid of some particular person or not.
—Aleister Crowley; *The Confessions of Aleister Crowley*, 1970

.4  Romance and poetry, ivy, lichens and wallflowers need ruin to make them grow.
—Nathaniel Hawthorne; *The Marble Faun*, "Preface," 1860

.5  And what's romance? Usually, a nice little tale where you have everything As You Like It, where rain never wets your jacket and gnats never bite your nose and it's always daisy time.
—D.H. Lawrence; *Studies in Classic American Literature*, 1924

.6  He loved the twilight that surrounds The borderland of old romance.
—Henry Wadsworth Longfellow; *Tales of a Wayside Inn*, "Prelude," 1863

.7  A romantic tale on her eyelashes.
—George Meredith; *The Egotist*, 1879

.8  Romantic love is the privilege of emperors, kings, soldiers and artists; it is the butt of democrats, traveling salesmen, magazine poets, and the writers of American novels.
—George Jean Nathan; *Testament of a Critic*, 1931

.9  As soon as histories are properly told there is no more need of romances.
—Walt Whitman; *Leaves of Grass*, "Preface," 1855

.10  Nothing spoils a romance so much as a sense of humor in the woman.
—Oscar Wilde; *A Woman of No Importance*, 1893

## 245 Rules

.1  No rule is so general, which admits not some exception.
—Robert Burton; *The Anatomy of Melancholy*, 1621

.2  What you do not want done to yourself, do not do to others.
—Confucius; *Analects*, c. 479 B.C.

.3  There's no rule so wise but what it's a pity for somebody or other.
—George Eliot; *Adam Bede*, 1859

.4  Nature provides exceptions to every rule.
—Margaret Fuller; "The Great Lawsuit. Man Versus Men. Woman Versus Women," *The Dial*, July 1843

**245**

.5  Rules and models destroy genius and art.
  —William Hazlitt; "Thoughts On Taste," *The Edinburgh Review*, 1818

.6  No rule so good as rule of thumb, if it hit.
  —James Kelly; *Scottish Proverbs*, 1721

.7  Experiences show that exceptions are as true as rules.
  —Edith Ronald Mirrielees; *Story Writing*, "The Substance of the Story," 1947

.8  There is only one rule for being a good talker; learn to listen.
  —Christopher Morley; *Works*, 1927

.9  The golden rule is that there are no golden rules.
  —George Bernard Shaw; *Man and Superman*, "Maxims for Revolutionists: The Golden Rule," 1903

.10 A story should aim to please, at least seem true, be apropos, well told, concise, and new; and whensoe'er it deviates from these rules, the wise will sleep, and leave applause to fools.
  —John Stillingfleet; Attributed

.11 General rules will bear hard on particular cases.
  —Harriet Beecher Stowe; *Uncle Tom's Cabin*, 1852

.12 When I read some of the rules for speaking and writing the English language correctly … I think
  Any fool can make a rule,
  And every fool will mind it.
  —Henry David Thoreau; *Winter*, February 3, 1860

.13 General rules are dangerous of application in particular instances.
  —Charlotte M. Yonge; *The Pillars of the House*, Vol. 2, 1889

# **246** Rumor

.1  Quick to perish is rumor by a woman voiced.
  —Aeschylus; *Agamemnon*, 458 B.C.

.2  Trying to squash a rumor is like trying to unring a bell.
  —Shana Alexander; *Talking Woman*, 1976

.3  Rumor is untraceable, incalculable, and infectious.
  —Margot Asquith; *More Or Less About Myself*, 1934

.4  Rumor have a nimbler foot than the mule.
  —James Fenimore Cooper; *The Headsman*, 1833

**246**

.5  Rumor, busy overmuch, persists in flitting and chattering about town. It hears all sorts of shocking things. It makes the world of five miles round, quite merry.
  —Charles Dickens; *Bleak House*, 1852–3

.6  Rumor, with her hundred babbling tongues.
  —Sarah Fielding; *The History of the Countess Dellwyn*, 1859

.7  "They say so" is half a lie.
  —Thomas Fuller II; *Gnomologia*, 1732

.8  Avoid the talk of men. For talk is mischievous light, and easily raised, but hard to bear and difficult to escape. Talk never wholly dies away when voiced by many people.
  —Hesiod; *Works and Days*, c. 800 B.C.

.9  Men have a natural passion for spreading rumors.
  —Livy; *Ab Urbe Condita*, c. 25 B.C.

.10 Rumor is seldom at a loss for answers.
  —Herman Melville; *The Confidence Man*, 1857

.11 A cruel story runs on wheels, and every hand oils the wheels as they run.
  —Ouida; *Wisdom, Wit and Pathos*, 1884

.12 No fleeter thing is known to man than the voice of rumor.
  —Plautus; *Fragments*, c. 200 B.C.

.13 I cannot tell how the truth may be; I tell the tale as 'twas said to me.
  —Sir Walter Scott; *The Lay of the Last Minstrel*, 1805

.14 This from Rumor's idle tongue I idly heard.
  —William Shakespeare; *King John*, 1595

.15 Rumor violently blows the sails of popular judgments.
  —Sir Philip Sidney; *Arcadia*, 1584

.16 Merely a drop of acid from rumor's unclean tongue.
  —Rex Stout; *The Unbroken Vase*, 1941

.17 What some invent the rest enlarge.
  —Jonathan Swift; *Journal of a Modern Lady*, 1711

.18 Rumor is not always wrong.
  —Tacitus; *Agricola*, c. A.D. 98

.19 Rumor, though she flies so fast and so far, is often slow in reaching those ears which would be most interested in her tidings.
  —Anthony Trollope; *Phineas Finn*, 1869

.20 A hundred tongues, a hundred mouths, a voice of iron.
  —Virgil; *Georgics*, 29 B.C.

# 247 Sadness

.1 Of all tales 'tis saddest—and more sad,
Because it makes us smile.
—Lord Byron; *Don Juan*

.2 Farewell sadness
Hello sadness.
—Paul Eluard; *Poesie et Verité*, "La vie immediate," 1942

.3 Listen to my tale of woe.
—Eugene Field; "The Little Peach," 1890

.4 This is the saddest story I have ever heard.
—Ford Madox Ford (originally Ford Hermann Hueffer); *The Good Soldier*, 1915
[This is the first line of the novel.]

.5 I cannot explain the sadness
That's fallen on my breast.
An odd, old fable haunts me,
And will not let me rest.
—Heinrich Heine; "Homecoming," 1823–4

.6 All the piteous tales that tears
Have water'd since the world was born.
—Thomas Hood; "Ode to Melancholy," 1825

.7 Melancholy shrinks from communication.
—Samuel Johnson; *Rasselas*, 1759

.8 There are few more melancholy sensations than those with which we regard scenes of past pleasure, when altered and deserted.
—Sir Walter Scott; *Rob Roy*, 1817

.9 I could a tale unfold whose lightest word
Would harrow up thy soul.
—William Shakespeare; *Hamlet*, 1600

.10 For God's sake, let us sit upon the ground
And tell sad stories of the death of kings!
—William Shakespeare; *Richard II*, 1595

.11 A sad tale's best for winter:
I have one of sprites and goblins.
—William Shakespeare; *Winter's Tale*, 1609

.12 Come listen to my mournful tale,
    Ye tender hearts and lovers dear;
Nor will you scorn to heave a sigh,
    Nor need you blush to shed a tear.
—William Shenstone; "Jenny Dawson," 1737

.13 She [Helen Keller] likes stories that make her cry—I think we all do, it's so nice to feel sad when you've nothing particular to be sad about.
—Annie Sullivan; Letter, 1887

.14 A lamentation and an ancient tale of wrong,
Like a tale of little meaning tho' the words are strong.
—Alfred, Lord Tennyson; *Poems*, "The Lotus-Eaters," 1832

# 247

.15 For of all sad words of tongue or pen,
The saddest are these: "It might have been!"
—John Greenleaf Whittier; "Maud Muller," 1856

# 248 Sarcasm

.1 I think I detect sarcasm. I can't be doing with sarcasm. You know what they say? Sarcasm is the greatest weapon of the smallest mind.
—Alan Ayckbourn; *Woman in Mind*, 1986

.2 What I claim is to live to the full the contradiction of my time, which may well make sarcasm the condition of truth.
—Roland Barthes; *Mythologies*, "Preface," 1957

.3 And that sarcastic levity of tongue,
The stinging of a heart the world have stung.
—Lord Byron; "Lara," 1814

.4 Sarcasm I now see to be, in general, the language of the Devil; for which reason I have long since as good as renounced it.
—Thomas Carlyle; *Sartor Resartus*, 1883–4

.5 Her sarcasm was so quick, so fine at the point—it was like being touched by a metal so cold that one doesn't know whether one is burned or chilled.
—Willa Cather; *My Mortal Enemy*, 1926

.6 Sarcasm is the questionable weapon of questionable intellects.
—Robert G. Dean; *Layoff*, 1942

.7 He has to learn that petulance is not sarcasm, and that insolence is not invective.
—Benjamin Disraeli; Speech, House of Commons, December 16, 1852
[The English Prime Minister refers to Sir Charles Wood.]

.8 Sarcasm: the last refuge of modest and chaste-souled people when the privacy of their soul is coarsely and intrusively invaded.
—Feodor Dostoyevsky; *Notes from the Underground*, 1864

.9 The arrows of sarcasm are barbed with contempt.... It is the sneer of the satire, the ridicule, that galls and wounds.
—Washington Gladden; *Things Old and New: Taming the Tongue*, 1909

.10 Keep a store of sarcasms, and know how to use them.
—Baltasar Gracian; *The Art of Worldly Wisdom*, 1647

**248**

.11 And I must twist my little gift of words
Into a scourge of rough and knotted cords
Unmusical, that whistle as they swing
To leave on shameless backs that purple
sting.
—J.R. Lowell; "Epistle to George William
Curtis"; *Letters*, Charles Eliot Norton,
ed. 1894

.12 Sarcasm confers a little aristocracy straightway and sharp on the source of the man who does not imagine that he is using it.
—George Meredith; *Beauchamp's Career*,
1876

.13 Many men have withstood an argument who fell before a sarcasm.
—Elizabeth Elton Smith; *The Three Eras of Woman's Life*, 1836

# **249** Satire

.1 One man's pointlessness is another man's barbed satire.
—Franklin P. Adams; *Nods and Becks*, 1944

.2 He that hath a satirical vein, as he maketh others afraid of his wit, so he had need be afraid of others' memory.
—Francis Bacon; *Essays*, "Of Discourse,"
1625

.3 Of all human dealings, satire is the very lowest, and most mean and common. It is equivalent in words for what bullying is in deeds; and no more bespeaks a clever man, than the other does a brave one.
—R.D. Blackmore; *Lorna Doone*, 1869

.4 But satire, ever moral, ever new,
Delights the reader and instructs him, too.
She, if good sense refine her sterling page,
Oft shakes some rooted folly of the age.
—Nicolas Boileau-Despreaux; *The Art of Poetry*, "Satire," 1674

.5 Satire is tragedy plus time. You give it enough time, the public, the reviewers will allow you to satirize it. Which is rather ridiculous when you think about it.
—Lenny Bruce; *The Essential Lenny Bruce*,
"Performing and the Art of Comedy,"
John Cohen, ed. 1967

.6 My satire shall be general. I would as much disdain to be personal with an anonymous pen, as to attack an unarmed man in the dark with the dagger I had kept concealed.
—Fanny Burney; *Cecilia*, 1782

**249**

.7 The satirist is prevented by repulsion from gaining a better knowledge of the world he is attracted to, yet he is forced by attraction to concern himself with the world that repels him.
—Italo Calvino; "Definitions of Territories: Comedy" in *Il Caffe*, Rome, February, 1967

.8 How terrible a weapon is satire in the hand of a great genius!
—Colley Cibber; *Apology for His Life*, 1740

.9 What arouses the indignation of the honest satirist is not, unless the man is a prig, the fact that people in positions of power or influence behave idiotically, or even that they behave wickedly. It is that they conspire successfully to impose upon the public a picture of themselves as so very sagacious, honest, and well-intentioned.
—Claud Cockburn; *Cockburn Sums Up*,
"The Worst Possible Taste," 1981

.10 By rights, satire is a lonely and introspective occupation, for nobody can describe a fool to the life without much patient self-inspection.
—Frank Moore Colby; *The Colby Essays*,
"Simple Simon," 1926

.11 I believe no satirist could breathe this air. If another Juvenal or Swift could rise up among us tomorrow, he would be hunted down. If you have any knowledge of our literature, and give me the name of any man, American born and bred, who has anatomized our follies as a people, and not as this or that party; and who has escaped the foulest and most brutal slander, the most inveterate hatred and intolerant pursuit; it will be a strange name in my ears, believe me.
—Charles Dickens; *Martin Chuzzlewit*,
1844

.12 Satire has always shone among the rest,
And is the boldest way, if not the best,
To tell men freely of their foulest faults;
To laugh at their vain deeds and vainer
thoughts.
—John Dryden; *Essay Upon Satire*, 1693

.13 It is the unkindness of the person who levels the satire at us, and not the satire itself, that pierces the soul.
—Sarah Fielding; *The Lives of Cleopatra and Octavia*, 1757

.14 Strange! that a Man who has wit enough to write a Satire should have folly enough to publish it.
—Benjamin Franklin; *Poor Richard's Almanack*, 1742

## 249

.15 The satire should be like the porcupine,
That shoots sharp quills out in every angry
line.
—Bishop Joseph Hall; *Virgidemiae*, 1598

.16 Satirists gain the applause of others through
fear, not through love.
—William Hazlitt; *Characteristics*, 1823

.17 Humor and satire are more effective techniques for expressing social statements than
direct comment.
—Kristin Hunter; in Claudia Tate, *Black
Women Writers at Work*, 1983

.18 It is difficult not to write satire.
—Juvenal; *Satires*, c. A.D. 120

.19 Satire must not be a kind of superfluous ill
will, but ill will from a higher point of view.
Ridiculous man, divine God. Or else, hatred
against the boggled-down vileness of average
man as against the possible heights that humanity might attain.
—Paul Klee; *The Diaries of Paul Klee
1898–1918*, 1957, a 1902 entry.

.20 Satires which censors can understand deserve
to be suppressed.
—Karl Kraus; *Poems*, "Controversy," 1930

.21 It is said that truth comes from the mouths of
fools and children: I wish every good mind
which feels an inclination for satire would
reflect that the finest satirist always has something of both in him.
—G.C. Lichtenberg; *Aphorisms*, "Notebook J" written, 1765–99.

.22 Satire should, like a polished razor keen,
Wound with a touch that's scarcely felt or
seen,
—Lady Mary Wortley Montagu; "To the
Imitator of the First Satire of Horace,"
1733

.23 Satire's my weapon, but I'm too discreet
To run amuck, and tilt at all I meet.
—Alexander Pope; *Horace: Satires*, 1733

.24 Satire must be founded in good nature, and directed by a right heart.
—Samuel Richardson; *Clarissa Harlowe*,
1747–8

.25 A fondness for satire indicates a mind pleased
with irritating others; for myself, I never could
find amusement in killing flies.
—Marie-Jeanne Roland; in Lydia Maria
Child, *Memoirs of Madame de Stael and
of Madame Roland*, 1847

## 249

.26 Satire is moral outrage transformed into comic
art.
—Philip Roth; *Reading Myself and Others*,
1975

.27 That is some satire, keen and critical.
—William Shakespeare; *A Midsummer
Night's Dream*, 1600

.28 Satire is a sort of glass, wherein beholders do
generally discover everybody's face but their
own.
—Jonathan Swift; *The Battle of the Books*,
"Preface," 1704

.29 The satirist who writes nothing but satire
should write but little—or it will seem that his
satire springs rather from his own caustic nature than from the sins of the world in which
he lives.
—Anthony Trollope; *Autobiography*, 1883

.30 If satire is to be effective, the audience must be
aware of the thing satirized.
—Gore Vidal; *Rocking the Boat*, 1962

.31 Satire lies about literary men while they live
and eulogy lies about them when they die.
—Voltaire; Lettre à Bordes, January 10,
1769

.32 Satire is always as sterile as it is shameful and
as impotent as it is insolent.
—Oscar Wilde; "The English Renaissance
of Art," Lecture, January 9, 1882

## 250 Sayings

.1 Give your ears, hear the sayings,
Give your heart to understand them;
It profits to put them in your heart.
—Amenemope; c. 11th century B.C.

.2 They say. What do they say? Let them say.
—Anonymous
[It is a Greek inscription on rings found at
Pompeii.]

.2 Do as we say, and not as we do.
—Giovanni Boccacio; *Decameron*, 1350

.3 Now I'll say something to remember.
—Robert Browning; *Works*, "A Soul's Tragedy," 1888–9

.4 It is better to be anxious about what I shall say,
than to suffer remorse for what I said.
—Buzurchimihr; *Maxim*, c. 570

.5 An old man's sayings are seldom untrue.
—Danish Proverb

## 250

.6   As the saying is.
—George Farquhar; *The Beaux' Stratagem*, 1548

.7   Don't you go believing in sayings, Picotee; they are all made by men, for their own advantage.
—Thomas Hardy; *Hand of Ethelberta*, 1876

.8   Saying things which should be said, and which should not be said.
—Horace; *Epistles*, 20 B.C.

.9   Do not ask who said this or that, but attend to what is actually said.
—Thomas à Kempis; *The Imitation of Christ*, c. 1413

.10  You know I say
Just what I think and nothing more nor less…
I cannot say one thing and mean another.
—Henry Wadsworth Longfellow; "Giles Corey"

.11  In saying what is obvious, never choose cunning. Yelling works better.
—Cynthia Ozick; "We Are the Crazy Lady and Other Feisty Feminist Fables," *The First Ms. Reader*, Francine Klagsbrun, ed., 1972

.12  Never say anything remarkable. It is sure to be wrong.
—Mark Rutherford (William Hale White); *Last Pages from a Journal*, 1915

.13  Almost every wise saying has an opposite one, no less wise, to balance it.
—George Santayana; *Little Essays*, 1920

.14  The ancient saying is no heresy,
Hanging and wiving go by destiny.
—William Shakespeare; *The Merchant of Venice*, 1600

.15  I can tell thee where that saying was born.
—William Shakespeare; *Twelfth Night*, 1600

.16  The common saying "Do as I say, not as I do," is usually reversed in the actual experience of life.
—Samuel Smiles; *Self-Help*, 1859

.17  A short saying oft contains much wisdom.
—Sophocles; *Aletes*, Fragment, c. 5th century B.C.

.18  There is an old-world saying current still,
"Of no man canst thou judge the destiny
To call it good or evil, till he die."
—Sophocles; *Trachinioe*, c. 5th century B.C.

## 250

.19  The saying that beauty is but skin-deep is but a skin-deep saying.
—Herbert Spencer; *Essays*, "Personal Beauty," 1863

.20  Have you heard of the terrible family They,
And the dreadful venomous things They say?
Why, half the gossip under the sun,
If you trace it back, you will find begun
In that wretched House of They.
—Ella Wheeler Wilcox; "They Say," 1883

# 251 Scandal

.1   Scandal is an importunate wasp, against which we must make no movement unless we are quite sure that we can kill it; otherwise it will return to the attack more furious than ever.
—Sebastien Nicolas Roche Chamfort; *Maximes et pensees*, 1805

.2   Scandal is what one half of the world takes pleasure inventing, and the other half in believing.
—Paul Chatfield; Attributed

.3   To converse with Scandal is to play at Losing Loadum; you must lose a good name to him, before you can win it for yourself.
—William Congreve; *Love for Love*, 1695

.4   Love and scandal are the best sweeteners of tea.
—Henry Fielding; *Love in Several Masques*, 1728

.5   Pleasant as it is to hear
Scandal tickling in our ear
Ev'n of our mothers;
In the chit chat of the day,
To us is pay'd, when we're away,
What we lent to others.
—John Gay; "The Lady's Lamentation," 1720

.6   The objection of the scandalmonger is not that she tells of racy doings, but that she pretends to be indignant about them.
—H.L. Mencken; *Notebooks*, 1956

.7   He's gone, and who knows how he may report
Thy words by adding fuel to the flame?
—John Milton; *Paradise Lost*, 1667

.8   A word of scandal spreads like a spot of oil.
—Marcel Proust; *Du Cote de Chez Swann*, 1913

## 251

.9  For my part, I believe there never was a scandalous tale without some foundation.
—Richard B. Sheridan; *The School for Scandal*, 1777

.10 Nor do they trust their tongue alone,
But speak a language of their own;
Can read a nod, a shrug, a look,
For better than a printed book;
Convey a libel in a frown,
And wink a reputation down.
—Jonathan Swift; *The Journal of a Modern Lady*, 1729

.11 Certain it is that scandal is good brisk talk, whereas praise of one's neighbor is by no means lively hearing. An acquaintance grilled, scored, devilled, and served with mustard and cayenne pepper excites the appetite; whereas a slice of cold friend with currant jelly is but a sickly, unrelishing meat.
—William Makepeace Thackeray; *The Roundabout Papers*, "On a Hundred Years Hence," 1863

.12 Scandal lied, as she so often does.
—Anthony Trollope; *The Warden*, 1855

## 252 Science

.1  Every great scientific truth goes through three stages. First, people say it conflicts with the Bible. Next they say it has been discovered before. Lastly they say they always believed it.
—Louis Agassiz; Attributed

.2  Science fiction is no more written for scientists than ghost stories are written for ghosts.
—Brian W. Aldiss; introduction to *Penguin Science Fiction*, 1962

.3  A modern poet has characterized the personality of art and the impersonality of science as follows: Art is I; science is we.
—Claude Bernard; *Bulletin of New York Academy of Medicine*, Vol. IV, 1928

.4  Science, after all, is only an expression for our ignorance of our own ignorance.
—Samuel Butler II; *Samuel Butler's Notebooks*, published 1951

.5  To understand a science it is necessary to know its history.
—Auguste Comte; *Positive Philosophy*, 1851–54

.6  Today the function of the artist is to bring imagination to science and science to imagination, where they meet, in myth.
—Cyril Connolly; *The Unquiet Grave*, 1944

## 252

.7  Most of the fundamental ideas of science are essentially simple, and may, as a rule, be expressed in a language comprehensible to everyone.
—Albert Einstein; *The Evolution of Physics*, 1938

.8  Myths are early science, the result of men's first trying to explain what they saw around them.
—Edith Hamilton; *Mythology*, 1942

.9  Science is an imaginative adventure of the mind seeking truth in a world of mystery.
—Cyril Hinshelwood; Address to Science Masters' Association, Oxford, England, 1953

.10 Equipped with his five senses, man explores the universe around him and calls the adventure Science.
—Edwin Powell Hubble; *The Nature of Science*, 1954

.11 Myths and science fulfill a similar function: they both provide human beings with a representation of the world and of the forces that are supposed to govern it. They both fix the limits of what is considered possible.
—Francois Jacob; *The Possible and the Actual*, 1982

.12 If science fiction is the mythology of modern technology, then its myth is tragic.
—Ursula K. Le Guin; "The Carrier Bag Theory of Fiction," 1986; appeared in *Women of Vision*, Denise M. Du Pont, ed., 1988

.13 Science fiction is not predictive; it is descriptive.
—Ursula K. Le Guin; *The Left Hand of Darkness*, 1969

.14 Science is all metaphor.
—Timothy Leary; interview, September 24, 1980

.15 The scientific mind does not so provide the right answers as ask the right questions.
—Claude Levi-Strauss; *The Raw and the Cooked*, "Overture," 1964

.16 Science must begin with myths, and with the criticism of myths.
—Karl Popper; in C.A. Mace, ed., *British Philosophy in the Mid–Century*, 1957

.17 A touch of science, even bogus science, gives an edge to the superstitious tale.
—V.S. Pritchett; *The Living Novel*, "An Irish Ghost," 1946

### 252

.18 Even if the open windows of science at first make us shiver after the cozy indoor warmth of traditional humanizing myths, in the end the fresh air brings vigor, and the great spaces have a splendor of their own.
—Bertrand Russell; *What I Believe*, 1925

.19 Ours is the first generation that has grown up with science-fiction ideas.
—Carl Sagan; *Cosmos*, 1980

.20 Science means simply the aggregate of all the recipes that are always successful. All the rest is literature.
—Paul Valery; *Moralities*, 1932

.21 Science is voiceless; it is the scientists who talk.
—Simone Weil; *On Science, Necessity, and the Love of God*, 1968

## 253 Secret

.1 Nothing is easier than to keep a secret: there needs no more but to shut one's mouth.
—Anonymous

.2 O fie miss, you must not kiss and tell.
—William Congreve; *Love for Love*, 1695

.3 When she knew a secret it no longer was.
—Marcelene Cox; in *Ladies' Home Journal*, 1948

.4 Three may keep a secret if two of them are dead.
—Benjamin Franklin; *Poor Richard's Almanack*, 1735

.5 He that tells a secret is another man's servant.
—George Herbert; *Jacula Prudentum*, 1640

.6 Secrets are things we give to others to keep for us.
—Elbert Hubbard; *Thousand and One Epigrams*, 1911

.7 No one keeps a secret so well as a child.
—Victor Hugo; *Les Miserables*, 1862

.8 The vanity of being known to be entrusted with a secret is generally one of the chief motives to disclose it.
—Samuel Johnson; *The Rambler*, May 1, 1750

.9 When a secret is revealed, it is the fault of the man who confided it.
—Jean de La Bruyere; *Les caractères ou les moeurs de ce siècle*, 1688

### 253

.10 How can we expect someone else to keep our secret if we have not been able to keep it ourselves?
—François de La Rochefoucauld; *Maximes*, 1665

.11 And that which you have spoken in the ear in closets shall be proclaimed upon the housetops.
—New Testament: Luke

.12 A good many men and women want to get possession of secrets just as spendthrifts want to get money—for circulation.
—George Dennison Prentice; *Prenticeana*, 1860

.13 If you would wish another to keep your secret, first keep it yourself.
—Seneca; *Hippolytus*, c. A.D. 60

.14 Seal up your lips, and give no words but mum:
The business asketh silent secrecy.
—William Shakespeare; *II Henry VI*, 1590

.15 Secrecy is the seal of speech, and occasion the seal of secrecy.
—Solon; *Maxim*, c. 575 B.C.

.16 A secret may be sometimes best kept by keeping the secret of its being a secret.
—Sir Henry Taylor; *The Statesman*, 1836

.17 I am full of leaks, and I let secrets out hither and yon.
—Terence; *Eunuchus*, 161 B.C.

.18 I usually get my stuff from people who promised somebody else that they would keep it a secret.
—Walter Winchell; Attributed

## 254 Sense

.1 There is no way in which to understand the world without first detecting it through the radar-net of our senses.
—Diane Ackerman; *A Natural History of the Senses*, 1990

.2 Common sense (which, in truth is very uncommon) is the best sense I know of.
—Lord Chesterfield; *Letter to His Son*, September 27, 1748

.3 There are times when sense may be unseasonable as well as truth.
—William Congreve; *The Double-Dealer*, 1694

## 254

.4 Good sense is a thing all need, few have, and
none think they want.
—Benjamin Franklin; *Poor Richard's Almanack*, 1746

.5 The knowledge we have comes from our senses.
—Joseph Glanvill; *The Vanity of Dogmatizing*, 1661

.6 He is quite devoid of common sense.
—Horace; *Satires*, 35 B.C.
[Horace is not using "common sense" in
the sense that we know it today. He was
speaking of what the French call *savoir
faire*, that is, social sense of propriety.]

.7 Sense-impression of Nature is the only true
foundation of human instruction, because it is
the only true foundation of human knowledge.
—Johann Pestalozzi; *The Method*, 1828

.8 He speaks sense.
—William Shakespeare; *The Merry Wives
of Windsor*, 1601

.9 He had what is roughly know as "horse-sense."
—C.D. Warner; *Backlog Studies*, 1884

## 255 Sentences

.1 Sentences which simply express moral judgements do not say anything. They are pure expressions of feeling and as such do not come
under the category of truth and falsehood.
—A.J. Ayer; *Language, Truth and Logic*,
1936

.2 Some sentences release their poisons only after
years.
—Elias Canetti; *The Human Province*, 1978

.3 The declared meaning of a spoken sentence is
only its overcoat, and the real meaning lies underneath its scarves and buttons.
—Peter Carey; *Oscar and Lucinda*, 1988

.4 He mouths a sentence as curs mouth a bone.
—Charles Churchill; *The Rosciad*, 1761

.5 The maker of a sentence launches out into the
infinite and builds a road into Chaos and old
Night, and is followed by those who hear him
with something of wild, creative delight.
—Ralph Waldo Emerson; *Journals*, 1834

.6 If sentences have little meaning when they are
writ, when they are spoken they have less.
—Henry Fielding; *Joseph Andrews*, 1742

.7 A sentence begins quite simply, then it undu-
lates and expands, parentheses intervene like
quick-set hedges, the flowers of comparison

## 255

bloom, and three fields off, like a wounded
partridge, crouches the principle verb, making
one wonder as one picks it up, poor little thing,
whether after all it was worth such a tramp, so
many guns, and such expensive dogs, and
what, after all, is its relation to the main subject, potted so gaily half a page back, and prov-
ing finally to have been in the accusative case.
—E.M. Forster; *Abinger Harvest*, "Proust,"
1936

.8 A sentence is a sound in itself on which other
sounds called words are strung.
—Robert Frost; Letter to John T. Bartlett,
February 22, 1914, in Lawrence Thompson, ed., *Selected Letters of Robert Frost*,
1946

.9 A sentence is not easy to define.
—Ernest Gowers; *The Complete Plain Words*,
1954

.10 Words have weight, sound and appearance; it
is only by considering these that you can write
a sentence that is good to look at and good to
listen to.
—W. Somerset Maugham; *The Summing
Up*, 1938

.11 Short sentences drive themselves into the
heart and stay there.
—Samuel Richardson; *Clarissa Harlowe*,
1747–48

.12 It is not so much consequence of what you say,
as how you say it. Memorable sentences are
memorable on account of some single irradi-
ating word.
—Alexander Smith; *Dreamthorp*, "On the
Writing of Essays," 1863

.13 Of sentences that stir my bile,
Of phrases I detest,
There's one beyond all others vile:
"He did it for the best."
—James Kenneth Stephen; *Lapsus Calami*,
"The Malefactor's Plea," 1891

.14 A sentence should contain no unnecessary
words, a paragraph no unnecessary sentences,
for the same reason that a drawing should have
no unnecessary lines and a machine no unnecessary parts.
—William Strunk, Jr.; *The Elements of
Style*, 1918

.15 The most attractive sentences are not perhaps
the wisest, but the surest and soundest.
—Henry David Thoreau; *Journal*, 1842

.16 Whenever the literary German dives into a
sentence, that is the last you are going to see

**255**

of him till he emerges on the other side of the Atlantic with his verb in his mouth.
—Mark Twain; *A Connecticut Yankee in King Arthur's Court*, 1889

.17 He only judges right, who weighs, compares, And, in the sternest sentence which his voice Pronounces, ne'er abandons charity.
—William Wordsworth; *Ecclesiastical Sonnets*, 1822

# 256 Sermons

.1 Everyone has at least one sermon in him.
—Anonymous

.2 A sermon, well delivered, is more uncommon even than prayers well read.
—Jane Austen; *Mansfield Park*, 1814

.3 Sermons remain one of the last forms of public discourse where it is culturally forbidden to talk back.
—Harvey Cox; Attributed

.4 A man likes to assume superiority over himself, by holding up his bad example and sermonizing on it.
—George Eliot; *Middlemarch*, 1872

.5 Go into one of our cool churches, and begin to count the words that might be spared, and in most places the entire sermon will go.
—Ralph Waldo Emerson; *Journals*, 1834

.6 The best sermon is preached by the minister who has a sermon to preach and not by the man who has to preach a sermon.
—William Feather; *The Business of Life*, 1949

.7 The Bell calls others to Church, but itself never minds the Sermon.
—Benjamin Franklin; *Poor Richard's Almanack*, 1747

.8 When a preacher reads his sermon with as much coldness and indifference as he would read a newspaper or an act of parliament, he must not be surprised if his audience discovers the same indifference, or even take a nap.
—Richard Graves; *The Spiritual Quixote*, 1773

.9 Sermons are not the only preaching which doth save souls.
—Richard Hooker; *Ecclesiastical Politie*, 1597

.10 That's all wants of a sermon. No possible relevance to anything but itself.
—P.D. James; *The Skull Beneath the Skin*, 1982

**256**

.11 Some plague the people with too long sermons; for the faculty of listening is a tender thing, and soon becomes weary and satiated.
—Martin Luther; *Table-Talk*, 1569

.12 Most sermons sound to me like commercials—but I can't make out whether God is the Sponsor or the Product.
—Mignon McLaughlin; *The Second Neurotic's Notebook*, 1966

.13 When Christ said, "The kingdom of heaven must suffer violence," he meant not the violence of long babbling prayers, nor the violence of tedious invective sermons without wit.
—Thomas Nashe; *The Unfortunate Traveller*, 1594

.14 Sermons are like pie-crust, the shorter the better.
—Austin O'Malley; *Keystones of Thought*, 1914–15

.15 The half-baked sermon causes spiritual indigestion.
—Austin O'Malley; *Keystones of Thought*, 1914–15

.16 Examples draw when precept fails, And sermons are less read than tales.
—Matthew Prior; "The Turtle and the Sparrow," early 18th century, in *Literary Works*, H.B. Wright and M.K. Spears, eds. 1959

.17 Preaching has become a by-word for a long and dull conversation of any kind; and whoever wishes to imply, in any piece of writing, the absence of everything agreeable and inviting, calls it a sermon.
—Sydney Smith; Quoted in Lady S. Holland's *Memoir*, 1855

.18 That anxious longing for escape is the common consequence of common sermons.
—Anthony Trollope; *Barchester Towers*, 1857

.19 He preached a prayer-meeting sermon that night that give him a rattling reputation [sic], because the oldest man in the world couldn't a understood it.
—Mark Twain; *Huckleberry Finn*, 1885

.20 The sermon edifies, the example destroys.
—Abbe de Villiers; *L'Art de Precher*, c. late 17th century

.21 He found in stones the sermons he had already hidden there.
—Oscar Wilde; *The Nineteenth Century*, "The Decay of Lying," 1989
[The reference is to William Wordsworth.]

# 257 Sigh

.1 A sigh breaks the body of a man.
—*Babylonian Talmud: Berachoth*, c. 450

.2 It made him easier to be pitiful,
And sighing was his gift.
—Elizabeth Barrett Browning; "Aurora Leigh," 1857

.3 A lonely man is a lonesome thing, a stone, a bone, a stick, a receptacle for Gilbey's gin, a stooped figure sitting at the edge of a hotel bed, heaving copious sighs like the autumn wind.
—John Cheever; *The Journals*, "The Sixties," 1966

.4 Drew a long, long sigh, and wept a last adieu!
—William Cowper; "On the Receipt of My Mother's Picture," 1796

.5 God is an unutterable Sigh in the Human Heart, said the old German mystic. And therewith said the last word.
—Havelock Ellis; *Impressions and Comments*, 1914

.6 When he is here, I sigh with pleasure—
When he is gone, I sigh with grief.
—W.S. Gilbert; *The Sorcerer*, 1877

.7 Most of the sighs we hear have been edited.
—Stanislaw Jerzy Lec; *More Unkempt Thoughts*, 1968

.8 Sighing was, he believed, simply the act of taking in more oxygen to help the brain cope with an unusual or difficult set of circumstances.
—Margaret Millar; *Spider Webs*, 1986

.9 Give nobody's heart pain so long as thou canst avoid it, for one sigh may set a whole world into a flame.
—Sa'Di; *Gulistan*, 1258

.10 Words may be false and full of art;
Sighs are the natural language of the heart.
—Thomas Shadwell; *Psyche*, 1675

# 258 Silence

.1 Silence never shows itself to so great an advantage, as when it is made the reply to calumny and defamation.
—Joseph Addison; *The Tatler*, 1709

.2 Keeping silent when proper, and speaking what is fit.
—Aeschylus; *Prometheus*, 475 B.C.

# 258

.3 Silence is talk too.
—African (Hausa) Proverb

.4 I kept silent because I approve the plan.
—Aristides; c. 480 B.C., Plutarch, *Lives*, "Aristides"
[Said, when Cleocritus accused him of being opposed to a plan of Temistocles because he remained silent.]

.5 I shall state silences more completely than ever a better man spangled the butterflies of vertigo.
—Samuel Beckett; *Dream of Fair to Middling Women*, written 1932; published 1992

.6 Silence is said to be golden, but the best fools the world has ever produced had nothing to say on the subject.
—Josh Billings; *Encyclopedia of Wit and Wisdom*, 1874

.7 Let him now speak, or else hereafter for ever hold his peace.
—Book of Common Prayer, 1548

.8 Silences can be as different as sounds.
—Elizabeth Bowen; *Collected Impressions*, 1950

.9 Silences have a climax, when you have got to speak.
—Elizabeth Bowen; *The House in Paris*, 1935

.10 There is no such thing as an empty space or an empty time. There is always something to see, something to hear. In fact, try as we may to make a silence, we cannot.
—John Cage; *Silence*, 1961

.11 He speaks badly who doesn't know how to be silent.
—Charles Cahier; *Quelques Six Mille Proverbes*, 1856

.12 How much one has to say in order to be heard when silent.
—Elias Canetti; *The Human Province*, 1978

.13 Silence is more eloquent than words.
—Thomas Carlyle; *Of Heroes and Hero-Worship*, 1840

.14 Under all speech that is good for anything there lies a silence that is better. Silence is deep as Eternity; speech is shallow as Time.
—Thomas Carlyle; *Critical and Miscellaneous Essays*, "Sir Walter Raleigh," 1838

.15 Mum's the word.
—George Colman the Younger; *Battle of Hexham*, c. 1789

258

.16 Speaking silence is better than senseless speech.
　　—Danish Proverb

.17 Silence is the ultimate weapon of power.
　　—Charles De Gaulle; Attributed

.18 Silence is all we dread.
There's Ransom in a Voice—
But Silence is Infinity.
　　—Emily Dickinson; *Poem*, 1873

.19 Who … tells a finer tale than any of us? Silence does.
　　—Isak Dinesen; *Last Tales*, "The Blank Page," 1957

.20 Let thy speech be better than silence, or be silent.
　　—Dionysius the Elder; *Fragments*, c. 1st century B.C.

.21 There are some silent people who are more interesting than the best talkers.
　　—Benjamin Disraeli; *Endymion*, 1880

.22 Speech may be barren; but it is ridiculous to suppose that silence is always brooding on a nestful of eggs.
　　—George Eliot; *Felix Holt, the Radical*, 1866

.23 I shall take your silence for consent.
　　—Henry Fielding; *The Fathers*, c. 1754

.24 That man's silence is wonderful to listen to.
　　—Thomas Hardy; *Under the Greenwood Tree*, 1872

.25 And Silence, like a poultice, comes
To heal the blows of sound.
　　—Oliver Wendell Holmes; "The Music-Grinders," 1848

.26 Silence is as full of potential wisdom and wit as the unhewn marble of a great sculpture.
　　—Aldous Huxley; *Point Counter Point*, 1928

.27 Silence is the reply adapted to folly.
　　—Solomon Ibn Gabriol; *Choice of Pearls*, c. 1050

.28 Silence propagates itself, and the longer talk has been suspended, the more difficult it is to find anything to say.
　　—Samuel Johnson; *The Adventurer*, 1754

.29 Silence isn't always golden, you know. Sometimes it is just plain yellow.
　　—Jan Kemp; in Sherry Ruth Anderson and Patricia Hopkins, *The Feminine Face of God*, 1991

258

.30 Silence at the right moment is a form of communication.
　　—George Kent; in Brooks, *Report from Part One*, 1972

.31 We will have to repent in this generation not merely for the vitriolic words and actions of the bad people, but for the appalling silence of the good people.
　　—Martin Luther King, Jr., *Letter from a Birmingham City Jail*, 1963

.32 It is good to speak, but better to keep still.
　　—Jean de La Fontaine; *Fables*, 1678

.33 Sometimes you have to be silent to be heard.
　　—Stanislaw Lec; *Unkempt Thoughts*, 1962

.34 Silence is the element in which great things fashion themselves.
　　—Maurice Maeterlinck; *The Treasure of the Humble*, "Silence," 1896

.35 Do not the most moving moments of our lives find us all without words?
　　—Marcel Marceau; in *Readers' Digest*, June, 1958

.36 Sticks and stones are hard on bones.
Aimed with angry art,
Words can sting like anything.
But silence breaks the heart.
　　—Phyllis McGinley; *The Love Letters of Phyllis McGinley*, "A Choice of Weapons," 1954

.37 Silence is the only Voice of our God.
　　—Herman Melville; *Pierre*, 1852

.38 Speech is the small change of silence.
　　—George Meredith; *The Ordeal of Richard Feverel*, 1859

.39 The deepest feelings always shows itself in silence;
not in silence, but restraint.
　　—Marianne Moore; "Silence," 1935

.40 That silence is one of the great arts of conversation is allowed by Cicero himself, who says that there is not only an art, but even an eloquence in it.
　　—Hannah More; *Essays*, "Conversation," c. 1800

.41 In Maine we have a saying that there's no point in speaking unless you can improve on silence.
　　—Edmund Muskie; Attributed

.42 Be silent or let thy words be worth more than silence.
　　—Pythagoras; *Florilegium*, c. 6th century B.C.

# 258

.43 An absolute silence leads to sadness: it is the image of death.
— Jean-Jacques Rousseau; *Reveries of a Solitary Walker*, 1782

.44 It is a great thing to know the season for speech and the season for silence.
— Seneca; *De Moribus*, c. 1st century A.D.

.45 I'll speak to thee in silence.
— William Shakespeare; *Cymbeline*, 1611

.46 Silence is the most perfect expression of scorn.
— George Bernard Shaw; *Back to Methuselah*, 1921

.47 I have often repented of speaking, but never of keeping silent.
— Simonides; *Apothegm*, c. 650 B.C.
[The remark has also been attributed to Greek philosopher Xenocrates, 396–315 B.C.]

.48 He had occasional flashes of silence that made his conversation perfectly delightful.
— Sydney Smith; Lady Holland's *A Memoir of the Reverend Sydney Smith*, 1855
[The reference is to Thomas Babington Macaulay.]

.49 The world would be happier if men had the same capacity to be silent that they have to speak.
— Baruch Spinoza; *Ethica*, 1677

.50 I have been breaking silence these twenty-three years and have hardly made a dent in it.
— Henry David Thoreau; *Journal*, February 9, 1841

# 259 Simile

.1 Similes should be sparingly used in prose, for they are at bottom poetical.
— Aristotle; *Rhetoric*, c. 4th century B.C., in Diogenes Laertius, *Lives of Eminent Philosophers*

.2 Threadbare is the simile which compares the world to a stage.
— Edward Bulwer-Lytton; *What Will He Do with It?*, 1859

.3 There's no simile for his lungs. Talking, laughing, or snoring, they make the beams of the house shake.
— Charles Dickens; *Bleak House*, 1852–53

.4 There are only certain words which are valid and similes … are like defective ammunition (the lowest thing I can think of at this time).
— Ernest Hemingway; letter to Bernard Berenson, March 20, 1953

# 259

.5 No simile runs on all fours.
— Latin Proverb

.6 One simile that solitary shines
In the dry desert of a thousand lines.
— Alexander Pope; *Imitations of Horace*, 1733–38

.7 In argument
Similes are like songs in love:
They must describe; they nothing prove.
— Matthew Prior; *Alma*, 1718

.8 Thou has the most unsavory similes.
— William Shakespeare; *I Henry IV*, 1598

.9 A simile committing suicide is always a depressing spectacle.
— Oscar Wilde; *A Critic in Pall Mall*, "Sententiae," 1919

.10 Oft on the dappled turf at ease
I sit, and play with similes
Loose type of things through all degrees.
— William Wordsworth; "To the Same Flower (the Daisy)," 1807

# 260 Sins and Sinners

.1 Cold preachers make bold sinners.
— American Proverb

.2 Confess your sins to the Lord, and you will be forgiven; confess them to men, and you will be laughed at.
— Josh Billings; *Josh Billings, His Sayings*, 1865

.3 A man may cry out against sin, of policy, but he cannot abhor it but by virtue of a godly antipathy against it.
— John Bunyan; *Pilgrim's Progress*, 1678

.4 Every sin has its own excuse.
— Czech Proverb

.5 Between these two, the denying of sins, which we have done, and the bragging of sins, which we have not done, what a space, what a compass is there, for millions of millions of sins!
— John Donne; *Sermons*, 1618

.6 Men perish with whispering sins, nay with silent sins, sins that never tell the conscience they are sins, as often with crying sins.
— John Donne; *Sermons*, 1624

.7 That which we call sin in others is experiment for us.
— Ralph Waldo Emerson; *Essays*, "Experience," 1849

## 260

.8    E'er you remark another's sin,
Bid your own conscience look within.
—Benjamin Franklin; *Poor Richard's Almanack*, 1741

.9    He that falls into sin is a man; that grieves at it, is a saint; that boasteth of it, is a devil.
—Thomas Fuller I; *Holy State*, 1642

.10    Should we all confess our sins to one another we would all laugh at one another for our lack of originality.
—Kahlil Gibran; *The Prophet*, 1923

.11    The loss of sin is a loss to literature. Without sin we shall never have anything except lyrical poetry.
—Saunders Lewis; in *Y Llenor*, Summer, 1927

.12    We don't call it sin today, we call it self-expression.
—Baroness Stocks; in Jonathan Green, *The Cynic's Lexicon*, 1984

.13    Nothing makes one so vain as being told that one is a sinner.
—Oscar Wilde; Attributed

## 261 Slander

.1    Slander, dog's eloquence.
—Appius Claudius; *Epigram*, c. 451 B.C.

.2    Slander slays three persons: the speaker, the spoken to, and the spoken of.
—Babylonian Talmud; *Arachin*, c. 450

.3    Hurl your calumnies boldly;
Something is sure to stick.
—Francis Bacon; *De Augumentis Scientiarum*, 1623

.4    The worse kind of slander is to speak well of everybody.
—Amelia Edith Barr; *The Maid of Maiden Lane*, 1900

.5    Character assassination is at once easier and surer than physical assault; and it involves far less risk for the assassin. It leaves him free to commit the same deed over and over again, and may indeed, win him the honors of a hero even in the country of his victims.
—Alan Barth; *Government by Investigation*, 1955

.6    Be not called "Master Two-tongues"; and slander not with thy tongue.
—Ben Sira; *Book of Wisdom*, c. 190 B.C.

## 261

.7    A slander is like a hornet; if you can't kill it dead the first time, better not strike at it.
—Josh Billings; *Josh Billings, His Sayings*, 1865

.8    Slander: a lot that often falls from bad men's mouths upon good men's names and professions.
—John Bunyan; *Pilgrim's Progress*, 1678

.9    If I tell a malicious lie, in order to affect any man's fortune or character, I may indeed injure him for some time; but I shall be sure to be the greatest sufferer myself at last.
—Lord Chesterfield; Letter to His Son, September 21, 1747

.10    The tongue of a viper is less hurtful than that of a slanderer.
—Henry Fielding; *Jonathan Wild*, 1743

.11    A Slander counts by Threes its victims, who
Are Speaker, Spoken Of, and Spoken To.
—Arthur Guiterman; *A Poet's Proverbs*, 1939

.12    If you speak evil, you yourself will soon be worse spoken of.
—Hesoid; *Works and Days*, c. 800 B.C.

.13    Slander is the revenge of a coward, and dissimulation of his defense.
—Samuel Johnson; Boswell's *Life of Johnson*, 1791

.14    Folks whose own behavior is most ridiculous are always to the fore in slandering others.
—Moliere; *Tartuffe*, 1664

.15    That they speak [evil of me] is not the point; that they do not speak it justly, that is the point.
—Plautus; *Trinummus*, c. 194 B.C.

.16    What is slander? A verdict of "guilty" pronounced in the absence of the accused, with closed doors, without defence or appeal, by an interested and prejudiced judge.
—Joseph Roux; *Meditations of a Parish Priest*, c. 1870

.17    Done to death by slanderous tongues,
Was the Hero that lies here.
—William Shakespeare; *Much Ado About Nothing*, 1598–99

.18    Slander,
Whose whisper o'er the world's diameter,
As level as the cannon to his blank,
Transports his poison'd shot.
—William Shakespeare; *Hamlet*, 1600–1

# 262 Slang

.1 Dialect tempered with slang is an admirable medium of communication between persons who have nothing to say and persons who would not care for anything properly said.
—Thomas Bailey Aldrich; *Ponkapog Papers*, "Leaves from a Notebook," 1903

.2 Slang is a conventional tongue with many dialects, which are as a rule unintelligible to outsiders.
—Albert Barrere; *A Dictionary of Slang, Jargon, and Cant*, "Preface," 1889

.3 Slang has no country, it owns the world… It is the voice of the god that dwells in the people.
—Ralcy Husted Bell; *The Mystery of Words*, 1924

.4 I've found that there are only two kinds that are any good: slang that has established itself in the language, and slang you make up yourself. Everything else is apt to be passé before it gets into print.
—Raymond Chandler; letter, March 18, 1949

.5 All slang is metaphor, and all metaphor is poetry.
—G.K. Chesterton; *A Defense of Slang*, 1901

.6 The one stream of poetry which is continually flowing is slang.
—G.K. Chesterton; *The Defendant*, 1901

.7 Correct English is the slang of prigs who write history and essays. And the strongest of all is the slang of poets.
—George Eliot; *Middlemarch*, 1872

.8 The language of the street is always strong. What can describe the folly and emptiness of scolding like the word jawing.
—Ralph Waldo Emerson; *Journals*, 1840

.9 Slang is … vigorous and apt. Probably most of our vital words were once slang; one by one timidly made sacrosanct in spite of ecclesiastical and other wraths.
—John Galsworthy; *Castles in Spain and Other Screeds*, 1927

.10 His slang … was always a little out of date, as though he had studied a dictionary of popular usage, but not in the latest edition.
—Graham Greene; *The Comedians*, 1966

.11 Down through the years certain fads had come and gone, and their vestiges could be found in

# 262

Janie's and Mabel's conversation, like mastodon bones in a swamp.
—Dolores Hitchens; *The Bank with the Bamboo Door*, 1965

.12 Slang is nothing more or less than a wardrobe in which language, having some bad deed to do, disguises itself. It puts on word-masks and metaphoric rags.
—Victor Hugo; *Les Miserables*, 1862

.13 I know only two words of American slang, "swell" and "lousy." I think "swell" is lousy, but "lousy" is swell.
—J.B. Priestley; *Thoughts in the Wilderness*, 1957

.14 Slang is a language that rolls up its sleeves, spits on its hands and goes to work.
—Carl Sandburg; in *The New York Times*, February 13, 1959

.15 The First Man introduced slang into the world & thus tacitly, by his high authority, made its use legitimate forever.
—Mark Twain; Letter to Helen Allen, c. 1910

.16 Slang in a woman's mouth is not obscene, it only sounds so.
—Mark Twain; *More Maxims of Mark*, Merle Johnson, ed. published 1927

.17 Slang, profoundly consider'd, is the lawless germinal element, below all words and sentences, and behind all poetry, and proves a certain perennial rankness and protestationism in speech.
—Walt Whitman; *November Boughs: Slang in America*, 1888

.18 Slang … is the wholesome fermentation or eructation of those processes eternally active in language, by which froth and specks are thrown up, mostly to pass away, though occasionally to settle and permanently crystallize.
—Walt Whitman; *November Boughs: Slang in America*, 1888

# 263 Sleep

.1 The world says that tales put people to sleep. I say that with tales you can rouse from their sleep.
—Nahman Bratzlav; Attributed

.2 There is much good sleep in an old story.
—German Proverb

**263**

.3 Sleep is when all the unsorted stuff comes flying out as from a dustbin upset in a high wind.
—William Golding; *Pincher Martin*, 1956

.4 One hour's sleep before midnight is worth three after.
—George Herbert; *Jacula Prudentum*, 1640

.5     Soft closer of our eyes!
Low murmur of tender lullabies!
—John Keats; "To Sleep," 1816

.6 The only time most women give their orating husbands undivided attention is when the old boys mumble in their sleep.
—Wilson Mizner; in Alva Johnson, *The Legendary Mizners*, 1953

.7 I never sleep comfortably except when I am at sermon or when I pray to God.
—François Rabelais; *Works*, c. 1550

.8 When I am in the pulpit, I have the pleasure of seeing my audience nod approbation while they sleep.
—Sydney Smith; Holland, *A Memoir of the Reverend Sydney Smith*, 1855

# **264** Society

.1 Society is held together by our needs; we bind it together with myth, legend, coercion, fearing that without it we will be hurled into that void, within which like the earth before the Word was spoken, the foundations of society are hidden.
—James Baldwin; *Notes of a Native Son*, 1955

.2 If we would please in society, we must be prepared to be taught many things we know already by people who do not know them.
—Sebastien Nicolas Roche Chamfort; *Maximes et pensees*, 1805

.3 The bond of human society is reason and speech.
—Cicero; *De Officiis*, c. 1st century B.C.

.4 At table, seated close together, there is a whole language in one's neighbor's elbow and an unlimited power of expression in its way of avoiding collisions.
—Frances Marion Crawford; *A Rose of Yesterday*, 1897

.5 God having designed man for a sociable creature, furnished him with language, which was to be the great instrument and cementer of society.
—John Locke; *II Civil Government*, 1690

**264**

.6 A decrepit society shuns humor as a decrepit individual shuns drafts.
—Malcolm Muggeridge; *The Most of Malcolm Muggeridge*, "Tread Softly for You Tread on My Jokes," 1966

.7 Human society is founded on mutual deceit; few friendships would endure if each knew what his friend said of him in his absence.
—Blaise Pascal; *Pensees*, 1670

.8 Teas,
Where small talk dies in agonies.
—Percy Bysshe Shelley; "Peter Bell the Third," 1819

.9 Society soon grows used to any state of things which is imposed upon it without explanation.
—Edith Wharton; *Old New York*, "The Spark," 1924

.10 If one could only teach the English how to talk and the Irish how to listen, society would be quite civilized.
—Oscar Wilde; *An Ideal Husband*, 1895

.11 Never speak disrespectfully of Society, Algernon. Only people who can't get into it do that.
—Oscar Wilde; *The Importance of Being Earnest*, 1895

# **265** Song and Singing

.1 Singers are saying things that the public wants to be able to say, but they don't know how to express themselves. We're like the voice of the public.
—Oleta Adams; in *Essence*, October, 1990

.2 Speech is a sound in which song is locked.
—Anonymous

.3 I do not know who sings my songs
Before they are sung by me.
—Mary Austin; "Whence" in *Poetry, a Magazine of Verse*, 1921

.4 Sing me the songs I delighted to hear,
Long, long ago, long ago.
—T.H. Bayly; "The Long Ago," early 19th century

.5 These days, what isn't worth saying is sung.
—Pierre de Beaumarchais; *Le Barbier de Seville*, 1775

.6 It is the best of all trades to make songs; and the second best is to sing them.
—Hillaire Belloc; "On Song," 1938

# 265

.7 Two people can sing together, but not speak together.
—Charles Cahier; *Quelques Six Mille Proverbes*, 1856

.8 To sing is an expression of your being, a being which is becoming.
—Maria Callas; in Arianna Stassinopoulos, *Maria Callas*, 1981

.9 All speech, even the commonest speech, has something of song in it: not a parish in the world but has its parish-accent—the rhythm or tune to which the people there sing what they have to say.
—Thomas Carlyle; *Heroes and Hero Worship*, 1840

.10 All the intelligence and talent in the world can't make a singer. The voice is a wild thing. It can't be bred in captivity.
—Willa Cather; *The Song of the Lark*, 1915

.11 Learn to say before you sing.
—John Clarke; *Paroemiologia*, 1639

.12 Swans sing before they die—'twere no bad thing
Did certain persons die before they sing.
—Samuel Taylor Coleridge; "Epigram on a Volunteer Singer," 1796

.13 Song: the licensed medium for bawling in public things too silly or sacred to be uttered in ordinary speech.
—Oliver Herford; *Neither Here Nor There*, 1922

.14 …men always prize that song the most, which rings newest in their ears.
—Homer; *Odyssey*, c. 700 B.C.

.15 This is a fault common to all singers, that among their friends they will never sing when they are asked; unasked, they will never desist.
—Horace; *Satires*, c. 35 B.C.

.16 There is delight in singing, though none hear Beside the singer.
—Walter Savage Landor; "To Robert Browning," 1846

.17 When in doubt, sing loud.
—Robert Merrill; *The Saturday Evening Post*, October 26, 1957

.18 The song that we hear with our ears is only the song that is sung in our hearts.
—Ouida; *Wisdom, Wit, and Pathos*, 1884

.19 If you have any soul worth expressing, it will show itself in your singing.
—John Ruskin; *Sesame and Lilies*, 1865

# 265

.20 Come sing me a bawdy song; make me merry.
—William Shakespeare; *I, Henry IV*, 1597–8

.21 Voltaire said that what was too silly to be said could be sung. Now you seem to think that what is too delicate to be said can be whistled.
—George Bernard Shaw; *Man and Superman*, 1903

.22 Our sweetest songs are those which tell of saddest thought.
—Percy Bysshe Shelley; "To a Skylark," 1821

.23 Singing … gives right joy to speech.
—Genevieve Taggard; *Calling Western Union*, "Definition of Song," 1936

.24 One man opens his throat to sing, the other sings in his mind.
—Rabindranath Tagore; "Broken Song," 1894

.25 There are German songs which can make a stranger to the language cry.
—Mark Twain; *A Tramp Abroad*, "The Awful German Language," 1880

.26 I am saddest when I sing. So are those who hear me; they are sadder even than I.
—Artemus Ward; Lecture, in Washington, 1863

# 266 Sorrow

.1 Excessive sorrow laughs. Excessive joy weeps.
—William Blake; *The Marriage of Heaven and Hell*, "Proverbs of Hell," 1790

.2 Sorrow makes silence her best orator.
—John Bodenham; *Belvedere*, 1600

.3 One often calms one's grief by recounting it.
—Pierre Corneille; *Polyeucte*, 1640

.4 Little sorrows are loud, great ones silent.
—Danish Proverb

.5 All sorrows can be borne if you put them into a story or tell a story about them.
—Isak Dinesen; in Hannah Arendt; *The Human Condition*, 1959

.6 I walked a mile with Sorrow
And ne'er a word said she;
But, oh, the things I learned from her
When Sorrow walked with me.
—Robert B. Hamilton, "Along the Road," early 20th century

.7 We weep to avoid the shame of not weeping.
—François de La Rochefoucauld; *Maxims*, 1665

## 266

.8  To speak of sorrow
works upon it
moves it from its
crouched place barring
the way to and from the soul's hall.
—Denise Levertov; *The Sorrow Dance*, "To Speak," 1967

.9  Sorrow is tranquility remembered in emotion.
—Dorothy Parker; *The Portable Dorothy Parker*, "Sentiment," 1944

.10  Grief can sometimes only be expressed in platitudes. We are original in our happy moments. Sorrow has only one voice, one cry.
—Ruth Rendell; *Shake Hands Forever*, 1975

.11  Give sorrow words. The grief that does not speak
Whispers the o'erfraught heart and bids it break.
—William Shakespeare; *MacBeth*, 1605–6

.12  The deeper the sorrow, the less tongue hath it.
—The Talmud

# 267 Sound

.1  I
fall into noisy abstraction
cling to sound as if it were the last protection
against what I cannot name.
—Paula Gunn Allen; *The Blind Lion*, "Shadows," 1974

.2  The appropriately beautiful or ugly sound of any word is an illusion wrought on us by what the word connotes. Beauty sounds as ugly as ugliness sounds beautiful.
—Max Beerbohm; *Yet Again*, 1909

.3  The three great elemental sounds in nature are the sound of rain, the sound of wind in a primeval wood, and the sound of outer ocean on a beach.
—Henry Beston; *The Outermost House*, "Lantern on the Beach," 1928

.4  Take care of the sense, and the sounds will take care of themselves.
—Lewis Carroll; *Alice's Adventures in Wonderland*, 1865

.5  No sound is dissonant which tells of Life.
—Samuel Taylor Coleridge; "The Lime-Tree Bower My Prison," 1797

.6  There is in souls a sympathy with sounds.
—William Cowper; *The Task*, 1785

## 267

.7  There is no sound but shall find some lovers, as the bitterest confections are grateful to some palates.
—Ben Jonson; *Explorata* "Conduetudo," 1636

.8  Not many sounds in life, and I include all urban and rural sounds; exceed in interest a knock at the door.
—Charles Lamb; *Essays of Elia*, "Valentine's Day," 1823

.9  The empty vessel giveth a greater sound than the full barrel.
—John Lyly; *Euphues*, 1579

.10  Becoming accustomed to certain sounds has a profound effect on character; soon one acquires the words and phrases and eventually also the ideas that go with these sounds.
—Friedrich Nietzsche; *The Gay Science*, 1882–87

.11  And empty heads console with empty sounds.
—Alexander Pope; *The Dunciad*, 1743

.12  More sound than sense.
—Seneca; *Ad Lucilium*, c. A.D. 64

.13  As they say of the blind,
Sounds are the things I see.
—Sophocles; *Oedipus at Colonus*, 401 B.C.

.14  "Sound" is a catch-all word which describes "all that we hear," in one lump, from music to noise.... We consider the kingdom of our eyes far more complex, and would not dream of trying to sum it all up in a word which would mean "all that we see."
—Anita T. Sullivan; *The Seventh Dragon*, 1985

.15  Sweet is every sound,
Sweeter thy voice, but every sound is sweet.
—Alfred, Lord Tennyson; "The Princess," 1847

.16  Sugar is not so sweet to the palate as sound to the healthy ear.
—Henry David Thoreau; Unpublished Manuscript, c. 1862

.17  With the sense of sight, the idea communicates the emotion, whereas, with sound, the emotion communicates the idea, which is more direct and therefore more powerful.
—Alfred North Whitehead; *Dialogues of Alfred North Whitehead*, June 10, 1943

# 268 Speech and Speaking

.1 Another good thing in the heart of God is to pause before speaking.
—Amen-Em-Apt; *Teaching How to Live*, c. 700 B.C.

.2 Much speaking is an abomination.
—Ani; *Maxims*, c. 1000 B.C.

.3 When you have spoken the word, it reigns over you. When it is unspoken you reign over it.
—Arabian Proverb

.4 Wherever the relevance of speech is at stake, matters become political by definition, for speech is what makes man a political being.
—Hannah Arendt; *The Human Condition*, "Prologue," 1958

.5 Speak less cleverly but more clearly.
—Aristophanes: *The Frogs*, 405 B.C.

.6 Princes have need, in tender matters and ticklish times, to beware what they say: especially in these short speeches, which fly abroad like darts, and are thought to be shot out of their secret intentions.
—Francis Bacon; *Essays*, "Of Empire," 1625

.7 The habit of common and continuous speech is a symptom of mental deficiency.
—Walter Bagehot; *Literary Studies*, 1879

.8 None love to speak so much, when the mood of speaking comes, as they who are naturally taciturn.
—Henry Ward Beecher; *Proverbs from Plymouth Pulpit*, 1887

.9 Whate'er is well-conceived is clearly said.
—Nicholas Boileau-Despreaux; *L'Art Poetique*, 1674

.10 I have not multiplied my speech overmuch.
—Book of the Dead; c. 4000 B.C.

.11 If a thing goes without saying, let it.
—Jacob M. Braude; *Treasury of Wit and Humor*, 1967

.12 Speak of what you understand.
—John Clarke; *Paroemiologia*, 1639

.13 Speech shows what a man is.
—John Clarke; *Paroemiologia*, 1639

.14 Speech is the voice of the heart.
—Kaibara Ekken; *Ten Precepts*, "On Speech," 1710

.15 Speech is but broken light upon the depth Of the unspoken.
—George Eliot; *The Spanish Gypsy*, 1868

# 268

.16 A man cannot speak but he judges himself.
—Ralph Waldo Emerson; *Essays*, "Compensation," 1841

.17 Speech is power: speech is to persuade, to convert, to compel. It is to bring another out of his bad sense into your good sense.
—Ralph Waldo Emerson; *Letters and Social Aims*, "Social Aims," 1876

.18 We should not speak merely to please the ear,
But to point the path that leads to noble fame
—Euripides; *Hippolytus*, c. 428 B.C.

.19 Human speech is like a cracked kettle on which we tap crude rhythms for bears to dance to, while we long to make music that will melt the stars.
—Gustave Flaubert; *Madame Bovary*, 1857

.20 He who speaks much is much mistaken.
—Benjamin Franklin; *Poor Richard's Almanack*, 1736

.21 You'll never move others, heart to heart, Unless your speech comes from your heart.
—Johann Wolfgang von Goethe; *Faust*, 1806

.22 I like people who refuse to speak until they are ready to speak.
—Lillian Hellman; *An Unfinished Woman*, 1969

.23 Think twice before you speak and then say it to yourself.
—Elbert Hubbard; *The Philistine*, 1909

.24 The Irish are a fair people; they never speak well of one another.
—Samuel Johnson; Boswell's *Life of Johnson*, 1775

.25 To speak and to offend, with some people, are but one and the same thing.
—Jean de La Bruyere; *Les Caracteres*, "Du Coeur," 1688

.26 It is never more difficult to speak well than when we are ashamed of keeping silent.
—François de La Rochefoucauld; *Maxims*, 1665

.27 He who talks more is sooner exhausted.
—Lao Tsu; *The Character of Tao*, c. 550 B.C.

.28 Speech is civilization itself. The word, even the most contradictious word, preserves contact—it is silence which isolates.
—Thomas Mann; *The Magic Mountain*, 1924

## 268

.29 A man's character is revealed by his speech.
—Menander; *The Flute Girl*, c. 300 B.C.

.30 Be skillful in speech, that you may be strong.
—Merikare; *The Teaching of Merikare*, c. 2135–2040 B.C.

.31 When we make ourselves understood, we always speak well.
—Molière; *Femmes Savantes*, 1672

.32 The unluckiest insolvent in the world is the man whose expenditure of speech is too great for his income of ideas.
—Christopher Morley; *Inward Ho!*, 1923

.33 Let your speech be always with grace, seasoned with salt, that ye may know how ye ought to answer every man.
—New Testament; Colossians

.34 If you your lips would keep from slips,
Five things observe with care;
To whom you speak, of whom you speak,
And how, and when, and where.
—W.E. Norris; "Thirlby Hall," 1884

.35 One who speaks aright never says his say at an unsuitable place or time, nor before one of immature faculties or without excellence. This is why his words are not spoken in vain.
—*Panchatantra*; Fragment, c. 400 A.D.

.36 There are some who speak well and write badly. For the place and the audience warm them, and draw from their minds more than they think of without that warmth.
—Blaise Pascal; *Pensées*, 1670

.37 Man does not speak because he thinks; he thinks because he speaks. Or rather, speaking is no different than thinking: to speak is to think.
—Octavio Paz; *Alternating Current*, "Andre Breton or the Quest of the Beginning," 1967

.38 People are ever prone to speak the worst.
—George Pettie; *Petite Palace*, 1576

.39 It is a tiresome way of speaking, when you should despatch the business, to beat around the bush.
—Plautius; *Mercator*, c. 200 B.C.

.40 It is easy to utter what has been kept silent, but impossible to recall what has been uttered.
—Plutarch; *Moralia*, "The Education of Children," c. A.D. 100

.41 Good speech is more hidden than malachite, yet it is found in the possession of women slaves at the millstones.
—Ptahotpe; *The Maxims of Ptahotpe*; c. 2350 B.C.

## 268

.42 Speech is the mirror of the soul: as a man speaks, so is he.
—Publilius Syrus; *Moral Sayings*, 1st century B.C.

.43 Speak fair and think what you will.
—John Ray; *English Proverbs*, 1670

.44 Here is the time of the tellable, here is its home. Speak and proclaim.
—Rainer Maria Rilke; *Duineser Elegien*, 1919

.45 The world does not speak. Only we do. The world can, once we have programmed ourselves with a language, cause us to hold beliefs. But it cannot propose a language for us to speak. Only other human beings can do that.
—Richard Rorty, *Contingency, Irony, and Solidarity*, 1989

.46 To speak much is one thing, to speak to the point is another.
—Sophocles; *Oedipus Coloneus*, c. 408 B.C.

.47 Most of do not use speech to express thought. We use it to express feelings.
—Jennifer Stone; *Stone's Throw*, "The Revisionist Imperative," 1988

.48 We are more anxious to speak than to be heard.
—Henry David Thoreau; *Journal*, 1841

.49 Lord, what an organ is human speech when it is played by a master!
—Mark Twain; Letter to Olivia Clemens, November 14, 1879

.50 Man is born with the faculty ... of speech, but why should he be able to speak before he has anything to say?
—Benjamin Whichcote; *Moral Aphorisms*, 1753

.51 Speech is an old torn net, through which the fish escape as one casts it over them.
—Virginia Woolf; "The Evening Party," 1918 in Susan Dick, ed. *The Complete Shorter Fiction of Virginia Woolf*, 1985

## 269 Speeches and Speechmaking

.1 Accustomed as I am to public speaking, I know the futility of it.
—Franklin Pierce Adams (F.P.A.); *F.P.A. Book of Quotations*, 1952

**269**

.2  When he killed a calf he would do it in high style, and make a speech.
—John Aubrey; *Brief Lives*, "William Shakespeare," c. 1693

.3  I do not object to people looking at their watches when I am speaking. But I strongly object when they start shaking them to make certain they are still going.
—Lord Birkett; Quoted in *The Observer*, October 30, 1960

.4  Speak softly, and be slow to begin your speech.
—Chinese Proverb

.5  There is no inspiration in evil and ... no man ever made a speech on a mean subject.
—Eugene V. Debs; *Efficient Expression*

.6  When a man is asked to make a speech, the first thing he has to decide is what to say.
—Gerald Ford; Attributed

.7  When a man gets up to speak, people listen, then look. When a woman gets up, people look; then, if they like what they see, they listen.
—Pauline Frederick; quoted in Jilly Cooper and Tom Hartman, *Violets and Vinegar*, "Mrs. Crankhurst," 1980

.8  Many have been the wise speeches of fools, though not as many as the foolish speeches of wise men.
—Thomas Fuller I; *The Holy State and the Profane State*, 1642

.9  Speeches in our culture are the vacuum that fills a vacuum.
—John Kenneth Galbraith; Commencement Address, American University, Washington D.C. June 18, 1984

.10  Speeches and fruit should always be fresh.
—Nikki Giovanni; *Sacred Cows ... and Other Edibles*, "In Sympathy with Another Motherless Child," 1988

.11  If no thought
your mind does visit
make your speech
not too explicit.
—Piet Hein; *Grooks*, "The Case for Obscurity," 1966

.12  I have never delivered a firebrand speech.
—Adolf Hitler; *The Observer*, "Sayings of Our Times," May 31, 1953

.13  His speech flowed from his tongue sweeter than honey.
—Homer; *Iliad*, c 700 B.C.

**269**

.14  Why don't th' feller who says, "I'm not a speechmaker," let it go at that instead o' givin' a demonstration.
—Frank McKinney Hubbard; *Abe Martin's Sayings*, 1915

.15  I never thought my speeches were too long; I've rather enjoyed them.
—Hubert Humphrey; Attributed

.16  Hubert, a speech does not need to be eternal to be immortal.
—Muriel Humphrey; in Max M. Kampelman, *Entering New Worlds*, 1991

.17  Speeches measured by the hour die with the hour.
—Thomas Jefferson; Letter to David Harding, April 20, 1824

.18  If you haven't struck oil in your first three minutes, *Stop boring!*
—George Jessel; Attributed

.19  There may be other reasons for a man's not speaking in public than want of resolution: he may have nothing to say.
—Samuel Johnson; Boswell's *Life of Johnson*, 1791

.20  It makes a great difference to a speaker whether he has something to say, or has to say something.
—Nellie L. McClung; *The Stream Runs Fast*, 1945

.21  Let your speech be always with grace, seasoned with salt.
—New Testament: Colossians

.22  A speech is poetry: cadence, rhythm, imagery, sweep! A speech reminds us that words, like children, have the power to make dance the dullest beanbag of a heart.
—Peggy Noonan; *What I Saw at the Revolution*, 1990

.23  Many public speakers are good extemporaneous listeners.
—Edgar Wilson "Bill" Nye; *Forty Liars and Other Lies*, 1882

.24  In our time, political speech and writing are largely the defense of the indefensible.
—George Orwell; *Shooting the Elephant*, "Politics and the English Language," 1946

.25  Speeches are often like eggs. You don't have to eat the whole of an egg or hear the whole of a speech to know that it is bad.
—Walter Hines Page; Burton J. Hendrick's *The Life and Letters of Walter Hines Page*, 1922–25

## 269

.26 A speech is like an airplane engine. It may sound like hell but you've got to go on.
—William Thomas Piper; *Time*, January 13, 1961

.27 Forgotten—like a maiden speech,
Which all men praise, but none remember.
—Winthrop Mackworth Praed; *Poems*, "To a Lady," 1864

.28 The most precious things in speech are pauses.
—Ralph Richardson, Attributed

.29 Be sincere; be brief; be seated.
—Franklin D. Roosevelt; Advice to his son James on making a speech, c. 1944

.30 Few speeches which have produced an electrical effect on an audience can bear the colorless photography of a printed record.
—Lord Rosebery; *The Life of William Pitt*, 1891

.31 Even the most timid man can deliver a bold speech.
—Seneca; *Epistle to Ludcilium, 269.31*

.32 I sometimes marvel at the extraordinary docility with which Americans submit to speeches.
—Adlai E. Stevenson; Speech to American Legion, Chicago, 1950

.33 There is but one pleasure in life equal to that of being called on to make an after-dinner speech, and that is not being called on to make one.
—Charles Dudley Warner; *The Complete Writings*, Thomas R. Lounsbury, ed. 1904

.34 If I am to speak for ten minutes, I need a week for preparation; if fifteen minutes, three days; if half an hour two days; if an hour, I am ready now.
—Woodrow Wilson; in Josephus Daniels *The Wilson Era*, 1946

## 270 Stories

.1 People create stories create people; or rather stories create people create stories.
—Chinua Achebe; "What Has Literature Got to Do with It?," 1986

.2 And nightly to the listening Earth
Repeats the story of her birth.
—Joseph Addison; *The Spectator*, August 23, 1712

.3 Stories ought not to be just little bits of fantasy that are used to while away an idle hour;

## 270

from the beginning of the human race stories have been used—by priests, by bards, by medicine men—as magic instruments of healing, of teaching, as a means of helping people come to terms with the fact that they continually have to face insoluble problems and unbearable realities.
—Joan Aiken; *The Way to Write for Children*, 1982

.4 History tells how it was. A story—how it might have been.
—Alfred Andersch; *Winterspelt*, 1974

.5 Stories are Beings. You invite them to live with you. They'll teach you what they know in return for being a good host. When they're ready to move on they'll let you know. Then you pass them on to someone else.
—Anonymous Cree Storyteller

.6 The announcement that you are going to tell a good story (and the chuckle that precedes it) is always a dangerous opening.
—Margot Asquith; *More Or Less About Myself*, 1934

.7 Our lives preserved. How it was; and how it be. Passing it along in the relay. That is what I work to do to produce stories that save our lives.
—Toni Cade Bambara; "Salvation Is the Issue," in Evans, ed. *Black Women Writers*, 1984

.8 Every life has a Scheherazadesworth of stories.
—John Barth; *Once Upon a Time*, "Program Note," 1994

.9 The story always old, and always new.
—Robert Browning; *The Ring and the Book*, 1868–69

.10 The Victorians expected every building, like every painting, to tell a story and preferably to point to a moral as well.
—Sir Hugh Maxwell Casson; *An Introduction to Victorian Architecture*, 1948

.11 There are only two or three human stories and they go on repeating themselves as fiercely as if they had never happened before.
—Willa Cather; *O Pioneers*, 1913

.12 A good story cannot be devised; it has to be distilled.
—Raymond Chandler; in *Raymond Chandler Speaking*, Dorothy Gardiner and Katherine S. Walker, eds., 1962

.13 Many a man would rather you heard his story than granted his request.
—Lord Chesterfield; *Letters to His Son*, published 1774

**270**

.14 The universal love of the marvelous, which causes most people to insist on having it introduced into a story, if it does happen to come in legitimately.
—James Fenimore Cooper; *The Chainbearers*, 1845

.15 A lost coin is found by means of a penny candle; the deepest truth is found by means of a simple story.
—Anthony de Mello; *One Minute Wisdom*, 1985

.16 The divine art is the story. In the beginning was the story.... But you will remember that the human characters do come forth on the sixth day only—by that time they were bound to come, for where the story is, the characters will gather!
—Isak Dinesen; *Last Tales*, "The Cardinal's First Tale," 1957

.17 Within our whole universe the story only has the authority to answer that cry of heart of its characters, the one cry of each of them: "*Who am I?*"
—Isak Dinesen; *Last Tales*, "The Cardinal's First Tale," 1957

.18 Stories are medicine.
—Clarissa Pinola Estes; *Women Who Run with the Wolves*, 1992

.19 A lie hides the truth, a story tries to find it.
—Paula Fox; *A Servant's Tale*, 1984

.20 There's only one story, the story of your life.
—Northrop Frye; in John Ayre; *Northrop Frye, A Biography*, 1989

.21 Telling ourselves our own stories ... has as much as any single factor been responsible for the survival of African-Americans and their culture.
—Henry Louis Gates, Jr., in Goss and Barnes, eds. *Talk That Talk*, 1989

.22 The destiny of the world is determined less by the battles that are lost and won than by the stories it loves and believes.
—Harold Goddard; *The Meaning of Shakespeare*, 1951

.22 There is one story and one story only
That will prove worth your telling,
Whether as learned bard or gifted child.
—Robert Graves; "To Juan at the Winter Solstice," in *Chief Modern Poets of Britain and America*, Gerald DeWitt Sanders, John Herbert Nelson and M.L. Rosenthal, eds., 1970

**270**

.23 These stories are suffused with the same purity that makes children appear so marvelous and blessed.
—Wilhelm Grimm; *Nursery and Household Tales*, "Preface," 1819

.24 The first recorded versions of the creation story, the flood story, the resurrection story, the story of Job, the story of the prodigal son, are to be found in ancient Egypt.
—W.J. Hardeman; Address, c. 1980

.25 And we can only tell stories truly, from the inside out. The outside of the story is simply its words—and why there should be so much fuss about the necessity of learning the words I do not understand. The hard thing is to understand a story from the inside....
—John Harrel; *Origins and Early Traditions of Storytelling*, 1983

.26 We may be willing to tell a story twice, never to hear it more than once.
—William Hazlitt; *Table-Talk*, 1821–22

.27 It's an old story, yet it remains forever new.
—Heinrich Heine; *Book of Songs*, "Lyrisches Intermezzo," 1822–23

.28 Soft as some song divine, thy story flows.
—Homer; *Iliad*, c. 700 B.C.

.29 Only change the name and the story is about you.
—Horace; *Satires*, c 35 B.C.

.30 Don't tell a good story even though you know one; its narration will simply remind your hearers of a bad one.
—Edgar Watson Howe; *Plain People*, 1929

.31 The fellow that tells a good story always has to listen to a couple of poor ones.
—Frank McKinney Hubbard; *Abe Martin's Wisecracks*, 1930

.32 There is no agony like bearing an untold story inside you.
—Zora Neale Hurston; *Dust Tracks on a Road*, 1942

.33 The Story is just the spoiled child of art.
—Henry James; *The Ambassadors*, "Preface," 1909

.34 Seldom any splendid story is wholly true.
—Samuel Johnson; *Works*, 1958

.35 If you don't like my story get out of the punt.
—James Joyce; *Finnegan's Wake*, 1939

.36 The difference between mad people and sane people ... is the sane people have variety when

**270**

they talk-story. Mad people have only one story that they talk over and over.
　　—Maxine Hong Kingston; *The Woman Warrior*, 1976

.37 But that's another story.
　　—Rudyard Kipling; *Soldiers Three*, 1988

.38 There are three kinds of stories. "Ha ha" stories to amuse and entertain, "Ah ha" stories for discovery of ideas and education, and "Ahhh" stories, where the tales are sublime and connect the teller and the listener with a golden thread.
　　—Arthur Koestler; *The Art of Creation*, 1964

.39 The story—from *Rumplestilskin* to *War and Peace*—is one of the basic tools invented by the human mind, for the purpose of gaining understanding. There have been great societies that did not use the wheel, but there have been no societies that did not tell stories.
　　—Ursula Le Guin; "Prophets and Mirrors" in *The Living Light*, 1970

.40 These are the stories that never, never die, that are carried like seed into a new country, are told to you and me and make in us new and lasting strengths.
　　—Meridel Le Sueur; *Nancy Hanks of Wilderness Road*, 1949

.41 As the pattern of every snowflake is unique, so also are the stories that nourish every single life.
　　—Helen Luke; *Kaleidoscope*, 1992

.42 If I were a tree, each story I would tell would be like a new root growing deep into the ground—nurturing, nourishing and grounding me. What a gift a story is!
　　—Dianne MacInnes; storyteller, oral quotation

.43 A person can be fully involved in a story without understanding it.
　　—Thomas Mann; *Joseph and His Brothers*, 1933

.44 Stories are like fairy gold. The more you give away the more you have.
　　—Polly McGuire; storyteller, oral quotation

.45 The word "story" comes from "storehouse." So a story is a store or storehouse. Things are actually stored in the story, and what tends to be stored there is *meaning*.
　　—Michael Meade; *Men and the Water of Life*, 1953

.46 In the thinking out of most stories, the thing the story is about, as apart from merely what

**270**

happens in it, is of utmost importance. For a story is not the sum of its happenings.
　　—Edith Ronald Mirrielees; *Story Writing*, "The Substance of the Story," 1947

.47 Earth and I gave you turquoise
When you walked singing
We lived laughing in my house
And told old stories.
　　—N. Scott Momaday; "Earth and I Gave You Turquoise," in *Carriers of the Dream Wheel*, Duane Niatum, ed., 1975

.48 A taste for dirty stories may be said to be inherent in the human mind.
　　—George Moore; *Confessions of a Young Man*, 1888

.49 Like an ebony phoenix, each in her own time and with her own season had a story.
　　—Gloria Naylor; *Women of Brewster Place*, 1988

.50 A story has to have muscle as well as meaning, and the meaning has to be in the muscle.
　　—Flannery O'Connor; in Sally Fitzgerald, ed., *The Habit of Being*, 1979

.51 Stories, like whiskey, must be allowed to mature in the cask.
　　—Sean O'Faolain; in *The Atlantic Monthly*, December, 1956

.52 A story you hear is a letter that comes to you from yesterday. It passes through many hands and each one adds his postscript. "So it was with me, brother." And when you tell it you send a letter to tomorrow, "How is it there with you?"
　　—George Papashivily; *Yes and No Stories*, 1946

.53 The difference between writing a story and simply relating past events is that a story, in order to be acceptable, must have shape and meaning. It is the old idea that art is the bringing of order out of chaos.
　　—Katherine Paterson; *The Spying Heart*, 1989

.54 The purpose of the stories is to put an adult mind in a child's heart and a child's eye in an adult head.
　　—Robert D. Pelton; *The Trickster in West Africa*, 1980

.55 From this story one learns that children,
Especially young lasses,
Pretty, courageous, and well-bred,
Are wrong to listen to any sort of man.
　　—Charles Perrault; *Perrault's Complete Fairy Tales*, A.E. Johnson, tr. 1961
　　[The French storyteller refers to "Little Red Riding Hood."]

**270**

.56 Socrates: Every discourse ought to be a living creature, having a body of its own and a head and feet; there should be a middle, beginning and end, adapted to one another and to the whole.
—Plato; *Phaedrus*, c. 4th century B.C.

.57 It is better to tell your own story than to have an adversary tell it for you.
—Samuel Richardson; *Clarissa Harlowe*, 1747–48

.58 The universe is made of stories,
not of atoms.
—Muriel Rukeyser; *The Speed of Darkness*, title poem, 1968

.59 If thou didst ever hold me in thy heart,
Absent thee from felicity awhile,
And in this harsh world draw thy breath in
pain,
To tell my story.
—William Shakespeare; *Hamlet*, 1600–1

.60 She told him stories to delight his ear.
—William Shakespeare; *The Passionate Pilgrim*, 1599

.61 For never was a story of more woe
Than this of Juliet and her Romeo.
—William Shakespeare; *Romeo and Juliet*, 1595

.62 The ancient people perceived the world and themselves within that world as part of an ancient continuous story composed of innumerable bundles of other stories.
—Leslie Marmon Silko; in Lorraine Anderson, ed., *Sisters of the Earth*, 1991

.63 The story was the important thing and little changes here and there were really part of the story. There were even stories about the different versions of stories and how they imagined the different versions came to be.
—Leslie Marmon Silko; *Storyteller*, 1981

.64 Every story can be symbolically unfolded for you through your Medicine Reflections and Seekings. As you do this, you will learn to see through the eyes of your Brothers and Sisters, and to share their perceptions.
—Hyemeyohsts Storm; *Seven Arrows*, 1972

.65 Some people think we're made of flesh and blood and bone. Scientists say we're made of atoms. But I think we're made of stories! When we die, that's what people remember, the stories of our lives and the stories that we told.
—Ruth Stotter; *The Storyteller's Calendar*, December, 1992

**270**

.66 Wherever men have lived there is a story to be told, and it depends chiefly on the story-teller or historian whether that is interesting or not.
—Henry David Thoreau; *Journal*, 1852

.67 What story was ever written without a demon?
—Anthony Trollope; *The Warden*, 1855

.68 The inner spaces that a good story lets us enter are the old apartments of religion.
—John Updike; Quoted by Anatole Broyard, *New York Times*, November 11, 1984

.69 I love the short story for being round, suggestive, insinuating, microcosmic. The story has both the inconvenience and the fascination of new beginnings.
—Luisa Valenzuela; in Janet Sternberg, ed. *The Habit of Being*, 1979

.70 We all see our lives as stories it seems to me, and I am convinced that psychologists and sociologists and historians and so on would find it useful to acknowledge that.
—Kurt Vonnegut; *Deadeye Dick*, 1985

.71 Make up your own
stories and believe
them if you want to
live the good life.
—Miriam Waddington; *Driving Home: Poems New and Selected*, "Advice to the Young," 1972

.72 Stories give people the feeling that there is meaning, that there is ultimately an order lurking behind the incredible confusion of appearances and phenomena that surrounds them…. Stories are substitutes for God. Or maybe the other way around.
—Wim Wenders; "Impossible Stories," 1982 in *The Logic of Images*, 1988

.73 Story is a sacred visualization, a way of echoing experience.
—Terry Tempest Williams; *Pieces of White Shell*, 1984

.74 The wonderful thing about stories is that they present deep psychological and metaphysical truths, but in a poetic form which is gripping, beautiful, and entertaining.
—Diane Wolkstein; *Parabola*, Vol. 2, No. 4, 1980

.75 We must give our own story to the world.
—Carter G. Woodson; *Negro Makers of History*, 1928

.76 I am not trying to tell a story. Yet perhaps it might be done that way. A mind thinking. They might be islands of light—islands in the

## 270

stream that I am trying to convey; life itself going on.
—Virginia Woolf; Diary entry, May 28, 1929

.77 But a story has to have two equal partners, tale teller and tale listener.
—Jane Yolen; *Touch Magic*, 1951

.78 But all stories have this in common: they beckon us out of the visible, providing alternative lives, modes of possibility.
—Paul Zweig; *The Adventurer*, 1974

# 271 Storytelling and Storytellers

.1 There is something musical about the way the storyteller weaves the ups and downs of experience into the fabric of life. We are captured, enamored, by the twist of language, the turn of the phrase, the indirection of the truth.
—Molefi Kere Asante; "Folk Poetry in the Storytelling Tradition," *Talk That Talk*, 1989

.2 The art of storytelling is reaching its end because the epic side of truth, wisdom, is dying out.
—Walter Benjamin; *The Storyteller*, 1936

.3 Death is the sanction of everything the storyteller can tell. He has borrowed his authority from death.
—Walter Benjamin; *The Storyteller*, 1936

.4 [The storyteller's] nesting places—the activities that are intimately associated with boredom—are already extinct in the cities and are declining in the country as well. With this the gift for listening is lost and the community of listeners disappear....
—Walter Benjamin; *The Storyteller*, 1936

.5 Storytelling is always the art of repeating stories, and this art is lost when the stories are no longer retained. It is lost because there is no more weaving and spinning to go on while they are being told.
—Walter Benjamin; *The Storyteller*, 1936

.6 It's all storytelling, you know.
That's what journalism is all about.
—Tom Brokaw; in Northwestern University *Byline*, Spring, 1982

.7 When you make a story your own and tell it, the listener gets the story, plus your appreciation of it. It comes to him filtered through your

## 271

own enjoyment. That is what makes the funny story thrice funnier on the lips of a jolly raconteur than in the pages of "Life." It is the filter of personality.
—Sara Cone Bryant; *How to Tell Stories to Children*, 1905

.8 Shakespeare's name, you may depend upon it, stands absurdly too high and will go down. He had no invention as to stories, none whatever. He took all his plots from old novels, and threw their stories into dramatic shape.... That he threw over whatever he did write some flashes of genius, nobody can deny; but this was all.
—Lord Byron; Letter to James Hogg, March 24, 1814

.9 I think you must remember that a writer is a simple-minded person to begin with and go on that basis. He's not a great mind, he's not a great thinker, he's not a great philosopher, he's a story-teller.
—Erskine Caldwell; in *The Atlantic Monthly*, July, 1958

.10 The storytellers of the Highlands are as varied in their subjects as are literary men and women elsewhere. One is a historian narrating events simply and concisely; another is a historian with a bias, coloring his narrative according to his leanings. One is an inventor, building fiction upon fact, mingling his materials, and investing the whole with the charm of novelty and the halo of romance. Another is a reciter of heroic poems and ballads, bringing the different characters before the mind as clearly as the sculptor brings the figure before the eye.
—Alexander Carmichael; *Carmina Gadelica*, 1928

.11 "Begin at the beginning," the King said, very gravely, "and go on until you come to the end: then stop."
—Lewis Carroll; *Through the Looking Glass*, 1872

.12 Here are the essentials for successful storytelling, identification with what we tell, a clear picture of events and a desire to share the story with others.
—Eileen Colwell; *A Storyteller's Choice*, 1963

.13 If, now, the library by chance has on its staff a few altruistic, emotional, dramatic, and irrepressible childlovers who do not find library work gives sufficient opportunities for altruistic indulgence, and if the library can spare

them from other work, let it set them at teaching the teachers the art of storytelling.
> —John Cotton Dana; "Storytelling in Libraries," in *Public Libraries 13*, November, 1908

.14 Whoever wants to tell a variety of stories ought to have a variety of beginnings.
> —Marie de France; *The Lais of Marie de France*, Robert Hannings and Joan Ferrante, trs., 1978

.15 [The storyteller] attracts narrative material like a magnet.
> —Linda Degh; *Folktales and Society; Storytelling in a Hungarian Peasant Community*, 1969

.16 Where the storyteller is loyal, eternally and unswervingly loyal to the story, there, in the end, silence will speak. Where the story has been betrayed, silence is but emptiness.
> —Isak Dinesen; *Last Tales*, "The Blank Page," 1957

.17 There are three essentials to a good story: humanity, a point, and the storyteller.
> —J. Frank Dobie; "Storytellers I Have Known," *Singers and Storytellers*, 1961

.18 It was impossible for me to repeat the same old story month after month and keep up my interest in it. It was an old story to me, and to go through with it night after night was a task together too mechanical for my nature. I was now reading and thinking. New views of the subject were being presented to my mind.
> —Frederick Douglass; *My Bondage and My Freedom*, 1855

.19 I was raised by and have raised people who regard telling one story when two would do as a sign someone is not really trying.
> —Linda Ellerbee; *And So It Goes*, 1986

.20 Listen, little Elia: draw your chair up close to the edge of the precipice and I'll tell you a story.
> —F. Scott Fitzgerald; *The Crackup*, "Notebook N," Edmund Wilson, ed., 1945

.21 What may be said of the style of story-telling in the South?... There were artists in narration but art no more was universal in this than in any other form of human endeavor, Herein is disappointment because in the rural South there was time enough for perfecting any embellishment the narrator devised ... but the regrettable fact stands: story-telling was not as artful as it should have been. It was too long-winded, and it had too much of the echo

of the political platform. Spontaneity was lost in the polishing of the paragraphs.
> —D.S. Freeman, "Forward" to Benjamin Botkin, *A Treasury of Southern Folklore*, 1949

.22 [Storytellers include] those who created the stories, and those who repeated them, the narrators who worked them over, the redactors who wrote them down, the compilers who collected them, and the translators who made them accessible in other languages.
> —Mia Gerhardt; *The Art of Story-Telling*, 1963

.23 Storytelling as an art means recreating literature—taking the printed words in a book and giving them life.
> —Ellen Greene; "Storytelling," in *World Book Encyclopedia*, Vol. 18, 1976

.24 Storytelling has been called the oldest and the newest of the arts. Human beings seem to have an inbuilt need to structure their world and to communicate their feelings and experiences through storying.
> —Ellen Greene and George Shannon; *Storytelling*, 1986

.25 If a nation loses its storytellers, it loses its childhood.
> —Peter Handke; in *The Independent*, June 9, 1988

.26 The action of a teller is wanted to give due effect to all stories of incident.
> —Thomas Hardy; *The Hand of Ethelberta*, 1876

.27 To sum up it would appear that national differences in the manner of storytelling are for the most part superficial.
> —Edwin S. Hartland; *The Science of Fairy Tales*, 1891

.28 Madame, all stories, if continued far enough, end in death, and he is no true story-teller who would keep that from you.
> —Ernest Hemingway; *Death in the Afternoon*, 1932

.29 Man is eminently a storyteller. His search for a purpose, a cause, and ideal, a mission and the like is largely a search for a plot and a pattern in the development of his life story—a story that is basically without meaning or pattern.
> —Eric Hoffer; *The Passionate State of Mind*, 1955

.30 Aunt Sue had a head full of stories.
Aunt Sue has a whole heart full of stories.
Summer nights on the front porch

Aunt Sue cuddles a brown-faced child to her
bosom
And tells him stories.
—Langston Hughes; *Selected Poems*, "Aunt
Sue's Stories," 1959

.31 Storytelling is an innovation, but how wonderful is that innovation! How many a prayer
is answered, request granted, companion won,
and how great is the knowledge received
through it! ... a jurist or reader of the Quran
is not capable of bringing to God a hundredth
of the people the [preacher] is capable of
bringing.
—Ibn al-Jawzi; *Kitab al qussas wa-al-mud-
hakkirin*, c. 1200, Merlin L. Swartz, trs.,
1971

.32 He was succinct because he had learned no
other way of expressing himself. The few
choices of things which could expressed were
items that had to be articulated with utmost
brevity. Such a blanket characteristic of literary style must have been maintained during
long eras because of several factors, including
the exhaustive familiarity with actors, plots,
and stylizations which adult villagers shared.
Therefore story content was not repeated *ad
nauseum* during formal recitals. Each person's
acquaintanceship with literature because of
formal recitals were heavily reinforced by a
year-round chitchat about and discussions of
stories.
—Melville Jacobs; *The Content and Style of
an Oral Literature*, 1959
[Jacobs speaks of the style and qualities of
storytellers of the North American
Clackamas Chinook tribes.]

.33 When you tell a story you automatically talk
about traditions, but they're never separate
from the people, the human implications.
You're talking about politics and morality and
economics and failure. You're talking about all
your connections as a human being.
—Gayl Jones; *Corregidora*, 1975

.34 But a good storyteller stirs up de old words to
make a new soup.
—Lynn Joseph; *The Mermaid's Twin Sister:
More Stories from Trinidad*, 1994

.35 One mark of a second-rate mind is to be always telling stories.
—Jean La Bruyere; *Characters*, "Of Opinions," 1688

.36 This feeling, an inexplicable renewal of enthusiasm after storytelling, is familiar to many
people.
—Barry Lopez; *Arctic Dreams*, 1986

.37 With weeping and with laughter
Still is the story told,
How well Horatius kept the bridge
In the brave days of old.
—Thomas Babington Macaulay; *Lays of
Ancient Rome*, "Horatius," 1842

.38 No two tellers present their tales in exactly the
same way. Each new teller brings another perspective, another way of telling the tale.
—Margaret Read MacDonald; *The Storyteller's Start-Up Book*, 1993

.39 ...such is the nature of storytelling, always
working to remind us that the human heart
has a mind of its own, and that the human
mind must likewise have a heart.
—Jack Maguire; *Creative Storytelling*, 1985

.40 Never tell a story because it is true: tell it because it is a good story.
—John Pentland Mahaffy; in W.B. Stan-
ford and R.B. McDowell *Mahaffy*, 1971

.41 You don't just get a story... You have to wait
for it to come to you.
—W. Somerset Maugham; in Robin
Maugham, *Conversation with Willie*,
1978

.42 I am a real storyteller. I identify myself with
those who are really listening and tell my story.
—Claude McKay; *Banjo*, 1929

.43 The purpose of every storyteller—to amuse.
—Herman Melville; *The Confidence-Man*,
1857

.44 Storytelling won an established place in the
life of the earliest hasidim and it became part
of the Shabbes ritual.... The Rebbes often
wove their teachings into an extended
metaphor or parable or told an illustrative
tale.... The telling of tales can be a mystical
expression on various levels. To tell tales of the
tsaddikim is one means of glorifying the tsaddikim and of contracting their piety and
power.... In this light, the hasidim believes
that tales, like prayers, contain the potential to
be active agents.
—Jerome R. Mintz; *The Legends of Hasidim*, 1968

.45 She was attracted by the art of storytellers
more than by any other—those Oriental storytellers who sit in the marketplace and hold
beneath their words a group of people who
have the faces of nurslings who are suckling.
The sand of time flows away and the whole
sun lies like a cloak upon the shoulders of the
storyteller.
—Adrienne Monnier; in Richard Mc-

**271**

Dougall, tr. *The Very Rich Hours of Adrienne Monnier*, 1976

.46 The art of a storyteller (and it is that which marks a genius) is to make his tale interminable, and still to interest his audience.
—James Justinian Morier; *The Adventures of Hajii Baba of Ispahan*, 1824

.47 Storytelling is one of the few truly universal human bonds; people in all times and places have sat down at night and told stories.
—Wendy Doniger O'Flaherty; *Other People's Myths*, 1988

.48 Most of the medieval regimes argue that a moderate cheerfulness is the best mental disposition to have in order to maintain well-being.... Conversation and storytelling in this view have medical relevance to people's health.
—Glending Olson; "Confabulatio: A Medieval View of Storytelling," *National Story-telling Journal*, 1987

.49 Whoever learns the work by heart,
Or through the storyteller's art
Becomes acquainted;
His life by sad defeat—although
The king of heaven be his foe—
Is never tainted.
—*Panchatantra*, c. A.D. 400

.50 ...a good storyteller recognizes his or her own peer, and it matters very little whether the stories have been learned entirely from oral sources or from printed or mechanically recorded sources.
—Anne Pellowski; *The World of Storytelling*, 1977

.51 One winter, I visited in turn every house in the entire village to tell my tales. I went out three nights a week. I would have gone more often, but I didn't want people to think I was a gadabout.
—Delia Poirier; Quoted by Luc Lacourciere "Canada," in *Folktales Told Around the World*, Richard Dobson, ed., 1975

.52 The sailor tells stories of winds, the ploughman of bulls; the soldier counts his wounds, the shepherd his sheep.
—Propertius; *Elegies*, c. 1st century B.C.

.53 At first there would be no professional storytellers. But it would not be long before ... there would be found some one whose adventures were always the pleasantest to hear, whose deeds were the most marvellous, whose realistic details the most varied.
—Arthur Ransome; *A History of Storytelling*, 1909

**271**

.54 That evening I strolled down to see the chief to ask him about the next day's ceremony. I found him sitting in the courtyard of his "palace" listening to a storyteller.... [the storyteller] derived his inspiration from his hat, round the entire rim of which were suspended articles that represented or reminded him of some proverb, story or riddle. You chose your little fancy, and he "was off."
—Robert S. Rattray; *The Ashanti*, 1923

.55 Fate is just even to rival storytellers, and balances matters.
—Charles Reade; *The Cloister and the Hearth*, 1861

.56 Storytellers are indispensable agents of socialization.
—David Riesman; *The Lonely Crowd*, 1950

.57 The way always seems shorter and easier if one tells stories—it's as if the storyteller were carrying his listener.
—Pinhas Sadeh; *Jewish Folktales*, "The Daughter Who Was Wiser Than Her Father," 1989

.58 She told him stories to delight his ear.
—William Shakespeare; *The Passionate Pilgrim*, 1599

.59 ...I pity the man who cannot enjoy Shakespeare. He has outlasted thousands of abler thinkers, and will outlast a thousand more. His gift of telling a story (provided some one else told it to him first); his enormous power over language, as conspicuous in his senseless and silly abuse of it as in his miracles of expression; his humor; his sense of idiosyncratic character; and his prodigious fund of that vital energy which is, it seems, the true differentiating property behind the faculties, good, bad, or indifferent, of the man of genius, enable him to entertain us so effectively that the imaginary scenes and people he has created become more real to us than our actual life.
—George Bernard Shaw; *Dramatic Opinions and Essays*, "Blaming the Bard," 1906

.60 It would be a truism to suggest that dramatic instinct and dramatic power of expression are naturally the first essentials for success in the art of storytelling, and that, without these, no storyteller would go very far; but I maintain that, even with these gifts, no high standard of performance will be reached without certain other qualities, among the first of which I place apparent simplicity, which is really the art of concealing art.
—Marie L. Shedlock; *The Art of the Story-Teller*, 1951

271

.61 Some people have taken exception on moral grounds to an art [storytelling] in which the perfect and imperfect are set side by side. But even in the discourses which Buddha in his bounty allowed to the recorded, certain passages contain what the learned call Upaya or "Adapted Truth"....
—Murasaki Shikibu; *The Tale of Genji*, 1001–15

.62 ...we find tranquil, measured epic poets ... also fantastic dreamers ... moralists, searching after truth ... realists specializing in the romantic tale dealing with everyday life ... jokers, jesters, humorists without malice ... bitter, sarcastic, satirical storytellers with exceedingly malicious and pointed social satire ... storytellers who relate chiefly "shameful," that is, indecent, or even downright cynical erotic tales ... storyteller-dramaturgists, for whom the center of interest and artistic invention lies in the manner of the narration, in the skill and animation of the handling of the dialogue ... bookish storytellers who had read plenty of cheap popular works or other novels of excitement and adventure, who were exceedingly avid for the "educated" bookish speech, and at other times overly zealous in transmitting it ... women who told stories for children....
—Yuri M. Sokolov; *Russian Folklore*, Catherine Ruth Smith, tr., 1950
[Sokolov details the many type of Russian storytellers.]

.63 Sabadu was unequalled in the art of storytelling; he was fluent and humorous, while his mimicry of the characters he described kept everybody's interest on the alert. To the Rabbit, of course, he gave a wee voice, to the Elephant he gave a deep bass, to the Buffalo a hollow mooing. When he attempted the Lion, the veins of his temple and neck were dreadfully distended as he made the effort; but when he mimicked the dog, one almost expected a little terrier-like dog to trot up to the fire, so perfect was his yaup-yaup. Everyone agreed as Sabadu began his story that his manner, even his style of sitting and smoothing his face, the pose of his head, betrayed a man of practice.
—Henry M. Stanley; *My Dark Companions and Their Strange Stories*, 1893

.64 I have often thought that a Story-teller is born, as well as a poet.
—Richard Steele; *The Guardian*, 1713

.65 We are lonesome animals. We spend all our life trying to be less lonesome. One of our ancient methods is to tell a story begging the lis-

271

tener to say—and to feel—"Yes, that's the way it is, or at least that's the way I feel it. You're not as alone as you thought."
—John Steinbeck; "In Awe of Words" in *Writers at Work*, Fourth Series, George Plimpton, ed., 1977

.66 Storytelling and copulation are the two chief forms of amusement in the South. They're inexpensive and easy to procure.
—Robert Penn Warren; *Newsweek*, August 25, 1980

.67 Storytelling is the oldest form of education.
—Terry Tempest Williams; *Pieces of White Shell*, 1984

.68 Storytelling is a personal art that makes public what is private and private what is public.
—Jane Yolen; ed. *Favorite Folktales from Around the World*, 1986

272 **Students and Studies**

.1 I must study politics and war that my sons may have liberty to study mathematics and philosophy. My sons ought to study mathematics and philosophy, geography, natural history, naval architecture, navigation, commerce, and agriculture, in order to give their children a right to study painting, poetry, music, architecture, statuary, tapestry, and porcelain.
—John Adams; Letter to Abigail Adams, May 12, 1780

.2 Histories make men wise; poets, witty; the mathematics, subtle; natural philosophy, deep; morals, grave; logic and rhetoric, able to contend.
—Francis Bacon; *Essays* "Of Studies," 1597

.3 The greatest significance of the present student generation is that it is through them that the point of view of the subjugated is finally and inexorably being expressed.
—James Baldwin; "They Can't Turn Back" in *Mademoiselle*, August, 1960

.4 The scholar teacheth his master.
—John Clarke; *Paroemiologia Anglo-Latina*, 1639

.5 Anyone who loves to make music knows that study is necessary.
—Duke Ellington; *Music Is My Mistress*, 1973

272

.6 We are students of words: we are shut up in schools and colleges and recitation-rooms for ten or fifteen years, and come out at least with a bag of wind, a memory of words, and do not know a thing.
—Ralph Waldo Emerson; *Essays*: Second Series, "New England Reformers"

.7 Make your friends your teachers and mingle the pleasures of conversation with the advantages of instruction.
—Baltasar Gracian; *The Art of Worldly Wisdom*, 1647

.8 Who learns by Finding Out has sevenfold The Skill of him who learned by Being Told.
—Arthur Guiterman; *A Poet's Proverbs*, 1924

.9 The secret of productive study is to avoid well.
—Thomas Hardy; *Two on a Tower*, 1882

.10 Beware of prosecuting study too excitedly.
—George Meredith; *The Ordeal of Richard Feverel*, 1859

.11 What is a student but a lover courting a fickle mistress who ever eludes his grasp?
—Sir William Osler; *Aequanamitas*, "The Student Life," 1906

.12 I have been filled through the ears, like a pitcher, from the wellsprings of another.
—Plato; *Phaedrus*, c. 375–368 B.C.

.13 Study depends on the good will of the student, a quality that cannot be secured by compulsion.
—Quintilian; *Institutes Oratoria*, A.D. 95 or 96

.14 Pedagogues ... what do they teach their pupils? Words, words, words. Among all their boasted subjects, none are selected because they are useful.
—Jean-Jacques Rousseau; *Emile*, 1762

.15 For every person wishing to teach there are thirty not wanting to be taught.
—W.C. Sellar and R.J. Yeatman; *And Now All This*, 1932

.16 We learn our lessons, not for life, but for the lecture-room.
—Seneca; *Epistulae ad Lucilium*, c. 1st century A.D.

.17 Apt scholars need little teaching.
—John Shebbeare; *The Marriage Act*, 1754

.18 I could undertake to be an efficient pupil if it were possible to find an efficient teacher.
—Gertrude Stein; *Q.E.D.: Adele*, 1903

272

.19 There are four types of characters among those who sit before the sages...: a sponge, which absorbs all; a funnel, which lets in at one end and lets out at the other; a strainer, which lets out the wine and retains the lees; a sieve, which lets out the coarse meal and retains the choice flour.
—Talmud; before A.D. 500

.20 No student knows his subject: the most he knows is where and how to find out the things he does not know.
—Woodrow Wilson; *New Freedom*, 1913

# 273 Stupidity

.1 No stupid man ever suspected himself of being anything but clever.
—Thomas Bailey Aldrich; *The Stillwater Tragedy*, 1880

.2 Perhaps there are not as many stupid things said as there are set down in print.
—Goncourt Brothers; *Journal*, 1866

.3 He was born stupid, and greatly increased his birthright.
—Samuel Butler II; *The Way of All Flesh*, 1903

.4 With stupidity and sound digestion man may front much.
—Thomas Carlyle; *Sartor Resartus*, 1833–34

.5 It's possible to say something stupid in Latin as well as in Spanish.
—Miguel de Cervantes; *Exemplary Novels*, "The Dialogue of Dogs," 1613

.6 Stupidity is the deliberate cultivation of ignorance.
—William Gaddis; *Carpenter's Gothic*, 1985

.7 We never really know what stupidity is until we have experimented on ourselves.
—Paul Gauguin; *Intimate Journals*, Van Wyck Brooks, tr., 1923

.8 Those people who appear stupid are stupid, as are half of those who don't.
—Baltasar Gracian; *Handbook-Oracle and the Art of Prudence*, 1647

.9 Ordinarily he was insane, but he had his lucid moments when he was merely stupid.
—Heinrich Heine; Comment, 1848
[Made when Savoye was appointed ambassador to Frankfurt by Lamartine.]

**273**

.10 It is so pleasant to come across people more stupid than ourselves. We love them at once for being so.
—Jerome K. Jerome; *The Idle Thoughts of an Idle Fellow*, "On Cats and Dogs," 1889

.11 He that reads and grows no wiser seldom suspects his own deficiency, but complains of hard words and obscure sentences, and asks why books are written which cannot be understood.
—Samuel Johnson; *The Idler*, 1758–60

.12 Nothing sways the stupid more than arguments they can't understand.
—Cardinal de Retz; *Memories*, 1718

.13 The trouble with the world is that the stupid are cocksure and the intelligent full of doubt.
—Bertrand Russell; *Skeptical Essays*, 1928

.14 Against stupidity the very gods
Themselves contend in vain.
—Friedrich von Schiller; *The Maid of Orleans*, 1801

.15 When a stupid man is doing something he is ashamed of, he always declares that it is his duty.
—George Bernard Shaw; *Caesar and Cleopatra*, 1901

.16 While he was not dumber than an ox he was not any smarter.
—James Thurber; *The Thurber Carnival*, 1945

.17 Better to keep your mouth shut and appear stupid than to open it and remove all doubt.
—Mark Twain; *Letters from the Earth*, 1905–9

.18 Strange as it may seem, no amount of learning can cure stupidity, and formal education positively fortifies it.
—Stephen Vizinczey: "Europe's Inner Demons," review of Norman Cohen, *An Inquiry Inspired by the Great Witch-Hunt* in *Sunday Telegraph*, London, March 2, 1975

# **274** Style

.1 Correct idiom is the foundation of good style.
—Aristotle; *Rhetoric*, c. 4th century B.C.

.2 Those who write as they speak, although they speak very well, write badly.
—Comte de Buffon; *Discours sur le style*, French Academy, August 25, 1753

**274**

.3 Style is the dress of thoughts.
—Lord Chesterfield; Letter to his son, November 24, 1749

.4 What is style? For many people, a very complicated way of saying very simple things. According to us, a very simple way of saying very complicated things.
—Jean Cocteau; *Le Rappel a l'ordre*, 1926

.5 Style is the perfection of a point of view.
—Richard Eberhart; Selected Poems, "Meditation Two," 1965

.6 A man's style is his mind's voice.
—Ralph Waldo Emerson; *Journals*, 1872

.7 Style is as much under the words as in the words.
—Gustave Flaubert; letter to Ernest Feydeau, 1860

.8 The style of an author should be the image of his mind, but the choice and command of language is the fruit of exercise.
—Edward Gibbon; *Miscellaneous Works*, 1796

.9 To me style is just the outside of content, and content is the inside of style, like the outside and the inside of the human body—both go together, they can't be separated.
—Jean-Luc Godard; quoted in *Godard*, "Introduction" by Richard Roud, 1970

.10 No style is good that is not fit to be spoken or read aloud with effect.
—William Hazlitt; *The Conversation of Authors*, 1821

.11 Which, of all defects, has been the one most fatal to a good style? The not knowing when to come to an end.
—Arthur Helps; *Companions of My Solitude*, 1851

.12 He has found his style, when he cannot do otherwise.
—Paul Klee; *The Diaries of Paul Klee, 1898–1918*, 1957, 1908 entry.

.13 Style is the physiognomy of the mind and is more unerring that that of the body. Imitating another's style is like wearing a mask.
—Arthur Schopenhauer; *Parerga and Paralipomena*, 1851

.14 I do not much dislike the matter, but
The manner of his speech.
—William Shakespeare; *Antony and Cleopatra*, 1606–7

**274**

.15 Effectiveness of assertion is the alpha and omega of style.
—George Bernard Shaw; *Man and Super-man*, 1903

.16 ...the fact that the ancients used the verb "sing" instead of the verb "tell" bears witness to this very thing, namely, that poetry was the source and origin of style.... For when poetry was recited, it employed the assistance of song.... Therefore since "tell" was first used in reference to poetic "style" and since among the ancients this poetic style was accompanied by song, the term "sing" was to them equivalent to the term "tell."
—Strabo; *Geography*, c. 7 B.C.–A.D. 18

.17 Proper words in proper places, make the true definition of a style.
—Jonathan Swift; Letter to a young clergyman, January 9, 1720

.18 A man's style is intrinsic and private with him like his voice or his gesture, partly a matter of inheritance, partly of cultivation. It is more than a pattern of expression. It is the pattern of the soul.
—Maurice Valency; *Jean Giraudoux: Four Plays*, "Introduction," 1958

.19 Clearness ornaments profound thoughts.
—Marquis de Vauvenargues; *Reflections and Maxims*, 1746

.20 In matters of grave importance, style, not sincerity, is the vital thing.
—Oscar Wilde; *The Importance of Being Earnest*, 1895

# **275** Subject

.1 When a man gets talking about himself, he seldom fails to be eloquent and often reaches the sublime.
—Josh Billings; *Josh Billings' Encyclopedia of Wit and Wisdom*, 1874

.2 The minutest animalcule on earth is a large subject to expatiate upon.
—Thomas Bridges; *The Adventures of a Bank-Note*, 1770–71

.3 Any subject can be taught effectively in some intellectually honest form to any child at any stage of development.
—Jerome Seymour Bruner; *The Process of Education*, 1960

.4 "The time has come," the Walrus said,
"To talk of many things;
Of shoes—and ships—and sealing-wax—

**275**

Of cabbages—and kings—
And why the sea is boiling hot—
And whether pigs have wings."
—Lewis Carroll; *Through the Looking Glass*, 1871

.5 Grasp the subject, the words will follow.
—Cato the Elder; Attributed
[Advice to orators.]

.6 O young artist, you search for a subject—everything is a subject. Your subject is yourself, your impressions, your emotions in the presence of nature.
—Eugene Delacroix; *Journal*, 1983–85

.7 Talk to a man about himself and he will listen for hours.
—Benjamin Disraeli; *Lothair*, 1870

.8 We reproach people for talking about themselves; but it is the subject they treat best.
—Anatole France; *La Vie Litteraire*, 1888

.9 You may talk too much on the best of subjects.
—Benjamin Franklin; *Poor Richard's Almanack*, 1753

.10 We prefer to speak evil of ourselves rather than not speak of ourselves at all.
—François de La Rochefoucauld, *Maxims*, 1678

.11 Don't talk about yourself; it will be done when you leave.
—Addison Mizner; A. Johnson, *The Legendary Mizners*, 1953

.12 Religious people spend so much time with their confessors because they like to talk about themselves.
—Marquise de Sevigne; *Letters of Madame de Sevigne to Her Daughter and Her Friends*, 1811

.13 Poetry is the subject of the poem.
—Wallace Stevens; *Opus Posthumous*, 1957

.14 It is the honorable characteristic of poetry that its materials are to be found in every subject which can interest the human mind.
—William Wordsworth; *Lyrical Ballads*, "Advertisement," 1798

# **276** Success

.1 No story of success ever starts with if and but.
—American Proverb

.2 Success supposes endeavor.
—Jane Austen; *Emma*, 1815

**276**

.3 Success is counted sweetest
By those who ne'er succeed.
—Emily Dickinson; *Complete Poems*, c. 1859, No. 67

.4 If A equals success, then the formula is A equals X plus Y plus Z, with X being work, Y play, and Z keeping your mouth shut.
—Albert Einstein; in *The Observer*, January 15, 1950

.5 Nothing recedes like success.
—Bryan Forbes; quoted in *The Observer*, London, December 19, 1971

.6 Everything is subservient to success, even grammar.
—Victor Hugo; *Les Miserables*, 1862

.7 Think of the really successful men and women you know. Do you know a single one who didn't learn very young the trick of calling attention to himself in the right quarters?
—Storm Jameson; *A Cup of Tea for Mr. Thorgill*, 1957

.8 The logic of worldly success rests on a fallacy: the strange error that our perfection depends on the thoughts and opinions and applause of other men! A weird life it is, indeed, to be living always in somebody else's imagination, as if that were the only place in which one could at last become real!
—Thomas Merton; *The Seven Storey Mountain*, 1948

.9 Success depends on three things: who says it, what he says, how he says it; and of these three things, what he says is least important.
—John Morley; *Recollections*, 1917

.10 Success has always been the worst of liars.
—Freidrich Nietzsche; Attributed

.11 Who wants to read about success? It is the early struggle which makes a good story.
—Katherine Anne Porter; "Gertrude Stein: Three Views," 1927, in *The Days Before*, 1952

.12 Dwells within the soul of every Artist
More than all his effort can express;
And he knows the best remains unuttered,
Sighing at what we call success.
—Adelaide Anne Procter; *Legends and Lyrics* "Unexpressed," 1858

.13 Success causes us to be more praised than known.
—Joseph Roux; *Meditations of a Parish Priest*, 1886

**276**

.14 People seldom see the halting and painful steps by which the most insignificant success is achieved.
—Anne Sullivan; letter, October 30, 1887, published in Helen Keller, *The Story of My Life*, 1903
[The educator of the deaf and blind refers to teaching Helen Keller.]

.15 God doesn't require us to succeed; he only requires that you try.
—Mother Teresa; quoted by Robert F. Kennedy, Jr., in *Rolling Stone*, December, 1992

.17 These success encourages: they can because they think they can.
—Virgil; *Aeneid*, c. 1st century B.C.

**277** Syllables

.1 He studies too much for words of four syllables.
—Jane Austen; *Pride and Prejudice*, 1813

.2    Philologists who chase
A panting syllable through time and space,
Start it at home, and hunt it in the dark
To Gaul, to Greece, and into Noah's ark.
—William Cowper; "Retirement," 1782

.3 He achieved that performance which is designated in melodramas "laughing like a fiend,"—it seems that fiends always laugh in syllables, and always in three syllables, never more nor less.
—Charles Dickens; *The Old Curiosity Shop*, 1840–41

.4 The quiet nonchalance of death
No daybreak can bestir;
The slow archangel's syllables
Must awaken her.
—Emily Dickinson; *Poems*, No. 5, c. 1858

.5 Love's stricken "why"
Is all that love can speak—
Built of but just a syllable
The huge hearts that break.
—Emily Dickinson; *Poems* No. 1368, c. 1876

.6 Still may syllables jar with time,
Still may reason war with rhyme,
Resting never!
—Ben Jonson; "A Fit of Rhyme Against Rhyme," 1616

.7    As some to church repair,
Not for the doctrine, but the music there.
These equal syllables alone require,
Though oft the ear the open vowels tire;

While expletives their feeble aid do join,
And ten low words oft creep in one dull line.
 —Alexander Pope; *An Essay on Criticism*,
 1711

.8  Syllables govern the world.
 —John Selden; *Table Talk*, "Power, State,"
 c. 1654

.9  A great many people think polysyllables are a
 sign of intelligence.
 —Barbara Walters; *How to Talk with Practically Anybody About Practically Anything*, 1970

# 278 Symbols

.1  Symbolism is the act of thinking in images, an
 act now lost to civilized man.
 —Anonymous African

.2  Symbols are the imaginative signposts of life.
 —Margot Asquith; *More Or Less About
 Myself*, 1934

.3  The symbolic view of things is a consequence
 of long absorption in images. Is sign language
 the real; language of Paradise?
 —Hugo Ball; *Flight Out of Time: A Dada
 Diary*, 1927, entry for April 8, 1917

.4  Nature is a temple in which living columns
 sometimes utter confused words. Man walks
 through it among forests of symbols, which
 watch him with knowing eyes.
 —Charles Baudelaire; *Les Fleurs du mal*,
 "Correspondences," 1857

.5  The triangle straight up symbolizes woman,
 the inverted triangle symbolizes man, and the
 two of them together are a six pointed star or
 the Star of David, which symbolizes life, because man and woman in their holy union
 symbolize life.
 —Claude Brown; *Manchild in the Promised
 Land*, 1965

.6  In a symbol there is concealment and yet revelation: here therefore, by silence and by
 speech acting together, comes a double
 significance.... In the symbol proper, what we
 can call a symbol, there is ever, more or less
 distinctly and directly, some embodiment and
 revelation of the Infinite; the Infinite is made
 to blend itself with the Finite, to stand visible,
 and as it were, attainable there. By symbols, accordingly, is man guided and commanded,
 made happy, made wretched.
 —Thomas Carlyle; *Sartor Resartus*, 1833–34

.7  A person gets from a symbol the meaning he
 puts into it, and what is one man's comfort and
 inspiration is another's jest and scorn.
 —Justice Robert Jackson; *West Virginia
 State Board v. Barnette*, 1943

.8  The stone remains, and the cross, to let us
 know
 Their unjust, hard demands, as symbols do.
 —Norman A. MacCaig; "Celtic Cross,"
 1960

.9  Great symbols swallow us whole. They lead
 us onto themselves ... we pursue ... but we
 never capture their whole meaning. Not because the symbol is mindlessly obscure
 (though there are literary vices of this kind
 too) but because it is radically, authentically
 enigmatic.
 —Theodore Roszak; *Where the Wasteland
 Ends*, 1972

# 279 Sympathy

.1  One cannot weep for the entire world, it is beyond human strength. One must choose.
 —Jean Anouilh; *Cecile*, 1949

.2  Needs there groan a world in anguish just to
 teach us sympathy?
 —Robert Browning; *La Saisiaz*, 1878

.3  Never does one feel oneself so utterly helpless
 as in trying to speak comfort for great bereavement.
 —Jane Welsh Carlyle; letter to Thomas
 Carlyle on the death of his mother,
 1853, in *Letters and Memorials of Jane
 Welsh Carlyle*, James Anthony Froude,
 ed. 1883

.4  "I weep for you," the Walrus said:
 "I deeply sympathize."
 With sobs and tears he sorted out
 Those of the largest size,
 Holding his pocket handkerchief
 Before his streaming eyes.
 —Lewis Carroll; *Through the Looking-
 Glass*, 1871

.5  Sympathy—the one poor word which includes
 all our best insight and our best love.
 —George Eliot; *Adam Bede*, 1859

.6  To be sympathetic without discrimination is
 so very debilitating.
 —Ronald Firbank; *Vainglory*, 1915

.7  Sympathy without relief is like mustard without beef.
 —R.L. Gales; *Vanished Country Folk*, 1914

## 279

.8 If all the people in the world should agree to sympathize with a certain man at a certain hour, they could not cure his headache.
—Ed Howe; *Country Town Sayings*, 1911

.9 A sympathizer is a fellow that's for you as long as it doesn't cost anything.
—Kin Hubbard; *Abe Martin's Sayings and Sketches*, 1915

.10 I can sympathize with people's pains, but not with their pleasures. There is something curiously boring about somebody else's happiness.
—Aldous Huxley; *Limbo*, 1920

.11 People in need never think that you feel enough.
—Samuel Johnson; Boswell's *Life of Johnson*, 1791

.12 We are all strong enough to hear the misfortunes of others.
—François de la Rochefoucauld; *Maximes*, 1678

.13 Is there anything more dangerous than sympathetic understanding.
—Pablo Picasso; quoted in Helene Parmelin, *Picasso Says…*, "Solitude," 1966

.14 There is nothing sweeter than to be sympathized with.
—George Santayana; *The Life of Reason* "Reason in Common Sense," 1905–6

.15 There are times when sympathy is as necessary as the air we breathe.
—Rose Pastor Stokes; in Herbert Shapiro and David Sterling, eds. "I Belong to the Working Class," 1992

.16 The old man said that what a man wanted that was down, was sympathy.
—Mark Twain; *Huckleberry Finn*, 1885

.17 A heart at leisure from itself,
To soothe and sympathize.
—Anna Letitia Waring; "Father, I Know That All My Life" late 19th century

.18 Anyone can sympathize with the sufferings of a friend, but it requires a very fine nature to sympathize with a friend's success.
—Oscar Wilde; "The Soul of Man under Socialism," *The Fortnightly Review*, 1891
[Wilde's work was published under the pseudonym of Sebastian Melmouth.]

## 280 Tact

.1 Silence is not always tact, and it is tact that is golden, not silence.
—Samuel Butler II; *Note-Books*, Higgledy-Piggledy," 1912

.2 'Tis ill talking of halters in the house of a man that was hanged.
—Miguel de Cervantes; *Don Quixote*, 1615

.3 Tact in audacity consists in knowing how far to go too far.
—Jean Cocteau; *Le Coq et l'Arlequin*, 1918

.4 Without tact you can learn nothing. Tact teaches you when to be silent.
—Benjamin Disraeli; *Endymion*, 1880

.5 Few persons have tact enough to perceive when to be silent.
—Sir Arthur Helps; *Essays*, "Secrecy," 1841

.6 Tact: to lie about others as you would have them lie about you.
—Oliver Herford; *The Deb's Dictionary*, 1931

.7 Don't flatter yourself that friendship authorizes you to say disagreeable things to your intimates. The nearer you come into relation with a person, the more necessary do tact and courtesy become.
—Oliver Wendell Holmes, Sr.; *The Autocrat of the Breakfast Table*, 1858

.8 Tact is after all a kind of mind reading.
—Sarah Orne Jewett; *The Country of the Pointed Firs*, 1896

.9 Tact is the ability to describe others as they see themselves.
—Mary Pettibone Poole; *A Glass Eye at a Keyhole*, 1938
[Poole's observation about tact has also been attributed to Abraham Lincoln.]

.10 Forbear to mention what thou canst not praise.
—Matthew Prior; *Carmen Seculare*, 1700

.11 Give thy thoughts no tongue,
Nor any unproportioned thought his act.
Be thou familiar but by no means vulgar.
—William Shakespeare; *Hamlet*, 1600–1
[Polonius advises his son Laertes advice on tact.]

.12 To have the reputation of possessing the most perfect social tact, talk to every woman as if you loved her, and to every man as if he bored you.
—Oscar Wilde; *A Woman of No Importance*, 1893

# 281 Tale

.1 But now the mystic tale that pleas'd of yore
Can charm an understanding age no more.
—Joseph Addison; *An Account of the Greatest English Poets*, 1694

.2 My tale is told.
—Aeschylus; *Agamemnon*, 458 B.C.

.3 Hear my tale and grave it on thy heart.
—Aeschylus; *Libation-Bearers*, 458 B.C.

.4 Various and strange was the long-winded tale.
—James Beattie; *The Minstrel*, 1771

.5 Put no faith in tale-bearers.
—H.G. Bohn, *Handbook of Proverbs*, 1855

.6 The tales are like rays of light, taking their colors from the medium through which they pass.
—W.A. Bone; *Children's Stories and How to Tell Them*, 1924

.7 I wrote tales beside,
Carved many an article on cherry-stones
To suit light readers
—Elizabeth Barrett Browning; *Aurora Leigh*, 1856

.8 Some men's whole delight ... is to talk of a Cock and Bull over a pot.
—Robert Burton; *The Anatomy of Melancholy*, 1621
[A cock-and-bull tale is either a long rambling, idle story, or an incredible one, concocted to deceive.]

.9 When we meet next we'll have a tale to tell.
—Lord Byron; *Don Juan*, 1820

.10 [A tale, no matter what its origin] tends to absorb something of the place where it is narrated—a landscape, a custom, a moral outlook, or else merely a very faint accent or flavor of the locality.
—Italo Calvino; *Italian Folktales*, George Martin, tr., 1980

.11 Oh! once the harp of Innisfail
Was strung full high to notes of gladness;
But yet it often told a tale
Of more prevailing sadness.
—Thomas Campbell; "O'Connor's Child," 1810

.12 For this thing do you know as well as I:
When one repeats a tale told by a man,
He must report, as nearly as he can,
Every least word, if he remember it.
—Geoffrey Chaucer; *The Canterbury Tales*, 1387

.13 Let every fellow tell his tale about.
—Geoffrey Chaucer; *Canterbury Tales*, "The Knight's Tale," 1387

.14 For though myself be a full vicious man,
A moral tale yet I you tell can.
—Geoffrey Chaucer; *Canterbury Tales*, "The Pardoner's Prologue," 1387

.15 Set forth thy tale, and tarry not the time.
—Geoffrey Chaucer; *Canterbury Tales*, "The Reeves Prologue," 1387

.16 This tale's a fragment from the life of dreams.
—Samuel Taylor Coleridge; "Phantom or Fact?" c. 1816

.17 By hearing the emblematic tales that spring from your heart and your love, your child will sense his own worthy being in your eyes, and perhaps sense a worthiness in the broader sweep of the human race.
—Chase Collins; *Tell Me A Story: Creating Bedtime Tales Your Child Dreams On*, 1992

.18 It's not superfluous and vain
To tell a good tale ov'r again.
—Samuel Colvil; *Whiggs Supplication*, 1681

.19 A tale should be judicious, clear, succinct;
The language plain, and incidents well
link'd;
Tell not as new what every body knows;
And new or old, still hasten to a close.
—William Cowper; *Conversation*, 1781

.20 If we take it for a Canterbury tale, why do we not refute it?
—Thomas Cranmer; *Sermon on Rebellion*, c. 1545
[A Canterbury tale is a story founded on legend or tradition, designed to interest and amuse, and frequently long-winded.]

.21 Very old men are we men:
Our dreams are tales
Told in dim Eden
By Eve's nightingales.
—Walter De La Mare; "All That's Past," 1912

.22 Such are the changes which a few years bring about, and so do things pass away, like a tale that is told.
—Charles Dickens; *The Old Curiosity Shop*, 1840–41

.23 A tale in the carrying is made more.
—Thomas Draxe; *Bibliotheca*, 1633

.24 Dead men tell no tales.
—John Dryden; *The Spanish Friar*, 1681

**281**

.25 A good tale ill told is marred in the telling.
—English Proverb

.26 Upon a mountain height, far from the sea,
  I found a shell,
  And to my listening ear the lonely thing
  Ever a song of ocean seemed to sing,
  Ever a tale of ocean seemed to tell.
    —Eugene Field; *Collected Works*, 1896

.27 What shall we tell you? Tales, marvelous
  tales
  Of ships and stars and isles where good men
  rest.
    —J.E. Flecker; *The Golden Journey to
    Samarkland*, "Prologue," 1913

.28 Beware of the porter's lodge for carrying tales
  out of school.
    —John Ford; *Fancies*, 1638
    [Tales out of school are gossip best left un-
    reported.]

.29 A tale without love is like beef without mustard: insipid.
    —Anatole France; *La Revolte des Anges*,
    1914

.30 The tale runs as pleases the teller.
    —Thomas Fuller II; *Gnomologia*, 1732

.31 Lest men suspect your tale untrue,
  Keep probability in view.
    —John Gay; *Fables*, "The Painter Who
    Pleased Nobody," 1727

.32 Tell-tale-tit, your tongue shall be slit,
  And all the dogs in the town shall have a
  little bit.
    —J.O. Halliwell; *The Nursery Rhymes of
    England*, 1842

.33 Nobody has any conscience about adding to
  the improbabilities of a marvelous tale.
    —Nathaniel Hawthorne; *The Marble Faun*,
    1860

.34 A tale of the times gone by.
    —Heinrich Heine; *Die Lorelei*, 1823–24

.35 Myself I do not believe the tale, but it is told.
    —Herodotus; *History*, c. 445 B.C.

.36 Pleasant it is at a feast and rich banquet to tell
  delightful tales.
    —Hesoid; *The Melampodia*, c. 650 B.C.

.37 Tales of Robin Hood are good among fools.
    —John Heywood; *Proverbs*, 1546
    [A tale of Robin Hood is an extravagant
    fiction usually told as such.]

.38 It is tedious to tell again tales already plainly
  told.
    —Homer; *The Odyssey*, c. 700 B.C.

**281**

.39 Soft as some song divine, thy tale flows.
    —Homer; *The Odyssey*, c. 700 B.C.

.40 He tells old wives' tales appropriate to the
  case.
    —Horace; *Satires*, 35 B.C.
    [An old wives' tale is any marvelous story
    or rumor. Even today idle and ridiculous
    stories continue to be called such.]

.41 A mere Tale of a Tub. Lend it no ear, I pray
  you.
    —Ben Jonson; *A Tale of a Tub*, 1633
    [A tale of a tub is like a cock-and-bull
    story, one concocted to deceive.]

.42 A tale never loses in the telling.
    —James Kelly; *Scottish Proverbs*, 1721

.43 We might as well spend that time in reading
  of profane histories, of Canterbury tales, or fit
  of Robin Hood.
    —Hugh Latimer; *Seven Sermons*, 1549

.44 In the tale, in the telling, we are all one blood.
  Take the tale in your teeth, then, and bite till
  the blood runs, hoping it's not poison; and we
  will all come to the end together, and even to
  the beginning, living, as we do, in the middle.
    —Ursula K. Le Guin; "It Was a Dark and
    Stormy Night; or, Why Are We Hud-
    dling About the Campfire?," speech,
    University of Chicago, 1989

.45 Every Shepherd tells his tale
  Under the Hawthorn in the vale.
    —John Milton; *L'Allegro*, 1632
    [That is, counts his sheep.]

.46 This is a fair tale of a tub told us of his election.
    —Sir Thomas More; *Confutation of Tyn-
    dale's Answers*, 1532

.47 Unwritten, half-forgotten tales of old.
    —William Morris; *Jason*, 1867

.48 And their words seemed to them as idle tales.
    —New Testament; Luke

.49 Thou shalt not go up and down as a tailbearer
  among thy people.
    —Old Testament; Leviticus

.50 For all our days are passed away in thy wrath:
  we spend our years as a tale that is told.
    —Old Testament: Psalms

.51 Often would he tell the same tale in other
  words.
    —Ovid; *Artis Amatoriae*, c. 1 B.C.

.52 Repeat your tale again to me.
    —Pacuvius; *Iliona*, c. 150 B.C.

**281**

.53 Many a tale hath been told in many a way.
   —Pindar; *Nemean Odes*, c. 459 B.C.

.54 From a mere nothing springs a mighty tale.
   —Propertius; *Elegies*, c. 24 B.C.

.55 A good tale ill told is a bad one.
   —John Ray; *English Proverbs*, 1678

.56 You will tell another tale when you are tired.
   —John Ray; *English Proverbs*, 1678

.57 An' all us other children, when the supper
   things is done,
   We set around the kitchen fire an' has the
   mostest fun
   A-list'nin to the witch-tales 'at Annie tells
   about
   An' the Gobble-uns 'at gits you Ef you don't
   watch out!
      —James Whitcomb Riley; "Little Orphant
      Annie," 1883

.58 A man is always a teller of tales, he lives surrounded by his stories and the stories of others, he sees everything that happens to him
   through them; and tries to live his life as if he
   were recounting it.
      —Jean-Paul Sartre; *Nausea*, "Saturday,
      Noon," 1938

.59 I cannot tell how the truth may be;
   I say the tale as 'twas said to me.
      —Sir Walter Scott; *The Lay of the Last
      Minstrel*, 1805

.60 'Tis an old tale and often told.
   —Sir Walter Scott; *Marmion*, 1808

.61 And so, from hour to hour we ripe and ripe,
   And then from hour to hour we rot,
   And thereby hangs a tale.
      —William Shakespeare; *As You Like It*,
      1600

.62 There comes an old man with his three sons—
   I could match this beginning with an old
   tale.
      —William Shakespeare; *As You Like It*,
      1600

.63 Mark now, how a plain tale shall put you
   down.
      —William Shakespeare; *I, Henry IV*, 1597

.64 Life is as tedious as a twice-told tale.
   Vexing the dull ear of a drowsy man.
      —William Shakespeare; *King John*, 1596

.65 I can ... mar a curious tale in telling it.
   —William Shakespeare; *King Lear*, 1605

.66 Aged ears play truant at his tales.
   —William Shakespeare; *Love's Labour's
   Lost*, 1595

**281**

.67 Life's but a walking shadow, a poor player
   That struts and frets his hour upon the
   stage,
   And then is heard no more; it is a tale
   Told by an idiot, full of sound and fury,
   Signifying nothing.
      —William Shakespeare; *Macbeth*, 1606

.68 For aught that ever I could read,
   Could ever hear by tale or history,
   The course of true love never did run
   smooth.
      —William Shakespeare; *A Midsummer
      Night's Dream*, 1600

.69 I will a round unvarnish'd tale deliver.
   —William Shakespeare; *Othello*, 1605

.70 An honest tale speeds best being plainly told.
   —William Shakespeare; *Richard III*, 1592

.71 A whispering tale in a fair lady's ear,
   Such as would please.
      —William Shakespeare; *Romeo and Juliet*,
      1595

.72 And thereby hangs a tale.
   —William Shakespeare; *The Taming of the
   Shrew*, 1594

.73 Your tale, sir, would cure deafness.
   —William Shakespeare; *The Tempest*, 1611

.74 By definition variants of a tale share the same
   essential story, but the overriding emotional
   tone of a specific variant may be quite different
   from the next. A change in key from major to
   minor or a change in tempo not only changes
   the song, it changes what is shared. The same
   is true of folktales.
      —George Shannon; *A Knock at the Door*,
      1992

.75 He cometh unto you with a tale which hold-
   eth children from play, and old men from the
   chimney corner.
      —Sir Philip Sidney; *An Apology for Poetrie*,
      1598

.76 Such wonderful tales as childhood loves to
   hear.
      —Robert Southey; *Joan of Arc*, 1796

.77 I do not care for hearing a Canterbury tale.
   —Richard Steele; *The Tatler*, December
   22, 1709

.78 I tell you my tale and my tale's author.
   —Jonathan Swift; *Polite Conversation*, 1738

.79 It's a winter's tale
   That the snow blind twilight ferries over the
   lakes

**281**

And floating fields from the farm in the cup of the vales.
—Dylan Thomas; "A Winter's Tale," 1946

.80 What cometh once in may never out, for fear of telling tales out of school.
—William Tyndale; *The Practice of Prelates*, 1530

.81 This is a tale of arms and of a man. Fated to be an exile, he was the first to sail from the land of Troy and reach Italy, at its Lavinian shore.
—Virgil; *Aeneid*, c. 1st century B.C.

.82 An old tale which every schoolboy knows.
—William Whitehead; *The Roman Father*, "Prologue," 1750

# **282** Talk and Talkativeness

.1 Spare thy flood of talk.
—Aeschylus; *Seven Against Thebes*, 467 B.C.

.2 He that talketh what he knoweth, will also talketh what he knoweth not.
—Francis Bacon; *Essays*, "Of Simulation," 1612

.3 Great talkers are great liars.
—Nathan Bailey; *Dictionary*, "Talker," 1736

.4 In dinner talk it is perhaps allowable to fling any faggot rather than let the fire go out.
—J.M. Barrie; *Tommy and Grizel*, 1900

.5 I don't care how much a man talks, if he only says it in a few words.
—Josh Billings; *Affurisms. From Josh Billings: His Sayings*, 1865

.6 Great talkers are like leaky pitchers, everything runs out of them.
—H.G. Bohn; *Handbook of Proverbs*, 1855

.7 [Henry] Miller is not really a writer but a nonstop talker to whom someone has given a typewriter.
—Gerald Brenan; *Thoughts in a Dry Season*, "Literature," 1978

.8 When you talk to the half-wise, twaddle; when you talk to the ignorant, brag; when you talk to the sagacious, look very humble, and ask their opinion.
—Edward Bulwer-Lytton; *Paul Clifford*, 1835

**282**

.9 He'd talk a horse's hind leg off.
—Henry Cockton; *Sylvester Sound*, 1844

.10 How often one talks not to hear what the other person has to say, but to hear what one has got to say oneself!
—Mary Coleridge; 1891, in Theresa Whistler, ed. *The Collected Poems of Mary Coleridge*, 1954

.11 Always look to those whom you are talking to, never at those you are talking about.
—C.C. Colton; *Lacon*, 1820

.12 Tomorrow I'll talk to them like a Dutch uncle.
—Joseph Conrad; *The Nigger of the Narcissus*, 1897
[That is, to talk sharply.]

.13 Be a hypocrite, if you like, but don't talk like one.
—Denis Diderot; *Rameau's Nephew*, 1761

.14 For more numerous was the herd of such, Who think too little, and who talk too much.
—John Dryden; *Absalom and Achitophel*, 1681

.15 To talk without thinking is to shoot without aiming.
—English Proverb

.16 True he can talk, and yet he is no speaker.
—Eupolis; *Demes*, c. 425 B.C.

.17 I believe they talked of me, for they laughed consumedly.
—George Farquhar; *The Beaux' Stratagem*, 1707

.18 He was talking at the top of his ego.
—Miles Franklin; *Childhood and Brindabella*, 1963

.19 Talking is a hydrant in the yard and writing is a faucet upstairs in the house. Opening the first takes all the pressure off the second.
—Robert Frost; *Collected Poems*, "Preface," 1939

.20 Everyone talks of what he loves.
—Thomas Fuller; *Gnomologia*, 1732

.21 In much of your talking, thinking is half murdered.
—Kahlil Gibran; *The Prophet*, "On Talking," 1923

.22 He who talks much cannot talk well.
—Carlo Goldoni; *Pamela*, 1750

.23 Every absurdity has a champion to defend it, for error is always talkative.
—Oliver Goldsmith; *The Deserted Village*, 1770

**282**

.24 Talking's just a nervous habit.
  —Martha Grimes; *The Deer Leap*, 1985

.25 I was plagy apt to talk turkey.
  —T.C. Haliburton, ed. *Traits of American Humor*, c. 1840
  [That is, to talk plainly.]

.26 I was talking through my hat.
  —Will N. Harben; *The Georgians*, 1904
  [That is, talking without knowing of what you talk.]

.27 The most fluent talkers or most plausible reasoners are not always the justest thinkers.
  —William Hazlitt; *Essays*, "On Prejudice," 1830

.28 He talked on for ever; and you wished him to talk on for ever.
  —William Hazlitt; *Letters on the English Poets*, "On the Living Poets," 1818
  [Hazlitt refers to Samuel Taylor Coleridge.]

.29 Lonely people talking to each other can make each other lonelier.
  —Lillian Hellman; *The Autumn Garden*, 1951

.30 Talk like water gushed from him; he might have been smitten by Aaron's rod.
  —O. Henry; *Hearts and Crosses*, 1907

.31 There is so much good in the worst of us,
  And so much bad in the best of us,
  That it hardly behooves any of us
  To talk about the rest of us.
  —Edward Wallis Hoch; "Good and Bad," *The Reader*, September 7, 1907
  [Hoch, the ex–Governor of Kansas disclaimed the verse attributed to him.]

.32 Talking is like playing on the harp; there is as much in laying the hands on the strings to stop the vibration as in twanging them to bring out their music.
  —Oliver Wendell Holmes, Sr.; *The Autocrat of the Breakfast Table*, 1858

.33 He began to talk Dutch to me. Well, I talked turkey to him.
  —Emerson Hough; *The Sagebusher*, 1919

.34 Every time I read where some woman gave a short talk I wonder how she stopped.
  —Kin Hubbard; *Abe Martin's Broadcast*, 1930

.35 Great talkers fire too fast to take good aim.
  —T.E. Hulme; *Proverb Lore*, 1902

**282**

.36 Let your reading aloud be good talk, and shun elocution and histrionics as you would the plague.
  —Holbrook Jackson; *The Anatomy of Bibliomania*, 1950

.37 Those that merely talk and never think,
  That live in the wild anarchy of drink.
  —Ben Jonson; "An Epistle," c. 1637

.38 He who talks to himself speaks to a fool.
  —James Kelly; *Scottish Proverbs*, 1721

.39 There are very few people who don't become more interesting when they stop talking.
  —Mary Lowry; in *The Pacific Sun*, 1985

.40 A table-talker rich in sense,
  And witty without wit's pretense.
  —Cotton Mather; *Epitaph on Anne Bradstreet*, 1672

.41 Who was ever cured by talk?
  —Herman Melville; *The Confidence-Man*, 1857

.42 You talk just like a book.
  —Moliere; *Don Juan*, 1655

.43 Those who have few things to attend to are great babblers; for the less men think, the more they talk.
  —Baron de la Brede et de Montesquieu; *Mes pensees*, c. 1722–55

.44 Like all good talkers, he knew how to delude his listeners into the belief that they were taking an important part in the conversation.
  —George Moore; *Evelyn Innes*, 1898

.45 My great-grandfather used to say to his wife, my great-grandmother, who in turn told her daughter, my grandmother, who repeated it to her daughter, my mother, who used to remind her daughter, my own sister, that to talk well and eloquently was a very great art, but that an equally great one was to know the right moment to stop.
  —Wolfgang Amadeus Mozart; Letter, November 4, 1787, published in *The Letters of Mozart and His Family*, Emily Anderson, ed., 1966

.46 One thing talk can't accomplish, however, is communication. This is because everybody's talking too much to pay attention to what anyone else is saying.
  —P.J. O'Rourke; *Modern Manners*, 1984

.47 The talkative man inflicts punishment.
  —Ovid; *Amores*, 13 B.C.

.48 To beguile with talk the slow-moving hours.
  —Ovid; *Tristia*, c. A.D. 9

# 282

.49 All sensible talk about vitally important topics must be commonplace, all reasoning about them unsound, and all study of them narrow and sordid.
—C.S. Peirce; *Collected Papers*, 1931–58

.50 You interrupt him with your talking.
—Plautus; *Pseudolus*, c. 200 B.C.

.51 Like all talkers, she thought other people talked too much.
—Katherine Anne Porter; "Gertrude Stein: Three Views," 1927, in *The Days Before*, 1952

.52 To be a convincing talker, I should be able to show my son just wherein Algebra is essential to his future success.
—George A. Posner; Attributed

.53 He's like a bagpipe, he never talks till his belly is full.
—John Ray; *English Proverbs*, 1678

.54 Talkative rather than eloquent.
—Sallust; *Histories*, c. 40 B.C.

.55 If only people would not talk till they knew, the world would be a nicer place.
—Olive Schreiner; *Undine*, 1876, published 1928

.56 A good old man, sir. He will be talking. As they say, when the age is in, the wit is out.
—William Shakespeare; *Much Ado About Nothing*, 1600

.57 How you do talk!
—William Shakespeare; *Henry VIII*, 1612

.58 Never talk for more that half a minute without pausing and giving others an opportunity to strike in.
—Sydney Smith; Lady Holland, *Memoir*, 1855

.59 You love to hear yourself talk.
—Jonathan Swift; *Polite Conversation*, 1738

.60 I should not talk so much about myself if there was anybody else whom I knew as well.
—Henry David Thoreau; *Walden*, "Economy," 1854

.61 Talk low, talk slow, and don't say too much.
—John Wayne, c. 1970
[Wayne's advice on acting.]

.62 Sometimes too much talking can kill a thing.
—Paulette C. White; *Love Poems to a Black Junkie*, "A Black Revolutionary Poem," 1975

.63 Men talk only to conceal the mind.
—Edward Young; *The Love of Fame, the Universal Passion*, 1725

# 283 Teachers

.1 A teacher affects eternity; he can never tell where his influence stops.
—Henry Adams; *The Education of Henry Adams*, 1907

.2 The true teacher defends his pupils against his own personal influence. He inspires self-distrust. He guides their eyes from himself to the spirit that quickens him. He will have no disciple.
—A. Bronson Alcott; *Orphic Sayings*, "The Teacher," 1840

.3 If the student fails to learn the teacher fails to teach.
—Anonymous

.4 For rigorous teacher seized my youth,
And purged its faith, and trimmed its fire,
Showed me the high, white star of Truth,
There bade me gaze, and there aspire.
—Matthew Arnold; *Poems: Second Series*, "Stanzas from the Grande Chartreuse," 1855

.5 A schoolmaster should have an atmosphere of awe, and walk wonderingly, as if he was amazed at being himself.
—Walter Bagehot; "Hartley Coleridge," 1852, reprinted in *Literary Studies*, Vol. 1, 1878

.6 He who makes himself his own teacher, makes himself pupil to a fool.
—St. Bernard; *Epistles*, c. 1140

.7 The world of knowledge takes a crazy turn
When teachers themselves are taught to learn.
—Bertolt Brecht; *The Life of Galileo*, Howard Brenton, tr., 1980

.8 Your teacher can lead you to the door; the acquiring of learning rests with each person.
—Chinese Proverb

.9 A good teacher, like a good entertainer, first must hold his audience's attention. Then he can teach the lesson.
—John Henrik Clarke; "A Search for Identity" in *Social Casework*, May, 1970

.10 No man, however conservative, can stand before a class day after day and refrain from saying more than he knows.
—Morris Cohen; *A Dreamer's Journey*, 1949

.11 It is the supreme art of the teacher to awaken joy in creative expression and knowledge.
—Albert Einstein; Motto for the Astronomy Building of Pasadena Junior College

.12 We love the precepts for the teacher's sake.
—George Farquhar; *The Constant Couple*, 1699

.13 I am not willing that this discussion should close without mention of the value of a true teacher. Give me a log hut, with only a simple bench. Mark Hopkins on one end and I on the other, and you may have all the buildings, apparatus and libraries without him.
—James A. Garfield; Address to Williams College Alumni, New York, December 28, 1871

.14 A good teacher feels his way, looking for response.
—Paul Goodman; *Growing Up Absurd*, 1960

.15 A schoolmaster spends his life telling the same people the same things about the same things.
—Greek Proverb

.16 Students rarely disappoint teachers who assure them in advance that they are doomed to failure.
—Sidney Hook; *Education for Modern Man*, 1946

.17 Better than a thousand days of diligent study is one day with a great teacher.
—Japanese Proverb

.18 The task of a teacher is not to work for the pupil nor to oblige him to work, but to show him how to work.
—Wanda Landowska; in *Landowska on Music*, Denise Restout, ed., 1964

.19 It is easier for a tutor to command than to teach.
—John Locke; *Some Thoughts Concerning Education*, 1693

.20 The evil of men is that they like to be teachers of others.
—Mencius; *Discourses*, c. 300 B.C.

.21 The average schoolmaster is and always must be essentially an ass, for how can one imagine an intelligent man engaging in so puerile an avocation?
—H.L. Mencken; *Prejudices*, 1922

.22 We teachers can only help the work going on, as servants wait upon a master.
—Maria Montessori; *The Absorbent Mind*, 1949

.23 What was the duty of the teacher if not to inspire.
—Bharati Mukherjee; *The Middleman*, "Buried Lives," 1988

.24 Few have been taught to any purpose who have not been their own teacher.
—Joshua Reynolds; *Discourses on Art*, December 11, 1769

.25 Teachers are more than any other class the guardians of civilization.
—Bertrand Russell; *Unpopular Essays*, "The Function of Teaching," 1950

.26 It is when the gods hate a man with uncommon abhorrence that they drive him into the profession of a school-master.
—Seneca; *Epistulae Morales*, c. 1st century A.D.

.27 I'm not a teacher: only a fellow-traveller of whom you asked the way. I pointed ahead—ahead of myself as well as of you.
—George Bernard Shaw; *Getting Married*, 1908

.28 A teacher should have maximal authority, and minimal power.
—Thomas Szasz; *The Second Sin*, "Education," 1973

.29 A teacher is one who brings tools and enables us to use them.
—Jean Toomer; *Essentials*, 1931

.30 The only good teachers for you are those friends who love you, who think you are interesting, or very important, or wonderfully funny.
—Brenda Ueland; *If You Want to Write*, 1938

.31 We schoolmasters must temper discretion with deceit.
—Evelyn Waugh; *Decline and Fall*. 1928

# 284 Teaching

.1 To know how to suggest is the great art of teaching.
—Henri-Frederic Amiel; *Journal*, November 16, 1864

.2 We all love to instruct, though we can teach only what is not worth learning.
—Jane Austen; *Pride and Prejudice*, 1813

.3 And gladly would he learn, and gladly teach.
—Geoffrey Chaucer; *Canterbury Tales*, "Prologue," c. 1386

.4 Who dares to teach must never cease to learn.
—John Cotton Dana; Motto composed for Kean College, New Jersey, c. 1924

## 284

.5 One might as well say he has sold when no one has bought as to say he has taught when no one has learned.
—John Dewey; in *Readings in the History of Education*, Edward A. Fitzpatrick, ed., 1936

.6 He teaches ill who teaches all.
—English Proverb

.7 You cannot teach a man anything, you can only help him find it within himself.
—Galileo Galilei; *Dialogue on the Great World Systems*, 1632

.8 If you want to teach a child to be good, don't tell him how bad he is. Tell him how good he can be.
—Kwasi Geiggar; in *Jet*, December 10, 1990

.9 Good teaching is one-fourth preparation and three-fourths theater.
—Gail Godwin; *The Odd Woman*, 1974

.10 More is often taught by a jest than by the most serious teaching.
—Balthasar Gracian; *The Art of Worldly Wisdom*, 1648

.11 The vanity of teaching often tempteth a man to forget he is a blockhead.
—Lord Halifax (George Savile), *Maxims*, 1693

.12 Everything I learn about teaching I learn from bad students.
—John Holt; *How Children Fail*, 1982

.13 You cannot teach what you do not know. You cannot give energy if you're not on fire on the inside.
—Jesse Jackson; "Reverend Jesse Jackson," *Ebony Man*, December, 1986

.14 To teach is to learn twice over.
—Joseph Joubert; *Pensées*, 1810

.15 I do not teach, I only tell.
—Michel de Montaigne; *Essays*, 1595

.16 Teaching consists of equal parts perspiration, inspiration, and resignation.
—Susan Ohanian; *Ask Ms. Class*, 1996

.17 Of what he knows nothing, nobody can teach anything.
—Ovid; *Trista*, c. A.D. 9

.18 People sometimes say, "I should like to teach if only pupils cared to learn." But then there would be little need of teaching.
—George Herbert Palmer; *The Teacher, Essays and Addresses on Education: The Ideal Teacher*, 1908

## 284

.19 Better untaught than ill taught.
—John Ray; *English Proverbs*, 1678

.20 Everybody is now so busy teaching that nobody has any time to learn.
—Agnes Repplier; *Essays in Miniature*, "Mr. Wilde's Intentions," 1982

.21 Even while they teach, men learn.
—Seneca; *Epistulae Morales*, c. 1st century A.D.

.22 When I am forgotten … say, I taught thee.
—William Shakespeare; *Henry VIII*, 1612–13

.23 He who can does. He who cannot, teaches.
—George Bernard Shaw; *Maxims for Revolutionists*, 1903

.24 One should always teach his pupil in concise terms.
—Talmud, Pesahim, before A.D. 500

.25 Children should be led into the right paths, not by severity, but by persuasion.
—Terence; *The Self-Tormentor*, 163 B.C.

.26 I want simply this world better taught.
—H.G. Wells; *The Undying Fire*, 1919

.27 Teaching is the royal road to learning.
—Jessamyn West; *The Life I Really Lived*, 1979

.28 Everybody who is incapable of learning has taken to teaching.
—Oscar Wilde; *The Decay of Lying*, 1889

## 285 Tears

.1 With the persuasive language of a tear.
—Charles Churchill; *The Times*, 1764

.2 Words that weep and tears that speak.
—Abraham Cowley; *Olney Hymns*, 1779

.3 Let no one pay me honor with tears, nor celebrate my funeral rites with weeping.
—Quintus Ennius; Fragment of *Iphigeneia*, c. 200 B.C.

.4 Tears are the noble language of the eye.
—Robert Herrick; *Hesperides*, 1648

.5 They say my verse is sad: no wonder;
Its narrow measure spans
Tears of eternity, and sorrow,
Not mine, but man's.
—A.E. Housman; *Last Poems*, "Fancy's Knell," 1922

.6 The Moving Finger writes; and, having writ,
Moves on: nor all your Piety nor Wit

**285**

Shall lure it back to cancel half a Line,
Nor all your Tears wash out a Word of it.
—Omar Khayyam; *Rubaiyat*, c. 1100, Edward Fitzgerald, tr., 1859

.7 Tears are sometimes as weighty as words.
—Ovid; *Ex Ponto*, A.D. 13

.8 I have asked to be left a few tears
And some laughter.
—Carl Sandburg; *Complete Poems*, 1950

.9 Of all the languages of earth in which the human kind confer
The Master Speaker is the Tear: it is the Great Interpreter.
—Frederic Ridgely Torrance; "The House of a Hundred Lights," c. 1928

.10 Tears are the silent language of grief.
—Voltaire; *A Philosophical Dictionary*, "Tears," 1764

**286** # Telephone

.1 Today the ringing of the telephone takes precedence over everything. It reaches a point of terrorism, particularly at dinnertime.
—Niels Diffrient; *New York Times*, October 16, 1986

.2 All phone calls are obscene.
—Karen Elizabeth Gordon; *The Well-Tempered Sentence*, 1983

.3 Remember that as a teenager you are at the last stage in your life when you will be happy to hear that the phone is for you.
—Fran Lebowitz; *Social Studies*, 1977

.4 Oh, how often I wished that Thomas A. Watson had laid a restraining hand on A.G. Bell's arm and had said to him, "Let's not and say we did."
—Jean Mercier; *Whatever You Do, Don't Panic*, 1961

.5 By inventing the telephone we've damaged the chances of telepathy.
—Dorothy M. Richardson; *Pilgrimage: Revolving Lights*, 1923

.6 It is impossible to read in America, except on a train, because of the telephone. Everyone has a telephone, and it rings all day and most of the night.
—Bertrand Russell; *Impressions of America*, 1924

.7 Confound a telephone, anyway. It is the very demon for conveying similarities of sound that

**286**

are miracles of divergence from similarity of sense.
—Mark Twain; *A Connecticut Yankee in King Arthur's Court*, 1889

.8 You should have contact with your closest friends through the most intimate and exclusive of all media—the telephone.
—Andy Warhol; *From A to B and Back Again*, 1975

**287** # Television

.1 The single biggest problem of television is that everyone talks so much.
—Roone Arledge; *Time*, August 22, 1977

.2 The charm of television entertainment is its ability to bridge the chasm between dinner and bedtime without mental distraction.
—Russell Baker; *All Things Considered*, "On with Mindlessness," 1962

.3 Television knows no night. It is perpetual day. TV embodies our fear of the dark, of night, of the other side of things.
—Jean Baudrillard; *Cool Memories*, 1987

.4 It is a medium of entertainment which permits millions of people to listen to the same joke at the same time, and yet remain lonesome.
—T.S. Eliot; *New York Post*, September 22, 1963

.5 If it was on TV, it must be so. Calendars were tricky and church bells might fool you, but if you heard Ed Sullivan's voice you *knew* it was Sunday night.
—Linda Ellerbee; *Move On*, 1991

.6 The contest between education and TV—between argument and conviction by spectacle—has been won by television.
—Robert Hughes; *Culture of Complaint*, 1993

.7 Television represents what happens to a medium when the artists have no power and the businessmen are in full, unquestioned control.
—Pauline Kael; *Reeling*, 1976

.8 Television despite its enormous presence, turns out to have added pitifully few lines to the communal memory.
—Justin Kaplan; Quoted in *Observer*, London, June 9, 1991
[Editor Kaplan found little from television to add to the 1992 edition of *Bartlett's Familiar Quotations*]

## 287

.9 Television—a medium. So called because it is neither rare nor well-done.
—Ernie Kovacs; Attributed

.10 Television has always been a convenient whipping boy for the ills that afflict society.
—Norman Lear; Quoted in *Playboy*, 1976

.11 For all its flexibility, television is more a mirror of taste than a shaper of it.
—Russell Lynes; *The Phenomenon of Change*, 1984

.12 It is television's primary damage that it provides ten million children with the same fantasy, ready made and on a platter.
—Marya Mannes; *More in Anger*, 1958

.13 I invite you to sit down in front of your television set when your station goes on the air and stay there without a book, magazine, newspaper, profit-and-loss sheet, or rating book to distract you—and you keep your eyes glued to that set until the station signs off. I can assure you that you will observe a vast wasteland.
—Newton Minow; speech, *National Association of Broadcasters*, May 9, 1961

.14 Man watches his history on the screen with apathy and an occasional passing flicker of horror or indignation.
—Conor Cruise O'Brien; Quoted in *Irish Times*, Dublin, July 16, 1969

.15 I'm always amazed that people will actually choose to sit in front of the television and just be savaged by stuff that belittles their intelligence.
—Alice Walker; in Brian Lanker, *I Dream a World*, 1989

.16 Disparagement of television is second only to watching television as an American pastime.
—George F. Will; *The Pursuit of Happiness and Other Sobering Thoughts*, "Prisoners of TV," 1978

.17 In television you don't have to fake real life.
—Oprah Winfrey; "Oprah Wonder Year," *Ladies Home Journal*, May, 1990

## 288 Theater

.1 In the theater lying is looked upon as an occupational disease.
—Tallulah Bankhead; *Tallulah*, 1952

.2 Theatergoing is a communal act, moviegoing a solitary one.
—Robert Brustein; *Who Needs Theater*, "The Humanist and the Artist," 1987

## 288

.3 In London, theatergoers expect to laugh; in Paris they wait grimly for proof that they should.
—Robert Dhery; *Look*, March 4, 1958

.4 Prologues precede the piece in mournful verse,
As undertakers walk before the hearse.
—David Garrick; *The Apprentice*, a Prologue, 1747

.5 Generally speaking, the American theater is the aspirin of the middle classes.
—Wolcott Gibbs; *More in Sorrow*, "Shakespeare, Here's Your Hat," 1958

.6 Theater is a verb before it is a noun, an act before it is a place.
—Martha Graham; in Arlene Croce, *Afterimages*, 1976

.7 The theatre is the best way of showing the gap between what is said and what is seen to be done, and that is why, ragged and gap-toothed as it is, it has still a far healthier potential that some poorer, abandoned arts.
—David Hare; "The Playwright as Historian," *Sunday Times Magazine*, November 26, 1978

.8 Drama assumes an order. If only so that it might have—by disturbing that order—a way of surprising.
—Vaclav Havel; *Disturbing the Peace*, 1986

.9 The novel is more of a whisper, whereas the stage is a shout.
—Robert Holman; *The Independent*, October 8, 1990

.10 The anomalous fact is that the theater, so called, can flourish in barbarism, but that any drama worth speaking of can develop but in the air of civilization.
—Henry James; Letter to C.E. Wheeler, April 2, 1911

.11 When we play the fool, how wide
The theatre expands! beside,
How long the audience sits before us!
How many prompters! what a chorus!
—Walter Savage Landor; "Plays," 1846

.12 The theater, when all is said and done, is not life in miniature, but life enormously magnified, life hideously exaggerated.
—H.L. Mencken; *Prejudices*, First Series, 1919

.13 Men go to the theater to forget; women to remember.
—George Jean Nathan; "The Theatre," *American Mercury*, July, 1926

.14 It hath evermore been the notorious badge
of prostituted
Strumpets and the lewdest Harlots, to
ramble abroad to
Plays, to Playhouses; whither no honest,
chaste or sober
Girls or Women, but only the branded
Whores and infamous
Adulteresses, did usually resort in ancient
times.
—William Prynne; *Histriomastix*, 1632

.15 The theatre for all its artifices, depicts life in
a sense more truly than history, because the
medium has a kindred movement to that of
real life, though an artificial setting and form.
—George Santayana; *Skepticism and the
Animal Mind*, 1955

.16 Good drama must be drastic.
—Friedrich Schlegel; *Dialogue on Poetry
and Literary Aphorisms*, 1968

.17 I hold the world but as the world, Gratiano,
A stage where every man must play a part.
—William Shakespeare; *The Merchant of
Venice*, 1597

.18 In a drama of the highest order there is little
food for censure or hatred; it teaches rather
self-knowledge and self-respect.
—Percy Bysshe Shelley; *A Defence of Poetry*, 1821

.19 The public voice in the theater today is crude
and raucous, and, all too often, weak-mined.
—Susan Sontag; *Against Interpretation*,
"Going to the Theater, Etc.," 1966

.20 In a good play every speech should be as fully
flavored as a nut or apple.
—John Millington Synge; *The Playboy of
the Western World*, "Introduction," 1907

.21 The stage is not merely the meeting place of
all the arts, but is also the return of art to life.
—Oscar Wilde; *Nineteenth Century*, May,
1885

.22 The theatre is supremely fitted to say: "Behold! These things are." Yet most dramatists
employ it to say: "This moral truth can be
learned from beholding this action."
—Thornton Wilder; Interview in *Writers
at Work*, First Series, Malcolm Cowley,
ed. 1958

# 289 Theology

.1 Dogmatic theological statements are neither
logical propositions nor poetic utterances.

They are "shaggy dog" stories; they have a
point, but he who tries too hard to get it will
miss it.
—W.H. Auden; *A Certain World*, "God,"
1970

.2 A theologian who has no joy in his work is not
a theologian at all. Sulky faces, morose
thoughts and boring ways of speaking are intolerable in this science.
—Karl Barth; Quoted in his Obituary, *The
New York Times*, December 11, 1968

.3 Theology is but our ideas of truth classified
and arranged.
—Harry Ward Beecher; *Proverbs from Plymouth Pulpit*, 1887

.4 First, I hate all theological controversy; it is
wearing to the temper, and is I believe (at all
events when viva voce) worse than useless.
—Lewis Carroll; *The Letters of Lewis Carroll*, Morton N. Cohen, ed., 1979

.5 Wandering in a vast forest at night, I have only
a faint light to guide me. A stranger appears
and says to me: 'My friend, you should blow
out your candle in order to find your way more
clearly.' This stranger is a theologian.
—Denis Diderot; *Addition aux Pensées
Philosophies*, 1746

.6 When Christian theology becomes traditionalism and men fail to hold and use it as they
do a living language, it becomes an obstacle,
not a help to religious conviction. To the
greatest of the early Fathers and the great
scholastics theology was a language which, like
all language, had a grammar and a vocabulary
from the past, but which they used to express
all the knowledge and experience of their own
time as well.
—Lily Dougall; "The Undiscovered Country" in B.H. Streeter, et al., *Immortality*,
1917

.7 The most tedious of all discourses are on the
subject of the Supreme Being.
—Ralph Waldo Emerson; *Journals*, 1836

.8 Theology is Anthropology.
—Ludwig Andreas Feuerbach; *The Essence
of Christianity*, 1841

.9 Theology is an attempt to explain a subject by
men who do not understand it. The intent is
not to tell the truth but to satisfy the questioner.
—Elbert Hubbard; *The Philistine*, 1905

.10 It is an old habit with theologians to beat the
living with the bodies of the dead.
—R.G. Ingersoll; "Reply to Archbishop
Farrar," 1890

**289**

.11 A theologian is born by living, nay dying and being damned, not by thinking, reading, or speculating.
    —Martin Luther; *Table Talk*, 1569

.12 Theology—An effort to explain the unknowable by putting it into terms of the not worth knowing.
    —H.L. Mencken; *A Mencken Chrestomathy*, "Sententiae: Arcana Coelestia," 1949

.13 My theology, briefly, is that the universe was dictated but not signed.
    —Christopher Morley; "Safe and Sane," 1931

.14 There was never a century nor a country that was short of experts who knew the Deity's mind and were willing to reveal it.
    —Mark Twain; "As Concerns Interpreting the Deity," 1905, appears in *What Is Man?*, Paul Baender, ed., 1973

# **290** Thinking

.1  To think is to say no.
    —Alain (Emile Auguste Chartier); *Le Citoyen contre les Pouvoirs*, c. 1920

.2  The most difficult thing in the world is to say thinkingly what everybody says without thinking.
    —Alain (Emile Auguste Chartier); *Les Cent et un propos d'Alain*, 1908–29

.3  To speak as the common people do, to think as wise men do.
    —Roger Ascham; *Toxophilus*, 1545

.4  She had the fluency of tongue and action meted out by divine providence to those who cannot think for themselves.
    —Djuna Barnes; *Nightwood*, 1937

.5  As soon as you say what you think and not what some other person has thought for you, you are on the way to being a remarkable man.
    —J.M. Barrie; *Tommy and Grizel*, 1900

.6  Think today and speak tomorrow.
    —H.G. Bohn; *Handbook of Proverbs*, 1855

.7  To think hard and persistently is painful.
    —Louis D. Brandeis; *Business—A Profession*, 1914

.8  To speak without thinking is to shoot without looking.
    —Charles Cahier; *Six Mille Proverbes*, 1856

**290**

.9  Why should I disparage my parts by thinking what to say? None but dull rogues think.
    —William Congreve; *The Double-Dealer*, 1693

.10 It is all right to say exactly what you think if you have learned to think exactly.
    —Marcelene Cox; in *Ladies' Home Journal*, 1945

.11 To think is to differ.
    —Clarence Darrow; from the court records of the Scopes trial, Dayton, Tennessee, July 13, 1925

.12 I think, therefore I am.
    —Rene Descartes; *Principes de la Philosophie*, 1637

.13 But far more numerous was the herd of such, Who think too little, and who talk too much.
    —John Dryden; *Absalom and Achitophel*, 1681

.14 There is no expedient to which a man will not go to avoid the real labor of thinking.
    —Thomas Alva Edison; *Apothegm*, c. 1895 [Edison had this apothegm posted on signs about his laboratory.]

.15 Thinking is the hardest work there is, which is the probable reason why so few engage in it.
    —Henry Ford; Interview, February, 1929

.16 How can I tell what I think until I see what I say.
    —E.M. Forster; *Aspects of the Novel*, 1927

.17 One may think that dares not speak.
    —Thomas Fuller II; *Gnomologia*, 1732

.18 In much of your talking, thinking is half murdered.
    —Kahlil Gibran; *The Prophet*, 1923

.19 Never be afraid to sit awhile and think.
    —Lorraine Hansberry; *A Raisin in the Sun*, 1959

.20 I say little (said she) but I think more.
    —John Heywood; *Proverbs*, 1546

.21 Why can't somebody give us a list of things that everybody thinks and nobody says, and another list of things that everybody says and nobody thinks?
    —Oliver Wendell Holmes, Sr.; *Professor at the Breakfast Table*, 1860

.22 A moment's thinking is an hour in words.
    —Thomas Hood; *Hero and Leander*, 1827

.23 Think twice before you speak and then say it to yourself.
    —Elbert Hubbard; *The Philistine*, 1895

**290**

.24 Thinking ... is a soundless dialogue, it is the weaving of patterns, it is a search for meaning. The activity of thought contributes to and shapes all that is specifically human.
—Vera John-Steiner; *Notebooks of the Mind*, 1985

.25 The reason there are so few good talkers in public is that there are so few good thinkers in private.
—Arthur C. Kasen; Attributed

.26 Think ten minutes before you answer a question.
—Edward Kimber; *The Juvenile Adventures of David Ranger*, 1757

.27 Think before you think!
—Stanislaw J. Lec; *Unkempt Thoughts*, 1962

.28 Thinkin' is cheap, but thinkin' wrong is expensive.
—Van Wyck Mason; *The Sulu Sea Murders*, 1933

.29 Thinking is the endeavor to capture reality by means of ideas.
—Jose Ortega y Gasset; *The Dehumanization of Art*, 1925

.30 Man is but a reed, the most feeble thing in nature, but he is a thinking reed.
—Blaise Pascal; *Pensees*, 1670

.31 If thou thinkest twice, before thou speakest once, thou wilt speak twice the better for it.
—William Penn; *Some Fruits of Solitude*, 1693

.32 They never taste who always drink;
They always talk, who never think.
—Matthew Prior; "Upon This Passage in Scaligerana," 1740

.33 The thinkers of the world should by rights be guardians of the world's mirth.
—Agnes Repplier; *In Pursuit of Laughter*, 1936

.34 I think, but dare not speak.
—William Shakespeare; *Macbeth*, 1606

.35 I am most fond of talking and thinking; that is to say, talking first and thinking afterward.
—Osbert Sitwell; *Laughter in the Next Room*, 1949

.36 To have ideas is to gather flowers. To think is to weave them into garlands.
—Anne-Sophie Swetchine; *The Writings of Madame Swetchine*, Count de Falloux, ed., 1869

**290**

.37 Miss says nothing; but I warrant she pays it off with thinking.
—Jonathan Swift; *Polite Conversation*, 1738

.38 Man was a feeling creature long before he was a thinking creature. The mind is younger than the body and younger than the emotions.
—Howard Thurman; *Meditations of the Heart*, 1953

.39 To think is to converse with oneself.
—Miguel de Unamuno; *The Tragic Sense of Life*, 1913

.40 How I love people who say what they think.
—Voltaire; *Lettres dur les Anglais*, 1733

# 291 Thoughts

.1 You are today where your thoughts have brought you; you will be tomorrow where your thoughts take you.
—James Allen; Attributed

.2 Thoughts left unsaid are never wasted.
—Anonymous

.3 Every thought is strictly speaking an afterthought.
—Hannah Arendt; *The Life of the Mind*, Vol. 1, 1978

.4 A thought which does not result in an action is nothing much, and an action which does not proceed from a thought is nothing at all.
—Georges Bernandos; *The Last Essays of George Bernandos*, "France Before the World of Tomorrow," 1955

.5 Thought itself needs words. It runs on them like a long wire. And if it loses the habit of words, little by little it becomes shapeless, somber.
—Ugo Betti; *Goat Island*, 1946

.6 Conversation is the legs on which thought walks; and writing, the wings by which it flies.
—Countess Blessington; *Desultory Thoughts and Reflections*, 1839

.7 Stung by the splendor of a sudden thought.
—Robert Browning; *Dramatis Personae*, "A Death in the Desert," 1864

.8 Words are the clothes that thoughts wear— only the clothes.
—Samuel Butler II; *The Notebooks of Samuel Butler*, H.F. Jones, ed., 1912

.9 Let not your tongue outrun your thought.
—Chilon; 6th century B.C., Diogenes Laertius *Chilon*, early 3rd century

**291**

.10 Learning without thought is labor lost.
—Confucius; *Analects*, c. 500 B.C.

.11 All we are is the result of what we have thought.
—Dhammapada; *Commentaries*, c. 475

.12 Thought is often bolder than speech.
—Benjamin Disraeli; *Ixion in Heaven*, 1834

.13 What was once thought can never be unthought.
—Friedrich Durrenmatt; *The Physicists*, 1962

.14 Thought was busy though the lips were silent.
—George Eliot; *The Mill on the Floss*, 1860

.15 The true use of speech is not so much to express our wants as to conceal them.
—Oliver Goldsmith; *The Bee*, 1759

.16 It is a great mistake to try to put our best thoughts into human language.
—Nathaniel Hawthorne; *The Marble Faun*, 1860

.17 Thought precedes action as lightning does thunder.
—Heinrich Heine; *History of Religion and Philosophy in Germany*, 1834

.18 The beginning of thought is in disagreement not only with others but with ourselves.
—Eric Hoffer; *The Passionate State of Mind*, 1955

.19 A thought is often original though you have uttered it a hundred times.
—Oliver Wendell Holmes, Sr.; *The Autocrat of the Breakfast Table*, 1858

.20 Little-minded people's thoughts move in such small circles that five minutes' conversation gives you an arc long enough to determine their whole curve.
—Oliver Wendell Holmes, Sr.; *The Autocrat of the Breakfast Table*, 1858

.21 Once you wake up thought in a man, you can never put it to sleep again.
—Zora Neale Hurston; *Moses, Man of the Mountain*, 1939

.22 There is thought, and there is thinking about thoughts, and they don't feel the same.
—Susanna Kaysen; *Girl, Interrupted*, 1993

.23 I've known countless people who were reservoirs of learning, yet never had a thought.
—Wilson Mizner; E.D. Sullivan, *The Fabulous Wilson Mizner*, 1935

.24 Speech was given to man to express his thought.
—Molière; *Le Mariage Force*, c. 1660

**291**

.25 But if thought corrupts language, language can also corrupt thought.
—George Orwell; *Politics and the English Language*, 1946

.26 What are words but the body and dress of thought?
—Samuel Richardson; *Clarissa Harlowe*, 1747–8

.27 To reflect is to disturb one's thoughts.
—Jean Rostand; *Pensées d'un Biologiste*, 1939

.28    Give thy thoughts no tongue
Nor any unproportion'd thought his act.
—William Shakespeare; *Hamlet*, 1600–1

.29 He gave man speech, and speech created thought,
Which is the measure of the universe.
—Percy Bysshe Shelley; *Prometheus Unbound*, 1820

.30 How often misused words generate misleading thoughts.
—Herbert Spencer; *Principles of Ethics*, 1879

.31 Speech was given to man to disguise his thoughts.
—Talleyrand; *Epigram*, c. 1790

.32 Said first and thought after
Brings many to disaster.
—H.W. Thompson; *Body, Boots and Britches*, 1940

.33 Thought is made in the mouth.
—Tristan Tzara; "Dada Manifesto on Feeble Love and Bitter Love" in *La Vie des Lettres*, 1921

.34 When a thought is too weak to be expressed simply, it should be rejected.
—Luc de Clapiers Vauvenargues; *Reflections and Maxims*, 1746

**292** Time

.1    Time is one's best friend, teaching best of all the wisdom of silence.
—A.B. Alcott; *Table-Talk*, "Learning," 1877

.2    Backward, turn backward, O Time, in your flight,
Make me a child again just for to-night!
—Elizabeth Akers Allen; "Rock Me To Sleep," 1860

# 292

.3 Time is a babbler, and speaks ever when no question is asked.
—Amelia Edith Barr; *The Squire of Sandal-Side*, 1886

.4 Time is a great teacher, but unfortunately it kills all its pupils.
—Hector Berlioz; *Almanach des lettres francaises*, 1870

.5 The hours of folly are measured by the clock, but of wisdom no clock can measure.
—William Blake; *The Marriage of Heaven and Hell*, "Proverbs of Hell," 1790

.6 Men talk of killing time, while time quietly kills them.
—Dion Boucicault; *London Assurance*, 1841

.7 Set forth thy tale, and tarry not the time.
—Geoffrey Chaucer; *The Canterbury Tales*, 1387

.8 There is never time to say our last word—the last word of our love, of our desire, faith, remorse, submission, revolt.
—Joseph Conrad; *Lord Jim*, 1900

.9 Time goes, you say? Ah, no!
Alas, Time stays, we go.
—Austin Dobson; "The Paradox of Time," 1877

.10 There is a time to speak, and a time to hold one's peace.
—Thomas Draxe; *Bibliotheca*, 1616

.11 No story is the same to us after the lapse of time; or rather we who [hear] it are no longer the same interpreter.
—George Eliot; *Letters and Journals*, G.S. Haight, ed., 1954–78

.12 The years teach much which the days never know.
—Ralph Waldo Emerson; *Essays: Second Series*, "Experience," 1844

.13 Once Upon a Time,
Once Upon a Time!
Everything that happened, happened
Once Upon a Time.
—Eleanor Farejon; *The Children's Bells*, "O Is for Once Upon a Time," 1960

.14 Time and Words can't be recalled.
—Thomas Fuller II; *Gnomologia*, 1732

.15 When you've got a thing to say,
Say it! Don't take half a day.
When your tale's got little in it,
Crowd the whole thing in a minute!
—Joel Chandler Harris; *Uncle Remus: His Songs and Sayings*, 1880

# 292

.16 Time has told me
less than I need to know.
—Gwen Harwood; *Bone Scan*, "Resurrection," 1988

.17 Time, you old gypsy man,
Will you not stay,
Put up your caravan
Just for one day?
—Ralph Hodgeson; "Time, You Old Gypsy Man," 1917

.18 There is a time for sleep, and time to take joy in hearing tales.
—Homer; *Odyssey*, c. 850 B.C.

.19 Even while we speak, envious Time has sped.
—Horace; *Odes*, 23 B.C.

.20 He talks like a watch which ticks away minutes, but never strikes the hour.
—Samuel Johnson; Boswell, *Life of Johnson*, 1791

.21 In general those who have nothing to say
Contrive to spend the longest time in doing it.
—James Russell Lowell; "An Oriental Apologue," 1849

.22 For tribal man space was the uncontrollable mystery. For technological man it is time that occupies the same role.
—Marshall McLuhan; *The Mechanical Bride*, "Magic That Changes Moods," 1951

.23 A time to keep silence, and a time to speak.
—Old Testament: Ecclesiastes

.24 The clock talked loud. I threw it away, it scared me what it talked.
—Tillie Olsen; *Tell Me a Riddle*, "I Stand Here Ironing," 1956

.25 While I am not speaking, the hour flies.
—Ovid; *Amores*, c. 1st century B.C.

.26 Time makes more converts than reason.
—Thomas Paine; *Common Sense*, "Introduction," 1776

.27 Time is the wisest counselor.
—Pericles; *Apothegm*, c. 450 B.C.

.28 O Time! thou tutor both to good and bad.
—William Shakespeare; *The Rape of Lucrece*, 1594

.29 O, call back yesterday, bid time return.
—William Shakespeare; *Richard III*, 1597

.30 If time can teach, I need not be told.
—Sophocles; *Oedipus at Colonus*, c. 408 B.C.

## 292

.31 Time and I against any two.
—Spanish Proverb

.32 No preacher is listened to but Time, which gives us the same train and turn of thought that elder people have in vain tried to put into our heads before.
—Jonathan Swift; *Thoughts on Various Things*, 1711

.33 As if you could kill time without injuring eternity.
—Henry David Thoreau; *Walden*, "Economy," 1854

.34 He knew the most effective time for speaking.
—Virgil; *Aeneid*, c. 1st century B.C.

.35 For time is the longest distance between two places.
—Tennessee Williams; *The Glass Menagerie*, 1945

## 293 Toasts

.1 My toast would be, may our country be always successful, but whether successful or otherwise, always right.
—John Quincy Adams; Letter to John Adams, August 1, 1816
[Adams' toast is in disagreement with the toast of naval hero Stephen Decatur: "Our country! In her intercourse with foreign nations may she always be in the right; but our country, right or wrong" (Given at Norfolk, April 1816).]

.2 When thou dost drink, beware the toast, For therein lies the danger most.
—Anonymous; *Berkeley MSS*, 1639

.3 Here's a sigh to those who love me
And a smile to those who hate;
And whatever sky's above me,
Here's a heart for every fate.
—Lord Byron; "To Thomas Moore," 1817

.4 To drink healths is to drink sickness.
—Thomas Dekker; *The Honest Whore*, 1635

.5 But the standing toast that pleased the most Was, "The Wind that blows, the ship that goes,
And the lass that loves a sailor!"
—Charles Dibdin; *The Round Robin*, 1811

.6 We drink one another's healths and spoil our own.
—Jerome K. Jerome; *Idle Thoughts of an Idle Fellow*, "On Eating and Drinking," 1889

## 293

.7 Drink to me only with thine eyes,
And I will pledge with mine;
Or leave a kiss but in the cup,
And I'll not look for wine.
—Ben Jonson; *The Forest*, "To Celia," 1616

.8 Here's mud in your eye!
—Van Wyck Mason; *The Bucharest Ballerina Murders*, 1940

.9 Luck to you, luck to us, luck to thee, luck to me.
—Plautus; *Stichus*, c. 200 B.C.

.10 Here's to the maiden of bashful fifteen;
Here's to the widow of fifty;
Here's to the flaunting, extravagant quean;
And here's to the housewife that's thrifty.
Let the toast pass,—
Drink to the lass,
I'll warrant she'll prove an excuse for the glass.
—Richard B. Sheridan; *The School for Scandal*, 1777

.11 May you live all the days of your life.
—Jonathan Swift; *Polite Conversation*, 1738

.12 There is an old toast which is golden for its beauty. "When you ascend the hill of prosperity may you not meet a friend."
—Mark Twain; "Pudd'nhead Wilson's New Calendar," 1897

## 294 Tongue

.1 A great ox stands on my tongue.
—Aeschylus; *Agamemnon*, 458 B.C.

.2 What among men is both good and bad? The tongue.
—Anacharsis, The Scythian; c. 590 B.C.; Diogenes Laertius, *Anacharsis*, c. 3rd. century A.D.

.3 A man is overthrown and ruined through his tongue. Take heed that thou dost not thyself produce thine own ruin.
—Ani; *Teaching*, c. 2000 B.C.

.4 The tongue of a woman is capable of producing sound, which admits of no comparison either for frightfulness or harmony.
—Anonymous

.5 Train thy tongue to say, "I do not know," lest thou be entrapped into falsehood.
—Babylonian Talmud: Berachoth; before A.D. 500

.6 Tongues are wagging like tails.
—Philip Barry; *The Philadelphia Story*, 1939

**294**

.7 Who hath not sinneth with his tongue?
—Ben Sira; *Book of Wisdom*, c. 190 B.C.

.8 Let not thy tongue cut your throat.
—H.G. Bohn; *Handbook of Proverbs*, 1855

.9 The magic of the tongue is the most dangerous of all spells.
—Lord Bulwer-Lytton; *Eugene Aram*, 1832

.10 The smaller the heart the longer the tongue.
—Charles Cahier; *Quelques Six Mille Proverbes*, 1856

.11 The first virtue, I think, is to rule the tongue.
—Cato; *Disticha*, c. 175 B.C.

.12 I preferred tongue-tied knowledge to ignorant loquacity.
—Cicero; *De Oratore*, 55 B.C.

.13 Whispering tongues can poison truth.
—Samuel Taylor Coleridge; *Christabel*, 1797

.14 Pardon me ... if my tongue do outslip my wit.
—Thomas Deloney; *Gentle Craft*, 1597

.15 Have you lost your tongue?
—Charles Dickens; *The Mystery of Edwin Drood*, 1870

.16 A false tongue will hardly speak truth.
—Thomas Draxe; *Bibliotheca*, 1633

.17 Keep watch upon thy tongue lest it cause mischief.
—Euripides; *Hippolytus*, c. 428 B.C.

.18 The tongue offends and the ears get the cuffing.
—Benjamin Franklin; *Poor Richard's Almanack*, 1757

.19 There is nothing that so much gratifies an ill tongue as when it finds an angry heart.
—Thomas Fuller II; *Gnomologia*, 1732

.20 The tongue is a wild beast; once let loose it is difficult to chain.
—Baltasar Gracian; *Oraculo Manual*, 1647

.21 He is not a fool who knows when to hold his tongue.
—William Hazlitt; *Characteristics*, 1823

.22 She has a tongue that scalds and bites like a bull whip.
—Ernest Hemingway; *For Whom the Bell Tolls*, 1940

.23 The tongue is no edge tool, but yet it will cut.
—John Heywood; *Proverbs*, 1546

.24 Sharpen your tongue for pleading.
—Horace; *Epistles*, 20 B.C.

**294**

.25 Her tongue is hung in de middle and works both ways.
—Zora Neale Hurston; *Mules and Men*, 1935

.26 A sharp tongue is the only edge tool that grows keener with constant use.
—Washington Irving; *The Sketch Book of Geoffrey Crayon, Gent.*, "Rip Van Winkle," 1819–20

.27 A man is hid under his tongue.
—Ali Ibn-Abi-Talib; *Sentences*, c. 7th century A.D.

.28 The tongue of man is his weapon, and speech is mightier than fighting.
—Khati I, King of Egypt; *Teaching*, c. 2500 B.C.

.29 "They are fools who kiss and tell"—
Wisely has the poet sung.
Man may hold all sorts of posts
If he'll only hold his tongue.
—Rudyard Kipling; "Pink Dominoes," 1892

.30 How like an angel speaks the tongue of woman
When pleading in another's cause her own!
—Henry Wadsworth Longfellow; *The Spanish Student*, 1843

.31 He must have leave to speak who cannot hold his tongue.
—George Meriton; *Yorkshire Ale*, 1683

.32 Keep thy tongue from evil, and thy lips from speaking guile.
—Old Testament: Psalms

.33 Let a fool hold his tongue and he will pass for a sage.
—Publilius Syrus; *Moral Sayings*, 1st century B.C.

.34 If thou desire to be held wise, be so wise to hold thy tongue.
—Francis Quarles; *Enchiridion*, 1640

.35 For I could tell you a story which is true,
I know a lady with a terrible tongue,
Blear eyes fallen from blue,
All her perfections tarnished—and yet it is not long
Since she was lovelier than any of you.
—John Crowe Ransom; "Blue Girls" in *The Cherry-Tree*, Geoffrey Grigson, comp. 1959

.36 You kin tame a bear. You kin tame a wild-cat and you kin tame a panther.... You kin tame anything, son, excusin' the human tongue.
—Marjorie Kinnan Rawlings; *The Yearling*, 1938

**294**

.37 My secrets cry aloud.
I have no need for tongue.
My heart keeps open house,
My doors are widely flung.
—Theodore Roethke; "Open House," 1941

.38 Many a man's tongue shakes out his master's undoing.
—William Shakespeare; *All's Well That Ends Well*, 1602

.39 Sweet, bid me hold my tongue,
For in this rapture I shall surely speak
The thing I shall repent.
—William Shakespeare; *Troilus and Cressida*, 1601

.40 A fluent tongue is the only thing a mother doesn't like her daughter to resemble her in.
—Richard Brinsley Sheridan; *St. Patrick's Day*, 1775

.41 I signified my contempt of him by thrusting my tongue in my cheek.
—Tobias Smollett; *Roderick Random*, 1748

.42 You have a glib tongue.
—Sophocles; *Oedipus at Colonus*, c. 408 B.C.

.43 Surely human affairs would be far happier if the power in men to be silent were the same as that to speak. But experience more than sufficiently teaches that men govern nothing with more difficulty than their tongues, and can moderate their desires more easily than their words.
—Baruch Spinoza; *Ethics*, 1677

.44 Swords are madmen's tongues, and tongues are madmen's swords.
—Jonathan Swift; "Ode to Dr. Sancroft," 1690

.45 Violence of the tongue is very real—sharper than any knife.
—Mother Teresa; in *In the Silence of the Heart*, Kathryn Spink, ed., 1983

.46 He can hardly speak, who cannot hold his tongue.
—Torriano; *Piazza Universale*, 1666

# **295** Tradition

.1 They that reverence too much old times are but a scorn to the new.
—Francis Bacon; *Essays*, "Of Innovations," 1625

.2 It is pure illusion to think that an opinion which passes down from century to century,

**295**

from generation to generation, may not be entirely false.
—Pierre Bayle; *Thoughts on the Comet*, 1682

.3 Tradition doesn't mean that the living are dead, but that the dead are living.
—Gilbert K. Chesterton; *Orthodoxy*, 1908

.4 Tradition! We scarcely know the word anymore. We are afraid to be either proud of our ancestors or ashamed of them. We scorn nobility in name and in fact. We cling to a bourgeois mediocrity which would make it appear we are all Americans, made in the image and likeness of George Washington.
—Dorothy Day; *The Long Loneliness*, 1952

.5 A tradition without intelligence is not worth having.
—T.S. Eliot; "After Strange Gods," 1934

.6 Tradition—which sometimes brings down truth that history has let slip, but is oftener the wild babble of the time, such as was formerly spoken at the fireside, and now congeals in newspapers—tradition is responsible for all contrary averments.
—Nathaniel Hawthorne; *The House of the Seven Gables*, 1851

.7 Tradition becomes our security, and when the mind is secure it is in decay.
—Jiddu Krishnamurti; *The Penguin Krishnamurti Reader*, 1970

.8 The traditions of all past generations weighs like an Alp upon the brain of all living.
—Karl Marx; *18th Brumaire*, 1852

.9 Tradition is a guide and not a jailer.
—W. Somerset Maugham; *The Summing Up*, 1938

.10 Traditions are group efforts to keep the unexpected from happening.
—Mignon McLaughlin; *The Neurotic's Handbook*, 1963

.11 Traditionalists are pessimists about the future and optimists about the past.
—Lewis Mumford; *The Brown Decades*, 1931

.12 Every tradition grows ever more venerable—the more remote is its origin, the more confused that origin is. The reverence due to it increases from generation to generation. The tradition finally becomes holy and inspires awe.
—Friedrich Wilhelm Nietzsche; *Human, All Too Human*, 1878

.13 Traditions that have lost their meanings are the hardest of all to destroy.
    —Edith Wharton; *Xingu*, "Autre Temps…," 1916

.14 Tradition wears a snowy beard.
    —John Greenleaf Whittier; "Mary Garvin," 1860

.15 If a race has no history, it has no worthwhile traditions, it becomes a negligible factor in the thought of the world. The American Indian left no continuous record. He did not appreciate the value of tradition; and where is he today? The Hebrew keenly appreciates the value of tradition.
    —Carter C. Woodson; *The Story of the Negro Retold*, 1935

# 296 Tragedy

.1  A perfect Tragedy is the noblest production of human nature.
    —Joseph Addison; *The Spectator*, 1712

.2  Tragedy is an imitation of an action that is serious, complete, and of a certain magnitude, effecting through pity and fear the proper katharsis or purgation, of emotions.
    —Aristotle; *Poetics*, c. 330 B.C.

.3  Tragedy on the stage is no longer enough for me, I shall bring it into my own life.
    —Antonin Artaud; quoted in *Memories for Tomorrow*, the memoirs of Jean-Louis Barrault, 1972

.4  Only a great mind overthrown yields tragedy.
    —Jacques Barzun; *The House of Intellect*, 1959

.5  There can be no tragedy without a struggle.
    —Ferdinand Brunetiere; *Questions de Critique*, 1888

.6  The tragedy of life is not so much what men suffer, but rather what they miss.
    —Thomas Carlyle; *Sartor Resartus*, 1833–34

.7  Tragedy is to say a certain story
    From ancient books which have preserved
        the glory
    Of one that stood in great prosperity
    And is now fallen out of high degree
    In misery, where he ends wretchedly.
    Such tales are versified most commonly
    In six feet, which men call hexameter.
    In prose are many written; some prefer
    A quantitative metre, sundry wise.
    —Geoffrey Chaucer; *The Canterbury Tales*, "The Prologue to the Monk's Tale," 1387

.8  Tragedy must be something bigger than life, or it would not affect us.
    —Lord Chesterfield; *Letter to His Son*, January 23, 1752

.9  The worst tragedy for a poet is to be admired through being misunderstood.
    —Jean Cocteau; *Le Coq et l'Arlequin*, 1918

.10 Show me a hero and I will write you a tragedy.
    —F. Scott Fitzgerald; *The Crack-Up*, "The Note-Books," 1945

.11 Everybody's tragedy is somebody's nuisance.
    —Winifred Holtby; in Vera Brittain, *Treatment of Friendship*, 1940

.12 And Tragedy should blush as much to stoop
    To the low mimic follies of a farce,
    As a grave matron would to dance with girls.
    —Horace; *Ars Poetica*, c. 19 B.C.

.13 I have spent more than half a lifetime trying to express the tragic moment.
    —Marcel Marceau; *The Guardian*, August 11, 1988

.14 The tragedy of love is indifference.
    —W. Somerset Maugham; *The Trembling of a Leaf*, 1921

.15 A tragic situation exists precisely when virtue does *not* triumph but when it is still felt that man is nobler than the forces which destroy him.
    —George Orwell; *Shooting an Elephant*, "Lear, Tolstoy and the Fool," 1950

.16 Modern discussions of the possibility of tragedy are not exercises in literary analysis; they are exercises in cultural diagnostics, more or less disguised.
    —Susan Sontag; *Against Interpretation*, "The Death of Tragedy," 1966

.17 The bad end unhappily, the good unluckily. That is what tragedy means.
    —Tom Stoppard; *Rosencrantz and Guildenstern Are Dead*, 1967

.18 Life is a tragedy wherein we sit as spectators for a while and then act our part in it.
    —Jonathan Swift; *Thoughts on Various Subjects*, 1711

.19 The essence of dramatic tragedy is not unhappiness. It resides in the solemnity of the remorseless working of things.
    —Alfred North Whitehead; *Science and the Modern World*, 1925

.20 One of the tragedies for many women is that our mothers told us nothing.
    —Oprah Winfrey; in *Woman's Day*, October 4, 1988

**296**

.21 You get tragedy where the tree, instead of bending, breaks.
—Ludwig Wittgenstein; *Culture and Value*, Journal entry, 1929, G.H. von Wright, ed., 1980

# **297** Trickery

.1 He had a thousand jadish tricks, Worse than a mule that flings and kicks.
—Samuel Butler I; *Hudibras*, 1663–78

.2 Women are like tricks of sleight of hand, Which, to admire, we should not understand.
—William Congreve; Valentine, *Love for Love*, 1695

.3 In trickery, evasion, procrastination, spoliation, botheration, under false pretenses of all sorts, there are influences that can never come to good.
—Charles Dickens; *Bleak House*, 1852–53

.4 When in doubt, win the trick.
—Edmond Hoyle; *A Short Treatise on the Game of Whist*, 1742

.5 Remember that all tricks are either knavish or childish.
—Samuel Johnson; Boswell's *Life of Johnson*, 1779

.6 It is a double pleasure to trick the trickster.
—Jean de la Fontaine; *Fables*, 1694

.7 What renders us so bitter against those who trick us is that they believe themselves to be more clever than we are.
—François de La Rochefoucauld; *Maxims*, 1665

.8 You can't teach an old dogma new tricks.
—Dorothy Parker; in Robert E. Drennan, *The Algonquin Wits*, 1968

.9 You fear some trick.
—Plautus; *Asinaria*, c. 200 B.C.

.10 He has more tricks than a dancing bear.
—John Ray; *English Proverbs*, 1732

.11 These are unsightly tricks.
—William Shakespeare; *King Lear*, 1605

.12 If I be served such another trick, I'll have my brains ta'en out and buttered, and give them to a dog for a new-year's gift.
—William Shakespeare; *The Merry Wives of Windsor*, 1602

.13 He hath as many tricks as a lawyer.
—William Walker; *Paroemiologia Anglo-Latina*, 1672

# **298** Truth

.1 Simple are the words of truth.
—Aeschylus; *Award of the Arms*, c. 458 B.C.

.2 The truth that makes men free is for the most part the truth which men prefer not to hear.
—Herbert Agar; *A Time for Greatness*, 1942

.3 A good mouth will love the truth and speak it.
—Ahikar; *Teachings*, c. 550 B.C.

.4 I have not spoken that which is not true knowingly, nor have I done anything with a false heart.
—Ani; *Papyrus: Book of the Dead*, c. 4000 B.C.

.5 If you want to annoy your neighbors, tell the truth about them.
—Pietro Aretino; *Sonetti Lussuriosi*, c. 1524

.6 Truth sits on the lips of dying men.
—Matthew Arnold; *Poems*, "Sohrab and Rustum," 1853

.7 There is at least one thing more brutal than the truth, and that is the consequence of saying less than the truth.
—Tri-Grace Atkinson; *Amazon Odyssey*, "The Older Woman," 1974

.8 Even a liar tells a hundred truths to one lie; he has to, to make the lie good for anything.
—Henry Ward Beecher; *Proverbs from Plymouth Pulpit*, 1870

.9 Truth can never be told so as to be understood, and not be believ'd.
—William Blake; *The Marriage of Heaven and Hell*, "Proverbs of Hell," 1808

.10 A truth that's told with bad intent Beats all the lies you can invent.
—William Blake; *Auguries of Innocence*, c. 1803

.11 "Telling the truth" ... is not solely a matter of moral character; it is also a matter of correct appreciation or real situations and of serious reflection upon them.
—Dietrich Bonhoeffer; *Ethics*, 1955

.12 There are grains of truth in the wildest fable.
—Charlotte Bronte; *Jane Eyre*, 1847

**298**

.13 So absolutely good is truth, truth never hurts the teller.
  —Robert Browning; "Fifine at the Fair," 1872

.14 'Tis strange—but true; for truth is always strange,
  Stranger than fiction.
  —Lord Byron; *Don Juan*, 1823

.15 What I tell you three times is true.
  —Lewis Carroll; *The Hunting of the Snark*, 1876

.16 Speak the truth freely, though the truth be hard.
  —Cato; *Dicta Catonis*, c. 175 B.C.

.17 There is no proverb which is not true.
  —Miguel de Cervantes; *Don Quixote*, 1605

.18 The truth often does sound unconvincing.
  —Agatha Christie; *Ordeal by Innocence*, 1959

.19 There are truths which one can say only after having won the right to say them.
  —Jean Cocteau; *Le Rappel a L'Ordre*, "Le Coq et l'Arlequin," 1926

.20 Veracity does not consist in saying, but in the intention of communicating truth.
  —Samuel Taylor Coleridge; *Biographia Literaria*, 1817

.21 Tell the truth and shame the devil.
  —Charles Cotton; *Scarronides*, 1670

.22 Truth is such a rare thing, it is delightful to tell it.
  —Emily Dickinson; Letter to Thomas Wentworth Higginson, August, 1870

.23 We swallow greedily any lie that flatters us, but we sip only little by little at a truth we find bitter.
  —Denis Diderot; *Le Neveu de Rameau*, 1761

.24 There are yet great truths to tell, if we had either the courage to announce them or the temper to receive them.
  —Benjamin Disraeli; *Coningsby*, 1844

.25 I never saw any good that came of telling the truth.
  —John Dryden; *Amphitryon*, 1690

.26 Truth disappears with the telling of it.
  —Lawrence Durrell; *Clea*, 1960

.27 Telling the truth often means no more than taking a liberty.
  —George Eliot; *Felix Holt the Radical*, 1866

**298**

.28 Plain and unvarnished are the words of truth.
  —Euripides; *Phoenissae*, c. 420 B.C.

.29 What everybody says, there must be some truth in it.
  —Henry Fielding; *Tom Jones*, 1749

.30 A lie hides the truth, a story tries to find it.
  —Paula Fox; *A Servant's Tale*, 1984

.31 Truth needs not many words, but a false tale a long preamble.
  —Thomas Fuller II; *Gnomologia*, 1732

.32 To be modest in speaking truth is hypocrisy.
  —Kahlil Gibran; *The Prophet*, 1923

.33 Truth from his lips prevailed with double sway,
  And fools, who came to scoff, remained to pray.
  —Oliver Goldsmith; *The Vicar of Wakefield*, 1766

.34 The truth is generally seen, rarely heard.
  —Baltasar Gracian; *The Art of Worldly Wisdom*, 1647

.35 A man ought to speak the truth to him that will hear it: but who is he!
  —Stefano Guazzo; *Civile Conversation*, 1574

.36 An honest man speaks the truth, though it may give offence; a vain man, in order that it may.
  —William Hazlitt; *Characteristics*, 1823

.37 I verily love to speak the truth.
  —Homer; *Odyssey*, c. 850 B.C.

.38 Many people would be more truthful were it not for their uncontrollable desire to talk.
  —Edgar Watson Howe; *Plain People*, 1929

.39 Lay thy hand on thy heart and speak the truth.
  —James Howell; *English proverbs*, 1659

.40 Truth *happens* to an idea. It *becomes* true, is *made* true by events. Its verity *is* in fact an event, a process, the process namely of its verifying itself; its veri-*fication*. Its validity is the process of its valid-*ation*.
  —William James; *Pragmatism*, 1907

.41 Every man has a right to utter what he thinks truth; and every other man has a right to knock him down for it.
  —Samuel Johnson; Boswell's *Life of Johnson*, 1780

.42 There's more things told than are true, and more things true than are told.
  —Rudyard Kipling; *Something of Myself*, 1937

**298**

.43 The teller of a mirthful tale has latitude allowed him. We are content with less than absolute truth.
—Charles Lamb; *Essays of Elia*, 1823

.44 The words of truth are always paradoxical.
—Lao-Tsze; *The Way of Virtue*, c. 550 B.C.

.45 Sometimes when we have to speak suddenly we come closer to the truth than when we have time to think.
—Madeleine L'Engle; *The Summer of the Great-Grandmother*, 1974

.46 Speak no more than the truth, utter no less.
—John Lyly; *Euphues and His England*, 1578

.47 I never know how much of what I say is true.
—Bette Midler; *A View from a Broad*, 1980

.48 A man must not always tell the whole truth.
—Michel de Montaigne; *Essays*, 1595

.49 And ye shall know the truth, and the truth shall make you free.
—The New Testament; John

.50 I shall not suffer defeat for my word is truth.
—Nu; *Papyrus: Book of the Dead*, c. 4000 B.C.

.51 There are only two ways to tell the one hundred percent truth: anonymously and posthumously.
—Susan Ohanian; *Ask Ms. Class*, 1996

.52 Truth often suffers more by the heat of its defenders than from the arguments of its opposers.
—William Penn; *Some Fruits of Solitude*, 1693

.53 Nothing is more advantageous to a man than to speak the truth.
—Phaedrus; *Fables*, c. 25 B.C.

.54 Truth is the pleasantest of sounds.
—Plato; Diogenes Laertius, *Plato*, c. 3rd century A.D.

.55 If you take truth from history what is left is but an idle unprofitable tale.
—Polybius; *History*, c. 2nd century B.C.

.56 Why do we not hear the truth? Because we do not speak it.
—Publilius Syrus; *Moral Sayings*, 1st century B.C.

.57 If anyone doubts my veracity, I can only say that I pity his lack of faith.
—Rudolph Erich Raspe; *Travels of Baron Munchausen*, 1785

**298**

.58 What everyone says, must be true.
—Samuel Richardson; *Clarissa Harlowe*, 1747–8

.59 Speaking truth is like writing fair, and only comes by practice.
—John Ruskin; *The Seven Lamps of Architecture*, 1849

.60 A man may in some circumstances, disguise the truth … for were it always to be spoken, and upon all occasions, this were no world to live in.
—Walter Scott; *Kenilworth*, 1821

.61 Who tells me true, though in his tale lie death,
I hear him as he flatter'd.
—William Shakespeare; *Antony and Cleopatra*, 1606–7

.62 My way of joking is to tell the truth; it's the funniest joke in the world.
—George Bernard Shaw; *John Bull's Other Island*, 1904

.63 The truth is always something that is told, not something that is known. If there were no speaking or writing, there would be no truth about anything. There would only be what is.
—Susan Sontag; *The Benefactor*, 1963

.64 The truth is always the strongest argument.
—Sophocles; *Phaedra*, c. 435–29 B.C.

.65 It takes two to speak the truth—one to speak, and another to hear.
—Henry David Thoreau; *A Week on the Concord and Merrimack Rivers: Wednesday*, 1849

.66 If you tell the truth you don't have to remember anything.
—Mark Twain; *Notebook*, 1935

.67 Few people have enough character to endure the truth, and to speak of it.
—Luc De Clapiers, Marquis de Vauvenargues; *Reflections and Maxims*, 1746

.68 The longest sword, the strongest lungs, the most voices, are false measures of truth.
—Benjamin Whichcote; *Sermons*, 1660

.69 If one tells the truth, one is sure, sooner or later, to be found out.
—Oscar Wilde; "Phases and Philosophies for the Use of the Young," 1894

.70 If you do not tell the truth about yourself you cannot tell it about other people.
—Virginia Woolf; *The Moment*, "The Leaning Tower," 1947

# 299 Understanding

**.1** But now the mystic tale that pleas'd of yore
Can charm an understanding age no more.
—Joseph Addison; *An Account of the Greatest English Poets*, 1694

**.2** The human understanding is like a false mirror, which, receiving rays irregularly, distorts and discolors the nature of things by mingling its own nature with it.
—Francis Bacon; *Norum Organum*, 1620

**.3** Fabulous Tales ought to be suited to the [Listener's] Understanding, being so contrived, that all Impossibilities ceasing, all great Accidents appearing feasible and the Mind wholly hanging in Suspense, they may at once surprise, astonish, please and divert; so that Pleasure and Admiration may go hand in hand.
—Miguel de Cervantes; *Don Quixote*, 1615

**.4** Shut up your mouth and chew the cud of understanding.
—William Congreve; *Love for Love*, 1695

**.5** If you understood everything I say, you'd be me.
—Miles Davis; *Music Is My Mistress*, 1973

**.6** It is not a bad thing in a tale that you understand only half of it.
—Isak Dinesen; *Seven Gothic Tales*, "The Dreamers," 1934

**.7** The growth of understanding follows an ascending spiral rather than a straight line.
—Joanna Field; *A Life of One's Own*, 1934

**.8** It is better to understand little than to misunderstand a lot.
—Anatole France; *Revolt of the Angels*, 1914

**.9** I'm glad I understand that while language is a gift, listening is a responsibility.
—Nikki Giovanni; in *Black Women Writers at Work*, Claudia Tate, ed., 1983

**.10** Whatever you cannot understand, you cannot possess.
—Johann Wolfgang von Goethe; *Spruche in Prosa*, 1819

**.11** Unless one is a genius, it is best to aim at being intelligible.
—Anthony Hope Hawkins; *The Dolly Dialogues*, 1894

**.12** Perfect understanding will sometimes almost extinguish pleasure.
—A.E. Housman; *The Leslie Stephen Lecture*, "The Name and Nature of Poetry," 1933

# 299

**.13** He who does not understand your silence will probably not understand your words.
—Elbert Hubbard; *Thousand and One Epigrams*, 1911

**.14** Men hate what they cannot understand.
—Moses Ibn Ezra; *Shirat Yisreal*, 12th century

**.15** I like people who understand what one says to them, and also what one doesn't say.
—Henry James; *The Princess Casamassima*, 1886

**.16** What provokes you to risibility, Sir. Have I said anything that you understand? Then I ask pardon of the rest of the company.
—Samuel Johnson; Remark, Richard Cumberland, *Recollections*, 1776

**.17** If one does not understand a person, one tends to regard him as a fool.
—Carl Jung; *Mysterium Coniunctions*, 1955–56

**.18** There is a great difference between knowing and understanding: you can know a lot about something and not really understand it.
—Charles F. Kettering; *Seed for Thought*, 1949

**.19** My words are easy to understand
and easy to put into practice.
Yet no one under heaven understands them
or puts them into practice.
—Lao-Tzu; *Tao-te ching*, c. 4th or 3rd century B.C.

**.20** And Jesus said, Are ye also yet without understanding?
—New Testament; Matthew

**.21** I am a barbarian here, because I am understood by no one.
—Ovid; *Trista*, A.D. 8

**.22** I still understand a few words in life, but I no longer think they make a sentence.
—Jean Rostand; *Pensees d'un Biologiste*, 1939

**.23** Myths are not believed in, they are conceived and understood.
—George Santayana; *The Life of Reason*, 1905–6

**.24** Here is something you can learn as you go along. Apply everything that comes your way to a better understanding and use of it. Be your own teacher and your own critic, develop that love and propensity for it that can bring such immeasurable returns. We can give you a starting-point; go on from here with a stout heart.
—Ruth Sawyer; *The Way of the Storyteller*, 1942

# 299

.25 To understand everything makes one very indulgent.
—Madame de Stael; *Corinne*, 1807

.26 Many men honestly do not know what women
want, and women honestly do not know why
men find what they want so hard to comprehend and deliver.
—Deborah Tannen; *You Just Don't Understand*, 1990

.27 A man must see before he can say.
—Henry David Thoreau; "Autumn," November 1, 1851

.28 Where misunderstanding serves others as an
advantage, one is helpless to make oneself understood.
—Lionel Trilling; *The Liberal Imagination*,
1950

.29 Speech is not what one should desire to un-
derstand. One should know the speaker.
—*Upanishads*, "Kaushitaki," c. 600 to 300
B.C.

.30 Nowadays to be intelligible is to be found out.
—Oscar Wilde; *Lady Windermere's Fan*,
1892

# 300 Universe and Universality

.1 Had I been present at the creation, I would
have given some helpful hints for the better or-
dering of the universe.
—Alfonso X, The Wise; *Apothegm*, c. 1275

.2 Since the Universe is defined as including all
that exists, it is useless to ask what lies beyond
it.
—Isaac Asimov; *Isaac Asimov's Book of Science and Nature Quotations*, Isaac Asimov and Jason A. Shulman, eds.

.3 Man cannot live without seeking to describe
and explain the universe.
—Sir Isaiah Berlin; *Sunday Times*, 1962

.4 The Universe is but one vast symbol of God.
—Thomas Carlyle; *Sartor Resartus*, 1833–4

.5 The notion of a universality of human experience is a confidence trick and the notion of
a universality of female experience is a clever
confidence trick.
—Angela Carter; *The Sadeian Woman*,
"Polemical Preface," 1979

# 300

.6 Sometimes I think we are alone in the universe, and sometimes I think we're not. In either case, the idea is quite staggering.
—Arthur C. Clarke; "Profiles of the Future," 1962

.7        —listen: there's a hell
of a good universe next door; let's go.
—E. E. Cummings; *1 × 1*, 1944

.8 The universe does not jest with us, but is in
earnest.
—Ralph Waldo Emerson; *Journals*, 1841

.9 In our general descriptions, we mean not universals, but would be understood with many
exceptions.
—Henry Fielding; *Joseph Andrews*, 1742

.10 The progress of the human race in understanding the universe has established a small
corner of order in an increasingly disordered
universe.
—Stephen W. Hawking; *A Brief History of
Time*, 1988

.11 The universe is not hostile, nor yet is it
friendly. It is simply indifferent.
—John R. Holmes; *The Sensible Man's View
of Religion*, 1933

.12 The universe begins to look more like a great
thought than a great machine.
—James Jeans; *Rede Memorial Lecture*,
Cambridge, November 4, 1930

.13 Do you know about the Eleventh Commandment? It says, "Thou shalt not bore God, or he
will destroy your universe."
—John Lilly; "Spiritualism," 1984

.14 The universe is a disymmetrical whole.
—Louis Pasteur; *Etudes sur la Biere*, c.
1856

.15 The universe ought to be presumed too vast to
have any character.
—Charles Sanders Peirce; *Collected Papers
of Charles Sanders Peirce*, 1931–34

.16 The universe is full of magical things, pa-
tiently waiting for our wits to grow sharper.
—Eden Phillpotts; *A Shadow Passes*, 1896

.17 The universe is in the business of making life.
—Cyril Ponnamperuma; Address, 1965

.18 The universe is one of God's thoughts.
—Johann von Schiller; *Essays, Aesthetical
and Philosophical*

.19 That the universe was formed by a fortuitous
concourse of atoms, I will no more believe than
that the accidental jumbling of the alphabet

# 300

would fall into a most ingenious treatise of philosophy.
  —Jonathan Swift; *Thoughts on Various Subjects*, 1911

.20 We who talk of the knowledge of the universe cannot sense the exact nature of an apple.
  —Jean Toomer; *Essentials*, 1931

.21 The entire universe is nothing but a great metaphor.
  —Simone Weil; *First and Last Notebooks*, 1970

.22 The more the universe seems comprehensible, the more it also seems pointless.
  —Steven Weinberg; *The First Three Minutes*, 1977

.23 The universe is duly in order, everything in its place.
  —Walt Whitman; *Leaves of Grass*, 1855–92

.24 Myths hook and bind the mind because at the same time they set the mind free: they explain the universe while allowing the universe to go on being explained.
  —Jeanette Winterson; *Boating for Beginners*, 1985

# 301 Vanity

.1 You will easily discover every man's prevailing vanity by observing his favorite topic of conversation; for every man talks most of that which he has most a mind to be thought to excel in.
  —Lord Chesterfield; Letter to his son, October 16, 1747

.2 There was never yet a true orator or poet who thought anyone better than him.
  —Cicero; *Epistolae ad Atticum*, c. 1st century B.C.

.3 Smart talk is my form of conceit.
  —Wilkie Collins; *I Say No*, 1884

.4 None of us are so much praised or censured as we think.
  —Charles Caleb Colton; *Lacon*, 1825

.5 Vanity plays lurid tricks with our memory.
  —Joseph Conrad; *Lord Jim*, 1900

.6 Vain men will speak well of him that does ill.
  —Oliver Cromwell; Letter to Richard Mayer, July 1651

.7 It may be that words are vain to save us; but feeble deeds are vainer far than words.
  —Benjamin Disraeli; *Sybil*, 1845

# 301

.8 We are so vain that we even care for the opinion of those we don't care for.
  —Marie von Ebner-Eschenbach; *Aphorisms*, 1893

.9 He was like a cock who thought the sun had risen to hear him crow.
  —George Eliot; *Adam Bede*, 1859

.10 If you want to succeed in the world it is necessary, when entering a salon, that your vanity should bow to that of others.
  —Madame de Genlis; *Tales of the Castle*, c. 1793

.11 A vain man finds it wise to speak good or ill of himself; a modest man does not talk of himself.
  —Jean de La Bruyere; *Les Caracteres*, 1688

.12 We talk little when vanity does not make us.
  —François de La Rochefoucauld, *Maxims*, 1665

.13 It is our own vanity that makes the vanity of others intolerable to us.
  —François de La Rochefoucauld; *Maximes*, 1665

.14 Most of us would be far enough from vanity if we heard all the things that are said about us.
  —Joseph Rickaby; Attributed

.15 We crave support in vanity, as we do in religion, and never forgive contradictions in that sphere.
  —George Santayana; *The Life of Reason in Society*, 1905–6

.16 He had only one vanity; he thought he could give advice better than any other person.
  —Mark Twain; *The Man That Corrupted Hadleyburg*, 1900

.17 However we may be reproached for our vanity we sometimes need to be assured of our merits and to have our most obvious advantages pointed out to us.
  —Luc de Clapiers Vauvenargues; *Reflections and Maxims*, 1746

.18 The inner vanity is generally in proportion to the outer self-depreciation.
  —Edith Wharton; *The House of Mirth*, 1905

# 302 Verbosity

.1 A plurality of words does not necessarily represent a plurality of things.
  —Joseph Albo; *Book of Principles*, 1428

**302**

.2 Your verbosity, founded upon your memory of what others have said, proves that you retain words without ever having considered their meaning.
  —Anonymous; *The Adventures of an Author*, 1767

.3 Piling verbose flights of stairs, one upon another, the Chadband style of oratory is widely received and much admired.
  —Charles Dickens; *Bleak House*, 1852–53

.4 A sophistical rhetorian [W.E. Gladstone], inebriated with the exuberance of his own verbosity, and gifted with an egotistical imagination that can at all times command an interminable and inconsistent series of arguments to malign an opponent and glorify himself.
  —Benjamin Disraeli; Speech, July 27, 1878

.5 A barren superfluity of words.
  —Samuel Garth; *The Dispensary*, 1699

.6 A glouton of wordes.
  —William Langland; *The Vision of Piers Plowman*, c. 14th century

.7 In general those who have nothing to say
  Contrive to spend the longest time in doing it;
  They turn and vary it in every way,
  Hashing it, stewing it, mincing it, ragouting it.
  —James Russell Lowell; *An Oriental Apologue*, 1849

.8 But there is one blanket statement which can be made about the world's schools: the teachers talk too much.
  —Martin Mayer; *The Schools*, 1961

.9 He multiplies words without knowledge.
  —The Old Testament: Job

.10 He that useth many words for the explaining any subject, doth, like the cuttle fish, hide himself for the most part in his own ink.
  —John Ray; *On Creation*, before 1705

.11 He draweth out the thread of his verbosity finer than the staple of his argument.
  —William Shakespeare; *Love's Labour's Lost*, 1594

# **303** Verse

.1 Though men in learned tongues do tie themselves to the ancient measures, yet in modern languages it seemeth to me as free to make new measures of verses as of dances: for a

**303**

dance is a measured pace, as a verse is a measured speech. In these things the sense is better than the art.
  —Francis Bacon; *The Advancement of Learning*, 1605

.2 Cheered up himself with ends of verse,
  And sayings of philosophers.
  —Samuel Butler I; *Hudibras*, 1663

.3 The fatal facility of the octosyllabic verse.
  —Lord Byron; *The Corsair*, "Preface," 1814

.4 The words I use
  Are everyday words and yet are not the same!
  You will find no rhymes in my verse, no magic.
  There are your very own phrases.
  —Paul Claudel; *La Muse Qui Est la Grace*, 1910

.5 Ye that are of good understanding, note the doctrine that is hidden under the veil of the strange verses.
  —Dante Alighieri; *The Divine Comedy*, c. 1310–20

.6 An artist who works in marble or colors has them all to himself and his tribe, but the man who moulds his thought in verse has to employ the materials vulgarized by everybody's use, and glorify them by his handling.
  —Oliver Wendell Holmes, Sr.; *The Poet at the Breakfast Table*, 1872

.7 No verses can please long, or live, which are written by water drinkers.
  —Horace; *Epistles*, c.19 B.C.

.8 They say my verse is sad: no wonder;
  Its narrow measure spans
  Tears of eternity, and sorrow,
  Not mine, but man's.
  —A.E. Housman; *More Poems*, "Foreword," 1936

.9 If nature refuses, indignation will produce verses.
  —Juvenal; *Satires*, c. A.D. 120

.10    'Tis verse that gives
  Immortal youth to mortal maids.
  —Walter Savage Landor; *Imaginary Conversations: Chesterfield and Rhodope*, 1829

.11 Great is the art of beginning, but greater the art is of ending;
  Many a poem is marred by a superfluous verse.
  —Henry Wadsworth Longfellow; "Elegiac Verse," 1881

## 303

.12 They praise those verses, yes, but read something else.
—Martial; *Epigrams*, c A.D. 90

.13 A Book of Verses underneath the Bough,
A Jug of Wine, a Loaf of Bread—and Thou
Beside me singing in the Wilderness—
Oh, Wilderness were Paradise enow!
—Omar Khayyam; *The Rubaiyat of Omar Khayyam*, c. 1100, Edward Fitzgerald, ed., 1859

.14 Curses be the verse, how well so'er it flow,
That tends to make one worthy man my foe.
—Alexander Pope; "An Epistle to Dr. Arbuthnot," 1735

.15 This be the verse you grave for me:
Here he lies where he longed to be;
Home is the sailor, home from the sea,
And the hunter home from the hill.
—Robert Louis Stevenson; *Underwoods*, "Requiem," 1887

.16 No one will get at my verses who insists upon viewing them as a literary performance, or attempt at such performance, or as aiming mainly toward art or aestheticism.
—Walt Whitman; *November Boughs*, 1888

## 304 Vocabulary

.1 I'm very anxious not to fall into archaism or "literary" diction. I want my vocabulary to have a very large range, but the words must be alive.
—James Agee; *Letters of James Agee to Father Flye*, 1962

.2 A person with a mind tidily stocked with a rich vocabulary feels adequate; and that sense of adequacy is the sense of power.
—Mauree Applegate; *Easy in English*, 1960

.3 For every man there is something in the vocabulary that would stick to him like a second skin. His enemies have only to find it.
—Ambrose Bierce; *The Devil's Dictionary*, 1911

.4 Thought makes everything fit for use. The vocabulary of an omniscient man would embrace words and images excluded from polite conversation.
—Ralph Waldo Emerson; *Essays, Second Series*, "The Poet," 1844

.5 I used to think I was poor. Then they told me I wasn't poor, I was needy. They told me it was self-defeating to think of myself as needy, I

## 304

was deprived. Then they told me underprivileged was over used. I was disadvantaged. I still don't have a dime. But I have a great vocabulary.
—Jules Feiffer; cartoon, in William Safire's *Safire's Political Dictionary*, 1965

.6 A country clergyman with a one-story intellect and a one-horse vocabulary.
—Oliver Wendell Holmes, Sr.; *The Autocrat of the Breakfast Table*, 1858

.7 Language was originally made by men who were not psychologists, and most men today employ almost exclusively the vocabulary of outward things. The cardinal passions of our life, anger, love, fear, hate, hope, and the most comprehensive divisions of our intellectual activity, to remember, expect, think, know, dream, with the broadest genera of aesthetic feeling, joy, sorrow, pleasure, pain, are the only facts of a subjective order which this vocabulary deigns to note by special words.
—William James; *The Principles of Psychology*, 1890

.8 Syntax and vocabulary are overwhelming constraints—the rules that run us. Language is using us to talk—we think we're using the language, but language is doing the thinking, we're its slavish agents.
—Harry Burchell Mathews; Interview in *City Limits*, May 26, 1988

.9 Each of us … is the possessor of not one vocabulary but three. The largest of your three vocabularies is your recognition vocabulary—the words whose meanings you recognize when you see them in print or hear them spoken. The next smaller vocabulary—usually about two-thirds the size of the recognition vocabulary—is your writing vocabulary. These are the words you not only can recognize but know thoroughly enough so that you can command them to use in your own writing. The smallest of your vocabularies—about sixty percent of your recognition vocabulary—is your speaking vocabulary. That's because you—like all the rest of us—will often hesitate to say a word aloud because of fear that you may mispronounce it.
—William Morris; *It's Easy to Increase Your Vocabulary*, 1957

.10 Those who prefer their English sloppy have only themselves to thank if the advertisement writer uses his mastery of vocabulary and syntax to mislead their weak minds.
—Dorothy Sayers; "The Psychology of Advertising," *The Spectator*, November 19, 1937

**304**

.11 The word Snob belongs to the sour-grape vocabulary.
—Logan Pearsall Smith; *Afterthoughts*, 1931

.12 One forgets words as one forgets names. One's vocabulary needs constant fertilizing or it will die.
—Evelyn Waugh; *Diaries*, December 25, 1962

# **305** Voice

.1 Great orators who are not also great writers become very indistinct shadows to the generations following them. The spell vanishes with the voice.
—Thomas Bailey Aldrich; *Ponkapog Papers*, 1903

.2 She had one of those high-pitched apologetic voices which seemed to make every pronouncement sound like a spirit message, inconclusive but faintly ominous.
—Margery Allingham; *Safer Than Love*, 1962

.3 The voice is the second face.
—Gerard Bauer; *Carnets Inedits*, mid–20th century

.4 How nice the human voice is when it isn't singing.
—Rudolf Bing; *Newsweek*, May 1, 1972

.5 Hear the voice of the Bard!
Who Present, Past, & Future, sees;
Whose ears have heard
The Holy Word
That walked among the ancient trees.
—William Blake; *Songs of Experience*, "Introduction," 1794

.6 The voice of Nature loudly cries,
And many a message from the skies,
That something in us never dies.
—Robert Burns; "New Year's Day," 1792

.7 The devil hath not, in all his quiver's choice,
An arrow for the heart like a sweet voice.
—Lord Byron; *Don Juan*, 1819–24

.8 All the intelligence and talent in the world can't make a singer. The voice is a wild thing. It can't be bred in captivity.
—Willa Cather; *The Song of the Lark*, 1915

.9 His voice is his great weapon. It is not an orator's voice. It is husky, and sometimes it fades to a whisper. Meanwhile, it is extraordinary

**305**

intimate. Mr. Reagan does not speak to audiences; he speaks to individuals.
—John Corry; *New York Times*, October 9, 1984
[Corry comments on Ronald Reagan in a televised debate with Democratic Presidential nominee Walter Mondale.]

.10 There is no index of character so sure as the voice.
—Benjamin Disraeli; *Tancred*, 1847

.11 His voice is soft as the upper air,
Or dying lovers' words.
—John Dryden; *The Rival Ladies*, 1664

.12 Thicken the thunders of man's voice, and lo! a world awakes.
—W.E.B. Du Bois; *The Souls of Black Folk*, 1903

.13 A man's style is his mind's voice. Wooden minds, wooden voices.
—Ralph Waldo Emerson; *Journals*, 1872

.14 Her voice is full of money.
—F. Scott Fitzgerald; *The Great Gatsby*, 1925

.15 The voice of the intellect is a soft one, but it does not rest until it has gained a hearing.
—Sigmund Freud; *Future of an Illusion*, 1928

.16 The voice which speaks in conformity with our dearest hopes will always be listened to.
—Emile Gaboriau; *File 113*, 1867

.17 Of all the musical instruments the human voice is the most beautiful, for it is made by God.
—Shusha Guppy; Attributed

.18 Our debt to the printing press is great—so great that it is vain to try to measure it—but it has not been all gain, and one of the losses to the people in general is that they no more hear the voice of poetry.
—Alexander Haddow; *On the Teaching of Poetry*, 1926

.19 When she gets excited, her voice rises to a pitch generally considered suitable only for hog-calling.
—Margaret Halsey; *Some of My Best Friends Are Soldiers*, 1944

.20 A good voice can transform the most conventional of sermons into something like a divine revelation.
—Aldous Huxley; *Collected Essays*, 1959

.21 The sweetest of all sounds is that of the voice of the woman we love.
—Jean de La Bruyere; *Les Characters*, 1688

## 305

.22 The voice is a celestial melody.
—Henry Wadsworth Longfellow; *The Masque of Pandora and other Poem*, title poem, 1875

.23 The melting voice through mazes running,
Untwisting all the chains that tie
The hidden soul of harmony.
—John Milton; "L'Allegro," 1631–32

.24 The angel ended, and in Adam's ear
So charming left his voice that he a while
Thought him still speaking.
—John Milton; *Paradise Lost*, published 1667

.25 The voice of one crying in the wilderness, Prepare ye the way of the Lord, make his paths straight.
—The New Testament: Matthew

.26 I am listening for the voices
Which I heard in days of old.
—Caroline Norton; "The Lonely Harp," 1862

.27 We have so many voices in us, how do we know which ones to obey?
—Edna O'Brien; *I Hardly Knew You*, 1978

.28 His voice was intimate as the rustle of sheets.
—Dorothy Parker; *The Collected Stories of Dorothy Parker*, "Dusk Before Fireworks," 1942

.29 The People's Voice is odd,
It is, and it is not, the voice of God…
—Alexander Pope; *Imitation of Horace*, 1737

.30 Her voice was like the voice the stars
Had when they sang together.
—Dante Gabriel Rossetti; "The Blessed Damozel," 1850

.31 The articulate voice is more distracting than mere noise.
—Seneca; *Epistles*, c. 1st century A.D.

.32 His voice was propertied
As all the tuned spheres.
—William Shakespeare; *Antony and Cleopatra*, 1606–7
[Propertied means "endowed with qualities."]

.33       Her voice was ever soft,
Gentle, and low, an excellent thing in woman.
—William Shakespeare; *King Lear*, 1605

.34 What's more enchanting than the voice of young people when you can't hear what they say?
—Logan Pearsall Smith; *Afterthoughts*, 1931

## 305

.35 My voice stuck in my throat.
—Virgil; *Aeneid*, c. 1st century B.C.

.36 Her voice had the sway of an aerialist crossing the high wire.
—Eudora Welty; *The Golden Apples*, "Moon Lake," 1949

.37 A clear sonorous voice, inaudible
To the vast multitude.
—William Wordsworth; "The Excursion," 1814

# 306 Wisdom

.1 Alcuin my name, wisdom I always loved,
Pray, reader, for my soul.
—Alcuin; *His Own Epitaph*, c. 804

.2 …even the lover of myth is in a sense a lover of wisdom, for the myth is composed of wonders.
—Aristotle; *Politics*, c. 4th century B.C.

.3 Think not Silence the Wisdom of Fools, but, if rightly timed the honor of wise Men.
—Sir Thomas Browne; *Christian Morals*, 1682

.4 With a profound reverence for the wisdom of our ancestors.
—Edmund Burke; *Conciliation with America*, 1775

.5 Be wiser than other people if you can; but don't tell them so.
—Lord Chesterfield; Letter to his son, November 19, 1745

.6 Great wisdom is generous; petty wisdom is contentious.
—Chuang-tzu; *On Leveling All Things*, c. 300 B.C.

.7 No one over thirty-five is worth meeting who has not something to teach us,—something more than we could learn for ourselves, from a book.
—Cyril Connolly; *The Unquiet Grave*, 1944

.8 The wisest people are the clowns; like Harpo Marx, who would not speak. If I could have anything I want I would like God to listen to what Harpo was not saying, and understand why Harpo would not talk.
—Philip K. Dick; *The Golden Man*, 1980

.9 Wisdom is a tree that grows in the heart, and its fruit appears upon the tongue.
—Friedrich Diez; *Asiatische Merkwurdigkeiten*, 1840

**306**

.10 Proverbs are the wisdom of the streets.
—English Proverbs

.11 Silence is true wisdom's best reply.
—Euripides; *Fragments*, c. 5th century B.C.

.12 The heart of a fool is in his mouth, but the mouth of a wise man is in his heart.
—Benjamin Franklin; *Poor Richard's Almanack*, 1732–57

.13 Wisdom doesn't always speak in Greek and Latin.
—Thomas Fuller II; *Gnomologia*, 1732

.14 Truth from his lips prevailed with double sway,
And fools, who came to scoff, remained to pray.
—Oliver Goldsmith; "The Deserted Village," 1770
[In his most famous poem, Goldsmith speaks of the village preacher.]

.15 Knowledge can be communicated, but not wisdom. One can find it, live it, be fortified by it, do wonders through it, but one cannot communicate and teach it.
—Hermann Hesse; *Siddhartha: Govinda*, 1923

.16 Such is the nature of men, that howsoever they may acknowledge many others to be more witty, or more eloquent, or more learned; yet they will hardly believe there be many so wise as themselves.
—Thomas Hobbes; *Leviathan*, 1651

.17 It is the province of knowledge to speak, and it is the privilege of wisdom to listen.
—Oliver Wendell Holmes, Sr.; *The Poet at the Breakfast Table*, 1872

.18 It is bad taste to be wise all the time, like being at a perpetual funeral.
—D.H. Lawrence; *Pansies*, "Peace and War," 1929

.19 We have no words for speaking of wisdom to the stupid. He who understands the wise is wise already.
—G.C. Lichtenberg; *Aphorisms*, "Notebook E" written 1765–99, R.J. Hollingdale, tr., 1990

.20 Anyone who follows a middle course is called a sage.
—Maimonides; *Guide to the Perplexed*, 1190

.21 Wisdom crieth without; she uttereth her voice in the streets.
—Old Testament: Proverbs

**306**

.22 The Athenians do not mind a man being clever, provided he does not impart his wisdom to others.
—Plato; *Euthyphro*, c. 4th century B.C.

.23 It is not wise to be wiser than necessary.
—Philippe Quinault; *Armide*, 1686

.24 Silence and reserve will give anyone a reputation for wisdom.
—Myrtle Reed; *Old Rose and Silver*, 1909

.25 Nine-tenths of wisdom is being wise in time.
—Theodore Roosevelt; Speech, Lincoln, Nebraska, June 14, 1917

.26 Wise men say nothing in dangerous times.
—John Selden; *Table-Talk*, "Wisdom," c. 1654

.27 Some folks are wise, and some are otherwise.
—Tobias Smollett; *Roderick Random*, 1748

.28 To be reconciled to the inevitable with good grace is wisdom.
—Rabindranath Tagore; Speech, Geneva, Switzerland, 1912

.29 Knowledge comes, but wisdom lingers.
—Alfred, Lord Tennyson; *Locksley Hall*, 1842

.30 Wisdom is not finally tested by the schools,
Wisdom cannot be pass'd from one having it to another not having it,
Wisdom is of the soul, is not susceptible of proof, is its own proof.
—Walt Whitman; *Song of the Open Road*, 1856

.31 The well-bred contradict other people. The wise contradict themselves.
—Oscar Wilde; "Phrases and Philosophies for the Use of the Young," 1891

# **307** Wit

.1 Melancholy men of all others are most witty.
—Aristotle; Quoted by Robert Burton in *Anatomy of Melancholy*, 1621

.2 Wit is cultured eloquence.
—Aristotle; *Rhetoric*, c. 330 B.C.

.3 I can say a neat thing myself if they will give me time.
—J.M. Barrie; *Farewell, Miss Julie Logan*, 1920

.4 Wit. The salt with which the American humorist spoils his intellectual cookery by leaving it out.
—Ambrose Bierce; *The Devil's Dictionary*, 1911

## 307

.5 You have to be wise before you can be witty.
—Josh Billings; *J.B. on Ice*, 1868

.6 Wit is a treacherous dart. It is perhaps the only weapon with which it is possible to stab oneself in one's own back.
—Geoffrey Bocca; *The Woman Who Would Be Queen*, 1954

.7 Use your wit as a buckler, not a sword.
—H.G. Bohn; *Handbook of Proverbs*, 1855

.8 The next best thing to being witty one's self, is to be able to quote another's wit.
—Christian Nestell Bovee; *Summaries of Thought*, 1862

.9 Humorous persons have pleasant mouths turned up at the corners…. But the mouth of a merely witty man is hard and sour until the moment of its discharge.
—Charles S. Brooks; *I Was Just Thinking*, "On the Difference Between Wit and Humor," 1959

.10 Never judge the heart of a wit by the tongue.
—Fanny Burney; *Camilla*, 1796

.11 Wit is like science, not of particulars but universals; for as arguments drawn from particulars signify little to universal nature, which is the proper object of science, so wit that is raised upon any one particular person goes no further unless it be from thence extended to all human nature.
—Samuel Butler I; *Hudibras*, 1663

.12 Don't put too fine a point on your wit, for fear it should be blunted.
—Miguel de Cervantes; *Exemplary Novels: Little Gypsy*, c. 1610

.13 A fool who has a moment's flash of wit is both astonishing and shocking, like cab horses at a gallop.
—Sebastien Nicolas Roche Chamfort; *Maximes et pensees*, 1805

.14 Humor is consistent with pathos, whilst wit is not.
—Samuel Taylor Coleridge; "Table Talk," 1821

.15 Wit ought be a glorious treat, like caviar, never spread it about like marmalade.
—Noel Coward; *Reader's Digest*, 1979

.16 He shows all his wit at once.
—Thomas Draxe; *Bibliotheca Scholastica Instructissima*, 1633

.17 A thing well said will be wit in all languages.
—John Dryden; *Essay of Dramatic Poetry*, 1668

.18 Wit makes its own welcome, and levels all distinctions. No dignity, no learning, no force of character, can make any stand against good wit.
—Ralph Waldo Emerson; *Letters and Social Aims*, "The Comic," 1876

.19 Borrowed wit becomes the mouth as ill as borrowed clothes the body.
—Sarah Fielding; *The Adventures of David Simple*, 1744

.20 Half wits talk much but say little.
—Benjamin Franklin; *Poor Richard's Almanack*, 1748

.21 Men never think their fortune too great, nor their wit too little.
—Thomas Fuller II; *Gnomologia*, 1732

.22 Many get the repute of being witty, but thereby lose the credit of being sensible. Jest has its little hour, seriousness should have all the rest.
—Baltasar Gracian; *The Art of Worldly Wisdom*, 1647

.23 There is so much wit necessary to make a skillful hypocrite that the faculty is fallen among bunglers, who make it ridiculous.
—Lord Halifax (George Savile); *Political, Moral and Miscellaneous Thoughts and Reflections*, 1750

.24 Wit is the salt of conversation, not the food.
—William Hazlitt; *Lectures on the English Comic Writers*, 1819

.25 Wit is an unruly engine, wildly striking
Sometimes a friend, sometimes the engineer.
—George Herbert; *The Church-Porch*, 1633

.26 Wit that is kindly is not very witty.
—Ed Howe; *Sinner Sermons*, 1926

.27 There is nothing breaks so many friendships as a difference of opinion as to what constitutes wit.
—Elbert Hubbard; *Epigrams*, 1911

.28 A flash of wit, like a flash of lightning, can only be remembered, it cannot be reproduced.
—Mary Clemmer Hudson; in Kate Sanborn, *The Wit of Women*, 1885

.29 Wit destroys eroticism and eroticism destroys wit, so women must choose between taking lovers and taking no prisoners.
—Florence King; *Reflections in a Jaundiced Eye*, 1989

.30 It is a great misfortune neither to have enough wit to talk well nor enough judgement to be silent.
—Jean de La Bruyere; *Les Caractères ou les moeurs de ce siècle*, 1688

**307**

.31 Wit sometimes enables us to act rudely with impunity.
   —François de La Rochefoucauld; *Maximes*, 1665

.32 Wit has a deadly aim and it is possible to prick a large pretense with a small pin.
   —Marya Mannes; *More in Anger*, 1958

.33 Impropriety is the soul of wit.
   —W. Somerset Maugham; *The Moon and Sixpence*, 1919

.34 That is not wit which needs explaining.
   —Herman Melville; *Redburn*, 1849

.35 A witty woman is a treasure; a witty beauty is a power.
   —George Meredith; *Diana of the Crossways*, 1885

.36 Wit consists in knowing the resemblance of things which differ, and the difference of things which are alike.
   —Charles de Montesquieu; *Epigram*, 1721
   [Madame de Stael quoted the epigram in *Germany*, 1810.]

.37 Wit is the epitaph of an emotion.
   —Friedrich Wilhelm Nietzsche; *Miscellaneous Maxims and Opinions*, 1879

.38 Wit is a happy and striking way of expressing a thought.
   —William Penn; *Some Fruits of Solitude*, 1693

.39 Wit when temperate is pleasing, when unbridled, it offends.
   —Phaedrus; *Fables*, c. 25 B.C.

.40 True Wit is Nature to advantage dress'd,
   What oft was thought, but ne'er so well expressed.
   —Alexander Pope; *Essay on Criticism*, 1709

.41 No one is as dull as a wit, when he does not hit off the scent at once.
   —Sir Walter Scott; *The Fair Maid of Perth*, 1828

.42 Look, he's winding up the watch of his wit; by and by it will strike.
   —William Shakespeare; *The Tempest*, 1611

.43 There's no possibility of being witty without a little ill-nature; the malice of a good thing is the barb than makes it stick.
   —Richard Brinsley Sheridan; *The School for Scandal*, 1777

.44 All human race would fain be wits,
   And millions miss for one that hits.
   —Jonathan Swift; *Polite Conversation*, 1738

**307**

.45 They had not much original wit, but had inherited a stock of cheerful sayings which passed as such.
   —Flora Thompson; *Over to Candleford*, 1941

.46 Somebody has said "Wit is a sudden marriage of ideas which before their union were not perceived to have any relation."
   —Mark Twain; *Notebooks & Journals*, Vol. 3, 1883–91
   [Twain is quoting Sydney Smith.]

**308** Witticisms

.1 I cheated in the final of my metaphysics examination: I looked into the soul of the boy sitting next to me.
   —Woody Allen; in his comedy routine in the film *Annie Hall*, 1977

.2 An epigram is a flashlight of a truth; a witticism, truth laughing at itself.
   —Minna Thomas Antrim; *Naked Truth and Veiled Illusions*, 1901

.3 Too bad all the people who know how to run the country are busy driving taxi cabs and cutting hair.
   —George Burns; Attributed

.4 A witty thing never excited laughter; it pleases only the mind, and never distorts the countenance.
   —Lord Chesterfield; Letter to his son, March 9, 1748

.5 Fasten your seatbelts, it's going to be a bumpy night.
   —Bette Davis gives guests at her party fair warning of what to expect in *All About Eve*, 1950 (screenplay by Herman Mankiewicz, story by Mary Orr)

.6 The telephone is a good way to talk to people without having to offer them a drink.
   —Fran Lebowitz; *Social Studies*, 1977

.7 Thou canst not serve cod and salmon.
   —Ada Leverson; in *The London Times*, 1970
   [Leverson comments on menu choices.]

.8 Never darken my Dior again!
   —Beatrice Lillie; *Every Other Inch a Lady*, 1972
   [It was her comment to a clumsy waiter who spilled soup on her.]

.9 Avoid witticisms at the expense of others.
   —Horace Mann; *Lectures and Reports on Education*, 1845

# 308

.10 Please accept my resignation. I don't care to belong to any club that will have me as a member.
—Groucho Marx; *Groucho and Me*, 1959

.11 Obviously the answer to oil-spills is to paper-train the tankers.
—Ralph Nader; Attributed

.12 You can lead a horticulture, but you can't make her think.
—Dorothy Parker; in John Keats, *You Might As Well Live*, 1970
[The witty Mrs. Parker was challenged to use "horticulture" in a sentence.]

.13 A witticism is a minor work that does not merit a second edition.
—Antoine Rivarol; *Pensees, traits et bon mots*, late 18th century

.14 Try to imagine a famous witty saying that is not immediately clear.
—James Thurber; Letter to Malcolm Cowley, March 11, 1954

.15 Let the meek inherit the earth—they have it coming to them.
—James Thurber; *Life*, 1960

.16 He who cannot shine by thought, seeks to bring himself into notice by a witticism.
—Voltaire; *Philosophical Dictionary*, "Wit, Spirit, Intellect," 1764

.17 One man's fish is another man's *poisson*.
—Carol Wells; *Folly for the Wise*, "More Mixed Maxims," 1904

# 309 Women

.1 A woman, especially, if she has the misfortune of knowing anything, should conceal it as well as she can.
—Jane Austen; *Letters*, R.W. Chapman, ed., 1952

.2 Ten measures of speech descended to the world: women took nine and men one.
—Babylonian Talmud: Kiddushin, c. 450

.3 A woman spins even when she talks.
—Babylonian Talmud; Megillah, c. 450
[That is, a woman schemes even while in idle chatter.]

.4 Sentences that begin with "all women" are never, never true.
—Margaret Culkin Banning; *A Week in New York*, 1941

# 309

.5 You see, dear, it's not true that woman was made from man's rib; she was made from his funny bone.
—J.M. Barrie; *What Every Woman Knows*, 1908

.6 The dogma of woman's complete historical subjection to man must be rated as one of the most fantastic myths ever created by the human mind.
—Mary Ritter Beard; *Woman as a Force in History*, 1946

.7 What a woman says to an eager lover, write it on running water, write it on air.
—Catullus; *Poems*, c. 1st. century B.C.

.8 I am a woman, needs must I speak.
—Geoffrey Chaucer; *The Canterbury Tales*, "The Marchantes Tale"

.9 Women are to be talked to as below men, and above children.
—Lord Chesterfield; Letter to his son, December 19, 1749

.10 The myth of the strong black woman is the other side of the coin of the myth of the beautiful dumb blonde.
—Eldridge Cleaver; *Soul on Ice*, 1968

.11 In all my experience, I never met a woman who declined to express an opinion.
—Wilkie Collins; *Blind Love*, 1890

.12 You are a woman, you must never speak what you think; your words must contradict your thoughts, but your actions may contradict your words.
—William Congreve; *Love for Love*, 1695

.13 If a man does something silly, people say, "Isn't he silly?" If a woman does something silly, people say, "Aren't women silly?"
—Doris Day; in *National Enquirer*, 1988

.14 The autobiographies of most famous women are a series of accounts of the outward existence, of petty details and anecdotes which give no realization of their real life. For the great moments of joy or agony they remain strangely silent.
—Isadora Duncan; *My Life*, 1942

.15 Half the sorrows of women would be averted if they could repress the speech they know to be useless—nay, the speech they have resolved not to utter.
—George Eliot; *Felix Holt*, 1866

.16 Once I tried to explain to a fellow feminist why I liked wearing makeup: she replied by

## 309

explaining why she does not. Neither of us understood a word the other said.
    —Nora Ephron; "On Never Having Been a Prom Queen," 1972

.17 'Tis woman's nature to bear her ills on lip and tongue with mournful pleasure.
    —Euripides; *Andromache*, c. 430 B.C.

.18 Women strive for the last word.
    —Thomas Fuller; *Church-History of Britain*, 1655

.19 Most men who run down women are running down one woman only.
    —Remy de Gourmont; *Promenades Philosophiques*, 1905

.20 What every woman says some women may feel.
    —Thomas Hardy; *Tess of the D'Urbervilles*, 1891

.21 A woman never forgets her sex. She would rather talk with a man than an angel, any day.
    —Oliver Wendell Holmes, Sr.; *The Poet at the Breakfast Table*, 1872

.22 Women always speak the truth, but not the whole truth.
    —Italian Proverb

.23 Women's liberation is not a debatable issue.
    —Jill Johnston; "A Dialogue on Women's Liberation," 1971

.24 Women speak because they wish to speak, whereas a man speaks only when driven to speech by something outside himself—like, for instance, he can't find any clean socks.
    —Jean Kerr; *The Snake Has All the Good Lines*, 1960

.25 How like an angel speaks the tongue of woman,
When pleading in another's cause her own.
    —Henry Wadsworth Longfellow; *The Spanish Student*, 1843

.26 Women who make men talk better than they are accustomed to are always popular.
    —E.V. Lucas; *Reading, Writing and Remembering*, 1932

.27 We don't love a woman for what she says, we like what she says because we love her.
    —Andre Maurois; *De La Conversation*, 1921

.28 Women have simple tastes. They get pleasure out of the conversation of children in arms and men in love.
    —H.L. Mencken; *A Book of Burlesques*, "Sententiae," 1920

## 309

.29 Whether they give or refuse, women are glad to have been asked.
    —Ovid; *Ars Amatoria*, c. A.D. 8

.30 The men are much alarmed by certain speculations about women; and well they may be, for when the horse and ass begin to think and argue, adieu to riding and driving.
    —Adelaide Anne Procter; Letter to Anna Jameson, 1838

.31 A woman's tongue is her sword.
    —Charles Reade; *The Cloister and the Hearth*, 1861

.32 Woman: the peg on which the wit hangs his jest, the preacher his text, the cynic his grouch and the sinner his justification.
    —Helen Rowland; *Reflections of a Bachelor Girl*, 1903

.33 For my part I distrust all generalizations about women, favorable and unfavorable, masculine and feminine, ancient and modern.
    —Bertrand Russell; *Unpopular Essays*, 1950

.34 Too many women in too many countries speak the same language—silence.
    —Anasuya Sengupta; "Silence," news item, 1995

.35 To be slow in words is a woman's only virtue.
    —William Shakespeare; *The Two Gentlemen of Verona*, 1594

.36 Women say so, That will say anything.
    —William Shakespeare; *A Winter's Tale*, 1610

.37 No is no negative in a woman's mouth.
    —Sir Philip Sidney; *Arcadia*, 1584

.38 It requires nothing less than a chivalric feeling to sustain a conversation with a lady.
    —Henry David Thoreau; *Journals*, entry for December 31, 1851

.39 It often happens that ladies mean that to be expressed which it does not become them to say out loud.
    —Anthony Trollope; *Ayala's Angel*, 1881

.40 What cannot a neat knave with a smooth tale
Make a woman believe?
    —John Webster; *The Duchess of Malfi*, 1623

## 310 Words

.1 Words are the physicians of a mind diseased.
    —Aeschylus; *Prometheus Bound*, c. 470 B.C.

**310**

.2 A word is like a bird: when he has sent it forth a man cannot recapture it.
—Ahikar; *Teachings*, c. 575 B.C.

.3 I like good strong words, that mean something.
—Louisa May Alcott; *Little Women*, 1868–69

.4 Words convey the mental treasures of one period to the generations that follow; and laden with this, their precious freight, they sail safely across gulfs of time in which empires have suffered shipwreck and the languages of common life have sunk into oblivion.
—Anonymous; quoted in Richard C. Trench, *On the Study of Words*, 1858

.5 Words are the tokens current and accepted for conceits, as moneys are for values.
—Francis Bacon; *On the Advancement of Learning*, 1605

.6 Words are all we have.
—Samuel Beckett; *New York Times*, 1974

.7 All words are pegs to hang ideas on.
—Henry Ward Beecher; *Proverbs from Plymouth Pulpit*, 1887

.8 Deliver your words not by number but by weight.
—H.G. Bohn; *Handbook of Proverbs*, 1855

.9 Words make love with one another.
—Andre Breton; *Surrealist Manifesto*, 1924

.10 The words! I collected them in all shapes and sizes, and hung them like bangles in my mind.
—Hortense Calisher; *Extreme Magic*, "Little Did I Know," 1964

.11 The smashers of language are looking for a new justice among words. It does not exist. Words are unequal and unjust.
—Elias Canetti; *The Human Province*, 1978

.12 "When I use a word," Humpty Dumpty said in rather a scornful tone, "it means just what I choose it to mean—neither more nor less."
—Lewis Carroll; *Through the Looking Glass*, 1872

.13 Words are the dress of thoughts; which should no more be presented in rags, tatters, and dirt, than your person should.
—Lord Chesterfield; Letter to his son, January 25, 1750

.14 Broadly speaking, the short words are the best, and the old words are the best of all.
—Winston Churchill; Speech in the House of Commons, January, 1952

**310**

.15 Our words are giants when they do us injury, and dwarfs when they do us service.
—Wilkie Collins; *The Woman in White*, 1860

.16 Words, as is well known, are the great foes of reality.
—Joseph Conrad; *Under Western Eyes*, "Prologue to Part 1," 1911

.17 Words pregnant with celestrial fire.
—William Cowper; *Boadicea*, 1780

.18 Words are made for a certain exactness of thought, as tears are for a certain degree of pain. What is least distinct cannot be named; what is clearest is unutterable.
—Rene Daumal; *A Night of Serious Drinking*, "Foreword," 1938

.19 By men's words we know them.
—Marie de France; c. 12th century, *The Lais of Marie de France*, Robert Hannings and Joan Ferrante, trs., 1978

.20 [A] source of our errors is, that we attach thoughts to words which do not express them with accuracy.
—Rene Descartes; *The Principles of Philosophy*, 1644

.21 Like a beautiful flower, full of color but without scent, are the fair but fruitless words of him who does not act accordingly.
—Dhammapala; *Commentaries*, c. 475

.22 A word in earnest is as good as a speech.
—Charles Dickens; *Bleak House*, 1852

.23 A word is dead
When it is said,
Some say.
I say it just
Begins to live
That day.
—Emily Dickinson; in *Letters of Emily Dickinson*, Mabel Loomis Todd, ed., 1933

.24 With words we govern men.
—Benjamin Disraeli; *Cotarini Fleming*, 1832

.25 Words are but the vague shadows of the volumes we mean. Little audible links, they are, chaining together great inaudible feelings and purposes.
—Theodore Dreiser; *Sister Carrie*, 1900

.26 Our words have wings, but fly not where we would.
—George Eliot; *Spanish Gypsy*, 1868

.27 For last year's words belong to last year's language

**310**

And next year's words await another
voice.
    —T.S. Eliot; *Four Quartets*, "Little Gid-
    ding," 1944

.28 If the word has the potency to revive and make
us free, it also has the power to blind, im-
prison, and destroy.
    —Ralph Ellison; unpublished essay, "Twen-
    tieth Century Fiction and the Black
    Mask of Humanity," 1946, reprinted in
    *Confluence*, December, 1953

.29 You can stroke people with words.
    —F. Scott Fitzgerald; *The Crack-Up*, "The
    Note-Books," 1945

.30 I haven't much opinion of words.... They're
apt to set fire to a dry tongue, that's what I say.
    —Ellen Glasgow; *The Deliverance*, 1904

.31 It's exactly where a thought is lacking
That just in time, a word shows up instead.
    —Johann Wolfgang von Goethe; *Faust*,
    1808

.32 Talk as if you were making your will: the fewer
words the less litigation.
    —Baltasar Gracian; *Oraculo Manual*, 1647

.33 Words have wings, and once let slip can never
be recalled.
    —Robert Greene; *Royal Exchange*, 1590

.34 Words are chameleons, which reflect the color
of their environment.
    —Learned Hand; Opinion, *Commissioner
    v. National Carbide*, 1948

.35 Articulate words are a harsh clamor and dis-
sonance. When man arrives at his highest perfection, he will again be dumb!
    —Nathaniel Hawthorne; *American Note-
    Books*, April, 1841

.36 Words are wise men's counters, they do but
reckon by them; but they are the money of
fools.
    —Thomas Hobbes; *Leviathan*, 1651

.37 I would never use a long word where a short
one would answer the purpose.
    —Oliver Wendell Holmes, Sr.; *Scholastic
    and Bedside Teaching*, 1867

.38 It has always been lawful, and always will be,
to issue words with the mint-mark of the
day.
    —Horace; *De Arte Poetica*, c. 20 B.C.

.39 Words. Frail beasts of burden that crashed
down to their knees under what she wanted to
say.
    —Fannie Hurst; *Lummox*, 1923

**310**

.40 Words form the thread on which we string our
experiences.
    —Aldous Huxley; *The Olive Tree*, 1937

.41 As long as a word is unspoken, you are its master; once you utter it, you are its slave.
    —Solomon Ibn Gabriol; *Choice of Pearls*,
    c. 1050

.42 As any custom is disused, the words that expressed it must perish with it; as any opinion
grows popular, it will innovate speech in the
same proportion as it alters practice.
    —Samuel Johnson; Boswell, *Life of John-
    son*, 1791

.43 And now we come to the magic of words. A
word, also, just like an idea, a thought, has the
effect of reality upon undifferentiated minds.
    —Erica Jong; *Animus and Anima*, "On the
    Nature of Anima," 1957

.44 Words are, of course, the most powerful drug
used by mankind.
    —Rudyard Kipling; Speech, February 14,
    1923

.45 Words can destroy. What we call each other
ultimately becomes what we think of each
other, and it matters.
    —Jeane J. Kirkpatrick; Speech, 1982

.46 Ours was a storytelling family even in pleasing times, and in those days my parents looked
on words as our sustenance, rich in their flavor
and wholesome for the soul.
    —Natalie Kusz; *Road Song*, 1990

.47 Sincere words are not grand; grand words are
not sincere.
    —Lao-Tsze; *The Way of Virtue*, c. 550 B.C.

.48 Words can have no single fixed meaning. Like
wayward electrons, they can spin away from
their initial orbit and enter a wider magnetic
field. No one owns them or has a proprietary
right to dictate how they will be used.
    —David Lehman; *Signs of the Times*, 1991

.49 We think because we have words, not the
other way around. The more words we have,
the better able we are to think conceptually.
    —Madeleine L'Engle; *Walking on Water*,
    1980

.50 Some words
bedevil me.
    —Audre Lorde; *Undersong*, "Coal," 1992

.51 How strangely do we diminish a thing as soon
as we try to express it in words.
    —Maurice Maeterlinck; *The Treasure of the
    Humble*, "Mystic Morality," Alfred Sutro,
    tr., 1896

# 310

.52 The word
   was born in the blood,
   grew in the dark body, beating,
   And flew through the lips and the mouth.
      —Pablo Neruda; *Plenos Poderes*, "La Pal-
      abra," 1962

.53 Every word is a preconceived judgement.
      —Freidrich Nietzsche; *Human, All Too
      Human*, 1878

.54 A trite word is an overused word which has
   lost its identity like an old coat in a second-
   hand shop. The familiar grows dull and we no
   longer see, hear, or taste it.
      —Anais Nin; *The Diary of Anais Nin*, Vol.
      5, 1974

.55 His word passeth not away.
      —Nu; *Papryus: Book of the Dead*, c. 4000
      B.C.

.56 Words differently arranged have a different
   meaning, and meanings differently arranged
   have different effects.
      —Blaise Pascal; *Pensees*, 1679

.57 He weigheth his words.
      —Pepi; *Papryus: Book of the Dead*, c. 4000
      B.C.

.58 A word to the wise is enough.
      —Plautus; *Persa*, c. 200 B.C.

.59 Far more effective [than books] is the spoken
   word. There is something in the voice, the
   countenance, the bearing, and the gesture of
   the speaker, that concur in fixing an impression upon the mind, deeper than can even vigorous writings.
      —Pliny the Younger; *Letters*, c. 1st. century
      A.D.

.60 A word unspoken is, like the sword in thy
   scabbard, thine; if vented, thy sword is in another's hand.
      —Francis Quarles; *Enchiridion*, 1640

.61 There is no greater impediment to the advancement of knowledge than the ambiguity
   of words.
      —Thomas Reid; *Essays on the Intellectual
      Powers of Man*, "Explication of Words,"
      1785

.62 Words once spoken cannot be recalled: but
   they may be contradicted by other words.
      —Samuel Richardson; *Clarissa Harlowe*,
      1747–48

.63 Never utter a word in private which you would
   regret to have heard in public.
      —Sa'Di; *Gulistan*, c. 1258

# 310

.64 Look out how you use proud words,
   When you let proud words go,
   It is not easy to call them back.
      —Carl Sandburg; *Primer Lesson*, 1920

.65 Words distract me more than noises, for words
   demand attention.
      —Seneca; *Ad Lucilium*, c. A.D. 65

.66 I understand the fury in your words,
   But not the words.
      —William Shakespeare; *Othello*, 1605

.67 Words, words, mere words, no matter from the
   heart.
      —William Shakespeare; *Troilus and Cres-
      sida*, 1601

.68 A fool and his words are soon parted.
      —William Shenstone; *On Reserve*, c.
      1763

.69 There are words that strike even harder than
   blows.
      —Samuel Smiles; *Character*, 1871

.70 Bright is the ring of words
   When the right man rings them,
   Fair the fall of songs
   When the singer sings them.
      —Robert Louis Stevenson; *Songs of Travel*,
      "If This Were Faith," 1887

.71 Fine words! I wonder where you stole them.
      —Jonathan Swift; *Polite Conversation*,
      1738

.72 That words have meaning is just the difficulty.
   That is why the poet has to turn and twist
   them in meter and verse, so that the meaning
   may be held in check, and the feeling allowed
   a chance to express itself.
      —Rabindranath Tagore; *My Reminiscences*,
      1917

.73 It is the man determines what is said, not the
   words.
      —Henry David Thoreau; *Journal*, July 11,
      1840

.74 For of all sad words of tongue or pen,
   The saddest are these: "It might have been!"
      —John Greenleaf Whittier; "Maud Mul-
      ler," 1856

.75 As though words could alter things.
      —Oscar Wilde; *The Picture of Dorian Gray*,
      1891

.76 A new word is like a fresh seed sown on the
   ground of the discussion.
      —Ludwig Wittgenstein; *Culture and Value*,
      1929

## 310

.77 The word-coining genius, as if thought plunged into a sea of words and came up dripping.
—Virginia Woolf; *The Common Reader*, "Notes on an Elizabethan Play," 1925 [Speaking of the merits of Elizabethan drama.]

.78 Words are always getting conventionalized to some secondary meaning. It is one of the works of poetry to take the truants in custody and bring them back to their right senses.
—W.B. Yeats; letter, February 3, 1889, in *Collected letters*, John Kelly, ed., 1986

# 311 The World

.1 Believe everything you hear said of the world; nothing is too impossibly bad.
—Honore de Balzac; *Comedie humaine*, 1842–48

.2 A myth is a fixed way of looking at the world which cannot be destroyed because, looked at through the myth, all evidence supports that myth.
—Edward de Bono; *Observer*, 1977

.3 The most incomprehensible thing about the world is that it is comprehensible.
—Albert Einstein; *Life Magazine*, 1950

.4 This is the way the world ends
Not with a bang but a whimper.
—T.S. Eliot; "The Hollow Men," 1925

.5 Shall I speak truly what I now see below?
The World is all a carcass, smoke and vanity,
The shadow of a shadow, a play
And in one word, just nothing.
—Owen Felltham; *Resolves*, 1696

.6 Half the world is composed of people who have something to say and can't, and the other half who have nothing to say and keep on saying it.
—Robert Frost, *Selected Letters*, L. Thompson, ed. 1965

.7 You can't reorder the world by talking to it.
—R. Buckminster Fuller; Quoted in *Contemporary Architects*, 1980

.8 The cynic says, "One man can't do anything." I say, "Only one man can do anything." One man interacting creatively with others can move the world.
—John W. Gardner; *Forbes*, 1977

## 311

.9 The world began without man, and it will complete itself without him.
—Claude Levi-Strauss; *Tristes Tropiques*, 1955

.10 We are told that when Jehovah created the world he saw that it was good. What would he say now?
—George Bernard Shaw; *Man and Superman*, "Maxims for Revolutionists," 1903

.11 We read the world wrong and say it deceives us.
—Rabindranth Tagore; *Gitanjali*, 1913

.12 We milk the cow of the world, and as we do
We whisper in her ear, "You are not true."
—Richard Wilbur; *Ceremony*, "Epistemology," 1950

.13 The world is a stage, but the play is badly cast.
—Oscar Wilde; *Lord Arthur Savile's Crime*, 1891

.14 The world is a funny paper read backwards—and that way it isn't so funny.
—Tennessee Williams; *The Observer*, 1957

# 312 Writers

.1 Every writer hopes or boldly assumes that his life is in some sense exemplary, that the particular will turn out to be universal.
—Martin Amis; *Observer*, London, August 30, 1987

.2 In Ireland, a writer is looked upon as a failed conversationalist.
—Anonymous

.3 If there is a category of human beings for whom his work ought to speak for itself, it is the writer.
—Isaac Asimov; *Contemporary Novelists*, 1976

.4 The responsibility of a writer its to excavate the experience of the people who produced him.
—James Baldwin; in conversation with Nikki Giovanni, November 4, 1971, London, published in *A Dialogue*, 1973

.5 For your born writer, nothing is so healing as the realization that he has come upon the right word.
—Catherine Drinker Bowen; *Adventures of a Biographer*, 1946

.6 I am a writer perhaps because I am not a talker.
—Gwendolyn Brooks; *Report from Part One*, 1972

## 312

.7 Authors before they write should read.
   —Fanny Burney; 1779, in *Diary and Letters of Madame D'Arblay*, Charlotte Bennett, ed. 1842

.8 The discipline of the writer is to learn to be still and listen to what his subject has to tell him.
   —Rachel Carson; Speech before American Association of University Women, June 22, 1956

.9 Most of the basic material a writer works with is acquired before the age of fifteen.
   —Willa Cather; in Rene Rapin, *Willa Cather*, 1930

.10 I think of an author as somebody who goes into the marketplace and puts down his rug and says, "I will tell you a story," and then he passes the hat.
   —Robertson Davies; *The Enthusiasms of Robertson Davies*, 1990

.11 The writer's language is to some degree the product of his own action; he is both the historian and the agent of his own language.
   —Paul de Man; *Blindness and Insight*, 1971

.12 I love being a writer. What I can't stand is the paperwork.
   —Peter De Vries; Attributed by Laurence J. Peter, 1977

.13 Writers should be read—but neither seen nor heard.
   —Daphne Du Maurier; Quoted in *The Wit of Women*, L. and M. Cowan, eds., 1969

.14 The novelist is the historian of the present. The historian is the novelist of the past.
   —Georges Duhamel; *Le Notaire du Havre*, 1933

.15 There are more truths in a good book than its author meant to put in it.
   —Marie von Ebner-Eschenbach; *Aphorisms*, 1893

.16 They're fancy talkers about themselves, writers. If I had to give young writers advice, I would say don't listen to writers talking about writing or themselves.
   —Lillian Hellman; *New York Times*, February 21, 1960

.17 The writer must write what he has to say, not speak it.
   —Ernest Hemingway; *Nobel Prize Speech*, 1954

## 312

.18 My function as a writer is not story-telling but truth-telling: to make things plain.
   —Laura Riding Jackson; *Progress of Stories*, 1935

.19 Every other author may aspire to praise; the lexicographer can only hope to escape reproach.
   —Samuel Johnson; *A Dictionary of the English Language*, "Preface," 1755

.20 A writer is someone who can make a riddle out of an answer.
   —Karl Kraus, in *Half-Truths and One-and-a Half Truths*, Heinrich Fischer, ed., 1955, Harry Zohn, tr., 1986

.21 A writer paradoxically seeks the truth and tells lies every step of the way.
   —Anne Lamont; *Bird by Bird*, 1994

.22 The great authors share their souls with us—"literally."
   —Ursula K. Le Guin; *Dancing at the Edge of the World*, "Where Do You Get Your Ideas From," 1989

.23 The role of the writer is not to say what we can all say, but what we are unable to say.
   —Anais Nin; 1954, *The Diary of Anais Nin*, Vol. 5, 1974

.24 An essayist is a lucky person who has found a way to discourse without being interrupted.
   —Charles Poore; *The New York Times*, May 31, 1962

.25 A good writer is basically a story-teller, not a scholar or a redeemer of mankind.
   —Isaac Bashevis Singer; *New York Times Magazine*, November 26, 1978

.26 Volume depends precisely on the writer's having been able to sit in a room every day, year after year, alone.
   —Susan Sontag; in *The New York Times Book Review*, 1986

.27 Every secret of a writer's soul, every experience of his life, every quality of his mind is written large in his works.
   —Virginia Woolf; *Orlando*, 1928

## 313 Writing

.1 A memorandum is written to protect the writer—not to inform the reader.
   —Dean Acheson; in the *Wall Street Journal*, September 8, 1977

.2 With pen and pencil we're learning to say Nothing, more clearly, every day.
   —William Allingham; "Blackberries," 1850

**313**

.3 It has been said that writing comes more easily if you have something to say.
—Sholem Asch; *New York Herald Tribune*, November 6, 1955

.4 Writing is an artificial activity. It is a lonely and private substitute for conversation.
—Brooks Atkinson; *Once Around the Sun*, "June 13," 1951

.5 It is a sad fact about our culture that a poet can earn more money writing or talking about his art than he can by practising it.
—W.H. Auden; *The Dyer's Hand*, "Foreword," 1963

.6 He writes dialogues by cutting monologues in two.
—Arthur "Bugs" Baer; Attributed

.7 To write is to make oneself the echo of what cannot cease speaking—and since it cannot, in order to become its echo I have, in a way, to silence it. I bring to this incessant speech the decisiveness, the authority of my own silence.
—Maurice Blanchot; *The Space of Literature*, 1955

.8 No one who cannot limit himself has ever been able to write.
—Nicolas Boileau-Despreaux; *L'Art Poetique*, 1674

.9 We speak naturally but spend all our lives trying to write naturally.
—Margaret Wise Brown; in Leonard S. Marcus, *Margaret Wise Brown*, 1992

.10 Less is more.
—Robert Browning; "Andrea del Sarto," 1855
[This became a popular aphorism of architect Ludwig Mies van der Rohe.]

.11 You don't write because you want to say something, you write because you have something to say.
—F. Scott Fitzgerald; *The Letters of F. Scott Fitzgerald*, Andrew Turnbull, ed. 1963

.12 Writing: I certainly do rewrite my central myth in every book, and would never read or trust any writer who did not also do so.
—Northrop Frye; *The Educated Imagination*, 1964

.13 Memoirs: the backstairs of history.
—George Meredith; *The Ordeal of Richard Feverel*, 1859

.14 I always write a good first line, but I have trouble in writing the others.
—Molière; *Les Precieuses Ridicules*, 1659

**313**

.15 One writes in order to feel.
—Muriel Rukeyser; *The Life of Poetry*, 1949

.16 Writing is a question of finding a certain rhythm. I compare it to the rhythms of jazz. Much of the time life is a sort of rhythmic progression of three characters. If one tells oneself that life is like that, one feels it less arbitrary.
—Francoise Sagan; interview, *Writers at Work*, Malcolm Cowley, ed. 1958

.17 You can't teach people to write well. Writing well is something God lets you do or declines to let you do.
—Kurt Vonnegut; *Wampeters, Foma, & Granfaloons*, 1974

.18 I never understand anything until I have written about it.
—Horace Walpole; *Letters*, W.S. Lewis et al, eds., 1937–81

.19 I put the words down and push them a bit.
—Evelyn Waugh; *The Essays, Articles and Reviews of Evelyn Waugh*, 1984

.20 Talent is helpful in writing, but guts are absolutely necessary.
—Jessamyn West; *The Woman Said Yes*, 1976

# **314** Youth

.1 The old repeat themselves and the young have nothing to say. The boredom is mutual.
—Jacques Bainville; *Lectures*, "Charme De La Conversation," 1937

.2 Oh, the soul keeps its youth!
—Amelia E. Barr; *The Belle of Bowling Green*, 1904

.3 Youth is the pollen
That blows through the sky
and does not ask why.
—Stephen Vincent Benet; *John Brown's Body*, 1928

.4 All my life I have worked with youth. I have begged for them and fought for them and lived for them and in them. My story is their story.
—Mary McLeod Bethune; Letter, c. 1920

.5 People are always talking about the joys of youth—but, oh, how youth can suffer!
—Willa Cather; *My Mortal Enemy*, 1926

.6 As long as you can still be disappointed, you are still young.
—Sarah Churchill; *The Observer*, 1981

**314**

.7 As I approve of a youth that has something of the old man in him, so I am no less pleased with an old man that has something of the youth. He that follows this rule may be old in body, but can never be so in mind.
—Cicero; *Old Age*, c. 1st century B.C.

.8 Youth is insolent; it is its right—its necessity; it has got to assert itself, and all assertion in this world of doubts is a defiance, is an insolence.
—Joseph Conrad; *Lord Jim*, 1900

.9 Youth is stranger than fiction.
—Marcelene Cox, in *Ladies Home Journal*, 1951

.10 You will stay young as long as you learn, form new habits and don't mind being contradicted.
—Marie von Ebner-Eschenbach; *Aphorisms*, 1893

.11 Cynicism is a sure sign of youth.
—Ellen Glasgow; *The Descendant*, 1897

.12 Grown people were always on the verge of telling you something valuable and then withdrawing it, a form of bully-teasing.
—Lillian Hellman; *Pentimento*, 1973

.13 A well-bred youth neither speaks of himself, nor, being spoken to, is silent.
—George Herbert; *Jacula Prudentum*, 1640

.14 Only the young die good.
—Oliver Herford; *Neither Here Nor There*, 1922

.15 Youth itself is a talent—a perishable talent.
—Eric Hoffer; *The Passionate State of Mind*, 1955

.16 You are young, gifted, and Black. We must begin to tell our young, There's a world waiting for you, Yours is the quest that's just begun.
—James Weldon Johnson; in Lorraine Hansberry *To Be Young, Gifted and Black*, 1959

.17 Ask the young: they know everything!
—Joseph Joubert; *Pensées*, 1842

.18 Even the youngest among us is not infallible.
—Benjamin Jowett; *Life and Letters of Benjamin Jowett*, Evelyn Abbott and Lewis Campbell, eds., 1897–9

.19 Fond youth flatters itself that all must heed its prayer.
—Jean de La Fontaine; *Fables*, "The Old Cat and the Young Mouse," 1668–94

.20 Youth is immortal;
'Tis the elderly only grow old!
—Herman Melville; *At the Hostelry*, "The Wise Virgins to Madam Mirror," 1925

**314**

.21 Youth has to do with spirit, not age. Men of seventy and eighty are often more youthful than the young. Theirs is the real youth.
—Henry Miller; "The Time of the Assassins," *The Henry Miller Reader*, Lawrence Durrell, ed., 1959

.22 Youth has a quickness of apprehension, which it is very apt to mistake for an acuteness or penetration.
—Hannah More; *Essays on Various Subjects*, "On the Danger of Sentimental or Romantic Connections," 1777

.23 I shall die very young ... maybe seventy, maybe eighty, maybe ninety. But I shall be very young.
—Jeanne Moreau; in Diana Vreeland, *D.V.*, 1984

.24 The response of teenagers to their idols is relevant. As an audience, they enjoy themselves, not by screaming with laughter, but screaming with screams.
—Desmond Morris; *The Human Zoo*, 1969

.25 It takes a long time to become young.
—Pablo Picasso; *Arts de France*, No. 6, 1946

.26 It's all the young can do for the old, to shock them and keep them up to date.
—George Bernard Shaw; *Fanny's First Play*, "Induction," 1912

.27 Don't laugh at youth for his affectations: he's only trying on one face after another till he finds his own.
—Logan Pearsall Smith; *Afterthoughts*, 1931

.28 What is more enchanting that the voices of young people when you can't hear what they say?
—Logan Pearsall Smith; *Afterthoughts*, 1931

.29 I must laugh and dance and sing,
Youth is such a lovely thing.
—Aline Thomas; "A Song of Youth," 20th century

.30 The deepest definition of youth is life as yet untouched by tragedy.
—Alfred North Whitehead; *Adventures of Ideas*, 1953

.31 Those whom the gods love grow young.
—Oscar Wilde; "A Few Maxims for the Instruction of the Over-Educated," *Saturday Review*, London, November 17, 1894

**314**

.32 The old believe everything, the middle-aged
suspect everything, the young know everything.
—Oscar Wilde; "Phrases and Philosophies
for the Use of the Young," 1891

**314**

.33 I was young and I learned by listening to my
elders and by drawing my own conclusions
through experience.
—Coleman Young; Quoted in *Detroit
News*, April 22, 1988

# Index of Authors

The number preceding the decimal refers to the topic; the number following the decimal locates the quotation within that topic.

Abbott, Sidney 211.1
Abelard, Pierre 227.1
Abrahams, Peter 232.1, 232.2, 270.1
Achebe, Chinua 203.1, 270.1
Acheson, Dean 313.1
Ackerman, Diane 116.1, 155.1, 160.1, 254.1
Ackroyd, Peter 191.1
Adams, Douglas 129.1
Adams, Franklin Pierce (F.P.A.) 249.1, 269.1
Adams, Henry Brooks 70.1, 119.1, 140.1, 206.1, 283.1
Adams, John 272.1
Adams, John Quincy 172.1, 293.1
Adams, Leonie 60.1
Adams, Oleta 265.1
Adams, Richard 71.1
Adams, Robert Martin 159.1
Adams, Thomas 171.1
Addison, Joseph 7.1, 7.2, 18.1, 30.1, 51.1, 74.1, 87.1, 87.2, 119.2, 148.1, 151.1, 164.1, 182.1, 225.1, 231.1, 243.1, 258.1, 270.2, 281.1, 296.1, 299.1
Ade, George 101.1, 109.1, 111.1, 140.2, 181.1, 220.1
Adebayo, Adesanya 218.1
Adler, Freda 82.1
Adler, Mortimer J. 231.2
Adler, Renata 180.1
Adorno, Theodor 83.1
Aeschylus 28.1, 38.1, 41.1, 46.1, 94.1, 107.1, 111.2, 142.1, 188.1, 194.1, 203.1, 246.1, 258.2, 281.2, 281.3, 282.1, 294.1, 298.1, 310.1
Aesop 26.1, 126.2, 143.1, 153.1, 222.1, 226.1, 232.3
African Proverb 72.1, 111.3, 168.1, 258.3
African Saying 224.1, 226.2
Agar, Herbert 298.2
Agassiz, Louis 252.1
Agee, James 148.2, 304.1
Agesilaus II 28.2
Aguilar, Grace 214.1
Ahikar 153.2, 179.1, 298.3, 310.2
Aiken, Conrad 156.1
Aiken, Joan 232.4, 270.3
Aird, Catherine 182.2
Akins, Zoe 191.2
Alain (Emile Auguste Chartier) 290.1, 290.2

Albo, Joseph 302.1
Alcott, A.B. (Amos Bronson) 65.1, 122.1, 123.1, 125.1, 228.1, 283.2, 292.1
Alcott, Louisa May 85.1, 105.1, 176.1, 239.1, 310.3
Alcuin 203.2, 306.4
Aldiss, Brian W. 252.2
Aldrich, Bess Streeter 129.2
Aldrich, Thomas Bailey 19.1, 22.2, 31.1, 36.1, 79.1, 262.1, 273.1, 305.1
Aldus (Manutius—Aldo Manuzio) 35.1
Alexander, Shana 246.2
Alfonso X, The Wise 300.1
Alger, William Rounseville 75.1
Allen, Arthur T. 158.1
Allen, Elizabeth Akers 292.2
Allen, Fred 229.1
Allen, James 291.1
Allen, Paula Gunn 116.2, 267.1
Allen, Woody 308.1
Allingham, Margery 305.2
Allingham, William 89.1, 313.2
Amen-Em-Apt 106.1, 268.1
Amenemope 250.1
American Anthropological Association 157.1
American Proverb 9.1, 22.1, 26.2, 181.2, 260.1, 276.1
Ames, E.S. 234.1
Amiel, Henri-Frederic 19.2, 124.1, 142.2, 284.1
Amis, Martin 312.1
Ammar, Hamed 38.2
Amory, Thomas 234.2
Anacharsis 294.2
Ancelet, Barry J. 197.1
Ancient Proverb 3.1
Andersch, Alfred 65.2, 270.4
Andersen, Hans Christian 90.1
Anderson, Brett 204.1
Anderson, Marian 21.1
Anderson, Mary 21.2
Anderson, Poul 218.2
Angelou, Maya 91.1, 147.1, 155.2, 158.2
Ani 12.1, 129.3, 153.3, 268.2, 294.3, 298.4
Anonymous 20.1, 22.3, 24.1, 25.1, 26.3, 29.1, 38.3, 47.1, 53.1, 68.1, 69.1, 82.2, 85.2, 97.1, 97.2, 97.3, 98.1, 101.2,

102.1, 105.2, 116.3, 117.1, 155.3, 156.2, 156.3, 164.2,
165.1, 172.2, 191.3, 196.1, 209.1, 210.1, 213.1, 213.2,
217.1, 224.2, 225.2, 235.1, 250.2, 253.1, 256.1, 265.2,
283.3, 291.2, 293.2, 294.4, 302.1, 310.4, 312.2
Anonymous African 278.1
Anonymous Cree Storyteller 270.5
Anouilh, Jean 155.4, 279.1
Antiphanes of Macedonia 109.2
Antisthenes 143.2, 206.2
Antrim, Minna Thomas 48.1, 126.1, 308.2
Appelfeld, Aharon 159.2
Appius Claudius 261.1
Applegate, Mauree 304.2
Apuleius 99.1
Arabian Proverb 87.3, 268.3
Arabic Saying 116.4
Arbuthnot, John 211.2
Arbuthnot, May Hill 98.2
Archias (Aulus Licinius) 35.2
Arendt, Hannah 148.3, 152.1, 166.1, 268.4, 291.3
Aretino, Pietro 298.5
Aristides 258.4
Aristophanes 28.3, 38.4, 57.1, 87.4, 180.3, 190.1, 205.1,
268.5
Aristotle 18.2, 18.3, 21.3, 38.5, 100.1, 145.1, 149.1, 151.2,
153.4, 153.5, 171.2, 196.2, 204.2, 205.2, 240.1, 259.1,
274.1, 296.2, 306.2, 307.1, 307.2
Arledge, Roone 287.1
Armenian Proverb 112.1
Armstrong, Louis (Satchmo) 97.5, 179.2
Arnold, Matthew 25.2, 60.2, 65.3, 208.1, 234.3, 283.4,
298.6
Artaud, Antonin 147.2, 161.1, 296.3
Asante, Molefi Kere 110.1, 271.1
Asch, Sholem 313.3
Ascham, Roger 213.3, 241.1, 290.3
Ashbery, John 181.4
Ashliman, D.L. 98.3
Asimov, Isaac 300.2, 312.3
Asquith, Margot 172.3, 246.3, 270.6, 278.2
Atherton, Gertrude 127.1, 207.1, 210.2
Atkinson, Brooks 191.4, 313.4
Atkinson, Tri-Grace 298.7
Attali, Jacques 189.1
Attlee, Clement 67.1, 175.1
Atwood, Margaret 90.2, 90.3, 106.2, 208.2
Aubrey, John 269.2
Auden, W.H. (Wystan Hugh) 42.1, 54.1, 90.4, 98.4,
116.5, 126.3, 148.4, 156.4, 167.1, 181.5, 208.3, 209.2,
219.1, 219.2, 225.3, 227.2, 231.3, 289.1, 313.5
August, Karl Friedrich 206.3
Augustine, Saint of Hippo 157.2
Aung San, Sun Kyi 64.1
Aulus Gellius 5.1
Aurelius, Marcus 128.1, 189.2
Austen, Jane 21.4, 46.2, 51.2, 74.2, 76.1, 96.2, 111.4,
116.6, 138.1, 140.3, 148.5, 158.3, 189.3, 211.12, 230.1,
244.1, 256.2, 276.2, 277.1, 281.2, 309.1
Auster, Paul 186.1
Austin, Mary 265.3
Ayckbourn, Alan 248.1
Ayer, Alfred Jules 68.2, 255.1

Babylonia Talmud Arachin 261.2
Babylonian Talmud Berachoth 257.1, 294.5
Babylonian Talmud Kethuboth 72.2

Babylonian Talmud Kiddushin 226.3, 309.2
Babylonian Talmud Megillah 309.3
Babylonian Talmud Nedarim 125.2
Babylonian Talmud Sanhedrin 153.6
Bachelard, Gaston 208.4
Bachmann, Ingeborg 93.1
Bacon, Francis 6.1, 13.1, 14.1, 14.2, 16.1, 18.4, 30.2, 49.1,
59.1, 83.2, 87.5, 99.2, 101.3, 139.1, 145.2, 172.4, 172.5,
174.1, 185.1, 187.1, 187.2, 203.3, 206.4, 213.4, 224.3,
227.3, 231.4, 249.2, 262.3, 268.6, 272.2, 282.2, 295.1,
299.2, 303.1, 310.5
Baer, Arthur "Bugs" 225.4, 313.6
Baez, Joan 227.4
Bagehot, Walter 123.2, 165.2, 268.7, 283.5
Bahr, Hermann 209.3
Bailey, F. Lee 150.1
Bailey, Nathan 282.3
Bailey, P.J. (Philip James) 5.2, 127.2, 209.4
Bailey, Pearl 158.4
Bainbridge, Beryl 109.3
Bainville, Jacques 314.1
Baker, Anita 212.1
Baker, Russell 287.2
Baldwin, Christina 169.1
Baldwin, James 38.6, 114.1, 152.2, 152.3, 161.2, 264.1,
272.3, 312.4
Baldwin, Stanley 207.2
Ball, George W. 191.5
Ball, Hugo 278.3
Ballantyne, Sheila 91.2
Ballard, J.G. (James Graham) 232.5
Ballou, Hoseau 38.7
Balzac, Honore de 29.2, 106.3, 137.1, 164.3, 181.6, 311.1
Bambara, Toni Cade 155.5, 168.2, 270.7
Bangs, Lester 204.4
Bankhead, Tallulah 4.1, 288.1
Banning, Margaret Culkin 309.4
Barnham, Rev. Richard Harris (Thomas Ingoldsby)
40.1, 103.1, 109.4
Baring, Maurice 21.5
Barker, Howard 21.6
Barker, Ronnie 69.2
Barkley, Alben W. 21.7
Barnes, Djuna 160.2, 290.4
Barr, Amelia Edith 20.2, 44.1, 95.1, 262.4, 292.3, 314.2
Barrere, Albert 262.2
Barres, Maurice 210.4
Barrett, Lawrence 4.2
Barrie, Sir J.M. (James Matthew) 86.1, 89.2, 89.3, 89.4,
145.3, 155.6, 163.1, 282.4, 290.5, 307.3, 309.5
Barry, Lynda 125.3
Barry, Philip 294.6
Barrymore, Ethel 4.3
Barth, Alan 261.5
Barth, John 270.8
Barth, Karl 289.2
Barthes, Roland 160.3, 183.1, 212.2, 248.2
Bartok, Bela 97.4
Baruch, Bernard 88.1, 111.2, 172.6, 210.5
Barzun, Jacques 44.2, 126.4, 155.7, 232.6, 296.4
Bashkirtseff, Marie 114.2
Bateson, Mary Catherine 130.1
Baudelaire, Charles 13.2, 278.4
Baudrillard, Jean 132.1, 210.6, 287.3
Bauer, Gerard 305.3
Bayle, Pierre 197.2, 295.2

Bayly, T.H. (Nathaniel Thomas Haynes) 13.3, 23.1, 265.4

Beard, Mary Ritter 309.6

Beaton, Cecil 31.2

Beattie, Ann 44.3

Beattie, James 281.4

Beaumarchais, Pierre-Augustin Caron de 18.5, 148.6, 265.5

Beaumont, Francis 34.1

Beauveau, Marie-Francise-Catherine de 34.2

Beauvoir, Simone de 192.1

Beckett, Samuel 161.3, 258.5, 310.6

Beddoes, Thomas Lovell 71.2

Beecher, Henry Ward 30.3, 145.4, 154.1, 158.5, 178.1, 203.4, 213.5, 216.1 268.8, 289.3, 298.8, 310.7

Beecher, Lyman 75.2

Beerbohm, Sir Max 50.1, 71.3, 91.3, 130.2, 206.5, 228.2, 267.2

Beethoven, Ludwig van 111.5

Behn, Aphra 160.4

Bell, Ralcy Husted 262.3

Belli, Melvin 150.2

Belloc, Hilaire 31.3, 76.2, 221.1, 241.2, 265.5

Belt, Harry H. 40.2

Ben Sira 224.4, 226.4, 261.6, 294.7

Benchley, Robert 1.1, 78.1, 140.4, 192.2

Benedict, Ruth 207.3

Benet, Stephen Vincent 75.3, 152.4, 314.3

Benjamin, Walter 145.5, 271.2, 271.3, 271.4

Bennett, Alan 57.2

Bennett, Emerson 187.3

Bennett, Gwendolyn A. 173.1

Benson, Robert Hugh 46.3

Bentham, Jeremy 223.1

Bentley, E.C. (Edmund Clerihew) 236.1

Bentley, Eric 92.1, 138.2

Bentley, Richard 157.3

Berardin de Saint-Pierre, Jacques-Henri 111.6

Berdyaev, Nicholas 183.2

Berger, John Peter 199.1, 231.5

Bergman, Ingrid 144.1

Berkeley, Bishop George 46.4, 117.2, 202.1

Berlin, Sir Isaiah 26.4, 300.3

Berlioz, Hector 292.4

Bernandos, Georges 291.4

Bernard, Claude 195.1, 252.3

Bernard, St. 283.6

Bernard, Tristan 21.8

Bernstein, Leonard 181.7

Besant, Annie 183.3

Beston, Henry 11.1, 267.3

Bethune, Mary McLeod 314.4

Betjeman, Sir John 234.4

Bettelheim, Bruno 90.5, 90.6, 91.4

Betti, Ugo 291.5

Bhartihari 114.3

Bibesco, Elizabeth 146.1, 204.5

Bierce, Ambrose 15.1, 17.1, 31.4, 33.1, 34.3, 66.1, 67.2, 74.3, 103.2, 115.1, 116.7, 150.3, 151.3, 184.1, 196.3, 206.6, 217.2, 228.3, 304.3, 307.4

Bigelow, Hilda 93.2

Billings, Josh (Henry Wheeler Shaw) 34.4, 46.5, 54.2, 75.4, 83.3, 99.3, 119.3, 119.4, 125.4, 140.5, 148.7, 154.2, 225.5, 258.6, 260.2, 261.7, 275.1, 282.5, 307.5

Bing, Rudolf 305.4

Birdseye, George 80.1

Birkenhead, 1st Earl of 130.3

Birkett, Lord 269.3

Birnbach, Lisa 58.1

Birney, Earle 232.7

Bishop, Morris 1.2, 156.5

Blackmore, R.D. (Richard Dodderidge) 249.3

Blake, William 24.2, 24.3, 38.8, 101.4, 127.3, 131.1, 266.1, 292.5, 298.9 298.10, 305.5

Blanchot, Maurice 313.7

Blanton, Smiley 56.1

Blessington, Countess of (Lady Marguerite) 31.5, 43.1, 96.3, 127.4, 172.7 291.6

Blinder, Alan 12.2

Bloom, Allan 12.3, 116.8, 145.6

Bly, Carol 42.2

Boardman, George Dana 216.2

Bocca, Geoffrey 307.6

Boccaccio, Giovanni 94.2, 250.2

Bodenham, John 266.2

Boerne, Ludwig 31.6

Bogan, Louise 171.3

Bogus, S. Diane 178.2

Bohn, H.G. (Henry George) 18.6, 25.3, 153.7, 165.3, 206.7, 281.5, 282.6, 290.6, 294.8, 307.7, 310.8

Bohr, Niels 227.5

Boileau (Despreaux), Nicolas 40.3, 237.1, 241.3, 249.4, 268.9, 313.8

Bombeck, Erma 158.6

Bone, W.A. 281.6

Bonhoeffer, Dietrich 174.2, 234.5, 298.11

Bonnefoy, Yves 191.6

Bonner, Anthony 159.3

Bonsenyor, Judah 12.4

Book of Common Prayer 258.7

Book of the Dead 268.10

Boorstein, Daniel J. 74.4

Booth, Shirley 4.4

Boothe, Clare (Luce) 154.3, 210.22

Borges, Jorge Luis 159.4, 183.4, 228.4

Borland, Hal 71.4

Borrow, George 73.1

Boswell, James 225.6

Bottome, Phyllis 154.4

Boucicault, Dion 292.6

Bovee, Christian Nestell 31.7, 53.1, 70.2, 142.3, 307.8

Bowdler, Thomas 82.3

Bowen, Catherine Drinker 181.8, 219.3, 312.5

Bowen, Elizabeth 38.9, 123.3, 147.3, 258.8, 258.9

Brabazon, Lord (Derek Charles Moore-Brabazon) 30.4

Brackenridge Hugh Henry 75.5, 75.6, 117.3, 165.4, 168.3, 172.8, 176.2, 177.1, 210.7, 224.5, 233.1, 239.2

Bradbury, Malcolm Stanley 151.4

Bradford, John 216.3

Bradlee, Ben C. 188.5

Bradley, F.H. (Francis Herbert) 14.3, 14.4, 80.2

Bradley, Shelland 41.2

Brahms, Johannes 135.1

Braley, Berton 109.5

Brandeis, Louis D. 88.2, 290.7

Bratzlav, Nahman 263.1

Braude, Jacob M. 268.11

Brautigan, Richard 76.3

Brecht, Bertolt 283.7

Brenan, Gerald 31.8, 42.3, 151.5, 281.7

Bresson, Robert 180.2

Breton, Andre 310.9

Breton, Nicholas 23.2
Brewer, J. Mason 158.7, 159.5
Brice, Fanny 21.9, 204.6
Bridges, Thomas 114.4, 275.2
Brien, Alan 236.2
Brinstead, Arthur 174.3
Brittain, Vera 211.4
Broadhurst 213.6
Brock, H.I. 156.6
Broder, David 210.8
Brokaw, Tom 271.6
Bronte, Anne 116.9
Bronte, Charlotte 36.2, 38.10, 82.4, 87.6, 148.8, 161.4,
    168.4, 182.3, 186.2, 187.4, 217.3, 298.12
Brooke, Frances Moore 196.4
Brookner, Anita 95.2, 244.2
Brooks, Charles S. 307.9
Brooks, Gwendolyn 208.5, 208.6, 312.6
Brooks, Louise 4.5, 9.2
Brooks, Phyllis 155.8
Broonzy, Big Bill 97.5
Brother Blue 112.3, 127.5, 145.7, 212.3
Brothers, Goncourt 273.2
Brothers, Joyce 96.4
Broun, Heywood 152.5, 236.3
Brown, Abbie Farwell 89.4
Brown, Claude 278.5
Brown, Craig 140.6
Brown, Himan 229.2
Brown, Margaret Wise 38.11, 313.9
Brown, Rita Mae 108.1, 119.5, 159.6, 237.2
Browne, Sir Thomas 13.4, 54.3, 68.3, 141.1, 205.3,
    222.2, 306.3
Browning, Elizabeth Barrett 160.5, 196.5, 257.2, 281.6
Browning, Robert 1.3, 19.3, 24.4, 60.3, 72.3, 142.4,
    172.9, 185.2, 202.2, 219.4, 250.3, 270.9, 279.2, 291.7,
    298.13, 313.10
Bruce, Lenny 249.5
Bruner, Jerome Seymour 49.2, 275.3
Brunetiere, Ferdinand 296.5
Bruno, Giordano 162.1
Brustein, Robert 288.2
Bryan, William Jennings 198.1
Bryant, Sara Cone 271.7
Bryant, William Cullen 187.5
Buber, Martin 11.2, 145.8, 183.5
Buchan, John 74.5
Buck, Pearl S. 44.4, 213.7
Budapest, Zsuzsanna E. 184.2
Buffon, Comte de 274.2
Bulgakov, Mikhail 118.1
Bultmann, Rudolf 184.3
Bulwer-Lytton, Edward George (Lord Lytton) 36.3,
    96.5, 119.6, 145.9, 155.9, 162.2, 175.2, 188.2, 201.1,
    202.3, 205.4, 223.2, 259.2, 282.8, 294.9
Bunner, Henry Cuyler 228.5
Bunyan, John 106.4, 120.1, 172.10, 199.2, 214.2, 260.3,
    261.8
Burckhardt, Johann L. 5.3, 28.4, 85.3
Burdette, Robert Joseph 202.4
Burger, Warren E. 150.4
Burgess, Gelett 83.4, 190.2, 225.7, 243.2
Burgess, Mrs. W.S. 156.7
Burke, Edmund 46.6, 135.2, 233.2, 306.4
Burney, Fanny 29.3, 56.2, 57.3, 140.7, 145.10, 165.5,
    249.6, 307.10, 312.7

Burnham, G.P. 35.3
Burnham, Sophie 10.1
Burns, George 308.3
Burns, Robert 138.3, 305.6
Burroughs, William 195.2
Burt, Struthers 148.9
Burton, John 27.1
Burton, Richard 82
Burton, Robert 5.4, 93.3, 99.4, 150.5, 245.1, 281.8
Butler, Samuel I 34.5, 46.7, 63.1, 68.4, 118.2, 190.3,
    190.4, 194.2, 202.5, 240.2, 241.4, 297.1, 303.2, 307.11
Butler, Samuel II 8.1, 15.2, 49.3, 61.1, 62.1, 68.5, 70.3,
    115.2, 137.2, 153.8, 153.9, 192.3, 196.6, 213.8, 252.4,
    273.3, 280.1, 291.8
Buzurchimihr 250.4
Byrom, John 37.1
Byron, Lord (George Gordon) 1.4, 6.2, 10.2, 17.2, 25.4,
    31.9, 64.2, 86.2, 120.2, 140.8, 145.11, 158.8, 171.4, 176.3,
    185.3, 222.3, 222.4, 223.3, 225.8, 228.6, 240.3, 241.5,
    247.1, 248.3, 271.8, 281.9, 293.3, 298.14, 303.3, 305.7
Byron, Mary G.C. 89.6

Cable, George Washington 187.6
Caesar Augustus 17.3
Cage, John 189.4, 208.7, 258.10
Cahier, Charles 84.1, 150.6, 258.11, 265.6, 290.7, 294.10
Calas, Nicolas 19.4
Caldwell, Erskine 271.9
Caldwell, Taylor 137.3
Calisher, Hortense 310.10
Callas, Maria 265.7
Callimachus 129.4, 132.2, 160.6
Calverley, Charles Stuart 23.3
Calvino, Italo 103.3, 159.7, 183.6, 249.7, 281.10
Cam, Helen M. 95.3
Campbell, George 109.6
Campbell, Joseph 85.4, 90.7, 98.5, 114.5, 155.10, 183.7,
    183.8, 184.4
Campbell, Thomas 129.5, 281.11
Camus, Albert 18.7, 60.4, 189.5
Canby, Vincent 229.3
Canetti, Elias 11.3, 14.5, 255.2, 258.12, 310.11
Capra, Frank 180.3
Carew, Thomas 209.5
Carey, Peter 166.2, 255.3
Carlin, Jerome E. 150.7
Carlyle, Jane Welsh 279.3
Carlyle, Thomas 1.5, 14.6, 26.5, 26.6, 27.2, 48.2, 62.1,
    80.3, 114.6, 116.10, 116.11, 124.2, 148.10, 157.4, 171.5,
    171.6, 181.9 182.4, 210.9, 219.5, 240.4, 248.4, 258.13,
    258.14, 265.8, 273.4, 278.6, 296.6, 300.4
Carmichael, Alexander 271.10
Carmody, Denise Lardner 106.5
Carneige, Dale 18.8, 76.4, 217.4
Carney, Julia Fletcher 142.5
Carroll, Lewis (Charles Dodgson) 26.7, 30.5, 32.1, 53.2,
    56.3, 86.3, 90.8, 140.9, 166.3, 166.4, 169.2, 176.4,
    185.4, 208.8, 208.9, 267.4, 271.11, 275.4, 279.4, 289.4,
    298.15, 310.12
Carson, Rachel 312.8
Carter, Angela Olive 43.2, 107.2, 183.9, 204.7, 300.5
Caruthers, William Alexander 208.10
Casson, Hugh Maxwell 270.10
Catullus 309.7
Cather, Willa 226.5, 237.3, 248.5, 265.9, 270.11, 305.8,
    312.9, 314.5

Catlin, Wynn 66.2
Cato (Dionysius) 26.8, 96.6, 294.11, 298.16
Cato, Marcus Porcius (The Elder) 198.2, 275.5
Cavendish, Margaret 188.3
Calverley, Charles Stuart 241.6
Cavour, Benso di 66.3
Centlivre Susannah 117.4, 238.1
Cerf, Bennett 148.11
Certeau, Michel de 26.9, 167.2
Cervantes, Miguel de 4.6, 36.4, 41.3, 45.1, 104.1, 117.5,
    139.3, 147.4, 216.4, 224.6, 224.7, 273.5, 280.2, 298.17,
    299.3, 307.12
Chambers, Robert 82.5
Chamfort, Sebastien Nicolas Roche De 148.12, 160.7,
    251.1, 264.2, 307.13
Champion, S.G. (Selwyn Gurney) 28.5, 111.7, 125.5,
    224.8
Chandler, Raymond 90.9, 262.4, 270.112
Chanel, Coco 152.6
Chang Chao 30.6
Channing, William Ellery 129.6
Chaplin, Charles 155.11, 180.4
Chapman, Robert William 228.7
Charles I 15.3
Charles V, Holy Roman Emperor 147.5
Charles, Elizabeth 145.12
Chase, Alexander 169.3
Chase, Ilka 21.10
Chase, Richard 30.7
Chatfield, Paul 251.2
Chaucer, Geoffrey 163.2, 176.5, 179.3, 281.12, 281.13,
    281.14, 281.15, 284.3, 292.7, 296.7, 309.8
Cheales, A.B. (Alan Benjamin) 112.4
Cheever, John 257.3
Chesterfield, Lord (Philip Dormer Stanhope) 5.5, 6.3,
    13.5, 14.7, 15.4, 34.6, 37.2, 46.8, 75.7, 135.3, 140.10,
    147.6, 153.10, 158.9, 159.8, 165.6, 205.5, 253.2, 261.9,
    270.13 274.3 296.8, 301.1, 306.5, 308.4, 309.9, 310.13
Chesterton, G.K. (Gilbert Keith) 18.9, 19.5, 31.10, 39.1,
    89.7, 95.4, 131.2, 140.11, 140.12, 145.13, 159.9, 171.7,
    187.7, 200.1, 226.6, 236.4, 262.5, 262.6, 295.3
Cheney, John Vance 173.2
Child, Julia 84.2
Chilon 291.9
Chinese Proverb 30.8, 51.3, 85.5, 128.2, 147.7, 185.5,
    205.6, 227.6, 269.4, 283.8
Chinweizu 110.2, 116.12, 203.5, 270.13
Choate, Joseph H. 214.3
Choerilus 24.5
Chomsky, Noam 147.8, 157.5, 157.6, 167.3, 222.5
Chopin, Kate 126.5
Chou En-Lai 66.4
Christie, Agatha 20.3, 76.5, 153.11, 298.18
Chuang-tzu (Chuang Tse) 123.4, 145.14, 147.9, 306.6
Churchill, Charles 165.7, 177.2, 198.3, 255.4, 285.1
Churchill, Sarah 314.6
Churchill, Winston 49.4, 66.5, 165.8, 220.2, 228.8,
    242.1, 310.14
Cibber, Colley 249.8
Cicero (Marcus Tullius) 18.10, 18.11, 26.10, 26.11, 34.7,
    51.4, 75.8, 75.9, 100.2, 107.3, 116.13, 125.6, 142.6,
    149.2, 190.5, 198.4, 222.6, 264.3, 294.12, 301.2, 314.7
Cioran, Emile M. 51.6
Clarke, John 188.4, 265.10, 268.12, 268.13, 272.4, 300.6
Clarke, John Henrik 77.1, 283.9
Claudel, Paul 303.4

Claudian 107.4
Cleaver, Elridge 107.5, 218.3, 309.10
Clement of Alexandria 214.4
Cobb, Irvin S. 63.2, 119.7, 169.4
Cobb, Richard 65.4, 116.14
Cockburn, Claud 249.9
Cockton, Henry 282.9
Cocteau, Jean 19.6, 65.5, 116.15, 153.12, 159.10, 209.6,
    241.7, 274.4, 280.3, 296.9, 298.19
Cody, Liza 135.4
Cohen, John 57.4
Cohen, Leonard 214.5
Cohen, Morris 283.10
Coke, Sir Edward 18.12
Colby, Frank Moore 31.11, 119.8, 249.10
Coleridge, Mary 282.10
Coleridge, Samuel Taylor 24.6, 24.7, 71.5, 80.4, 92.2,
    95.5, 131.3, 139.4 150.8, 158.10, 165.9, 189.6, 194.3,
    202.6, 222.7 223.4, 265.11, 267.5, 281.16, 294.13,
    298.20, 307.14
Colette (Sidonie Gabrielle Colette) 119.9, 181.10, 209.7
Collins, Chase 281.17
Collins, Mortimer 13.6
Collins, Wilkie 99.5, 131.4, 223.5, 301.3, 309.11, 310.15
Collins, William 89.8
Colman, George the Younger 258.15
Colton, C.C. (Charles Caleb) 128.3, 133.1, 158.11, 202.7,
    219.6, 240.5
Coltrane, John 181.11
Colvil, Samuel 281.18
Colwin, Laurie 108.2
Colyer, Mary 57.5
Colton, C.C. (Charles Caleb) 5.6, 17.4, 30.9, 192.4,
    217.5, 226.7, 238.2, 282.11, 301.4
Colwell, Eileen 271.12
Combe, William 225.9
Comte, Auguste 252.5
Comtesse Diane (Marie Josephine de Suin de Beausacq)
    54.4
Confucius (K'ung fu-tzu) 3.2, 13.7, 40.4, 145.15, 145.16,
    147.10, 245.2, 291.10
Congreve, William 160.8, 164.4, 202.8, 208.11, 251.3,
    253.2, 254.3, 290.8, 297.2, 299.4, 309.12
Connolly, Cyril 39.2, 164.5, 252.6, 306.7
Conrad, Joseph (Tedor Josef Konrad Korzeniowski)
    88.3, 88.4, 126.6, 205.7 212.4, 232.8, 282.12, 292.8,
    301.5, 310.16, 314.8
Conway, M.D. (Moncure Daniel) 163.3
Cook, Eliza 58.2, 122.2
Cooke, Alistair 229.4
Coolidge, Calvin 237.4
Cooper, James Fenimore 51.7, 120.3, 214.6, 246.5,
    270.14
Coover, Robert Lowell 186.3
Corneille, Pierre 135.5, 194.4, 266.3
Cornford, F.M. 221.2
Cornish Prayer 103.4
Corry, John 305.9
Cosby, Bill 5.7
Cotgrave, Randle 37.3
Cotton, Charles 298.21
Coupland, Douglas 169.5
Cousins, Norman 148.13
Coward, Noel 307.15
Cowley, Abraham 213.9, 285.2
Cowley, Hannah 25.5, 225.10

Cowper, William 17.5, 27.3, 138.4, 164.6, 189.7, 257.4, 267.6, 277.2, 281.19, 310.17
Cox, Coleman 2.1
Cox, Harvey 256.3
Cox, Marcelene 253.3, 290.9, 314.9
Cozzens, F.S. (Frederick Swartwout) 224.9
Crabbe, George 7.3, 91.5, 165.10
Craik, Dinah Mulock 26.12
Cranch, Christopher Pearse 76.6
Crane, Stephen 163.4, 187.8
Cranmer, Thomas 281.20
Crashaw, Richard 87.7
Cratinus 24.8
Crawford, Frances Marion 164.7, 264.4
Crisp, Quentin 82.6, 149.3, 153.13
Crist, Judith 180.5
Croce, Benedetto 127.6
Cromwell, Olvier 301.6
Cross, Amanda 150.9
Crowley, Aleister 244.3
Cummings, E.E. (Edward Estlin) 145.17, 210.10, 227.7, 300.7
Cuomo, Mario 210.11
Curran, John Philpot 171.8
Cutting, Bronson 219.7
Czech Proverb 260.4

Dahlberg, Edward 161.5
Daley, Richard J. 207.4
Dalmon, Charles 103.5
Dana, Charles A. 103.6
Dana, John Cotton 271.13, 284.4
Daniel, Samuel 1.6, 240.6
Daninos, Pierre 102.2
Danish Proverb 68.6, 112.5, 150.10, 250.5, 258.16, 266.4
Dante Alighieri 37.4, 158.12, 303.5
Darling, Charles John 47.2, 48.3
Darnton, Robert 90.10, 98.6
Darrow, Clarence 290.10
Darwin, Charles Robert 19.7, 187.9
Daumal, Rene 310.18
Davenport, Robert 144.2
Davidson, John 176.6
Davies, John 129.7
Davies, Robertson 154.5, 228.9, 312.10
Davis, Bette 4.7, 308.5
Davis, Dorothy Salisbury 116.16
Davis, Miles 152.7, 299.5
Davis, Rebecca Harding 209.8
Davis, Tony 97.6
Day, Clarence 30.10, 90.12, 176.7, 219.8
Day, Doris 309.13
Day, Dorothy 295.4
Day, John 83.5
Day, Lillian 14.8, 146.2
de Bono, Edward 119.10, 183.10, 311.2
De Forest, John W. 164.8
de France, Marie 75.10, 271.14, 310.19
De Gaulle, Charles 210.12, 258.17
De Goncourt, Jules 219.9
De La Mare, Walter 71.6, 281.21
de Man, Paul 60.5, 147.11, 171.9, 312.11
De Mello, Anthony 270.15
De Mille, Agnes 59.2, 204.8
De Morgan, Augustus 27.4
DePalma, Brian 180.6

De Sales, St. Francis 34.8, 215.1
De Sica, Vittorio 131.5
De Vries, Peter 31.12, 50.2, 80.5, 164.9, 210.13, 312.12
Dean, Robert G. 248.6
Debord, Guy 228.10
Debs, Eugene V. 269.5
Defoe, Daniel 216.5, 233.3
Degh, Linda 98.7, 271.15
Dekker, Thomas 153.14, 293.4
Delacroix, Eugene 275.6
Deland, Margaret 230.2
Delius, Frederick 181.12
Deloney, Thomas 294.14
Demacatus 99.6
Demieville, Paul 159.11
Demosthenes 3.3
Denning, Lord 66.6
Dennis, John 225.11
Deor 173.3
Descartes, Rene 30.11, 68.7, 70.4, 206.8, 290.11, 310.20
Dewar, Thomas Robert 140.13
Dewey, John 74.6, 284.5
Dhammapada 291.12, 310.21
Dhery, Robert 288.3
Dibdin, Charles 293.5
Didacus Stella 104.2
Dick, Philip K. 306.8
Dickens, Charles 18.13, 56.4, 82.7, 90.13, 123.5, 124.3, 127.7, 132.3, 138.5, 170.1, 176.8, 209.9, 219.10, 246.5, 249.11, 259.3 277.3, 281.22, 294.15, 297.3, 302.3, 310.22
Dickinson, Emily 36.5, 64.3, 127.8, 258.18, 276.3, 277.4, 277.5, 298.22, 310.23
Diderot, Denis 282.13, 289.5, 298.23
Didion, Joan 155.12
Dietrich, Marlene 160.9
Diez, Friedrich 306.9
Diffrient, Niels 286.1
Dillard, Annie 187.10, 226.8
Dillon, Wentworth 82.8, 209.10
Dimner, Ernest 141.2
Dimond, William 140.14
Dinesen, Isak (Karen Blixen) 19.8, 124.4, 258.19, 266.5, 270.16, 270.17, 271.16, 299.6
Diodorus of Sicily 24.9
Diogenes 210.14
Dionysius the Elder 258.20
Diop, Birago 110.3, 158.13
Disraeli, Benjamin 9.3, 15.5, 18.14, 18.15, 26.13, 31.13, 37.5, 46.9, 51.8, 75.11, 75.12, 86.4, 109.7, 114.7, 125.7, 143.3, 154.6, 196.7, 211.5, 227.8, 236.5, 240.7, 248.7, 258.21, 275.7, 280.4, 291.12, 298.24, 301.7, 302.4, 305.10, 310.24
D'Israeli, Isaac 228.11
Dixon, C. Madeleine 134.1
Dobie, J. Frank 271.17
Dobson, Austin 292.9
Doctorow, E.L. (Edgar Lawrence) 116.17, 186.4
Dodsley, Robert 144.3
Donaldson, William 217.6
Donne, John 60.6, 151.6, 160.10, 170.2, 174.4, 260.6
Doolittle, Hilda 137.4
Doolittle, Justus 165.11, 179.4
Dostoyevsky, Fyodor 44.5, 148.14, 248.8
Dougall, Lily 289.6
Douglas, George 14.9

Douglass, Frederick  271.18
Dove, Rita  9.4, 185.6
Dow, Lorenzo  27.5
Doyle, Arthur Conan  116.18
Drabble, Margaret  228.12
Draxe, Thomas  181.13, 281.23, 292.10, 294.16, 307.16
Dreiser, Theodore  39.3, 147.12, 310.25
Dryden, John  13.8, 18.16, 23.4, 27.6, 59.3, 62.2, 79.2,
    105.3, 107.6, 127.9, 149.4, 176.9, 190.6, 196.8, 249.12,
    281.24, 282.14, 290.12, 298.25, 305.11, 307.17
Du Bois, W.E.B. (William Edward Burghardt)  148.15,
    305.12
Du Maurier, Daphne  312.13
Ducey, Jean Sparks  158.14
Dudek, Louis  14.10
Duhamel, Georges  312.14
Dumas, Alexandre  214.7
Dumas, Alexandre (Fils)  101.5
Dumas, Henry  209.11
Dunbar, Paul Laurence  121.1
Duncan, Isadora  74.7, 309.14
Dundes, Alan  98.8
Dundy, Elaine  4.8
Dunham, Barrows  126.7
Dunn, Katherine  147.13
Dunne, Finley Peter ("Mr. Dooley")  26.14, 57.6, 63.3,
    198.5, 198.6, 222.8
Duran, Fray Diego  87.8
Durant, Ariel  184.5
Durant, Will  66.7, 74.8, 177.3, 184.5, 192.5
Durrell, Lawrence  127.10, 144.4, 298.26
Durrenmatt, Friedrich  49.5, 232.9, 291.13
Dutch Proverb  224.10
Dvorak, Antonin  97.7
Dworkin, Andrea  90.14, 108.3
Dylan, Bob  97.8, 97.9

Early, Eleanor  82.9
Eastman, Max  236.6
Eban, Abba  210.15
Eberhart, Richard  274.5
Ebner-Eschenbach, Marie von  14.11, 50.3, 301.8, 312.15,
    314.10
Eco, Umberto  114.8
Edgeworth, Maria  31.14, 228.13
Edison, Thomas Alva  145.18, 290.13
Edwards, Richard  166.5
Edwards, Tyron  87.9
Egyptian Verse  160.11
Ehrmann, Max  158.15
Einstein  Albert  56.5, 91.6, 127.11, 252.7, 276.4, 283.11,
    311.3
Ekken, Kaibara  268.14
Eliade, Mircea  183.11
Eliot, George (Mary Ann Evans)  8.2, 11.4, 18.17, 25.6,
    36.6, 73.2, 104.3, 108.4, 111.8, 127.12, 140.15, 141.3,
    169.6, 171.10, 187.11, 196.9, 200.2, 222.9, 226.9, 230.3,
    243.3, 245.3, 256.4, 258.12, 262.7, 268.15, 279.5,
    291.14, 292.11, 298.27, 301.9, 309.15, 310.26
Eliot, T.S. (Thomas Stearns)  27.7, 63.4, 76.7, 166.6,
    170.3, 208.12, 287.4, 295.5, 310.27, 311.4
Elizabeth I of England  143.4
Ellerbee, Linda  271.19, 287.5
Ellington, Duke (Edward Kennedy Ellington)  272.5
Elliott, Ebenezer  88.6
Ellis, Havelock  257.5

Ellison, Ralph  43.3, 46.10, 127.13, 310.28
Emerson, Ralph Waldo  3.4, 3.5, 3.6, 15.6, 17.6, 19.9,
    24.10, 24.11, 25.7, 27.8, 27.9, 28.6, 31.15, 39.4, 44.6,
    51.9, 51.10, 51.11, 52.1, 58.3, 72.4, 75.13, 75.14, 83.6,
    87.10, 87.11, 87.12, 94.3, 102.3, 106.6, 107.7, 114.9,
    116.19, 118.3, 122.3, 131.6, 136.1, 147.14, 149.5, 174.5,
    177.4, 187.12, 196.10, 196.11, 204.9, 208.13, 212.5,
    216.6, 224.11, 226.10, 228.14, 228.15, 228.16 230.4,
    234.6, 234.7, 240.8, 242.2, 255.5, 256.5, 260.7, 262.8,
    268.16, 268.17, 272.6, 274.6, 289.7, 292.12, 300.8,
    304.4, 305.13, 307.18
English Proverb  38.12, 47.3, 51.12, 72.5, 99.7, 111.9,
    111.10, 111.11, 112.6, 136.2, 233.4, 281.25, 282.15, 284.6,
    306.10
Ennius, Quintus  285.3
Enzensberger, Hans Magnus  211.6
Ephron, Nora  180.7, 309.16
Epictetus  50.4, 101.6, 135.6, 151.7, 166.7, 206.9
Epicurus  68.8, 183.12
Epstein, Joseph  204.10
Erasmus, Desiderius (Gerard Didier)  34.9, 62.3, 83.7,
    111.22, 153.15
Erskine, John  181.14
Esson, Louis  219.11
Estes, Clarissa Pinkola  168.5, 270.18
Estonian Proverb  224.12
Ethiopian Proverb  124.5
Eluard, Paul  247.2
Eupolis  37.6, 205.8, 282.16
Euripides  76.8, 87.13, 99.8, 107.8, 108.5, 141.4, 154.7,
    161.6, 179.5, 194.5, 222.10, 268.18, 294.17, 298.28,
    306.11, 309.17
Evodus  73.3

Faber, Frederick W.  189.8
Fairfax, Edward  240.9
Falk, Marcia  171.11
Farejon, Eleanor  292.13
Farquhar, George  57.7, 250.6, 282.17, 283.11
Faulkner, William  12.5, 163.5
Feather, William  256.6
Feiffer, Jules  304.5
Felltham, Owen  311.5
Fenelon, François  34.10, 46.11, 215.2
Fenton, James  128.4, 178.3
Ferber, Edna  145.19
Ferguson, James  143.5
Ferris, William  110.4
Feuerbach, Ludwig Andreas  289.8
Field, Eugene  22.4, 247.3, 281.26
Field, Joanna  299.7
Fielding, Henry  18.18, 50.5, 62.4, 96.7, 120.4, 138.6,
    144.5, 165.12, 166.8, 191.7, 208.14, 224.13, 233.5, 251.4,
    255.6, 258.23 261.10, 298.29, 300.9
Fielding, Sarah  171.12, 246.6, 249.13, 307.19
Finney, Charles G.  215.3
Finnish Proverb  73.4
Firbank, Ronald  279.6
Fischer, Martin Henry  26.15, 74.9
Fisher, Sir John  15.7
Fitzgerald, Edward  68.9
Fitzgerald, F. Scott  47.4, 271.12, 296.10, 305.14, 310.29,
    313.11
Fitzherbert, William  29.4
Fitzpatrick, Jean Grasso  106.7
Flanagan, Hallie  229.5

Flaubert, Gustave 13.9, 268.19, 274.7
Flecker, James Elroy 108.6, 209.12, 281.27
Fletcher, Andrew (of Saltoun) 23.5
Fleischer, Lenore 229.6
Fleming, Ian 229.7
Fletcher, John 3.7, 34.1, 36.7, 57.8, 62.5
Florio, John 85.6
Fontane, Theodor 147.15
Forbes, Bryan 276.5
Ford, Ford Madox 247.4
Ford, Gerald 269.6
Ford, Henry 290.14
Ford, John 139.5, 281.28
Ford, Paul Leicester 158.16
Ford, Richard 164.10
Forster, E.M. (Edward Morgan) 108.7, 163.6, 255.7,
    290.15
Fosdick, Harry Emerson 216.7
Foster, George G. 150.11
Fowles, John 209.13
Fox, Paula 270.19, 298.30
Frame, Janet 205.9
France, Anatole (Jean-Jacques-Francois Thibault) 56.6,
    137.5, 145.20, 154.8, 161.7, 275.8, 281.29, 299.8
Frank, Anne 122.4, 229.8
Frankfurter, Felix 150.12
Frankl, Victor 166.9
Franklin, Benjamin 6.4, 51.13, 54.5, 68.10, 81.1, 96.8,
    115.3, 139.6, 147.16, 150.13, 179.6, 186.5, 190.7, 198.7,
    205.10, 220.3, 226.11, 233.6, 234.8, 239.3, 249.14,
    253.4, 254.4, 256.7, 260.8, 268.20, 275.9, 294.18,
    306.12, 307.20
Franklin, John Hope 76.9
Franklin, Miles 158.17, 282.18
Franz, Marie-Louise von 90.15, 90.16
Frayn, Michael 228.17
Frederick, Pauline 269.7
Freeman, D.S. 271.21
French Proverb 30.12, 33.2, 139.7
Frere, John Hookham 1.7
Freud, Sigmund 8.3, 79.3, 90.17, 162.3, 172.11, 184.6,
    234.9, 305.15
Friel, Brian 59.4
Froebel, Friedrich 128.5
Fromm, Erich 31.16
Frost, Robert 74.10, 109.8, 140.16, 155.13, 160.12, 208.15,
    208.16, 255.8 270.20, 282.19, 311.6
Froude, J.A. (James Anthony) 85.7
Fry, Christopher 43.4, 207.5, 208.17
Fry, Stephen 229.9
Frye, Northrop 14.12, 98.9, 155.14, 159.12, 183.13, 184.7,
    270.21, 313.12
Fulbright, J. William 70.5
Fuller, R. Buckminster 106.8, 311.7
Fuller, Margaret 245.4
Fuller, Thomas I 45.2, 150.14, 181.15, 198.8, 214.8,
    224.14, 260.9, 269.8 309.18
Fuller, Thomas II 5.8, 18.19, 22.5, 38.13, 38.14, 46.12,
    47.5, 51.14, 68.11, 75.15, 96.9, 102.4, 104.4, 108.8,
    125.8, 139.8, 140.17, 158.18, 160.13, 179.7, 196.12, 205.11,
    209.14, 224.15, 227.9, 233.7, 240.10, 246.7, 281.30,
    282.20, 290.16, 292.14, 294.19, 298.31, 306.13, 317.21
Fyleman, Rose 89.9


Gaboriau, Emile 137.6, 305.16
Gaddis, William 273.6

Gaelic Proverb 224.16
Galbraith, John Kenneth 66.8, 152.8, 190.8, 198.9, 211.7,
    269.9
Galen (or Galenus, Claudius) 40.5, 147.17
Gales, R.L. 279.7
Galileo Galilei 284.7
Gallico, Paul 135.7
Galsworthy, John 262.9
Gandhi, Indira 227.10
Gardner, Erle Stanley 166.10
Gardner, Howard 33.3
Gardner, John W. 311.8
Garfield, James A. 283.12
Garibaldi, Giuseppe 3.8
Garnett, Richard 160.14
Garrick, David 288.4
Garrison, Theodosia 103.7
Garth, Samuel 138.7, 302.5
Garvey, Marcus 221.3
Gary, Roman 119.11
Gaskell, Elizabeth 233.8
Gass, William 95.6, 171.13
Gates, Henry Louis, Jr. 232.10
Gauguin, Paul 273.7
Gautier, Theophile 181.16
Gawain, Shakti 218.4
Gay, John 37.7, 95.7, 99.9, 139.9, 150.15, 153.16, 226.12,
    251.5, 281.31
Gayle, Addison, Jr. 117.6
Geiggar, Kwasi 284.8
Gellhorn, Martha Ellis 140.18
Gellius, Aulus 158.19
Genlis, Madame Stephanie Felicite de 301.10
Gerhardt, Mia 271.22
German Proverb 5.9, 195.3, 215.4, 263.2
Gerould, Katharine Fullerton 83.8
Gibbon, Edward 107.9, 116.20, 174.6, 184.8, 247.8
Gibbs, Wolcott 180.8, 288.5
Gibran, Kahlil 83.9, 260.10, 282.21, 290.17, 298.32
Gide, Andre 158.20, 217.7, 226.13
Gilbert, Sir W.S. (William Schwenk) 28.7, 37.8, 41.4,
    47.6, 156.8, 173.4, 186.6, 207.6, 242.3, 257.6
Giles, Herbert 16.2
Gill, Brendan 200.2
Gilliatt, Penelope 43.5, 140.19, 180.9
Gilman, Charlotte Perkins 21.11, 155.15
Gilmore, Dame Mary 46.13
Ginott, Haim G. 135.8, 136.3
Ginsberg, Allen 7.4
Giono, Jean 219.12
Giovanni, Nikki 45.3, 158.21, 269.10, 299.9
Girardin, Delphine de 35.4
Giraudoux, Jean 25.8, 74.11, 150.16
Giroud, Françoise 183.14
Gissing, George 41.5, 92.3, 95.8
Gladden, Washington 248.9
Glanvill, Joseph 125.9, 202.9, 254.5
Glasgow, Ellen 90.18, 121.2, 123.6, 125.10, 137.7, 201.3,
    310.30, 314.11
Glaspell, Susan 141.5
Glass, George 4.9
Glassie, Henry 98.10
Gluck, Christoph 187.13
Godard, Jean-Luc 152.9, 180.10, 274.9
Goddard, Harold 270.22
Godden, Rumer 18.20

Godwin, William  44.7, 284.9
Goethe, Johann Wolfgang von  4.10, 44.8, 70.6, 86.5,
    111.23, 126.8, 129.8, 138.8, 141.6, 147.18, 147.19, 148.16,
    268.21, 299.10, 310.31
Goforth, Frances S.  38.15, 98.11
Goldberg, Arthur J.  66.9
Golding, William  263.3
Goldoni, Carlo  282.22
Goldsmith, Oliver  4.11, 18.21, 30.13, 48.4, 139.10, 150.17,
    153.17, 225.12, 282.23, 291.15, 298.33, 306.14
Goldsmith, Bonnie Zucker  160.15
Goldwyn, Samuel  42.4, 180.11
Gonzales Prada, Manuel  202.10
Goode, Mort  97.10
Goodman, Paul  283.13
Goodrich, S.G. (Samuel Griswold)  89.10
Gordon, Karen Elizabeth  147.20, 286.2
Gorky, Maxim  206.10
Gosson, Stephen  84.3
Goudge, Eileen  150.18
Gourmont, Remy de  61.2, 309.19
Gowers, Ernest  255.9
Gracian, Baltasar  18.22, 51.15, 53.3, 74.12, 83.10, 83.11,
    86.6, 99.10, 104.5, 248.10, 272.7, 273.8, 284.10, 294.20,
    298.34, 307.2, 310.32
Graham, Katharine  227.11
Graham, Martha  59.5, 161.8, 288.6
Graham, Philip L.  188.5
Graham, Winston  220.3
Grahame, Kenneth  127.14
Grant, Cary  69
Grass, Gunther  26.16
Graves, Richard  225.13, 256.8
Graves, Robert  74.13, 89.11, 151.8, 208.18, 223.6,
    270.22
Gray, Thomas  176.10
Greek Proverb  53.4, 57.9, 135.9, 283.14
Greenaway, Peter  180.12
Greenberg, Joanne  82.10
Greene, Ellen  271.23, 271.24
Greene, Graham  153.18, 177.5, 262.10
Greene, Robert  160.16, 310.33
Greer, Germaine  124.6
Gregory, Dick  116.21
Greville, Richard Fulke  50.6
Grigson, Geoffrey  219.13
Grimes, Martha  282.24
Grimke, Francis James  217.8
Grimm, Jacob  97.11
Grimm, Wilhelm  97.11, 270.23
Grumbach, Doris  213.10
Guazzo, Stefano  51.16, 68.12, 96.10, 102.4, 111.24,
    298.35
Guedalla, Philip  1.8, 115.4
Guest, Edward A.  215.5
Guest, Judith  126.9
Guinon, Albert  158.22
Guiterman, Arthur  145.21, 226.14, 261.11, 272.8
Guitry, Sacha  125.11
Gummere, Francis B.  156.9
Guppy, Shusha  305.17
Gussow, Mel  148.17
Guthrie, Woody  97.12, 97.13
Gyraldus, Lilius  80.6

Haddow, Alexander  305.18

Haecker, Theodor  86.7
Hafiz (Shams-Ed-Dinmuhammad)  160.17
Haig, Alexander  154.9
Haley, Alex  110.5
Haliburton, Thomas Chandler (Sam Slick)  139.11,
    213.11, 282.25
Halifax, Lord (George Savile)  18.23, 64.4, 86.8, 196.13,
    222.11, 238.3, 284.11, 307.23
Halisham, Lord (Quintin Hogg)  18.24
Hall, Bishop Joseph  84.4, 249.15
Halleck, Fitz-Greene  222.12
Halliwell, J.O. (James Orchard)  281.32
Halsey, Margaret  98.12, 305.19
Hamilton, Alexander  233.9
Hamilton, Edith  25.9, 27.10, 83.12, 252.8
Hamilton, Richard  183.15
Hamilton, Robert B.  266.6
Hampl, Patricia  171.14, 208.19
Hand, Learned  40.6, 67.3, 150.19, 310.34
Handke, Peter  271.25
Hansberry, Lorraine  290.18
Hanslick, Eduard  181.17
Harben, Will N.  282.26
Hardeman, W.J.  27.11, 270.24
Hardwicke, Cedric  4.12
Hardy, Thomas  18.25, 20.4, 48.5, 63.5, 95.9, 176.11,
    208.20, 209.15, 235.2, 236.7, 250.7, 258.24, 271.26,
    272.9, 309.20
Hare, Augustus William  47.7, 153.19, 202.11, 215.6,
    234.10
Hare, David  288.7
Hare, Julius Charles  47.7
Harkness, Georgia  234.11
Harper, Ralph  95.10
Harrel, John  270.25
Harris, Joel Chandler  34.11, 145.23, 292.15
Harris, Sydney J.  17.7, 58.4, 155.16, 210.16
Harrison, Barbara Grizzuti  91.7
Harrison, Benjamin  240.11
Hart, Moss  137.8
Hartland, Edwin Sydney  65.6, 271.27
Harwood, Gwen  292.16
Hathaway, Katharine Butler  42.5
Havel, Vaclav  42.6, 166.11, 288.8
Havner, Vance  183.16
Hawking, Stephen W.  300.10
Hawkins, Anthony Hope  299.11
Hawthorne, Nathaniel  21.12, 40.7, 73.5, 76.10, 114.10,
    147.21, 155.17, 197.3, 244.4, 281.33, 291.16, 295.6,
    310.35
Haydon, B.R. (Benjamin Robert)  112.7
Hayes, Helen  152.10
Haynes, Lemuel B.  62.6
Hazlitt, William  6.5, 6.4, 51.17, 51.18, 68.13, 108.9,
    140.20, 163.7, 185.7, 196.13, 198.10, 202.12, 217.9,
    243.4, 245.5, 249.16, 270.26, 274.10, 282.27, 282.28,
    294.21, 298.36, 307.24
Healy, Eugene  224.17
Heard, H.F.  102.5
Heath, Robert  21.13
Hebert, Anne  208.21
Hebrew Proverb  26.17
Hecht, Anthony  90.19
Hecht, Ben  180.13
Heilbrun, Carolyn G.  191.8, 212.6
Hein, Piet  269.11

Heine, Heinrich 87.14, 90.20, 99.11, 144.6, 181.18, 247.5, 270.27, 273.9, 281.34, 291.17
Heisenberg, Werner Karl 195.4
Hellman, Lillian 58.5, 154.10, 181.19, 268.22, 282.29, 312.16, 314.12
Helps, Sir Arthur 95.11, 158.23, 274.11, 280.5
Hemans, Felicia Dorothea 89.12
Hemingway, Ernest 140.21, 259.4, 271.28, 294.22, 312.17
Henry, Marguerite 152.11
Henry, Matthew 46.14
Henry, O. (William Sidney Porter) 155.18, 176.12, 282.30
Herberg, Will 58.6
Herbert, Sir Alan Patrick 1.9, 9.5
Herbert, George 3.9, 25.10, 28.8, 53.5, 72.6, 72.7, 93.4, 108.10, 128.6, 139.12, 147.22, 171.15, 179.8, 188.6, 194.6, 208.22, 224.18, 233.10, 253.5, 263.4, 307.25, 314.13
Herford, Oliver 66.11, 153.20, 225.14, 233.11, 265.12, 280.6, 314.14
Herodotus 107.10, 115.5, 281.35
Herold, Don 38.16, 177.6
Herrick, Robert 5.10, 87.15, 285.4
Heschel, Abraham Joshua 182.5
Hesiod 108.11, 163.8, 246.8, 261.12, 281.36
Hesse, Hermann 306.15
Heuscher, Julius E. 90.21
Heywood, John 27.12, 37.9, 72.8, 281.37, 290.19, 294.23
Higginson Thomas Wentworth 109.9
Hillman, Sidney 211.8
Hindemith, Paul 181.20
Hindustan Proverb 11.5
Hinshelwood, Cyril 252.9
Hippocrates 21.14, 151.9, 194.7
Hirsch, Mary 119.12
Hitchcock, Alfred 64.5, 76.11
Hitchens, Dolores 262.11
Hitler, Adolf 221.4, 269.12
Hoban, Russell 44.9, 147.23
Hobbes, Thomas 13.10, 113.1, 145.24, 169.7, 306.16, 310.36
Hoch, Edward Wallis 282.31
Hocking, William Ernest 183.17
Hodgeson, Ralph 292.17
Hoffer, Eric 46.15, 101.7, 124.7, 128.7, 221.5, 271.29, 291.18, 314.15
Hoffman, Abbie 91.8
Hofmannsthal, Hugo von 160.18
Hofstadter, Richard 42.7
Hogan, Linda 158.24
Holland, J.G. (Josiah Gilbert) 224.19
Hollien, Harry 11.6
Holman, Robert 288.9
Holmes, John R. 300.11
Holmes, Oliver Wendell, Jr. 150.20, 206.11
Holmes, Oliver Wendell, Sr. 15.8, 21.15, 45.4, 101.8, 121.3, 144.7, 145.25, 147.24, 149.6, 154.11, 158.25, 160.19 161.9, 196.14, 196.15, 207.7, 212.7, 215.7, 225.15, 237.5, 241.8, 258.25, 267.7, 280.7, 282.32, 290.20, 291.19, 303.6, 304.6, 306.17, 309.21, 310.37
Holt, John 284.12
Holtby, Winifred 152.12, 296.11
Holter, Ronald K. 225.16
Holyday, Barten 150.21
Homer 24.12, 25.11, 28.9, 34.12, 36.8, 48.6, 77.2, 107.11, 107.12, 107.13 120.5, 186.7, 194.8, 205.12, 205.13, 205.14, 209.16, 237.6, 265.13, 269.13, 270.28, 281.38, 281.39, 292.18, 298.37

Hood, Thomas 76.12, 89.13, 142.7, 151.10, 160.20, 219.14, 225.17, 247.6, 290.21
Hook, Sidney 283.15
Hooker, Richard 256.9
Hooton, E.A. (Earnest Albert) 116.22
Hopkins, Mark 147.25
Hopper, Hedda 108.12
Horace (Quintus Horatius Flaccus) 5.11, 13.11, 13.12, 24.13, 24.14, 28.10, 34.13, 40.8, 51.19, 56.7, 74.14, 75.16, 76.13, 81.2, 92.4, 95.12, 111.25, 119.13, 133.2, 157.7, 165.13, 170.4, 172.12, 203.7, 250.8, 254.6, 265.14, 270.29, 281.40, 292.19, 294.24, 296.12, 303.7, 310.38
Horne, Richard Hengest 214.9
Hough, Emerson 282.33
Household, Geoffrey (Edward West) 50.7
Housman, A.E. (Alfred Edward) 208.23, 285.5, 299.12, 303.8
Howe, Edgar Watson "Ed" 15.9, 46.16, 77.3, 131.7, 148.18, 158.26, 190.9, 238.4, 270.30, 279.8, 298.38, 307.26
Howe, Lord Geoffrey 66.12
Howe, Irving 92.5
Howell, James 224.20, 298.39
Howells, William Dean 189.9, 233.12, 242.4
Howitt, Mary 89.14, 176.13
Hoyle, Edmond 297.4
Hubbard, Elbert 18.26, 84.5, 86.9, 86.10, 108.13, 109.10, 125.12, 150.22, 153.21, 174.7, 198.11, 215.8, 219.15, 226.15, 236.8, 238.5, 253.6, 268.23, 289.9, 290.22, 299.13, 307.27
Hubbard, Kin (Frank McKinney) 22.6, 32.2, 36.9, 47.8, 51.20, 77.4, 88.5, 108.14, 108.15, 150.23, 210.17, 269.14, 270.31, 279.9, 282.34
Hubble, Edwin Powell 252.10
Hudson, Helen 164.11
Hudson, Mary Clemmer 207.28
Hufstedler, Shirley M. 138.9
Hughes, Langston 119.14, 208.24, 271.30
Hughes, Richard 95.13
Hughes, Robert 82.11, 287.6
Hugo, Victor 47.9, 75.17, 79.4, 130.4, 181.22, 214.10, 253.7, 262.12, 276.6
Hulme, T.E. (Thomas Ernest) 147.26, 179.9, 215.9, 282.35
Humboldt, Wilhelm von 141.7
Humphrey, Hubert H. 113.2, 269.15
Humphrey, Muriel 269.16
Huneker, James G. 150.24
Hunt, Lamar 150.25
Hunt, Leigh 144.8
Hunter, Kristin 249.17
Hurst, Fannie 310.39
Hurston, Zora Neale 30.14, 76.14, 86.11, 98.13, 145.26, 153.22, 160.21, 179.10, 224.21, 270.32, 291.21, 294.25
Hutchins, Robert Maynard 74.15
Huxley, Aldous 84.6, 85.8, 88.6, 125.13, 131.8, 169.8, 181.23, 198.12, 200.3, 221.6, 224.22, 231.6, 258.26, 279.10, 305.20, 310.40
Huxley, T.H. (Thomas Henry) 40.9, 88.7, 151.11, 177.7
Hyde, Robin 191.9

Ibn-Abi-Talib, Ali 294.27
Ibn al-Jawzi 271.31
Ibn Ezra, Moses 80.7, 109.11, 299.14
Ibn Gabriol, Solomon 34.14, 158.27, 227.12, 258.27, 310.41

Ibsen, Henrik 122.5, 126.10, 154.12
Imagist Manifesto 208.25
Ingalls, John 211.9
Inge, W.R. (William Ralph) 99.12, 234.12
Ingeland, Thomas 111.26
Ingersoll, R.G. (Robert Green) 24.15, 113.3, 129.9, 174.8, 289.10
Ionesco, Eugene 183.18
Irish Proverb 112.8, 235.3
Irving, Washington 26.18, 116.23, 159.13, 294.26
Isherwood, Christopher 195.5
Isocrates 133.3
Issa, Kobayashi 226.16
Italian Proverb 33.4, 96.11, 149.7, 309.22
Ivory Coast Saying 172.13

Jabotinsky, Vladimir 147.27
Jackson, Holbrook 202.13, 282.36
Jackson, Jesse 145.27, 284.13
Jackson, Laura Riding 232.11, 312.18
Jackson, Robert 278.7
Jacob, François 252.11
Jacobs, Melville 271.32
Jacoby, Johann 143.6
James, C.L.R. 211.10
James, Clive 95.14
James, Henry 120.6, 140.22, 140.23, 164.12, 270.33, 288.10, 299.15
James, P.D. (Phyllis Dorothy) 95.15, 210.18, 256.10
James, William 71.8, 80.8, 123.7, 147.28, 151.12, 298.40, 304.7
Jameson, Anna 147.29
Jameson, Storm 40.10, 147.30, 276.7
Janeway, Elizabeth 61.3, 191.10, 206.12, 218.5
Japanese Proverb 65.7, 75.18, 114.11, 283.16
Jarrell, Randall 71.9
Jeans, James 300.12
Jefferson, Thomas 68.14, 87.16, 150.26, 198.13, 219.16, 269.17
Jeffrey, Lord Francis 217.10
Jenkins, David 106.9
Jenner, Charles 44.10, 141.8, 219.17, 240.12
Jenyns, Soame 75.19
Jerome, Jerome K. 46.17, 273.10, 293.6
Jerome, Saint 75.20, 96.12, 158.28
Jerrold, Douglas 65.8, 89.15
Jespersen, Otto 2.2
Jessel, George 269.18
Jewett, Sarah Orne 280.8
Jewish Proverb 28.11, 227.13
Jimenez, Juan Ramon 91.9
John-Steiner, Vera 290.23
Johnson, Charles 206.13
Johnson, Claudia "Lady Bird" 210.19
Johnson, Georgia Douglas 112.9
Johnson, James Welden 24.16, 209.17, 314.16
Johnson, Jill 124.8
Johnson, Joyce 152.13
Johnson, Ralph Underwood 31.17
Johnson, R.W. 218.6
Johnson, Samuel 6.7, 17.8, 18.27, 22.7, 24.17, 26.19, 28.12, 40.11, 48.7, 51.21, 54.6, 55.1, 68.15, 81.3, 85.9, 96.13, 96.14, 96.15 109.12, 116.24, 117.7, 125.14, 133.4, 135.10, 139.13, 145.28, 147.31, 150.27, 151.13, 153.23, 157.8, 161.10, 163.9, 164.13, 169.9, 176.14, 177.8, 181.24, 185.8, 186.8, 192.6, 198.14, 202.14, 209.18, 216.8, 225.18, 227.14, 228.18, 239.5, 247.7, 253.8, 258.28, 261.13, 268.24, 269.19, 270.34, 273.1, 279.11, 292.20, 297.5, 298.41, 299.16, 310.42, 312.19
Johnson, Sonia 147.32, 218.7
Johnston, Jill 309.23
Johnstone, Charles 96.16, 150.28
Jolson, Al 192.7
Jones, Gayl 271.33
Jones, Rufus M. 113.4
Jong, Erica 108.16, 108.17, 164.14, 223.7, 249.18, 310.43
Jonson, Ben 17.9, 19.11, 72.9, 75.21, 89.16, 108.18, 111.27, 111.28, 150.29, 153.24, 155.19, 157.9, 179.11, 267.7, 277.6, 281.41, 282.37, 293.7
Joseph, Lynn 271.34
Jordan, Sara Murray 168.6
Joubert, Joseph 18.28, 29.5, 75.22, 127.15, 130.5, 159.14, 165.14, 196.16 206.14, 227.15, 284.14, 314.17
Jowett, Benjamin 314.18
Joyce, James 270.35
Joyce, P.W. (Patrick Weston) 179.12
Julian 145.29
Jung, Carl 26.20, 99.13, 107.14, 299.17
Junius 109.13
Junot, Laure 217.11
Juvenal 131.9, 150.30, 187.14, 249.18, 303.9

Kael, Pauline 180.15, 221.7, 287.7
Kaiser, Henry 218.8
Kalidasa 219.18
Kant, Immanuel 165.15, 165.16
Kaplan, Justin 287.8
Kaplan, Mordecai M. 221.8
Kasen, Arthur C. 290.24
Kaufman, Judge Irving R. 150.31
Kavanaugh, Ted 164.15
Kaye-Smith, Sheila 155.20
Kaysen, Susanna 161.11, 291.22
Keats, John 7.5, 13.13, 24.18, 51.22, 80.9, 124.9, 127.16, 129.10, 150.32 152.14, 224.23, 226.17, 263.5
Keble, John 14.13
Keenan, Deborah 12.7
Keenan, Henry Francis 199.3
Keillor, Garrison 188.7, 229.10
Keller, Helen 88.8, 159.15
Kellogg, Marjorie 158.29
Kelly, James 245.6, 281.45, 282.38
Kemp, Jan 258.29
Kempis, Thomas A 106.10, 250.9
Kempton, Murray 183.19
Kendrick, Bayard 179.13
Kennedy, John F. 54.7
Kent, George 258.30
Kenyan Saying 197.4
Kerr, Jean 168.7, 309.24
Kettering, Charles F. 299.18
Keynes, John Maynard 135.11, 218.9
Khati 224.24, 294.28
Khrushchev, Nikita 210.20
Kierkegaard, Soren 214.11, 219.19, 219.20
Kimber, Edward 290.25
King, Florence 191.11, 207.29
King, Martin Luther, Jr. 124.10, 125.15, 258.31
King, Yolanda 155.22
Kingsley, Charles 89.17, 149.8, 174.9, 233.13
Kingsmill, Hugh 82.12
Kingsolver, Barbara 237.7

Kingston, Maxine Hong  203.7, 270.36
Kinsella, W.P. (William Patrick)  114.12
Kipling, Rudyard  162.4, 168.8, 227.16, 228.19, 270.37, 294.29, 298.42, 310.44
Kirkland, Gelsey  214.12
Kirkpatrick, Jeane J.  310.45
Klee, Paul  249.19, 274.12
Knowles, Frederic Lawrence  144.9
Knowles, F.M.  153.25, 239.6
Knox, Ronald  22.8
Koestler, Arthur  171.16, 225.19, 270.38
The Koran  10.3, 148.19, 194.9, 199.4
Korda, Michael  108.19
Kouyate, D'Jimo  110.6
Kouyate, Mamadou  110.7
Kovacs, Ernie  287.9
Kraus, Karl  14.14, 14.15, 74.16, 137.9, 249.20, 312.20
Kreble, John  158.30
Kreymborg, Alfred  105.4
Krishnamurti, Jiddu  26.21, 295.7
Kroll, Jack  148.20
Kronenberger, Louis  43.6, 108.20, 136.4
Krutch, Joseph Wood  4.13, 11.7, 82.13, 163.10, 240.13
Kundera, Milan  148.21, 171.17, 185.9, 189.10
Kung, Hans  60.7, 183.20, 184.9
Kunitz, Stanley Jasspon  64.6
Kusz, Natalie  310.46
Kyd, Thomas  219.21

La Bruyere, Jean de  25.12, 29.6, 48.8, 243.5, 253.9, 268.15, 271.35, 301.11, 305.21, 307.30
La Fontaine, Jean de  96.17, 145.30, 160.22, 208.26, 258.32, 297.6, 314.19
La Grange, A.E. Lelievre de  96.18
La Rochefoucauld, François de  1.10, 3.10, 23.6, 28.13, 31.18, 31.19, 41.6, 51.23, 75.23, 75.24, 96.19, 96.20, 99.14, 103.8, 128.8, 136.5, 141.9, 169.10, 213.12, 226.18, 253.10, 266.7, 268.26, 275.10, 279.12, 297.7, 301.12, 301.13, 307.31
Lacordaire, Jean-Baptiste  36.10
Lacroix, Christian  200.4
Lafarge, Father John  174.10
Laharpe, Jean-Francois de  83.13
Laird, Charlton  22.9, 39.5, 109.14, 147.33
Lamartine, Alphonse de  106.11, 163.11
Lamb, Charles  6.8, 13.14, 18.29, 119.15, 150.33, 189.11, 217.12, 225.20, 225.21, 225.22, 231.7, 267.8, 298.43
Lamb, Mary  213.13
Lamont, Anne  312.21
Landon, L.E. (Letitia Elizabeth Landon Maclean)  17.10, 22.10, 101.9
Landon, Melville D.  31.20
Landor, Walter Savage  23.7, 55.2, 213.14, 223.8, 225.23, 231.8, 265.15, 288.11, 303.10
Landowska, Wanda  283.17
Lang, Andrew  23.8
Langer, Susanne K.  181.25, 206.15, 227.17
Langford, N.P. (Nathaniel Pitt)  179.14
Lanier, Sidney  181.26, 181.27
Langland, William  302.6
Lao-Tsze (Lao Tzu or Lao Tsu)  28.14, 56.9, 226.19, 268.27, 298.44, 299.19, 310.47
Lapham, Lewis  212.8
Larkin, Philip  208.27
Lardner, Ring  82.14, 86.12, 153.26

Lasch, Christopher  145.31, 191.12
Lathrop, Rose Hawthorne  60.8
Latimer, Hugh  281.43
Latin Proverb  259.5
Lavater, Johann Kaspar  14.16
Law, Vernon S.  85.10
Lawrence, George Alfred  164.16, 215.10
Lawrence, D.H. (David Herbert)  19.12, 221.9, 244.5, 281.43, 306.18
Lawrence, Herbert  228.20
Lawrence, Kathleen Rockwell  30.15
Laye, Camara  197.5
Layton, Irving  14.17, 122.6
Le Bon, Gustave  31.21
Le Carre, John (David John Moore)  3.11, 66.13
Le Gallienne Richard  54.8
Le Guin, Ursula K.  91.10, 91.11, 91.12, 95.16, 117.8, 183.21, 223.9, 227.18, 231.9, 252.12, 252.13, 270.39, 281.44, 312.22
Le Sueur, Meridel  152.15, 270.40
Leacock, Stephen  119.16, 151.14, 219.22, 219.23, 219.24, 225.24
Lean, David  12.8
Lean, V.S.  150.34
Lear, Edward  156.10
Lear, Norman  287.10
Leary, Timothy  252.14
Lebowitz, Fran  51.24, 76.15, 158.31, 229.11, 286.3, 308.6
Lec, Stanislaw J.  183.22, 257.7, 258.33, 290.26
Lee, Gerald Stanley  35.5, 114.13
Leflar, Robert A.  150.35
Lehman, David  138.10, 310.48
Lehmann-Haupt, Christopher Charles Herbert  186.9
Leifchild, Rev. John  216.9
Leigh, Henry Sambrooke  9.6
Leitch, Mary Sinton  23.9
Lemaitre, François  54.9
Lenclos, Ninon de  96.21
L'Engle, Madeleine  74.17, 298.45, 310.49
Lenin, Nikolai (Vladimir Ilich Ulyanov)  219.25
Lennon, John  232.12
Lennox, Charlotte  186.10, 239.7
Leonard, George B.  31.22
Leonardo Da Vinci  145.32
Leslie, Eliza  96.22
Lessing, Gotthold Ephraim  90.22, 112.10
Levant, Oscar  12.9, 80.10, 225.25
Leverson, Ada  308.7
Levertov, Denise  266.8
Levi-Strauss, Claude  183.23, 252.15, 311.9
Levinas, Emmanuel  174.11
Lewes, G.H. (George Henry)  20.5
Lewis, C.S. (Clive Staples)  140.24
Lewis, D.B. Wyndham  86.13
Lewis, John L.  28.15
Lewis, Saunders  260.11
Lewis, Sinclair  135.12, 219.26
Lewisohn, Ludwig  53.6
Lichtenberg, Georg Christoph  171.19, 195.6, 216.10, 249.21, 306.19
Liddon, E.S. (Eloise Liddon Soper)  82.15
Lieberman, Gerald F.  150.36
Lillie, Beatrice  308.8
Lilly, John  300.13
Lincoln, Abraham  18.30, 86.14, 99.15, 123.8, 150.37, 216.11

Lindbergh, Anne Morrow 21.16, 232.13
Lindsay, Vachel 62.7, 79.5, 185.10
Lipman, Maureen 4.14
Lippmann, Walter 167.4, 188.8, 190.10
Lively, Penelope 184.10
Livy (Titus Livius) 246.9
Llewellyn, Caroline 148.22, 234.13
Lloyd, David 196.17
Lloyd George, David 75.24
Locke, John 6.9, 30.16, 61.4, 68.16, 109.15, 123.9, 157.10,
    264.5, 283.18
Long, Earl 210.21
Longfellow, Henry Wadsworth 10.4, 23.10, 24.19, 25.13,
    51.25, 76.16, 91.13, 107.15, 152.16, 158.32, 160.23,
    182.6, 231.10, 244.6, 250.10, 281.45, 294.30, 303.11,
    305.22, 309.25
Longworth, Alice Roosevelt 108.21
Lopez, Barry 271.36
Lorde, Audrey 123.10, 178.4, 310.50
Lover, Samuel 23.11
Lowell, James Russell 31.23, 32.3, 85.11, 91.14, 166.12,
    178.5, 224.25, 248.11, 292.21, 302.7
Lowry, Mary 282.39
Lucas, E.V. 309.26
Lucas, George 19.13
Luce, Clare Boothe see Boothe, Clare
Lucretius (Titus Lucretius Carus) 13.15
Luke, Helen 270.41
Lundberg, Ferdinand 150.38
Lunn, Arnold 216.12
Lurie, Alison 90.23
Luther, Martin 7.7, 34.15, 113.5, 256.11, 289.11
Luthi, Max, 98.14, 98.15
Lydgate, John 40.12
Lyly, John 28.16, 99.16, 160.24, 164.17, 173.5, 187.15,
    267.9, 298.46
Lynch, David 180.16
Lynes, Russell 135.13, 146.3, 287.11
Lysander 194.10

Mabley, Jack 138.11
MacArthur, Douglas 81.4
Macaulay, Rose 227.19
Macaulay, Thomas Babington 13.16, 16.3, 27.13, 39.6,
    52.2, 67.4, 83.14, 101.10, 165.17, 271.37,
MacCaig, Norman A. 278.8
MacDonald, Margaret Read 38.17, 271.38
MacDowell, Edward 181.28
Machado, Antonio 147.34
Machiavelli, Niccolo 33.5, 101.11
MacInnes, Dianne 270.42
Mackintosh, James 165.18
Mackenzie, Henry 6.10, 118.4, 139.14, 158.33, 164.18,
    226.20
MacLaine, Shirley 59.6
MacLeish, Archibald 12.10, 86.15, 149.9, 172.14, 185.11,
    208.28, 209.19
Madhubuti, Haki 232.14
Maeterlinck, Maurice 258.34, 310.51
Maguire, Jack 271.39
Mahaffy, John Pentland 271.40
Mahone, Barbara 178.6
Mailer, Norman 114.14, 169.11, 207.8
Maimonides (Moses) 113.6, 145.33, 174.12, 237.8,
    306.20
Makeba, Miriam 234.14

Makin, Bathsua 81.5
Malamud, Bernard 91.15, 95.17, 152.17, 171.20
Malesherbes, Chretien de 165.19
Mallarme, Stephane 208.29, 208.30
Mallet, Carl-Heinz 90.24, 90.25
Malory, Thomas 57.10, 143.7
Malraux, Andre 192.8
Mandela, Nelson 26.22, 197.6
Mann, Horace 195.7, 308.9
Mann, Thomas 39.7, 123.11, 130.6, 186.11, 196.18,
    268.28, 270.43
Mannes, Marya 44.11, 196.19, 204.11, 210.23, 287.12,
    307.32
Manrique, Don Jose 185.12
Mansfield, Katherine 51.26
Mansfield, Lord 141.10
Manton, M.T. 159.16
Marceau, Marcel 258.35, 296.13
Marcus, Griel 183.24
Marcus Manilius 107.16
Marcuse, Herbert 167.5
Marishall, Jean 18.31
Marks, Edward B. 4.15
Marlowe, Christopher 144.10, 174.13
Marquis, Don 80.11, 103.9, 139.15, 207.9, 208.31, 210.24,
    226.21
Marshall, Sybil 208.32
Marti, Jose 24.20
Martial (Marcus Valerius Martialis) 150.39, 173.6, 303.12
Martin, D.E. (Dwight Edwards) 165.20
Martin, Judith ("Miss Manners") 15.10
Martineau, Harriet 18.32, 101.12
Martinez Ten, Carmen 157.11
Marx, Groucho (Julius) 117.9, 164.19, 308.10
Marx, Karl 295.8
Masefield, John 111.29
Mason, Van Wyck 290.27, 293.8
Massie, Suzanne 218.10
Massinger, Philip 111.30, 117.5, 204.12
Mather, Cotton 282.40
Mathews, Harry Burchell 304.8
Mathews, Shailer 80.12
Matthau, Carol 164.20
Maugham, W. Somerset 21.17, 51.27, 54.10, 58.7, 92.6,
    109.16, 126.11, 127.17, 240.14, 255.10, 271.41, 295.9,
    296.14, 307.33
Maupassant, Guy de 51.28
Maurois, Andre 51.29, 309.27
Maxwell, Elsa 119.17
May, Rollo 160.25
May, Thomas 149.10
Mayer, Martin 302.8
Mayor, Federico 54.11
McCarthy, Mary 82.16, 114.15, 125.16
McClung, Nellie L. 131.10, 269.20
McCullers, Carson 130.7
McEvoy, J.P. (Joseph Patrick) 158.34
McEwan, Ian 211.11
McGinley, Phyllis 108.22, 208.33, 258.36
McGuire, Polly 270.44
McIlvanney William 154.13
McInerney, Jay 44.12
McIntyre, Joan 11.8
McKay, Claude 271.42
McLaughlin, Mignon 50.8, 123.12, 136.6, 158.35,
    256.12, 295.10

McLuhan, Marshall  36.11, 75.26, 140.25, 167.6,
    292.22
McMillan, Harold  42.8
Mead, Margaret  40.13, 132.4
Meade, Michael  270.45
Melville, Herman  7.8, 8.4, 52.3, 85.12, 140.26, 148.23,
    173.7, 182.7, 186.12, 213.15, 219.27, 246.10, 258.37,
    271.43, 282.41, 307.34, 314.20
Menander  44.13, 75.27, 214.13, 268.29
Mencius  283.19
Mencken, H.L. (Henry Louis)  31.24, 31.25, 32.4, 35.6,
    80.13, 97.14, 115.6, 122.7, 144.11, 176.15, 208.34, 218.11,
    251.6, 283.20, 288.12, 289.12, 309.28
Menninger, Karl A.  158.36
Mercier, Jean  286.4
Meredith, George  9.7, 12.11, 14.18, 92.7, 108.23, 160.26,
    166.13, 166.14, 171.21, 186.13, 198.15, 214.14, 219.28,
    223.10, 224.26, 224.27, 240.15, 244.7, 248.12, 258.38,
    272.10, 307.35, 313.13
Merikare  268.30
Meriton, George  294.31
Merker, Hannah  157.12, 158.37
Merman, Ethel  21.18
Merrick, Rev. James  195.8
Merrill, James  164.21
Merrill, Robert  265.16
Merton, Thomas  18.33, 183.25, 276.8
Meurier, Gabriel  84.7
Mexican Proverb  144.12
Meynell, Alice  63.6
Michaelis, C.F.  181.29
Michelangelo (Buonarroti)  25.14
Midler, Bette  298.47
Mikes, George  228.21
Mill, John Stuart  198.16, 208.35
Millar, Margaret  84.8, 175.3, 185.13, 257.8
Millay, Edna St. Vincent  91.16, 155.23, 178.7
Miller, Casey  147.35, 185.14
Miller, Harlan  164.22
Miller, James Nathan  227.20
Miller, Kelly  116.25
Miller, Henry  116.26, 127.18, 162.5, 183.26, 314.21
Millet, Kate  148.24, 161.12
Milosz, Czeslaw  230.5
Milne, A.A. (Alan Alexander)  33.6
Milton, John  10.5, 15.11, 15.12, 24.21, 28.17, 72.10, 73.6,
    87.17, 91.17, 140.27, 165.21, 179.15, 188.9, 205.15,
    233.14, 240.16, 241.9, 251.7, 281.45, 305.24
Minchin, J.G.C.  211.12
Minow, Newton  287.13
Mintz, Jerome R.  271.44
Mirrielees, Edith Ronald  245.7, 270.46
Mistinguett (Jeanne Bourgeois)  144.13
Mitchell, Susan  144.14
Mizner, Addison  275.11
Mizner, Wilson  96.23, 99.17, 145.34, 148.25, 263.6,
    291.23
Mohammed  153.27, 222.13
Moliere (Jean-Baptiste Poquelin)  17.12, 74.18, 109.17,
    130.8, 130.9, 135.14, 148.26, 192.9, 223.11, 230.6,
    243.6, 261.14, 268.31, 282.42, 291.24, 313.14
Momaday, N. Scott  270.47
Monnier, Adrienne  271.45
Monroe, Marilyn  91.18
Montagu, Ashley  233.15
Montagu, Lady Mary Wortley  75.28, 202.15, 249.22

Montale, Eugenio  200.5
Montaigne, Michel de  13.17, 28.18, 36.12, 67.5, 71.10,
    87.18, 92.8, 109.18, 190.11, 206.16, 213.16, 228.22,
    284.15, 298.48
Montesquieu, Charles Louis (Baron de la Brede et de
    Montesquieu)  198.17, 282.43, 307.36
Montessori, Marie  74.19, 283.21
Mooneyham, W. Stanley  160.27
Moore, George  122.8, 270.48, 282.44
Moore, Gerald  204.13
Moore, Marianne  178.8, 258.39
Moore, Melba  237.9
Moore, Thomas  32.5, 51.30, 68.17, 73.7, 173.8, 177.9
Moraga, Cherrie  208.36
More, Hannah  29.7, 127.19, 258.40, 314.22
More, Sir Thomas  281.46
Moreau, Jeanne  4.16, 314.23
Morgan, Robin  171.22
Morgenstern, Christian  119.18
Morier, James Justinian  271.46
Morita, Akio  56.10
Morley, Christopher  18.34, 80.14, 123.13, 155.24, 163.12,
    216.13, 245.8, 268.32, 289.13
Morley, John  18.35, 276.9
Moroccan Proverb  133.6
Morris, Desmond  56.11, 314.24
Morris, William  60.9, 281.47, 304.9
Morrison, Blake  169.12
Morrison, Toni  147.36, 159.17, 183.27, 227.21
Morrow, Dwight  141.11
Mortimer, John  21.19, 92.9
Mother Goose  105.5
Motherwell, William  103.10
Mozart, Wolfgang Amadeus  282.45
Muggeridge, Malcolm  167.7, 264.6
Mugo, Micere Githae  178.9
Mukherjee, Bharati  283.22
Mumford, Lewis  295.11
Mu-mon  71.11
Murasaki, Shikibu  155.25
Murdoch, Iris  19.14, 19.15, 181.30, 232.15
Murray, D.C.  194.11
Murray, Les A.  152.18
Murrow, Edward R.  147.37, 217.13, 229.12
Muskie, Edmund  258.41
Mydral, Gunnar  147.38
Myson of Chen  88.9

Nabokov, Vladimir  14.19, 67.6, 200.6, 223.12
Nader, Ralph  308.11
Nash, Ogden  5.12, 41.7, 108.24, 157.13
Nashe, Thomas  256.13
Nathan, George Jean  43.7, 54.12, 198.18, 244.8,
    288.13
National Storyteller's League, The  98.16
National Storytelling Press  116.27
Native American Proverb  141.12
Naylor, Gloria  183.28, 270.49
Near, Holly  123.14
Needham, Richard J.  117.10
Nehru, Jawaharlal  94.4
Neilson, John Shaw  207.10
Neruda, Pablo  147.39, 209.20, 310.52
Nevill, Dorothy  51.31, 211.13
New England Primer  60.10
New England Proverb  150.40

New Testament: Colossians 268.33, 269.21
New Testament: I Corinthians 38.18, 78.3
New Testament: James 111.31
New Testament: John 27.14, 106.12, 298.49
New Testament: Luke 128.9, 141.13, 150.41, 238.6, 253.11, 281.48
New Testament: Mark 72.12
New Testament: Matthew 199.5, 222.14, 237.10, 299.20, 305.25
New Testament: I Timothy 87.19, 87.20
Newman, Edwin 1.11, 123.15
Newman, John Henry 102.6, 215.11
Newton, Sir Isaac 104.6
Nichols, David 98.17
Nicholson, Godfrey 207.11
Nicolson, Harold 16.4
Nietzsche, Friedrich 16.5, 34.16, 40.14, 44.14, 46.18, 48.9, 51.32, 97.15, 111.32, 141.14, 153.28, 201.4, 210.25, 233.16, 267.10, 276.10, 295.12, 307.37, 310.53
Nin, Anais 310.54, 312.23
Nizer, Louis 135.15, 150.42
Noda, Kesaya E. 178.10
Noonan, Peggy 81.6, 229.13, 269.22
Norman, Diana 103.11
Norris, W.E. (William Edward) 268.34
Norton, Caroline 305.26
Novalis (Friedrich Leopold von Hardenberg) 208.37
Nu 298.50, 310.55
Nursery Rhyme 22.11, 32.6, 193.1, 193.2, 193.3, 193.4, 193.5, 193.6, 193.7, 193.8, 193.9, 193.10, 193.11, 193.12, 193.13, 193.14, 193.15, 193.16, 193.17, 193.18. 193.19. 193.20
Nye, Edgar Wilson "Bill" 158.38, 181.31, 269.23
Nyerere, Julius 59.7

Oakley, Ann 183.29
Oates, Joyce Carol 208.38
O'Brien, Conor Cruise 287.14
O'Brien, Edna 305.27
O'Brien, Flann 61.5
O'Connor, Flannery 166.15, 270.50
Odets, Clifford 164.23
Odetta (Odetta Felious Gordon) 97.16
O'Faolain, Sean 270.51
O'Flaherty, Wendy Doniger 271.47
Ogden, C.K. 166.16
Ohanian, Susan 284.16, 298.51
Old Testament: Apocrypha, Ecclesiasticus 34.17, 99.18, 141.15, 181.32, 219.29
Old Testament: Apocrypha, II Maccabees 34.18
Old Testament: Ecclesiastes 292.23
Old Testament: Genesis 104.7, 147.40, 163.13
Old Testament: Hebrews 77.5
Old Testament: Isaiah 131.11, 188.10, 195.9
Old Testament: Job 187.16, 302.9
Old Testament: Leviticus 281.49
Old Testament: Proverbs 12.12, 28.19, 99.19, 142.8, 306.21
Old Testament: Psalms 22.12, 27.16, 72.13, 179.16, 199.6, 281.50, 294.32
Old Testament: 2 Samuel 134.2
Oliphant, Margaret 20.6, 127.20
Olivier, Lord Laurence 4.17, 21.20
Olsen, Tillie 292.24
Olson, Glending 271.48
O'Malley, Austin 38.19, 102.7, 256.14, 256.15

Omar Khayyam 285.6, 303.13
Orlando, Vittorio Emanuele 198.19
O'Rourke, P.J. 282.46
Ortega y Gasset, Jose 51.33, 61.6, 171.23, 208.39, 240.17, 290.28
Orwell, George 140.28, 140.29, 147.41, 211.14, 221.10, 223.13, 269.24, 291.25, 296.15
Osler, William 195.10, 272.11
Otway, Thomas 160.28
Ouida (Marie Louise de la Ramee) 17.13, 108.25, 205.16, 246.11, 265.17
Overbury, Thomas 160.29
Ovid (Publius Ovidius Naso) 17.14, 75.29, 107.17, 154.14, 160.30, 164.24, 208.40, 214.15, 226.22, 281.51, 282.47, 282.48, 284.17, 285.7, 292.25, 299.21, 309.29
Ozick, Cynthia 88.10, 158.39, 161.13, 250.11

Pacuvius (Marcus) 34.19, 281.52
Page, Walter Hines 269.25
Paine, Thomas 88.11, 292.26
Palacio Valdes, Armando 198.20
Palladas 155.26, 213.17
Palmer, George Herbert 284.18
Palmer, Samuel 37.10, 179.17, 224.28, 224.29
Panchatantra 19.16, 268.35, 271.49
Pankhurst, Christabel 210.26
Papashivily, George 270.52
Parker, Dorothy 4.18, 34.20, 80.15, 82.17, 160.31, 243.7, 266.9, 297.8, 305.28, 308.12
Parker, Edward G. 198.21
Parker, Martin 13.18
Parsons, Eliza 103.12
Pascal, Blaise 26.23, 75.30, 75.31, 112.11, 153.29, 158.40, 165.22, 166.17, 187.17, 264.7, 268.36, 290.29, 310.56
Pasternak, Boris 76.17
Pasteur, Louis 300.14
Pater, Walter 136.7
Paterson, Katherine 270.53
Patten, Brian 60.11
Patterson, Joan 91.19
Paulding, J.K. (James Kirke) 93.5
Pavese, Cesare 38.20, 46.19
Paz, Octavio 54.13, 166.18, 183.30, 208.41, 230.7, 268.37
Peacock, Thomas Love 21.21, 30.17, 76.18, 148.27
Pearson, Carol 114.16
Pegler, Westbrook 179.18
Peguy, Charles 195.11
Pei, Mario 158.41
Peirce, Charles Sanders 40.15, 282.49, 300.15
Pellowski, Anne 77.6, 173.9, 197.7, 271.50
Pelton, Robert D. 270.54
Penn, William 68.18, 96.24, 153.30, 240.18, 290.30, 298.52, 307.38
Pepi 310.57
Pepys, Samuel 63.7
Perez Galdos, Benito 202.16
Pericles 292.27
Perlman, Mildred 35.7
Perrault, Charles 270.55
Persian Proverb 45.5, 80.16
Pestalozzi, Johann 254.7
Peters, Elizabeth 83.15, 119.19
Peterson, Virgilia 146.4
Petrarch (Francesco Petrarca) 18.36, 147.42, 160.32
Petre, Maud 50.9
Petronius 107.18

Pettie, George 268.38
Peyser, Joan 108.26
Pfeiffer, John 127.21
Phaedrus 2.3, 26.24, 28.20, 33.7, 298.53, 307.39
Pheilmon 45.6
Philippine Proverb 114.17
Phillips, Stephen 173.10
Phillips, William 31.26
Phillpotts, Eden 300.16
Philo 56.12
Picasso, Pablo 19.17, 77.7, 279.13, 314.25
Pickard, Nancy 10.6
Pickford, Mary 180.17
Piglia, Ricardo 200.7
Pindar 107.19, 281.53
Pinter, Harold 206.17
Piozzi, Hester Lynch Thrale 51.34
Piper, William Thomas 269.26
Pirandello, Luigi 232.16
Pitt, William the Younger 75.33
Plato 7.9, 18.37, 38.21, 41.8, 99.20, 104.8, 111.33, 148.28,
    172.15, 209.21, 240.20, 270.56, 272.12, 298.54, 306.22
Plautus (Titus Maccius) 37.11, 47.10, 96.25, 135.16,
    139.16, 154.15, 188.11, 206.18, 246.12, 261.15, 268.39,
    282.50, 293.9, 297.9, 310.58
Pliny the Elder (Caius Plinius Secundus) 72.14, 154.16
Pliny the Younger (Caius Plinius Caecilius Secundis)
    34.21, 158.42, 169.13, 198.22, 310.59
Plutarch 82.18, 130.10, 268.40
Poe, Edgar Allan 67.7, 109.19, 208.42, 225.26, 225.27
Pogrebin, Letty Cottin 180.18
Poirier, Delia 271.51
Polybius 9.8, 298.55
Pomfret, John 138.12
Ponnamperuma, Cyril 300.17
Poole, Mary Pettibone 41.9, 148.29, 228.23, 280.9
Poore, Charles 312.24
Popcorn, Faith 42.9
Pope, Alexander 24.22, 38.22, 43.8, 53.7, 68.19, 73.9,
    79.6, 82.19, 92.10, 107.20, 120.7, 171.24, 189.12, 189.13,
    238.7, 242.5, 249.23, 259.6, 267.12, 277.7, 303.14,
    305.29, 307.40
Popper, Sir Karl 125.17, 183.31, 252.16
Porter, Katherine Anne 22.13, 276.11, 282.51
Portuguese Proverb 37.12
Posner, George A. 282.52
Pound, Ezra 101.13, 147.43, 159.18, 223.14
Pound, Roscoe 149.11
Powdermaker, Hortense 77.8
Praed, Winthrop Mackworth 269.27
Prentice, George Dennison 253.12
Priestley, J.B. (John Boynton) 43.9, 262.13
Primus, Pearl 110.8
Prior, Matthew 228.24, 256.16, 259.7, 280.10, 290.31
Pritchett, Sir V.S. (Victor Sawdon) 155.27, 252.17
Procter, Adelaide Anne 276.12, 309.30
Propertius 192.10, 271.52, 281.54
Propp, Vladimir 98.18
Proust, Marcel 172.16, 239.8, 251.8
Prynne, William 288.14
Ptahotpe 268.41
Publilius Syrus 5.13, 18.38, 50.10, 55.3, 75.34, 125.18,
    158.43, 226.23, 268.42, 294.33, 298.56
Publius Nigidius 153.31
Pushkin, Alexander 160.33, 162.6, 169.14
Putnam, Emily James 146.5

Puttenham, George 157.14
Puzo, Mario 150.43
Pyle, Ernie 180.19
Pythagoras 214.16, 258.42

Quarles, Francis 294.34, 310.60
Quasimodo, Salvatore 208.43
Quillen, Robert 18.39
Quinault, Philippe 306.23
Quine, Willard Van Orman 157.15
Quinn, Jane Bryant 150.44
Quintilian (Marcus Fabius Quintilanus) 75.35, 87.21,
    153.32, 272.13

Raban, Jonathan 140.30
Rabelais, François 26.25, 92.11, 148.30, 263.7
Racine, Jean 160.34
Radcliffe, Ann 38.23, 51.35
Radner, Gilda 43.10
Raine, Kathleen 187.18
Raleigh, Walter the Younger 163.14
Rand, Ayn 5.14
Ransom, John Crowe 294.35
Ransome, Arthur 271.53
Raper, John W. 18.40
Raspe, Rudolph Erich 298.57
Rassias, John A. 157.16
Rattray, Robert S. 271.54
Rausching, Herman 154.17
Rawlings, Marjorie Kinnan 93.6, 294.36
Ray, John 13.19, 28.21, 38.24, 57.11, 99.21, 112.12, 139.17,
    148.31, 158.44, 179.19, 216.14, 268.43, 281.55, 281.56,
    282.53, 284.19, 297.10, 302.10
Reade, Charles 99.22, 113.7, 116.28, 155.28, 186.14,
    205.17, 224.30, 271.55, 309.31
Reagan, Ronald 211.15
Redmond, Eugene 110.9
Reed, H. Langford 156.11
Reed, Myrtle 306.24
Reed, Thomas B. 99.23
Reid, Thomas 310.61
Renan, Ernest 79.7, 115.7
Renard, Jules 137.10, 148.32, 182.8, 209.22
Renault, Mary 26.26
Rendell, Ruth 164.25, 266.10
Repplier, Agnes 21.22, 54.14, 119.20, 123.16, 137.11,
    148.33, 148.34, 158.45, 229.14, 284.20, 290.32
Reston, James 188.12, 211.15
Retz, Cardinal de 273.12
Reyner, Edward 137.12
Reynolds, Joshua 128.10, 283.23
Rhyne, George 150.45
Rhys, Jean 55.4
Rich, Adrienne 20.7, 153.33, 209.23
Richards, I.A. 166.16
Richardson, Derek 123.14
Richardson, Dorothy M. 286.5
Richardson, Sir Ralph 4.19, 4.20, 269.28
Richardson, Samuel 6.11, 52.4, 56.13, 84.9, 96.26, 113.8,
    120.8, 139.18, 145.35, 172.17, 214.17, 216.15, 217.14,
    224.31, 224.32, 224.33, 235.4, 249.24, 255.11, 270.57,
    291.26, 298.58, 310.62
Richter, Jean Paul 31.27, 93.7, 106.13, 237.11
Rickaby, Joseph 301.14
Ricker, Marilla M. 154.18
Riding, Laura 106.14

Ridley, James 219.30
Riesman, David 271.56
Riis, Jacob 38.25
Riley, James Whitcomb 103.13, 281.57
Rilke, Ranier Maria 164.26, 268.44
Rimbaud, Arthur 155.29
Rinehart, Dana Gillman 210.27
Rinehart, Mary Roberts 150.46
Ristad, Eloise 204.14
Rivarol, Antoine 308.13
Rivers, Caryl 183.32
Roberts, Richard 160.35
Robeson, Paul 197.8
Robinson, Edwin Arlington 160.36, 208.44
Robinson, James 233.17
Robinson, Marilynne, 88.12
Robinson, Pat 183.33
Roche, Boyle 171.25
Roethke, Theodore 111.34, 294.37
Rogers, Samuel 181.33, 208.45
Rogers, Will 108.27, 114.18, 119.21, 125.19, 180.20, 211.17,
    213.18
Roland, Marie-Jeanne 249.25
Rooney, Andy 51.36
Roosevelt, Eleanor 56.14, 167.8
Roosevelt, Franklin D. 166.19, 269.29
Roosevelt, Theodore 210.28, 212.9, 306.25
Root, Elihu 150.47
Rorem, Ned 181.34
Rorty, Richard 268.45
Rosebery, Lord 269.30
Rosen, Marjorie 180.21
Rosen, Richard Dean 138.13
Rosenzweig, Franz 174.14
Rossetti, Dante Gabriel 305.30
Rossini, Gioacchino, 181.34
Rossner, Judith 232.17
Rostand, Edmond 144.15
Rostand, Jean 34.22, 159.19, 187.19, 213.19, 226.24,
    291.27, 299.22
Rosten, Leo 44.15
Roszak, Theodore 183.34, 278.9
Roth, Philip 249.26
Rougemont, Denis de 232.18
Rousseau, Jean-Jacques 1.12, 50.11, 133.8, 145.36,
    258.43, 272.14
Roux, Joseph 165.23, 213.21, 217.15, 228.25, 261.16,
    276.13
Rowland, Helen 47.11, 65.8, 309.32
Rubinstein, S. Leonard 56.15
Rukeyser, Muriel 163.15, 184.11, 270.58, 313.15
Rule, Jane 177.10
Runbeck, Margaret Lee 127.22
Runes, Dagobert D. 72.15, 125.20
Runick, Margaret Lee 15.13
Rushdie, Salman 147.44, 152.19, 185.15
Rusk, Dean 205.18
Ruskin, John 265.18, 298.59
Russell, Bertrand 31.28, 55.5, 70.7, 108.28, 129.11, 177.11,
    221.11, 231.11, 252.18, 273.13, 283.24, 286.6, 309.33
Russell, George William (AE) 152.20
Russell, Lord John 224.34
Russian Proverb 35.8, 39.8, 96.27, 112.13, 142.9, 203.9,
    214.18, 224.35
Rutherford, Mark 250.12
Ryle, Gilbert 183.35

Sabatini, Rafael 148.35
Sackville-West, Vita 49.7
Sacred Books of the East 199.7
Sadeh, Pinhas 271.57
Sa'Di or Saadi (Shaikh-'A-Din) 11.9, 51.37, 202.17,
    205.19, 257.9, 310.63
Safire, William 21.23
Sagan, Carl 252.19
Sagan, Françoise 313.16
Saguisag, Rene 167.10
Saint-Exupery, Antoine de 38.26, 166.20
St. John, Henry 182.9
St. Johns, Adela Rogers 180.22
Saki (Hector Hugh Munro) 86.16
Sallust 282.54
Samuel, Harold 181.35
Samuel, Lord 177.12
Samuelson, Paul A. 227.22
Sanchez, Sonia 208.46
Sand, George (Amandine-Aurore Lucille Dupin,
    Baronne Dudevant) 155.8, 131.12, 135.17
Sandburg, Carl 150.48, 153.4, 208.47, 241.10, 262.14,
    285.8, 310.64
Santayana, George 8.5, 18.41, 20.8, 27.17, 34.23, 184.13,
    206.19, 227.23, 234.15, 237.12, 250.13, 279.14, 288.15,
    299.23, 301.15
Sappho 160.37
Saroyan, William 106.15
Sartre, Jean-Paul 44.16, 281.58
Sarton, May 138.14
Satit, Virginia 44.17
Sawyer, Ruth 299.24
Saxe, J.G. (John Godfrey) 73.10
Sayers, Dorothy 228.26, 304.10
Scarborough, William 103.14, 179.20
Schelling, Friedrich von 234.16
Schiller, Johann Friedrich von 87.22, 90.26, 139.19,
    166.21, 233.18, 273.14, 300.18
Schlegel, August Wilhelm von 159.20
Schlegel, Friedrich von 115.9, 288.16
Schnabel, Artur 17.15, 21.24
Schneiders, Sandra M. 106.16
Schomburg, Arthur A. 87.23, 158.46, 197.9
Schopenhauer, Artur (Arthur) 6.12, 11.10, 48.10, 141.16,
    155.30, 189.14, 237.13, 274.13
Schrader, Paul 180.23
Schreiner, Olive 234.17, 282.55
Scott, Hazel 38.27
Scott, Robert Falcon 52.5
Scott, Sarah 56.16
Scott, Sir Walter 24.23, 99.24, 136.8, 173.11, 202.18, 208.48,
    237.14, 243.8, 246.13, 247.8, 281.59, 281.60, 298.60, 307.41
Scudery, Madeleine de 160.38
Seathe, Chief of the Duwamish Indians 197.10
Seeger, Alan 60.12
Seeger, Pete 97.17
Seferis, George 242.6
Segal, Erich 160.39
Segal, Lore 71.12
Selden, John 27.18, 89.18, 215.12, 216.16, 239.9, 240.21,
    277.8, 306.26
Seldes, Gilbert 43.11
Sellar, W.C. 272.15
Seneca (Marcus Annaeus) 28.22, 51.38, 56.17, 106.17,
    108.29, 135.18, 155.31, 155.32, 253.13, 258.44, 267.12,
    269.31, 272.16, 283.25, 284.21, 305.31, 310.65

Senegaleze Proverb 145.37
Sengupta, Anasuya 309.34
Serling, Rod 4.21
Serov, A.N. 97.18
Sevigne, Marie de 189.15, 205.20, 275.12
Sexton, Anne 93.8
Shadwell, Thomas 257.10
Shaftesbury, Lord 148.36
Shakespeare, William 1.13, 1.14, 1.15, 2.4, 3.12, 3.13,
    3.14, 4.22, 5.15, 6.13, 10.7, 12.13, 17.16, 18.42, 23.13,
    25.15, 25.16. 25.17, 26.27, 28.24, 34.24, 36.13, 49.8,
    55.6, 57.12, 57.13, 62.8, 64.7, 64.8, 72.16, 72.17, 75.36,
    75.37, 86.17, 89.19, 89.20, 89.21, 91.20, 91.21, 93.9,
    104.9, 105.6, 107.21, 107.22, 107.23, 109.20, 111.35,
    117.11, 118.6, 126.12, 127.23, 133.9, 134.3, 139.2, 139.20,
    139.21, 139.22, 139.23, 139.24, 141.17, 143.8, 144.16,
    144.17, 144.18, 147.45, 150.49, 150.50, 153.5, 155.33,
    155.34, 157.17, 160.40, 160.41, 160.42, 160.43, 161.14,
    163.16, 166.22, 170.5, 170.6, 170.7, 176.16, 176.17,
    179.21, 181.36, 185.16, 188.13, 188.14, 192.11, 192.12,
    194.12, 195.12, 198.23, 202.19, 213.22, 220.4, 224.36,
    224.37, 226.25, 240.22, 240.23, 243.9, 246.14, 247.9,
    247.10, 247.11, 249.27, 250.14, 250.15, 253.14, 254.8,
    258.45, 259.8, 261.17, 261.18, 265.19, 266.11, 270.59,
    270.60, 271.58, 274.14, 280.11, 281.61, 281.62, 281.63,
    281.64, 281.65, 281.66, 281.67, 281.68, 281.69, 281.70,
    281.71, 281.72, 281.73, 282.56, 282.57, 284.22, 288.17,
    290.33, 291.28, 292.28, 292.29, 294.38. 294.39, 297.11,
    297.12, 298.61, 302.11, 305.32, 305.33, 307.42, 309.35,
    309.36, 310.66, 310.67
Shannon, George 281.74
Shapiro, Karl 224.38
Sharp, Cecil 97.19
Sharpe, Tom 111.36
Shaw, George Bernard 25.18, 26.28, 30.18, 31.29, 31.30,
    54.15, 57.14, 59.8, 96.28, 109.21, 144.19, 153.6, 177.13,
    199.8, 209.24, 210.29, 214.19, 219.31, 226.26, 227.24,
    228.27, 234.18, 245.9, 258.46, 265.20, 271.59, 273.15,
    274.15, 283.26, 284.23, 298.62, 311.10, 314.26
Shays, Ruth 138.15
Shebbeare, John 272.17
Shedlock, Marie L. 271.60
Sheen, Fulton J. 17.17
Shelley, Mary 163.17
Shelley, Percy Bysshe 1.16, 37.13, 67.8, 158.47, 209.25,
    242.7, 264.8, 265.21, 288.18, 291.29
Shenstone, William 99.25, 111.27, 202.20, 225.28,
    247.12, 310.68
Shepard, Sam 180.24, 183.36
Sheridan, Richard Brinsley 109.22, 169.15, 219.32,
    226.27, 251.9, 293.10, 294.40, 307.43
Sherman, Frank Dempster 79.8
Shikibu, Murasaki 271.61
Shirley, James 72.18
Shorthouse, Joseph H. 201.5
Siddons, Sarah 204.15
Sidney, Sir Philip 85.13, 160.44, 243.10, 246.15, 281.75,
    309.37
Siegfreid, Andre 238.8
Sienkiewicz, Henryk 206.20
Sierra, Judy 90.27, 90.28
Silko, Leslie Marmon 13.20, 169.16, 270.62
Simms, William Gilmore 34.25
Simon, Paul 130.11, 168.9
Simonides 258.47
Singer, Isaac Bashevis 63.8, 77.9, 159.21, 312.25

Sioux Saying 116.29
Sitwell, Edith 31.31, 208.49
Sitwell, Osbert 159.22, 290.34
Skelton, John 145.38
Skelton, Robin 70.8
Skinner, B.F. (Burrhus Frederic) 74.20, 231.12
Smart, Elizabeth 242.8
Smiles, Samuel 250.16, 310.69
Smith, Adam 219.33
Smith, Alexander 228.28, 255.12
Smith, Betty 12.14, 226.28
Smith, Elizabeth Elton 248.13
Smith, Horatio (Horace) 47.12, 73.12
Smith, Jimmy Neil 197.11
Smith, Liz 108.30, 108.31, 108.32
Smith, Logan Pearsall 14.20, 17.18, 97.20, 216.17, 304.11,
    305.34, 314.27, 314.28
Smith, Stevie 1.17, 126.13
Smith, Sydney 51.39, 74.21, 148.37, 188.15, 216.18,
    225.29, 243.11, 256.17, 258.48, 263.8, 282.58
Smith, W.C. (Walter Chambers) 79.9
Smith, Wolfman Jack 229.15
Smollett, Tobias 150.51, 202.21, 294.41, 306.27
Socrates 18.43, 68.20, 214.20, 226.29
Sokolov, Yuri M 271.62
Solon 3.15, 253.15
Solow, Robert M. 20.9
Sontag, Susan 14.21, 31.32, 218.12, 288.19, 296.16,
    298.63, 312.26
Sophocles 72.19, 188.16, 205.21, 242.9, 250.17, 250.18,
    267.13, 268.46, 292.30, 294.42, 298.64
South, Robert 224.39
Southey, Robert 38.28, 81.7, 281.76
Spacks, Patricia Meyer 108.33
Spanish Proverb 111.38, 134.4, 135.19, 164.27, 292.31
Spark, Muriel 27.19, 74.22, 205.22
Spellman, Francis Cardinal 214.21
Spencer, Herbert 76.19, 114.19, 215.16, 250.19, 291.30
Spender, Dale 147.46, 232.19
Spillman, Carolyn V. 38.15, 98.11
Spinoza, Baruch 258.49, 294.43
Spolin, Viola 21.25, 130.12
Sproles, Judy 88.13
Spurgeon, C.H. (Charles Haddon) 28.25, 135.20,
    154.19, 215.13
Stael, Madame (Anne-Louise-Germaine Necker) de
    208.50, 299.25
Stailey, Jay 162.7
Stamp, Sir Josiah Charles 18.44
Stanley, Henry M. 271.63
Stanton, Edwin M. 81.8
Stanton, Elizabeth Cady 150.52
Starhawk (Miriam Simos) 61.7, 162.8, 183.37, 185.17
Stark, Freya 93.10
Statius 94.5
Steele, Richard 6.14, 51.40, 51.41, 51.42, 271.64, 281.77
Stein, Gertrude 100.3, 119.22, 132.5, 235.5, 272.18
Steinbeck, John 271.65
Steiner, George 147.47, 206.2
Steinmetz, Charles 227.25
Stendhal (Henri Beyle) 211.18
Stephen, J.K. (James Kenneth) 225.30, 255.13
Stephens, James 112.14
Stern, Philip Van Dorn 10.8
Sterne, Laurence 54.16, 111.39, 205.23, 206.22, 216.19,
    242.10

Stevens, Wallace 25.19, 95.18, 98.20, 151.15, 171.26, 183.38, 191.13, 209.26, 275.13
Stevenson, Adlai E. 2.5, 154.20, 210.30, 269.32
Stevenson, Robert Louis 1.18, 35.9, 38.29, 42.10, 105.7, 106.18, 111.40, 126.14, 137.13, 140.31, 154.21, 164.28, 200.8, 208.51, 211.19, 231.13, 303.15, 310.70
Stewart, R.J. 183.39
Still, John 116.30
Stillingfleet, John 245.10
Stinnett, Caskie 66.14
Stocks, Baroness (Mary Danvers Brinton) 260.12
Stoddard, Richard Henry 207.12
Stokes, Rose Pastor 279.15
Stoll, Clarice Stasz 116.31
Stone, Jennifer 76.20, 146.7, 180.25, 268.47
Stoppard, Tom 4.23, 64.9, 157.18, 167.10, 228.29, 240.24, 296.17
Storm, Hyemeyohsts 270.64
Stotter, Ruth 270.65
Stout, Rex (Todhunter) 246.16
Stowe, Harriet Beecher 95.19, 178.11, 245.11
Strabo 24.24, 74.23, 94.6, 274.16
Strachey, Lytton 80.17, 115.10, 147.48
Stravinsky, Igor 11.11, 158.48
Strunk, William, Jr. 255.14
Strunsky, Simeon 228.30, 235.6
Sturluson, Snorri 209.27
Suetonius (Carius Tranquillius) 52.6
Sullivan, Anita T. 267.14
Sullivan, Annie 247.13, 276.14
Sullivan, Leon 217.17
Sundermann, Herman 158.49
Surtees, R.S. (Robert Smith) 102.8
Sutro, Alfred 41.10, 166.23
Swahili Proverb 154.22
Swetchine, Anne-Sophie 290.35
Swift, Jonathan 5.16, 6.15, 18.45, 19.18, 27.20, 34.26, 75.38, 75.39, 84.10, 96.29, 139.25, 143.9, 144.20, 148.38, 153.7, 154.23, 155.35, 164.29, 169.17, 179.22, 202.22, 214.22, 225.31, 231.14, 240.25, 241.11, 246.17, 249.28, 251.10, 274.17, 281.78, 282.59, 290.36, 292.32, 293.11, 294.44, 296.18, 300.19, 307.44, 310.71
Swift, Kate 147.35, 185.14
Swinburne, Algernon 19.19, 238.9
Symons, Michael Brooke 42.11
Szasz, Thomas 84.11, 106.19, 124.11, 161.15, 283.27
Synge, John Millington 288.20

Tacitus 13.21, 75.40, 107.24, 198.24, 203.9, 246.18
Taggard, Genevieve 265.22
Tagore, Rabindranath 28.26, 163.18, 213.23, 265.23, 306.28, 310.72, 311.11
Talleyrand (-Perigord, Charles Maurice) 291.31
Talmud 266.12, 272.19, 284.24
Talmud Kiddushin 93.1
Talmud Sukkah 128.11
Tam'si, Tchigaya U 169.18
Tannen, Deborah 44.18, 299.26
Tapahonso, Luci 116.32
Tarkington, Booth 18.46, 211.20
Tartar, Maria 90.29. 90.30, 90.31
Taylor, Ann 178.12
Taylor, Bert Leston 31.33
Taylor, Elizabeth Wray 101.14
Taylor, Sir Henry 47.13, 158.50, 226.30, 253.16
Tedlock, Dennis 183.40

Temple, Sir William 30.19, 224.40
Tennyson, Alfred Lord 37.14, 73.13, 79.10, 85.14, 87.24, 90.32, 111.41, 151.16, 152.21, 160.45, 165.24, 170.8, 170.9, 173.12, 176.18, 198.25, 243.12, 247.14, 267.15, 306.29
Terence (Publius Terentius) 5.17, 17.19, 34.27, 36.14, 108.34, 154.24, 192.13, 253.17, 284.25
Teresa, Mother Of Calcutta (Agnes Gouxha Bojaxhui) 142.10, 276.15, 294.45
Tey, Josephine 150.53
Thackeray, William Makepeace 51.43, 148.39, 178.13, 226.31, 251.11
Thai Proverb 40.16
Thalberg, Irving 180.26
Thatcher, Margaret 207.13, 211.21
Thayer, Lee 34.28
Theocritus 25.20
Thirkell, Anglea 158.51
Thomas, Aline 314.29
Thomas, Caitlin 243.13
Thomas, D.M. 183.41
Thomas, Dylan 24.25, 31.34, 60.13, 182.10, 199.9, 208.52, 278.79
Thomas, Gwyn 208.53
Thomas, Lewis 42.12, 181.37
Thomas, Norman 198.26
Thompson, C.W. (Charles Willis) 80.18
Thompson, Dorothy 126.15
Thompson, Flora 307.45
Thompson, H.W. (Harold William) 292.32
Thompson, Hunter S. 183.42
Thomson, James 24.26, 30.20, 67.9
Thoreau, Henry David 5.18, 8.6, 34.29, 73.14, 74.24, 75.41, 81.9, 91.22, 109.23, 111.42, 114.20, 114.21, 133.10, 145.39, 147.49, 151.17, 165.25, 174.15, 181.38, 206.23, 208.54, 231.15, 237.15, 240.26, 245.12, 255.15, 258.50, 267.16, 268.48, 270.66, 282.60, 292.33, 298.65, 299.27, 309.38, 310.73
Thorne-Thomsen, Gundrun 134.5
Thurber, James 44.19, 67.10, 119.23, 135.21, 148.40, 227.26, 273.16, 308.15
Thurman, Howard 290.37
Tibullus (Albius) 107.25, 139.26, 160.46
Tillich, Paul 158.52
Tolkien, J.R.R. (John Ronald Reuel) 7.10
Tolson, Marvin P. 215.14
Tomlin, Lily 106.19
Toomer, Jean 97.21, 283.28, 300.20
Torrance, Frederic Ridgely 285.9
Torriano 148.41, 294.46
Tourgee, Albion W. 8.7
Tracy, Spencer 4.24
Travers, P.L. (Pamela Lyndon) 90.33
Tree, Sir Herbert Beerbohm 31.35, 58.8, 128.12
Trench, Richard Chenevix 37.15
Trillin, Calvin Marshall 12.15
Trilling, Lionel 91.23, 98.21, 299.28
Triolet, Elsa 222.15
Trollope, Anthony 37.16, 48.11, 81.10, 83.16, 86.18, 151.18, 172.18, 182.11, 208.55, 216.20, 243.14, 246.19, 249.29, 251.12, 256.18, 270.67, 309.39
Truman, Harry S. 5.19
Trump, Donald 83.17
Tuchman, Barbara 115.11
Turnbull, Agnes Sligh 66.15
Turner, Mark 199.10, 199.11

Twain, Mark (Samuel Langhorne Clemens)  4.25, 5.20,
    15.14, 21.26, 27.21, 33.8, 40.17, 45.7, 47.14, 47.15,
    48.12, 51.44, 52.7, 53.8, 54.17, 57.15, 57.16, 60.14, 62.9,
    65.9, 65.10, 75.42, 76.21, 86.19, 102.9, 109.24, 111.43,
    114.22, 116.33, 118.7, 119.24, 119.25, 119.26, 126.16,
    130.13, 132.6, 136.9, 140.32, 140.33, 147.50, 148.42,
    149.12, 151.19, 151.20, 153.38, 153.39, 165.26, 172.19,
    176.19, 186.15, 188.17, 198.27, 201.6, 207.14, 210.31,
    214.23, 220.5, 220.6, 222.16, 223.15, 235.7, 236.9,
    255.16, 256.19, 262.15, 262.16, 265.24, 268.49, 273.17,
    279.16, 286.7, 289.14, 293.12, 298.66, 301.16, 307.46
Tyndale, William  281.80
Tyndall, John  134.6
Tzara, Tristan  291.33

Ueland, Brenda  158.53, 283.29
Unamuno, Miguel de  43.12, 70.9, 126.17, 202.23, 207.15,
    290.38
Unknown  24.28, 29.8
Untermeyer, Louis  225.32
Upanishads  299.29
Updike, John  31.36, 71.13, 180.27, 270.68
Ustinov, Peter  43.13, 148.43

Valency, Maurice  274.18
Valenzuela, Luisa  270.69
Valery, Paul  135.22, 208.56, 252.20
Van der Post, Laurens  181.39
Van Dyke, Henry  51.45, 173.13, 219.34
Van Loon, H.W. (Hendrik Willem)  80.19
Vanbrugh, Sir John  148.44
Vauvenargues, Luc De Clapiers, Marquis de  40.18,
    145.40, 153.40, 165.27, 165.28, 213.24, 274.19, 291.34,
    298.67, 301.17
Vaughn Williams, Ralph  97.22
Veeck, Bill  150.54
Vidal, Gore  153.41, 210.32, 249.30
Viguers, Ruth Hill  38.30
Villiers, Abbe de  256.20
Villiers, George  192.14
Virgil or Vergil (Publius Vergilius Maro)  24.27, 45.8,
    72.20, 85.15, 94.7, 246.20, 276.17, 281.81, 292.34,
    305.35
Vizinczey, Stephen  273.18
Voltaire (François-Marie Arouet)  13.22, 13.23, 31.37,
    61.8, 81.11, 83.18, 87.25, 112.15, 113.9, 168.10, 192.15,
    196.20, 197.12, 205.24, 206.24, 214.24, 227.27, 238.11,
    249.31, 285.10, 290.39, 308.16
Vonnegut, Kurt, Jr.  148.45, 270.70, 313.17

Waddington, Miriam  270.71
Wagner, Jane  147.51
Wagner, Richard  181.40, 181.41
Wagner, Robert F., Jr.  70.10
Wain, John Barrington  223.16
Walker, Alice  163.20, 178.14, 287.15
Walker, Margaret  208.57
Walker, William  297.13
Walpole, Horace  43.14, 186.16, 222.17, 313.18
Walter, Bruno  181.42
Walter, Eugene  145.41
Walters, Barbara  277.9
Walton, Izaak  108.35
Ward, Artemus (Charles Farrar Browne)  210.33, 265.25
Ward, Mrs. Humphrey (Mary Augusta)  83.19, 181.14
Warhol, Andy  286.8

Waring, Anna Letitia  279.17
Warner, Anna  27.22
Warner, Charles Dudley  9.9, 151.20, 196.21, 254.9,
    269.33
Warner, Marina  90.34, 197.13
Warren, Robert Penn  116.34, 208.58, 271.66
Watson, William  173.14, 201.7
Watts, Isaac  27.23
Waugh, Evelyn  158.53, 159.23, 229.16, 283.30, 304.12,
    313.19
Wayne, John  180.28, 282.61
Weber, Eugen  90.35
Webster, Daniel  75.24
Webster, Jean  51.46
Webster, John  139.27, 309.40
Webster, Noah  147.52, 225.33
Wedgewood, C.V. (Dame Cicely Veronica)  115.12
Weil, Simone  219.35, 252.21, 300.21
Weinberg, Steven  300.22
Weinreich, Max  63.9
Weiss, John  137.14, 148.46
Weissman-Chajes, Marcus  12.16
Welles, Orson  77.10
Wellington, Duke of (Arthur Wellesley)  214.25
Wells, Carol  308.17
Wells, Carolyn  3.16, 80.20, 156.12
Wells, H.G. (Herbert George)  116.35, 117.12, 131.13,
    147.53, 154.25, 219.36, 237.16, 284.26
Wells, Kenneth A.  158.54
Welty, Eudora  30.21, 91.24, 231.16, 305.36
Wenders, Wim  270.72
West, Dorothy  116.36
West, Jessamyn  137.15, 148.47, 150.55, 284.27, 313.20
West, Mae  69
West, Rebecca  19.20, 44.20, 175.4
Westcar Papyrus  162.9
Wharton, Edith  51.47, 64.10, 264.9, 295.13, 301.18
Whatley, Richard  216.21
Wheatley, Phyllis  127.24
Whichcote, Benjamin  268.50, 298.68
Whipple, E.P. (Edwin Percy)  137.16
Whistler, James McNeill  18.47, 92.12
White, E.B. (Elwyn Brooks)  119.27, 209.28, 229.17
White, Paulette C.  282.62
White, Theodore H.  211.22
Whitehead, Alfred North  8.8, 74.25, 76.22, 125.21,
    127.25, 159.24, 219.37, 267.17, 296.19, 314.30
Whitehead, William  281.82
Whitehorn, Katherine  158.55
Whitelaw, William  41.11
Whitman, Cedric  184.15
Whitman, Walt  15.15, 18.48, 20.10, 21.27, 116.37, 147.54,
    151.21, 244.9, 262.17, 262.18, 300.23, 303.16, 306.30
Whittier, John Greenleaf  25.21, 187.20, 215.15, 247.15,
    295.14, 310.74
Wickham, Anna  141.18
Wiener, Norbert  219.38
Wiesel, Elie  106.20, 191.14
Wilbur, Richard  311.12
Wilcox, Ella Wheeler  146.8, 148.48, 181.43, 250.20
Wilde, Oscar  5.21, 18.49, 18.50, 21.28, 26.29, 36.15,
    47.16, 51.48, 51.49, 54.18, 56.18, 93.12, 95.20, 101.15,
    108.36, 108.37, 115.13, 120.9, 128,13, 145.42, 153.42,
    153.43, 155.36, 164.30, 169.19, 176.20, 185.18, 192.16,
    207.16, 223.17, 227.28, 238.12, 239.10, 239.11, 244.10,
    249.32, 256.21, 259.9, 260.13, 264.10, 264.11, 274.20,

279.18, 280.12, 284.28, 288.21, 298.69, 299.30, 306.31, 310.75, 311.13, 314.31, 314.32
Wilder, Thornton 11.12, 159.25, 288.22
Will, George 210.34, 287.16
Willard, Nancy 153.44
Williams, Hank 97.23
Williams, Patricia J. 124.12
Williams, Raymond 19.21
Williams, Robin 161.16
Williams, Tennessee (Thomas Lanier) 55.7, 182.12, 292.35, 311.14
Williams, Terry Tempest 74.26, 270.73, 271.67
Wilmot, John 143.10
Wilson, Colin 126.17
Wilson, Earl 108.38
Wilson, Edward O. 8.9
Wilson, John 60.15
Wilson, Spencer 215.16
Wilson, Thomas 160.47, 205.25
Wilson, Woodrow 108.39, 269.34, 272.20
Winchell, Walter 108.40, 253.18
Winfrey, Oprah 287.17, 296.20
Winter, William 187.21
Winters, Yvor 219.39
Winterson, Jeanette 160.48, 183.43, 300.24
Wiseman, Adele 19.22
Wittig, Monique 87.27
Wittgenstein, Ludwig 12.17, 40.19, 147.55, 153.45, 296.21, 310.76
Wodehouse, Sir P.G. (Pelham Grenville) 15.16, 148.49, 236.10
Wolcot, John ("Peter Pindar") 24.29, 75.45, 82.20
Wolfe, Tom 183.44, 229.18
Wolkstein, Diane 60.16, 270.74
Wollstonecraft, Mary 146.9
Woodberry, George Edward 74.27
Woodhouse, Barbara 11.13
Woodson, Carter C. 115.14, 270.75, 295.15
Woolf, Virginia 82.21, 94.8, 119.28, 151.22, 196.22, 223.18, 228.31, 268.51, 270.76, 298.70, 310.77, 312.27

Wordsworth, William 17.20, 23.14, 24.30, 25.22, 32.7, 64.11, 89.22, 94.9, 173.15, 182.13, 255.17, 259.10, 275.14, 305.37
Wotton, Sir Henry 1.19, 66.16
Wouk, Herman 27.24
Wright, Frances 120.10, 176.21
Wright, Richard 231.17
Wyatt, Sir Thomas the Elder 241.12
Wycherley, William 165.29, 241.13
Wyse, Lois 35.10, 123.18

Xenocrates 258.47
Xenophon 213.25

Yeatman, R.J. 272.15
Yeats, William Butler 89.23, 91.25, 98.22, 184.16, 208.59, 226.32, 310.78
Yellow Wolf of the Nez Perce 221.12
Yezierska, Anzia 131.14
Yiddish Proverb 11.14, 12.18, 72.21, 90.36, 112.16
Ying-yai Sheng-lan 21.29
Yolen, Jane 270.77, 271.68
Yonge, Charlotte M. 245.13
Young, Andrew 190.12, 215.17
Young, Coleman 314.33
Young, Edward 28.27, 126.18, 129.12, 228.32, 282.63
Younger, Evelle J. 150.56

Zaidi, Sajida 166.24
Zangwill Israel 41.12
Ze Ami 4.26, 128.14
Zeldin, Theodore 151.23
Zeno 72.22
Zephaniah, Benjamin 208.60
Zinnemann, Fred 64.12
Zipes, Jack 90.37, 90.38, 90.39, 197.14
Zuni Storyteller 112.17
Zweig, Paul 270.78

# Key Word Index

The number preceding the decimal refers to the topic; the number following the decimal locates the quotation within that topic.

ability: a. to hold converse with myself, 206.2

abstraction: quarreled about an a., 226.5; fall into noisy a., 267.1

absurd, absurdity: flatterer never seems a., 96.8; no a. so palpable but that it may be firmly planted in the human head, 237.17; ridicule often checks what is a., 243.8; every a. has a champion, 282.23

accent: of despair, 1.4; dwells in the mind and heart, 1.10 English, 1.11; soul of language, 1.12; of Christians, 1.14; Scots, 1.18;

acrobat: politician is an a., 210.4

act: theatergoing is a communal a., 288.2

action, actions: follow speeches and votes, 3.3; great minds, 3.7; like rhymes, 3.10; questions, not answers, 3.11; to the word, 31.12; is eloquence, 3.14; lie louder than words, 3.16; a. of a teller, 271.26; thought which does not result in a. is nothing much, 291.4; thought precedes a., 291.17

acting: form of confession, 4.1; just a trade, 4.7; requires absorption, 4.14; love of spoken word, 4.16; masochistic ... exhibitionism, 4.17; controlled dream, 4.20; not the noblest thing, 4.24

actor: sculptor carves in snow, 4.2; should be overheard, 4.4; to be successful, 4.5; saying the same thing, 4.8; ain't listening, 4.9; can instruct a priest, 4.10; good, 4.12; dull, 4.22; opposite of people, 4.23; followed ... advice, 4.25; effect lies with his audience, 21.2; a. enunciated very clearly, 78.1

actress: to be a success, 4.3

admire: find not much in ourselves to a., 114.22

advance: denounced as unnatural, 39.8

adventure: strange a. among strange people, 232.2; science ... imaginative a. of the mind, 252.9; calls the a. science, 252.10

advertising: all our a. is propaganda, 221.7

advice: best, 5.2; midst of crowd, 5.3; religion and matrimony, 5.5; approbation, 5.6; brief, 5.11; altered, 5.13; from seniors, 5.18; no a. to give young poets, 209.20; thought he could give a. better than any other person, 301.16

advise: fellow loved to a., 111.39; comic lecturers, 140.5

Aesop: fables, 87.21; the fable of A., 87.23

affectation: necessary, 6.5; distinguished from hypocrisy,

6.7; pleasure, 6.8; awkward and forced, 6.9; recognized, 6.12; terrible enemy, 6.14; don't laugh at youth for its a., 314.27

afraid: of expressing honest emotion, 76.2

age: every a. is fed on illusions, 126.6; of substitutes, 138.2

agreed, agreement: communication means a., 44.15; religion ... least a. upon phenomenon, 234.11

allegorical, allegory: tracts of light, 7.2; fine ornaments, 7.7; cordially dislike, 7.10; speech of feeling is a., 76.17

amazement: poetry is the language in which man explores his own a., 208.17

ambiguity, ambiguous: confronting social a., 43.3; all knowledge is a., 145.22

Americans: feel inferior, 1.11; A. respects convictions, 210.3

amusement: find a. in killing flies, 249.25; two chief forms of a. in the South, 271.66

analogy: often misleading; 8.1; hopeful, 8.2; prove nothing, 8.3; past may furnish, 8.7

analysis, analyze: a. is partially effected in thought, 38.10; of character, 77.9; linguistic a., 157.18

ancestors: lofty deeds of my father's a., 197.5; tales of wars fought by our a., 197.6; my a. in Africa reckoned sound of major importance, 197.8; afraid to be either proud of our a. or ashamed of them, 295.4

ancients: what unsuspected a. say, 13.8; praise of, 13.10; left us ideas, 123.1

anecdote: tall tale, 9.1; tasty, 9.2, fell into anecdotage, 9.3; poor man's history, 9.4; portable, 9.7

angel: mistake for a ghost, 10.1; singing out of tune, 10.2; bends over a dying man, 10.3; circle his throne, 10.5; eloquent as a., 158.11; in action so like an a., 163.16; music is ... the speech of angels, 181.9; parody of an a., 200.8; how like an a. speaks the tongue of woman, 294.30; how like an a. speaks the tongue of woman, 309.25

anger: never without argument, 18.23

animals: not measured by man, 11.1; eyes ... speak great language, 11.2; less worries, 11.3; agreeable friends, 11.4; dumbness in eyes, 11.5; don't talk much, 11.12; man ... talking a., 163.3; man ... a make-believe a., 163.7; the paragon of a., 163.16

announcement: a. that you are going to tell a good story, 270.6

answers: violent, 12.1; worthy of consideration, 12.3; speedily, 12.4; simple, 12.5; dusty, 12.11; soft, 12.12; express, 12.17; sweet the a. makes, 73.7; such an a. would stop them all, 179.21; what we name must a. to us, 185.17; a. the questions of common people, 206.20

antiquities: history defaced, 13.1; fond of, 13.7; cliched and boring, 13.9; full of eulogies, 13.23; volumes of a., 30.13; a. … created to provide professors with their bread, 219.9

anxieties: maps for coping with a., 90.29

anxious: to convince his hearers of his own assertions, 111.33; more a. to speak than to listen, 268.48

aphorism: vulgar, 14.7; cliches, 14.8; states too much, 14.9; more for your time and money, 14.10; last link in a long chain, 14.11; translate a. into continuous prose, 14.12; like a burr, 14.17; salted, 14.20; proverb is a racial a., 224.8

Apollo: the songs of A., 107.23

apology: lay foundation for future offense, 15.1; desperate habit, 15.9; best, 15.11; lovely perfume, 15.13; never apologize, 15.16; a. for his occupation, 35.6

apothegms: pointed speeches, 16.1; not given to a., 16.4; food for every epoch, 16.5

applause: echo of a platitude, 17.1; spur of noble minds, 17.4; sweet, seducing charms, 17.5; of a single human being, 17.8; thundering 17.11; a receipt, 17.15; bold is thy a., 202.18; gain a. through fear, 249.16

apprehension: youth has a quickness of a., 314.22

argue, argument: out of pretty mouths, 18.1; incisive, 18.3; derived from authority, 18.12; gift of nature, 18.13; knock-down a., 18.16, take wrong side of a., 18.22; powerless against bias, 18.25, over-refines, 18.36; bag full of a., 18.43; worst sort of conversation, 18.45; vulgar, 18.49, convincing, 18.50; see all a. for, 26.28; convincing the other by a., 68.14; more ancient than formal a., 87.9; upon the vast interests of vast bodies, 101.12; beating down your adversary's a., 198.14; generally quarrel because they cannot a., 226.6; reason … only argument that belong to man, 233.1; finding a. for going on believing as we already do, 233.17; a. they can't understand, 273.12; truth … always the strongest a., 298.64

Aristotle: a pedantic blockhead, 202.21

arrogance, arrogant: more a. than honesty?, 117.8; height of a. to make average music, 204.1

art: selects and paraphrases, 19.1; speaking the truth, 19.3; communication that insinuates, 19.4; themes in new light, 19.13; speaks truth, 19.15; a lie … realizes the truth, 19.17; start an argument, 19.20; communicates, 19.21; celebration, 19.22; ruled … by the imagination, 127.6; a. of telling lies skillfully, 153.5; a. of memory, 169.9; a. of mythmaking, 183.15; a. of telling you nothing in a great harangue, 192.9; a. of observation, 195.10; poetry is a spoken … a., 208.25; professor of the a. of puffing, 219.32; a. of storytelling, 271.2; a. of repeating stories, 271.5

articulate: how a. once can become when alone and raving at a radio, 229.9

artist: simplifier, 19.2; speaking about his work, 19.6; unhappy lover, 19.14; should be articulate, 19.19; a. is making something exist by observing it, 195.2; bad performance haunts the a., 204.13; great preacher is a great a., 215.14

ass: lives like an a., 124.5; average schoolmaster is … essentially an a., 283.20

assassination: jokes … act of assassination, 140.19; character a., 261.5

assertion: convince his hearers of his own a., 68.20; sweeping a. are erroneous, 101.9; effectiveness of a., 274.15

assumption: dangerous things, 20.3; adopt the most powerful a., 20.9; assume the bad is more potent, 101.7; questioning yesterday's a., 159.1

attention: calling a. to himself, 276.7

audience: keep from coughing, 4.19; cheers of uncomprehending a., 17.18; can't fool an a., 21.1; best a., 21.7; wants to be surprised, 21.8; gives you everything you need, 21.9; pleased with a smart retort, 21.11; can't exchange thoughts with an a., 21.16; practically infallible, 21.22; coughing and non-coughing, 21.24; make a see nearly anything, 26.26; seeing my a. nod appropriation while they sleep, 263.8; first must hold his a.'s attendance, 283.9

authenticity: a. of the miracles, 174.3

author: style of an a., 274.8; tell … my tale's a., 281.78

authority: greatest enemy of a., 148.3; a. to answer that cry of heart, 270.17

autobiography: a. of most famous women, 309.14

baby: sound of a new-born b., 22.3; bald head and pair of lungs, 22.4; not want to hear about b., 22.7; when the first b. laughed, 89.4; put it in the oven for b. and me, 193.13; Rock-a-bye baby on the tree top, 193.15

bad: when she was b., she was horrid, 105.5

bagpipe: like a b. … never talks till his belly is full, 282.53

ballad: don't sing English b., 23.1; sang b from a cart, 23.4; air full of b notes, 23.8; flings a Romany b., 23.9; expect to find lies in, 23.11; of Sir Patrick Spence, 24.6

barbarian: I am a b. here, 299.21

bard: in song-crated skilled, 24.5; lyric poets … sing to accompaniment of instruments, 24.9; smite the chords rudely, 24.10; Olympian, 24.11; share of honor and revenge, 24.12; black and unknown b, 24.16; turns a Persian tale, 24.22; scorn pedantic laws, 24.23; singers and poets, 24.24; shepherds call me b, 24.27; clever b for friends, 24.29; of angels sing, 24.30; all the b. of earth were dead, 187.21; b. shall scorn pedantic laws, 202.18; hear the voice of the b., 305.5

battles: b. of giants, 104.8

bear: b. of very little brain, 33.6

beauty: eloquent beyond … words, 25.1; spark of beauty's heavenly ray, 25.4, a talisman, 25.5; language by which goodness speaks, 25.6; flowering of virtue, 25.7; first to hear, 25.8; dwells on high, 25.10; purgation of superfluities, 25.14; mute deception, 25.20; saying that b. is but skin-deep, 250.19

beginning: in the b. was the story, 270.16; fascination of new b., 270.69; begin. at the b., 271.11; have a variety of b., 271.14

behavior: folks whose b. is most ridiculous, 261.14

belief, believe, believing: kill: b. of fathers, 26.4; compel the soul … to believe, 26.5; nothing rashly, 26.8; act of saying it … as true, 26.9; only half what you see, 26.12; only what I understand, 26.13; what you hear, 26.14; b our own lies, 26.16; who we do not know, 26.19; drunk with a certain b., 75.14; do you b. in fairies, 89.2; don't believe in ghosts, 103.6; b. in gods in some form, 107.14; b. … he has a sense of humor, 119.27; any lie will be believed, 154.17; b. that words have a meaning, 166.16; mythology is what grown-ups b., 184.15; do not b. a word we are saying, 196.22; nothing that you may not get people to b., 205.16; easy to b. that praise is sincere, 213.20; b. whatever it is comfortable to b., 230.2; don't go b. in sayings, 250.7; do not b. the tale, 281.35; knave … make a woman b., 309.40; b. everything you hear said of the world, 311.1

bell, bells: it tolls for thee, 60.6; b. calls others to church, 256.7

bible: book divine, 27.1; clash and contradict itself, 27.5; monument over grave of Christianity, 27.7; like an old Cremona, 27.8; English b., 27.13; is literature, 27.17; full of interest, 27.21; men talk about b. miracles, 174.15

bigot, bigotry: there is too much b., 217.17; b. delights in public ridicule, 243.11

biography: all b. is ultimately fiction, 95.16; gossip … the very stuff of b., 108.26; history … innumerable b., 116.10

bitter: renders us so b. against those who trick us, 296.7

blind: ears are eyes, 72.19; three b. mice, 193.18

blood: smell the b. of an Englishman, 193.2; b. is compulsory, 240.24

boast, boastful, boasting: never be b., 28.5; overweeningly, 28.10; in one street, 28.12; has no merit, 28.14; not of what thou would'st have done, 28.17; dignity begins, 28.27; of his openness, 48.1; b. of honesty, 117.4

body, bodies: never lie, 59.2

bon mot: represents a thing everyone thinks, 29.1; surprise those from whose lips they fall, 29.5; runs risk of being thrown away, 29.6; olives of the martini age, 29.8

bones: jest breaks no. b., 139.131

book: sacred, 27.3; skims cream of others' b., 29.7; legacies … a great genius leaves, 30.1; speak plain, 30.2; good company, 30.3; do not exhaust words, 30.81; bottled chatter, 30.10; receive chief value, 30.19; written by people, 30.21; words in our hearts, 112.17; b of history, b. of sermons, 116.18; I hate b., 145.36; don't need b. to make films, 180.12; you talk just like a b., 282.42

borderline: b. between prose and poetry, 223.9;

bore, boredom, boring: worse crime is b., 31.2; person who talks, 31.5; people who talk of themselves, 31.5; farmer-generals, 31.6; to oneself, 31.8; to death, 31.12; things world only interested in one subject, 31.13; considered a harmless creature, 31.14; roasted, 31.23; a nonentity, 31.24; capacity … to b, 31.25; form of criticism, 31.26; problem for moralist, 31.28; susceptible to disgust, 31.29; inspire b., 31.31; reverse side of fascination, 31.32; secret of being a b., 31.37; eternal paradise would be very b., 91.9; not only b. those nearby, 229.14

boys: fresh, 32.2; beggarly, 32.3; small talk of b., 32.4; b. made of, 32.6; deceive b. with toys, 194.10

brag, braggart, bragging: is they bravery, 28.1; of knowing something, 28.6; be found an ass, 28.23; b with my tongue, 28.24

brain: half a b., 33.4; three kinds of b., 33.5; stored power, 33.8; use b of other people, 41.5; rub and polish our b., 67.5

breeding: concealing how much we think of ourselves, 48.12; test of a man or woman's breeding, 226.6

brevity, brief, briefly: laconic b., 34.1; best recommendation of speech, 34.7; soul of lingerie, 34.20; don't deserve to be said b., 34.22; of being inspired, 34.23; soul of wit, 34.24; soul of eloquence, 75.5

brutally: b. honest, 117.10

brutes: superiority, 11.9; education makes us more stupid than b., 74.11

bugs: that secretly bite the eloquent, 109.2

Burns, Robert: love's sweetest bard, 24.15

business: meant b., 35.3; other people's money, 35.4; persuading crowds, 35.5; everybody's b is nobody's b., 108.35; historian's b., 115.12; b. of the law, 149.9; b. as usual, 165.8; b. of making life, 300.17

camera: I am a c. with its shutter open, 195.5

campaign: you c. in poetry, 210.11

candor: rewards of c., 36.2; my tepid friend, 36.5; anything unpleasant to say, 36.15

cant: of hypocrisy … cant of criticism, 54.16

care: good movies make you c., 180.14

castles: build c. in the air, 91.22

catechism: book of nature is a c., 187.6

cats: ask for what you want, 11.7; c has only nine lives, 65.9; c. and the fiddle, 193.4

cause: clearness of c., 18.11; need not be patroned by passion, 68.3; rhetoric in a worthy c., 240.15

celebrate, celebration; I c. myself, 20.10

censors: satire c. can understand, 249.20

censure: no man can justly c. … another, 141.1

change: only people … who cannot change, 123.18; prayer does not c. God, 214.11

changed: rather be ruined than c., 126.3

chanting: a kind of, 1.5;

character: maxims of men reveal their c., 165.27; mystery … left in the revelation of c., 182.12; man's reputation would not know his c., 238.5; man's c. is revealed by his speech, 268.29; universe … too vast to have any c., 300.15; index of c., 305.10

charm: conversation has a kind of c., 51.38; to incite to learning, 74.23; c. us orator, 198.25; c. an understanding age no more, 281.1

chat, chatter: sort of chit-chat, 37.2; evening's c, 37.3; leave world to c., 37.4; hare-brained c., 37.5; on various subjects, 37.8; not worth a chuet, 37.9; as I flow, 37.14; insignificant c., 37.16; c. of a beggar's teeth, 147.2

child, children: advice to c., 5.19; cruel to bore a c., 31.22; voices of immorality, 38.1; seen and not heard, 38.4; violations committed by c., 38.9; spake as a c., 38.18; pick up words, 38.24; always say what's true, 38.29; birth of an Aztec c., 87.8; solutions … child can grasp, 90.5; fairy tales of my childhood, 90.26; give c. "roots and wings," 98.11; what the c. imitates, 128.5; listens like a three years' c., 158.10; miracles are the c. of mendacity, 174.8; are natural mythologists, 184.12; c. is fed with milk and praise, 213.13; became a c. on earth for me, 234.4; spoiled c. of art, 270.33; tales as c. loves to hear, 281.76; teach a c. to be good, 284.8; c. should be led into the right paths, 284.25; make me a child again just for to-night, 292.2

church: I like the silent c. before the service begins, 216.6

civilization: essential ingredients, 22.9; manure of the next, 39.2; not exist until … written language, 39.5; speech is c. itself, 268.28

classes: familiar and sentimental, 51.35

clear, clearly, clarity; as mud, 40.1; as a London fog, 40.7; crystall, 40.12; speak c., 78.2

clearness: c. is everything, 147.10; chief merit of language is c., 147.17; c. ornaments profound thoughts, 274.19

clever, cleverness: too c. is dumb, 41.7; impart c to others, 41.8; do not mind a man being c., 306.22

cliche: c are sociable, 42.2; dead poetry, 42.3; have new c., 42.4; like cat's fleas, 42.5; organizes life, 42.6

clown: c. is often deadpan, 148.17; wisest people are the c., 306.8

clues: Myths ... c. to the spiritual potentialities, 183.8

comedian: test of real c., 43.7

comedy: is tragedy, 43.2; an escape, 43.4; criticism, 43.6; society protecting itself, 43.9; farce is nearer c., 92.2; speaks for civilization, 92.5; appeals to the collective mind, 92.6

comic: smile at c. powers, 43.1

command: easier ... to c. than to teach, 283.18

commandment: eighth, not made for bards, 24.7; do you know the eleventh c., 300.13

communicative, communication: a c who has nothing to c., 31.7; improvement in c., 31.11; too much c., 44.3; mass, 44.11; evil, 44.13; balancing act, 44.18; listening is not always auditory c., 158.37; complex things are c. to great masses of people, 167.4; prayer is power within us to c., 214.14; melancholy shrinks from c., 247.7; silence ... is a form of c., 258.30; talk can't accomplish ... c., 282.46

community: heirlooms of the c., 110.9; c. of those who seek the truth, 145.6; your standing in the community, 238.4

company: of clever, well-informed people, 51.2

comparisons: are odious, 45.1, 45.7; make enemies, 45.6

complain, complaining, complaint: delightful to c., 46.4; of the age we live in, 46.6; never c., 46.9; no point in c., 46.10; c. is cheap, 46.13; inner need to c., 147.51; c. is the largest tribute Heaven receives, 214.22

complicated: any problem, however c. ... looked at in the right way ... become more c., 218.2

compliment, complementing: forensic anaesthetic, 47.2; is lying, 47.3; cost nothing, 47.5

compromise: printed texts of folktales are c., 98.10

conceal, concealment: c. inmost thoughts, 48.6; capacity for c. ... away the truth, 211.13; men talk only to c., 282.63

conceive, conceived: c. well is expressed clearly, 40.3

concise: strive to be c., 40.8

conclusion: jumping to c., 49.6; cannot come to any c., 49.7; foregone c. 49.8

confess, confession: c. a defect, 50.1; good for the soul, 50.2; saddest of all c., 99.5; a lack of humor?, 119.8; man who c. his ignorance, 125.5; not ashamed to c., 125.6

confidence: causes more conversation, 51.23

Confucius: anticipated the apothegm, 16.2

confused: may be c. but not convinced, 205.11

conscience: bid your c. look within, 260.8

consent: take your silence for c., 258.23

contempt: remains entirely concealed, 48.10; dash of c. for the opinions of his audience, 198.11; signified my c., 294.41

content: is the inside of style, 274.9

contest: c. between education and TV, 287.6

contradict, contradiction: old Con would c. him!, 18.34; respectable way of c. myself, 64.9; spirit of c., 68.7; risk no c., 95.6; wise c. themselves, 306.31

controversy: scores most in c., 68.5

conversation: accents firm and loud in c., 1.7; to enliven the c., 18.31; use of book without pictures or c., 30.5; with finest men of past centuries, 30.11; with mighty

dead, 30.20; with a superior man, 51.3; no rules for c., 51.4; three cannot take part in a c., 51.11; completes [a gentleman], 51.12; strikes the hour, 51.13; teaches more than meditation, 51.14; beginning and end of knowledge, 51.16; polite, 51.24; like a dear little baby, 51.26; interpretation of worlds, 51.30; socializing instrument, 51.33; is feminine, 65.1; marriage is one long c., 164.28; most c. are simply monologues, 175.3; no such thing as c., 175.4; c. between friends, 181.8; interrupts to c. of others, 202.17; poetry is subconscious c., 208.46; often praise and dispraise in c., 213.2; prayer is c. with God, 214.4; good pun ... among the smaller excellencies of lively c., 225.6; followed c. as a shark follows a ship, 225.24; questions ... breath of life for a c., 227.20; reading ... silent c., 231.8; preaching ... by- word for a long and dull c., 256.17; silence is one of the great arts of c., 258.40; made his c. perfectly delightful, 258.48; c. is the legs on which thought walks, 291.6; wit is the salt of c., 307.24; sustain a c. with a lady, 309.38; writer ... failed conversationalist, 312.2

convenience: of a general statement, 101.8; generalizations are merely c., 101.14

conviction: seem open to c. yourself, 205.6

convince, convincing: argument seldom c., 18.19; others by our arguments, 18.28; best way to c. a fool, 99.3; to be a c. talker, 282.52

counsel, counseling: bad, 5.1; good, 5.4; cease thy, 5.15; personal c. on a group scale, 16.7

counselors: irony and pity are two good c., 137.5

countenance: confessed, 50.5

country: may our c. be always successful, 293.1

courage: destitute of c., 2.3; destitute of c., 28.20; to ask questions, 52.1; most reliable and useful c., 52.3

courtesies, courtesy: small c. sweeten life, 53.1; politic witchery, 53.3

craft: magic is the c. of shaping, 162.8

creation: first recorded stories, 27.11; criticism: sincere, 47.10; language is a process of free c., 157.6; c. of musical language, 181.42; myth ... must be the collective creation of ... anonymous people, 183.27

creative: listens to a story one is being c., 158.1

credulity: progress of c., 174.6

criticism: casual conversation, 54.1; meant as a standard of judging well, 54.6; art of praise, 54.8; acid that dissolves images, 54.13; c. other people, 54.17; to love without c., 160.2

crowds: speak in heroes, 114.13

cruelty: the most intolerable, 55.2; c. story runs on wheels, 108.25

cry, crying: gets the milk, 22.1; likes stories that make her c., 247.13; c. out against sin, 260.3; voice of one c. in the wilderness, 305.25

culture: an instrument wielded by professors, 219.35

cured: who was ever c. by talk, 282.41

curiosity: key to creativity, 56.10; begets c., 56.13

curse, cursing: a little friendly c. 57.3; fruit of c., 57.8; like a donkey, 57.9; with bell, book and candle, 57.10; pure ornamental c. 57.16; c. be the verse, 303.14

custom: c. is the most important mistress of language, 157.9; motion pictures presents our c., 180.26; as any c. is disused, 310.42

cynics: c. can chill and dishearten, 58.3;

cynicism: unpleasant way of telling the truth, 58.5; idealism gone sour, 58.6; humor of the hatred, 58.8; sure sign of youth, 314.11

damage: television's primary d., 287.12

dance, dancing: a measured pace, 59.1; hidden language of soul, 59.5; perpendicular expression, 59.8; fairies left off d., 89.18

danger, dangerous: all generalizations are d., 101.5; sincere ignorance, 125.15; d. in being persuaded, 205.25; d. to say things that people might remember, 210.8; general rules are d., 245.13

day, days: most completely lost of all d., 148.12; brave d. of old, 271.37

daydream: is an evasion, 183.26

dead: all gods dead except god of war, 107.5

death: animals hear about d., 11.10; cruel note, 60.1; pale priest, 60.3; linguistic predicament, 60.5; dialogue between death and love, 64.3; less hideous than explanations; 86.13; grumbling is the d. of love, 160.9; like a man who talks me to d., 163.17; defend to the d. your right to say it, 196.20; d. is the sanction of everything, 271.3; all stories … end in d., 271.28; quiet nonchalance of d., 277.4

debate: is masculine, 65.1; better to d. a question without settling it, 227.15

debt: by disputation, 68.4

deceit, deceive: a liar … doesn't know how to d., 153.40; propaganda doesn't d. people, 221.5; human society is founded on mutual d., 264.8; temper discretion with d., 283.30

decision: give me your d., 141.10

defect: no curiosity, 56.18

defense: in d. of the indefensible; 211.14; d. of the indefensible, 269.24

deficiency: symptom of mental d., 268.7

definition; enclosing of a wilderness, 61.1; sack of flour, 61.2; cannot afford narrow d., 61.7; d. overlap but they almost never coincide, 146.3

delude: knew how to d. his listeners, 282.44

demon: story … written without a d., 270.67

demythologizing: essay on the d. of the New Testament, 234.5

democracy: government by discussion, 67.1

designs: narrative of d. which have failed, 186.8

describe, description: d. what we have not seen, 85.9; accurate d. of what has never occurred, 115.13; set out to d. the indescribable, 159.9; tact … ability to d. others as they see themselves, 280.9

deserve: better to d. honors, 118.7; uncontrollable d. to talk, 298.38

desire: to be cruel and to hurt, 55.4; man who conquers his d., 114.3

detective story: about restoration of order, 95.14

devil: apology for the d., 15.2; shame the d., 36.7; give the d his due, 62.2; d. is the father of lies, 154.2; to tense the d., 158.4; never so black as painted, 173.7; sarcasm … the language of the d., 248.4; tell the truth and shame the d., 298.21

dialect: speech of the people, 63.1; Irish, 63.3; Babylonia d., 202.5; d. tempered with slang, 262.1

dialogue: sound among other sounds, 64.5, wooden, 64.8; reserved for culminating moments, 64.10; mute d. with Mother's heart, 64.11; writes d. by cutting monologues in two, 313.6

diary: life of every man is a d., 155.6; life of every man is a d., 163.1; memory … is the diary, 169.19

dictionary: defining what is unknown, 61.5; masterpiece in literature … a d. out of order, 159.10; need no d. of quotations, 228.2

die: d. of laughing, 148.38; legends d. hard, 152.10; stories that never, never d., 270.40; shall d. very young, 314.23

difference: between courage and bluster, 52.4; between what one hears and sees, 65.7; between a cat and a lie, 65.9; of taste in jokes, 140.15; between a lecture and a speech, 151.19; between mad people and sane people, 203.8; between gossip and philosophy, 206.10; between a common man and a poet, 209.15; between mad people and sane people, 270.36; d. between knowing and understanding, 299.18

difficulty: men govern nothing with more d. than their tongues, 294.43

dignity: humor … an affirmation of d., 119.11; no man's d. can be asserted without being impaired, 226.30

diplomacy: lying for your country, 66.1; art of saying "nice doggie," 66.2; rules of d., 66.8; lying in state, 66.11

diplomats: when a diplomat says yes, 66.6; open mouth, 66.9; only decent d., 66.13

disagree, disagreement: d. without being disagreeable, 102.1; beginning of thought is in d., 291.18

discourse: nothing can be retrenched, 34.8; long d. argueth folly, 99.16; every d. ought to be a living creature, 270.56; d. without being interrupted, 312.24

discovered: meanings are d., 166.9

discretion: more important than eloquence, 51.15

discussion: confirming others in their errors, 67.2; in America means dissent, 67.10

disease: imagination is a contagious d., 127.25

dispute: about trifles, 18.18; no and yes cause, 68.6; long d., 68.10; make an end of, 68.11; philosophical d., 206.12

disguise: wear some d., 6.6

distrust: public regards lawyers with great d., 150.1

doctor: disease killed him not the d., 168.3; are so opinionated, 168.4

doctrine: sure to seek, 27.4; d. hidden under the veil, 303.5

dog: barking d., 3.1; little d. laughed, 193.4; to fetch her poor d. a bone, 193.12; prose books are the show dog, 223.6

dogma: can't teach an old d. new tricks, 297.8

double-entendre: horrible d.e., 69.1; shows double sense, 69.3

doubt: father of invention, 70.2; d. … all things, 70.4; keep your d. to yourself, 70.6

drama: life is a d., 155.9; good d. must be drastic, 288.16; d. … teaches … self-knowledge, 288.18

dreams: individual's folk-tales, 71.1; to sell, 71.2; regarded as revelations, 71.8; faithful interpreters, 71.10; myths … are public d., 183.7; fragment from the life of d., 281.16; our d. are tales, 281.21

drunkenness: not a heresy, 113.7

duel: repartee is a d. fought with the point of jokes, 236.6

duty: first d. of a lecturer, 151.22; first duty of love, 158.52; every man content that his neighbor may neglect his d., 219.33; always declares it is his d., 273.15

ear: lend e. in many a secret place, 25.22; e. troubles mouth, 72.1; little pitchers, 72.7; in one e., 72.8; hang your e., 72.9; all e., 72.10; e. burns, 72.14; e. pricked up, 72.20; social sewerage in his e., 108.23; think … of my whole body as an e., 147.1; use e. as boltingcloth, 158.5; mermaid did their e. entice, 170.7; await your tidings, 188.11; e. believe other people, 195.3; as I read my ears are opened, 231.17; not speak merely to please the e., 268.18; stories to delight his e., 270.60; filled through the e., 272.12; whispering tale in a fair lady's e., 281.71

earnest: word in e., 310.22

earth; giants in the e., 104.7; speak to the e., 187.16

easy, easier: lover than a husband, 29.2

eat, eating: e. a Christmas pie, 193.9

echo: mockery in it, 73.2; the mimic, 73.3; knows all languages, 73.4; e. are truly endless, 142.10; make one the e. of what cannot cease speaking, 313.7

education: commences at mother's knee, 38.7; begins a gentleman, 51.12; ability to listen, 74.10; continuing dialogue, 74.15; natural process, 74.19; a leading out, 74.22; all entertainment is e., 77.8; only one thing can kill the movies … education, 180.20; e. altereth nature, 187.15; prejudice of e., 217.1

effect, effective: e. which lectures produce, 151.2; satire … to be e., 249.30; fit to be spoken or read aloud with e., 274.10

effort: to listen is an e., 158.48

ego; egotism: e. … salt of conversation, 51.45; talking at the top of his e., 282.18

ejaculations: short prayers darted up to God, 214.8; religions of the world are the e. of a few imaginative men, 234.6

elephants; arguments are like e., 18.20; fly into e., 28.21

eloquence, eloquent: of the bar, 34.21; child of knowledge, 75.12; well-rounded phrase, 75.16; like a razor whetted with oil, 75.39; does not consist in speech, 75.44; language of nature, 240.5; dumb e., 240.6; called e. in the forum, 240.26; talkative rather than e., 282.54; wit is cultured e., 307.2

emotions: from A to B, 4.18; convey an e., 76.11; positive e. put to work, 148.13; nostalgia is a dangerous e., 191.8; wit … epitaph of an e., 307.37

enchanter: spell operates … upon the imagination, 19.10

end: decline to accept the e. of men, 163.5

enemy: of long explanations, 86.5; a flatterer, 96.12; joke never gains over an e., 140.17; kinder the e. who must malign us, 141.8; O Lord make my e. ridiculous, 214.24

English: language of imaginative race, 42.3; standard, 147.49; correct E. … slang of prigs, 262.7

entertain, entertainment: bard was to provide e., 24.1; hardly e. an echo in it, 73.14; e. all comers, 77.2

enthusiasm: oratorical e., 198.27; renewal of e. after storytelling, 271.36

epic: no e. with artillery, 79.7; is the sea, 79.8

epigram: stiffen in cold e., 80.2; a dwarfish whole, 80.4; compared to the scorpion, 80.6; rapier-pointed, 80.9; flashlight of a truth, 308.21

epitaph: let no man write my e., 81.7; rarest quality in an e. is truth, 81.9; were an e. to be my story, 160.12

equivocation: half-way to lying, 153.30

eroticism: wit destroys e., 307.29

error: new maxim … brilliant e., 165.19

escape: anxious longing for e., 256.18

eternity: teacher effects e., 283.1

ethic: to find a perfect e., 177.3

etiquette: apologies for unfortunate occurrence, 15.10

eulogy, eulogies: most moving kind of speech, 81.6; invariably dull, 81.10

euphemisms: like fashion have their day, 82.1; secret agents on a delicate mission, 82.6; national passion for e., 82.15

evangelists: knew they had to write down Christ's teachings, 197.13

evasion: nothing like a metaphor for an e., 171.21

evil: dialogue a necessary e., 64.12; cause of all human e., 101.6; e. news rides post, 188.9; resolution to avoid all e., 239.4; if you speak e., 261.12; prefer to speak e. of ourselves, 275.10; e. of men, 283.19; keep thy tongue from e., 294.32

exactness: words are made for a certain e. of thought, 310.18

exaggeration: every concept is an e., 61.6; false eloquence is e., 75.1; people addicted to e., 83.3; Roman trait, 83.12; cheapest form of humor, 119.19

examples: e. draw when precept fails, 256.16; e. destroys, 256.20

exceptional: think ourselves e., 54.4

exceptions: are as true as rules, 245.7

excite, excitement: of an untold story, 76.9; e. the spectators, 77.10

excuses: bad excuse … better than none, 84.3; more than tacit confessions, 84.9

exercise: imagination grows by e., 127.17

exhausted: talks more is sooner e., 268.27

existence: beings with superhuman powers, 26.22; noting e. until .. it is observed, 195.2

expediency: e. wearing a long white dress, 149.3

experience, experiencing: fixed in aphorisms, 14.3; e. in common, 44.14; severe mistress 85.2; with the facts of life, 146.4; life of the law, 149.6; of popular lecturing, 151.11; e. things that you are not familiar with, 180.6; all tragic human e. gain in pathos, 201.6; prisoner of his own e., 217.13; proverbs are the deductions of our e., 224.5; proverbs … daughters of daily e., 224.10; notion of a universality of human e., 300.5; string our e., 310.40

explain, explanation: best argument, 18.8; why they're born, 38.27; never e., 46.9; loathe e., 86.1; explain his e., 86.2; facts e. nothing 88.12; can't e. one's marriage, 164.12; for those who believe in God, no e. is necessary, 174.10; every m. can be e. after the event, 174.14; poetry cannot be e., 208.21; cannot e. the sadness, 247.5; not wit which needs e., 307.34

expresses, expressing: music e. that which cannot be said, 181.22; nearest to e. the inexpressible is music, 181.23; quote others .. the better to e. myself, 228.22

expression: most of our e. are metaphorical, 171.19; the utmost facility and copiousness of e., 198.22; executive e. of human immaturity, 211.4; dramatic power of e. 271.60

eye, eyes: say one thing, 44.6; e. have ears, 64.2; he who has e. sees something in everything, 171.18; music is the e. of the ear, 181.13; e. believe themselves, 195.3; heavenly rhetoric of thine e., 240.22; soft closer of our e., 263.5; drink to me only with thine e., 293.7; here's mud in your e., 293.8

fable: allegorical, 7.3; first pieces of wit, 87.1; bridge … leads to the truth, 87.3; old f. haunts me, 87.14; bearers of f., 87.27; gods of f., 107.7; history fades into f., 116.23; national literature begins with f., 159.14; grains of truth in the wildest f., 298.12

facts: stubborn things, 88.6; ventriloquist's dummies, 88.6; more powerful than arguments, 88.11; all f. created equal, 150.12; f. are fine, far as they go, 152.11

failings: to talk about, 36.6

fairies, fairy: see the f. riding, 8.6; at the bottom of the garden, 89.9; knock g. castles down, 122.2; land of literature is a f. land, 159.13; stories are like f. gold, 270.44

fairy tales: not proper to tell children f.t., 38.25; told in the books, 89.10; represent archetypes, 90.16; effective when told from memory, 90.21; popular poetry, 90.25; mass-mediated f.t., 90.39; invent f.t. about everything, 126.13; myth is not a f.t.a, 183.35; literary f.t. was being institutionalized, 197.14; don't ask questions of f.t., 227.13

fairyland: sunny country of common sense, 89.7

faith: points of f., 68.17; in our fairy tales, 90.18; that moves mountains, 137.8; prayer is the voice of f., 214.9

falsehood: fiction is not f., 95.10; lying is father to f., 153.14; difference between telling a f. and lying, 153.31; one f. treads on the heels of another, 154.24

fame: a goddess capricious is f., 156.10

family: terrible f. They, 250.20; ours was a storytelling f., 310.46

fanatics: infallible way of making f., 205.24

fancy: a person's real mind, 20.4; loves about the world to stray, 91.5; full of shapes is f., 91.21; power of f. over reason, 161.10

fantasy: solid base in reality, 91.3; reality can easily become the current f., 232.17

farce: appeals to ... their collective belly, 92.6; is played out, 92.11; will go on, 92.12; life is the f., 155.29

farewell: first f. has pathos in it., 201.2

fate: defy f. with mocking laughter, 92.3; f. is just even to rival storytellers, 271.55

father: gloomy, 93.1; who my f. was, 93.8; never seen nor heard, 93.12; hear the instruction of thy f., 133.6; recitals of the f. to the children, 197.12

faults: of our own, 46.11; confessed a f., 50.3; confess f. in plural, 50.6; to take up all the discourse, 51.41; defend yourself for your f., 84.1; tell men of their foulest f., 249.12

fear: constant assertion of belief, 26.21; courage is resistance to f., 52.7; ghost ... visible sign of an inward f., 103.2; brought gods into the world, 107.18; nostalgic about old f., 191.1; deeper the nostalgia and the more complete the f., 191.14; you f. some trick, 297.9

feel, feelings: hoard up our f., 46.19; talking what they f., 75.43; no more than I express, 76.1; sensation of f. good all over, 148.7; poetry is the revelation of a f., 208.43; deepest f. always shows itself in silence, 258.39; f. allowed to express itself, 310.72; writes in order to f., 313.15

fiction: show a better life, 95.1; historical, 95.3; what f. means, 95.19; history is agreed upon f., 116.1; no longer any such thing as f. or non-f., 186.4; poetry is a comforting piece of f., 208.34; truth is ... stranger than f., 298.14

fight, fighting: act as if he were f. bees, 216.11

figures of speech: based on sports, 44.12

first: f. ... who mixed narration and dialogue, 186.5

flatterer, flattery: applause ... from unwilling throats, 17.13; mistake f. for truth, 38.23; grace in f., 47.13; f. tells you your opinion, 96.1; always acceptable, 96.3; sits in the parlor, 96.9; incense ... offered to female beauty, 96.16; swallow greedily any lie that f. us. 298.23; fond youth f. itself, 314.19

flatulency: bravos but induce f., 213.15

fluently: knows so little ... f., 125.10

folk: wee f., good f., 89.1; some f. are wise, 306.27

folk music: bunch of fat people, 97.8; thought f.m. was something old, 97.17; expression of the human mind, 97.19

folk tales: collective dreams, 71.1; stories that never run out of editions, 98.1; a narrative of adventures, 98.15

folklore: give expression to deep universal emotions, 98.2; collection of ridiculous notions, 98.12; pot-likker of human living, 98.13

folksinger: sings through his nose, 97.1; sings songs nobody ever wrote, 97.2

folly: proclaims the general f. first ... passes for a prophet, 99.13

food: of popular applause; 17.20

fool, foolish: two f. in every marker, 35.8; wise to seem f., 41.1; has no dialogue with himself, 64.4; may talk, 75.21; flattery the food of f., 96.29; treasure of a f. ... his tongue, 99.1; two kinds of f., 99.12; any f. can make a rule, 109.23; heart of a f. is on his tongue, 112.1; fool ... first invented kissing, 144.20; let the f. talk, 145.30; any f. can tell the truth, 153.8; greatest f. are the greatest liars, 153.10; he's a f. that marries, 165.29; every f. believes what his teachers tell him, 177.13; he who asks a question is a f. for five minutes, 227.6; f.'s remark ... a thorn concealed in mud, 235.3; any f. can make a rule, 245.12; wise speeches of f., 269.8; talks to himself speaks to a f., 282.38; when we play the f., 288.11; not a f. who knows how to hold his tongue, 294.21; f. who kiss and tell, 294.29; let a f. hold his tongue, 294.33; heart of a f. is in his mouth, 306.12; f. and his words ... soon parted, 310.68

foot: poetry of the f., 59.3

force: listening is ... a creative f., 158.36

Foreign Secretary: poised between a cliche, 42.8

forensics: eloquence and reduction, 100.3

forgive, forgiveness: forgive those who bore, 31.18

France: despotism tempered by epigrams, 80.3

frankness: cruel people describe themselves ... paragons of f., 55.7

freedom: shall awhile repair, 89.8

friend: tell ... disagreeable truths, 36.3; are dreams and fables, 87.10; persuasion of a f. is a strong thing, 205.13; poetry ... friend to whom you can say too much, 208.6; lying and poetry are always f., 208.26; people-pleaser is not always the f. of the people, 210.7; make your f. your teachers, 272.7; sympathize with a f.'s success, 279.18; only good teachers ... are those f. who love you, 283.29

fun: to make fun of a person, 243.2

function: what is the real f. ... of language?, 147.50; f. of the artist, 252.6

funeral: good f. needs a joke, 140.1; never joke at f., 140.26

funny: everything is f., 119.21; difficult to like anybody's else ideas of being funny, 119.22; whatever is f. is subversive, 140.29

future: must be clothed in imagery, 183.17

game: parody is a g., 200.6

garden: how does your g. grow, 193.10

generality; generalization: vague g. is a lifesaver, 101.1; necessary to advancement of knowledge, 101.10; distrust all g. about women, 309.33

genius: in every madman a misunderstood g., 161.1; requires a g. to make a good pun, 225.10; g. for repartee is a gift, 236.7; write some flashes of g., 271.8; word-coining g., 310.77

gentleman: what sort of g. is the devil, 62.4; never rude unintentionally, 102.5;

geography: history is all explained by g., 116.34

gesture: language in their very g., 147.45

ghost: go back to their quiet graves, 103.7

giants: not g. but windmills, 104.1;

gift: most useful g. ... curiosity, 56.14; of fantasy ... meant more, 91.6; divine g. of laughter, 148.15; g. of laughter, 148.35; narrative g., 186.15; what a g. a story is, 270.42

girl: drive man out of his wits, 105.1; little g. made of, 105.2

glass: satire is a sort of g., 249.28

God: ashamed, 28.26; whispers in the ear, 72.3; is the poet, 106.3; disposes, 106.10; cannot alter the past, 115.2; language ... the immediate gift of G., 147.52; G. said ... make man in our image, 163.13; has coined a parable, 199.4; G. knows what is good for us, 214.20; pray as if everything depended upon G., 214.21; one of the chief pretenders to the throne of G. is radio, 229.17; an unutterable sigh in the human heart, 257.5; silence ... voice of our G., 258.37; doesn't require us to succeed, 276.15

goddesses: mother, 107.2

gods: fear first made g., 94.5; boastful g. of ancient myths, 98.9; father 107.2; every g. did seem to set his seal, 107.22; whom the g. wish to destroy, 161.6; man is a fallen g., 163.11; follow the myths about the g., 183.12; tricky or boastful g. of ancient myths, 183.13 poetry, language of the g., 208.45; g. ... is moved by the voice of prayer, 214.15; very g. contend in vain., 273.14; whom the g. love grow young, 314.31

good: for your own g., 205.9; say nothing g. of yourself, 213.21; much g. in the worst of us, 282.31

goodbye: how to say g., 65.8

good-nature: more agreeable in conversation, 51.1

goodness: we may ... speak of g. as love in conduct, 160.35; g. of the true pun, 225.26

gospel: all is not g., 27.12; written for people thinking mythologically, 184.9; does not know how to preach the g., 216.1; 'tis not preaching the g., but ourselves, 216.19

gossip: irresponsible communication, 108.1; emotional speculation, 108.2; are frogs, 108.10; opiate of the oppressed, 108.17; all literature started as g., 159.6

grace: g. of listening, 158.42

grammar: death ... grammatically correct full-stop, 60.11; business of g., 109.6; can be a little ungrammatical, 109.8; discovered but not invented, 109.14; social criticism begins with g., 166.18

gratifies: nothing so much g. an ill tongue, 294.19

greatness: exaggeration ... companion of g., 83.18

greedy: g. of getting information, 132.2

Greeks: held novelty in such disdain, 13.11

grief: to weep ... first feel g., 76.13; patch g. with proverbs, 224.37; sigh with g., 257.6; calms one's g. by recounting it, 266.3; sometimes expressed in platitudes, 266.10; g. that does not speak, 266.11

grievance: purpose in life, 46.15; obsessed and consumed with my g., 131.14; jokes are g., 140.25

Grimm: fairy tales, 90.2; rank next to Bible in importance, 90.4

griot: have transmitted the classics of African societies, 110.2; oral historian, 110.6; men of the spoken word, 110.7

growth: g. of understanding, 299.7

grumble, grumbling: believe in g., 46.16; g with the rest, 46.17

guesser: best g. the best prophet, 222.6

habit: talking is just a nervous h., 282.24

hair: stood upright like porcupine's quills, 94.2

hand: ready, 3.8

happiness: gods have no thoughts for our h., 107.24; enjoy h. in silence, 129.8; h. which is not also noise, 189.8

hate: explanations, 86.19; imagine we h. flattery, 96.20; careless flattery, 96.23; plain speech breeds h., 213.17; h. some people because we do not know them, 217.5; h. what they cannot understand, 299.14

hated: rather be h. than laughed at., 148.37

hatred: propaganda so much more successful when it stirs up h., 221.11

head: h. does not hear anything until the heart has listened, 112.14; uneasy lies the h. that wears a crown, 143.8; crams our h. with learned lumber, 202.7; empty h. console with empty sounds, 267.11; h. full of stories, 271.30

health: to drink h. is to drink sickness, 293.4; drink another's h., 293.6

hear, heard, hearing: h what he does not like, 36.14; h. by the fire, 38.13; hearing as well as being heard, 51.18; hear you, or ... hear him, 51.40; not permit ears to h. improper words, 72.2; hearing ear, 72.4; ears to h., 72.12; h. more, speak less, 72.22; h something you like, 108.38; terrible to h. such things, 111.1; h. one side only, 111.20; h. a different drummer, 111.42; h. by the fire, 128.6; if people are unwilling to h. you, 158.9; in normal conversation the h. really h. only about fifty per cent, 158.41; best h. aids ... attentive wife, 164.19; h. a mermaid on a dolphin's back, 170.6; deafest man can h. praise, 213.14; if you will not h. reason, 233.6; have to be silent to be h., 258.33; h. the misfortunes of others, 279.12; not h. the truth, 298.56; h. all the things that are said about us, 301.14

hearer: willing and prepared h., 111.40

heart: sound as a bell, 36.13; makes man eloquent, 75.35; full of emotion, 76.16; on my lips, 76.18; grown brutal, 91.25; fear no more, says the h., 94.8; music which sounds like ... voice of the human h., 97.20; embittered h. talks a lot, 112.16; h. speaks many ways, 160.34; hurt you to the h., 188.17; Queen of hearts ... made some tarts, 193.14; winning words to conquer willing h., 205.15; ask God to give you an endearing h., 214.13; sighs ... natural language of the h., 257.10; silence breaks the h., 258.36; song sung in our h., 265.17; speech comes from the h., 268.21; hold me in thy h., 270.59; huge h. that break, 277.5; h. at leisure, 279.17; tales that spring from your h. 281.17; here's a h. for every fate, 293.3; smaller the h. the longer the tongue, 294.10

heat: is in inverse proportion to knowledge, 211.12

heaven: hear in h., 111.5; learn the language of h., 113.8; admits no jest, 139.6

hell: diplomat ... tell you to go to hell, 66.14

heresy: signifies no more than a private opinion, 113.1

heretics:: of one generation, ... of one country, 113.4; not backed with a sufficient array of battalions, 113.9

hero: a bore at last, 31.15; can be found less in large things, 114.1; a man who would argue with the gods, 114.14; nobody should come to movies unless he believes in h., 180.28; show me a h. and I will write you a tragedy, 296.10

heroic: invented the h. myth, 79.3; believe in the h., 114.7
hillbilly: sing like a h., 97.23
hire: h. out their words and anger, 150.40
historian: object, 9.8; a broad-gauge gossip, 115.1; relate .. what they would have believed, 115.3; novelist of the past, 312.14
history: fables agreed upon, 13.22; tells how it was, 65.2; facts which become legend, 65.5; always an epic, 79.9; the recital of facts, 87.26; about human beings, 95.3; without hiatus, 95.5; entrusted with the exact cultural h., 110.8; biography of heroes, 114.6; repeats itself, 115.4; an account, mostly false, 116.7; is the present, 116.17; fiction is h. without ... is better than prophecy, 116.23; forget the h. of its own life, 172.18; homilies: juggling h., 120.2; miracles exist as ancient h., 174.5; myth is far truer than h., 182.3; myths make h., 183.34; mythology ... grandmother of history, 184.2; news is the first rough draft of history, 188.5; recreated h. giving it life, 197.4; first foundations of all h., 197.12; parody has completely replaced h., 200.7; h. are properly told 244.9; take truth from h., 298.55
honest: h. man speaks the truth, 298.36
honor: word of h., 118.1; but a word, 118.2; owe h. to poets, 209.16; h. in the Bible were the false prophets, 222.5; prophet is not without h. except in his own country, 222.14; to ruin one's self over poetry is an h., 223.17; h. of wide men, 306.3
Hoosier: will talk politics after he's dead, 211.20
hospital: specialize in poets and singers, 161.11; most difficult things to contend with in a h., 168.7
hostility: expressed in a number of ways, 148.24
hours: slow-moving h., 282.48
humor: by affectation spoil'd, 6.15; tragedy standing on its head, 119.7; kindly contemplation of the incongruities of life, 119.16
human: everything h. is pathetic, 119.24
human beings, humans: h.b. who talked like asses, 99.11; all normal h. acquire language, 157.5; fundamental needs of h.b., 158.17
human nature: hunter for aphorisms on h.n., 14.4
humanity: sphinxlike, 44.20; irony ... h's sense of propriety, 137.10; literature is the memory of humanity, 159.21
humbug: politician is requires to listen to h., 210.18
humiliate: boast of little things, 28.13
humor: exaggeration cheapest form of h., 83.15; a rubber sword, 119.12; cuts the knot of serious questions, 119.13; emotional chaos, 119.23; brings insight and tolerance, 137.1; in all true h. lies its germ, pathos, 201.1; pun is the lowest form of h., 225.25; decrepit society shuns h., 264.7
humorist: world dwindles daily for the h., 140.6
hunt, hunting: h. down a tired metaphor, 171.4; Daddy's gone a-h., 193.1; h. for a wild negation, 233.11
husband: should not insult his wife publicly, 135.21
hyperbole: perpetual, 83.2; little h. never hurts, 83.17
hypocrite, hypocrisy: a man who moralizes is usually a h., 176.20; be a h. if you like, 282.13; modest in speaking the truth is h., 298.32; make a skillful h., 307.23

iconoclasm: only way to get at truth, 121.3
idea, ideas: interrupt the easy flow of her conversation, 51.46; same i. under different names, 61.4; i. communicates the emotion, 76.22; mistake facts for i., 88.10; history of i., 116.35; was ... once modern, 123.6; no new i., 123.10; wherever new i. emerge, 123.14; when the i. is expressed, 147.9; language ... shaper of i.,

147.46; great minds discuss i., 172.2; fundamental i. of science are essentially simple, 252.7; i. communicates the emotion, 267.17; too great for his income of i., 268.32; to have i. is to gather flowers, 290.35; truth happens to an i., 298.40; wit ... sudden marriage of i., 307.46
ideal: better than ourselves, 122.1; foreign word i., 122.5; proverb ... halfway house to an i., 224.27
idealist: cynic in the making, 122.6
identity: preserve and cultivate its i., 124.2; who am I?, 124.4; what you say you are, 124.8; trite word ... has lost its i., 310.54
idiom: correct i. ... foundation of good style, 274.1
idiot: to generalize is to be an i., 101.4
idols: dead metaphors make strong i., 171.11
ignorance: bear without emotion, 6.10; affected, 6.11; enemy of art, 19.11; art of hiding i., 41.2; curiosity ... confession of i., 56.15; progressive discovery of i., 74.8; a blind giant, 104.3; first requisite of the historian, 155.10; never settles a question, 125.7; vincible i., 125.13; when ... voluntary, is criminal, 125.14; i. must necessarily be infinite, 125.17; quotations are useful in periods of i., 228.10
ignorant: malady of the i., 125.1; discuss medicine before the i., 168.8
illiterate: proverbs ... the literature of the i., 224.9
illusion: dust the devil throws, 126.1; some i. creates disillusion, 126.4; i. multiply, 126.7; don't part with your i., 126.16; religion is an i., 234.9
imagery: mythology is the use of i., 184.3
imagination: all acts ... begin in the i., 91.7; air of the mind, 127.2; the Eldorado of the poet, 127.4; more important than knowledge, 127.11; a licensed trespasser, 127.12; frames events unknown, 127.19; politics ... enemy of the imagination 211.11
imitation: act of, 4.26; sincerest of flattery, 128.3; tragedy is an i. of an action that is serious, 296.2
immortal: make me i. with a kiss, 144.10; thing they grow i. as they quote, 228.32; youth is i., 314.20
immortality: children are voices of i., 38.1; i. to conversation, 51.44; thing said walks in i., 75.45; glorious discovery of Christianity, 129.6
imperfections: conceal their i., 48.8
impossible: believe ... impossible things, 26.7
impotence: insults ... are signs of i., 135.22
impression: to create an unfavorable i., 108.9
impromptu: make... impromptu at my leisure, 130.8; the touchstone of wit, 130.9
impropriety: soul of wit, 307.33
improvisation: way of evoking creativity, 130.1; essence of good talk, 130.2; i. of human experience, 130.7; too good to leave to chance, 130.11
impulse: narrative i. is always with us, 186.3; i. to ask questions, 227.19
inconvenient: lie even when i., 153.41
incredible: believe anything ... i., 26.29
indifference; speak of beauty, 25.9; based on the i. of the majority, 211.16
indignation: truth in i., 75.17; pours righteous i., 131.2; moral i., 131.5; most passionate forms of love., 131.12; i. of the honest satirist, 249.9; pretends to be i., 251.6; i. will produce verses, 303.9
individual, individuality: boiling up i. into the species, 124.2; most personal map of our i., 169.1
indoctrination: i. ... exercised through the mass media., 167.3

inevitable: reconciled to the i., 306.28

infants: converse with angels, 22.5

inferiority: quotations confess i., 228.16

infinity: silence is i., 258.18

information: ask for i., 56.4; can tell us everything, 132.1; add to the sum of accurate i., 132.4; business of not giving i., 219.7

injured, injury: sooner forgotten than an insult, 135.3; men sometimes feel i. by praise, 213.24

inquiry: strangled the holy curiosity of i., 56.5

inquisitive: do not be i., 56.17

insane, insanity: often the logic of ... mind overtasked, 161.9; ordinarily he was i., 273.9

inspire, inspiration: derived his i. from his hat, 271.54; duty of the teacher is to i., 283.22

instinct: divine, 46.3

instruct, instruction: steady and regular i., 74.2; severity of i., 87.2; increases in born worth, 133.2; make i. useful, 133.4; chief subjects of i., 147.53; earliest i. was imparted orally, 158.46; all love to i., 284.2

instructors: poets, the first i. of mankind, 209.10

instrument: what an i. is the human voice, 76.10; fear ... i. of great sagacity, 94.3; i. of information and entertainment, 167.5; magic i. of healing, 270.3

insult: a stiff apology, 15.4; i. him with their malevolence, 135.2; received i. with a glow, 135.4; two i. no human will endure, 135.12; like bad coins, 135.20; irony is an i. ... in the form of a compliment, 137.16; pun is prima facie an insult, 225.15

intellect, intelligence: voice of the i., 172.11; think polysyllables are a sign of i., 277.9; voice of the i., 305.15

intelligible: aim at being i., 299.11; to be i. is to be found out, 299.30

interest: speak of i., not of reason, 205.10; exceed in i. a knock at the door, 267.8

interesting: a teacher ... has an obligation to be i., 136.3; test of i. people, 136.4; become more i. when they stop talking, 282.39

interestingly: say everything i., 51.28

interests: will not lie, 136.2; speak all sorts of tongues, 136.5

interrupt, interruption: don't object to applause, 17.7; you i. him with your talking, 282.50

intoxicated: with my own eloquence, 75.11

intrinsic: man's style is i., 274.18

invent: human beings have ... right to i. themselves, 124.6

investigators: admirable i. who are bad lecturers, 151.12

Irishman: bore an I., 31.30

irony: generally unconscious, 137.2; a bitter truth, 137.4; sentimental i. 137.9

irrationality: miracle entails a degree of i., 174.11

irrationally: human beings ... able to behave i. in the name of reason, 233.15

Janus: forward I look, and backward, 107.15

jargon: your j. o' your schools, 138.3; verbal sleight of hand, 138.10

jealousy: moral indignation is j. with a halo, 131.13

jest, jesting: more ... taught by j., 74.12; irony is a nipping j., 137.12; irony is j. hidden behind gravity, 137.14; j. at scars, 139.2; more is often taught by a j., 284.10

jester: j. a fool is not far off, 139.8; wear the j.'s motley garb, 139.15

Jesus: loves me, 27.22

jog: my j. to make them comfortable, 204.6

joke, joking: with a double meaning, 69.2; at their own expense, 119.1; j. is on you. 119.14; takes irony to appreciate a j. ... on oneself, 137.15; only three basic j., 140.2; got hold of a vulgar j., 140.12; bitter cosmic j., 140.18; aim of a j., 140.28; soak them in a j. for a month, 203.4; my way of j., 298.62

journalism: storytelling ... what j. is all about, 271.6

Jove: laughs at lovers' perjuries, 160.46

joy: one inch of j., 148.30; excessive j. weeps, 266.1

judge, judgement: j. for yourself, 141.3; ourselves by our motives, 141.11; exhibiting our power of j., 141.14; hasty j. 141.15; j. a fellow by what he laughs at, 148.25; j. a man by his questions, 227.27; blows the sails of popular j., 246.15; sentences which simply express moral j., 255.1; man cannot speak but he j. himself, 268.16; never j. the heart of a wit, 307.10; every word is a preconceived j., 310.53

judges: of humor ... don't agree, 119.4; j. must also be performers, 204.2

Juno: the goddess of marriage, 164.29

Jupiter: his bolts and power of thunder, 107.16; laughs at the perjuries of lovers, 107.25

justice: a drum major for j., 124.10; do j. for one another, 149.1

kill: first thing ... let's k. all the lawyers, 150.51; who k. Cock Robin, 193.20; too much talking can k. a thing, 282.62; as if you could k. time, 292.33

kind, kindness: cruel to be k., 55.6; make haste to be k., 142.2; little deeds of k., 142.5; law of k., 142.8

kings: converse with k. should be rare, 143.1; will not hear the truth, 143.6; k. ... have long hands, 143.9; tell sad stories of the death of k., 247.10

kiss, kissed, kissing: through a veil, 47.9; one fond k. before we part, 144.3; Jenny k. me, 144.8; some k. and tell, 144.14; k. me Kate, 144.17; k. the place and make it well, 178.12; kiss kiss bang bang, 180.15; k. the girls and made them cry, 193.3; must not k. and tell, 253.2

know: k. ourselves chiefly by hearsay, 124.7; people ... k. so much that ain't so., 125.4; only the ignorant k. everything, 125.20; what a man k., 145.14; I do not k. much, 145.19; to k. that we do not k., 145.39; k. a man from his laugh, 148.14; remember that the Lord k. something, 214.3; tell me what you k., 228.15; k. when to come to an end, 274.11; k. how far to go too far, 280.3; people would not talk until they k., 282.55; refrain from saying more than he k., 283.10; cannot teach what you do not k., 284.13; less than I need to k., 292.16; I do not know, 294.5; men honestly do not k. what women want, 299.26; misfortune of k. anything, 309.1; ask the young, they k. everything, 314.17

knowledge: in distinct and disjointed aphorisms, 14.2; know it—don't need to believe it, 26.20; I do not know, 51.29; display of k., 51.37; the utilization of k., 74.25; contained in fairy tales, 90.24; subtracting from the sum of human k., 99.23; extreme prejudice of k., 101.3; k. can only be finite, 125.17; death of k., 125.21; great impediments of k., 145.9; essence of k., 145.15; sum of human k., 147.43; province of k. to speak, 158.25; pedantry is the dotage of k., 202.13; if we would have new k. we must get new ... questions, 227.17; k. ... come from our senses, 254.5; world of k. makes a crazy turn, 283.7; prefer tongue-tied k., 294.12; talk of k. of the universe, 300.20; multiplies words without k., 302.9; k. can be communicated,

306.15; province of k. to speak, 306.17; impediment for the advancement of k., 310.61

label: first step toward action, 61.3
lady: when a l. says nor, 31.9; talk so much in s., 44.8; never shows her underwear intentionally, 146.2; l. mean that to be expressed, 309.39
lament: one's ill fortune, 46.1
language: learned his great, 1.3; the bud, 3.5; spoken by angels, 10.4; an art, 19.7; inflated, 28.10; clearness is everything, 40.4; chief virtue ... clearness, 40.5; speak the same l., 44.9; dancing, l given way to movement, 59.4; dialect that has an army, 63.9; concentrating emotion, 76.3; l. of facts, 88.4; fantasy is the l. of the inner self, 91.11; l. used extensively in the educational profession, 138.11; kindness is a l. the dumb can speak, 142.3; process of free creation, 147.8; raison-d'etre of l. 147.9; l. of the stones, 147.12; not acquainted with foreign l., 147.19; both hides and reveals, 147.20; little better than the croak and cackle of fowls, 147.21; l. is memory and metaphor, 147.30; a living thing, 147.33; life is a foreign l., 155.24; every living l. ... is in perpetual motion, 157.3; l. most shows a man, 163.9; men converse by means of l., 172.4; l. of my mother, 178.6; l. is a species of music, 181.27; Nature ... speaks a various l., 187.5; l. of Nature, 187.13; quotation contributes to ... enlargement of the l., 228.18; helps form the limits of our reality, 232.19; l. of the street is always strong, 262.8; language ... disguises itself, 262.12; whole l. in one's neighbor's elbow, 264.5; persuasive l. of a tear, 285.1; thought corrupts l., 291.25; l. is using us to talk, 304.8; smashers of l., 310.11; last year's words belong to last year's l., 310.27; writer's l., 312.11
laugh, laughter, laughing: making people l., 43.10; l. broke into a thousand pieces, 89.4; l. at a jest, 139.14; died l. over one of his own jokes, 140.4; loud l. reduce him to a buffoon, 140.10; four main grades of l., 148.2; l. ... a by-product, 148.9; hearty "belly" l., 148.11; l. or die, 148.23; l. best who l. last, 148.44; penetrating sort of l., 148.49; fitting ... to l. at life, 155.31; l. at one another for our lack of originality, 260.10; they l. consumedly, 282.17; witty thing never excited l., 308.4
law, laws: elementary l. never apologize, 15.15; language of the l, 40.6; a silent magistrate, 149.2; l. is blind, 149.10; l does not exist for the lawyers, 150.36
lawyer: our wrangling l., 150.5; saw a l. killing a viper, 150.8; shyster l., 150.11; like morticians, 150.18; spend ... time .. shoveling smoke, 150.20; l. with a briefcase, 150.44; hauling a l. away, 150.49; l.'s business to consider remote contingencies, 150.54; many tricks as a l., 297.13
learn, learning: careful what ... children l., 38.5; love of l. is ... curious, 56.12; nothing l. ... in a dispute, 68.13; education is l. what you didn't know, 74.4; what has been l. has been forgotten, 74.20; always safe to l., 133.1; listen and you will l., 158.27; if you listen you may l. something, 158.34; unseasonable ostentation of l., 202.14; enough l. to misquote, 228.6; l. by finding out, 272.8; no amount of l. can cure stupidity, 273.18; gladly l. and gladly teach, 284.3; never cease to l., 284.4; l. from bad students, 284.12; even while they teach men l., 284.21; l. without thought is labor lost, 291.10
lecture: applause, 171.17; for the sake of a crowded audience, 21.14; curtain l., 151.1; better to practise shop-

lifting than to give l., 151.5; sensible people never go to l., 151.14
leer: l. about his lips, 148.8
legend: asleep in lap of l., 13.13; lies which become history, 65.5; l. die, dreams end, 71.4; believe all the fables in l., 87.5; past exudes l., 95.16; as much a part of the real history of a country, 152.4; consecration of fame, 15.6; lap of l. old, 152.14; l. of the green chapels, 199.9
lend: his ears, 72.16
lesson: intended by an author; 30.18; best l. ... those that are lived, 155.22; learn our l. ... for the lecture-room, 272.16
letter: story you hear is a l. ... from yesterday, 270.52
liability: no greater l. than a command of language, 210.23
liar: not believed, when speaks truth, 26.1; boaster and l, first cousins, 28.25; throne set up for the l., 153.2; most mischievous l., 153.19; aim of a l., 156.42; always lavish of oaths, 194.4; great talkers are great l., 282.3; even a l. tells a hundred truths to one l., 298.8
liberation: women's l. ... not a debatable issue, 309.23
lie, lies, lying: compliments are l., 47.1; can't l when ... dance, 59.6; ambassador ... sent to lie abroad, 66.16; exaggeration a branch of l.; 83.10; excuse is a l. guarded, 84.10; have not l. willingly, 153.3; makes the smallest amount of l. go the longest way, 153.9; entered the territory of l., 153.18; optimistic l., 153.36; universal practice, 153.37; 869 different forms of l., 153.39; l. ... beyond reproach, 153.43; l. so simple and lovely, 154.3; three kinds of l., 154.6; red hot l., 154.15; l. mouth is a stinking pit, 179.11; there's myth in the sense of a l., 183.36; Nature will tell you a direct l., 187.9; more oath-taking, the more l., 194.3; parables are not l., 199.8; you can't pray a l., 214.23; necessary to l. damnably, 221.1; all propaganda is l., 221.10; proverb does not tell a l., 224.12; satire l. about literary men, 249.31; tell a malicious l., 261.9; l. hides the truth, 270.19; l. is looked upon as an occupational disease, 288.1; l. hides the truth, 298.30
life, lives, living: heroes and villains, 4.13, continual allegory, 7.5; worth living, 20.8; art of drawing sufficient conclusions, 49.3; is doubt, 70.9; l.'s sweet fable, 87.7; is eating us up, 87.12; a huge farce, 92.3; imitates art, 128.13; l which is everlasting, 129.3; is a jest, 139.9; makes l. not a jest, 139.18; meaning of l., 147.36; l. ... goes on, 155.13; made up of sobs, sniffles, 155.18; l. is a drama, 175.2; take l. without mythology, 184.5; conceive of our l. as narratives, 186.9; condition of l. as a narrative, 186.11; everything must be larger than l., 200.4; pathos of l., 201.3; philosophy of l 206.3; poetry is l, distilled, 208.5; quarreled about ... their life, 226.8; l. itself is a quotation, 228.4; only riddle that we shrink from giving up, 242.3; stories that save our l., 270.7; every l. has a Scheherazadesworth of stories, 270.8; story of your l., 270.21; providing alternate l., 270.78; l. is tedious, 281.64; l.'s but a walking shadow, 281.67; don't have to fake real l., 287.17; theatre ... depicts life in a sense more truly than history, 288.15; tragedy of l., 296.6; l. is a tragedy, 296.18; assumes that his l. is in some sense exemplary, 312.1; l. untouched by tragedy, 314.30
light: candle ... gives a lovely l., 155.23; golden l. of metaphor, 171.14
limerick: a whale of a tale in perverse form, 156.1; an art form complex, 156.2; l packs laughs anatomical, 156.3; furtive and mean, 156.5

limit: l. of my language, 147.55; who cannot l. himself, 313.8

linguist, linguistics: l. habits condition our view of the world, 157.11; l. becomes an ever eerier area, 157.13; the manifold l., 157.17;

lip, lips: spoken 1.16; of books, 30.14; witchcraft in your l., 75.36; lyric ever on the lip, 79.1; voiceless l. of the unreplying dead, 129.9; those l. that I have kissed, 139.20; our l. found ways of speaking, 144.9; upon his l. persuasion sate, 205.8; from whom l divine persuasion flows, 205.12; sober l. then did he softly part, 240.9; seal up your l., 253.14; l. keep from slips, 268.34; l. were silent, 291.14; truth from the l. prevailed, 298.33

listen, listening: l to their elders, 38.6; entertain some folk is to l. to them, 77.4; sincerest form of flattery, 96.4; before linguistics ... there was l., 157.12; seldom l. ... for more than half a minute, 158.3; who l. once will l. twice, 158.8; l. more slowly, 158.14; you seldom l. to me, 158.29; no one really l. to anyone else, 158.35; Neanderthal man l. to stories, 163.6; learn my son to l., 166.20; l. to my mother's stories of her life, 178.14; l. to a human mind, 181.37; l. how they say your name, 185.6; trains the mind to l., 197.9; make the periodical duty of l. to them as hard as possible, 215.10; l. to other people's problems, 218.10; radio ... something people l. to while they are doing something else, 229.18; not so much to like as to l., 231.10; learn to l., 245.8; silence is wonderful to l. to, 258.24; good extemporaneous l., 269.23; is a responsibility, 299.9; l. to my elders, 314.33

listener: good l. is not only popular, 145.34; good extraneous l., 158.38; good l. is a good talker with a sore throat, 158.55; eagerness of the l., 186.2; a congregation of l., 197.11

literature: sharing folk l. in classrooms, 38.16; carried on within small limits, 98.21; folk l. ... delights in unbounded and immortal things, 98.22; life comes before l., 155.8; the immortality of speech, 159.20; appropriate use of language, 159.23; art of l., 159.24; beginning of l. is myth, 183.4; conscious mythology, 184.7; professors of l. ... are always more ridiculous, 219.13; like their l. clear, cold, pure and very dead, 219.26; pass from hearing l. to reading it, 231.13; recreating l., 271.23

live, living: lot of l. ... done in the imagination, 127.13; l. in hearts, 129.5; l. the width of life, 155.1; l. no longer in the faith of reason, 233.18; among riddles and mysteries, 242.10; may you l. all the days of your l., 293.11

logic: lesson that l. shall teach us, 40.15; l. on fire, 75.2; l. chiefest e., 174.13; speak l., 240.10; l. of worldly success, 276.8

lonely, lonesome: l. man is a lonesome thing, 257.3; we are l. animals, 271.65; l. people talking to each other, 282.29

love: rules of l., 5.17; makes world go around, 42.11; being in l. is great, 47.4; l. gift of a fairy tale, 90.8; true l. is like ghosts, 103.8; God is l., 106.12; no one can agree on what it is, 160.1; ceases to be a pleasure, 160.4; how do I l. thee?, 160.5; is like singing, 160.21; a cruel conqueror, 160.22; l. demonstrated is irresistible, 160.27; I do love you so much, my mother, 178.7; l. the man who knows it all, 202.4; poets are all who l., 209.4; we l. a man who damns us, 216.16; tired f l., 241.2; can bear anything better than r., 243.13; essence of romantic l., 244.2; l. the twilight, 244.6;

similes are like songs in l., 259.7; tale without l., 281.29; everyone talks of what he l., 282.20; tragedy of l., 296.14; words make l. with one another, 310.9

lover: no tongue flatters like a l., 96.5; l. vows, 160.6; easier to be a l. than a husband, 164.3

loyal: where the storyteller is l., 271.16

lucidity: adds beauty, 40.18; supreme l. ... called madness, 161.8

luck: l. to you, l. to us, 293.9

lullabies: low murmur of tender l., 263.5

lunatics: all are l., 206.6

mad, madness: grew a little m., 1.17; rules of m., 5.17; when confronting m., 161.2; all born m., 161.3; m. north-north-west, 161.14; little spark of m., 161.16

made: we're m. of stories, 270.65

madmen: useful of m., 161.13; swords are m.'s tongues, 294.44

magic: believer in the m. of language, 147.13; dealer in m. and spells, 156.8; m. of the tongue, 162.2; m. of the tongue, 294.9; m. of words, 310.43

magicians: tell tales of the deeds of m., 162.9

majority: always the best repartee, 236.5

make, maker: m. of a sentence, 255.5; m. up your own stories, 270.71

man: lies by believing, 26.6; only animal that can be bored, 31.16; lives ... by catchwords, 42.10; eager to learn, 74.23; talking about himself, 75.4; leave story better than he found it, 83.19; is fed with fables, 87.16; has a right to his opinion, 88.1; m. life is a fairy tale, 90.1; proposes, 106.10; who hears badly, 111.32; no such thing as an honest m., 117.2; sensible m doesn't tear down idols, 121.2; ignorant m. ... the first to be heard, 125.2; wise m. superior to any insults, 135.14; to judge a m. means, 141.7; m does not know what he is saying, 145.13; is distinguished from all other, 148.1; God having designed m. for a social creature, 157.10; takes a great m. to make a good listener, 158.23; when a m. talks of love, 160.28; m. will ... endure, 163.5; every m. speak his maxim, 165.5; m. of maxims, 165.9; noisy m. is always in the right, 189.7; there was a crooked m., 193.17; m.'s opinions, 196.15; asserted by a m. is an opinion, 196.19; praise any m. who will praise me, 213.22; first m. introduced slang, 262.15; timid m. can deliver a bold speech, 269.31; m. is eminently a storyteller, 271.29; inverted triangle symbolizes m., 278.5; m. watches his history on the screen, 287.14; m. is ... a thinking reed, 290.29; wake a t. in a man, 291.21; time you old gypsy m., 292.17; m. is hid under his tongue, 294.27; m. determines what is said, 310.73; only one m. can do anything, 311.8; world began without m., 311.9

mankind: divided into two sects, 122.3; history of m., 186.8; politician divides m. into two classes, 210.25

manner: Socratic m. is not a game, 206.5; dislike ... the m. of his speech 274.14

manners: correct my m., 1.2; if m. had not existed, would have invented them, 102.3; lie is the building block of good m., 153.13

marriage, marry: better to m. a quiet fool, 164.2; particular charm of m., 164.5; proper time to m., 164.6; worth all the disadvantages of m., 164.14; comedies and romances ... end with a marriage, 164.18; m. on the rocks, 164.21; wit is a sudden m. of ideas, 307.46

martyr: m. to mild enthusiasm, 219.4

marvelous: universal love of the m., 270.14; makes children appear so m., 270.23

master: of everything I can explain, 86.7; mighty m. of unmeaning rhyme, 241.5; many a tongue shakes out his m.'s undoing, 294.38; as long as the word is unspoken, 310.41

mathematics: worst subject, 12.15

mature, maturity: taken the fairy tale of childhood into m., 90.14; language study is a route to m., 157.16; stories ... must be allowed to m., 270.51

maxim: cruel m. taught by knowledge of the world, 145.10; unalterable m., 165.1; never out of season, 165.3; narrow m. which enslave mankind, 165.7

meaning, meant: in a nutshell, 34.28; doesn't matter, 37.8; epigram ... beautiful m. in few and clear words, 80.7; m. have our lightest fantasies, 91.14; even a joke should have some m., 140.9; no word is used with more m., 160.25; real m. lies underneath its scarves and buttons, 166.2; take things as they are m., 166.5; subtle as odor, 166.13; what's your m.?, 166.14; where shall we seek for m. 166.24; must a name m. something, 185.4; a poem should not m. but be, 208.28; reason always m. what someone else has to say, 233.8; declared m. of a spoken sentence, 255.3; it m. just what I choose it to m., 310.12; words can have no single fixed m., 310.48; that words have m. is just the difficulty, 310.72

media: what the mass m. offer is not popular art, 167.1; transforms the great silence, 167.2; most intimate and exclusive of all m., 286.8

medical, medication: m. without explanation is obscene, 168.2; m. relevance to human health, 271.48

medicine: does not depend on the incantations of the sorcerer, 168.1; stories are m., 270.18

mediocre, mediocrity: public insist on having ... m. information, 167.8; media is the plural of m., 167.9; m. in politics is not to be despised, 211.6; m. prose might be read as an escape, 223.7

medium: m. is the message, 167.6; m. is the legend, 167.7; unsuited to moral lessons, 180.1

melody: made still a blund'ring kind of m., 190.6

memoirs: backstairs of history, 313.13

memorable: m. sentences are m. on account, 255.12

memorandum: law is only a m., 149.5; written to protect the writer, 313.1

memory: of having been read to, 30.15; is a sacred trust, 110.4; drug their hearts with false m., 116.12; m. of men are too frail, 116.30; everyone complains of his m., 141.9; liar should have a good m., 153.32; poor sort of m., 169.2; thing you forget with, 169.3; man's m. ... his private literature, 169.8; selective m., 169.12; the best qualifications of a prophet is to have a good m., 222.12; added pitifully few lines to the communal m., 287.8

men: flatterers of themselves, 96.10; like stone jugs, 96.14; wise m. ... resolve and execute, 99.24; crafty m. deal in generalizations, 101.2; ghosts fear m., 103.14; all m. hold to some divine power, 107.3; gossip among men ... is called theory, 108.3; always detested women's gossip, 108.16; all m. ... desire knowledge, 145.1; m. must have legends, 152.18; some m. were born to lie, 153.16; m. are mad most of their lives, 161.5; golden race of speaking m. 163.8; must cherish our old m., 163.20; lower classes of m., 195.6; m. who live their creeds, 215.5; six honest serving-men, 227.16; talent of turning m. into ridicule, 243.1; dead

m. tell no tales, 281.24; m. go the theater to forget, 288.13; m. talk of killing time, 292.6; truth sits on the lips of dying men, 298.6; such is the nature of m., 306.16; melancholy m. ... are most witty, 307.1; by m.'s words we know them. 310.19

merciless: movies are m., 180.27

Mercury: words of M., 107.23

merged: illusion and reality often m., 232.1

mermaid: so much of a m. as is not a woman must be a fish, 170.1

message: always find a messenger, 44.1; should be delivered by Western Union, 180.11; problems are m. 218.4

messenger: m. of good news, 188.15

metaphor, metaphorical: for God drawn from human experience, 106.16; maze of m. confusion, 109.13; run like a coach on four wheels, 171.1; once a glowing m., 171.6; all m. is poetry, 171.7; more tenacious than facts, 171.9; can give birth to love, 171.17; provides two loaves where there seems to be one, 171.20; science is all m., 252.14; all slang is m., 262.5

midnight: iron tongue of m., 89.21

mind: flaw in understanding, 6.3; ruling idea of any m., 20.2; characteristic of small m., 31.17, nonconformist m., 43.11; live close to great m., 74.5; m. of man compared to a musical instrument, 134.6; fashion a jest with a sad m., 139.26; men's m. are conciliated by a kind manner, 142.6; feudal habit of m., 146.5; let the joy bells ring in your receptive m., 158.7; the m. of man, 165.2; old m. are like horses, 172.1; m. bent upon the causes of events, 186.13; m. pleased with irritating others, 249.26; imaginative adventure of the m., 252.9; put an adult's m. in a child's heart, 270.54; mark of a second-rate m., 271.34; tact ... kind of m. reading, 280.8; knew the Deity's mind, 289.14; m. is younger than the body, 290.37; great m. overthrown yields tragedy, 296.4

ministers: some m. would make good martyrs, 215.13

minority: heresy is what the m. believes, 113.3

minstrel: wandering m. I, 173.4; m. of the unfulfilled desire, 173.13; pilgrim of the sky, 173.14

miracle: church speaks of m. because it speaks of God, 174.2; in every m. a silent chiding of the world, 174.4; m. seem impossible, 174.9

mirth, mirthful: like a flash of lightning, 119.2; teller of a m. tale, 119.15; pick out the tales of m., 139.12; thinkers of the world ... guardians of the world's m., 290.32

misery: hardly any mental m. worse, 243.3

mistake, mistaken: more apt to be m. in their generalizations, 101.11; hero by m., 114.8; m. at the top of one's voice, 196.3; prophecy is the most gratuitous, 222.9; speaks much is m., 268.20

misunderstanding: most quarrels amplify a m., 226.13

mock, mockery: achievements m. me, 2.4; m. is often poverty of wit, 243.5; fume of little hearts, 243.12

models: of virtuous thoughts, 7.9

moment: most moving m. of our lives, 258.35; trying to express the tragic m., 296.13

money: no m. in poetry, 208.18; proverbs ... ready m. of human experience, 224.25; gives me pleasure all the time, 241.2

monologue: is not a decision, 175.1

monsters: natural history of m., 150.32; we have many m. to kill, 242.6

moon: cow jumped over the m. 193.4

moral, morals: generalities in m. mean nothing, 101.5; m. don't sell nowadays, 176.1; everything's got a m.,

176.4; to point a m. 176.14; tell a story and point a m. as well, 270.10

moralist: cursed the canting m., 176.6; begin with a dislike of reality, 176.7; teach the rustic m. to die, 176.10

morality: rules of m., 177.1; was held a standing jest, 177.2; comes with the sad wisdom of age, 177.6; takes no account of the art in life, 240.13

moralize: moralizing; to denounce m. out of hand, 176.15; m. two meanings in one word, 176.16

mother: take me on your knee m., 89.14; what the m. sings to the cradle, 178.1; name for God in the lips and hearts of little children, 178.13; the universal m., nature, 187.4

motive: m. for metaphor, 171.26; persons attempting to find a m. in this narrative, 176.19; two m. for reading a book, 231.11

mouth: out of the m. of babes, 22.12; mustard in a young child's m., 51.34; m. of the Congo, 79.5; fool's m. … his destruction, 99.19; m. obeys poorly, 112.15; humor must fall out of a man's m., 119.3; stop his m. with a kiss, 144.16; lawyer's m. without a fee, 150.21; words I remember from my mother's m., 178.4; keep watch over thy m. 179.1; hold your m., 179.3; utters lilies, 179.4; m. for every matter, 179.7; shooting off your m., 179.14; open my m. in a parable, 199.6; tells it with his tiresome m., 202.4; m. a sentence, 255.4; keep your m. shut, 273.17; thought is made in the m., 291.33; good m. will love the truth, 298.3; pleasant m. turned up at the corners, 307.9

movies: my m. is born first in my head, 180.2; suddenly become "film" and "cinema," 180.5; are about people who do things, 180.23; m have mirrored our moods and myths, 180.25

murder, murdered: m. with jargon, 138.7; thinking is half m., 282.21

murmur: because I had no shoes, 45.5; at what they call the injustice, 46.8; never touch the gods, 107.4

muscle: story has to have m., 270.50

music: understood by children and animals, 11.11; sent up to God by lover and bard, 24.4; drown [bad m.] in conversation, 51.48; for m. any words are good enough, 181.3; m. is immediate, 181.5; wild sounds civilized, 181.15; myth of the inner life, 181.25; love in search of a word, 181.26; art of expressing sensations, 181.29; kind of harmonious language, 181.34; crystallization of sound, 181.38; people would compose m. skillfully enough, 219.31; loves to make m., 272.5

musicians: borrowed from the songs of the common people, 97.7

mutes: love makes m. 160.38

mystery: married life requires shared m., 164.10; will lead millions by the nose, 182.9; space was the uncontrollable m., 292.22

mystify: seek not to m. the mystery, 182.7

myth: everyone accepts, 26.3; a new language, 74.23; poets not alone in sponsoring m., 94.6; American history is a m., 116.21; history is a m., 116.26; language of the Jewish m., 145.8; m. are clues to the spiritual potentialities, 155.10; beginning of literature is m., 159.4; basing morals on m., 177.12; neither a lie nor a confession, 183.1; contains the story … preserved in popular memory, 182.2; deal in false universals, 183.9; rises to fill a need, 183.28; primary function of m., 183.29; test of a true m., 183.37; set the mind free, 183.43; "the good old days" were a m., 191.4; m. are a way of solving the problem of making intelligible, 218.1; free m.

from reality, 232.7; story which describes and illustrates dramatic form, 232.18; someone else's religion, 234.13; are early science, 252.8; lover of m., 306.2; m. of the strong black woman, 309.10; a fixed way of looking at the world, 311.2; do rewrite my central m. in every book, 313.12

mythologists: m. wrote for the feeble soul, 145.29

mythology: literature is conscious m., 159.12; body of primitive people's beliefs, 184.1; womb of mankind's initiation to life and death, 184.4; m. of self, 184.13; is not religion, 234.10; religious sentiment growing wild, 234.16

name, named: music can n. the unnameable, 181.7; glory and nothing of a n., 185.3 what's in a name, 185.16; thankful my n. is obnoxious to no pun, 225.28; better never n. than to be ill spoken of, 238.1; invisible thing called a good n., 238.3; only change the n., 270.29

names: call your opponent n., 18.26; I don't want to mention n., 108.15; called them by the wrong n., 185.2; n. will never hurt me, 185.13; n. are everything, 185.18; pronounce foreign n. as he chooses, 220.2

narration: history … the inaccurate n. of events, 116.22; n. always going backward, 186.16; n. will … remind your hearers of a bad one, 270.30

narrative: n sparkled like ale, 156.7; construct a n. for ourselves, 186.1 bald and unconvincing n., 186.6; attracts n. material like a magnet, 271.15

narrator: tale cultivated by a n., 90.39

nation: genius, wit, and spirit of a n., 224.3; proverbs of a n., 224.19; proverbs are the wisdom of whole n., 224.31; if a n. loses its storytellers, 271.25

naturally: most difficult performance … is acting n., 204.7

nature: lawless part of our n., 148.34; in all private quarrels the duller nature is triumphant, 226.9; satire … founded in good n., 249.24; n. of storytelling, 271.39

Nature: no rebel like N., 121.1; N.'s instructions, 133.8; interpret N. as freely as a lawyer, 150.16; N. cures the disease, 168.10; about N. consists N. itself, 187.1; cannot command N., 187.2; has a language of her own, 187.11; can speak of everything, 187.17; what N. wishes should be said, 187.21; N. provides exceptions to every rule, 245.4; sense-impression of N., 254.7; great elemental sounds in N., 267.3; is a temple, 278.4

necessity: making things plain, 40.9

need: for a movie is a gun and a girl, 180.10; good sense is a thing all n., 254.4

neighbors: make sport of our n., 148.5; quarrelsome man has no good n., 226.11; annoy your n., 298.5

Neptune: flatter N for his trident, 107.21

nervous: there's nothing to get n. about, 204.14

new: remains forever n., 270.27; tell not as n. what everybody knows, 281.19

news: few words as possible, 34.25; gossip is just n. running ahead, 108.30; gossip is a n. story, 108.32; I have wonderful n. to tell, 188.2; ill n. has wings, 188.3; good n. may be told at any time, 188.6; n. from Lake Wobegon, 188.7; nature of bad n., 188.13; first bringer of unwelcomed n., 188.14; radio n. is bearable, 229.11

nickname: of all eloquence a n. is the most concise, 185.7

night: do not go gentle, 60.13; little fairy comes at n., 89.13; things that go bump in the n., 103.4; my vision in the n., 160.20; television knows no n., 287.3

nobler: man is n. that the forces which destroy him, 296.15

noise: a baby, a loud n., 22.8; proves nothing, 75.42; music ... the most widely beloved of all n., 181.16; music is meaningless n. unless, 181.20; music the least disagreeable, 181.24; nothing essential happens in the absence of n., 189.1; taste in n., 189.3; like of a hidden brook, 189.6; drowns out words, 189.10

nonsense: heard in the schools, 26.11; n. you talk, 74.18; to appreciate n., 190.2; daring n. seldom fails to hit, 190.3; firm anchor in n., 190.8; learn to make n. eloquently, 215.17; rhyme often makes mystical n., 241.13

nostalgia: of what has been, 191.2; seductive liar, 191.5

nothing: art of saying n., 108.40; n. can be known, 145.11; say n. in the most words, 192.3; n. to say, say n., 192.4; often a good thing to say, 192.5; every quarrel begins in n., 226.15; saying n. more clearly every day, 313.2

novelist: historian, an unsuccessful n., 115.6; , who could interpret the common feelings of commonplace people, 242.4; historian of the present, 312.14

novels: n. often end in m., 164.7; n. is more of a whisper, 288.9

oath: with a swaggering accent, 1.15; o. of love, 160.40; not surety for man, 194.1; but words, 194.2; stinging rhetoric of a rattling o., 240.8

object: to mention a loved o. is to invest that o. with reality, 232.13

obligation: sense of o., 163.4

obscene: slang in a woman's mouth is not o., 262.16; all phone calls are o., 286.2

obscure, obscurity: ornate o., 40.17; o. because excessively discussed, 67.7

observation, observer: a passive science, 195.1; what we o. is not nature in itself, 195.4; activity of both eyes and ears, 195.7; difficult to report an o., 195.10; he is a great o., 195.12

occupation: satire is a lonely ... o., 249.10

offend: speak an o. ... one and the same thing, 268.25

old testament: record of man's conviction, 27.10

Olympus: the deities of O., 107.9; abode of the gods, 107.11

opinion: unsolicited, 5.14; arguments confirm people in their own o., 18.46; which justify cruelty, 55.5; dispute about o., 68.9; not bound by the o. of men, 113.5; blotting out the traces of their o., 113.6; satisfied with your o., 125.12; express many absurd o., 190.9; make proselytes to our o., 196.1; truth of their o., 196.2; same o. with ourselves, 196.4; stiff in o., 196.8; making you a present of his o., 196.9; borrow their o., 196.13; o. which passes down from century to century, 197.2; prejudice is a vagrant o., 217.2; o. founded on prejudice, 217.10 backed his o. with quotations, 228.24; o. which passes down from century to century, 295.2; difference of o. as to what constitutes w., 307.27; never met a woman who declined to express an o., 309.11; haven't much o. of words, 310.30

opportunities, opportunity: theirs for the taking, 38.30; problems are ... o. in work clothes, 218.8; o. to learn from eager youths, 219.37; giving others an o. to strike in, 282.58

oppressed: o. speak a million tongues, 161.15

optimism: movies ... sounding a note of cautious o., 180.7; o. about the past, 295.11

oracles: God's o. can never lie, 129.7

oral: sacred appeal of o. transmission remains crucial, 197.13

oral tradition: fairy tales form the o.t., 90.27; folklore ... recorded from the o.t., 98.8; studies of Cajun and Creole o.t., 197.1; o.t. kept the ears rather than the eyes sharpened, 197.8; wandered so far from the o.t., 197.11; continued to feed the writers with material, 197.14

orally: taken back to a time when the story, transmitted orally, was all there was, 197.11; preacher is one who works o., 215.8

orators: dumb when beauty pleadeth, 25.17; love makes all men o., 160.16; man who ... feels what he says, 198.1; good man ... skilled in speaking, 198.2; is obliged to instruct, 198.4; what the o. want in depth, 198.17; o. persuades and carries all with him, 240.4

oratory: hide art, 19.18; more easily heard than understood, 22.10; unbelievable ... acceptable, 26.10, rules for o., 51.4; aim of forensic o. is to teach, 100.2; commencement o., 198.9; will not work against the stream, 198.15; just like prostitution, 198.19

order: invented structure for concerning and communicating o., 177.10; o. lurking behind the incredible confusion, 270.72; drama assumes an o., 288.8

original: thought os often o., 291.19

outrage: satire is moral o., 249.26

owl: o. is sort of a college professor, 219.15

ox: not dumber than an o., 273.16; great o. stands on my tongue, 294.1

pain, painful: gentleman ... never inflicts p., 102.6; of a new idea, 123.2; jests that give p., 139.3; soothe the p. 165.13; give nobody's heart p., 257.9; can sympathize with people's p., 279.10; to think hard ... is painful, 290.7

palace: built upon sand, 91.16

parable: in which lay hid that gold, those pearls, 199.2, all p. end—incomplete, disappointing, 199.3, p. of sunlight, 199.9; conveniently combines story and projection, 199.10

paradise: deserves p., 148.19

paradox, paradoxical: take away p. from the thinker, 219.20; confronts the p. exposes himself to reality, 232.9; words of truth are always p., 298.44

parody: fighting and profane p. of the Old Testament, 200.1; homage gone sour, 200.2; most penetrating of criticisms, 200.3; originality in a second-hand suit, 200.5

part: cast for a p. we do not even know we are playing, 204.5; either p. of the solution or p. of the problem, 218.3

partners: story has to have two equal p., 270.77

passion: for ballads, 23.10; slept, 24.17; bards of p, 24.18; grows by gratification, 56.16; love is a talkative p., 160.45; with me poetry has been ... a passion, 208.42; men have a natural p. for spreading rumors, 246.9

past: make the p. alive, 116.8; exudes legend, 152.17; best prophet of the future is the p., 222.4

pastime: watching television as an American p., 287.16

pathetic: a forgetful liar, 153.25

pathos: true humor ... its germ, p., 119.6; of distance, 201.4; infinite p. of human life, 201.5; humor is consistent with p., 307.14

pauses: most precious thing in speeches, 269.28

peace: p. propaganda makes war seem imminent, 221.9

pedagogues: what do they teach their pupil, 272.14

pedant, pedantry: p. of courts and schools, 202.1; plague all your p., 202.2; p. can hear nothing but in favor of the conceits, 202.9; p. must cry out loud, 202.10; vacant skull of a p., 202.30

people: never preachers, 3.4; know what they want, 5.12; resemble ballads, 23.6; inquisitive, 51.42; ask for criticism, 54.10; not creatures of logic, 76.4; who have a different point of view, 88.2; little p. live in nuts, 89.5; p. without history, 116.29; do not care to be taught what they do not already know, 125.16; two kinds of fascinating p., 145.42; making decent p. laugh, 148.26; literature exists for the sake of the p., 159.16; myths galvanize p., 183.33; most nostalgia p. in the world, 191.9; don't recite other p.'s opinions, 196.11; kind of p. we become, 203.5; can say anything, 203.8; p. start parades, 210.27; common p. do not pay, they only beg, 214.19; Irish are a fair p., 268.24; p. create stories, 270.2; who appear stupid, 273.8; p. more stupid than ourselves, 273.10; religious p. spend so much time with their confessors, 275.12; p. in need, 279.11; love p. who say what they think, 290.39; be wiser that other p., 306.5; stroke p. with words, 310.29

perceive: p. when to be silent, 280.5

perform, performance: when you p. ... you are out of yourself, 204.8; no strong p. without a little fanaticism, 204.9; resolve to p. what you ought, 239.3

Persians: no images of the gods, 107.10

personal: disdain to be p. with an anonymous pen, 249.6

personalities, personality: people who disintegrate as p., 186.1; filter of p., 271.7

persuade, persuasion, persuasive: beauty itself doth ... p., 25.16; eloquence is a p. thing, 75.27; by sweetness, 75.30; p. only shrine is eloquent speech, 205.1; modes of p. ... there are three kinds, 205.2; every man naturally p. himself that he can keep his resolutions, 239.5; p. men to action, 240.14; speech is to p., 268.17

perversion: p. of the mind, 172.14

pessimist: synonymous with a p., 165.23; to be a prophet it is sufficient to be a p., 222.15; p. about the future, 295.11

petulance: not sarcasm, 248.7

philologists: who chase a panting syllable, 277.2

philosophers: most mothers are instinctive p., 178.11; are as jealous as women, 206.19; what the first p. taught the last, 237.15

philosophy: traditional disputes of p., 68.2; p. dispute, 68.8; unitelligible answers to insoluble problems, 206.1; you can't do without p., 206.10; has a fine saying for everything, 206.22

phoenix: like an ebony p., 270.49

phrases: well-chosen p., 147.27; repeated a p. a great many times, 237.16

physician: P. aphorism, 14.6; words are the p. of a mind diseased, 310.1

pity, pitied: do not complain ... never p., 46.2

plague: p. the people with too long sermons, 256.11

platitude: epigram, p. with wine-leaves in its hair, 80.13; solemn p. gone to a masquerade ball, 80.17; literature is the orchestration of p., 159.25; art of saying p., 198.21; a truth repeated until people get tired of hearing it, 207.2; to higher and higher p. 207.4; not fond of uttering p., 207.6; stroke a p. until it purrs like an epigram, 207.9; nothing produces such an effect as a good p., 207.16; proverbs are always p., 224.22

play: theories of what is a good p., 21.5; great success, 21.28; kissing is a prologue to a p., 144.5; life is like a p., 155.19

pleading: sharpen your tongue with p., 294.24

please, pleasing: praise is always p., 213.16; if we would p. in society, 264.2; with when temperate is p., 307.39

pleasure: conversation is one of the greatest p., 51.27; speak one's mind ... becomes a p., 54.18; listen ... with pleasure, 75.31; talk entirely for their own p., 158.53; remembrances of past p. 191.7; sigh with p., 257.6; double p. to trick the trickster, 297.6

Pluto: the grisly god, 107.12

poem: traced a p to a dream, 90.17; p. ... must charm, 172.12; my p. are indelicate, 208.24; to read a p. is to hear it with our eyes, 208.41 that prolonged hesitation between sound and sense, 208.56

poet: loiter'd in green lanes, 23.7; unsatisfied child, 74.13; first teachers, 74.14; business of the p., 76.7; in command of his fantasy, 91.23; gives to life the supreme fictions, 95.17; p. ... most unpoetical of anything in existence, 124.9; lecturing on a live p. is all wrong, 151.8; p. may praise many, 164.13; p. must become more and more comprehensive, 166.6; passionately in love with language, 209.2; p. is a nightingale, 209.25; priest of the invisible, 209.26; should be a professor of hope, 219.12; p. are needed to sing the dawn, 223.10; good p. have a weakness for bad puns, 225.3; every p. knows the pun is Pierian, 225.32; intelligible forms of ancient p., 233.18; tranquil, measured epic p., 271.62; worst tragedy for a p., 296.9

poetry: work of the bard, 24.20; necessarily declines, 39.6; genuine p is conceived ... in the soul, 65.3; form of speech, 76.19; fantasy is nearer to p., 91.10; p. is reflective, 181.5; most ... widely effective way of saying things, 208.1; where language is renewed, 208.2; eldest sister of all arts, 208.11; can communicate before it is understood, 208.12; what is lost in translation, 208.15; what Milton saw when he went blind, 208.31; being a professor of p. is ... like being a Kentucky colonel, 219.2; p.—the best words in their best order, 223.4; sinks and swoons under a moderate weight of prose, 223.8; must be as well written as prose, 223.14; stream of p. which is continually flowing, 262.6; p. was the source and origin of style, 274.16; p. is the subject of the poem, 275.13; honorable characteristic of p., 275.14

point: speak to the p., 268.46; too fine a p. on your wit, 307.12

poison: flattery is p., 96.18; some sentences release their p. only after years, 255.2

polite, politeness: exceedingly p., 47.6; p consists in being one's self, 53.7; p. in speech—euphemism, 82.5

political: methodical engineering of myth for p. ends, 183.32; no p. gain in silence and submission, 211.1

politician: can sit on a fence and keep both ears to the ground, 210.1; never beliefs what he says, 210.12; ought to be born a foundling, 210.19; p. ... approaches every question with an open mouth., 210.30; to what extent any p. believes what he says, 210.32

politics: science of how who gets what, 211.8; purification of p., 211.9; just like show business, 211.15; is apple sauce, 211.17

portraits: of famous bards, 24.25

possessed: by an idea, 123.11

possible, possibility: politics is the art of the p., 211.7; discussions of the p. of tragedy, 296.16; no p. of being witty, 307.43

poverty: don't joke about your p., 140.22

power: knowledge is ... p., 145.2; p. of magic should not be under- estimated, 162.8; p. over our inmost being,

181.6; visionary p. 182.13; connection between naming and p., 185.14; wondrous p. of noise, 189.12; p. of sound, 205.7; p. of the spoken word, 212.1; great p. constitutes its own argument, 212.8; p. of the radio, 229.5; silence ... ultimate weapon of p., 258.17; speech is p., 268.17; witty beauty is a p., 307.35

practice: we should p. what we preach, 216.17

praise: thyself, 3.9; fortune and manners of men of old, 13.12; the past time, 13.17; just p. is only a debt, 96.15; flattery ... p. without foundation, 96.22; p. others extravagantly, 213.1; if we p. ourselves ... something will always stick, 213.4; advantage of doing one's own p., 213.8; requires constant renewal, 213.10; p. to the face is open disgrace, 213.11; we p. only to be p., 213.12; nothing people can't contrive to p., 230.6; more p. than known, 276.13; author may aspire to p., 312.19

pray, prayer: p. the Lord my soul to keep, 60.10; language of the heart, 214.1; p. is translation, 214.5; do not p. for yourself, 214.16; Lord's p. contains the sum total of religion and morals, 214.25

preach, preaching: to the educated, 21.4; p. viciously and act virtuously, 120.10; p. a respectable mythology, 184.14; p. well that lives well, 216.4; p. to death by wild curates, 216.18; p. ... because you have something to say, 216.21; p. which doth save souls, 256.9; p. a prayer-meeting sermon, 256.19

preacher: devil is a very successful p., 62.6; you talk for a living, 190.12; a black poet is a p., 209.11; test of a p., 215.1; many p. don't hear themselves, 215.4; must have a definite point, 215.11; number of good p. may have decreased, 215.16; when a p. reads his sermon, 256.8; cold p. make bold sinners, 260.1; no p. is listened to but time, 292.32

precision: of communication, 44.19

prefer, preference: beauty of inflections or ... of innuendoes, 25.19; people p. illusion to reality, 126.9

prejudice: driving out of p. down your throat, 74.9; p. ... grow, firm as weeds among stones, 217.3; deluded by vulgar p., 217.6; p. are the props of civilization, 217.7; squints when it looks, 217.11; a bundle of p., 217.12; we all decry p., 217.16

present: flattery is a p., 96.15

Press: never lose your temper with the P., 210.26

presumption: I acquired a certain pedantic p., 202.16

pretense: little p. served the wolf, 120.8

price: p. of your voice?, 150.20

pride, proud: p. of not being a liar, 153.28; look out how you use p. words, 310.64

probability: keep p. in view, 281.31

problem: of the actor, 21.20: p. that presents itself as a dilemma, 218.5; if you mention a p., you caused it., 218.7

profanity: furnishes a relief, 57.15

professor; professing: one who talks in someone else's sleep, 219.1; guard the glory that was Greece, 219.8; p. emeritus, 219.22; liberals ... professors of the practicable, 219.28

projection: parable is the p. of story, 199.11

prologue: courtship ... witty p., 164.4; p. precede the piece in mournful verse, 288.4

promise: I can p. to be sincere, 141.6; p. to build a bridge where there is no river, 210.20

pronounce, pronunciation: spare my p. vagaries, 1.2; p. with the vulgar, 147.16; take care to p. correctly the words usually mis—p., 220.1

proper: p. words in p. places, 274.17

proof, prove: never assume that incapable of p., 20.5; p. against p., 103.11; gossip p. nothing, 108.4; miracle cannot p. what is impossible, 174.12

propaganda: consists in nearly deceiving your friends, 221.2; done more to defeat the good intentions of nations, 221.3

propagandist: p.'s purpose, 221.6

prophet: word unto p. spoken, 27.9; historian, a p. in reverse, 115.9; p. of the past, 222.3

prophecy: heresy often turns out to be p., 113.2; study prophecy when they are become histories, 222.2

proposal: impracticable, 18.44

prose: a regular feature ... was the mixture of p. and verse, 159.11; p. is discourse, 208.38; all the lines except the last go to the end, 223.1; words in their best order, 223.4; p. can paint evening and moonlight, 223.10; good p. is like a window pane, 223.13; takes the mold of the body and mind entire, 223.18

prosperity: jest's p. lies in the ear, 139.24

proud: we are ridiculously proud, 185.9

proverb: the horse of conversation, 224.1; sanctuary of the intuitions, 224.11; short aphorisms, 224.13; much matter decocted into few words, 224.14; no p. which is not true, 298.17; wisdom of the street, 306.10

psychoanalysis: nothing true except exaggerations, 83.1; beautiful modern myth of p., 183.41

psychobabble: a set of repetitive verbal formalities, 138.13

psychological: fairy tales represent p. triumphs, 90.7; height of p. luxury, 131.8

public: accustomed to p. speaking, 269.1

punishment: p. of a liar, 153.6; talkative man inflicts p., 282.47

punning, puns: seeds of p ... in the minds of all men, 225.1; short quip followed by a long groan, 225.2; sort of a literary prostitution, 225.5; make so vile a p., 225.11; two strings of thought tied with an acoustic knot, 225.19; noble thing per se, 225.20; pistol left off at the ear, 225.21

pupils: seven p. in the class, 219.34; to be an efficient p., 272.18; true teacher defends his p. against his own ... influence, 283.2; makes himself p. to a fool, 283.6; if only p. cared to learn, 284.18; teach his p. in concise terms, 284.24

purpose: listens to good p., 158.12

pygmies: on the shoulders of giants, 104.2

quarrel: interrupts an argument, 18.9; lover's q. with the world, 160.12; the dowry which married folk bring to each other, 164.24; q. with ourselves, poetry, 208.59; q. of friends, 226.1; q. not with a long-tongued man, 226.4; better to q. with a knave than a fool, 226.7; takes two to make a q., 226.29; men have q. about religion, 234.8

queen: I am your anointed q., 143.4

question: never answer q. until asked, 12.8; q. ... we do not know, 12.10; blind man's q. to ask, 25.3; believer asks no q., 26.17; curiosity leads to disagreeable q., 56.2; avoid a questioner, 56.7; every q. leads to another q., 56.11; settle a q., 67.4; dares to ask difficult q., 74.13; fiction's business to ask, 95.12; history is ... the study of q., 116.5; great q. of all choosers and adventurers, 155.20; question is ... which is to be master, 166.4; asking of q., 206.13; ask the hard q., 227.2; hypothetical q. get hypothetical answers, 227.4; q. are always easy, 227.8; power to q., 227.10; some q. don't have a., 227.11; q. you ask yourself, 227.18; a great many of searching q., 227.24; better to ask some of the q., 227.26; q. are never indiscreet, 227.8; ask the right q., 252.15

quiet: to keep q. and listen, 158.19; so q. you could hear a pun drop, 225.4

quote, quotation, quoting: work contains nothing worth q., 30.17; "I love you" is always a q., 160.46; husband q. the wife, 164.23; don't q. your proverb, 224.16; good pun deserves to be drawn and q., 225.16; the act of repeating erroneously the word of another, 228.3; to be apt in q. is a splendid and dangerous gift, 228.9; one may q. till one compiles, 228.11; we all quote, 228.14; wrapped himself in q., 228.19; often q. myself, 228.27; better to be q. than honest, 228.29

race: if a r. has no history, 295.15

radio: r. was fraught with politeness, 229.1; r. involves you., 229.2; from talk r. to insult r., 229.6; gives birth to a million images, 229.13; something people listen to while ... doing something else, 229.18

rationalization, rationalized: contemporary man has r. the myths, 183.30

read, reading: aphorisms ... affect you agreeably in r., 14.16; some r. to think, 30.9; my little fable, 87.24; what do our clergy lose by r. their sermons, 215.6; r. books of quotations, 228.8; basic tool in living of a good life, 231.2; r. some of the rules for speaking and writing, 245.12; r. and grows no wiser, 273.11; who wants to r. about success, 276.11; let your r. aloud be good talk, 282.36

reader: a wise r. to quote wisely, 228.1; satire delights the r., 249.4

Reagan, Ronald: rhetorical roundheels, 21.23

realities, reality: r. sandwiches, 7.4; transform one million r., 91.1; fantasy discourages r., 91.19; produce the illusion of a loftier r., 126.8; copy of r. that we can recognize, 145.31; r. becomes too complex for oral communication, 152.9; legends make r., 152.19; external r. is a fiction, 232.5; leaves a lot to the imagination, 232.12; not the same to the doer as to the sayer, 232.14; much not count overmuch on your r., 232.16; story, which was the r., 270.1; endeavor to capture r. by means of ideas, 290.28; words ... great foes of r., 310.16

reason, reasoned: law is experience developed by r., 149.11; only argument that belongs to man, 233.1; r. me out of my r., 233.3; hearken to r., 233.10

reasons: heart has its r., 112.11; people will hunt for r. to confirm first impressions, 217.14; quick come the r. for approving what we like, 230.1; poor men's r. are not heard, 233.4

recall: impossible to r. what has been uttered, 268.40

recipes: science ... r. that are always successful, 252.20

reflect: to r. is to disturb one's thoughts, 291.27

refuse: like people to r. to speak, 268.22

relation, relationship: of our typical dreams to fairy tales, 90.17; make the r. between particular and universal fully explicit, 199.1

relevance: no possible r. to anything but itself, 256.10; r. of speech is at stake, 268.4

religion: avoid all arguments about r., 18.33; issue bibles against him, 62.9; Christian r. doubted, 70.3; mythology is the mother of r., 184.2; politics ... is the binding secular r., 211.22; fair humanities of old r., 233.18; speak the language of the heart, 234.1; r. we call false were once true, 234.7; is like love, 234.17; only one r., 234.18; old apartments of r., 270.68

remarks: good r. surprise their author, 75.22; silly r., 147.4; famous r. are seldom quoted correctly, 228.30; enough truth to make the r. unbearable, 235.2; are not literature, 235.5; very seldom quoted correctly, 235.6

remember, remembrance: all knowledge is r., 145.24; what people r., 270.65

remorse: suffer r. for what I said, 250.4

rendezvous; with death, 60.12

repartee: cannot think of any r., 236.1; what you wish you'd said, 236.3; something we think of twenty-four hours too late, 236.9

repeat, repeated, repetition: r. too often becomes insipid, 237.1; thinking r. will substitute for proof, 237.2; r. is the mother ... of education, 237.11; only form of permanence nature can achieve, 237.12; r. the same old story, 271.18; r. a tale told by a man, 281.12

repent, repented: often r. of speaking, 258.47; speak the thing I shall r., 294.39

reply: r. to calumny and defamation, 258.1

reputation: biting people's r., 37.10; for being good company, 108.20; two modes of establishing our r., 238.2; wink a r. down, 251.10; r. for wisdom, 306.24

repute: puns are in very bad repute, 225.29; men get the r. of being witty, 307.22

reserve: always more interesting, 76.5

resolved, resolution: r. to take fate by the throat, 239.1; r. is necessary to decision, 239.2; easily formed when the heart suggest them, 239.7; never tell your r. before hand, 239.9; useless attempts to interfere with scientific laws, 239.11

respect: to rhyme with renewed r., 241.7

responsibility: listening is a r., 158.21; r. of a writer, 312.4

result, results; give only r., 18.14; we are the r. of what we have thought, 291.9

retract: those who never r. their opinions, 196.16

revelation: idea ... must come with the force of a r., 123.7

revenge: r. in every complaint, 46.18; slander is the r. of a coward, 261.13

reverence: r. too much old times, 295.1; r. for the wisdom of our ancestors, 306.4

revolution: fear ... herald of all r., 94.3

reward: acclaimed by applause, 17.12

rhetoric: in the study, 75.41; r. wherewith I persuade another, 205.3; we have let r. do the job of poetry, 208.36; quarrel with others, 226.32; observing ... the available means of persuasion, 240.1; sophistical r., 240.7; pluck ... some flower of r., 240.11; truth and beauty in r., 240.19; art of ruling the minds of men, 240.20

rhyme, rhyming: beautiful old r., 25.15; ring out my mournful r., 173.12; misliking of r., 241.1; scarce in this world of ours, 241.6; troublesome an modern bondage of r., 241.9

rhythm: writing is a question of finding a certain r., 313.16

riddle: key to a r. is another r., 242.2

ridicule: may be a shield, 243.7; often checks what is absurd, 243.8; ounce of ridicule, 243.14

Robin Hood: English ballad-singer's joy, 23.14; tales of R.H., 281.37

romance: unreliable consolations of r., 90.34; no need of r., 116.37; learned r. as she grew older, 244.1; usually a nice little tale, 244.5; nothing spoils a r. so, 244.10

royalty: r. ... is badly spoken of, 143.2

rude, rudely: ghosts are very r., 103.12; as calculatedly r. as the British, 135.7; act r. with impunity, 307.31

rule: grammar has a r. absurd, 109.5; grammar is not a set of r., 109.14, no r. in filmmaking, 180.3; rhetorican's r., 240.2; admits some exception, 245.1; r. .. destroy genius and art, 245.5; r. of thumb, 245.6; golden r., 245.9; general r. ... bear hard on particular cases, 245.11

rumor: history ... distillation of r., 116.11; trying to squash a r., 246.2; is untraceable, 246.3; have a nimbler foot than a mule, 246.4; seldom at a loss for answers, 246.10

Russia: riddle wrapped in a mystery inside an enigma, 242.1

sad, saddest, sadness: meaning of s., 90.20; of all tales tie s., 247.1; s. story I have ever heard, 247.4; cannot explain the s., 247.5; absolute silence leads to s., 258.43; sweetest songs ... tell of s. thought, 265.21; s. when I sing, 265.25; told a tale of more prevailing s., 281.11; s. words of tongue or pen, 310.74

sages: s. whom we understand less, 133.5; maxims of the s., 165.11; may pour out their wisdom's treasure, 176.3; four types ... sit before the s., 272.19; any on who follows a middle course, 306.20

salt: Attic s., 225.8

sarcasm: language of the devil, 62.1; think I detect s., 248.1; arrows of s., 248.9; keep a store of s., 248.10; fell before a s., 248.13

satire: to enliven an eulogy., 81.11; is a lesson, 200.6; praise undeserved is s. in disguise, 213.6; man's barbed s., 249.1; of all human dealings, s. is the very lowest, 249.3; be like the porcupine, 249.15; impotent as it is insolent, 249.32

savage, savaged: is a slave, 39.1; s. by stuff that belittles their intelligence, 287.15

say, said: s what you have to s., 30.4; more you s., 34.10; s in sentences, 34.16; can be s. clearly, 40.19; things left unsaid, 44.5; what you have to say, 49.4; leave unsaid the wrong thing, 51.31; s. nothing, art of diplomacy, 66.7; all that should be said, 75.24; well s. as if I s. it myself, 75.38; father s. to his children, 93.7; what God s. is best, 106.4; saying things ... that are absolutely ... true, 108.37; to know how to s. what others only know, 145.12; s. anything for their fee, 150.28; everything has been s. before, 158.20; leaving three or four things ... unsaid, 164.22; should s. what you mean, 166.3; learn the meaning of what you s., 166.7; she s. what she means, 166.10; nothing is s. that has not been s. before, 192.13; nothing more to s., 227.21; read to s. what we have read, 231.7; don't s. anything, you won't be called on to repeat it, 237.4; what people s. behind your back, 238.4; what do they s., 250.1; do as we s., 250.2; s. something to remember, 250.3; s. things that should be s., 250.8; attend to what is actually s., 250.9; cannot s. one thing and mean another, 250.10; s. what is obvious, 250.11; never s. anything remarkable, 250.12; what isn't worth s. is sung, 265.5; learn to s. before you sing, 265.10; well-conceived is clearly s., 268.9; goes without s., 268.11; first ... decide what to s., 269.6; I say little ... but think more, 290.19; s. first and thought after, 291.32; thing well s., 307.17

sayings: soft and flattering s., 96.6; hear the s., 250.1; old man's s. are seldom untrue, 250.5; as the s. is, 250.6; every wise s. has an opposite, 250.13; ancient s. is no

heresy, 250.14; where that s. was born, 250.15; inherited a stock of cheerful s., 307.45

scandal: gossip isn't s., 108.22; an importunate wasp, 251.1; half of the world takes pleasure in inventing, 251.2; s. tickling in our ear, 251.5; spreads like a spot of oil, 251.8

schizophrenic: when God talks to us, we're s., 106.19

scholar; knows no boredom, 31.27; s often a fool, 202.3; s. teacheth his master, 272.4; apt s. need little teaching, 272.17

scholarship: not ... a property, but as a devotion, 219.38

school, schooling: a spirit of curiosity, 56.1; sounding jargon of the s., 138.4; noisy jargon of the s., 138.12; life is a s., 155.28; such nonsense is often heard in s., 190.5; carrying tales out of s., 281.28

science: authority depend on ... analogy, 8.5; offers analogies, 8.9; fairy tales of s., 90.32; of folklore and literary criticism, 98.18; lying is done ... also with silence, 153.33; language is the only instrument of s., 157.8; myths are early s., 183.19; must begin with myths, 183.31; professors of the dismal s., 219.5; s. is we, 252.3; an expression of our ignorance, 252.4; begin with myths, 252.16; open windows of s., 252.18; is voiceless, 252.21; ashamed of keeping s., 268.26; wit is like s., 307.11

science fiction: the mythology of modern technology, 95.15; no more written for scientists, 252.2; mythology of modern technology, 252.12; not predicate, ... descriptive, 252.13; grown up with s.f. ideas, 252.19

scoffing: s. comes not of wisdom, 243.10

scorn: silence ... most perfect expression of s., 258.46

scriptures: uncorrupt, sufficient, clear, 27.6; search the s., 27.14; quoted the s., 27.19; open town in time of war, 27.20; devil can cite s., 62.8

sculpture: to a block of marble, 74.1

season: s. for silence, 258.44

secret: imagination is a guilty s., 127.22; a kiss ... a s. told to the mouth, 144.15; no language can utter the s. of love, 160.17; great s. of managing the mind, 172.8; Nature tells every s. once, 187.12; to keep a s., 253.1; three may keep a s., 253.4; things we give to others, 253.6; when a s. is revealed, 253.9; get possession of s., 253.12; my s. cry aloud, 294.37; every s. of a writer's soul, 312.27

see, seeing: hearing is not s., 111.3; others s. as well as you, 195.8; s. many things, 195.9; always tell what one s., 195.11; sounds are the things I s., 267.13

self: something one creates, 124.11

self-confidence: humor comes from s-c., 119.5

self-expression: pass into communication, 44.4

sell, selling: lives by s. something, 35.9

sense, senses: reduce s. almost to nil, 74.7; good s. expressed in clear language, 75.6; rich grape of good s., 75.20; condensed good s. of nations, 165.18; can't talk s., talk metaphor, 171.8; making s. out of experience, 206.15; radar-net of our s., 254.1; common s. ... the best s., 254.2; s. may be unseasonable, 254.3; devoid of common s., 254.6; horse-s., 254.9; take care of the s., 267.4; more sound than s., 267.12

sensations: few more melancholy s., 247.8

sentences: s. have little meaning, 166.8; mouths a s. as curs mouth a bone, 198.3; men of talents ... convinced by short s., 216.15; proverb is a short s. based on long experience, 224.6; proverb is an instructive s., 224.28; every s. I utter must be understood ... as a question, 227.5; if s. have little meaning when they are writ,

255.6; begins quite simply, 255.7; not easy to define, 255.9; short s. drive themselves, 255.11; s. that stir my bile, 255.13; should contain no unnecessary words, 255.14; most attractive s., 255.15; s. that begin with "all women," 309.4

sentiments: calm quiet interchange of s., 51.21

seriousness: increasing s. of things, 140.23

sermon: shook the s. out of my mind, 172.10; great s. lead the people to praise the preacher, 215.3; asked for reasons, not s., 233.13; everyone has at least one s. in him, 256.1, s. well delivered is … uncommon, 256.2; best s. is preached by the minister, 256.6; most s. … sound like commercials, 256.12; like pie-crust, 256.14 half-baked s., 256.15; s. edifies, 256.20

servant: tells a secret is another man's s., 253.5

severe: too s. a moraler, 176.17

sex, sexes: rift between the s., 105.7; woman never forgets her s., 309.21

shadow: live in the s. of an idea, 122.3; grasping at the s., 126.2; life's but a walking s., 155.33; lose the substance by grasping the s., 232.3; words are but the vague s., 310.25

shame, ashamed: not a. to think, 36.12; s. the devil, 62.5; praise s. me, 213.23

sheep: Little Bo-Peep has lost her s., 193.8

shortage: suffer from a s. of listeners., 158.6

shoulders: standing on s. of giants, 104.6

sick: use this treatment to help the s., 194.7

sigh, sighing: God is an utterable s., 106.13; glad heart seldom s., 112.5; breaks the body of a man, 257.1; s. was his gift, 257.2; most of the s. … have been edited, 257.7; s. at what we call success, 276.12

silence, silent: highest applause, 17.6; converted a man, 18.35; sudden, 51.6; great art of conversation, 51.16; flashes of s., 51.39; idiot's eloquence, 75.18; virtue of fools, 99.2; honors … purchase s., 118.5; when s. speaks for love, 160.14; man has in him the s. of the air, 16.18; hovers over all the mountain peaks, 182.5; Nature's s. is its one remark, 187.10; s. that spoke, 205.14; unbearable repartee, 236.4; s. is said to be golden, 258.6; as different as sounds, 258.8; s. have a climax, 258.9; doesn't know how to be s., 258.11; more e. than w., 258.13; speaking s., 258.16; propagates itself, 258.28; appalling s. of good people, 258.31; improve on s., 258.41; capacity to be s., 258.49, breaking s. these twenty-three years, 258.50; s. is not always tact., 280.1; time to keep s., 292.23; true wisdom's best reply, 306.11; judgement to be s., 307.30

silly: to give advice, 5.21; palaver is s., 34.2; too s. to be said, 265.20; aren't women s., 309.13

simile: has been superseded by the metaphor, 171.3; are at bottom poetical, 259.1; no s. for his lungs, 259.3; like defective ammunition, 259.4; no s. runs on all fours, 259.5; most unsavory s., 259.8;

simple, simplicity: makes the uneducated more effective, 18.2; s. are the words of truth, 298.1

sin, sinners: in wine or wantoness, 28.8; epigrams cover a multitude of s. 80.20; cry out against s., 120.1; has many tools, 154.11; ultimate s. of any performer, 204.4; only the s. has the right to preach, 216.13; every s. has its own excuse, 260.4; millions of millions of s., 260.5; being told that one is a s., 260.13; s. with his tongue, 294.7

sincere, sincerity: criticism sounds more s. 54.15; grand words are not s., 310.47

sing, singing: of knights and paladins, 1.6; faster than

you'll tell money, 23.13; teach me to hear mermaids s., 170.2; I have heard the mermaids s., 170.3; minstrel s. us now a tender song, 173.10; sing a song of sixpence, 193.16; two people can s. together, 265.6, to sing … expression of your being, 265.7; delight in s., 265.15; when in doubt, s. loud, 265.16

skillful: be s. in speech, 268.30

slander: dog's eloquence, 261.1; slays three persons, 261.2; like a hornet 261.7

slang: accent of Chicago, 1.9; all s. is metaphor, 171.7; conventional tongue with many dialects, 262.2; has no country, 262.3; s. you make up yourself, 262.4; language that rolls up its sleeves, 262.14

sleep: s. o brave-hearted, 185.10; s. in continual noise, 189.9; much good s. in an old story, 263.2; hour's sleep before midnight, 263.4; mumble in their s., 263.6; never s. comfortably except, 263.7

smile: hidden by a minstrel-s., 173.1; a man who does not disagree, but s. 205.22

Socrates: calling S to an argument, 18.37

social, sociable: expressing s. statements, 249.17; designed man for a s. creature, 264.6

society: bores and bored, 31.9; talk so much in s., 44.8; held together by our needs, 264.1; bond of human s., 264.4; never speak disrespectfully of s., 264.12

sociology: black literature is taught as s., 159.17

soldiers: as soon as you have s. the story is called history, 116.2

solitude: guardian of his s., 164.26

solution: any s. to a problem changes the problem, 218.6; always an easy s. to every problem, 218.11; problems … solved … by extinction or duplication, 218.12

songs: fashion laborious s, 24.14; child learn sooner, 38.22; all s. are folk songs, 97.5; folk s. composes itself, 97.11; s. of the singer, 112.9; s. of love, 160.23; s. of the brides, 164.16; s. of tears is dead, 169.14; s. my mother and yours always sang, 178.9; I made my s. a coat, 184.16; do not know who sings my s., 265.3; sing me the s. 265.4; I delighted to hear, 265.4; licensed medium for bawling in public, 265.12; prize that s. most, 265.13; sing me a bawdy s., 265.19; soft as some s. divine, 270.28; ever a s. of ocean seemed to sing, 281.26

sonnets: defiant love s., 105.4

sorrow: s. comes to explain … the sublime language by means of which he speaks to God., 214.7; hush all our s. in a moment, 233.5; excessive s. laughs, 266.1; makes silence her best orator, 266.2, little s. are loud, 266.4; all s. can be borne, 266.5; half the s. of women, 309.15

sorry: love means never having to say you're s., 160.39

soul: changed in the telling, 50.9; echoes roll from s. to s., 73.13; folk tale … primer of the picture-language of the s., 98.5; story of the s., 152.20; Old King Cole was a merry old s., 193.11; shall I lay perjury on my s., 194.12; each religion … proposes some method of fortifying the human s., 234.15; would harrow up thy s., 247.9; unkindness … pierces the s., 249.13; s. worth expressing, 265.18; speech is the mirror of the s., 268.42; wisdom is of the s., 306.30; great authors share their s. with us, 312.22; s. keeps its youth, 314.2

sound: animal communication, 11.6; empty vessel, 28.16; shadow of a s., 73.12; making folk-songs from soul s., 97.21; s. of a kiss, 144.7; s. of laughter, 148.21; full of s. and fury, 155.33; first s. in the song of love, 160.23; ordered s., 181.35; s of music creep into our ears, 181.36; s. of their environment constitute a music, 189.4;

learned nonsense has a deeper s., 190.4; sweetest of all s. is praise, 213.25; sentence is a s. in itself, 255.8; heal the blows of s., 258.25; appropriately beautiful or ugly s., 267.2; no s. is dissonant, 267.5; catch-all word, 267.14; sweet is every s., 267.15 truth often does s. unconvincing, 298.18; truth is the pleasantest of s., 298.54

soup: stirs up de old words to make a new s., 271.34

space: no such thing as empty s., 258.10

speak, speaking: English without an accent, 1.1; with a slightly American accent, 1.8; so loud, 3.6; when to s., 5.10; bright angel, 10.7; of the moderns, 13.5; without book, 30.16, much and s. well, 34.9; s the word he meant, 36.1; unable to s., 37.6; till he had something to say, 44.10; to s. kindly, 53.4; s. a dialect with an accent, 63.2; manner of s., 75.7; eloquence in s., 75.10; s. right on, 75.37; s into the air, 78.3; s. from experience, 85.15; forensic s. either attacks or defends, 100.1; ghosts ... never speak till spoke to, 103.1; like a green girl, 105.6; God s. in a whisper, 106.7; s. to God as if men were listening, 106.17; where the heart dares to s., 112.10; s. like a rouge, 117.1; s. honestly, 117.6; s. educationese, 138.9; she s. academese, 138.14; s. in jest, 139.16; s. of me as I am, 141.7; province of knowledge to s., 145.25; s. the language of the company, 147.6; s. the language of the place, 147.7; s. the same language, 147.23; s. to an unwilling listener, 158.28; s. that I may see thee, 163.9; I would s. if only I had memories, 169.18; mother ... s. with her life, 178.10; s. boldly when one has nothing to say, 192.16; I only s. right on, 198.23; s. on every question with grace, 198.24; s. I to them in parables, 199.5; s. with more safety, 203.3; on the side of those who s. last, 205.30; s. softly and carry a big stick, 212.9; for ... forty years ... s. prose without knowing it, 223.11; when all men s. well of you, 238.6; you love to s. in riddles, 242.9; he s. sense, 254.8; s. what is fit, 258.2; let him now s., 258.7; s. to thee in silence, 258.45; s. well of everybody, 261.4; to s. of sorrow, 266.8; pause before s., 268.1; much s. is an abomination, 268.2; s. the worst, 268.38; s. and proclaim, 268.44; able to s. before he has anything to say,m 268.50; s. softly, 269.4; s. comfort for great bereavement, 279.3; s. as the common people do, 290.3; must have leave to s., 294.31; s. the truth freely, 298.16; love to s. the truth, 298.37; when we have to s. suddenly, 298.45; s. no more than the truth, 298.46; well-bred youth never s. of himself, 314.13

speaker: true relation with his audience, 21.12; he is no s., 282.16

speech: uncorrupted, 1.9; modest in 3.2; mirror of action, 3.15; be short, 34.17; is civilization, 39.7; power of s., 44.7; art of concealing thought, 48.2; true use of s., 48.4; courteous s. from children, 53.8; s. to express thoughts, 76.20; fool's s. ... bubble of air, 99.7; grammar is common s. formulated, 109.16; to prepare a good impromptu s., 130.13; s. of man stops short, 181.41; device for saying nothing, 192.1; oaths are the flash-notes of s., 194.11; poetry ... destinies of s., 208.4; speak the s., I pray you, 220.4; fine example of rhetoric, 240.3; secrecy ... seal of s., 253.15; utter all s. that is good, 258.14; s. be better than silence, 258.20; s. may be barren, 258.22; small change of silence, 258.38; protestationism in s., 262.17; s. is a sound in which song is locked, 265.2; all s. has something of song in it., 265.8; s. ... makes man a political being, 268.4; s. less cleverly, 268.5; shows what a man is,

268.13; voice of the heart, 268.14; but broken light, 268.15; like a cracked kettle, 268.19; true use of s., 291.15; created thought, 291.29; given to man to disguise his thoughts, 291.31

speeches: should always be fresh, 45.3; impromptu s., 130.3; extemporaneous s., 130.10; persuasive s. to fuddle the mental apparatus, 172.19; leave it to men's charitable s., 185.1; short s. which fly aboard like darts, 268.6; should always be fresh; 269.10; make your s. not too explicit, 269.11; never delivered a firebrand s., 269.12; measured by the hour, 269.17; s. is poetry, 269.22; often like eggs, 269.25; like an airplane engine, 269.26; every s. should be ... fully flavored, 288.20

speechmaker: I'm not a s., 269.14

spell: foreigners always s. better than they pronounce, 220.5

spirit: capable of compassion and sacrifice, 163.5; youth has to do with s., 314.21

spiritualism: media ... sounds like a convention of s., 167.10

spontaneity: through s. we are re-formed, 130.12

sport: fosters international hostility, 21.19

stage: life is a s. and a play, 155.26; s. is a shout, 288.9; s. where every man must play his part, 288.17; the return of art to life, 288.21; tragedy on the s., 296.3; world is a s., 311.13

stars: instruction to give, 27.23

steps: halting and painful s., 276.14

still: better to keep s., 258.32

stimulation: all s. generates a memory, 169.5

stones: found in stones ... sermons, 256.21

story: innumerable bundles of other stories, 13.20; divine art, 19.8; believe s that ought to be truth, 26.2; how much to believe, 26.18; short in s., 34.18; make long s. short, 34.19; make s. shorter, 34.26; need to be long, 34.29; child's s. is a dream, 38.11; heart of story, 38.17; brought to its conclusion, 49.5; still the s. is told, 52.2; all that remained was the s., 60.16; tells how it might have been, 65.2; long, blind, dreaming s., 71.9; s. operate like dreams, 71.12; s. to delight his ear, 72.17; bearing an untold s., 76.14; s. ... help him cope with life's problems, 91.4; gentleman never heard the s. before, 102.8; God ... loves s., 106.20; rhythmic s. that possessed the special quality of moral ... resolution, 110.1; about the great and powerful, 111.6; we are the hero of our own s., 114.15; history is indeed our s., 116.27; s. is the thing, 134.5; tell the untold s., 147.44; s. that never, never die, 15.15; making a s. better than it happened, 153.34; false s. has seven endings, 154.22; life is a handful of short s., 155.3; s. are important they keep us alive, 155.5; tell ourselves s. in order to live, 155.12; s. of your life, 155.14; s. do recount what life has been, 155.25; whenever s. and storytellers are together, 162.7; s. has to have muscle, 166.15; s. are medicine, 168.5; like a s. with a bad moral, 176.11; s. with a moral appended, 176.12; modern detective s., 182.2; myth ... the hidden part of every s., 183.6; elders telling s. of the old days, 197.6; s. shall swarm with the invisible dead of my tribe, 197.10; internalize the s., 212.3; power consists ... in deciding what s. will be told, 212.6; when we read a s. we inhabit it, 231.5; unread s. is not a s., 231.9; s. ought to be just little bits of fantasy, 232.4; behave reasonably in s., 233.12; two or three human s., 237.3; never get tired of telling our s., 237.9; love s. are only fit for the solace of people, 244.3; cruel s. runs on wheels, 246.11; s. are beings, 270.5; s. always old and always new, 270.9; only two or three human s., 270.11; good s. cannot be devised, 270.12; outside of a s. is simply its words, 270.25; willing to tell a s. twice, 270.26; bearing an untold s. inside you, 270.32; but that's another s., 270.37; three kinds of s., 270.38; s. that nourish every single life, 270.41; word s. comes from storehouse, 270.45; not the sum of its happenings, 270.46; must have shape and meaning, 270.53; better to tell your own s., 270.57; part of an ancient continuous s., 270.62; essentials to a good s., 271.17; I'll tell you a s., 271.20; tell it because it is a good s., 271.40; don't just get to a s., 271.41; s. to delight his ear, 271.58; no story is the same ... after the lapse of time, 292.11; could tell you a s. which is true, 294.35; I will tell you a s., 312.10; my s. is their s., 314.4

storyteller: s. art, 19.16; repeat their stories to ... listeners, 21.13; fairy tales first told by gifted tellers, 90.37; history, a far more daring s., 116.28; plays like a wind on the s.'s instrument, 134.1; person who has a good memory, 169.4; stimulation of the s.'s voice, 197.13; depends chiefly on the s. 270.66; weaves the ups and downs of experience, 271.1; nesting place, 271.4; s. of the Highlands, 271.10; include those who created the stories, 271.22; oldest and newest of the arts, 271.24; I am a real s., 271.42; purpose of every s., 271.43; attracted by the art of s., 271.45; good s. recognizes his or her peer, 271.50; at first no professional s., 271.53; indispensable agents of socialization, 271.56; s. were carrying his listener, 271.57; s. is born, 271.64; good writer is basically a s., 312.25

storytelling: oldest form of education, 74.26; encourage the art of s., 98.16; given my life to s., 112.3; as an art means recreating literature, 159.3; reveals meaning, 166.1; s. is subject to two unavoidable defects, 169.17; first practiced by ordinary persons, 197.7; essentials for successful s., 271.12; s. is an innovation, 271.31; s. won an established place, 271.44; one of the few truly universal human bonds, 271.47; unequalled in the art of s., 271.63; oldest form of education, 271.67; a personal art, 271.68

stream: islands in the s., 270.76

strength: giant's, 104.9

struggle: literature is ... a s. to escape from the confines of language, 159.7; no tragedy without a s., 296.5

student: a lover courting a fickle mistress, 272.11; if a s. fails to learn, 283.3; s. rarely disappoint teachers, 283.15

study: must s. politics and war, 272.1; secret of productive s., 272.9; beware of prosecuting s., 272.10; depends on the good will of the student, 272.13

stupid, stupidity: need advice, 5.7; argument with a man so s., 18.40; way of asking makes people very s., 233.16; not as many s. things said, 273.2; born s., 273.4; with s. ... man may front much, 273.4 say something s., 273.5; deliberate cultivation of ignorance, 273.6; never know what s. is, 273.7

style: to have a command of metaphor, 171.2; s. of storytelling in the South, 271.21; dress of thoughts, 274.3; simple way of saying very complicated things, 274.4; perfection of a point of view, 274.5; found his s., 274.12; physiognomy of the mind, 274.13; s. not sincerity is the vital thing, 274.20

subject: any s. can be made interesting, 31.3; particular s. of conversation, 51.7; discussion of any s. is a right,

67.8; honor is the s. of my story, 118.6; everyone is ignorant ... on different s., 125.19; chief effect of talking on any s., 196.21; s. ... always should agree with rhyme, 241.3; no man ever made a speech on a mean s., 269.5; no student knows his s., 272.20; large s. to expatiate upon, 275.2; grasp the s., 275.5; you search for a s., 275.6; talk too much on the best of s., 275.9; s. of the Supreme Being, 289.7; explain a s. by men who do not understand it, 289.9

subservient: everything is s. to success, 276.6

success: story of s., 276.1; supposes endeavor, 276.2, counted sweetest, 276.3; nothing recedes like s., 276.5; depends on three things, 276.9; always been the worst of liars, 276.10

succinct: he was s. because he had learned no other way, 271.32

suffer, suffered: professor of the fact that another s., 219.19; how youth can s.

suggest: know how to s. ... great art of teaching, 284.1

suicide: s. committing s., 259.9

superiority: man likes to assume s. over himself, 256.4

surprise: music takes us by s., 181.17

survival: responsible for the s. of African-Americans, 270.21

suspected, suspects, suspicion: his own tediousness, 31.1; s. himself of being anything but clever, 273.1

suspense: soul of narrative, 186.14

superstitious: s. and rationalizing at the same time, 230.3

swan: the minstrel of its own death, 173.6; sing before they die, 265.11

swear, swearing: shows lack of vocabulary, 57.2; compromise between running and fighting, 57.6

sweat: s. of their browbeating, 150.24

syllables: seems fiends always laugh in s., 277.3; s. govern the world, 277.8

symbol, symbolic, symbolism: language as s., 147.32; nature speaks in s., 187.20; every story can be s. unfolded, 270.64; s. ... act of thinking in images, 278.1; imaginative signposts of life, 278.2; s. view of things, 278.3; in a s. there is concealment, 278.6; great s. swallow us whole, 278.9

symmetry: s. of form attainable in pure fiction, 186.12

sympathetic, sympathy: lose your audience s., 21.10; s. with sounds, 267.6; one poor word which includes all our best insight, 279.5; to be s. without discrimination, 279.6; s. without relief, 279.7; as necessary as the air we breathe, 279.15

taciturn: none love to speak ... as they who are naturally t., 268.8

tact: teaches you when to be silent., 280.4; to lie about others, 280.6; possessing the most perfect social t., 280.12

talent: catch the flame, 17.14; of flattering, 96.2; requires no extraordinary t. to lie, 153.23; punning is a t. which no man affects, 225.31; helpful in writing, 313.20; youth itself is a t., 314.15

tales: were so dear, 13.3; of a tub, 26.25; crowd ... in a minute, 34.11; childhood loves to hear, 38.28; dead bodies must tell the t., 52.5; of cruelty, 55.1; t of woe, 60.9; dead ... tell no t., 60.15; fragment from life of dreams, 71.5; dreams are t., 71.6; piteous t., 76.12; of cock and bull, 83.5; old wives' foolish t., 83.7; from Arabian Nights, 90.12; runic t. to sigh and sing, 108.6; genius of t. telling, 110.8; worth the hearing, 111.30; t.

so sad, so tender, 111.37; shallow village t., 116.19; honest t., 117.11; live beyond any t. we happen to enact, 155.27; t. told by an idiot, 155.33; tedious as a twice-told t., 155.34; moral t. yet I you telle can, 176.5; t. of the Spider and the Fly, 176.13; t. out of season, 181.2; mystic t. that pleas'd of yore, 182.1; have their t. believed for their oaths, 194.6; romantic t. of her eyelashes, 244.7; tell the t. as twas told to me, 246.13; listen to my mournful t., 247.12; never a scandalous t. without some foundation, 251.9; sermons are less read than t., 256.16; tells a finer t., 258.19; t. put people to sleep, 263.1; another way of telling the t., 271.38; make his t. interminable, 271.46; my t. is told, 281.2; hear my t., 281.3; long-winded t., 281.4; like rays of light, 281.6; have a t. to tell, 281.9; let every fellow tell his t., 281.13; set forth thy t., 281.15; tell a good t. ov'r again, 281.18; take it for a Canterbury t., 281.20; t. in the carrying is made more, 281.23; t. of ships and stars, 281.27; mere tale of a tub, 281.41; and thereby hangs a t., 281.61; tale told by an idiot, 281.67; this moral t. can be learned, 288.22; when your t.'s got little in it, 292.15; time to take joy in hearing t., 292.18; teller of mirthful t., 298.43

talk, talkers, talking: learned to t., 2.2; sense to American people, 2.5; no good doers, 3.13; well in hand, 9.9; to angels, 10.6; to animals, 11.13; too big, 28.3; often but not long, 34.6; of nothing but business, 35.1; plainly, 36.10; t dies in agony, 37.13; t. like that forever, 41.4; like playing a harp, 45.4; about oneself, 48.9; bravely about death, 60.7; t of the devil, 62.3; t. along the walls, 73.8; t. of dreams, 91.20; father t. to me, 93.2; t. ... like a father, 93.5; too much t. ... indice of a fool, 99.6; t. to oneself when alone is folly, 99.10; t. of a fool, 99.18; not being t. about, 108.36; t. bad grammar, 109.7; t. of the child in the marketplace, 128.11; t. about language, 147.18; life is a wonderful thing to t. about, 155.4; t. to the unborn, 155.7; opposite of t. is waiting, 158.31; t. who alternately absorbs and expresses ideas, 158.45; listen when clever men are t., 158.49; t. with my mind, 172.9; t. of mere morality, 177.4; t. like a Sphinx, 182.3; you're t. nonsense 190.1; maintain an opinion for the sake of t., 196.13; to despise the popular t., 203.6; t. like philosophers, 206.7; poets ... talk to themselves out loud, 209.24; if you're a preacher, you t. for a living, 215.17; race prejudice can't be t. down, 217.8; possible to t. to the unborn, 232.6; not being t. about, 238.12; practice r. in your common t., 240.23; I t. in riddles, 242.8; rule for being a good t., 245.8; avoid the t. of men, 246.8; scandal is a good brisk t., 251.11; edge to the superstitious t., 252.17; culturally forbidden to t. back, 256.3; silence is t. too, 258.3; more interesting than the best t., 258.21; small t. dies in agonies, 264.9; man gets t. about himself, 275.1; t. to a man about himself, 275.7; reproach people for t. about themselves, 275.8; don't t. about yourself, 275.11; t. of a Cock and Bull, 281.8; spare thy flood of t., 282.1; i dinner t., 282.4; don't care how much a man t. 282.5; non-stop t., 282.7; t. a horse's hind leg off, 282.9; t. ... like a Dutch uncle, 282.12; t. is a hydrant in the yard, 282.19; apt to t. turkey, 282.25; t. through my hat, 282.26; most fluent t., 282.27; t. is like playing on the harp, 282.32; always t. who never think, 290.31; t. like a watch, 292.20; clock t. loud, 292.24; can't reorder the world by t. about it, 311.7; fancy t. about themselves, 312.16

taste; public r. ... ghetto of good t., 229.10; t. for dirty stories, 270.48; bad t. to be wise all the time, 306.18; women have simple t., 309.28

taught: under the shape of a parable, 199.7; any subject can be t. effectively, 275.3; t. when no one has learned, 284.5; better untaught than ill t., 284.19; simply want this world better t., 284.26

taunt: a graceful t., 135.15

teach, teaching: the truth, 26.15; both please and t., 43.8; awakening natural curiosity, 56.6; experience t. slowly, 85.7; teaches ... also his son's son, 93.11; cannot t. what you don't know, 145.27; t. is ... a performing art, 204.10; t. a love of reading, 231.12; t. the English how to talk, 264.11; t. ... the art of storytelling, 271.13; t. us sympathy, 279.2; cannot t. a man anything, 284.7; good t. ... three-fourths theater, 284.9; to t. is to learn twice over, 284.14; I do not t, I only tell, 284.15; nobody can t. anything, 284.17; t. is the royal road to learning, 284.27; time can t., 292.30; who has not something to t. us, 306.7; can't t. people to write well, 313.17

teacher, teachers: animals, 11.8; g., 66.13; t. of morality discourse like angels, 177.8; disposes a man to become a University t., 219.36; t. can lead you to the door, 283.8; supreme art of the t., 283.11; love the precepts for the t.'s sake, 283.11; good t. feels his way, 283.13; one day with a great t., 283.16; task of a t., 283.17; t. can only help the work going on, 283.21; been their own t., 283.23; guardians of civilization, 283.4; t. brings tools, 283.28; time is a great t., 292.4

tears: strongest figure in female rhetoric ... is a flood of t., 240.12; have water'd since the world was born, 247.6; t. that speak, 285.2; no one pay me honor with t., 285.3; noble language of the eye, 285.4; sometimes as weighty as words, 285.7; asked to be left a few t., 285.8; the great interpreter, 285.9; silent language of grief. 285.10

tedious: t. as a twice-told tale, 237.6

telepathy: damaged the chances of t., 286.5

telephone: ringing of the t. takes precedence; 286.1; happy to hear the phone is for you, 286.3

television: biggest problem of t., 287.1; charm of t. entertainment, 287.2; convenient whipping boy, 287.10; more a mirror of taste, 287.11

temperament: a disease that afflicts amateurs, 19.5

temple: every l. is a t., 147.24

temptation: to vivify the tale, 83.4

terms: define your t., 61.8

terrors: flock to fill the void, 91.12

theater: take its audience seriously, 21.6; without audience, no t., 21.25 my kind of t. can be presented anywhere, 127.5; radio ... creative t. of the mind, 229.15; can flourish in barbarism, 288.10; life hideously magnified, 288.12

theological, theology: dramatic t. statements are ... "shaggy dog" stories, 289.1; ideas of truth classified, 289.3; hate all t. controversy, 289.4; when Christian t. becomes traditionalism, 289.6; an effort to explain the unknowable, 289.12

theologian: who has not joy in his work is not a t., 289.2; stranger is a t., 289.5; old habit with t., 289.11

theories, theory: professors ... prefer their own t. to truth, 219.6; make a t. to prove our performance the best, 230.4

thief, thieves: flatterers ... are t. in disguise, 96.24; a t. said the last kind thing to Christ, 142.4

things: listen more often to t., 158.13; learn to look at all t. with a sort of mental squint, 208.8; say the same t. … over and over, 237.5; great t. fashion themselves, 258.34; to say disagreeable t., 280.7; most difficult t. in the world, 290.2; more t. told than are true, 298.42

think, thinking: nature of aphoristic t., 14.21; t we t., 33.1; what the heart thinketh, 112.12; when the mind is t., 172.15; men t. in myths, 183.23; the ability to t. in quotations, 228.12; t. twice before you speak, 268.23; t. because he speaks, 268.37; they can because they t. they can, 276.17; who t. too little, 282.14; talk without t., 282.15; merely talk and never t., 282.37; less men t. the more they talk, 282.43; to t. is to say no, 290.1; as soon as you say what you t., 290.5; t. today and speak tomorrow, 290.6; none but dull rogues t., 290.8; learned to t. exactly, 290.9; to t. is to differ, 290.10; I think therefore I am, 290.11; t. too little, 290.12; avoid the real labor of t., 290.13; how can I tell what I think, 290.15; one may t. that dares not speak, 290.16; t. is half murdered, 290.17; moment's t. is an hour in words, 290.21; soundless dialogue, 290.24; t. … before you answer a question, 290.25; t. before you t., 290.26; t. wrong is expensive, 290.27; often bolder than speech, 291.12; once t. can never be unthought, 291.13; t. about thoughts, 291.22; we t. because we have words, 310.49

thinker: t. at work, 49.2

thought: the blossom, 3.5; conscious utterance of t., 19.9; hide not thy t., 36.8; deeper than all speech, 76.6; better … be t. a fool, 99.15; picture and counterpart of t., 147.25; means for communicating t., 147.28; justness of t., 165.6; certain t. are prayers, 214.10; lumbering poor vehicle … for the conveying of great t., 223.15; classics … the noblest t. of man, 231.15; use speech to express t., 268.47; give thy t. no tongue, 280.11; t. other people talked to much, 282.51; where your t. have brought you, 291.1, t. left unsaid are never wasted, 291.2; splendor of a sudden t., 291.7; reservoirs of learning … yet never had a t. 291.23; wit … striking way of expressing a t., 307.38; words are the dress of t., 310.13; where a t. is lacking, 310.31

throat: opens his t. to sing, 265.23; let not your tongue cut your t., 294.8

thriller: extension of the fairy tale, 90.9; question raised by the t., 95.9

time: antiquates antiquities, 13.4; Homeric, 13.6; killing t., 43.12; waste of t., 86.4; few things happen at the right t., 115.5; has lost all meaning in that nightmare alley, 191.11; how easily that man can pass his t., 226.20; t. has come, 275.4; syllables may jar with t., 277.6; t. to learn, 284.20; one's best friend, 292.1; is a babbler, 292.3; t. stays we go, 292.9; t. to hold one's peace, 292.10; once upon a t., 292.13; t. and words can't be recalled, 292.14; envious t. has sped, 292.19; makes more converts than reason, 292.26; wisest counselor, 292.27; most effective t. for speaking, 292.34; longest distance between two places, 292.35; being wise in t., 306.25; takes a long t. to become young, 314.25

times: t. of heroism … t. of terror, 114.10; tale of the t. gone by, 281.34; say nothing in dangerous t., 306.26

tired: we grow t. of everything but, 243.4

tiresome: t. way of speaking, 268.39

toast: beware the t., 293.2; standing t. that pleased the most, 293.5; let the t. pass, drink to the lass, 293.10; old t. which is golden, 293.12

tone: eloquence in t. of voice, 75.23; language of t., 181.40

tongue: acquire Southern knack, 1.18; ready 3.8; animals have long t., 11.14; hold my t., 37.1; committed a little perjury, 57.1; silver on his t., 75.15; t. of experience, 85.2; nobody gets old and bitter of t., 89.23; airy t. that syllable men's names, 91.17; fear runs away with my t., 94.1; t. long enough to cut his own throat, 99.21; what the t. is, … the man is, 124.3; t. must be confuted by his conscience, 150.14; a t. folk, 158.2; true love lacketh a t., 160.24; each t. best tells his own story, 160.29; knit the knot with our t., 164.17; music … only universal t., 181.33; name dwells on every t., 185.12; quickens the t. of a narrator, 186.2; my t. has sworn it, 194.5; persuasion to cut his own throat, 99.21; use a sweet t., 205.19; it is the t. that wins and not the deed, 205.21; prophet in his own t., 222.13; his t. dropped manna, 233.14; rumor with her hundred babbling t., 246.6; from rumor's idle t., 246.14; rumor's unclean t., 246.16; done to death by slanderous t., 261.17; speech flowed from his t., 248.3; slander not with thy t., 261.6; your t. shall be split, 281.32; she had the fluency of t., 290.4; not outrun your thought, 291.7; man is overthrown … through his t., 294.3; t. are wagging like tails, 294.6; lost your t., 294.15; false t., 294.16; keep watch upon thy t., 294.17; t. offends, 294.18; is a wild beast, 294.20; t. that scalds and bites like a bull whip, 294.22; t. hung in the middle, 294.25; glib t., 294.42; woman's t. is her sword, 309.31

tomorrow: boast not of t., 28.19

tool: story … basic t. invented by the human mind, 270.39; tongue is no edge t., 294.23; edge t. that grows keener with constant use, 294.26

topics: sensible talk about vitally important t., 282.49

touched: touched by a metal so cold, 248.5

trade: t. is talking, 150.26; best of all t. to make songs, 265.5

tradition: imagination continually frustrates t., 127.21; oftener the wild babble of the time, 197.3; automatically talk about t., 271.33; t. doesn't mean that the living are dead, 295.3; t. without intelligence, 295.5; the wild babble of the time, 295.6; becomes our security, 295.7; guide and not a jailer, 295.9; to keep the unexpected from happening, 295.10; t. … becomes holy and inspires awe, 295.12; that have lost their meanings, 295.13; wears a snowy beard, 295.14

tragedy: should blush, 92.4; farce is t. played at a thousand revolutions 92.9; life is a t. in close-up, 155.11; life is a t. wherein we sit as spectators, 155.35; satire is t. plus time, 249.5; noblest production of human nature, 296.1; to say a certain story from ancient books, 296.7; something bigger than life, 296.8; somebody's nuisance, 296.11; should blush as much as stoop, 296.12

tranquility: sorrow is t. remembered in emotion, 266.9

translate, translation: t. … at best at echo, 73.1; to read is to t., 231.3

travel: part of our national folklore, 98.17

treachery: in politics … abstract words conceal t., 211.10

treasure: witty woman is a t., 307.35; words convey the mental t., 310.4

tree: instead of bending, breaks, 296.21; wisdom is a t. that grows in the heart, 306.9

trial: delay a trial for years or months, 150.57

tribe: purify dialect of the t., 63.4

trick, trickery: kiss is a lovely t., 144.1; t. the writer into something other than the urge at the beginning,

241.10; had a thousand jadish t., 297.1; when in doubt, win the t., 297.4; all t. are either knavish or childish, 297.5; more t. than a dancing bear, 297.10; unsightly t., 297.11

triviality: we remember the least t., 169.10

trouble: telling one's t., 38.20; become inquisitive and have t., 56.9; world's t. ... due to questions of grammar, 109.18; learn to laugh at t., 148.18; poetry is t. dunked in tears, 208.53; prophet ... a man who foresees t., 222.8; t. with the world, 273.13

trust: the man who hesitates in his speech, 18.41; t the tale, 19.12; distrust the incommunicable, 44.16; t. a person entirely or not at all, 165.12; infinite pathos of human t., 201.7; put his t. in the right word, 205.7

true, truth: perception of t., 8.6; aphorism and t., 14.14; lose sight of t., 18.38; must not say that thou wert t; swears she is made of t, 26.27; children and fools speak t., 38.12; cliches ... tell deepest t., 42.9; hard to confess t., 50.7; look t. in the face, 58.8; mean between two opinions, 68.7; disputation ... sifter out of t., 68.12; dreams come t., 71.13; translate t. into language, 75.13; t. in wildest fables, 87.6; fantasy, the only t., 91.8; fantasy ... springs from a t., 91.24; stranger than fiction, 95.4; fools and madmen tell ... t., 99.4; naked t. in the presence of ladies, 102.9; no statement about God is ... t., 106.9; where hearts are t., 112.4; instruments of darkness tell us t., 134.3; tell me what you know is t., 145.21; t. beyond realities, 152.1; every legend contains its residuum of t., 152.3; t. is man's slave, 154.4; speak your t. quietly and clearly, 158.15; in love everything is t., 160.7; eternal t. will be neither t. nor eternal, 166.19; there is no moral t., 176.2; moral t., 176.21; to get into the t. of anything 182.4; nothing t. than myth, 183.18; t. ... will always have its ragged edges, 186.12; poets that wrapt t. in tales, 209.5; penchant for telling the t., 210.16; poetry of everyday t., 223.5; t. comes in a well rubbed-down state, 224.24; in quarreling, the t. is always lost, 226.23; does not become greater by frequent repetition, 237.8; make sarcasm the condition of t., 248.2; t. comes from the mouth of fools, 249.21; scientific t. goes through three stages, 252.1; deepest t. found ... by a simple story, 270.15; seldom any splendid story is wholly t., 270.34; present deep psychological and metaphysical t., 270.74; adapted t., 271.61; cannot tell how the t. may be, 281.59; tutor: t. both to good and bad, 292.28; whispering tongues can poison t., 294.13; t. that makes men free, 298.2; more brutal than the t., 298.7; t. told with bad intent, 298.10; t. never hurts the teller, 298.13; such a rare thing, 298.22; great t. to tell, 298.24; not always tell the whole t., 298.48; t. shall make you free, 298.49; disguise the t., 298.60; always something that is told, 298.63; takes two to speak the t., 298.65; do not tell the t. about yourself, 298.70; t. from his lips prevailed, 306.14; women always speak the t., 309.22; more t. in a good book, 312.15; writer paradoxically seeks the t., 312.21

tydings: make either glad or sad, 188.4

tyranny: t. of the "rat race," 183.42

understanding, understood: not necessary to u. ... to argue, 18.5; the assumptions in which we are drenched, 20.7; brevity is very good, 34.5; grown-ups never u., 38.26; speaks and writes to be u., 40.11; disguises ... lack of u., 74.3; understood his time, 77.7; hears only what he u., 111.23; life can only be u. back-

wards, 155.21; good listener tires to understand ... what the other person is saying, 58.54; we don't u. out name at all, 185.9; last recourse of nostalgia, 191.6; religion is so far from being u., 234.2; u. a science, 252.5; speak of what you u., 268.12; make ourselves u., 268.31; sympathetic u., 279.13; who u. the wise is wise already, 306.19; u. the fury in your words, 310.66

universe: vast u. serves for a theatre, 92.8; man explores the u. around him, 252.10; is made of stories, 270.58; u. was dictated but not signed, 289.13

universities: sophistry and affectation, 6.1; need black market u., 151.23; servant to bred at an u., 202.8

use: u. of poetry, 208.49

Utopia: literature is my U., 159.15

utter, utterances: sound clever, 41.10; u. have no meaning, 166.23; u. dark sayings of old, 199.6; prophecies boldly u., 222.16; u. what he thinks is truth, 298.41

validity: denied the v. of our ancient religions, 234.14

valor: in a false quarrel there is no true v., 226.25

value: mention of the v. of a true teacher, 283.12

vain, vanity: v. to give advice, 5.20; 'tis v. to speak reason, 233.7; use not v. repetitions, 237.10; v. of being ... entrusted with a secret, 253.8; v. of teaching, 284.11

vehemence: all v. springs from the will, 141.16

vein: hath a satirical v., 249.2

Venus: the goddess of love, 164.29

veracity: the heart of morality, 177.7; intention of communicating truth, 298.20; anyone doubts my v., 298.57

verb: god is a v., 106.8; life is a v., 155.15; with a v. in his mouth, 255.16; theater is a v., 288.6

verbose, verbosity: thread of his v., 18.42; v. in fewer words than anyone else, 210.13

verdict: v. of guilty pronounced in the absence of the accused, 261.16

verses: all good v. are like impromptus, 130.5; indignation will produce v., 131.9; they never made sense, 156.6; minstrel ... did continue to narrate stories in v., 173.9; v. may find him who a sermon flees, 208.22; prose is v., and v. is merely prose, 223.3; rhyme the rudder is of v., 241.4; v. without rhyme, 241.11

versions: stories about the different v. of stories, 270.63

vertigo: spangled the butterflies of v., 258.5

vessel: empty v. giveth a greater sound, 267.9

vice: can v. atone for crimes, 1.4; gossip, a v. enjoyed vicariously, 108.13; amplification is the v. of the modern orator, 198.13; most effective way of attacking v., 243.6

victims: slander counts by three its v., 261.11

views: v. of the mob, 203.9

villainy: v. you teach me, 133.9

violations: committed by children, 38.9

violence: repartee of the illiterate, 236.2; the kingdom of heaven must suffer v., 256.13; v. of the tongue, 294.45

viper: tongue of a v., 261.10

virtue: gathered from fable or allegory, 7.1; clarity, an excellent v., 40.10; first v. ... is to rule the tongue, 294.10; woman's only v. 309.35

virtuous: most v. men can hardly ever fully say why they are v., 216.10

visited: v. every house in the entire village, 271.51

visualization: story is a sacred v., 270.73

voice: doth raise, 1.19; spoilt by affectation, 6.2; raise your v., 18.27; in a loud v. gives an explanation, 21.29; of the bard, 24.2; beauty of thy v., 25.13; of children heard, 38.8; unique tone of v., 51.32; always be dissident v.,

54.7; era unto my v., 72.13; echo is the v. of reflection, 73.6; v. is still living, 73.10; woo the v., 85.14; sound of his father's v., 93.6; imagination is the v. of daring, 127.18; v. of honest indignation, 131.1; v. of the inanimate, 147.12; hear the v. of water, 158.13; v. is sweet with deep mysterious accords, 169.6; listen to the v. in the upper air, 182.6; bloodless race that sends a feeble v., 186.7; nature ever has a v., 187.3; people's v. is a mighty power, 203.1; voice of the people, 203.2; discovered the v. of an innermost self, 214.12; ancestral v. prophesying war, 222.7; v. sounds like a prophet's word, 222.12; v. of the story or the poem itself, 231.16; v. of reason is stifled, 233.2; religion ... voice of the deepest human experience, 234.3; v. of rumor, 246.12; v. of iron, 246.20; ransom in a v., 258.18; singers are ... like the v. of the public., 265.1; v. is a wild thing, 265.9; man's style ... his mind's v., 274.6; public v. in the theater ... crude and raucous, 288.19; v. of young people, 314.28

vote: v. for the man who promises the least., 210.5

walk, walked, walking: religion is a way of w., 234.12; when sorrow w. with me, 266.6; when you w. singing, 270.47

walls: ooze ghosts, 103.3; Humpty Dumpty sat on a w., 193.5

war: diplomacy ... a continuation of w., 66.4; minstrel boy to the w. is gone, 173.8

warfare: jungle w. is a stately minuet, 150.55

warning: take 5.16;

waste: definition of utter w., 150.25

wasteland: television ... a vast wasteland, 287.13

water: talk like w. gushed from him, 282.20

weakness: in argument, 18.32; of any habitual fallacy, 20.6

weapons: w. worthy of the strong, 137.6; sarcasm ... questionable w., 248.6; terrible w. is satire, 249.8; tongue of man is his w., 294.28

weather: don't knock the w., 51.20

weep: obliged to w., 148.6; w. and you w. alone, 148.48; to avoid the shame of not w., 266.7; cannot w. for the entire world, 279.1; I w. for you, the Walrus said, 279.4

welcome: wit makes its own w., 307.18

wheel: squeaks loudest, 46.5

whirlwind: god is the w., 106.2

whisper, whispering: what he w. sounds like what it is, 138.5; w. to each other half in fear, 170.9; teases you by its provoking inaudibility, 189.11

wicked: get punished, 95.2

wife, wives: clever enough to appreciate, 41.12; old w. fables, 87.20; w. who preaches in her gown, 151.10; fear repartee in a w., 236.10; tells old w.'s tales, 281.40

will: to doubt, 70.7; ill w. from a higher point of view, 249.19

wine: to a gifted bard, 24.8; w. turned to sound, 181.43; preaching is heady w., 216.12; avoid quarrels caused by w., 226.22

wings; bell rings ... angel got w., 10.8; words have w., 310.26

winter: sad tale's best for w., 247.11; it's a w.'s tale, 281.79

wise, wisdom: appear to be more clever, 41.11; dreams and fables of the sky; 71.7; w. man speaks, 75.21; lip-w., 85.13; fairy w., 89.15; from hearing comes w., 111.21; w. make jests, 139.17; privilege of w. to listen, 158.25; w. in love, 160.45; reputed w. for saying nothing, 192.12; w. prophets make sure of the event first, 222.17; discerneth the proverbs of the w., 224.4; w.

men make proverbs, 224.29; proverb ... the wisdom of many, 224.34; first key to w., 227.1; prudent question is one-half of w., 227.3; being made w. by the remarks of our friends, 235.1; no rule so w., 245.31 short saying oft contains much w., 250.17; foolish speeches of w. men, 269.8; histories make men w., 272.2; think as w. men do, 290.3; of w. no clock can measure, 292.5; be so w. to hold thy tongue, 294.34; w. I always loved, 306.1; great w. is generous, 306.6; doesn't always speak in Greek and Latin, 306.13; w. crieth without, 306.21; w. than necessary, 306.23; w. lingers, 306.29; w. before you can be witty, 307.5; word to the w. is enough, 310.58

wisecrack: epigram, a w. played Carneige Hall, 80.13

wish, wishes: farces ... disguised fulfillment of repressed w., 92.1; I w. I loved the Human Race, 163.14

wit, witty: aphorisms ... show much real w., 14.13; desire commendation of w., 18.4; to match thy beauty, 25.11; keep w. about you, 38.19; w. backbiter, 41.3; conversation is seldom w., 51.43; more malice than love in the hearts of all w., 112.7; don't try for w., 119.17; is the lightning of the mind, 172.7; no such whetstone to sharpen a good w., 213.3; punning is a low species of w., 225.33; quotation is a diamond on the finger of a man of w., 228.25; enjoy your dear w. 240.16; w. enough to write a satire, 249.14; w. without w's pretense 282.49; my tongue do outslip my w., 294.14; treacherous dart, 307.6; use your w. as a buckler, 307.7; moment's flash of w., 307.13; glorious treat, 307.15; shows all his w. at once, 307.16; borrowed w. 307.19; half w. talk much, 307.20; an unruly engine, 207.25; w. that is kindly, 307.26; has a deadly aim, 307.32; true w. is Nature to advantage dress'd, 307.40; winding up the watch of his w., 307.42

witticism: minor work ... does not merit a second edition, 308.13; brings himself into notice by a w., 308.16

witches: A-list'nin' to the w-tales, 281.57

woe: tale of w., 247.3; never a story of more w., 270.61

woman: asks you to apologize, 15.14; allows that another is beautiful, 25.12; boast of her chastity, 28.18; accounted chatterboxes, 37.11; w's h. and tongue, 112.6; basic spelling that every w. should know, 144.13; that grand word w., 146.8; one syllable of a w.'s speech, 160.19; w. seldom asks advice, 164.1; conceived Nature to be a w., 187.8; asserted by a w. is opinionated, 196.19; want something done ask a w., 211.21; w.'s preaching is like a dog's walking on his hind legs, 216.8; quick to perish is rumor by a w. voiced, 246.1; triangle straight up symbolizes w., 278.5; w. gave a short talk, 282.34; t. of a woman ... capable of producing sound, 294.4; w. spins even when she talks, 309.3

women: never disarmed by compliments, 47.16; often more powerful than men, 90.23; gossip among w. is universally ridiculed, 108.3; history ... having a collective forgetfulness about w., 116.31; when w. kiss, 144.11; w. all want to be ladies, 146.9; if w. had but written stories, 163.2; when you say man ... you include w., 163.15; w. ... are like riddles, 242.5; tragedies of many w., 296.20; w. are like tricks of sleight of hand, 297.2; strive for the last word, 309.18; glad to have been asked, 309.29

wonder: w. is the foundation of all philosophy, 206.16

word: to the action, 3.12; use soft w., 18.6; have the last w., 18.7; specious and fantastic arrangements of w., 18.30; beautiful w. for doing things tomorrow, 25.18;

of the Lord, 27.15; lamp unto my feet, 27.16; need an army, 28.2; great power in w., 34.4; few w, but wonderfully clear, 34.12; superfluous, 34.13; fewer w., fewer errors, 34.14; fewer w., better prayer, 34.15; dangerous words in business, 35.10; preserves contact, 39.7; smallest number of w, 44.2; annihilate a man with w., 54.2; dialect w., 63.5; right w. and the almost right w., 65.10; signs of our ideas, 68.16; modest w. to express immodest things, 82.2; are threads, 85.8; w. can change you, 90.3; father could not put in w., 93.10; folk s. are written, 97.14; new w. to fit no situations, 97.17; foolishly w. are not always foolish, 99.22; fool and his w. ... soon parted, 99.25; w. that men say, 106.1; God is but a w., 106.11; w. were placed in the mouths of folk poets, 110.1; be ye doers of the w., 111.31; heroes in w., 114.4; honest man's w., 117.5; honor ... w. of fools, 118.4; signs of our ideas, 123.9; for whom w have lost their value, 123.15; jargon of w., 138.6; true w. said in jest, 139.11; w. that to be kind must lie, 142.1; a w. of kindness, 142.9; be king of your w., 143.5; knowing the force of w., 145.16; left us the w., 147.39; twist w. and meaning as you please, 150.15; w. pass away ... as they strike upon the air, 157.2; w. are the weak support of cold indifference, 160.8; pleasant w. ... food of love, 160.30; w. contain much of their magical power, 162.3; magic of the necessary w., 162.4; w. divested of their magic, 162.5; same meaning changes with the w., 166.17; w. are sometimes the most powerful drugs, 168.6; w. of his mouth were smoother than butter, 179.16; w. are wearisome and worn, 181.10; mystery of having been moved by w., 182.10; make in your mouths the w. that were our names, 185.11; flood of w. and his drop of reason, 198.7; w. unsuitable to the time place and company, 202.6; poetry is the renewal of w. forever and ever., 208.16; weird power in the spoken w., 212.4; often more groans than w., 214.2; professor is ... not afraid of w. at all, 219.3; w. spoken never die, 226.3; magic of the spoken w., 231.17; the great foes of reality, 232.8; at every w. a reputation dies, 238.7; lies in his w. and gets a bad reputation, 238.10; sad w. of tongue and pen, 247.15; twist my little gift of w., 248.11; w. have weight, sound and appearance, 255.10; count the w. that might be spared, 256.5; w. may be false, 257.10; mums the w., 258.15; let thy w. be worth more than silence, 258.42; most of out vital w. were once slang, 262.9; give sorrow w., 266.11; w. not spoken in vain, 268.35; students of w., 272.6; w. of four syllables, 277.1; ten low w. oft creep in one dull line, 277.7; w. seemed ... as idle tales, 281.48; tell the same tale in other w., 281.51; thoughts itself needs w., 291.5; w. are the clothes that thoughts wear, 291.8; the body and dress of t., 291.26; never time to say out last w., 292.8; truth needs not many w., 298.31; my w. is truth, 298.50; w. is like a bird, 310.2; like good strong w., 310.3; tokens ... accepted for conceits, 310.5; w. are all we have, 310.6; pegs to hang ideas on, 310.7; deliver you w. not by number, 310.8; short w. are the best, 310.14; w. are giants when they do us injury, 310.15; with w. we govern men, 310.24; w. are chameleons, 310.34; wise men's counters, 310.36; never use a long w., 310.37; frail beasts of burden, 310.39; most powerful drug used by mankind, 310.44; some w. bedevil me, 310.50; w. was born in blood; 310.52; his w. passeth not away, 310.55; weigheth his w., 310.57; w. demand attention, 310.65; w. that strike even harder than blows, 310.69; bright is the ring of w., 310.70

work: best thing you can sing about, 97.12; what a piece of w. is man, 163.16; good w. is like a good tree, 199.4; w. as if everything depended upon man, 214.21; selling retail the w. of other men, 219.18; few professors ever completer their w., 219.23; learns the w. by heart, 271.49; thinking is the hardest w. there is, 290.14

world: allegory, 7.8; loveliest fairy in the w., 89.17; mysterious w. of might be, 91.3; slowly changing the w., 122.4; in the w. to laugh, 148.32; w. is mad, 148.35; whole w. loved man when he smiled, 163.19; all my movies are about strange w., 180.16; w. ... is for the hearing, 189.1; w. is never quiet, 189.5; intellectual w. is divided into two classes, 202.23; stories we tell ourselves ... function to order the w., 232.10; we live in a fantasy w., 232.15; w. does not speak, 268.45; give our story to the w., 270.75; w. ... is comprehensible, 311.3; way the w. ends, 311.4; w. is all a carcass, 311.5; milk the cow of the w., 311.12; funny paper read backwards, 311.14; a w. waiting for you, 314.16

worship: pseudosimplicities of brutal directness, 36.11

worth: determined by the stories and songs ... knows, 116.32; opinion is w. expressing, 196.4

wound: w. with a touch that's scarcely felt, 249.22

write: w. with the learned, 147.16; to try to w. love, 160.3; learned fool w. his nonsense, 190.7; he who w. prose builds his temple to fame, 223.2; w. in prose you say what you mean, 241.8; difficult not to w. satire, 249.18; speak well and w. badly, 268.36; w. as they speak, 274.2; I w. tales beside, 281.7; moving finger w., 285.6; w. it on running water, 309.7; can make a riddle out of an answer, 312.20; w. because you have something to say, 313.11; always w. a good first line, 313.14

writers: frustrated actor, 4.21; of the babel, 27.24; has become a voice of his tribe, 158.2; what a w. asks of his reader, 231.10; simple-minded person to begin with, 271.9; for your born w., 312.5; w. because I am not a talker, 312.6; discipline of the w., 312.8; basic material a w. works with, 312.9; love being a w., 312.12; should be read, 312.13; w. must write, 312.17; function as a w., 312.18; role of the w., 312.23

writing: for antiquity, 13.14; simply talking on paper, 109.3; depends ... upon the force of imagination, 127.9; w. things to quote, 228.5; w. comes more easily if you have something to say, 313.3; artificial activity, 313.4; trying to w. naturally, 313.9

wrong: those who disagree with us are w., 70.5; our own opinion is never w., 196.12; quarrels do not last long if the w. is only on one side, 226.18; bad quarrels come when two people are w., 226.28; rumor is not always w., 246.18; ancient tale of w., 247.14; w. to listen to any sort of man, 270.55; we read the world w., 311.11

yawn: silent shout, 31.10

years: y. teach much which the days never know, 292.12

yesterday: call back y., 292.29

Yiddish: is sick, 63.8

young, youth: allowances are made for the illusions of y., 126.14; not y. enough to know everything, 145.3; education of y. is professed by many, 219.30; rigorous teacher seized my y., 283.4; y. have nothing to say, 314.1; pollen that blows through the sky, 314.3; y. is insolvent, 314.8; stranger than fiction, 314.9; only the y. die good, 314.14; such a lovely thing, 314.29

Zeus: guided men to think, 107.1; no mortal can vie with Z., 107.13